COMPLETE FAT COUNTER

Also by Peter Cox & Peggy Brusseau

LifePoints

LifePoints Diet

LifePoints for Kids

LifePoints Cookbook

LifePoints Counter & Meal Planner

Linda McCartney's Home Cooking
(with Linda McCartney)

THE COMPLETE FAT COUNTER

Peter Cox & Peggy Brusseau

BLOOMSBURY

Publisher's Note
The information in this book was correct to the best of the Editor's and Publisher's belief at the time of going to press. While no responsibility can be accepted for errors and omissions, the Editor and Publisher would welcome corrections and suggestions for material to include in subsequent editions of this book.
This book may include words, brand names and other descriptions of products which are or are asserted to be proprietary names or trademarks. No judgement concerning the legal status of such words is made or implied thereby. Their inclusion does not imply that they have acquired for legal purposes a non-proprietary or general significance nor any other judgement concerning their legal status.
Please note that food products frequently change in composition, and this may substantially affect the ratings herein. A free update to the information in this book can be obtained from: BM Box Superliving, London WC1M 3XX, England. Please enclose a stamped addressed envelope.

First published in 1998 by
Bloomsbury Publishing Plc
38 Soho Square
London W1V 5DF

International management by the Alta Vista Corporation Ltd
A copy of the CIP entry for this book is available from the British Library

ISBN 0 7475 3444 6

1 3 5 7 9 10 8 6 4 2

Typeset by Palimpsest Book Production Ltd., Polmont, Stirlingshire
Printed and bound in Great Britain by Clays Ltd, St Ives plc

CONTENTS

IMPORTANT NOTICE

All diets should begin with a medical check-up to make certain that no special health problems exist and to confirm that there are no medical reasons why you should not undertake a change of diet. Because the diagnosis and treatment of medical conditions is a responsibility shared between you and your medical advisors, neither the authors nor publisher of this book can accept responsibility for the individual consequences of dietary treatment based on the recommendations described herein.

Fat counting as described in this book has been created to be used by healthy adults. It does not apply to pregnant or lactating women. Women who are pregnant or lactating should not consider any weight-reduction diet until they have returned to a non-pregnant, non-lactating condition. A reduction in protein intake is emphatically not recommended for a woman who is pregnant or lactating, as the health of her child relies on both a higher-protein and a higher-calorie intake during this time.

TRADE NAMES

This book may include words, brand names and other descriptions of products which are or are asserted to be proprietary names or trademarks. No judgement concerning the legal status of such words is made or implied thereby. Their inclusion does not imply that they have acquired for legal purposes a non-proprietary or general significance nor any other judgement concerning their legal status.

UPDATE

If you would like to receive a free update to the information in this book, please send an A4 size stamped self-addressed envelope to: BM Box Superliving, London WC1M 3XX, England.

ACKNOWLEDGEMENTS

Grateful appreciation is due to our tireless principal researcher and data-hound, Miranda Creed-Miles, for her sterling work in tracking down so much product information. Thanks are also due for all the co-operation we have received from many kind people within the food manufacturers and retailers who supplied us with data about their products. We would also like to express our gratitude to everyone at Bloomsbury for their enthusiasm, in particular to Kathy, Sarah, Sarah, Lisa and Stephen. Finally, to Louis and Beau – who can finally see what their parents have been up to for months on end!

Peter & Peggy

READ THE LABEL!

The fat content of food products is constantly changing. This reflects the fact that new products are introduced, existing products are reformulated and some products are discontinued. While we have taken great care to ensure the information in this book is as accurate as it can be, it is inevitable that some products will no longer accord with the information presented here. It is therefore very important for you to read the nutritional information presented on the product's label, and for you to form your judgement on the basis of that information alone.

THE GOLDEN PROMISE OF FAT COUNTING

Life is painful, Your Highness – anyone who says differently is selling something.

How truthful that remark is! It comes from a brilliant film of a few years back called 'The Princess Bride', and if you ever get the chance, do see it – it's great fun for kids and adults alike.

If you've ever tried to go on a diet, you'll know from personal experience that there really is no such thing as a free lunch – despite all the promises made by fad diets and their proponents. The truth is it's *hard* to change the way you eat. And calorie counting – which many people still believe is the *only* way to lose weight – is especially difficult. Keeping track of all those impossible numbers requires that you have the mental powers of an Einstein – and sticking to a regime which makes you feel hungry most of the time demands nothing short of Mother Teresa's willpower. But calorie-restricted diets have even more serious health drawbacks, too, including:

- bloating and distended stomach
- constipation
- depression
- failure to produce collagen, the major protein of all connective tissues
- feeling cold all the time
- hair loss
- headaches
- lack of energy
- loss of lean tissue
- low blood pressure, leading to dizziness
- menstrual difficulties
- sleep disruption
- water retention
- yeast infections

All these problems have been associated with dieting in the scientific literature. In fact, there are enough scientific studies around now for us to come to the conclusion that dieting, as it is usually attempted, is ineffective in any long-term sense. For example, a highly significant Dutch study observed men who had gained weight in response to stressful life events (many of us put on weight when we're under stress – perhaps you've done so). A year later, this weight gain had disappeared in all the men – with the exception of those who had consciously *tried* to lose weight by dieting, they'd actually *gained* even more weight!

Many scientific studies now confirm that, if you want to *put on* weight, a great way to do it is to go on a diet. Weight gain is particularly provoked by 'diet cycling' (continual diet/binge cycles), and it is such a well-accepted phenomenon that it is sometimes used in a clinical situation to help underweight patients to put on bulk. How, precisely, does this happen? It's probably connected to the production of an enzyme called lipoprotein lipase (LPL), which is responsible for storing bodily fat. When you start a diet, LPL levels initially drop, then remorselessly rise again – sometimes to twenty-five times the normal level.

When you diet by drastically reducing your calorie intake your body, not unreasonably, concludes that you're in danger of starving. And since this is a threat which our ancestors have successfully coped with in the past, your body already has an excellent survival strategy lined up, ready to be implemented at the drop of a calorie. The first thing it does is to lower your metabolism in order to conserve energy. The longer your food intake continues to be below what it has been used to receiving, the harder your body tries to preserve that precious energy locked up as fat. That's why the first week or so of *any* diet always produces an impressive result, yet subsequent weeks achieve much less. Your body's deep-rooted instincts are fighting you all the way – and, usually, they win!

One particularly notorious way in which your instincts triumph over your willpower is through the binge impulse. Anyone who's ever attempted dieting will be familiar with it. You may know the scenario – your diet's lasted a few days, and so far it's gone well. Then, in one insane and unrestrained moment, you find yourself behaving like a shark in a crowded swimming pool. Eat! Eat! Eat! As you madly consume everything that could possibly have a calorie or two associated with it, you start to feel helpless and – yes – ashamed. How could you possibly be so weak? How could you have ruined all your hard work in a momentary feeding frenzy? This sort of negative self-talk can sometimes even lead to serious eating disorders such as bulimia. But take it easy on yourself for a moment. When you think about it, the binge impulse is – yet again – a very logical and successful feeding strategy. Your body thinks that there is a severe food shortage which is causing you to starve. Trying to protect you, your instincts become super-sensitive to any potential source of food – and, of course, in today's society there are *unlimited* sources of food everywhere. Drop your guard for just one instant, and those ancient survival instincts take over.

If calorie-restricted diets worked effectively, then there would be few people in the Western world with an obesity problem. In their recent paper entitled 'Diet and Health: Implications For Reducing Chronic Disease Risk', the Committee on Diet and Health of the National Research Council pointed out that 'food intake has declined over the past decade when body weight and presumably fat stores have, on average, increased'. In other words, our growing fatness can*not* be explained by the fact that we're eating more calories – because we're *not*! Other studies have confirmed that Westerners today take in fewer calories than we did at the beginning of the twentieth century – while the level of obesity has stubbornly climbed.

So let's make one thing clear. Fat counting – which you're going to learn about here – is not just one more diet. In fact, it isn't a diet at all. A 'diet' implies restricting your food intake, usually in ways that you don't like. Fat counting, on the other hand, is all about *eating*. It's about choosing to eat positively good food, with a low fat content. It's not about self-denial, pain and suffering. Big difference – we think you'll agree!

Controlling your fat intake brings you two huge benefits. First must be the fact that, as a nation, we simply consume far too much fat – with very serious health consequences. If you are at all concerned about improving your diet, controlling the amount of fat you consume must be your number one priority. Official government surveys show that fat comprises about 42 per cent of the average diet.[1] This excessive fat consumption (official recommendations suggest that fat should comprise no more than 33 per cent of the average diet[2]) is one major factor in the development of a host of severe health problems, many of which are interconnected. For example, consuming too much fat (especially saturated fat) can lead to an increase in your blood cholesterol level, which in turn increases your risk of cardiovascular disease. *Reducing your fat intake not only can make you feel slimmer and trimmer, it will also substantially reduce your risk of many serious diseases*. As a result of continuing public health education campaigns, many people are now aware of the need to reduce their risk of cardiovascular disease (heart attacks, strokes, angina, thrombosis) by eating less fat, and less saturated fat, in their diets. But the health benefits don't stop there. Cancer – which kills nearly one in four people in the UK – is also linked to fat consumption: particularly breast cancer, prostate cancer, large bowel cancer and pancreatic cancer.[3] While there are certainly other important factors in the development of cancer – such as the clear causative role of cigarette smoking, for example – too much fat plays its destructive part here, too. When the American National Cancer Institute examined the diets of *non-smoking* women whose diets were high in saturated fat – from foods such as meat, butter and cheese – they found that their risk of developing lung cancer was *four times higher* than normal.[4] 'Our study finds a strong increasing trend in lung cancer risk associated with increased saturated fat consumption among non-smoking women,' said Dr Michael Alavanja, who directed the study. Among women, the disease now kills more people than breast cancer. This is probably due to the fact that the amount of fat in your diet can raise the levels of the hormone oestrogen, which is known to have a cancer-promoting effect.

Apart from the substantial health benefits associated with controlling your fat intake, there is also one very major lifestyle advantage – it can help to keep you slim and trim! And, even here, there's a health benefit too: people who avoid gaining weight as they approach middle age dramatically lower their heart disease risk and may entirely prevent diabetes, according to researchers at the University of Maryland.[5] Many studies have shown the health benefits of losing weight, but the University of Maryland study was the first to demonstrate conclusively the value of *preventing* weight gain. 'People are not paying attention to their weight until they get to a point where they feel uncomfortable, unattractive or they've had a heart attack,' commented scientist Barbara Hansen. 'The time to take action is much earlier. People typically eat more as they age and begin to gain weight. To keep weight stable, people don't have to diet; they merely have to avoid overeating. This is not starvation or restriction.'

How does fat counting help you to control or lose weight? The answer is: in several entirely natural ways. First, you'll be effortlessly reducing your calorie intake – in effect, controlling the calories without the bother of counting them. This is because fat contributes more calories to your diet than any other nutrient. One gram of fat yields about 9 calories – protein and carbohydrates yield less than half this (about 4 calories). So reducing your fat consumption will naturally tend to reduce your calorie intake too!

But there's even better news. Fat counting doesn't mean reducing the *quantity* of food you eat – it simply means choosing to eat lower-fat foods. When you switch from high-fat foods to high-complex-carbohydrate ones, something rather wonderful happens to your body's hunger mechanism. You can prove this for yourself right now. First, imagine yourself with ten chips on a plate in front of you. Ten chips isn't very much, is it? Well, go ahead and eat them anyway! Now, do you still feel hungry? Of course you do! Actually, you've just mentally consumed about 12g of fat – a significant amount. Let's do the experiment again, but, this time, imagine a large baked potato in front of you. Eat it all up, and ask yourself if you've still got room for more. Almost certainly not! Both foods had the same calorie yield. But the baked potato contained a mere 0.2g of fat – sixty times less than the chips! Those ten chips didn't make you feel full, did they? But the entire baked potato *did*, didn't it? You've just proved to yourself a fact that scientists now accept: that fatty foods do *not* tell your body when to stop eating (scientists call this satiation), nor do they prevent you from starting eating when you shouldn't (satiety).[6] Yo for fat counting!

But we're not finished yet. When you eat low-fat, complex-carbohydrate foods, they actually *change your body*. This is how our friend and nutrition expert Professor Neal Barnard explains it:

> Carbohydrate-rich meals are not just low in calories. They readjust your hormones, which in turn boost your metabolism and speed the burning of calories. One of these hormones is thyroid hormone. Below your Adam's apple, your thyroid gland manufactures a hormone called T4, so named because it has four iodine atoms attached. This hormone has two possible fates: it can be converted into the active form of thyroid hormone called T3, which boosts your metabolism and keeps your body burning calories, or it can be converted to an inactive hormone, called *reverse* T3. When your diet is rich in carbohydrates, more of the T4 is converted to T3, and your metabolism gets a good boost. If your diet is low in carbohydrate, more of the T4 is turned into reverse T3, resulting in a slowed metabolism. The same thing occurs during periods of very low calorie dieting or starvation. Less of the T4 is

> converted to T3 and more to the useless reverse T3. This is presumably the body's way of guarding its reserves of fat; when not much food is coming in, the body conserves fat and turns down production of the fat-burning hormone, T3. But a diet generous in carbohydrates keeps T3 levels high and keeps the fat fires burning.[7]

And there's more! Have you ever wondered why smokers are often so thin? Perhaps you've even wondered about taking up the weed just to trim down a bit? Well, now you can *look* like a slender smoker, without that hacking cough! As carbohydrate-rich foods gradually release sugars into the body, this stimulates the production of a neurohormone called noradrenalin, which plays an important role in instructing your body's brown fat cells (also known as brown adipose tissue) to consume stored fat. The basic function of brown fat cells is to warm the blood and distribute heat through your body, and they do this by burning fat, which is good news for slimmers! Scientists estimate that – when stimulated – brown fat can burn up 200–400 calories a day, which would equate to a useful weight loss of about 2 lbs a month.[8] Now, smokers stimulate their brown fat cells by releasing noradrenalin into their systems. The good news is that researchers have found that the glucose released by carbohydrate-rich foods can raise your noradrenalin level by about the same amount as do cigarettes![9] So next time you may be tempted to reach for a coffin nail, reach for a carrot instead!

The key question that everyone wants answered when they first start fat counting is: how much weight will I lose? Of course, this does rather depend on you. Most diet books make rather outrageous claims about their potential for weight loss, yet most of them fail to back those claims up with independent scientific evidence. As a change from that, we'd like to mention some recent research which was independent, scientific and may prove encouraging to you. In 1991 the results of the world's longest controlled human-feeding study ever to be undertaken were published. Scientifically speaking, it was a beautifully designed study.[10] Thirteen women aged between 22 and 56 were randomly put into one of two groups. The first ate a low-fat diet (about 45g of fat a day) while the second group ate a 'normal' control diet (about 85g of fat a day – close to the average). Both groups ate the same type of food, but the low-fat group ate reduced-fat versions (e.g. low-fat yoghurt instead of normal yoghurt). Significantly, although the low-fat group could eat as much food as they wanted to, they actually chose to consume about 250 fewer calories a day. After eleven weeks, the subjects were given a complete break for seven weeks (a so-called 'washout' period) and then the tables were turned – the low-fat group went on to the control diet, and the former control group ate low-fat foods. This sort of study is called a 'crossover' study, and is a powerful way of eliminating error.

The results were fantastic! The women on the low-fat diet had lost *twice as much* weight as those on the calorie-controlled diet – about $^1/_2$ lb a week, 2.5 kg in eleven weeks. All that without calorie counting, and without food restriction!

Now, of course, your mileage may vary. This degree of weight loss may not be the fastest in the world, but it's pretty close to painless – and there's good evidence to believe that it *lasts*. As the scientists wrote:

> There is a great deal of evidence that conscious reduction in the amount of food consumed results in rapid losses of body weight; but almost invariably this lost weight is regained. Reductions in the fat content of the diet with no limitation on the amount of food consumed may lead to a more permanent weight loss than can be achieved through [conventional] dieting.

These, then, are the golden promises of fat counting. Yes, it's an easy system to use – far easier than counting calories. Yes, it's a healthy way to reduce your risk of today's most common afflictions. Yes, it can help you keep (or achieve) a trim figure without a massive dose of willpower – or masochism!

So is it the first entirely painless diet in the world? No. As the prince might have said, all changes to your diet are a bit painful – anyone who says differently is selling something. To begin with, you *will* notice that you're eating lower-fat food, and you *might* miss the taste of double cream on your jam butty! But take heart. The evidence shows that your tastebuds can be retrained in a remarkably short period of time – actually just a week or two – to shun high-fat food in favour of more tempting lower-fat fare. And there's never been a better time to start fat counting – as you'll see in the Counter, the range of tasty low-fat foods has never been wider. We also want to pass on to you some of our favourite hints and tips, which we think will help you especially when you're making the transition to lower-fat eating. You'll find them a little later on in this section. Together, we'll conquer that fat tooth for good!

ALL ABOUT FAT

Many people are confused about fat. Is margarine better than butter? Or should we all be eating olive oil instead? We seem to get one message one week, and the opposite the next. This makes it very difficult for anyone to understand what to do any more. So let's start with some basics . . .

WHAT IS FAT?

Fats are solid at room temperature; oils are liquid. But scientists now use the term 'fat' to include all oils and fats, whether or not they're solid or liquid. So we will, too.

Chemically, fats are made up of three molecules of fatty acids and one of an alcohol called glycerol. What's a fatty acid? We'll come to that in a moment. You'll also hear the word 'triglycerides' used to describe fat – it means three fatty acid molecules ('tri') plus glycerol – 'tri-glyceride'.

WHAT'S A FATTY ACID?

Fatty acids are – not surprisingly – acids that are found in fats. That's why they're called fatty acids! There are four major fatty acids: palmitic, stearic, oleic and linoleic. Remember, each molecule of fat contains three of these four fatty acids. Now it's the *combination* of these acids in the fat molecule that determines whether the fat is saturated, unsaturated or polyunsaturated – words we've all heard a great deal in the past few years. So let's explain them.

All fats consist of long chains of carbon and hydrogen atoms. When all the available sites on the carbon atoms are filled with hydrogen atoms the fat is saturated. If there are unfilled spaces the fat is unsaturated. The more empty spaces, the more unsaturated the fat is.

Saturated

Palmitic fatty acid has sixteen carbon atoms and no unsaturated carbon bonds. So it is called 'saturated'.

Stearic fatty acid has eighteen carbon atoms and no unsaturated carbon bonds. So it is also called 'saturated'.

Saturated fat is known to raise the level of cholesterol in your blood. The more you eat, the higher your cholesterol level, and the greater your chances of suffering a stroke or heart attack. As a guide, saturated fat is usually solid at room temperature – animal fat contains lots of saturated fat: lard, meat, butter and so on. A few plant fats also contain significant amounts – principally coconut and palm oil. Although this book only gives the total amount of fat found in a food, it's important to remember that you should try to shift your diet away from saturated fats in particular. There's no need to add up both total fat and saturated fat – just reducing or eliminating the animal fat will be enough to keep your saturated fat intake low.

Monounsaturated

Oleic fatty acid has eighteen carbon atoms and one unsaturated carbon bond. So it is called 'mono-unsaturated'.

Ongoing research suggests that monounsaturated fat is much healthier than saturated fat. A major source is olive oil. Experiments on humans show that switching to monounsaturated fat from the saturated kind not only can decrease the risk of heart disease, but may also be able to lower your blood pressure. It is also less prone to go rancid than other types of fat, and rancidity is believed by some scientists to promote cancer.

Polyunsaturated

Linoleic fatty acid has eighteen carbon atoms and two unsaturated carbon bonds. So it is called 'poly-unsaturated'.

Early research indicated that polyunsaturated fats lowered total and LDL cholesterol (low-density lipoprotein – the 'bad' form of cholesterol) more than did monounsaturated fats. The latest research, however, finds no difference in their cholesterol-lowering ability. However, the more polyunsaturated an oil is, the more it can be damaged by excess heat, air and light. Most polyunsaturated oils should only be used raw because, once damaged, they form free radicals. Good sources of polyunsaturated fats include sunflower and corn oil. We all need a little linoleic acid in our diets every day because, of the four major fatty acids, this is the only one we can't synthesize for ourselves internally.

TRANS-FATTY ACIDS

By bubbling hydrogen through vegetable oil, food manufacturers can add some hydrogen to the fatty acids, in a process called hydrogenation. The result – partially hydrogenated vegetable oils – can be used in a semi-solid spread like margarine. Because of the particular chemical configuration they take, some of the fatty acids in hydrogenated oils are known as trans-fatty acids, or trans fat. However, there are concerns that trans fat may raise blood cholesterol, just like saturated fat. Scientists don't know for certain at the moment whether trans fat is a health hazard, but the official advice is not to increase trans fat in the diet any further.[11] This is one reason why it makes sense to reduce your total fat consumption, rather than just switching from one type of fat to another.

BUTTER OR MARGARINE?

Fierce advertising wars have tried to persuade us over the years that one or other of these fats is healthier. In fact, some margarines can contain as much total fat as butter, although their saturated fat content would be less. Advertising has also tried to persuade us to increase the amount of polyunsaturated margarine we eat, which, if we didn't reduce our other fat consumption, would simply result in us eating more fat than ever. So what should you do?

In reality, there is probably little practical difference between butter and most of the mass-market margarines. Butter will certainly be higher in saturated fat, but margarines can contain hydrogenated oils (see Trans-fatty Acids above). The process of hydrogenation fills some unsaturated bonds of the fat molecule with hydrogen atoms, making it more similar to a saturated fat. For example, soya bean oil in its natural state is only 15 per cent saturated, but when it's partially hydrogenated it is closer to 25 per cent saturated, similar to vegetable shortenings. We think it prudent to avoid hydrogenated fats where you can.

One alternative is to buy margarines which specifically state that they are *not* hydrogenated; these often contain high-quality oils such as cold-pressed sunflower oil and olive oil. Another is simply to cut down your intake of both types of fat. For example, do you really need to eat quite so much margarine or butter? If you want something to put on your toast in the morning, why not try lightly brushing a little olive oil on to it? Similarly, when cooking, use our low-fat sauté (see page 000).

CHOOSING OILS

There are three methods of extracting oil from plants:

- Cold pressing: this is the traditional hydraulic pressing process, where the temperature is kept low throughout and which therefore preserves temperature-sensitive vitamins. The end product is expensive, mainly because there is a high percentage of waste in the discarded pulp, but the oil is nutritious and tastes and smells good. Buy it – so what if it's more expensive, you consume less! Which is what we all need to do, in any case!

- Screw or expeller: this process involves high-pressure pressing, which generates high temperatures. Vitamins are destroyed during this process, and although it enables more oil to be extracted it is dark, strong smelling and needs further refining and deodorizing.
- Solvent extraction: this is the most common process because it produces the highest yields. The grains or seeds are ground, steamed and then mixed with solvents. The solvents used are either the petroleum-based benzene, hexane or heptane. The mixture is then heated to remove the solvents and washed with caustic soda. This has the effect of destroying its valuable lecithin content. After this it is bleached and filtered, which removes precious minerals as well as any coloured substances. Finally, it is heated to a high temperature to deodorize it. One other aspect of vegetable oils produced by solvent extraction is that they have lost their vitamin E. This vitamin helps stop the oil from going rancid. Rancid oils are dangerous because they provide the raw material for producing free radicals in our bodies. Sometimes chemical retardants are added to stop the oil from turning rancid, but it would seem to be much more sensible to stick with the cold-pressed oils which can keep well, if properly stored, for up to six months.

ESSENTIAL FATTY ACIDS

The two classes of essential fatty acids (EFAs) are named omega-6 and omega-3. They are both necessary for good health because they provide the catalysts for various metabolic functions (e.g. they can activate prostaglandins, or cell regulators). Through a complicated transformation process, essential fatty acids become biologically active and therefore become useful links in many metabolic systems. They are called 'essential' because the body cannot make them and they must be obtained from food sources. Most vegetable oils provide the EFAs to a greater or lesser extent, but they are not significantly present in meat.

- Omega-6 fatty acids (e.g. linoleic acid) are found in vegetable seeds and the oils produced from them. Good sources include oils made from safflower, sunflower, corn, soya, evening primrose, pumpkin, walnut and wheat germ.

- Omega-3 fatty acids (e.g. alpha linoleic acid) are found in deep-water fish oils and are alleged to have near-miraculous properties – hence the popularity of fish oil supplements. They are also, however, found in linseed, rapeseed (canola) and soya bean oil, so vegetarians do not need to consume fish if they wish to increase their omega-3s. The food supplement spirulina also contains both linoleic and linolenic acids. In fact, flaxseed (linseed) oil actually contains about twice as much omega-3 essential fatty acids as is found in fish oil. According to nutritionist Ann Louise Gittleman, co-author of *Beyond Pritikin*, flaxseed oil's greatest attribute is its ranking as the vegetable source highest in omega-3 fatty acids. 'Fish is the best-known source of the omega-3's' she says, 'but flaxseed oil contains 55 to 60 per cent omega-3 – about twice as much as is found in fish oil.'[12] Flaxseed is also rich in omega-6 fatty acids.

HOW TO USE THE COMPLETE FAT COUNTER

Congratulations – this is the easy bit! You'll be pleased to know that there are no rules to memorize, instructions to learn or commands to follow slavishly. It really is easy – *just use the Counter to pick the lowest-fat food you'd like to eat!*

For your convenience, we've divided the foods into natural groupings. Within each group, you'll see that we've used one standard serving size for all the foods in that group. This is because you will want to compare one food with another, and the only fair way to do that is to compare like with like. However, bear in mind that although the serving sizes we've given are fairly common portion sizes, they may well *not* be the pack size of the food as sold. It is possible, therefore, for you to eat a *smaller* portion of a high-fat food and actually consume less than if you ate a larger portion of a lower-fat food! On balance, we think it is more important consistently to choose lower-fat food, rather than try to eat smaller amounts of high-fat food. Eating high-fat food does nothing to retrain your tastebuds, and, as you've seen, high-fat food doesn't make you feel full and doesn't flick your appetite's 'off' switch (satiation and satiety, mentioned earlier).

For example, in the Biscuits section, the standard serving size we've used is 90g/3oz. Biscuits vary quite considerably in their weight. A digestive biscuit weighs about 20g, so a typical serving of digestives would be about four biscuits. Brownies, on the other hand, can weigh 60g or more – so in this case the typical serving would be just one and a half brownies. At the other end of the scale, rice cakes weigh only about 10g, and very thin crackers or wafers can weigh as little as 4 or 5g. But since all the serving sizes in this section have been uniformly standardized, all you really need to do is go for the lowest-fat cookie you can find! If you want to be super-precise about it, get your kitchen scales out, and use the conversion tables in the Appendix to work out quickly how many biscuits you can have with your morning cuppa! Instructions for doing this are also in the Appendix (see page 386).

- Fat grams are calculated for foods 'as sold' unless otherwise specified, e.g. braised, boiled, baked, etc.
- You don't want to be bothered with decimal points, so all calculations have been rounded to the nearest whole number. Because of this, and also because of the natural variation in food and analysis techniques, a few grams difference either way isn't very significant in the Counter. It's much more important to reduce the major sources of fat in your diet, rather than waste time fussing over which prawn will give you 1g of fat rather than 2g!
- A knob of butter is about 5g, as is a teaspoonful of margarine. Since most people are a little bit generous with the yellow stuff, we've set the standard serving size in this section to be 10g.
- The standard serving size for cakes is 90g, which conveniently represents one slice of fruit cake (a slice of sponge cake weighs about half – 50g), a large-ish doughnut or a Danish pastry.
- The standard serving for breakfast cereal is about 30g; for a dense food, such as muesli, it's 40g or more. When you've chosen your cereal, remember to add (low-fat!) milk.
- A small wedge of hard cheese such as cheddar is about 30g (1 oz). Half a cup of grated cheddar (not packed down) is about 60g. Half a cup of cottage cheese (not packed) is about 120g.
- For chips the serving we've given – 60g – is a rather small portion: a normal portion is 75g or more. We've chosen this because if you're fat counting you shouldn't really be eating mammoth portions of fried foods – but as an occasional garnish or side order with a main meal they're OK.

SETTING YOUR FAT COUNTING GOALS

You don't *need* to keep a running count of your fat intake in order to benefit from fat counting. As we've said, the most important thing is to use the Counter consistently to choose the lowest-fat option which pleases you. However, if you want to be sure that you're keeping within acceptable limits – and frankly, most people have no idea how much of their diet consists of fat – then you'll want to plan and record your day's intake from time to time. Use the following guidelines to adjust your day's total fat intake limit, probably starting at about the 50g a day level, and use the planning form below (photocopy it or draw up something similar in your organizer or diary) to check on your day's progress.

Maximum total daily fat intake (g)	% of day's calories (assumes 2,000 cal./day)	Comment
30	13.5	The lowest suggested limit – lower not advised
40	18	Maintains weight loss
50	22.5	Many experts feel this is an appropriate level for adults. Gradual weight loss still occurs[13]
65	30	Government's recommendation for adults
90	40	Average adult intake

FAT COUNTER DAILY PLANNER

Food	Grams of fat

Food	Grams of fat
YOUR DAILY TOTAL:	

ADAPTING THE COUNTER TO YOUR NEEDS – THE FAT CONVERTER

What do you do if you want to eat a different serving size from the one given in the Counter? Easy! Simply turn to the Conversion Tables in the Appendix, and in no time at all you'll be able to calculate the amount of fat in a range of different serving sizes.

Also, you may want to compare foods in the Counter with foods which *aren't* listed (comprehensive as it is!). Again, this is easy. Using the nutritional information box you'll find on all foodstuffs, you can quickly work out how many grams of fat are in any chosen serving size – and use that information to compare foods that aren't listed with foods that are. Here's how you do it. From the food's label, find out how many grams of fat there are in 100g of the food. Go down the left column of the table until you find the closest number – for example, 9g of fat per 100g of product is closest to 10g on the table.

Next, decide for yourself which of the seven serving sizes listed in the table below you want to eat. All you have to do now is look across the table and see where the row and column cross. For example: your chosen food has 10g of fat per 100g product. You want to eat a 6 oz serving. Look across the table until you see when the '10' row crosses the '170g/6oz' column – you can instantly see that the serving contains 17g of fat.

FAT CONVERTER

	FAT IN EACH SERVING SIZE						
Fat per 100g	10g/ 0.3 oz	30g/ 1 oz	60g/ 2 oz	90g/ 3 oz	110g/ 4 oz	170g/ 6 oz	280g/ 10 oz
1	0	0	0	1	1	2	3
5	1	2	4	5	6	9	14
10	1	3	6	9	11	17	28
15	2	5	10	14	17	26	42
20	2	6	12	18	22	34	56
25	3	8	16	23	28	43	70
30	3	9	18	27	33	51	84

Fat per 100g	10g/ 0.3 oz	30g/ 1 oz	60g/ 2 oz	90g/ 3 oz	110g/ 4 oz	170g/ 6 oz	280g/ 10 oz
35	4	11	22	32	39	60	98
40	4	12	24	36	44	68	112
45	5	14	28	41	50	77	126
50	5	15	30	45	55	85	140
55	6	17	34	50	61	94	154
60	6	18	36	54	66	102	168
65	7	20	40	59	72	111	182
70	7	21	42	63	77	119	196
75	8	23	46	68	83	128	210
80	8	24	48	72	88	136	224
85	9	26	52	77	94	145	238
90	9	27	54	81	99	153	252
95	10	29	58	86	105	162	266
100	10	30	60	90	110	170	280

THE QUICK FAT CHECK QUIZ

Fat is one of the most pervasive ingredients in today's food, and especially in fast food. You can quickly become addicted to a high-fat diet, to the extent that you'll search out high-fat foods in preference to more healthy offerings. You can check the degree to which you may be a 'fat addict' by taking the following quiz, devised by clever researchers at Seattle's Fred Hutchinson Cancer Research Center. Here's how to do it:

Think about your diet over the past three months and answer each of the questions by choosing a number from 1 to 4. If a question doesn't apply to your diet, leave it blank (for instance, if you don't eat red meat, don't answer questions 5, 6 and 19 – your score is based on the rest of your diet).

1 Always	2 Often	3 Occasionally	4 Rarely or never

	In the past three months, when you . . .	Circle answer 1 to 4
1	ate fish, did you avoid frying it?	1 2 3 4
2	ate chicken, did you avoid frying it?	1 2 3 4
3	ate chicken, did you remove the skin?	1 2 3 4
4	ate spaghetti or noodles, did you eat it plain or with a meatless tomato sauce?	1 2 3 4
5	ate red meat, did you trim all the visible fat?	1 2 3 4
6	ate ground beef, did you choose extra lean?	1 2 3 4
7	ate bread, rolls or muffins, did you eat them without butter or margarine?	1 2 3 4

8	drank milk, was it skimmed milk instead of whole?	1 2 3 4
9	ate cheese, was it a reduced-fat variety?	1 2 3 4
10	ate a frozen dessert, was it sorbet, ice milk, or non-fat yoghurt or ice cream?	1 2 3 4
11	ate cooked vegetables, did you eat them without adding butter, margarine, salt pork or bacon fat?	1 2 3 4
12	ate cooked vegetables, did you avoid frying them?	1 2 3 4
13	ate potatoes, were they cooked by a method other than frying?	1 2 3 4
14	ate boiled or baked potatoes, did you eat them without butter, margarine or sour cream?	1 2 3 4
15	ate green salads with dressing, did you use a low-fat or non-fat dressing?	1 2 3 4
16	ate dessert, did you eat only fruit?	1 2 3 4
17	ate a snack, was it raw vegetables?	1 2 3 4
18	ate a snack, was it fresh fruit?	1 2 3 4
19	cooked red meat, did you trim all the fat before cooking?	1 2 3 4
20	used mayonnaise or a mayonnaise-type dressing, was it low fat or non fat?	1 2 3 4

Now it's time to learn the truth! First, transfer the numbers above to the score sheet below. Disregard questions that were left blank. You'll see that the items are arranged within five fat-lowering strategies rather than according to their order in the quiz. Add up the total for each strategy, then whip out your calculator and follow the instructions . . .

Strategy 1: How well do you avoid frying your food?

Question 1 ____

Question 2 ____

Question 12 ____

Question 13 ____

Subtotal ____

Now divide by 4 to learn your average: ____

Strategy 2: How well do you avoid fatty meat?

Question 3 ____

Question 5 ____

Question 6 ____

Question 19 ____

Subtotal ____

Now divide by 4 to learn your average: ____

Strategy 3: How well do you avoid fat as flavouring?

Question 4 ____

Question 7 ____

Question 11 ____

Question 14 ____

Subtotal ____

Now divide by 4 to learn your average: ____

Strategy 4: How well do you substitute low-fat or non-fat versions of foods?

Question 8 ____

Question 9 ____

Question 10 ____

Question 15 ____

Question 20 ____

Subtotal ____

Now divide by 5 to learn your average: ____

Strategy 5: How well do you replace fatty foods with fresh produce?

Question 16 ____

Question 17 ____

Question 18 ____

Subtotal ____

Now divide by 3 to learn your average: ____

Now add up all your averages and write the grand total here ____. Lastly, divide this figure by 5 to calculate your overall score, and write it here ____. Then check the chart below:

If your overall average is . . .	Your percentage of fat from calories is . . .	And we say . . .
1.0 to 1.5	under 25%	Excellent!
1.5 to 2	25 to 29%	Better than most people – a few small tweaks and you're there
2 to 2.5	30 to 34%	Some of your eating habits need attention
2.5 to 3	35 to 39%	Most people's score – start fat counting now!
3 to 3.5	40 to 44%	Unhealthy – your diet's putting you at risk
3.5 to 4	45% or more	You're a Fat Addict! But there's hope . . . start re-training your tastebuds to enjoy less fatty food

HINTS & TIPS FOR FAT COUNTERS

Here we want to share with you some of the tips and tricks we've found useful in our journey from high-fat gorging to low-fat living. The first one concerns a cooking technique we use a lot – the sauté.

Sautéing is one of the most enticing cooking methods because, in addition to producing those lovely appetizing aromas, it also creates sensual sizzling sounds that start us all salivating with anticipation! However, even though sautéing adds less fat to food than deep frying or pan frying, it still adds enough fat to put a dent in your fat goal for the day. The problem we faced was how to replace this attractive method of food preparation. It took us a lot of tastings to discover the best alternative, but we think you'll agree that the following technique really does preserve all the lusciousness of a traditional sauté, without the fat! Try it once or twice and you'll quickly get the hang of it – so you can use it in all the recipes you see which use sautéing as part of their technique.

- Dissolve 1–2 teaspoons of yeast extract in 60–90ml (2–3 fl. oz) water and bring this to a quick simmer in a frying pan or saucepan over a medium heat. Add the onions, garlic or whatever is to be sautéed and stir for 2–5 minutes (or the recommended time, if you're following a recipe). The aroma is enticing, the sizzle is there and the flavour and texture created are excellent.

Once you get used to this low-fat sauté, adjust it by trying other liquids, such as tomato sauce, in place of the yeast extract dilution.

FLAVOUR TO THE MAX!

You're not going to succeed in reducing the amount of fat you consume if all you do is pine for the taste and texture that fat gives food. Instead, we strongly urge you to start to experiment with other techniques and dishes. Start cooking with fresh herbs, spices, garlic, onion, scallions, flavoured vinegars and high-quality mustard to boost your food's flavour – there's a whole world of flavour out there, just waiting for you to explore! Try using herbs and spices to add gorgeous new flavour combinations to food while it's being steamed (a very good way to preserve nutrients and protect natural juices). And if you really want to enjoy the taste of oil, buy strongly flavoured ones – such as walnut or basil olive oil – and use a pastry brush to apply it thinly to food after the cooking process. This really makes a little oil go a long way!

Also, actively experiment with new sauces and dressings. Fruits, vegetables and legumes can all be used to create purees, relishes, coulis and compotes. Relishes – known as salsa in Mexico, chutneys in India, and sambals in Indonesia and Malaysia – can be hot or cold, chunky or smooth. Add them to rice, pasta, steamed vegetables or meats.

Herbs

Dried herbs are best added during cooking so that their essential oils distribute through the food. If fresh, they are often best added towards the end of cooking or just before serving so as not to lose the delicate flavours fresh herbs produce. For instance, fresh basil may be added to a tomato sauce almost as a garnish when you serve it, yet it will still impart that exquisite aroma and flavour to the whole dish. Experiment in your own cooking and even try growing a pot of basil, parsley or thyme on your windowsill or terrace so that you have these otherwise expensive condiments to hand.

Spices

Spices are often best added at the sauté stage so that their essential oils distribute well but also 'mature' during the rest of the cooking process. Some spices, such as black pepper, are especially good added at this stage. Others, such as the curry collection of spices, are often best added just before the end of cooking so that their flavours do not deteriorate. Again, experiment – with a light hand to begin with – until you get to know the results you may expect.

Warming Spice and Herb Blend

This is a robust blend which we love – it may be used alone or in combination with Mild and Fresh Spice Blend in savoury dishes. The ingredients may be adjusted to suit your taste.

Makes 140g (5 oz)
Serves 4
Preparation time: 15 minutes

5 spring onions, finely chopped
3 cloves garlic, finely chopped
1 tbsp fresh ginger, grated
1–2 fresh hot chillies, finely chopped
2 tbsp fresh basil, chopped
1 tsp freshly ground cardamom
1 tsp freshly ground black pepper
1/4 tsp ground nutmeg

Blend all the ingredients and add to the dish during sauté stage.

Mild and Fresh Spice Blend
This mixture can be used to flavour soups, stews and other dishes; adjust it to suit your taste.

Makes 3–4 tbsp (1 dish)
Preparation time: 10 minutes

1 tbsp caraway seeds
3 cloves garlic, crushed
2 tsp fresh ginger, grated
1 tsp freshly ground black pepper
1 tsp ground coriander
1/2 tsp salt
1/4 tsp ground allspice

Grind all the ingredients in a mortar and pestle until the caraway seeds are slightly crushed. Stir into the dish, either during the sauté stage or shortly before serving, and adjust to taste.

Garam Masala
This spice mixture may be changed to suit your tastes. Use a mortar and pestle, a hand-turned peppermill or an electric grinder, such as a coffee grinder, to grind your spices. It is best, and noticeably different in flavour and aroma, to use whole spices – grinding them only when you need them. We all have need for little short cuts now and again, however, so simply store any surplus ground spices in a labelled, airtight jar in a dark cupboard.

Makes 2–3 tbsp (1 dish)
Preparation time: 5 minutes

2 tsp freshly ground coriander
1 tsp freshly ground black pepper
1 tsp freshly ground cumin

$^1/_2$ tsp freshly crushed cardamom
$^1/_2$ tsp freshly ground cloves
$^1/_2$ tsp freshly ground cinnamon

If you can, grind these spices individually, measure them, then mix them. Alternatively, if you know that you will cook with garam masala again within the next 7–10 days, prepare a double or triple recipe, blend the spices and simply use half or one-third of it today. Garam masala is traditionally used in Indian cookery.

THE FAT COUNTER'S RECIPE UPGRADE

When you adopt low-fat living, your old and much-loved favourite recipes need not necessarily become things of the past. You can often transform these old favourites into low-fat dishes by performing one or two simple amendments. Here is a ten-point recipe upgrade programme we think will work with most of your past glories:

1 Does it include pastry? Substitute with New Pastry (see page 27).
2 Does it include a sauté stage? Use the low-fat sauté (see page 23).
3 Does it include eggs? If for texture and colour, use mashed tofu and turmeric. If for binding purposes, use a little agar powder, breadcrumbs or a tablespoon of rice flakes. If for raising purposes, use egg substitute plus an agent such as baking powder, as appropriate.
4 Does it include high-fat meat or fish? Try using Quorn instead, which is available from most supermarkets.
5 Does it include fatty meat? Use textured vegetable protein (TVP) or a product such as VegeMince instead. This is now widely available, both from supermarkets and health food shops, and is available in mince and chunk form. It is also available in plain, beef or chicken flavours.
6 Does it include milk? Use skimmed milk or soya milk, or substitute another liquid such as fruit juice or vegetable stock.
7 Does it include cream? Usually low-fat plain yoghurt will do instead.
8 Does it include cheese? First, reduce the amount asked for by three-quarters, adding rice flakes or lentils to make up for the texture and binding qualities. Second, try eliminating it entirely and use tofu or nutritional yeast flakes instead (available from health food shops). Remember that a robust cheese flavour can often be produced by using a small amount of very strongly flavoured cheese, such as parmesan.

9 Does it include sugar? Try using a small amount of blackstrap molasses instead. While sugar doesn't contain any fat, we don't want you to substitute a sweet tooth for a fat one!

10 Is it deep fried? Sorry, find a new favourite! Deep frying, for a fat counter, is the same as deep trouble!

New Pastry
Serves 6
Makes sufficient for one 12-in. flan

285g (10 oz) Grape Nuts breakfast cereal
115g (4 oz) oat flakes
2 tsp spice, to taste (ie. freshly ground black pepper for a savoury flan; spices such as cinnamon, nutmeg, cloves or allspice for a sweet flan)
200ml (7 fl. oz) water

Blend the dry ingredients in a bowl. Add the liquid, stir well and leave to stand for 10 minutes, stirring once or twice in that time. Turn the mixture into a lightly oiled flan or pie dish and press into place. Bake blind for 20 minutes in a hot oven; or fill and bake as per recipe.

This pastry works well for a raised pie: simply reserve about one-quarter of the mixture and press the remaining pastry into place in a deep pie dish. Lightly flour a board and roll the reserved pastry to fit the pie dish. Lift very carefully on to the filled pie, press the edges together and bake.

MAKEOVERS FOR LEFTOVERS

In all probability, when you start fat counting, you'll be buying new types of food. This can become rather expensive if you don't use your leftovers properly! The most vital aspect of using leftovers effectively is using them *as soon as possible*.

Fruit

There are times when you over-purchase and then realize you can't eat it all before it will start to go off, or times when you arrive home with a bag full of squashed peaches because the bus driver braked too hard and sent you and your bag hurtling into another passenger! For those times, and many others you can probably think of, it is useful to have an easy way of salvaging the situation, and the damaged fruit. Here are some tips we have found useful.

Fresh but otherwise unattractive fruit can be mixed with soya or skimmed milk in a blender to make a milkshake. Add a little ground spice of your choice (try coriander, nutmeg or allspice) to give it some zing and serve chilled, if possible. Here is our favourite:

Banana NutriShake

Most milkshakes are far too high in fat. This one *isn't* – because we use soya milk, and because we don't add anything apart from bananas and a hint of spice. Choose a good brand of soya milk, which includes extra calcium and vitamin B12. Try adjusting the flavouring to your taste – we've found ¼–½ tsp of vanilla extract combines gorgeously with the bananas, or alternatively you could try the same amount of rum extract.

Serves 4
Preparation time: 10 minutes

1l (2 pints) soya milk, chilled
4 very ripe bananas, peeled
¼ tsp ground nutmeg

Purée the soya milk, bananas and nutmeg together in a blender. Divide the mixture between four large tumblers (preferably pre-chilled), stir briskly and serve at once.

Fresh peelings, cores and sundry pieces of fruits such as apples, pears, rhubarb, plums and berries can be turned into a yummy Fruit Butter. Wash the fruit and turn it into a large enamel saucepan, with a tiny amount of water added to the mixture. Cover and place over a low flame, stirring frequently, until the mixture is very soft and the separate fruits have lost their shape. Add a little brown sugar and some ground spice to taste, and cook for a further 5 minutes. Then rub the mixture through a sieve, discard the rough pulp and eat the rest today! Children and adults alike are fond of this surprise fruit butter. And it is especially wonderful because it uses whatever you have to hand, so no two batches are alike. We like it warmed, but it is delicious cold as well.

Bruised or dented pears and apples may be peeled and sliced, then left in the fridge to marinate in a mixture of wine or fruit juice and fresh herbs or spices. Try adding a cup of red wine, gently warmed in a pot with whole cloves and a small piece of cinnamon, then poured over the fruit slices. Make sure the fruit is covered, then leave the dish to cool before chilling it in the fridge until you are ready to serve it.

Bananas that look too ripe for your children's tastes can be diced into a tahini and banana sandwich instead – before they ever get to see the brown speckles. Of course, to some people the speckled sort is the perfect sort, but even then it's worth making this sandwich – it's delicious!

Vegetables

You bought the broccoli on Friday and by noon on Saturday you realize it is not going to fit into your ever-changing plans. Do you helplessly watch as it turns yellow? Never! Steam it right now until just tender and still bright green, then remove it from the heat and leave it to cool. An hour later, when you fancy a little snack, arrange the broccoli on a plate with a little low-fat French dressing or some spicy salsa. Instant! Alternatively, you could add the steamed broccoli to a salad for extra depth and robustness. Or again, you could marinate a collection of vegetables. Once you start to think inventively and creatively, there's really no limit to what can be done. Here, for example, is our favourite Vegetable Marinade:

Vegetable Marinade
Serves 8
Preparation time: 45 minutes plus cooling and chilling time

for the marinade:
285ml (10 fl. oz) cider vinegar
juice of 2 lemons
whole cloves
whole peppercorns
1 tsp caraway seed
140ml (5 fl. oz) apple juice
bay leaves
small pieces cinnamon stick
425ml (15 fl. oz) water

the vegetables:
225g (8 oz) carrots, scrubbed and thinly sliced
450g (1 lb) green beans (fresh, tinned or frozen)
1 small red pepper, chopped
1 small green pepper, chopped
1 small onion, thinly sliced
1 medium cauliflower, trimmed and cut into florets
450g (1 lb) broccoli, trimmed and cut into florets

Gently heat all the marinade ingredients together in a large enamel saucepan while you prepare the vegetables. Do not bring to the boil yet. Add all the vegetables to the marinade, stir well and bring to a low boil. Cover the pan and simmer gently for 15 minutes. Remove the pan from the heat and allow the mixture to cool, stirring the mixture once or twice as it does so. Serve immediately or keep chilled in the fridge for 3–4 days. This marinade improves in flavour for being chilled. It is excellent as a lunch, picnic or light evening meal.

More ideas: steam some root vegetables with the broccoli – parsnips, potatoes and carrots, for instance – then mash the whole lot together with some skimmed milk and pepper for an exquisite, colourful mash that your children, especially, will love.

Take all the clean peelings, tops and tails, outer leaves and unpresentable veg and put them into a giant pot along with a handful each of barley, oats and fresh herb. Bring to the boil, then cover and simmer gently for about an hour. Leave to cool, then strain this broth and measure into soup-sized portions. Keep one in the fridge and freeze the rest for your later convenience. Here is our favourite recipe for Vegetable Stock:

Vegetable Stock
Serves 8
Makes approximately 2l (4 pints)
Preparation time: 2 hours plus cooling time

55g (2 oz) barley or scotch broth mixture
3l (6 pints) water
450–675g (1–1½ lbs) root vegetables or parts (i.e. peels, tops and tails, chunks), washed
225–450g (½–1 lb) greens or outside leaves (i.e. unsightly leaves, green parts of cauliflower, leaves of celery, coarse lettuce leaves, cabbage hearts), washed
2 large onions, coarsely chopped and including the skins
1 bulb garlic, coarsely chopped and including the skins
bay leaf
any chopped fresh herb or bouquet garni
1 tsp whole peppercorns
1 tsp whole cloves
1 piece of cinnamon stick

Measure the barley and water into a large saucepan and place over a high heat. Bring the mixture to a boil, stirring frequently. Add the remaining ingredients and stir well. Cover the pan, reduce the heat and leave to simmer for 45–60 minutes, stirring just occasionally and skimming any froth from the surface.

Leave the mixture to cool, then strain the stock through a colander or sieve and discard the vegetable matter. Use the stock at once or measure it into portions for freezing and later use.

Certain classic or traditional dishes are actually based on leftovers, so don't feel shy about conserving your scraps. Here are two you are sure to recognize:

Bubble 'n' Squeak
This consists of pre-cooked vegetables that are roughly chopped the next morning and low-fat sautéed (see page 23) together over a medium heat. We like ours with freshly ground black pepper and tomato ketchup.

Vegetable Patties
Pre-cooked vegetables can be finely chopped and mixed with spices, rolled oats or cooked rice and a little water. Once they are shaped into patties, they can be grilled or low-fat sautéed and served as part of a warming breakfast or lunch.

Even more ideas: add vegetable pieces to a sauce before you purée it to improve its texture and add depth to its flavour.

Lightly steam the vegetable pieces, then douse them in a spicy tomato sauce, cover the dish and leave to cool. Suddenly, you have a scrumptious vegetable marinade that can be served as a side dish, chutney or dressing for a main dish.

Cereals

Leftover rice, millet, couscous and pasta may all be put to excellent use, providing you use them quickly. Here are some inspirations for you:

Most salads are enhanced when a *little* of any of these cereal products is tossed in with the vegetable mixture.

A bean or vegetable soup is also enhanced when small amounts of rice or pasta are stirred in towards the end of cooking.

Rice, millet and couscous – as well as odds and ends of rolled oats, rice flakes or puffed-grain breakfast cereals – are easily converted into a useful Grain Loaf. Simply stir them together with a packaged vegetable sausage or burger dry mix, some strong spices and dried herbs, and a blend of water and tomato paste until the mixture has a firm but moist texture. Press it into a loaf tin and bake in a hot oven for about 30 minutes.

Now pour a little tomato sauce over the loaf and bake for a further 10 minutes. Remove from the oven, leave to cool in the pan for about 5 minutes, then turn it on to a plate to slice and serve. This is delicious hot, with rice, a collection of steamed or baked vegetables and a light sauce. We thinly slice a cooled loaf to make sandwiches or fill pitta breads.

Speaking of breads – if you make your own bread, you can add a little cooked rice or millet to the dough. Work it in well, so that the grains are held by the dough, then bake in the usual way.

Nuts and Beans

Yes! Even these can be used. Here are a few ideas:

Dried beans often lurk in the cupboard in cellophane bags, each one containing precisely twelve beans. What good is that? Get them all out, pour them together into a bowl and cover them in water. Later today or tomorrow, drain them, rinse them and add them to a soup or stew. Or if you have a pressure cooker, cook them, cool them and add them to a salad.

Cooked beans can also be mashed together with spices and sautéed onions and garlic to make a sandwich spread or dip. Here is a recipe that is wonderfully close to refried beans, of Mexican cuisine fame:

Red Bean Paste
Serves 4
Preparation time: 40 minutes plus cooling and chilling time

115g (4 oz) dried kidney or pinto beans, washed and soaked overnight
1 tsp yeast extract
3 tbsp water
5 cloves garlic, finely chopped
2 small onions, finely chopped
1 tsp chilli powder
1 tbsp soy sauce
2 tbsp cider vinegar
285–425ml (10–15 fl. oz) vegetable stock or water

Drain and rinse the beans and pressure cook them for 25 minutes.

Drain them immediately. Dissolve the yeast extract in the water, pour into a large pan and place over a medium to high flame. When the mixture begins to bubble, add the garlic and onion and sauté for 2 mintues, stirring often. Add the chilli powder and stir for a further 1 minute.

Add the soy sauce, vinegar and the cooked beans to the sauté and mash them slightly as you gradually add the stock. Aim for a thick, rough paste. Serve hot or allow to cool and chill in its serving dish. Useful as a dip, pâté or sandwich spread.

Another all-time favourite of ours, which tastes as if it's very high in fat but in fact has none, is:

Bean Pâté
Serves 8
Preparation time: 45 minutes plus cooling and chilling time

225g (8 oz) dried red lentils, washed and drained
1 tsp yeast extract
570ml (1 pint) water
1 tsp turmeric
85g (3 oz) rice flakes
1 tsp freshly ground black pepper or ½–1 tsp chilli powder
2 tsp ground ginger

Turn the lentils into a saucepan. Dissolve the yeast extract in the water, pour over the lentils, place on a medium to high flame and bring to a soft boil. Cover the pan, reduce the heat and simmer for 30 minutes, stirring occasionally.

Add the turmeric, rice flakes, pepper and ginger and cook over a low flame for a further 5–10 minutes. Remove from the heat and spoon into a serving dish. Press the paté well down into the dish. Allow the paté to cool, then cover and chill before serving. This looks wonderful garnished with parsley or lemon slices.

This recipe can be altered to make use of pre-cooked beans of any sort. Simply cook the beans in with the remaining ingredients and press into a ramekin or pudding bowl before leaving to cool.

Shelled nuts should be used as soon as possible. Any leftovers may be ground and added to bread, cake or biscuit recipes. Alternatively, they may be stirred together with leftover grains, vegetables and beans to make burgers or a loaf. Add a little tomato sauce to the mix then sauté, grill or bake in the usual way.

Pre-cooked beans may be mixed together and cooked in a marinade. Kept chilled, this marinade can provide snacks and lunches for three to five days.

Five-bean Salad
Serves 12
Preparation time: 30 minutes plus cooling and chilling time

450g (1 lb) cooked kidney beans
450g (1 lb) cooked green beans
450g (1 lb) cooked chickpeas
450g (1 lb) cooked butter beans
450g (1 lb) cooked borlotti or pinto beans
5 spring onions, thinly sliced
1 eating apple, grated
5 cloves garlic, crushed
1 tbsp fresh ginger, grated
1 tsp brown sugar
2 tsp freshly ground black pepper
5 whole cloves
1 piece stick cinnamon
285ml (10 fl. oz) cider vinegar
juice of 4 lemons

Measure all the ingredients, except the lemon juice, into a glass or enamel saucepan and stir well. Place the pan over a medium heat, cover and bring to a slow boil. Reduce the heat and simmer, covered, for 10 minutes.

Leave the pan covered and remove from the heat. Allow to cool then stir in the lemon juice and turn the salad into a separate dish to chill in the refrigerator. This salad improves as it cools and may be kept, chilled, for two to three days.

Grind leftover nuts and mix some ground spices in with them. Freshly ground black pepper and cumin seed make a wonderful savoury mixture; ground allspice and coriander make a delectable sweet mixture. Sprinkle the ground nuts over a salad or bowl of fresh fruit, or lightly roast the mixture in a frying pan (without oil) for 3–4 minutes over a medium flame. Serve the same day on to lightly steamed greens or freshly steamed rice or couscous.

ESCAPING FROM THE KITCHEN

Even the most ardent home cook wants to escape from the kitchen at some time or other and sit down to a meal cooked by someone else. And for other people whose jobs involve an element of business entertainment, restaurant dining can become an occupational hazard. It can sometimes be difficult to find low-fat food in some restaurants, so here are some valuable tips which work for us and which will help you get maximum pleasure from your meal out.

Know the No-No's

These are some foods and dishes that seem, on first glance at the menu, to be healthy, but are secretly a storehouse for fat. Here's our shortlist:

- Potato: sautéed potatoes and potato salads are probably best avoided, as are mashed potatoes, which are made with lots of milk and butter. Baked potato is a good food that is often spoiled by being doused in butter. Order baked or steamed potatoes without the fat.
- Ratatouille: this delicious dish is made with large quantities of olive oil. Perhaps there is a vegetable soup or pickle on the menu instead?
- Risotto: a wonderful rice dish but, again, made with large quantities of olive oil. How about a simple mixture of steamed rice and wild rice instead?
- Pastries: sorry, most are rather high in fat. Would a toasted crumpet or bagel do instead?
- Nuts: watch for these high-fat foods in muesli, nut butters, savoury snack mixes, snack bars and biscuits.
- Cheese: for some reason, professional chefs find it hard to be sparing when cooking with cheese, so try not to order a dish that contains it. Pizza parlours usually have one or two options already on the menu – we've always enjoyed tomato sauce with olive and fresh basil topping – and no cheese. If you don't see it on the menu, ask for it.
- Aubergine: this food is a sponge for oils and fats. Try to avoid it.
- Soufflé: somehow this dish is always a combination of milk, cheese, cream and eggs. Whoa!
- Cream of . . .: anything that says "cream of" is a bit of a no-no, although some manufacturers now produce excellent low-fat "cream-of" soups (see the Counter on page 341).

- Sauces and dressings: these must be taken carefully and with a light hand. Many low-fat dressings and sauces are available, so ask for them. Otherwise, a squeeze of fresh lemon will enhance most salads and steamed vegetables, and *a few drops* of a sesame or walnut oil will give deep flavour. Low-fat or no-fat dressings are widely available in supermarkets (see the Counter on page 184) – so they should be available in restaurants, too. Again, ask!

Plan ahead

If you can, learn the type of restaurant and style of food it serves before you go out. This isn't always possible and, in any case, you should think ahead and plan what you will order if it is on the menu. Here are some dishes we suggest you bear in mind as likely to be low or moderate in fat:

Starters
In-season melon or fresh mango
Any fruit juice
Gazpacho or Minestrone soup
Steamed asparagus spears with low-fat dressing
Mixed salad (no fish, meat or cheese) with low-fat dressing
Note: By all means, have a starter. It is easy to find one with little or no fat and you'll feel better for it.

Main course
Couscous with chickpea and vegetable stew
Pasta with simple tomato sauce, no cheese
Sweet pepper stuffed with rice, vegetable and tomato mixture, but no cheese
Steamed rice and dhal with spinach and potato (*Note*: this meal will vary according to the chef; go for one not floating in ghee)
Pizza with tomato sauce, olives and fresh basil, but no cheese

Desserts
Fruit salad, from fresh or dried fruits
Iced yoghurt
Sorbet
Baked apple
Fresh figs, lychees, mango, melon, strawberries, raspberries or poached pears
Note: No cream or ice cream, please!

Most restaurants are aware of a growing interest in healthy eating and will happily cater for your needs. We happen to think, however, that going with plenty of information and ideas like those we have just suggested will make your meal out a more satisfying and pleasant one.

Bon appétit!

Beans & Lentils

NOTE: The standard serving size in this section is 170g/6oz. If you wish to consume more or less than this amount (e.g. if you are going to consume a pack of food whose weight differs from the standard serving size) use the conversion tables on page 386 to calculate the new amount of fat in the food.

Adzuki Beans, boiled *serving 170g/6oz*	0
Baked Beans (Holland & Barrett) *serving 170g/6oz*	0
Baked Beans (Marks & Spencer) *serving 170g/6oz*	1
Baked Beans (Waitrose) *serving 170g/6oz*	1
Baked Beans with Bacon (Heinz) *serving 170g/6oz*	3
Baked Beans Brunch (Tesco) *serving 170g/6 oz*	1
Baked Beans & Burgers in Tomato Sauce (Tesco) *serving 170g/60z*	3
Baked Beans with Chicken Nuggets (Heinz) *serving 170g/6oz*	5
Baked Beans, Curried (Tesco) *serving 170g/60z*	1
Baked Beans, Healthy Balance, in Tomato Sauce (Heinz) *serving 170g/6oz*	0
Baked Beans, Healthy Balance, & Vegetable Sausages (Heinz) *serving 170g/6oz*	6
Baked Beans, Healthy Choice, Lower in Sugar & Salt (Asda) *serving 170g/6oz*	1
Baked Beans, Healthy Eating, No Saccharin (Tesco) *serving 170g/6oz*	1
Baked Beans, Healthy Selection, in Tomato Sauce (Somerfield) *serving 170g/6oz*	0
Baked Beans & Hot Dogs (Tesco) *serving 170g/6oz*	7
Baked Beans Hot Pot (Tesco) *serving 170g/6oz*	5
Baked Beans & Jumbo Sausages (Tesco) *serving 170g/6oz*	8
Baked Beans with Pepperoni (Heinz) *serving 170g/6oz*	3
Baked Beans with Pork Sausages (Heinz) *serving 170g/6oz*	7
Baked Beans, Reduced Sugar & Salt (Waitrose) *serving 170g/6oz*	0
Baked Beans & Sausages in Tomato Sauce (Somerfield) *serving 170g/6oz*	3
Baked Beans in Tomato Sauce *serving 170g/6oz*	1
Baked Beans in Tomato Sauce (Heinz) *serving 170g/6oz*	0
Baked Beans in Tomato Sauce (Somerfield) *serving 170g/6oz*	1
Baked Beans in Tomato Sauce (Tesco) *serving 170g/6oz*	1

Baked Beans in Tomato Sauce, Basics (Somerfield) *serving 170g/6oz* 0
Baked Beans in Tomato Sauce with Burgers *serving 170g/6oz* 5
Baked Beans in Tomato Sauce, Home Made *serving 170g/6oz* 9
Baked Beans in Tomato Sauce, No Added Sugar (Heinz Weight Watchers) *serving 170g/6oz* 0
Baked Beans in Tomato Sauce with Pork Sausages *serving 170g/6oz* 8
Baked Beans in Tomato Sauce, Reduced Sugar *serving 170g/6oz* 1
Baked Beans with Vegetable Sausages (Heinz) *serving 170g/6oz* 6
Balor Beans, raw or tinned *serving 170g/6oz* 0
Barbecue Beans (Heinz) *serving 170g/6oz* 1
Beans & Bites (Holland & Barrett) *serving 170g/6oz* 4
Beans with 4 Pork Sausages (Tesco) *serving 170g/6oz* 5
Beans with 8 Pork Sausages (Tesco) *serving 170g/6oz* 5
Beansprouts, Mung, Boiled *serving 170g/6oz* 1
Beansprouts, Mung, Raw *serving 170g/6oz* 1
Beansprouts, Mung, Stir Fried in Blended Oil *serving 170g/6oz* 10
Beansprouts, Mung, Tinned *serving 170g/6oz* 0
Black Bean Stir Fry (Marks & Spencer) *serving 170g/6oz* 4
Black Beans, Boiled *serving 170g/6oz* 1
Black Eye Beans, Boiled *serving 170g/6oz* 1
Black Gram Bengali Curry *serving 170g/6oz* 5
Black Gram Gujerati Curry *serving 170g/6oz* 11
Broad Beans, Boiled *serving 170g/6oz* 1
Broad Beans, Raw *serving 170g/6oz* 2
Burrito, Beans, Cheese & Beef *serving 170g/6oz* 11
Butter Beans, Boiled or Tinned *serving 170g/6oz* 1
Butter Beans, Tinned *serving 170g/6oz* 0
Cannellini Beans, Canned *serving 170g/6oz* 1
Chick Pea Curry *serving 170g/6oz* 13
Chick Pea Dahl *serving 170g/6oz* 10
Chick Pea Dahl & Spinach with Butter *serving 170g/6oz* 20
Chick Pea & Potato Curry *serving 170g/6oz* 9
Chick Pea Rissoles, Fried in Sunflower Oil *serving 170g/6oz* 29
Chick Pea & Tomato Gujerati Curry *serving 170g/6oz* 25
Chick Pea & Tomato Punjabi Curry *serving 170g/6oz* 7
Chick Peas, Boiled or Tinned *serving 170g/6oz* 4
Chilli Beans, Tinned *serving 170g/6oz* 1

Cluster Beans, Raw *serving 170g/6oz* 0
Cowpeas, Boiled or Tinned *serving 170g/6oz* 1
Cranberry (Roman) Beans, Tinned *serving 170g/6oz* 0
Curried Beans (Heinz) *serving 170g/6oz* 3
Flageolet Beans (Waitrose) *serving 170g/6oz* 1
French Beans: *see* Green Beans
Garbanzo Beans: *see* Chick Peas
Gram Black Chilki Urad Dahl, Boiled *serving 170g/6oz* 1
Green Beans/French Beans, Boiled *serving 170g/6oz* 1
Green Beans/French Beans, Raw *serving 170g/6oz* 1
Haricot Beans, Boiled *serving 170g/6oz* 1
Kidney Bean Gujerati Curry *serving 170g/6oz* 10
Kidney Bean & Mung Bean Curry *serving 170g/6oz* 21
Kidney Bean Punjabi Curry *serving 170g/6oz* 10
Kidney Beans, Boiled *serving 170g/6oz* 1
Kidney Beans, Tinned *serving 170g/6oz* 1
Lentil Curry, Red/Masoor Dahl *serving 170g/6oz* 11
Lentil Curry, Red/Masoor Dahl, Punjabi *serving 170g/6oz* 8
Lentil Curry Red/Masoor Dahl & Tomato *serving 170g/6oz* 8
Lentil Curry, Red/Masoor Dahl & Tomato with Vegetable Oil
serving 170g/6oz 10
Lentil Soups: *see under* Soups
Lentils, Green & Brown, Boiled *serving 170g/6oz* 1
Lentils, Red, in Tomato Sauce, Timmed *serving 170g/6oz* 0
Lentils, Sprouted, Raw *serving 170g/6oz* 1
Lentils, Sprouted, Stir Fried *serving 170g/6oz* 1
Lilva Beans, Tinned *serving 170g/6oz* 1
Lima Beans, Boiled *serving 170g/6oz* 1
Mixed Bean Salad (Tesco) *serving 170g/6oz* 2
Mixed Beans in Curry Sauce (Tesco) *serving 170g/6oz* 7
Mixed Beans in Curry Sauce (Waitrose) *serving 170g/6oz* 8
Mixed Beans in Sauce (Waitrose) *serving 170g/6oz* 1
Mixed Beans in a Spicy Tomato Sauce (Tesco) *serving 170g/6oz* 1
Mixed Beans in Taco Sauce (Tesco) *serving 170g/6oz* 1
Mixed Beans in Tomato Sauce (Tesco) *serving 170g/6oz* 0
Mixed Chilli Beans (Heinz) *serving 170g/6oz* 1
Mothbeans, Boiled *serving 170g/6oz* 1

Mung Bean Dahl, Bengali *serving 170g/6oz*	6
Mung Bean Dahl, Punjabi *serving 170g/6oz*	5
Mung Bean Dahl & Spinach *serving 170g/6oz*	5
Mung Bean Dahl & Tomato *serving 170g/6oz*	6
Mung Bean Gujerati Curry *serving 170g/6oz*	10
Mung Bean Punjabi Curry *serving 170g/6oz*	5
Mung Bean Seeds, Boiled *serving 170g/6oz*	1
Mung Beansprouts *see* Beansprouts, Mung	
Natto *serving 170g/6oz*	19
Navy Beans, Boiled *serving 170g/6oz*	1
Navy Beans, Tinned *serving 170g/6oz*	1
Navy Beans, Sprouted, Boiled *serving 170g/6oz*	1
Navy Beans, Sprouted, Raw *serving 170g/6oz*	1
Papri Beans, Tinned *serving 170g/6oz*	0
Pea Dishes: *see under* Vegetables & Vegetable Dishes	
Pea Soups: *see under* Soups	
Peas: *see under* Vegetables & Vegetable Dishes	
Pinto Beans, Boiled, *serving 170g/6oz*	1
Pinto Beans, Refried, *serving 170g/6oz*	2
Pinto Beans, Sprouted, boiled *serving 170g/6oz*	1
Pinto Beans, Sprouted, raw *serving 170g/6oz*	2
Pinto Beans, Tinned *serving 170g/6oz*	1
Refried Beans, Tinned *serving 170g/6oz*	2
Runner Beans, Boiled *serving 170g/6oz*	1
Runner Beans, Raw *serving 170g/6oz*	1
Shellie Beans, Tinned *serving 170g/6oz*	0
Snap Beans, Tinned *serving 170g/6oz*	0
Soya Beans, Boiled *serving 170g/6oz*	12
Soya Beans, Green, Boiled *serving 170g/6oz*	11
Soya Beans, Roasted and Toasted *serving 170g/6oz*	41
Soya Beans, Sprouted, Raw *serving 170g/6oz*	11
Soya Beans, Sprouted, Steamed *serving 170g/6oz*	8
Soya Beans, Sprouted, Stir Fried *serving 170g/6oz*	12
Soya Chunks, Flavoured (Holland & Barrett) *serving 170g/6oz*	1
Soya Chunks, Unflavoured (Holland & Barrett) *serving 170g/6oz*	1
Soya Mince, Flavoured (Holland & Barrett) *serving 170g/6oz*	1
Soya Mince, Unflavoured (Holland & Barrett) *serving 170g/6oz*	1

Soya Mince Granules *serving 170g/6oz*	9
Sword Beans, Raw *serving 170g/6oz*	1
Tempeh *serving 170g/6oz*	11
Tofu, Dried Frozen (Koyadofu) *serving 170g/6oz*	52
Tofu, Fried *serving 170g/6oz*	34
Tofu Fujuk *serving 170g/6oz*	28
Tofu, Marinated (Cauldron Foods) *serving 170g/6oz*	6
Tofu, Naturally Smoked (Cauldron Foods) *serving 170g/6oz*	10
Tofu Okara, *serving 170g/6oz*	3
Tofu Original Soya Bean Curd (Cauldron Foods) *serving 170g/6oz*	5
Tofu, Raw, Firm *serving 170g/6oz*	15
Tofu, Raw, Regular *serving 170g/6oz*	8
Tofu, Salted & Fermented (Fuyu) *serving 170g/6oz*	14
Tofu Soya Bean, Steamed *serving 170g/6oz*	7
Tofu Soya Bean, Steamed Fried *serving 170g/6oz*	30
Tuscan Beans, Vegetable Meal (Marks & Spencer) *serving 170g/6oz*	7
White Beans, Boiled *serving 170g/6oz*	1
White Beans, Tinned *serving 170g/6oz*	0
Winged Beans, Boiled *serving 170g/6oz*	10
Yambean, Boiled *serving 170g/6oz*	0
Yardlong Beans, Boiled *serving 170g/6oz*	0
Yellow Beans, Boiled *serving 170g/6oz*	2

BEEF & VEAL

NOTE: The standard serving size for beef in this section is 280g/10oz, and for veal 110g/4oz. If you need to compare the fat content of different cuts of beef and veal, use the conversion tables on page 386. Also use the conversion tables if you wish to consume more or less than these amounts (e.g. if you are going to consume a pack of food whose weight differs from the standard serving size) to calculate the new amount of fat in the food.

Aberdeen Angus Beef (Waitrose) *serving 280g/10oz*	31
Angus Beef Joint, Prepared, Fresh (Marks & Spencer) *serving 280g/10oz*	13

Beef in Blackbean Sauce, Frozen, Microwave (Iceland) *serving 280g/10oz* 7
Beef Bourguignon, Chilled Ready Meal (Tesco) *serving 280g/10oz* 7
Beef Burgundy (Waitrose) *serving 280g/10oz* 15
Beef Casserole, Individual, Main Meal (Marks & Spencer) *serving 280g/10oz* 17
Beef Casserole, Quick Cook, Frozen, Boiled (Iceland) *serving 280g/10oz* 26
Beef Cubes, Quick Cook, Frozen, Boiled (Iceland) *serving 280g/10oz* 45
Beef Curry *serving 280g/10oz* 18
Beef Curry (Marks & Spencer) *serving 280g/10oz* 16
Beef Curry Dinner Supreme (Findus) *serving 280g/10oz* 13
Beef Curry, Fresh, Microwaved (Iceland) *serving 280g/10oz* 13
Beef Curry & Rice, Frozen, Pan Boil (Iceland) *serving 280g/10oz* 17
Beef Curry with Rice (Birds Eye) *serving 280g/10oz* 6
Beef Curry with Rice, Frozen (Asda) *serving 280g/10oz* 10
Beef Curry with Rice, Frozen Ready Meal (Safeway) *serving 280g/10oz* 8
Beef Curry with Rice, Lunch Bowl Ready Meal (Heinz) *serving 280g/10oz* 7
Beef Goulash, Ready Meal, Tinned (Tesco) *serving 280g/10oz* 6
Beef Goulash (Marks & Spencer) *serving 280g/10oz* 15
Beef in Gravy, Cooked, Sliced, Frozen (Asda) *serving 280g/10oz* 7
Beef in Gravy, Sliced, Frozen (Iceland) *serving 280g/10oz* 7
Beef in Gravy, Slices (Princes) *serving 280g/10oz* 8
Beef Hot Pot (Birds Eye) *serving 280g/10oz* 14
Beef Jerky, Chopped and Formed *serving 280g/10oz* 36
Beef Joint, Prepared, Fresh (Marks & Spencer) *serving 280g/10oz* 13
Beef Kebabs in a Red Wine Marinade, Chilled (Tesco) *serving 280g/10oz* 7
Beef Madras, Canned Ready Meal (Tesco) *serving 280g/10oz* 17
Beef Mince, Mexican (Waitrose) *serving 280g/10oz* 47
Beef in Peppercorn Sauce, Main Meal (Marks & Spencer) *serving 280g/10oz* 31
Beef Ragu (Waitrose) *serving 280g/10oz* 15
Beef Roast, Seasoned (Waitrose) *serving 280g/10oz* 25

Beef, Sliced, Quick Cook (Waitrose) *serving 280g/10oz* 30
Beef Stew: *see under* Soups
Beef Stir Fry, Quick Cook (Waitrose) *serving 280g/10oz* 30
Beef Stroganoff *serving 280g/10oz* 32
Beef Stroganoff (Crosse & Blackwell) *serving 280g/10oz* 32
Beef Stroganoff, Chilled Ready Meal (Tesco) *serving 280g/10oz* 27
Beef Stroganoff (Waitrose) *serving 280g/10oz* 18
Beef & Vegetable Casserole (Waitrose) *serving 280g/10oz* 11
Beef Wellington (Waitrose) *serving 280g/10oz* 45
Bologna: *see under* Sausages
Braised Steak, Low-Fat Main Meal (Marks & Spencer) *serving 280g/10oz* 12
Braising, Aberdeen Angus (Waitrose) *serving 280g/10oz* 30
Braising Beef Steak (Waitrose) *serving 280g/10oz* 30
Braising Steak, Braised Lean *serving 280g/10oz* 27
Braising Steak, Braised Lean & Fat *serving 280g/10oz* 36
Braising Steak, Sliced, Extra Lean, Chilled (Tesco) *serving 280g/10oz* 4
Brisket, Aberdeen Angus (Waitrose) *serving 280g/10oz* 57
Brisket, Braised Lean *serving 280g/10oz* 31
Brisket, Braised Lean & Fat *serving 280g/10oz* 49
Brisket of Beef, Traditional, Delicatessen (Marks & Spencer) *serving 280g/10oz* 9
Brisket Roast, British (Waitrose) *serving 280g/10oz* 57
Burrito with Beans & Meat *serving 280g/10oz* 22
Burrito with Beef *serving 280g/10oz* 26
Burrito, Beef, Cheese & Chilli Peppers *serving 280g/10oz* 23
Burrito Beef & Chilli Peppers *serving 280g/10oz* 23
Casserole Beef, Select Choice (Somerfield) *serving 280g/10oz* 31
Casserole Steak, Scotch (Waitrose) *serving 280g/10oz* 16
Casserole Steak, Sliced (Waitrose) *serving 280g/10oz* 13
Cheeseburger, Frozen, Microwaveable (Tesco) *serving 280g/10oz* 27
Chilli with Beans, Tinned *serving 280g/10oz* 15
Chilli Con Carne *serving 280g/10oz* 24
Chilli Con Carne (Marks & Spencer) *serving 280g/10oz* 7
Chilli Con Carne (Somerfield) *serving 280g/10oz* 5
Chilli Con Carne, Chilled Ready Meal (Safeway) *serving 280g/10oz* 12

Chilli Con Carne, Chilled Ready Meal (Tesco) *serving 280g/10oz* 14
Chilli Con Carne, Frozen (Asda) *serving 280g/10oz* 15
Chilli Con Carne (Hot), Tinned (Tesco) *serving 280g/10oz* 13
Chilli Con Carne (Mild) Ready Meal, Tinned (Tesco) *serving 280g/10oz* 14
Chilli Con Carne, Microwave Ready Meal (Safeway) *serving 280g/10oz* 12
Chilli Con Carne with Rice (Birds Eye) *serving 280g/10oz* 6
Chilli Con Carne with Rice, Chilled Ready Meal (Safeway) *serving 280g/10oz* 22
Chilli Con Carne with Rice, Lunch Bowl Ready Meal (Heinz) *serving 280g/10oz* 5
Chilli Con Carne with Rice, Microwave Ready Meal (Safeway) *serving 280g/10oz* 10
Chilli, Mexican with Deep Fried Potato Wedges, Frozen Ready Meal (Heinz Weight Watchers) *serving 280g/10oz* 8
Chilli & Rice, Main Meal (Marks & Spencer) *serving 280g/10oz* 12
Chimichanga with Beef *serving 280g/10oz* 32
Chimichanga, Beef & Cheese *serving 280g/10oz* 36
Chimichanga, Beef, Cheese & Red Chilli Peppers *serving 280g/10oz* 27
Chimichanga, Beef & Red Chilli Peppers *serving 280g/10oz* 28
Chow Mein *serving 280g/10oz* 17
Chuck, Aberdeen Angus (Waitrose) *serving 280g/10oz* 30
Chunky Beef Bourguignon, Canned Ready Meal (Tesco) *serving 280g/10oz* 8
Corned Beef (Libby's) *serving 280g/10oz* 10
Corned Beef (Princes) *serving 280g/10oz* 36
Corned Beef (Somerfield) *serving 280g/10oz* 34
Corned Beef (Waitrose) *serving 280g/10oz* 39
Corned Beef, Brazilian (Marks & Spencer) *serving 280g/10oz* 31
Corned Beef Crispbreaks (Somerfield) *serving 280g/10oz* 34
Corned Beef, Ease Rosti (Tesco) *serving 280g/10oz* 15
Corned Beef & English Mustard (Princes) *serving 280g/10oz* 31
Corned Beef Hash, Family, Main Meal (Marks & Spencer) *serving 280g/10oz* 18
Corned Beef Hash, Findus Dinner Supreme *serving 280g/10oz* 13
Corned Beef Hash, Frozen Ready Meal (Tesco) *serving 280g/10oz* 10

Corned Beef Hash (Somerfield) *serving 280g/10oz*	13
Corned Beef, Lean (Princes) *serving 280g/10oz*	28
Corned Beef Loaf *serving 280g/10oz*	17
Corned Beef & Onion (Princes) *serving 280g/10oz*	36
Corned Beef, Peppered (Princes) *serving 280g/10oz*	36
Corned Beef, Premium (Princes) *serving 280g/10oz*	35
Corned Beef, Premium (Waitrose) *serving 280g/10oz*	34
Corned Beef, Spicy (Princes) *serving 280g/10oz*	28
Corned Beef & Sweet Pickle (Princes) *serving 280g/10oz*	35
Cubed Casserole Steak, Extra Lean, Chilled (Tesco) *serving 280g/10oz*	4
Cured Beef (Waitrose) *serving 280g/10oz*	24
Diced Beef, Frozen, Stewed (Iceland) *serving 280g/10oz*	30
Diced Beef Steak (Waitrose) *serving 280g/10oz*	13
Diced Braising Steak, Scotch (Waitrose) *serving 280g/10oz*	30
Diced Steak & Kidney (Waitrose) *serving 280g/10oz*	12
Enchilada, Cheese & Beef *serving 280g/10oz*	26
Enchirito, Cheese, Beef & Beans *serving 280g/10oz*	23
Escalopes, Chilli & Lime, Delicatessen (Marks & Spencer) *serving 280g/10oz*	8
Fillet, Aberdeen Angus (Waitrose) *serving 280g/10oz*	13
Fillet Steak, Fried Lean *serving 280g/10oz*	22
Fillet Steak, Fried Lean & Fat *serving 280g/10oz*	25
Fillet Steak, Grilled Lean *serving 280g/10oz*	22
Fillet Steak, Grilled Lean & Fat *serving 280g/10oz*	27
Fillet Steak, Select Choice (Somerfield) *serving 280g/10oz*	20
Flank, Pot Roasted Lean *serving 280g/10oz*	32
Flank, Pot Roasted Lean & Fat *serving 280g/10oz*	57
Frying Steaks, Quick Grill, Fresh (Iceland) *serving 280g/10oz*	31
Gravy, tinned *serving 280g/10oz*	7
Grillsteaks (Birds Eye) *serving 280g/10oz*	74
Grillsteaks (Somerfield) *serving 280g/10oz*	66
Grillsteaks, Chargrilled Flavour (Somerfield) *serving 280g/10oz*	50
Grillsteak, Aberdeen Angus, Main Meal (Marks & Spencer) *serving 280g/10oz*	54
Grillsteaks, Chilled (Tesco) *serving 280g/10oz*	45
Grillsteaks, Frozen (Tesco) *serving 280g/10oz*	67
Ground Beef (Waitrose) *serving 280g/10oz*	28

Ground Beef, Extra Lean (Waitrose) *serving 280g/10oz* 8
Ground Beef, Fat 10% (Waitrose) *serving 280g/10oz* 28
Ground Steak, Scotch Beef (Waitrose) *serving 280g/10oz* 20
Indian Beef Mince (Waitrose) *serving 280g/10oz* 47
Italian Beef Mince (Waitrose) *serving 280g/10oz* 47
Kheema *serving 280g/10oz* 106
Koflas *serving 280g/10oz* 77
Lasagnes: *see under* Pasta & Noodles
Leek/Cheese Topped Steak, Main Meal (Marks & Spencer) *serving 280g/10oz* 33
Leg Beef, Sliced (Waitrose) *serving 280g/10oz* 30
Leg, Sliced, Aberdeen Angus (Waitrose) *serving 280g/10oz* 30
Leg, Sliced, British (Waitrose) *serving 280g/10oz* 13
Lemon Pepper Steaks (Waitrose) *serving 280g/10oz* 4
Lunch Tongue, Deli (Asda) *serving 280g/10oz* 29
Luncheon Meat, Thin Sliced *serving 280g/10oz* 11
Meat Balls in Bolognese Sauce (Somerfield) *serving 280g/10oz* 31
Mince (9%) Healthy Eating, Chilled (Tesco) *serving 280g/10oz* 22
Mince, Aberdeen Angus (Waitrose) *serving 280g/10oz* 45
Mince, Prime, Fat 20% (Waitrose) *serving 280g/10oz* 48
Mince, Stewed, Lean *serving 280g/10oz* 38
Minced Beef, British (Waitrose), *serving 280g/10oz* 45
Minced Beef, Extra Lean, Fresh Stewed (Iceland) *serving 280g/10oz* 25
Minced Beef, Extra Lean (Somerfield) *serving 280g/10oz* 20
Minced Beef, Fresh (Iceland) *serving 280g/10oz* 45
Minced Beef, Frozen (Iceland) *serving 280g/10oz* 46
Minced Beef, Healthy Eating, Chilled (Tesco) *serving 280g/10oz* 11
Minced Beef, Large (Marks & Spencer) *serving 280g/10oz* 24
Minced Beef, Scotch (Waitrose) *serving 280g/10oz* 52
Minced Beef, Small (Marks & Spencer) *serving 280g/10oz* 20
Minced Beef, Super Value, Frozen, Fried (Iceland) *serving 280g/10oz* 67
Minced Beef Casserole (Waitrose) *serving 280g/10oz* 18
Minced Beef Cobbler (Birds Eye) *serving 280g/10oz* 22
Minced Beef Crispbreak (Somerfield) *serving 280g/10oz* 36
Minced Beef & Onion in Gravy, tinned (Tesco) *serving 280g/10oz* 29

Item	Fat (g)
Minced Beef & Onion (Princes) *serving 280g/10oz*	34
Minced Beef & Onion Slices (Waitrose) *serving 280g/10oz*	60
Minced Beef & Onions, tinned (Tesco) *serving 280g/10oz*	26
Minced Beef Steak, Frozen, Shallow Fry (Iceland) *serving 280g/10oz*	46
Minced Beef Steak, Lean & Tender, Frozen (Iceland) *serving 280g/10oz*	28
Minced Beef & Veg & Gravy (Birds Eye) *serving 280g/10oz*	10
Minced Beef & Veg & Gravy & Potato (Birds Eye) *serving 280g/10oz*	14
Minced Beef & Veg & Yorkshire Pudding (Waitrose) *serving 280g/10oz*	27
Mini Diced Steak (Waitrose) *serving 280g/10oz*	8
Mixed Grill Beef, Slicing (Somerfield) *serving 280g/10oz*	69
Moussaka (Crosse & Blackwell) *serving 280g/10oz*	21
Moussaka, Chilled Ready Meal (Tesco) *serving 280g/10oz*	18
Moussaka (Waitrose) *serving 280g/10oz*	27
Moussaka, Meat (Waitrose) *serving 280g/10oz*	28
Osso Bucco, Farmhouse (Waitrose) *serving 280g/10oz*	28
Ox Hearts (Somerfield) *serving 280g/10oz*	10
Ox Liver (Somerfield) *serving 280g/10oz*	22
Ox Tail (Service Meat) Waitrose *serving 280g/10oz*	28
Ox Tongue (Marks & Spencer) *serving 280g/10oz*	47
Ox Tongue (Somerfield) *serving 280g/10oz*	37
Ox Tongue (Waitrose) *serving 280g/10oz*	48
Ox Tongue, Cured (Waitrose) *serving 280g/10oz*	37
Ox Tongue, Deli (Asda) *serving 280g/10oz*	37
Ox Tongue, Traditional, Delicatessen (Marks & Spencer) *serving 280g/10oz*	60
Pork & Beef, Main Meal (Marks & Spencer) *serving 280g/10oz*	67
Potted Beef (Marks & Spencer) *serving 280g/10oz*	32
Prime Rib, Aberdeen Angus (Waitrose) *serving 280g/10oz*	70
Prime Rib, British (Waitrose) *serving 280g/10oz*	70
Prime Rib, Scotch Beef (Waitrose) *serving 280g/10oz*	70
Rib, Carvery, Scotch Beef (Waitrose) *serving 280g/10oz*	64
Rib, Prime (Waitrose) *serving 280g/10oz*	70

Rib Roast, Roasted Lean *serving 280g/10oz* 32
Rib Roast, Roasted Lean & Fat *serving 280g/10oz* 57
Roast Beef, Aberdeen Angus, Delicatessen (Marks & Spencer) *serving 280g/10oz* 17
Roast Beef, Scottish, Delicatessen (Marks & Spencer) *serving 280g/10oz* 8
Roast Beef, Sliced, Cold Meats (Tesco) *serving 280g/10oz* 9
Roast Beef, Wafer Thin, Delicatessen (Marks & Spencer) *serving 280g/10oz* 5
Roast Beef in Gravy (Birds Eye) *serving 280g/10oz* 5
Roast Beef in Gravy, Sliced, Frozen Ready Meal (Tesco) *serving 280g/10oz* 10
Roast Beef Platter (Birds Eye) *serving 280g/10oz* 8
Roast Beef, Yorkshire Pudding & Potatoes, Main Meal (Marks & Spencer) *serving 280g/10oz* 12
Roast, Mini, Aberdeen Angus (Waitrose) *serving 280g/10oz* 31
Roasting Beef, British (Waitrose) *serving 280g/10oz* 31
Roasting Beef, Scottish (Waitrose) *serving 280g/10oz* 47
Roasting Joint, Fresh (Iceland) *serving 280g/10oz* 34
Rolled Brisket, Scotch Beef (Waitrose) *serving 280g/10oz* 57
Rolled Brisket Roast (Waitrose) *serving 280g/10oz* 57
Rolled Rib, British (Waitrose) *serving 280g/10oz* 30
Rolled Rib (Waitrose) *serving 280g/10oz* 30
Rolled Sirloin, Scotch Beef (Waitrose) *serving 280g/10oz* 64
Rump Steak, Fried Lean *serving 280g/10oz* 18
Rump Steak, Fried Lean & Fat *serving 280g/10oz* 36
Rump Steak, Grilled Lean *serving 280g/10oz* 17
Rump Steak, Grilled Lean & Fat *serving 280g/10oz* 32
Salami: *see under* Sausages
Salt Beef, Cold Meats (Tesco) *serving 280g/10oz* 11
Sandwich Steaks (Waitrose) *serving 280g/10oz* 13
Scottish Beef, Traditional (Waitrose) *serving 280g/10oz* 38
Shepherd's Pie: *see under* Pies, Pasties, Flans & Quiches
Silverside, Aberdeen Angus (Waitrose) *serving 280g/10oz* 20
Silverside Beef Joint, Select Choice (Somerfield) *serving 280g/10oz* 34
Silverside, Cooked & Roasted (Somerfield) *serving 280g/10oz* 21
Silverside of Beef, Peppered, Cold Meats (Tesco) *serving 280g/10oz* 9

Silverside of Beef, Peppered, Deli (Asda) *serving 280g/10oz* 12
Silverside of Beef, Premium, Chilled (Iceland) *serving 280g/10oz* 22
Silverside, Pot Roasted Lean *serving 280g/10oz* 18
Silverside, Pot Roasted, Lean & Fat *serving 280g/10oz* 38
Sirloin, Aberdeen Angus (Waitrose) *serving 280g/10oz* 64
Sirloin, Scotch Beef (Waitrose) *serving 280g/10oz* 64
Sirloin Steak, Fresh, Roasted (Iceland) *serving 280g/10oz* 64
Sirloin Steak, Prime (Waitrose) *serving 280g/10oz* 64
Sirloin Steak, Select Choice (Somerfield) *serving 280g/10oz* 59
Sirloin Steak, Thin Cut (Waitrose) *serving 280g/10oz* 64
Sirloin Steak (Waitrose) *serving 280g/10oz* 64
Spiced Beef & Rice (Birds Eye) *serving 280g/10oz* 10
Spicy Beef Calzone (Waitrose) *serving 280g/10oz* 29
Steak, Aberdeen Angus (Waitrose) *serving 280g/10oz* 31
Steak au Poivre, Fresh (Marks & Spencer) *serving 280g/10oz* 31
Steak Casserole (Marks & Spencer) *serving 280g/10oz* 7
Steak Casserole, Scottish, Main Meal (Marks & Spencer) *serving 280g/10oz* 7
Steak & Kidney Fresh Casserole (Iceland) *serving 280g/10oz* 30
Steak Mince, Select Choice (Somerfield) *serving 280g/10oz* 43
Steak Pudding *serving 280g/10oz* 34
Steak in Red Wine Platter, Healthy Options (Birds Eye) *serving 280g/10oz* 6
Stewed Steak (Princes) *serving 280g/10oz* 10
Stewed Steak, Premium (Princes) *serving 280g/10oz* 15
Stewed Steak & Kidney (Princes) *serving 280g/10oz* 13
Stewed Steak in Gravy, Tinned (Tesco) *serving 280g/10oz* 10
Stewing Steak (Waitrose) *serving 280g/10oz* 30
Stewing Steak, Stewed Lean *serving 280g/10oz* 18
Stewing Steak, Stewed Lean & Fat *serving 280g/10oz* 27
Suet: *see under* Oils & Cooking Fats
Swiss Air Dried Beef, Sliced (Waitrose) 14
T-Bone Steak, British (Waitrose) 22
T-Bone Steak, Scotch Beef (Waitrose) *serving 280g/10oz* 64
Tenderised Steak, Select Choice (Somerfield) *serving 280g/10oz* 22
Top Rump Beef Joint, Select Choice (Somerfield) *serving 280g/10oz* 34

Topside, Cooked & Flash Roasted (Somerfield) *serving 280g/10oz* 11
Topside, Cooked (Somerfield) *serving 280g/10oz* 5
Topside of Beef, British, Roast, Deli (Asda) *serving 280g/10oz* 25
Topside of Beef, Cooked, Cold Meats (Tesco) *serving 280g/10oz* 6
Topside of Beef, Roast, Premium (Somerfield) *serving 280g/10oz* 7
Topside of Beef, Roast (Somerfield) *serving 280g/10oz* 14
Topside Beef Joint, Select Choice (Somerfield) *serving 280g/10oz* 34
Topside Joint, South American, Large, Frozen, Roasted (Iceland) *serving 280g/10oz* 31
Topside Joint, South American, Medium, Frozen, Roasted, (Iceland) *serving 280g/10oz* 31
Topside Joint, South American, Small, Frozen (Iceland) *serving 280g/10oz* 31
Tostada, Beans, Beef & Cheese *serving 280g/10oz* 21
Tostada, Beef & Cheese *serving 280g/10oz* 28
Veal, Brain, Braised *serving 110g/4oz* 11
Veal, Brain, Pan Fried *serving 110g/4oz* 18
Veal, Breaded Escalope (Marks & Spencer) *serving 110g/4oz* 12
Veal, Diced (Waitrose) *serving 110g/4oz* 3
Veal, Diced, Farmhouse (Waitrose) *serving 110g/4oz* 3
Veal Escalope, Farmhouse (Waitrose) *serving 110g/4oz* 3
Veal, Ground, Broiled *serving 110g/4oz* 8
Veal, Ground, Farmhouse *serving 110g/4oz* 3
Veal, Heart, Braised *serving 110g/4oz* 7
Veal, Housed, Topside (Waitrose) *serving 110g/4oz* 3
Veal, Kidneys, Braised *serving 110g/4oz* 6
Veal, Leg, Separable, Lean & Fat, Braised *serving 110g/4oz* 7
Veal, Leg, Separable, Lean & Fat, Pan Fried, Breaded *serving 110g/4oz* 10
Veal, Leg, Separable, Lean & Fat, Pan Fried, Not Breaded *serving 110g/4oz* 9
Veal, Leg, Separable, Lean & Fat, Roasted *serving 110g/4oz* 5
Veal, Leg, Separable, Lean Only, Braised *serving 110g/4oz* 6
Veal, Leg, Separable, Lean Only, Pan Fried, Breaded *serving 110g/4oz* 7
Veal, Leg, Separable, Lean Only, Pan Fried, Not Breaded *serving 110g/4oz* 5

Veal, Leg, Separable, Lean Only, Roasted *serving 110g/4oz* 4
Veal, Liver, Braised *serving 110g/4oz* 8
Veal, Liver, Pan Fried *serving 110g/4oz* 13
Veal, Loin, Separable, Lean & Fat, Braised *serving 110g/4oz* 19
Veal, Loin, Separable, Lean & Fat, Roasted *serving 110g/4oz* 14
Veal, Loin, Separable, Lean Only, Braised *serving 110g/4oz* 10
Veal, Loin, Separable, Lean Only, Roasted *serving 110g/4oz* 8
Veal, Lungs, Braised *serving 110g/4oz* 3
Veal, Medallions, Chilled, Healthy Eating (Tesco) *serving 110g/4oz* 2
Veal, Pancreas, Braised *serving 110g/4oz* 16
Veal, Rib, Separable, Lean & Fat, Braised *serving 110g/4oz* 14
Veal, Rib, Separable, Lean & Fat, Roasted *serving 110g/4oz* 15
Veal, Rib, Separable, Lean Only, Braised *serving 110g/4oz* 9
Veal, Rib, Separable, Lean Only, Roasted *serving 110g/4oz* 8
Veal, Sirloin, Farmhouse (Waitrose) *serving 110g/4oz* 3
Veal, Sirloin, Separable, Lean & Fat, Braised *serving 110g/4oz* 14
Veal, Sirloin, Separable, Lean & Fat, Roasted *serving 110g/4oz* 11
Veal, Sirloin, Separable, Lean Only, Braised *serving 110g/4oz* 7
Veal, Sirloin, Separable, Lean Only, Roasted *serving 110g/4oz* 7
Veal, Spleen, Braised *serving 110g/4oz* 3
Veal, Thymus, Braised *serving 110g/4oz* 5
Veal, Tongue, Braised *serving 110g/4oz* 11
Wafer Thin Beef, Chilled (Iceland) *serving 280g/10oz* 7

Biscuits

NOTE: Biscuits and cookies often vary considerably in weight. A 'diet' or low calorie biscuit may weigh as little as 11g; whereas brownies or other substantial cookies can weigh as much as 60g. As always, you should check the information on the packet to find out just how many biscuits are included in our standard 90g/3oz portion.

All Butter Biscuits (Asda) *serving 90g/3oz* 20
All Butter Biscuits (Somerfield) *serving 90g/3oz* 20
All Butter Biscuits (Tesco) *serving 90g/3oz* 22
All Butter Fruit Biscuits (Tesco) *serving 90g/3oz* 19
All Butter Madeira Thins (Marks & Spencer) *serving 90g/3oz* 18

All Butter Scottish Shortbread Thick Fin (Tesco) *serving 90g/3oz* 25
All Butter Shortbread Fingers (Asda) *serving 90g/3oz* 26
All Butter Thins (Somerfield) *serving 90g/3oz* 16
All Butter Viennese (Marks & Spencer) *serving 90g/3oz* 24
Almond Biscuits (Waitrose) *serving 90g/3oz* 21
Almond Shortie (Asda) *serving 90g/3oz* 21
Almond Shorties (Tesco) *serving 90g/3oz* 24
Almond Thin Biscuits (Waitrose) *serving 90g/3oz* 22
Almond Thins (Tesco) *serving 90g/3oz* 22
Amarettini Biscuits (Marks & Spencer) *serving 90g/3oz* 8
Apple & Sultana Flapjack (Waitrose) *serving 90g/3oz* 14
Apricot Oat Snackbar (Waitrose) *serving 90g/3oz* 18
Bakewell Creams (Fox's) *serving 90g/3oz* 21
Beatrix Potter's Countline (Marks & Spencer) *serving 90g/3oz* 25
Beatrix Potter's Pencil Tin (Marks & Spencer) *serving 90g/3oz* 25
Biscuits for Cheese, Brown Wheat Cracker (Tesco) *serving 90g/3oz* 16
Biscuits for Cheese, Cornish Wafer (Tesco) *serving 90g/3oz* 28
Biscuits for Cheese, Cream Cracker (Tesco) *serving 90g/3oz* 13
Biscuits for Cheese, Poppy Snack (Tesco) *serving 90g/3oz* 20
Biscuits for Cheese, Sesame (Tesco) *serving 90g/3oz* 28
Biscuits for Cheese, Small High Bake Water (Tesco) *serving 90g/3oz* 7
Biscuits for Cheese, Wholegrain (Tesco) *serving 90g/3oz* 17
Blackcurrant Viennese (Marks & Spencer) *serving 90g/3oz* 31
Bourbon Biscuits, Grocery (Iceland) *serving 90g/3oz* 19
Bourbon Creams (Asda) *serving 90g/3oz* 18
Bourbon Creams (Somerfield) *serving 90g/3oz* 19
Bourbon Creams (Tesco) *serving 90g/3oz* 18
Bourbon (Waitrose) *serving 90g/3oz* 18
Brandy Snaps *serving 90g/3oz* 18
Brandy Snaps (Fox's) *serving 90g/3oz* 13
Brandy Snap Basket (Marks & Spencer) *serving 90g/3oz* 16
Break in Biscuits (Marks & Spencer) *serving 90g/3oz* 26
Brownies *serving 90g/3oz* 15
Brownies (Betty Crocker) *serving 90g/3oz* 18

Butter Almond Shortbread (Waitrose) *serving 90g/3oz*	28
Butter Biscuits (Waitrose) *serving 90g/3oz*	20
Butter Crinkle Crunch (Fox's) *serving 90g/3oz*	16
Butter Puff Biscuits (Marks & Spencer) *serving 90g/3oz*	22
Butter Shortbread Fingers (Waitrose) *serving 90g/3oz*	26
Butter Tea (Fox's) *serving 90g/3oz*	19
Buttercrisp Creams (Fox's) *serving 90g/3oz*	27
Cappuchino Sticks (Somerfield) *serving 90g/3oz*	27
Caramel Wafers (Marks & Spencer) *serving 90g/3oz*	21
Cheese Crackers *serving 90g/3oz*	23
Cheese Crackers (Waitrose) *serving 90g/3oz*	32
Cheese Digestive (Marks & Spencer) *serving 90g/3oz*	21
Cheese Sandwich (Somerfield) *serving 90g/3oz*	34
Cheese Sandwich (Tesco) *serving 90g/3oz*	24
Cheese Sandwich (Waitrose) *serving 90g/3oz*	26
Cheese Thin Biscuits (Asda) *serving 90g/3oz*	29
Cheese Thins (Tesco) *serving 90g/3oz*	29
Cheese Thins (Waitrose) *serving 90g/3oz*	29
Cheese Thins, Savoury (Somerfield) *serving 90g/3oz*	29
Cherry & Almond Biscuits (Waitrose) *serving 90g/3oz*	24
Children's Novelty Biscuits (Waitrose) *serving 90g/3oz*	12
Chocolate Biscuits, Full Coated *serving 90g/3oz*	25
Chocolate Brownie Biscuit (Waitrose) *serving 90g/3oz*	26
Chocolate Brownies (Waitrose) *serving 90g/3oz*	22
Chocolate Chip Chewy Bars (Asda) *serving 90g/3oz*	21
Chocolate Chip Chopblock (Somerfield) *serving 90g/3oz*	15
Chocolate Chip & Coconut (Tesco) *serving 90g/3oz*	26
Chocolate Chip Cookies (Asda) *serving 90g/3oz*	21
Chocolate Chip Cookies (Marks & Spencer) *serving 90g/3oz*	23
Chocolate Chip Cookies (Somerfield) *serving 90g/3oz*	23
Chocolate Chip Cookies (Tesco) *serving 90g/3oz*	22
Chocolate Chip Cookies (Waitrose) *serving 90g/3oz*	21
Chocolate Chip Flapjack (Waitrose) *serving 90g/3oz*	19
Chocolate Chip & Hazelnut (Tesco) *serving 90g/3oz*	26
Chocolate Chip & Hazelnut (Fox's) *serving 90g/3oz*	27
Chocolate Chip Shortbread (Somerfield) *serving 90g/3oz*	25
Chocolate Chip Shortbread (Tesco) *serving 90g/3oz*	24

Chocolate Crunch Creams (Fox's) *serving 90g/3oz* 20
Chocolate Digestive (Holland & Barrett) *serving 90g/3oz* 21
Chocolate & Nut Cookies (Waitrose) *serving 90g/3oz* 22
Chocolate & Orange Cookies (Waitrose) *serving 90g/3oz* 21
Chocolate Orange Flapjack (Somerfield) *serving 90g/3oz* 24
Chocolate Peanut Cookies (Waitrose) *serving 90g/3oz* 29
Chocolate Sandwich Biscuits, Grocery (Iceland) *serving 90g/3oz* 23
Chocolate Shortbread (Waitrose) *serving 90g/3oz* 25
Chocolate Shortbread Bar (Waitrose) *serving 90g/3oz* 26
Chocolate Shortbread Selection (Waitrose) *serving 90g/3oz* 26
Chocolate Snap Biscuit (Waitrose) *serving 90g/3oz* 24
Chocolatier, Milk Chocolate (Fox's) *serving 90g/3oz* 24
Chocolatier, Plain Chocolate (Fox's) *serving 90g/3oz* 23
Chocolatier, White Chocolate (Fox's) *serving 90g/3oz* 27
Classic Biscuits (Fox's) *serving 90g/3oz* 19
Classic Creams (Fox's) *serving 90g/3oz* 23
Coconut Cookies (Waitrose) *serving 90g/3oz* 21
Coconut Crinkle Crunch (Fox's) *serving 90g/3oz* 22
Coconut Crumble Cream Biscuits (Somerfield) *serving 90g/3oz* 26
Coconut Crumble Creams (Waitrose) *serving 90g/3oz* 26
Coconut Crunch Cream (Fox's) *serving 90g/3oz* 26
Coconut Crunch (Tesco) *serving 90g/3oz* 24
Coconut Macaroons, Prepared from Recipe *serving 90g/3oz* 11
Coconut Rings (Tesco) *serving 90g/3oz* 21
Coconut Rings (Waitrose) *serving 90g/3oz* 20
Cookies Animal Crackers *serving 90g/3oz* 12
Country Oat Bakes (Tesco) *serving 90g/3oz* 20
Cream Crackers *serving 90g/3oz* 15
Cream Crackers (Asda) *serving 90g/3oz* 13
Cream Crackers (Somerfield) *serving 90g/3oz* 13
Cream Crackers (Tesco) *serving 90g/3oz* 12
Cream Crackers (Waitrose) *serving 90g/3oz* 13
Crispbread Rye *serving 90g/3oz* 2
Crispbreaks Cheese (Somerfield) *serving 90g/3oz* 11
Crispy Cheese Crackers (Marks & Spencer) *serving 90g/3oz* 20
Custard Cream Biscuits (Marks & Spencer) *serving 90g/3oz* 22
Custard Cream Biscuits (Somerfield) *serving 90g/3oz* 22

Custard Creams (Asda) *serving 90g/3oz* 22
Custard Creams (Iceland) *serving 90g/3oz* 22
Custard Creams (Tesco) *serving 90g/3oz* 22
Custard Creams (Waitrose) *serving 90g/3oz* 22
Custard Creams, Healthy Choice 25% Less Fat (Asda) *serving 90g/3oz* 15
Dark Chocolate Ginger Cookie (Marks & Spencer) *serving 90g/3oz* 21
Dark Treacle Cookies (Heinz Weight Watchers) *serving 90g/3oz* 14
Devon Creams (Fox's) *serving 90g/3oz* 21
Digestive, Basics (Somerfield) *serving 90g/3oz* 21
Digestive Biscuits Chocolate *serving 90g/3oz* 22
Digestive Biscuits (Holland & Barrett) *serving 90g/3oz* 19
Digestive Biscuits, Plain *serving 90g/3oz* 19
Digestive Biscuits, Healthy Choice 25% Less Fat (Asda) *serving 90g/3oz* 15
Digestive Biscuits, Fat Reduced (Somerfield) *serving 90g/3oz* 18
Digestive Biscuits, Reduced Fat (Sainsbury's) *serving 90g/3oz* 14
Digestive Biscuits, Reduced Fat (Waitrose) *serving 90g/3oz* 15
Digestive Cream Biscuits (Somerfield) *serving 90g/3oz* 20
Digestive Creams (Asda) *serving 90g/3oz* 20
Digestive Creams (Tesco) *serving 90g/3oz* 20
Digestive Finger Biscuits (Somerfield) *serving 90g/3oz* 17
Digestives, High Fibre (Marks & Spencer) *serving 90g/3oz* 21
Digestive Sweetmeal (Asda) *serving 90g/3oz* 21
Digestive Sweetmeal (Waitrose) *serving 90g/3oz* 20
Digestives (Iceland) *serving 90g/3oz* 20
Digestives (Tesco) *serving 90g/3oz* 20
Digestives, Reduced Fat (Marks & Spencer) *serving 90g/3oz* 16
Double Chocolate Chip Cookies (Fox's) *serving 90g/3oz* 28
Double Chocolate Chip Cookies (Somerfield) *serving 90g/3oz* 23
Double Chocolate Chip Cookies (Waitrose) *serving 90g/3oz* 23
Double Chocolate & Orange Cookies (Somerfield) *serving 90g/3oz* 22
Dutch Shortcake Chocolate (Marks & Spencer) *serving 90g/3oz* 28
Easter Lamb Biscuits (Waitrose) *serving 90g/3oz* 25
Economy Chocolate Chip (Tesco) *serving 90g/3oz* 21

Economy Shortie (Tesco) *serving 90g/3oz*	20
Family Fruit Shortcake Biscuits (Tesco)*serving 90g/3oz*	16
Father Christmas Biscuits (Waitrose) *serving 90g/3oz*	20
Fig Bars *serving 90g/3oz*	7
Fig Rolls (Asda) *serving 90g/3oz*	7
Finger Moulded Wafer (Waitrose) *serving 90g/3oz*	25
Flapjack (Waitrose) *serving 90g/3oz*	17
Flapjack *serving 90g/3oz*	24
Flapjack, Cherry & Coconut (Somerfield) *serving 90g/3oz*	22
Flapjack Cookies (Marks & Spencer) *serving 90g/3oz*	24
Flapjack Plain (Holland & Barrett) *serving 90g/3oz*	25
French Macaroon Biscuit (Waitrose) *serving 90g/3oz*	8
Fresh Celery Cracker (Marks & Spencer) *serving 90g/3oz*	22
Fruit Country Oatbakes (Tesco) *serving 90g/3oz*	18
Fruit Flapjack (Holland & Barrett) *serving 90g/3oz*	22
Fruit & Nut Cookies (Marks & Spencer) *serving 90g/3oz*	24
Fruit & Nut Creams (Tesco) *serving 90g/3oz*	20
Fruit Shortcake Biscuit (Asda) *serving 90g/3oz*	19
Fruit Shortcake Biscuit (Holland & Barrett) *serving 90g/3oz*	21
Fruit Shortcake Biscuit (Iceland) *serving 90g/3oz*	18
Fruit Shortcake Biscuit (Somerfield) *serving 90g/3oz*	18
Fruit Shortcake (Tesco) *serving 90g/3oz*	19
Fruit Shortcake (Waitrose) *serving 90g/3oz*	18
Fruit Shrewsbury (Waitrose) *serving 90g/3oz*	16
Garibaldi Biscuits (Asda) *serving 90g/3oz*	8
Garibaldi Biscuits (Tesco) *serving 90g/3oz*	8
Garibaldi Biscuits (Waitrose) *serving 90g/3oz*	10
Ginger Cookies (Waitrose) *serving 90g/3oz*	20
Ginger Creams (Fox's) *serving 90g/3oz*	19
Ginger Crinkle Crunch (Fox's) *serving 90g/3oz*	12
Ginger Crunch Biscuits (Somerfield) *serving 90g/3oz*	13
Ginger Crunch Biscuits (Tesco) *serving 90g/3oz*	21
Ginger Crunch Creams (Fox's) *serving 90g/3oz*	23
Ginger Nuts (Asda) *serving 90g/3oz*	13
Ginger Nuts (Tesco) *serving 90g/3oz*	14
Ginger Snap (Fox's) *serving 90g/3oz*	12
Ginger Snap Biscuits (Marks & Spencer) *serving 90g/3oz*	12

Ginger Thins (Asda) *serving 90g/3oz*	15
Ginger Thins Biscuits (Somerfield) *serving 90g/3oz*	15
Ginger Wafer Biscuit (Holland & Barrett) *serving 90g/3oz*	21
Gingerbread, Homemade *serving 90g/3oz*	15
Gingerbread Men (Waitrose) *serving 90g/3oz*	8
Gingerbread, Novelty (Waitrose) *serving 90g/3oz*	12
Gingernut Biscuits, Homemade *serving 90g/3oz*	17
Gingersnaps *serving 90g/3oz*	9
Gold Ribbon Wafer Biscuits, Grocery *serving 90g/3oz*	24
Golden Crunch Cream (Fox's) *serving 90g/3oz*	23
Golden Crunch (Fox's) *serving 90g/3oz*	17
Hazelnut Cookies (Waitrose) *serving 90g/3oz*	26
High Bake Biscuits (Waitrose) *serving 90g/3oz*	7
High Bake Water Biscuits (Somerfield) *serving 90g/3oz*	7
High Bake Water Biscuits (Tesco) *serving 90g/3oz*	7
Highland Shorties Biscuits (Marks & Spencer) *serving 90g/3oz*	20
Highland Shorties (Waitrose) *serving 90g/3oz*	20
Homestyle Lemon Cookies (Marks & Spencer) *serving 90g/3oz*	18
Honeycombe Biscuits (Marks & Spencer) *serving 90g/3oz*	24
Ice Topped Bar (Waitrose) *serving 90g/3oz*	9
Indulgence Cookies, Chocolate Chunk & Hazelnut (Asda) *serving 90g/3oz*	30
Indulgence Cookies, Chocolate Coated Fruit & Nut (Asda) *serving 90g/3oz*	26
Indulgence Cookies, Chocolate Orange (Asda) *serving 90g/3oz*	25
Indulgence Cookies, Double Chocolate Chunk (Asda) *serving 90g/3oz*	29
Indulgence Cookies, Ginger & Lemon Flavour (Asda) *serving 90g/3oz*	22
Indulgence Cookies, Maple & Walnut Flavour (Asda) *serving 90g/3oz*	27
Jaffa Cakes *serving 90g/3oz*	9
Jaffa Cakes (Asda) *serving 90g/3oz*	7
Jaffa Cakes (Iceland) *serving 90g/3oz*	7
Jaffa Cakes (Marks & Spencer) *serving 90g/3oz*	7
Jaffa Cakes (Somerfield) *serving 90g/3oz*	9
Jaffa Cakes (Waitrose) *serving 90g/3oz*	7

Jam Sandwich Cream Biscuits (Marks & Spencer) *serving 90g/3oz*	21
Jam Sandwich Creams (Fox's) *serving 90g/3oz*	21
Lemon & Almond Shortcake (Waitrose) *serving 90g/3oz*	29
Lemon Crunch Biscuits (Marks & Spencer) *serving 90g/3oz*	21
Lemon Crunch Cream Biscuits (Somerfield) *serving 90g/3oz*	22
Lemon Curd Sandwich Creams (Fox's) *serving 90g/3oz*	21
Lemon Puff Biscuits (Somerfield) *serving 90g/3oz*	27
Lemon Puffs (Tesco) *serving 90g/3oz*	27
Lemon Shortcake (Asda) *serving 90g/3oz*	20
Lemon Thins (Tesco) *serving 90g/3oz*	16
Luxury Shortbread Assortment (Somerfield) *serving 90g/3oz*	27
Luxury Shortbread Assortment (Waitrose) *serving 90g/3oz*	27
Macaroons *serving 90g/3oz*	18
Malted Milk Biscuits (Asda) *serving 90g/3oz*	20
Malted Milk Biscuits (Somerfield) *serving 90g/3oz*	20
Malted Milk Biscuits (Waitrose) *serving 90g/3oz*	20
Malted Milk Creams (Tesco) *serving 90g/3oz*	21
Marie Biscuits (Asda) *serving 90g/3oz*	13
Matzo Crackers *serving 90g/3oz*	2
Matzo Crackers, Whole Wheat *serving 90g/3oz*	1
Melba Toast *serving 90g/3oz*	3
Milk Chocolate Butter Biscuit (Marks & Spencer) *serving 90g/3oz*	23
Milk Chocolate Butter Tea (Fox's) *serving 90g/3oz*	22
Milk Chocolate Caramel Wafers (Marks & Spencer) *serving 90g/3oz*	21
Milk Chocolate Coconut Fingers (Marks & Spencer) *serving 90g/3oz*	21
Milk Chocolate Coconut Rings (Asda) *serving 90g/3oz*	23
Milk Chocolate Digestive Finger Biscuits (Somerfield) *serving 90g/3oz*	19
Milk Chocolate Digestives (Somerfield) *serving 90g/3oz*	23
Milk Chocolate Digestives (Iceland) *serving 90g/3oz*	22
Milk Chocolate Digestives (Marks & Spencer) *serving 90g/3oz*	23
Milk Chocolate Digestives (Waitrose) *serving 90g/3oz*	22
Milk Chocolate Digestives, Healthy Choice, 25% Less Fat (Asda) *serving 90g/3oz*	16

Milk Chocolate Digestives, Premium (Tesco) *serving 90g/3oz* 22
Milk Chocolate Malted Milk Biscuits – Puffin (Asda) *serving 90g/3oz* 23
Milk Chocolate Mint Sandwich Bars – Puffin (Asda) *serving 90g/3oz* 22
Milk Chocolate Nice Biscuits (Asda) *serving 90g/3oz* 20
Milk Chocolate Nice Biscuits (Somerfield) *serving 90g/3oz* 20
Milk Chocolate Orange Sandwich Bars (Tesco) *serving 90g/3oz* 22
Milk Chocolate Orange Wafer Fingers (Tesco) *serving 90g/3oz* 27
Milk Chocolate Party Rings (Fox's) *serving 90g/3oz* 21
Milk Chocolate Rich Tea Biscuits (Somerfield) *serving 90g/3oz* 21
Milk Chocolate Sandwich (Tesco) *serving 90g/3oz* 22
Milk Chocolate Sandwich Bars – Puffin (Asda) *serving 90g/3oz* 22
Milk Chocolate Shortcake (Tesco) *serving 90g/3oz* 23
Milk Chocolate Syrup Crunch (Tesco) *serving 90g/3oz* 18
Milk Chocolate Wafer Bars (Waitrose) *serving 90g/3oz* 24
Milk Chocolate Wafers (Asda) *serving 90g/3oz* 27
Milk Wafer Fingers (Waitrose) *serving 90g/3oz* 26
Mini Caramel Wafer Bag (Marks & Spencer) *serving 90g/3oz* 21
Mini Chocolate Chip Cookies (Asda) *serving 90g/3oz* 21
Mini Finger Chocolate Wafer (Waitrose) *serving 90g/3oz* 25
Mini Meringue (Waitrose) *serving 90g/3oz* 22
Molasses Cookies *serving 90g/3oz* 12
Montana Caramel (Fox's) *serving 90g/3oz* 22
Montana Chocolate (Fox's) *serving 90g/3oz* 26
Montana Orange (Fox's) *serving 90g/3oz* 25
Morning Coffee Biscuits (Asda) *serving 90g/3oz* 13
Morning Coffee Biscuits (Iceland) *serving 90g/3oz* 13
Morning Coffee Biscuits (Somerfield) *serving 90g/3oz* 13
Morning Coffee Biscuits (Waitrose) *serving 90g/3oz* 13
Multigrain Crackers (Tesco) *serving 90g/3oz* 17
Nice Biscuits (Fox's) *serving 90g/3oz* 18
Nice Biscuits (Somerfield) *serving 90g/3oz* 21
Nice Biscuits (Tesco) *serving 90g/3oz* 17
Nice Biscuits (Waitrose) *serving 90g/3oz* 15
Nice Cream Biscuits (Tesco) *serving 90g/3oz* 22
Nice Cream Biscuits (Asda) *serving 90g/3oz* 22

Oat Crunch Biscuits (Somerfield) *serving 90g/3oz*	20
Oatcakes, Homemade *serving 90g/3oz*	16
Oatcakes, Retail *serving 90g/3oz*	16
Oatflake & Honey Cookies (Waitrose) *serving 90g/3oz*	19
Oatmeal Bran With Sesame (Fox's) *serving 90g/3oz*	33
Oatmeal Cookies *serving 90g/3oz*	16
Onion & Sesame Thins (Waitrose) *serving 90g/3oz*	26
Orange Oat Snackbar (Waitrose) *serving 90g/3oz*	18
Orange Snap Biscuit (Waitrose) *serving 90g/3oz*	23
Original Thick Tea (Fox's) *serving 90g/3oz*	8
Party Rings (Fox's) *serving 90g/3oz*	12
Peanut Butter Cookies *serving 90g/3oz*	21
Peanut Butter Cookies (Waitrose) *serving 90g/3oz*	32
Peanuts & Raisins Chocolate Chip (Waitrose) *serving 90g/3oz*	24
Petit Beurre (Fox's) *serving 90g/3oz*	16
Petticoat Tails (Waitrose) *serving 90g/3oz*	25
Pizza Crackers (Waitrose) *serving 90g/3oz*	29
Plain Chocolate Digestives (Iceland) *serving 90g/3oz*	22
Plain Chocolate Digestives (Somerfield) *serving 90g/3oz*	24
Plain Chocolate Digestives (Waitrose) *serving 90g/3oz*	22
Plain Chocolate Ginger Biscuit (Marks & Spencer) *serving 90g/3oz*	20
Plain Chocolate Ginger Biscuit (Waitrose) *serving 90g/3oz*	21
Plain Chocolate Half Coated Ginger Rings (Tesco) *serving 90g/3oz*	19
Plain Chocolate Mint Sandwich (Tesco) *serving 90g/3oz*	23
Plain Chocolate Orange Biscuit (Waitrose) *serving 90g/3oz*	20
Plain Chocolate Rich Tea Biscuits (Somerfield) *serving 90g/3oz*	21
Plain Chocolate Wafer Break Biscuits (Somerfield) *serving 90g/3oz*	25
Plain Chocolate Wafer Break (Waitrose) *serving 90g/3oz*	25
Plain Chocolate Wafer Fingers (Tesco) *serving 90g/3oz*	25
Plain Wafer Fingers (Waitrose) *serving 90g/3oz*	26
Poppy & Sesame Thin Biscuits (Asda) *serving 90g/3oz*	26
Poppy & Sesame Thins Savoury Biscuits (Somerfield) *serving 90g/3oz*	25

Poppy & Sesame Thins (Tesco) *serving 90g/3oz*	27
Poppy & Sesame Thins (Waitrose) *serving 90g/3oz*	25
Raspberry Viennese Sandwich (Marks & Spencer) *serving 90g/3oz*	31
Real Chocolate Chip Cookies (Heinz Weight Watchers) *serving 90g/3oz*	14
Rice Cakes, Brown Rice *serving 90g/3oz*	3
Rice Cakes, Brown Rice & Buckwheat *serving 90g/3oz*	3
Rice Cakes, Brown Rice & Corn *serving 90g/3oz*	3
Rice Cakes, Brown Rice & Multigrain *serving 90g/3oz*	3
Rice Cakes, Brown Rice & Rye *serving 90g/3oz*	3
Rice Cakes, Brown Rice & Sesame Seed *serving 90g/3oz*	3
Rich Highland Shortie Biscuits (Somerfield) *serving 90g/3oz*	20
Rich Shortie (Asda) *serving 90g/3oz*	21
Rich Shortie Biscuits (Tesco) *serving 90g/3oz*	21
Rich Tea Biscuits (Asda) *serving 90g/3oz*	13
Rich Tea Biscuits (Iceland) *serving 90g/3oz*	13
Rich Tea Biscuits (Marks & Spencer) *serving 90g/3oz*	14
Rich Tea Biscuits, Healthy Choice 25% Less Fat (Asda) *serving 90g/3oz*	9
Rich Tea Biscuits (Waitrose) *serving 90g/3oz*	14
Rich Tea Biscuits, Reduced Fat (Marks & Spencer) *serving 90g/3oz*	10
Rich Tea Biscuits, Reduced Fat (Sainsbury's) *serving 90g/3oz*	9
Rich Tea Cream, Large (Marks & Spencer) *serving 90g/3oz*	19
Rich Tea Cream Biscuits (Marks & Spencer) *serving 90g/3oz*	19
Rich Tea Finger Biscuits (Marks & Spencer) *serving 90g/3oz*	13
Rich Tea Finger (Waitrose) *serving 90g/3oz*	13
Rich Tea Finger Biscuits (Somerfield) *serving 90g/3oz*	13
Rich Tea Finger Creams (Tesco) *serving 90g/3oz*	19
Rich Tea Fingers (Asda) *serving 90g/3oz*	13
Rich Tea Fingers (Tesco) *serving 90g/3oz*	13
Rocky (Fox's) *serving 90g/3oz*	25
Rocky Caramel (Fox's) *serving 90g/3oz*	19
Rough Griddle Oatcakes (Waitrose) *serving 90g/3oz*	17
Rye Crackers with Cheese Filling *serving 90g/3oz*	20
Rye Crispbread Crackers *serving 90g/3oz*	1

Rye Wafers *serving 90g/3oz* 1
Sandwich Biscuits *serving 90g/3oz* 23
Scotch Abernethy Biscuits (Asda) *serving 90g/3oz* 19
Scottish Abernethy Biscuits (Marks & Spencer) *serving 90g/3oz* 19
Scottish Oat Cakes (Marks & Spencer) *serving 90g/3oz* 11
Scottish Shortbread Fingers (Marks & Spencer) *serving 90g/3oz* 26
Seasalt Crackers (Marks & Spencer) *serving 90g/3oz* 23
Sesame & Onion Crackers (Tesco) *serving 90g/3oz* 26
Sesame & Onion Thins Savoury Biscuits (Somerfield) *serving 90g/3oz* 26
Sesame & Poppy Crackers (Waitrose) *serving 90g/3oz* 28
Shortbread *serving 90g/3oz* 23
Shortbread, Home Made with Butter *serving 90g/3oz* 30
Shortbread Assortment (Marks & Spencer) *serving 90g/3oz* 22
Shortbread Assortment (Somerfield) *serving 90g/3oz* 26
Shortbread Biscuit (Holland & Barrett) *serving 90g/3oz* 24
Shortbread Bunnies (Waitrose) *serving 90g/3oz* 20
Shortbread Faces on a Stick (Waitrose) *serving 90g/3oz* 20
Shortbread Fingers (Somerfield) *serving 90g/3oz* 26
Shortbread Fingers (Tesco) *serving 90g/3oz* 25
Shortbread Guy Fawkes (Waitrose) *serving 90g/3oz* 20
Shortbread Mums & Dads (Waitrose) *serving 90g/3oz* 20
Shortbread Petticoat Tails (Somerfield) *serving 90g/3oz* 25
Shortbread Rocket Lollies (Waitrose) *serving 90g/3oz* 20
Shortbread Santas/Snowmen (Waitrose) *serving 90g/3oz* 20
Shortbread Thins (Marks & Spencer) *serving 90g/3oz* 20
Shortcake (Somerfield) *serving 90g/3oz* 22
Shortcake (Tesco) *serving 90g/3oz* 21
Shortcake (Waitrose) *serving 90g/3oz* 22
Sponge Fingers (Somerfield) *serving 90g/3oz* 4
Sponge Fingers (Waitrose) *serving 90g/3oz* 3
Spring Onion Cracker (Marks & Spencer) *serving 90g/3oz* 23
Stem Ginger Biscuits (Marks & Spencer) *serving 90g/3oz* 20
Stem Ginger Cookies (Heinz Weight Watchers) *serving 90g/3oz* 12
Stem Ginger Cookies (Somerfield) *serving 90g/3oz* 20
Stem Ginger Shortbread (Waitrose) *serving 90g/3oz* 20
Stollen Fingers (Somerfield) *serving 90g/3oz* 17

Stollen Fingers (Waitrose) *serving 90g/3oz*	29
Stollen with Marzipan (Waitrose) *serving 90g/3oz*	17
Sultana & Cinnamon Cookies (Heinz Weight Watchers) *serving 90g/3oz*	11
Sultana Cookies (Marks & Spencer) *serving 90g/3oz*	17
Swiss Crispy Almond Thins (Marks & Spencer) *serving 90g/3oz*	34
Swiss Praline Wafers (Marks & Spencer) *serving 90g/3oz*	28
Teacakes, Milk Chocolate (Marks & Spencer) *serving 90g/3oz*	15
Teacakes, Orange (Marks & Spencer) *serving 90g/3oz*	14
Teddy Bear Biscuits (Waitrose) *serving 90g/3oz*	19
Thick Chocolate Wafer Bars (Marks & Spencer) *serving 90g/3oz*	28
Thistle Shortbread (Tesco) *serving 90g/3oz*	24
Toffee Break Biscuits (Marks & Spencer) *serving 90g/3oz*	18
Traditional Crumbly Shortbread Rounds (Somerfield) *serving 90g/3oz*	28
Treacle Cookies (Waitrose) *serving 90g/3oz*	25
Treacle Crunch Creams (Fox's) *serving 90g/3oz*	22
Triple Chocolate Chip Cookies (Marks & Spencer) *serving 90g/3oz*	25
Two Finger Moulded Chocolate Wafer Bars (Tesco) *serving 90g/3oz*	25
Viennese Creams Chocolate (Fox's) *serving 90g/3oz*	27
Viennese Creams (Fox's) *serving 90g/3oz*	26
Viennese Fancies (Somerfield) *serving 90g/3oz*	24
Viennese Fingers (Waitrose) *serving 90g/3oz*	26
Viennese Sandwich Chocolate (Fox's) *serving 90g/3oz*	29
Viennese Sandwich Double Chocolate (Fox's) *serving 90g/3oz*	28
Viennese Sandwich (Marks & Spencer) *serving 90g/3oz*	28
Wafer Filled Biscuits *serving 90g/3oz*	27
Water Biscuits *serving 90g/3oz*	11
Wheat Biscuits (Somerfield) *serving 90g/3oz*	2
Wheat Crackers *serving 90g/3oz*	19
Wheat Crackers with Cheese Filling *serving 90g/3oz*	23
Wheaten Crackers (Marks & Spencer) *serving 90g/3oz*	20
White Chocolate Fingers (Tesco) *serving 90g/3oz*	26
Whole Wheat Cereal Biscuits (Iceland) *serving 90g/3oz*	2
Whole Wheat Crackers *serving 90g/3oz*	15
Wholemeal Biscuits, Home Made *serving 90g/3oz*	8
Wholemeal Bran Biscuits (Fox's) *serving 90g/3oz*	18
Wholemeal Crackers *serving 90g/3oz*	10

BREAD

NOTE: The standard serving size in this section is 90g/3oz. If you wish to consume more or less than this amount (e.g. if you are going to consume a pack of food whose weight differs from the standard serving size) use the conversion tables on page 386 to calculate the new amount of fat in the food.

Allinson Sliced (Marks & Spencer) *serving 90g/3oz*	3
Allinson Unsliced (Marks & Spencer) *serving 90g/3oz*	3
Bagel (Marks & Spencer) *serving 90g/3oz*	2
Bagel (Waitrose) *serving 90g/3oz*	3
Bagel, Cinnamon & Raisin *serving 90g/3oz*	2
Bagel, Egg *serving 90g/3oz*	2
Bagel, Oat Bran *serving 90g/3oz*	1
Bagel, Onion (Waitrose) *serving 90g/3oz*	3
Bagel, Plain (including Onion, Poppy, Sesame) *serving 90g/3oz*	1
Baguette (Marks & Spencer) *serving 90g/3oz*	0
Baguette, (Tesco) *serving 90g/3oz*	1
Baguette, Cheese (Somerfield) *serving 90g/3oz*	17
Baguette, Cheese (Waitrose) *serving 90g/3oz*	14
Baguette, Cheese, Chilled (Tesco) *serving 90g/3oz*	18
Baguette, Cheese & Bacon (Somerfield) *serving 90g/3oz*	19
Baguette, Cheese & Chive Chilled (Tesco) *serving 90g/3oz*	13
Baguette, Cheese & Garlic, Hot (Marks & Spencer) *serving 90g/3oz*	20
Baguette, Cheese & Onion (Somerfield) *serving 90g/3oz*	22
Baguette, French Style (Waitrose) *serving 90g/3oz*	1
Baguette, Garlic (Somerfield) *serving 90g/3oz*	16
Baguette, Garlic (Waitrose) *serving 90g/3oz*	16
Baguette, Garlic, Chilled & Prepacked (Asda) *serving 90g/3oz*	14
Baguette, Garlic, Frozen, Baked (Iceland) *serving 90g/3oz*	19
Baguette, Garlic, Frozen, Unbaked (Iceland) *serving 90g/3oz*	17
Baguette, Garlic & Herb, Chilled (Tesco) *serving 90g/3oz*	16
Baguette, Garlic, Hot (Marks & Spencer) *serving 90g/3oz*	22
Baguette, Garlic Harvester (Somerfield) *serving 90g/3oz*	17
Baguette, Half (Marks & Spencer) *serving 90g/3oz*	0

Baguette, Ham & Pineapple Hot (Marks & Spencer) *serving 90g/3oz* 6
Baguette, Herb (Somerfield) *serving 90g/3oz* 16
Baguette, Homebake (Marks & Spencer) *serving 90g/3oz* 0
Baguette, Homebake Fresh Ovenbake (Iceland) *serving 90g/3oz* 1
Baguette, Malted Brown, Garlic Frozen (Tesco) *serving 90g/3oz* 20
Baguette, Part Bake, Large (Waitrose) *serving 90g/3oz* 1
Baguette, Part Bake, Small (Waitrose) *serving 90g/3oz* 1
Baguette, Part Baked, Garlic Frozen (Tesco) *serving 90g/3oz* 18
Baguette, Part Baked, Garlic, White (Tesco) *serving 90g/3oz* 14
Baguette, Reduced Fat, Garlic (Waitrose) *serving 90g/3oz* 10
Baguette, Sausage, Hot (Marks & Spencer) *serving 90g/3oz* 6
Baguette, Tomato & Herb (Waitrose) *serving 90g/3oz* 17
Baguette, Twin Pack, Garlic (Waitrose) *serving 90g/3oz* 16
Baguette, White, Half (Somerfield) *serving 90g/3oz* 1
Bap, Cheese with Herbs (Waitrose) *serving 90g/3oz* 7
Bap, Floured (Marks & Spencer) *serving 90g/3oz* 6
Bap, Floured (Waitrose) *serving 90g/3oz* 3
Bap, Granary (Waitrose) *serving 90g/3oz* 3
Bap, Granary (Tesco) *serving 90g/3oz* 3
Bap, Large White (Tesco) *serving 90g/3oz* 2
Bap, Multi Seeded White (Waitrose) *serving 90g/3oz* 3
Bap, Salad, Granary, Malted Brown (Somerfield) *serving 90g/3oz* 0
Bap, Salad, White (Somerfield) *serving 90g/3oz* 5
Bap, Stoneground Wholemeal (Somerfield) *serving 90g/3oz* 4
Bap, White Farmhouse (Somerfield) *serving 90g/3oz* 3
Bap, White, Floured (Waitrose) *serving 90g/3oz* 4
Bap, Wholemeal (Tesco) *serving 90g/3oz* 2
Bap, Wholemeal (Waitrose) *serving 90g/3oz* 5
Batch Brown (Marks & Spencer) *serving 90g/3oz* 1
Batch Loaf, Seeded (Marks & Spencer) *serving 90g/3oz* 10
Baton Loaf, White Seeded, Baked Off (Somerfield) *serving 90g/3oz* 2
Baton, White Seeded (Somerfield) *serving 90g/3oz* 2
Baton, White Sesame (Somerfield) *serving 90g/3oz* 2
Bhaji, Ethnic Bread (Waitrose) *serving 90g/3oz* 13

Bloomer (Tesco) *serving 90g/3oz*	2
Bloomer (Waitrose) *serving 90g/3oz*	2
Bloomer, Crusty (Tesco) *serving 90g/3oz*	3
Bloomer, Sliced (Marks & Spencer) *serving 90g/3oz*	2
Bloomer, Soft (Somerfield) *serving 90g/3oz*	2
Bloomer, White (Waitrose) *serving 90g/3oz*	2
Bloomer/Vienna (Marks & Spencer) *serving 90g/3oz*	2
Bloomer, White Large (Somerfield) *serving 90g/3oz*	2
Bloomer, White Poppy Seed (Waitrose) *serving 90g/3oz*	2
Bloomer, White Seeded (Somerfield) *serving 90g/3oz*	2
Bloomer, White Seeded (Waitrose) *serving 90g/3oz*	2
Bloomer, White Small (Somerfield) *serving 90g/3oz*	2
Bloomer, Wrapped (Waitrose) *serving 90g/3oz*	2
Box Split Loaf (Somerfield) *serving 90g/3oz*	2
Breadcrumbs, Dry *serving 90g/3oz*	5
Breadcrumbs, Golden (Somerfield) *serving 90g/3oz*	1
Breadsticks *serving 90g/3oz*	8
Breadsticks, Plain (Waitrose) *serving 90g/3oz*	6
Breadsticks, Sesame (Waitrose) *serving 90g/3oz*	10
Brittany Brown Bread (Waitrose) *serving 90g/3oz*	1
Brown Bread, Fresh as Sold (Iceland) *serving 90g/3oz*	1
Brown Bread, Malted Wheat Grains (Waitrose) *serving 90g/3oz*	2
Brown Bread, Medium Sliced (Somerfield) *serving 90g/3oz*	1
Brown Bread, Medium Sliced (Tesco) *serving 90g/3oz*	2
Brown Malted Wheat, Sliced (Waitrose) *serving 90g/3oz*	2
Bun, Bath (Marks & Spencer) *serving 90g/3oz*	11
Bun, Chelsea/Bath *serving 90g/3oz*	12
Bun, Chelsea (Somerfield) *serving 90g/3oz*	7
Bun, Chelsea (Waitrose) *serving 90g/3oz*	8
Bun, Cherry & Walnut (Marks & Spencer) *serving 90g/3oz*	8
Bun, Chocolate Iced (Waitrose) *serving 90g/3oz*	9
Bun, Cinnamon & Raisin (Waitrose) *serving 90g/3oz*	6
Bun, Cluster Iced (Tesco) *serving 90g/3oz*	5
Bun, Currant *serving 90g/3oz*	7
Bun, Currant (Somerfield) *serving 90g/3oz*	5
Bun, Currant (Tesco) *serving 90g/3oz*	4
Bun, Currant Basics (Somerfield) *serving 90g/3oz*	1

Bun, Fruit (Waitrose) *serving 90g/3oz*	6
Bun, Hot Cross *serving 90g/3oz*	6
Bun, Hot Cross (Somerfield) *serving 90g/3oz*	5
Bun, Hot Cross (Waitrose) *serving 90g/3oz*	5
Bun, Hot Cross, Chilled (Iceland) *serving 90g/3oz*	7
Bun, Hot Cross, Traditional (Tesco) *serving 90g/3oz*	7
Bun, Hot Cross, White (Tesco) *serving 90g/3oz*	6
Bun, Hot Cross, Wholemeal (Somerfield) *serving 90g/3oz*	7
Bun, Hot Cross, Wholemeal (Waitrose) *serving 90g/3oz*	6
Bun, Iced Fruit (Marks & Spencer) *serving 90g/3oz*	7
Bun, Iced Fruit (Waitrose) *serving 90g/3oz*	4
Bun, Iced (Marks & Spencer) *serving 90g/3oz*	8
Bun, Marlborough (Waitrose) *serving 90g/3oz*	5
Bun, Mini Fruit (Somerfield) *serving 90g/3oz*	7
Bun, Mini Hot Cross (Somerfield) *serving 90g/3oz*	7
Bun, Mini Hot Cross (Waitrose) *serving 90g/3oz*	5
Bun, Mini Spiced (Marks & Spencer) *serving 90g/3oz*	6
Bun, Mini Spiced Fruit (Waitrose) *serving 90g/3oz*	5
Bun, Raspberry Iced (Marks & Spencer) *serving 90g/3oz*	7
Bun, Spiced Fruit (Marks & Spencer) *serving 90g/3oz*	6
Bun, Spiced Fruit (Somerfield) *serving 90g/3oz*	6
Bun, Spiced Fruit (Tesco) *serving 90g/3oz*	6
Bun, Spiced Fruit (Waitrose) *serving 90g/3oz*	5
Bun, Spiced Wholemeal (Waitrose) *serving 90g/3oz*	6
Bun, Wholewheat Spiced Fruit (Tesco) *serving 90g/3oz*	7
Burger Bap, Sesame (Waitrose) *serving 90g/3oz*	4
Burger Bun, Fresh as Sold (Iceland) *serving 90g/3oz*	6
Burger Bun, Frozen, Defrosted (Iceland) *serving 90g/3oz*	1
Burger Bun, Large Seeded (Tesco) *serving 90g/3oz*	4
Burger Bun, Seeded (Somerfield) *serving 90g/3oz*	5
Burger Bun, Sesame (Waitrose) *serving 90g/3oz*	4
Burger Bun, White (Somerfield) *serving 90g/3oz*	4
Burger Roll (Somerfield) *serving 90g/3oz*	6
Cheese Bread (Safeway) *serving 90g/3oz*	7
Ciabatta (Marks & Spencer) *serving 90g/3oz*	5
Ciabatta (Somerfield) *serving 90g/3oz*	2
Ciabatta (Waitrose) *serving 90g/3oz*	2

Ciabatta, Cheese & Tomato & Spinach, Hot (Marks & Spencer)
serving 170g/6oz 12
Ciabatta, Garlic Mushroom, Chilled & Prepacked (Asda)
serving 90g/3oz 10
Ciabatta, Half (Marks & Spencer) *serving 90g/3oz* 5
Ciabatta, Smoked Cheese & Ham, Chilled & Prepacked (Asda)
serving 90g/3oz 15
Ciabatta, Tomato (Waitrose) *serving 90g/3oz* 4
Ciabatta, Vegetable, Chargrilled, Hot (Marks & Spencer)
serving 170g/6oz 12
Cob, Crusty White (Somerfield) *serving 90g/3oz* 1
Cob, Granary (Tesco) *serving 90g/3oz* 3
Cob, Malted Brown Granary (Waitrose) *serving 90g/3oz* 2
Cob, Multigrain (Holland & Barrett) *serving 90g/3oz* 1
Cob, Wholemeal (Somerfield) *serving 90g/3oz* 4
Coburg Loaf, White (Somerfield) *serving 90g/3oz* 2
Cornbread, Home Made with Whole Milk *serving 90g/3oz* 7
Cottage Loaf (Somerfield) *serving 90g/3oz* 2
Cracked Wheat Bread *serving 90g/3oz* 4
Crispbread, Light *serving 90g/3oz* 5
Croissant (Somerfield) *serving 90g/3oz* 24
Croissant (Waitrose) *serving 90g/3oz* 28
Croissant, All Butter (Marks & Spencer) *serving 90g/3oz* 18
Croissant, All Butter (Tesco) *serving 90g/3oz* 18
Croissant, All Butter (Waitrose) *serving 90g/3oz* 24
Croissant, All Butter Mini (Tesco) *serving 90g/3oz* 18
Croissant, All Butter Mini (Waitrose) *serving 90g/3oz* 28
Croissant, Almond (Marks & Spencer) *serving 90g/3oz* 22
Croissant, Almond (Waitrose) *serving 90g/3oz* 20
Croissant, Butter (Marks & Spencer) *serving 90g/3oz* 23
Croissant, Cheese Mini (Marks & Spencer) *serving 90g/3oz* 27
Croissant, Egg & Bacon (Waitrose) *serving 90g/3oz* 21
Croissant, French Butter (Waitrose) *serving 90g/3oz* 20
Croissant, Ham & Cheese (Waitrose) *serving 90g/3oz* 21
Crostini, (Waitrose) *serving 90g/3oz* 4
Crostini, Cheese & Onion (Waitrose) *serving 90g/3oz* 27
Croutons, Plain *serving 90g/3oz* 6

Croutons, Toasted (Waitrose) *serving 90g/3oz* 26
Crumpet (Marks & Spencer) *serving 90g/3oz* 1
Crumpet (Tesco) *serving 90g/3oz* 1
Crumpet, English Toasting (Somerfield) *serving 90g/3oz* 2
Crumpet, Large Toaster (Tesco) *serving 90g/3oz* 1
Crumpet, Round (Somerfield) *serving 90g/3oz* 1
Crumpet, Toasted *serving 90g/3oz* 1
Crumpet, Traditional (Tesco) *serving 90g/3oz* 1
Crumpet Finger (Somerfield) *serving 90g/3oz* 1
Danish Bread, Light (Asda) *serving 90g/3oz* 2
Danish Bread, Malted Grain, Thick Sliced (Tesco) *serving 90g/3oz* 2
Danish Cinnamon & Raisin Swirl (Waitrose) *serving 90g/3oz* 22
Danish Loaf, Floured (Somerfield) *serving 90g/3oz* 2
Danish Loaf, Medium Sliced (Tesco) *serving 90g/3oz* 2
Danish Loaf, Thick Sliced (Tesco) *serving 90g/3oz* 2
Danish Loaf, White (Waitrose) *serving 90g/3oz* 2
Danish Pastry, Almond & Custard (Waitrose) *serving 90g/3oz* 17
Danish Pastry, Apple (Waitrose) *serving 90g/3oz* 18
Danish Pastry, Cheese *serving 90g/3oz* 20
Danish Pastry, Lemon & Sultana (Waitrose) *serving 90g/3oz* 16
Danish Pastry, Toffee Pecan (Waitrose) *serving 90g/3oz* 19
Danish Toaster (Waitrose) *serving 90g/3oz* 4
Danish Twists, Mincemeat (Waitrose) *serving 90g/3oz* 15
Danish White Bread, Medium Sliced (Somerfield) *serving 90g/3oz* 2
Danish White Bread, Thick Sliced (Somerfield) *serving 90g/3oz* 2
Date & Walnut Teabread (Marks & Spencer) *serving 90g/3oz* 12
Egg Bread, Toasted *serving 90g/3oz* 6
Farmhouse (Tesco) *serving 90g/3oz* 3
Farmhouse Crusty Wholewheat (Tesco) *serving 90g/3oz* 3
Farmhouse Loaf (Somerfield) *serving 90g/3oz* 2
Farmhouse Loaf, Sliced (Marks & Spencer) *serving 90g/3oz* 2
Farmhouse Loaf, Soft (Somerfield) *serving 90g/3oz* 2
Farmhouse Loaf, White (Waitrose) *serving 90g/3oz* 2
Farmhouse Tin, Wholemeal (Waitrose) *serving 90g/3oz* 3
Farmhouse, White Sesame (Waitrose) *serving 90g/3oz* 2

Farmhouse, White (Somerfield) *serving 90g/3oz*	2
Farmhouse, White (Waitrose) *serving 90g/3oz*	1
Farmhouse, Wholemeal Bread (Marks & Spencer) *serving 90g/3oz*	3
Flatbread, Cheese & Tomato (Marks & Spencer) *serving 90g/3oz*	7
Flatbread, Garlic & Herb (Marks & Spencer) *serving 90g/3oz*	16
Flute, Part Baked, Large (Waitrose) *serving 90g/3oz*	1
Focaccia, Garlic & Basil, Chilled & Prepacked (Asda) *serving 90g/3oz*	21
Focaccia, Mediterranean (Waitrose) *serving 90g/3oz*	9
Focaccia, Mixed Pack (Waitrose) *serving 90g/3oz*	3
Focaccia, Mushroom & Garlic (Waitrose) *serving 90g/3oz*	8
Focaccia, Rosemary (Waitrose) *serving 90g/3oz*	5
French or Vienna Bread (includes Sourdough) *serving 90g/3oz*	3
French Stick, Brown (Somerfield) *serving 90g/3oz*	4
French Stick, Harvester (Somerfield) *serving 90g/3oz*	4
French Stick, Seeded (Somerfield) *serving 90g/3oz*	2
French Stick, White (Somerfield) *serving 90g/3oz*	1
French Style Stick (Waitrose) *serving 90g/3oz*	2
French Toast, Frozen, Ready to Heat *serving 90g/3oz*	5
French Toast, Prepared from Recipe, Made with Low-fat (2%) Milk *serving 90g/3oz*	10
French Toast, Prepared from Recipe Made with Whole Milk *serving 90g/3oz*	10
French Toast with Butter *serving 90g/3oz*	13
French Toast Sticks *serving 90g/3oz*	19
Fruit Batch Loaf (Somerfield) *serving 90g/3oz*	3
Fruit Loaf (Somerfield) *serving 90g/3oz*	6
Fruit Loaf, Sliced (Somerfield) *serving 90g/3oz*	5
Fruit Loaf, Thick Sliced (Tesco) *serving 90g/3oz*	6
Fruit Plait (Waitrose) *serving 90g/3oz*	6
Garlic Bread (Asda) *serving 90g/3oz*	15
Garlic Bread (Safeway) *serving 90g/3oz*	7
Garlic Bread, Healthy Choice, Chilled & Prepacked (Asda) *serving 90g/3oz*	10
Garlic Bread, Stonebake, Hot (Marks & Spencer) *serving 170g/6oz*	20

Garlic Breadsticks (Waitrose) *serving 90g/3oz*	6
Garlic Harvester Bread, Frozen, Oven Baked (Iceland) *serving 90g/3oz*	14
Garlic Knots, Wholemeal (Waitrose) *serving 90g/3oz*	13
Garlic & Mozzarella Bread (Marks & Spencer) *serving 90g/3oz*	19
Garlic Toastie (Marks & Spencer) *serving 90g/3oz*	10
Goldgrain/Sesame Bread (Waitrose) *serving 90g/3oz*	3
Granary Baton, Bake Off (Waitrose) *serving 90g/3oz*	1
Granary Bread, Sesame Seed (Waitrose) *serving 90g/3oz*	2
Granary, Lite (Marks & Spencer) *serving 90g/3oz*	2
Granary, Long Tin (Waitrose) *serving 90g/3oz*	3
Granary, Malted Bread, Tin (Waitrose) *serving 90g/3oz*	2
Granary, Malted Brown (Tesco) *serving 90g/3oz*	2
Granary, Malted Brown, Tin (Waitrose) *serving 90g/3oz*	3
Granary, Malted Stick (Waitrose) *serving 90g/3oz*	3
Granary, Tin (Waitrose) *serving 90g/3oz*	3
Greek Olive Bread (Waitrose) *serving 90g/3oz*	7
Greek Salad Flatbread (Waitrose) *serving 90g/3oz*	5
Harvest Brown (Marks & Spencer) *serving 90g/3oz*	2
Harvester Tin Loaf (Somerfield) *serving 90g/3oz*	2
Heyford Tin Bread (Waitrose) *serving 90g/3oz*	4
Hi Bran (Marks & Spencer) *serving 90g/3oz*	3
Hovis (Waitrose) *serving 90g/3oz*	2
Hovis (Marks & Spencer) *serving 90g/3oz*	2
Hovis Handy (Tesco) *serving 90g/3oz*	2
Italian Bread *serving 90g/3oz*	3
Italian Tomato Bread (Waitrose) *serving 90g/3oz*	3
Knot, White Seeded (Somerfield) *serving 90g/3oz*	0
Knot Rolls, Seeded (Waitrose) *serving 90g/3oz*	1
Knots, Frozen, Part Bake (Waitrose) *serving 90g/3oz*	1
Large Flute, Bake Off (Waitrose) *serving 90g/3oz*	1
Laverbread *serving 90g/3oz*	3
Lincolm Plum Bread (Waitrose) *serving 90g/3oz*	3
Lincoln Plum Teabread (Marks & Spencer) *serving 90g/3oz*	7
Long Split Tin (Waitrose) *serving 90g/3oz*	2
Long White Tin, Part Bake (Waitrose) *serving 90g/3oz*	1
Malt Loaf (Tesco) *serving 90g/3oz*	2

Maltbread *serving 90g/3oz*	2
Milk Bread *serving 90g/3oz*	8
Mixed Fruit Loaf (Somerfield) *serving 90g/3oz*	5
Mixed Grain Bread (includes Whole Grain) *serving 90g/3oz*	3
Mixed Grain, Medium Sliced (Waitrose) *serving 90g/3oz*	2
Mixed Grain Bread, Toasted (includes Whole Grain) *serving 90g/3oz*	4
Mixed Grain Seed, Wholemeal (Waitrose) *serving 90g/3oz*	6
Mozzarella Pesto Bread (Waitrose) *serving 90g/3oz*	11
Muffin *serving 90g/3oz*	6
Muffin (Marks & Spencer) *serving 90g/3oz*	2
Muffin (Somerfield) *serving 90g/3oz*	2
Muffin, Apple Cinnamon (Betty Crocker) *serving 90g/3oz*	8
Muffin, Blackcurrant (Waitrose) *serving 90g/3oz*	18
Muffin, Blueberry (Betty Crocker) *serving 90g/3oz*	8
Muffin, Blueberry (Somerfield) *serving 90g/3oz*	19
Muffin, Blueberry (Tesco) *serving 90g/3oz*	20
Muffin, Chocolate Chip & Frosting (Betty Crocker) *serving 90g/3oz*	12
Muffin, Chocolate Dairy Cream (Somerfield) *serving 90g/3oz*	25
Muffin, Country Carrot (Somerfield) *serving 90g/3oz*	22
Muffin, Double Berry (Somerfield) *serving 90g/3oz*	19
Muffin, Double Chocolate (Somerfield) *serving 90g/3oz*	21
Muffin, Double Chocolate (Waitrose) *serving 90g/3oz*	21
Muffin, Raisin & Bran (Waitrose) *serving 90g/3oz*	18
Muffin, Spiced Fruit (Somerfield) *serving 90g/3oz*	2
Muffin, Strawberry Flavoured (Somerfield) *serving 90g/3oz*	21
Muffin, Toffee & Banana (Somerfield) *serving 90g/3oz*	18
Muffin, Traditional (Tesco) *serving 90g/3oz*	1
Muffin, Traditional Wholemeal (Tesco) *serving 90g/3oz*	3
Muffin, White (Tesco) *serving 90g/3oz*	1
Muffin, White (Waitrose) *serving 90g/3oz*	2
Muffin, Wholemeal (Somerfield) *serving 90g/3oz*	2
Muffin, Wholemeal (Waitrose) *serving 90g/3oz*	2
Multigrain Bread (Marks & Spencer) *serving 90g/3oz*	6
Naan, Garlic (Waitrose) *serving 90g/3oz*	15
Naan, Mini (Marks & Spencer) *serving 90g/3oz*	5

Naan Bread *serving 90g/3oz*	11
Naan Bread (Marks & Spencer) *serving 90g/3oz*	7
Nan Bread (Tesco) *serving 90g/3oz*	12
Naan Bread, Herb & Garlic (Marks & Spencer) *serving 90g/3oz*	4
Nan Bread, Peshwari (Tesco) *serving 90g/3oz*	12
Oat Bran Bread *serving 90g/3oz*	4
Oatmeal, Medium Sliced (Tesco) *serving 90g/3oz*	3
Oatmeal, Thick Sliced (Tesco) *serving 90g/3oz*	3
Pain au Chocolat, (Tesco) *serving 90g/3oz*	25
Pain au Chocolat (Waitrose) *serving 90g/3oz*	26
Pain au Chocolat, Mini (Tesco) *serving 90g/3oz*	25
Pain au Chocolat, Mini (Waitrose) *serving 90g/3oz*	26
Pain au Raisin (Marks & Spencer) *serving 90g/3oz*	15
Pain au Raisin, Mini (Marks & Spencer) *serving 90g/3oz*	18
Pain au Raisin, Mini (Somerfield) *serving 90g/3oz*	17
Pain de Bordeaux (Waitrose) *serving 90g/3oz*	1
Pain de Campagne (Waitrose) *serving 90g/3oz*	2
Pain Fermier (Waitrose) *serving 90g/3oz*	1
Pain Raisin, Traditional French (Waitrose) *serving 90g/3oz*	13
Pain Rustique, Bake Off (Waitrose) *serving 90g/3oz*	1
Papadums, Fried *serving 90g/3oz*	15
Papadums, Raw *serving 90g/3oz*	2
Paratha *serving 90g/3oz*	13
Paysan Rustique (Waitrose) *serving 90g/3oz*	2
Petit Pain, Frozen, Part Baked (Waitrose) *serving 90g/3oz*	1
Petit Pain, Homebake, Fresh, Ovenbake (Iceland) *serving 90g/3oz*	1
Petit Pain, Part Baked (Waitrose) *serving 90g/3oz*	1
Petit Parisienne (Waitrose) *serving 90g/3oz*	1
Pikelets (Tesco) *serving 90g/3oz*	1
Pitta (Marks & Spencer) *serving 90g/3oz*	2
Pitta Bread, Spicy (Tesco) *serving 90g/3oz*	1
Pitta, Mini White (Tesco) *serving 90g/3oz*	1
Pitta, White *serving 90g/3oz*	1
Pitta, White (Somerfield) *serving 90g/3oz*	2
Pitta, White (Tesco) *serving 90g/3oz*	1

Pitta, White Picnic (Waitrose) *serving 90g/3oz* 1
Pitta, White Traditional (Waitrose) *serving 90g/3oz* 1
Pitta, Wholemeal (Somerfield) *serving 90g/3oz* 2
Pitta, Wholemeal (Tesco) *serving 90g/3oz* 2
Pitta, Wholemeal (Waitrose) *serving 90g/3oz* 2
Pitta, Whole Wheat *serving 90g/3oz* 2
Pitta, Whole Wheat (Tesco) *serving 90g/3oz* 2
Pitta, Wholemeal Picnic (Waitrose) *serving 90g/3oz* 2
Ploughmans Plait (Waitrose) *serving 90g/3oz* 12
Popovers, Prepared from Recipe, Made With Low-fat (2%) Milk *serving 90g/3oz* 7
Popovers, Prepared from Recipe, Made with Whole Milk *serving 90g/3oz* 8
Poppadums (Marks & Spencer) *serving 90g/3oz* 26
Poppy Seed Bread (Waitrose) *serving 90g/3oz* 5
Potato Cake, Traditional (Tesco) *serving 90g/3oz* 5
Premium Loaf, Medium (Marks & Spencer) *serving 90g/3oz* 3
Premium Loaf, Thick (Marks & Spencer) *serving 90g/3oz* 3
Protein Bread (includes Gluten) *serving 90g/3oz* 2
Pumpernickel Bread *serving 90g/3oz* 3
Pumpernickel Bread, Toasted *serving 90g/3oz* 3
Puri Punjabi *serving 90g/3oz* 32
Raisin Bread *serving 90g/3oz* 4
Rice Bran Bread *serving 90g/3oz* 4
Rich Fruit Loaf (Marks & Spencer) *serving 90g/3oz* 6
Roll, Aberdeen (Marks & Spencer) *serving 90g/3oz* 28
Roll, Breakfast Morning (Marks & Spencer) *serving 90g/3oz* 5
Roll, Bridge (Waitrose) *serving 90g/3oz* 5
Roll, Bridge White (Somerfield) *serving 90g/3oz* 3
Roll, Bridge White (Waitrose) *serving 90g/3oz* 4
Roll, Bridge Wholemeal (Waitrose) *serving 90g/3oz* 5
Roll, Brown (Waitrose) *serving 90g/3oz* 2
Roll, Burger or Hotdog, Mixed Grain *serving 90g/3oz* 5
Roll, Burger or Hotdog, Plain *serving 90g/3oz* 5
Roll, Burger or Hotdog, Reduced Calorie *serving 90g/3oz* 2
Roll, Ciabatta (Marks & Spencer) *serving 90g/3oz* 5
Roll, Ciabatta (Waitrose) *serving 90g/3oz* 2

Roll, Cob White (Waitrose) *serving 90g/3oz* 1
Roll, Continental (Tesco) *serving 90g/3oz* 1
Roll, Cottage White (Waitrose) *serving 90g/3oz* 4
Roll, Crusty White (Marks & Spencer) *serving 90g/3oz* 0
Roll, Crusty White (Waitrose) *serving 90g/3oz* 2
Roll, Dinner, Egg *serving 90g/3oz* 6
Roll, Dinner, Oat Bran *serving 90g/3oz* 4
Roll, Dinner, Plain, Commercially Prepared (includes Brown and Serve) *serving 90g/3oz* 7
Roll, Dinner, Rye *serving 90g/3oz* 3
Roll, Dinner, Wheat *serving 90g/3oz* 6
Roll, Dinner, Whole Wheat *serving 90g/3oz* 4
Roll, Finger (Marks & Spencer) *serving 90g/3oz* 3
Roll, Finger White (Somerfield) *serving 90g/3oz* 3
Roll, French *serving 90g/3oz* 4
Roll, Garlic (Somerfield) *serving 90g/3oz* 10
Roll, Garlic, Chilled (Tesco) *serving 90g/3oz* 12
Roll, Garlic, Chilled & Prepacked (Asda) *serving 90g/3oz* 16
Roll, Garlic, Frozen (Tesco) *serving 90g/3oz* 18
Roll, Garlic, White (Safeway) *serving 90g/3oz* 4
Roll, Granary (Marks & Spencer) *serving 90g/3oz* 3
Roll, Granary (Waitrose) *serving 90g/3oz* 2
Roll, Granary, Malted Brown (Waitrose) *serving 90g/3oz* 4
Roll, Hard *serving 90g/3oz* 4
Roll, Healthy Eating White Batch (Tesco) *serving 90g/3oz* 2
Roll, Large Petit Pain Harvester (Somerfield) *serving 90g/3oz* 2
Roll, Large Petit Pain White (Somerfield) *serving 90g/3oz* 1
Roll, Large Soft Brown Split (Somerfield) *serving 90g/3oz* 3
Roll, Milk, Knot (4) (Marks & Spencer) *serving 90g/3oz* 8
Roll, Milk, Scroll (Waitrose) *serving 90g/3oz* 4
Roll, Milk, White (Tesco) *serving 90g/3oz* 4
Roll, Milk, Wholemeal Sliced (Tesco) *serving 90g/3oz* 4
Roll, Mini Brown (Marks & Spencer) *serving 90g/3oz* 6
Roll, Morning (Somerfield) *serving 90g/3oz* 3
Roll, Old English/Scotch (Marks & Spencer) *serving 90g/3oz* 2
Roll, Old Fashioned White (Waitrose) *serving 90g/3oz* 3
Roll, Old Fashioned Wholemeal (Waitrose) *serving 90g/3oz* 2

Roll, Premium White (Marks & Spencer) *serving 90g/3oz*	2
Roll, Scotch Wholemeal (Somerfield) *serving 90g/3oz*	3
Roll, Scottish White (Waitrose) *serving 90g/3oz*	1
Roll, Soft Brown (Somerfield) *serving 90g/3oz*	3
Roll, Soft White Finger (Waitrose) *serving 90g/3oz*	4
Roll, Soft White (Marks & Spencer) *serving 90g/3oz*	3
Roll, Soft White (Somerfield) *serving 90g/3oz*	2
Roll, Soft White (Waitrose) *serving 90g/3oz*	3
Roll, Soft White Snack (Waitrose) *serving 90g/3oz*	3
Roll, Soft White Split (Somerfield) *serving 90g/3oz*	3
Roll, Soft Wholemeal (Marks & Spencer) *serving 90g/3oz*	4
Roll, Split (Marks & Spencer) *serving 90g/3oz*	3
Roll, Stoneground (Marks & Spencer) *serving 90g/3oz*	6
Roll, Submarine (Marks & Spencer) *serving 90g/3oz*	4
Roll, Sweet Cheese *serving 90g/3oz*	16
Roll, White (Marks & Spencer) *serving 90g/3oz*	2
Roll, White Assorted (Waitrose) *serving 90g/3oz*	3
Roll, White Basics (Somerfield) *serving 90g/3oz*	1
Roll, White Crusty (Tesco) *serving 90g/3oz*	1
Roll, White Homebake (Marks & Spencer) *serving 90g/3oz*	0
Roll, White Mini (Marks & Spencer) *serving 90g/3oz*	10
Roll, White, Organic Flour (Waitrose) *serving 90g/3oz*	2
Roll, White Soft (Waitrose) *serving 90g/3oz*	4
Roll, Wholemeal Assorted (Waitrose) *serving 90g/3oz*	5
Roll, Wholemeal (Holland & Barrett) *serving 90g/3oz*	2
Roll, Wholemeal Mini (Tesco) *serving 90g/3oz*	4
Roll, Wholemeal, Organic Flour (Waitrose) *serving 90g/3oz*	2
Rustique, Flat, Bake Off (Waitrose) *serving 90g/3oz*	1
Rye Bread (Tesco) *serving 90g/3oz*	1
Rye Bread (100%) (Waitrose) *serving 90g/3oz*	1
Rye Bread, Light (Waitrose) *serving 90g/3oz*	2
Rye Bread, Toasted *serving 90g/3oz*	3
Rye, Light Seedless (Waitrose) *serving 90g/3oz*	2
Rye, Malted (Waitrose) *serving 90g/3oz*	4
Rye Stick (Waitrose) *serving 90g/3oz*	2
Rye Stick with Onion (Waitrose) *serving 90g/3oz*	2
Sandwich Loaf, Medium (Marks & Spencer) *serving 90g/3oz*	2

Sandwich Loaf, Soft (Somerfield) *serving 90g/3oz* 2
Sandwich Loaf, Thick (Marks & Spencer) *serving 90g/3oz* 2
Schiacciata (Marks & Spencer) *serving 90g/3oz* 6
Scone, Bramley Apple, Sultana & Cinnamon (Somerfield) *serving 90g/3oz* 8
Scone, Cheese *serving 90g/3oz* 16
Scone, Cheese (Tesco) *serving 90g/3oz* 11
Scone, Cheese (Waitrose) *serving 90g/3oz* 11
Scone, Cream (Somerfield) *serving 90g/3oz* 11
Scone, Dairy Cream (Somerfield) *serving 90g/3oz* 11
Scone, Devon (Tesco) *serving 90g/3oz* 14
Scone, Fruit *serving 90g/3oz* 9
Scone, Fruit (Somerfield) *serving 90g/3oz* 9
Scone, Fruit Basics (Somerfield) *serving 90g/3oz* 8
Scone, Fruit, White (Waitrose) *serving 90g/3oz* 6
Scone, Individual Derby (Tesco) *serving 90g/3oz* 11
Scone, Individual Devon (Tesco) *serving 90g/3oz* 12
Scone, Individual Sultana (Tesco) *serving 90g/3oz* 9
Scone, Individually Wrapped Giant Cheese (Tesco) *serving 90g/3oz* 10
Scone, Large Cheese (Tesco) *serving 90g/3oz* 14
Scone, Plain *serving 90g/3oz* 13
Scone, Plain (Waitrose) *serving 90g/3oz* 11
Scone, Potato *serving 90g/3oz* 13
Scone, Potato (Marks & Spencer) *serving 90g/3oz* 4
Scone, Strawberry (Marks & Spencer) *serving 90g/3oz* 20
Scone, Sultana (Waitrose) *serving 90g/3oz* 11
Scone, Sultana, Round (Marks & Spencer) *serving 90g/3oz* 10
Scone, Traditional Sultana (Tesco) *serving 90g/3oz* 10
Scone, Wholemeal *serving 90g/3oz* 13
Scone, Wholemeal (Tesco) *serving 90g/3oz* 9
Scone, Wholemeal (Waitrose) *serving 90g/3oz* 9
Scone, Wholemeal Fruit *serving 90g/3oz* 12
Scottish Square Bread (Tesco) *serving 90g/3oz* 1
Soda Bread *serving 90g/3oz* 2
Soda Bread, Brown (Marks & Spencer) *serving 90g/3oz* 3
Soda Bread, Brown (Tesco) *serving 90g/3oz* 2

Soda Bread, Irish, Home Made *serving 90g/3oz* 5
Soda Bread, White (Waitrose) *serving 90g/3oz* 3
Soft Bake Bread (Somerfield) *serving 90g/3oz* 1
Soft Bake White Farmhouse Bread (Somerfield) *serving 90g/3oz* 0
Soft Bake White Tin Bread (Somerfield) *serving 90g/3oz* 0
Soft Baked Bread (Somerfield) *serving 90g/3oz* 1
Soft Grain Bread, Healthy Choice (Asda) *serving 90g/3oz* 1
Soft Grain Bread, Medium (Marks & Spencer) *serving 90g/3oz* 2
Softgrain Bread, Medium Sliced (Somerfield) *serving 90g/3oz* 1
Softgrain Bread, Medium Sliced (Tesco) *serving 90g/3oz* 1
Softgrain Bread, Thick Sliced (Somerfield) *serving 90g/3oz* 1
Softgrain Bread, Thick Sliced (Tesco) *serving 90g/3oz* 1
Sour Dough Loaf (Somerfield) *serving 90g/3oz* 2
Split Loaf, Soft (Somerfield) *serving 90g/3oz* 2
Split Tin Loaf (Marks & Spencer) *serving 90g/3oz* 3
Split Tin (Tesco) *serving 90g/3oz* 3
Square Loaf (Marks & Spencer) *serving 90g/3oz* 1
Sunflower & Honey Loaf (Marks & Spencer) *serving 90g/3oz* 8
Taco Shells, Baked *serving 90g/3oz* 20
Tandoori, Ethnic Bread (Waitrose) *serving 90g/3oz* 12
Teacakes (Marks & Spencer) *serving 90g/3oz* 4
Teacakes (Tesco) *serving 90g/3oz* 4
Teacakes, Fresh *serving 90g/3oz* 7
Teacakes, Fruited (Somerfield) *serving 90g/3oz* 4
Teacakes, Fruited (Tesco) *serving 90g/3oz* 4
Teacakes, Toasted *serving 90g/3oz* 7
Three Seed Loaf (Waitrose) *serving 90g/3oz* 6
Tin Loaf, Soft White (Somerfield) *serving 90g/3oz* 2
Toaster Pastries, Fruit (includes Apple, Blueberry, Cherry, Strawberry) *serving 90g/3oz* 9
Tortillas, Made with Wheat Flour *serving 90g/3oz* 1
Tortillas, Ready to Bake or Fry, Corn *serving 90g/3oz* 2
Triple Grain Mini Stick (Waitrose) *serving 90g/3oz* 1
Waffles, Plain, Home Made *serving 90g/3oz* 13
Walnut Bread, Marbled (Waitrose) *serving 90g/3oz* 10
Wheat Bran Bread *serving 90g/3oz* 3
Wheat Bran Bread, Toasted *serving 90g/3oz* 3

Wheat Bread, Reduced Calorie *serving 90g/3oz*	2
Wheat Bread, Reduced Calorie, Toasted *serving 90g/3oz*	2
Wheat Bread (includes Wheat Berry) *serving 90g/3oz*	4
Wheat Bread, Toasted (includes Wheat Berry) *serving 90g/3oz*	4
Wheat Germ Bread *serving 90g/3oz*	3
Wheat Germ Bread, Toasted *serving 90g/3oz*	3
Wheat Sandwich Bread, Malted (Waitrose) *serving 90g/3oz*	2
Wheatgerm Bread, Average *serving 90g/3oz*	2
Whiskey Loaf (Marks & Spencer) *serving 90g/3oz*	3
White Bread, Bakers Choice (Marks & Spencer) *serving 90g/3oz*	2
White Bread, Batch Soft (Marks & Spencer) *serving 90g/3oz*	4
White Bread, Commercially Prepared (includes Soft Bread Crumbs) *serving 90g/3oz*	3
White Bread, Commercially Prepared, Toasted *serving 90g/3oz*	4
White Bread, Farmhouse (Marks & Spencer) *serving 90g/3oz*	2
White Bread, Healthy Eating, Medium Sliced(Tesco) *serving 90g/3oz*	1
White Bread, Healthy Eating, Thick Sliced (Tesco) *serving 90g/3oz*	1
White Bread, Heyford (Waitrose) *serving 90g/3oz*	2
White Bread, Lite (Marks & Spencer) *serving 90g/3oz*	2
White Bread, Premium, Medium Sliced (Somerfield) *serving 90g/3oz*	2
White Bread, Medium Sliced (Somerfield) *serving 90g/3oz*	1
White Bread, Premium, Medium Sliced (Tesco) *serving 90g/3oz*	2
White Bread, Premium, Thick Sliced (Tesco) *serving 90g/3oz*	2
White Bread, Premium (Waitrose) *serving 90g/3oz*	2
White Bread, Soft Farmhouse (Marks & Spencer) *serving 90g/3oz*	3
White Bread, Soft (Waitrose) *serving 90g/3oz*	1
White Bread, Premium, Thick Sliced (Somerfield) *serving 90g/3oz*	2
White Bread, Thick Sliced (Somerfield) *serving 90g/3oz*	1
White Bread, Thick Sliced (Waitrose) *serving 90g/3oz*	2
White Bread, Thin Sliced (Waitrose) *serving 90g/3oz*	2
White Bread, Toasting Loaf (Marks & Spencer) *serving 90g/3oz*	4
White Bread, Traditional (Waitrose) *serving 90g/3oz*	3
White Loaf, Medium Sliced (Waitrose) *serving 90g/3oz*	2
White, Medium Sliced (Tesco) *serving 90g/3oz*	2
White Organic Bread (Waitrose) *serving 90g/3oz*	2

White Sandwich Tin (Waitrose) *serving 90g/3oz* 2
White Sliced Toaster (Tesco) *serving 90g/3oz* 2
White, Thick Sliced (Tesco) *serving 90g/3oz* 2
White, Thin Sliced (Tesco) *serving 90g/3oz* 2
White Toaster Bread, Premium, Medium Sliced (Somerfield) *serving 90g/3oz* 2
White Toasting Bread (Waitrose) *serving 90g/3oz* 3
Whole Wheat Bread, Commercially Prepared *serving 90g/3oz* 4
Whole Wheat Bread, Commercially Prepared, Toasted *serving 90g/3oz* 4
Whole Wheat Bread, Home Made *serving 90g/3oz* 5
Whole Wheat Bread, Home Made, Toasted *serving 90g/3oz* 5
Wholemeal, Bakers Choice (Marks & Spencer) *serving 90g/3oz* 3
Wholemeal Batch, Soft (Marks & Spencer) *serving 90g/3oz* 5
Wholemeal Bread, Multigrain, Medium Sliced (Somerfield) *serving 90g/3oz* 3
Wholemeal Bread, Medium Sliced (Somerfield) *serving 90g/3oz* 2
Wholemeal Bread, Medium Sliced (Waitrose) *serving 90g/3oz* 2
Wholemeal Bread, Sandwich, Medium Sliced (Marks & Spencer) *serving 90g/3oz* 2
Wholemeal Bread, Sandwich, Thick Sliced (Marks & Spencer) *serving 90g/3oz* 2
Wholemeal Bread, Thick Sliced (Somerfield) *serving 90g/3oz* 2
Wholemeal Bread, Thick Sliced (Waitrose) *serving 90g/3oz* 2
Wholemeal Bread, Traditional (Waitrose) *serving 90g/3oz* 1
Wholemeal Breadcrumbs (Somerfield) *serving 90g/3oz* 2
Wholemeal, Continental (Waitrose) *serving 90g/3oz* 4
Wholemeal, Healthy Eating (Tesco) *serving 90g/3oz* 2
Wholemeal, Healthy Eating, Medium Sliced (Tesco) *serving 90g/3oz* 3
Wholemeal, Healthy Eating, Thick Sliced (Tesco) *serving 90g/3oz* 3
Wholemeal, Heyford Premium (Waitrose) *serving 90g/3oz* 4
Wholemeal, Lite (Marks & Spencer) *serving 90g/3oz* 4
Wholemeal Loaf (Holland & Barrett) *serving 90g/3oz* 2
Wholemeal Loaf (Somerfield) *serving 90g/3oz* 4
Wholemeal Loaf, Continental Style (Holland & Barrett) *serving 90g/3oz* 2

Wholemeal Loaf with Oats (Waitrose) *serving 90g/3oz* 2
Wholemeal, Long Tin (Waitrose) *serving 90g/3oz* 3
Wholemeal, Medium Sliced (Tesco) *serving 90g/3oz* 2
Wholemeal, Multigrain (Tesco) *serving 90g/3oz* 3
Wholemeal, Natures Choice (Tesco) *serving 90g/3oz* 3
Wholemeal, Organic Tin (Waitrose) *serving 90g/3oz* 2
Wholemeal, Organic Wrapped (Waitrose) *serving 90g/3oz* 2
Wholemeal, Plain Stoneground (Waitrose) *serving 90g/3oz* 2
Wholemeal, Premium, with Added Wheatgerm (Tesco) *serving 90g/3oz* 3
Wholemeal Sandwich (Waitrose) *serving 90g/3oz* 2
Wholemeal, Seeded Batch (Waitrose) *serving 90g/3oz* 2
Wholemeal Bread, Sliced (Waitrose) *serving 90g/3oz* 2
Wholemeal Loaf, Sliced (Waitrose) *serving 90g/3oz* 2
Wholemeal, Soft, Medium Sliced (Tesco) *serving 90g/3oz* 2
Wholemeal, Stoneground, Medium Sliced (Tesco) *serving 90g/3oz* 2
Wholemeal, Soft, Thick Sliced (Tesco) *serving 90g/3oz* 2
Windmill, Fruited (Tesco) *serving 90g/3oz* 6
Wrapped Tin (Waitrose) *serving 90g/3oz* 2

Burgers

NOTE: The standard serving size in this section is 110g/4oz. If you wish to consume more or less than this amount (e.g. if you are going to consume a pack of food whose weight differs from the standard serving size) use the conversion tables on page 386 to calculate the new amount of fat in the food.

100% Beef Burger (Birds Eye) *serving 110g/4oz* 32
100% Beefburger (Waitrose) *serving 110g/4oz* 24
Aberdeen Angus Burger (Waitrose) *serving 110g/4oz* 15
Aduki Beanburger, Fried in Vegetable Oil *serving 110g/4oz* 8
American Style Beefburger (Somerfield) *serving 110g/4oz* 18
American Style Quarter Pounders (Somerfield) *serving 110g/4oz* 19
Bean Burger, Spicy (Cauldron Foods) *serving 110g/4oz* 18

Bean Nuggett, Mexican Selection, Frozen, Ovenbaked (Iceland) *serving 110g/4oz* 17
Beef Burger (Marks & Spencer) *serving 110g/4oz* 19
Beef Burger (Somerfield) *serving 110g/4oz* 24
Beefburger 100%, Frozen (Asda) *serving 110g/4oz* 24
Beefburger, Chilled (Tesco) *serving 110g/4oz* 22
Beefburger 80%, Frozen (Tesco) *serving 110g/4oz* 28
Beefburger (Waitrose) *serving 110g/4oz* 27
Beefburger, Fresh (Waitrose) *serving 110g/4oz* 19
Beefburger, Thin (Marks & Spencer) *serving 110g/4oz* 18
Beef Grills (6), Frozen (Asda) *serving 110g/4oz* 23
Burger, Economy (Birds Eye) *serving 110g/4oz* 24
Burger, Extra Lean (Birds Eye) *serving 110g/4oz* 13
Butter Bean Beanburger, Fried in Vegetable Oil *serving 110g/4oz* 12
Chargrill Flavour Quarter Pounders (Somerfield) *serving 110g/4oz* 27
Chargrill Quarterpounders (4), Frozen (Asda) *serving 110g/4oz* 23
Chargrilled $^{1}/_{4}$ lb (Waitrose) *serving 110g/4oz* 21
Cheeseburger, Regular Double, Patty & Bun with Condiments & Vegetables *serving 110g/4oz* 17
Chicken Burger (Marks & Spencer) *serving 110g/4oz* 8
Chicken Burger (Somerfield) *serving 110g/4oz* 19
Chicken Burger, Fuzzy (Marks & Spencer) *serving 110g/4oz* 15
Chicken Classic Burger, Chilled, Raw (Tesco) *serving 110g/4oz* 11
Chicken Classic Burger, Chilled, Cooked (Tesco) *serving 110g/4oz* 17
Classic Burger in a Bun, Chilled (Tesco) *serving 110g/4oz* 11
Classic Burger with Cheese, Chilled (Tesco) *serving 110g/4oz* 19
Classic Cheese Burger, Chilled (Tesco) *serving 110g/4oz* 11
Cod Burger & Fries, Frozen, Microwave (Iceland) *serving 110g/4oz* 12
Cutlets, Rice, Mushrooms & Broccoli, Crispy (Somerfield) *serving 110g/4oz* 12
Flaming Good Burger, (Birds Eye) *serving 110g/4oz* 13
Fun Pots Burger (CPC) *serving 110g/4oz* 16
Hamburger, Chilled (Safeway) *serving 110g/4oz* 13

Hamburger, Large Single, Meat Patty with Condiments & Vegetables *serving 110g/4oz* 14
Hamburgers with Onion & Gravy, Tinned (Tesco) *serving 110g/4oz* 8
Healthy Eating Burger, Chilled (Tesco) *serving 110g/4oz* 10
Healthy Eating Burger, Frozen (Tesco) *serving 110g/4oz* 12
Kidney Bean Beanburger, Fried in Vegetable Oil *serving 110g/4oz* 12
Meat Free Chunky Burgers (Birds Eye) *serving 110g/4oz* 11
Mega Burger (Birds Eye) *serving 110g/4oz* 25
Mexican Bean Quarter Pounder, Frozen (Tesco) *serving 110g/4oz* 11
Nut Cutlets (Goodlife Foods) *serving 110g/4oz* 16
Nut Cutlets (Safeway) *serving 110g/4oz* 8
Original Burger (Birds Eye) *serving 110g/4oz* 26
Pork Quarter Pounders (Somerfield) *serving 90g/3oz* 19
Quarter Pounders (Birds Eye) *serving 110g/4oz* 24
Quarterpound Beefburgers, Frozen (Tesco) *serving 110g/4oz* 25
Quarterpounders (4), Frozen (Asda) *serving 110g/4oz* 23
Sausage Burger, Frozen (Tesco) *serving 110g/4oz* 28
Southern Fried Burger, Chilled (Iceland) *serving 110g/4oz* 28
Southern Fried Chicken Burger in a Bun, Frozen (Tesco) *serving 110g/4oz* 10
Soya Beanburger, Fried in Vegetable Oil *serving 110g/4oz* 12
Strike Burger (Somerfield) *serving 110g/4oz* 10
Strike Cheese Burger (Somerfield) *serving 110g/4oz* 12
Strike Reduced Fat Burger (Somerfield) *serving 110g/4oz* 6
Tempeh Burger, Made with Rice, Fried in Vegetable Oil *serving 110g/4oz* 9
Tofu Burger, Baked *serving 110g/4oz* 5
Tofu Burger, Chilli Flavour (Cauldron Foods) *serving 110g/4oz* 14
Tofu Burger, Savoury (Cauldron Foods) *serving 110g/4oz* 12
Vegeburger Mix, Made up with Water & Egg, Fried in Vegetable Oil *serving 110g/4oz* 14
Vegeburger Mix, Made up with Water & Egg, Grilled *serving 110g/4oz* 7
Vegeburger Mix, Made up with Water, Fried in Vegetable Oil *serving 110g/4oz* 13

Vegeburger Mix, Made up with Water, Grilled *serving 110g/4oz* 6
Vegetable Burger (Birds Eye) *serving 110g/4oz* 10
Vegetable Burger, Frozen (Holland & Barrett) *serving 110g/4oz* 9
Vegetable Burger, Frozen, Grilled (Iceland) *serving 110g/4oz* 13
Vegetable Quarter Pounders, Country Club Cuisine (Birds Eye) *serving 110g/4oz* 10
Vegetarian Burger, Frozen (Tesco) *serving 110g/4oz* 12
Vegetarian Burger, Low Fat Chargrilled (Tivall) *serving 110g/4oz* 6
Vegetarian Char Grilled Quarter Pounder (Tivall) *serving 110g/4oz* 10
Wild Boar Apple Burger (Waitrose) *serving 90g/3oz* 4

Butter, Margarine & Spreads

NOTE: The standard serving size in this section is 10g/0.3oz. If you wish to consume more or less than this amount (e.g. if you are going to consume a pack of food whose weight differs from the standard serving size) use the conversion tables on page 386 to calculate the new amount of fat in the food.

Believe It or Not Spread (Somerfield) *serving 10g/0.3oz* 7
Blended Spread, 70% Fat, Savers (Safeway) *serving 10g/0.3oz* 7
Blended Spread, Basics (Somerfield) *serving 10g/0.3oz* 7
Blue Band (Van Den Bergh) *serving 10g/0.3oz* 8
Butter, Blended (Safeway) *serving 10g/0.3oz* 8
Butter, Cointreau (Waitrose) *serving 10g/0.3oz* 4
Butter, Cornish (Somerfield) *serving 10g/0.3oz* 8
Butter, Creamery (Asda) *serving 10g/0.3oz* 8
Butter, Creamery (Somerfield) *serving 10g/0.3oz* 8
Butter, Creamery, Healthy Eating Half Fat (Tesco) *serving 10g/0.3oz* 8
Butter, Dairy (Waitrose) *serving 10g/0.3oz* 8
Butter, Danish (Safeway) *serving 10g/0.3oz* 8
Butter, Easy Spread, Unsalted (Marks & Spencer) *serving 10g/0.3oz* 8

Butter, English (Safeway) *serving 10g/0.3oz* 8
Butter, English (Waitrose) *serving 10g/0.3oz* 8
Butter, English, Salted (Marks & Spencer) *serving 10g/0.3oz* 8
Butter, English Churn (Marks & Spencer) *serving 10g/0.3oz* 7
Butter, Garlic (Safeway) *serving 10g/0.3oz* 8
Butter, Garlic (Somerfield) *serving 10g/0.3oz* 8
Butter, Half Fat (Sainsbury's) *serving 10g/0.3oz* 4
Butter, Light Half Fat (Waitrose) *serving 10g/0.3oz* 4
Butter, Low Fat (Marks & Spencer) *serving 10g/0.3oz* 4
Butter, Normandy (Marks & Spencer) *serving 10g/0.3oz* 8
Butter, Salted or Unsalted *serving 10g/0.3oz* 8
Butter, Slightly Salted (Marks & Spencer) *serving 10g/0.3oz* 8
Butter, Somerset (Waitrose) *serving 10g/0.3oz* 8
Butter, Spreadable, (Tesco) *serving 10g/0.3oz* 8
Butter, Spreadable, Salted (Marks & Spencer) *serving 10g/0.3oz* 8
Butter, Touch of (Marks & Spencer) *serving 10g/0.3oz* 7
Butter, Touch of, Low Fat (Marks & Spencer) *serving 10g/0.3oz* 4
Butter, Welsh (Tesco) *serving 10g/0.3oz* 8
Butter, Whisky (Somerfield) *serving 10g/0.3oz* 4
Country Blend Spread (Somerfield) *serving 10g/0.3oz* 7
Delight, Diet (Van Den Bergh) *serving 10g/0.3oz* 2
Delight, Low Fat (Van Den Bergh) *serving 10g/0.3oz* 4
Echo (Van Den Bergh) *serving 10g/0.3oz* 8
Flora Buttery (Van Den Bergh) *serving 10g/0.3oz* 7
Flora, Low Salt (Van Den Bergh) *serving 10g/0.3oz* 7
Flora, 70% Vegetable Fat Spread (Van Den Bergh) *serving 10g/0.3oz* 7
Ghee *serving 10g/0.3oz* 10
Gold Extra Light (St Ivel) *serving 10g/0.3oz* 3
Gold Light (St Ivel) *serving 10g/0.3oz* 4
Gold Light, Unsalted (St Ivel) *serving 10g/0.3oz* 4
Golden Churn (St Ivel) *serving 10g/0.3oz* 7
High Fibre Sunflower Spread (Somerfield) *serving 10g/0.3oz* 4
I Can't Believe It's Not Butter! (Van Den Bergh) *serving 10g/0.3oz* 7
I Can't Believe It's Not Butter! Light! (Van Den Bergh) *serving 10g/0.3oz* 4
Icing Butter *serving 10g/0.3oz* 3

Ideal Reduced Fat Spread (Somerfield) *serving 10g/0.3oz* 6
Krona, Soft Tub Vegetable Fat Spread (Van Den Bergh) *serving 10g/0.3oz* 6
Krona Gold (Van Den Bergh) *serving 10g/0.3oz* 7
Light Soft Spread, Luxury (Tesco) *serving 10g/0.3oz* 7
Low Fat Golden Spread (Somerfield) *serving 10g/0.3oz* 4
Lowest Ever 95% Fat-Free Spread, Healthy Eating (Tesco) *serving 10g/0.3oz* 1
Margarine, Baking (Safeway) *serving 10g/0.3oz* 8
Margarine, Baking (Somerfield) *serving 10g/0.3oz* 8
Margarine, Blended, 60% Corn Oil & 40% Butter *serving 10g/0.3oz* 8
Margarine, Block (Asda) *serving 10g/0.3oz* 8
Margarine, Dairy Free Soya (Somerfield) *serving 10g/0.3oz* 8
Margarine, Soft (Asda) *serving 10g/0.3oz* 8
Margarine, Soft (Safeway) *serving 10g/0.3oz* 8
Margarine, Soft (Somerfield) *serving 10g/0.3oz* 8
Margarine, Soft (Tesco) *serving 10g/0.3oz* 8
Margarine, Soft, Chilled (Iceland) *serving 10g/0.3oz* 8
Margarine, Soft Tub (Waitrose) *serving 10g/0.3oz* 7
Margarine, Soya (Safeway) *serving 10g/0.3oz* 8
Margarine, Sunflower (Waitrose) *serving 10g/0.3oz* 8
Margarine, Sunflower, Chilled (Iceland) *serving 10g/0.3oz* 8
Mello (St Ivel) *serving 10g/0.3oz* 6
Mono (St Ivel) *serving 10g/0.3oz* 8
Olivani Spread (Somerfield) *serving 10g/0.3oz* 6
Olive Gold, A Lower Fat Spread with Olive Oil (Asda) *serving 10g/0.3oz* 6
Olive Gold, Extra Light (Sainsbury's) *serving 10g/0.3oz* 4
Olive Gold Spread (Somerfield) *serving 10g/0.3oz* 6
Olive Oil Spread (Tesco) *serving 10g/0.3oz* 6
Olive Reduced Fat Spread (Safeway) *serving 10g/0.3oz* 6
Olive Spread (Marks & Spencer) *serving 10g/0.3oz* 6
Olivio (Van Den Bergh) *serving 10g/0.3oz* 6
Premium Blend Spread (Waitrose) *serving 10g/0.3oz* 7
Pure Gold Spread (Asda) *serving 10g/0.3oz* 4
Reduced Fat Spread, Chilled (Iceland) *serving 10g/0.3oz* 6

Soft Spread, Reduced Fat 60%, Savers (Safeway) *serving 10g/0.3oz* 6
Soft Spread (Somerfield) *serving 10g/0.3oz* 6
Soft Spread (Waitrose) *serving 10g/0.3oz* 7
Soya Spread (Waitrose) *serving 10g/0.3oz* 8
Stork, Packet (Van Den Bergh) *serving 10g/0.3oz* 8
Stork, Rich Blend (Van Den Bergh) *serving 10g/0.3oz* 8
Stork, Special Blend (Van Den Bergh) *serving 10g/0.3oz* 8
Summer County (Van Den Bergh) *serving 10g/0.3oz* 6
Sunflower 60% Fat Spread, Savers (Safeway) *serving 10g/0.3oz* 6
Sunflower 70% Spread, Low Trans Fatty Acids (Somerfield) *serving 10g/0.3oz* 7
Sunflower Extra Light Spread (Sainsbury's) *serving 10g/0.3oz* 4
Sunflower Light (Sainsbury's) *serving 10g/0.3oz* 6
Sunflower Light Spread (Safeway) *serving 10g/0.3oz* 4
Sunflower Spread (Asda) *serving 10g/0.3oz* 8
Sunflower Spread (Marks & Spencer) *serving 10g/0.3oz* 7
Sunflower Spread (Safeway) *serving 10g/0.3oz* 7
Sunflower Spread (Somerfield) *serving 10g/0.3oz* 7
Sunflower Spread, 38% (Tesco) *serving 10g/0.3oz* 4
Sunflower Spread, 40% (Waitrose) *serving 10g/0.3oz* 4
Sunflower Spread, 70% (Waitrose) *serving 10g/0.3oz* 7
Sunflower Spread, Extra Rich (Somerfield) *serving 10g/0.3oz* 7
Sunflower Spread, Low Fat (Safeway) *serving 10g/0.3oz* 4
Sunflower Spread, Low Fat (Somerfield) *serving 10g/0.3oz* 4
Sunflower Spread, Very Low Fat (Somerfield) *serving 10g/0.3oz* 2
Utterly Butterly (St Ivel) *serving 10g/0.3oz* 7
Very Low Fat Spread, Healthy Eating (Tesco) *serving 10g/0.3oz* 2
Vitalite (St Ivel) *serving 10g/0.3oz* 7
You'd Butter Believe It, a Lower Fat Dairy Spread (Asda) *serving 10g/0.3oz* 6

CAKES, GATEAUX, SWEET PIES & TARTS

NOTE: The standard serving size in this section is 90g/3oz. If you wish to consume more or less than this amount (e.g. if you are going to consume a pack of food whose weight differs from the standard

serving size) use the conversion tables on page 386 to calculate the new amount of fat in the food.

Almond Fingers (Tesco) *serving 90g/3oz*	13
Almond Slice (Mr Kipling) *serving 90g/3oz*	12
Angel Cake (Marks & Spencer) *serving 90g/3oz*	15
Angel Cake (Waitrose) *serving 90g/3oz*	15
Angel Layer Cake (Somerfield) *serving 90g/3oz*	17
Angel Layer Cut Cake (Tesco) *serving 90g/3oz*	18
Angelfood Cake *serving 90g/3oz*	1
Apple Amber (Sara Lee) *serving 90g/3oz*	7
Apple Bakewell, Dutch (Mr Kipling) *serving 90g/3oz*	15
Apple & Blackberry Crumble (Somerfield) *serving 90g/3oz*	5
Apple & Blackberry Pie (Somerfield) *serving 90g/3oz*	11
Apple & Blackberry Pie (Waitrose) *serving 90g/3oz*	11
Apple & Blackberry Pie, Deep Filled, Chilled (Asda) *serving 90g/3oz*	13
Apple & Blackberry Pie, Frozen (Tesco) *serving 90g/3oz*	10
Apple & Blackberry Shortcrust Pie (Marks & Spencer) *serving 90g/3oz*	10
Apple & Blackcurrant Pie, Individual (Mr Kipling) *serving 90g/3oz*	11
Apple Buttercrust Pie, Frozen (Marks & Spencer) *serving 90g/3oz*	8
Apple Cake (Marks & Spencer) *serving 90g/3oz*	13
Apple Crumble, Chilled (Asda) *serving 90g/3oz*	8
Apple Crumble, Frozen (Asda) *serving 90g/3oz*	8
Apple Crumble, Frozen (Tesco) *serving 90g/3oz*	8
Apple Crumble, Frozen, Oven Baked (Iceland) *serving 90g/3oz*	7
Appble Danish, Frozen (Marks & Spencer) *serving 90g/3oz*	4
Apple Flan, Open (Waitrose) *serving 90g/3oz*	9
Apple & Mincemeat Strudel, Frozen (Tesco) *serving 90g/3oz*	15
Apple Pie, Deep Dish, Frozen, Oven Baked (Iceland) *serving 90g/3oz*	10
Apple Pie, Bramley (Somerfield) *serving 90g/3oz*	11
Apple Pie, Deep Fill, Chilled (Tesco) *serving 90g/3oz*	6
Apple Pie, Deep Filled (Waitrose) *serving 90g/3oz*	10

Apple Pie, Frozen (Tesco) *serving 90g/3oz* 9
Apple Pie, Home Made *serving 90g/3oz* 11
Apple Pies (Asda) *serving 90g/3oz* 12
Apple Pies (Hales) *serving 90g/3oz* 15
Apple Pies (Lyons) *serving 90g/3oz* 14
Apple Pies (Tesco) *serving 90g/3oz* 9
Apple Pies, Bramley (Somerfield) *serving 90g/3oz* 15
Apple Pies, Mini (Waitrose) *serving 90g/3oz* 13
Apple in Pyjamas (Waitrose) *serving 90g/3oz* 5
Apple & Raspberry Shortcrust Pie (Marks & Spencer) *serving 90g/3oz* 9
Apple Strudel (Waitrose) *serving 90g/3oz* 4
Apple Strudel, Frozen (Tesco) *serving 90g/3oz* 13
Apple & Sultana Cake Bites (Mr Kipling) *serving 90g/3oz* 14
Apple & Sultana Lattice Pie, Frozen (Tesco) *serving 90g/3oz* 12
Apple Sundaes (Asda) *serving 90g/3oz* 14
Apple Turnover (Holland & Barrett) *serving 90g/3oz* 6
Apple/Almond Lattice Flan (Waitrose) *serving 90g/3oz* 10
Apricot Peach & Apple Lattice Tart (Somerfield) *serving 90g/3oz* 9
Apricot & Raisin Flapjacks (Mr Kipling) *serving 90g/3oz* 20
Apricot Roll (Marks & Spencer) *serving 90g/3oz* 9
Assorted Fruit Pies, Apple & Blackcurrant (Tesco) *serving 90g/3oz* 11
Assorted Fruit Pies, Apple (Tesco) *serving 90g/3oz* 11
Assorted Fruit Pies, Apricot (Tesco) *serving 90g/3oz* 11
Assorted Fruit Pies (Asda) *serving 90g/3oz* 12
Assorted Pies (Hales) *serving 90g/3oz* 15
Assorted Pies (Lyons) *serving 90g/3oz* 12
Assorted Tarts (Asda) *serving 90g/3oz* 12
Bailey's Gateau, Frozen (Tesco) *serving 90g/3oz* 19
Bakewell Cake Bars, Strawberry (Mr Kipling) *serving 90g/3oz* 16
Bakewell Slices (5) (Asda) *serving 90g/3oz* 22
Bakewell Slices (Mr Kipling) *serving 90g/3oz* 6
Bakewell Tart (Marks & Spencer) *serving 90g/3oz* 25
Bakewell Tart (Mr Kipling) *serving 90g/3oz* 17
Bakewell Tart (Somerfield) *serving 90g/3oz* 17

Bakewell Tart, Cherry (Asda) *serving 90g/3oz*	14
Bakewell Tart, Fluted (Waitrose) *serving 90g/3oz*	19
Bakewell Tart, Frozen (Tesco) *serving 90g/3oz*	21
Bakewells, Cherry (Lyons) *serving 90g/3oz*	15
Bakewells, Cherry (Tesco) *serving 90g/3oz*	19
Bakewells, Santa (Mr Kipling) *serving 90g/3oz*	14
Balloon Cake (Iceland) *serving 90g/3oz*	13
Banana Bread, Made with Margarine *serving 90g/3oz*	9
Banana Bread, Made with Vegetable Shortening *serving 90g/3oz*	11
Banana Cream Pie, Frozen (Asda) *serving 90g/3oz*	18
Banana Cream Pie, Home Made *serving 90g/3oz*	12
Banana Loaf (Marks & Spencer) *serving 90g/3oz*	21
Banoffee Cake Bars (Mr Kipling) *serving 90g/3oz*	8
Banoffee Corner House Cake (Lyons) *serving 90g/3oz*	17
Banoffi Tart (Waitrose) *serving 90g/3oz*	28
Battenberg (Lyons) *serving 90g/3oz*	10
Battenberg (Marks & Spencer) *serving 90g/3oz*	9
Battenberg (Mr Kipling) *serving 90g/3oz*	10
Battenberg (Somerfield) *serving 90g/3oz*	9
Battenberg Cakes, Mini (Mr Kipling) *serving 90g/3oz*	7
Battenberg, Family (Somerfield) *serving 90g/3oz*	10
Battenberg Treats (Lyons) *serving 90g/3oz*	16
Battenbergs, Mini Orange & Lemon (Mr Kipling) *serving 90g/3oz*	6
Battenberg *serving 90g/3oz*	16
Battenberg (Tesco) *serving 90g/3oz*	9
Belgian Buns (Tesco) *serving 90g/3oz*	3
Berry Pie, Deep Filled (Waitrose) *serving 90g/3oz*	10
Best Wishes Cake (Waitrose) *serving 90g/3oz*	16
Birthday Cake, Happy, Chocolate (Tesco) *serving 90g/3oz*	17
Birthday Cake (Waitrose) *serving 90g/3oz*	15
Birthday Cake, 6in. Round (Waitrose) *serving 90g/3oz*	21
Birthday Cake, Child's (Waitrose) *serving 90g/3oz*	16
Birthday Cake, Chocolate (Marks & Spencer) *serving 90g/3oz*	24
Birthday Cake, Elephant (Marks & Spencer) *serving 90g/3oz*	14
Birthday Cake, Happy 6 (Waitrose) *serving 90g/3oz*	6
Birthday Cake, Happy, Yellow 8 (Waitrose) *serving 90g/3oz*	17

Birthday Cake (Iceland) *serving 90g/3oz*	13
Birthday Cake, Large Chocolate (Marks & Spencer) *serving 90g/3oz*	22
Birthday Cake, Lilac Flowers (Waitrose) *serving 90g/3oz*	14
Birthday Cake, Poppy (Waitrose) *serving 90g/3oz*	21
Birthday Cake, Rose (Marks & Spencer) *serving 90g/3oz*	14
Birthday Cake, Small (Marks & Spencer) *serving 90g/3oz*	15
Birthday Cake, Sponge (Waitrose) *serving 90g/3oz*	14
Birthday Cake, Yellow 6 (Waitrose) *serving 90g/3oz*	16
Black Forest Gateau (Somerfield) *serving 90g/3oz*	15
Black Forest Gateau (Waitrose) *serving 90g/3oz*	15
Black Forest Gateau, Frozen (Marks & Spencer) *serving 90g/3oz*	14
Black Forest Gateau, Frozen (Tesco) *serving 90g/3oz*	16
Black Forest Slices, Festive Selection (Mr Kipling) *serving 90g/3oz*	19
Blackcurrant & Apple Pies (Lyons) *serving 90g/3oz*	14
Blueberry Pie (Waitrose) *serving 90g/3oz*	14
Blueberry Pie, Home Made *serving 90g/3oz*	11
Boston Cream Pie *serving 90g/3oz*	8
Bramley Apple & Custard Pies (Mr Kipling) *serving 90g/3oz*	14
Bramley Apple Pie (Waitrose) *serving 90g/3oz*	11
Bramley Apple Pie, Frozen (Tesco) *serving 90g/3oz*	12
Bramley Apple Pie, Individual (Mr Kipling) *serving 90g/3oz*	11
Bramley Apple Pies (Marks & Spencer) *serving 90g/3oz*	11
Bramley Apple Pies (Mr Kipling) *serving 90g/3oz*	11
Bramley Apple Slices (Mr Kipling) *serving 90g/3oz*	11
Bun, Chocolate Choux (Waitrose) *serving 90g/3oz*	19
Buttercream Sandwich (Lyons) *serving 90g/3oz*	16
Butterscotch Pie, Pudding-Type, Home Made *serving 90g/3oz*	13
Cake Bar, Chocolate & Nut (Lyons) *serving 90g/3oz*	29
Cappuccino Corner House Cake (Lyons) *serving 90g/3oz*	17
Captain Rainforest Cake, Grocery (Iceland) *serving 90g/3oz*	14
Caramel Cake Bar, Chocolate Coated, Single (Asda) *serving 90g/3oz*	21
Caramel Cake Bars (Cadbury's) *serving 90g/3oz*	16
Caramel Crunch (Marks & Spencer) *serving 90g/3oz*	24

Caramel Shortcakes (Mr Kipling) *serving 90g/3oz* 25
Caramel Supremes (Lyons) *serving 90g/3oz* 23
Carrot Cake (Betty Crocker) *serving 90g/3oz* 12
Carrot Cake (Holland & Barrett) *serving 90g/3oz* 7
Carrot Cake (Marks & Spencer) *serving 90g/3oz* 18
Carrot Cake (Somerfield) *serving 90g/3oz* 27
Carrot Cake (Waitrose) *serving 90g/3oz* 7
Carrot Cake, Home Made *serving 90g/3oz* 24
Carrot Cake T/bake (Marks & Spencer) *serving 90g/3oz* 15
Carrot Corner House Cake (Lyons) *serving 90g/3oz* 19
Carrot & Orange Cake (Waitrose) *serving 90g/3oz* 14
Carrot & Orange Sponge Sandwich (Asda) *serving 90g/3oz* 11
Carrot Slices (Tesco) *serving 90g/3oz* 18
Caterpillar Cake (Marks & Spencer) *serving 90g/3oz* 18
Cats & Dogs Cake (Marks & Spencer) *serving 90g/3oz* 12
Cel Cake, Hard Iced (Waitrose) *serving 90g/3oz* 12
Celebration Gateau, Frozen (Iceland) *serving 90g/3oz* 15
Cheeky Monkey Cake (Marks & Spencer) *serving 90g/3oz* 14
Cheeky Monkey Chocolate Cake (Marks & Spencer) *serving 90g/3oz* 21
Cheesecake: *see under* Desserts
Cherry Cake (Marks & Spencer) *serving 90g/3oz* 11
Cherry Genoa (Tesco) *serving 90g/3oz* 9
Cherry Genoa (Waitrose) *serving 90g/3oz* 12
Cherry Genoa Cake (Marks & Spencer) *serving 90g/3oz* 6
Cherry Genoa Cake (Somerfield) *serving 90g/3oz* 10
Cherry Madeira Cakebars (Mr Kipling) *serving 90g/3oz* 14
Cherry Pie (Somerfield) *serving 90g/3oz* 11
Cherry Pie, Deep Dish, Frozen, Oven Baked (Iceland) *serving 90g/3oz* 11
Cherry Pie, Deep Filled, Chilled (Asda) *serving 90g/3oz* 13
Cherry Pie, Home Made *serving 90g/3oz* 11
Cherry Shortcrust Pie (Marks & Spencer) *serving 90g/3oz* 10
Cheryl Cheeky Monkey Cake (Marks & Spencer) *serving 90g/3oz* 13
Chinese Cakes & Biscuits *serving 90g/3oz* 19
Chocolate Cake *serving 90g/3oz* 24

Chocolate Cake (Cadbury's) *serving 90g/3oz* 14
Chocolate Cake (Waitrose) *serving 90g/3oz* 18
Chocolate Cake, Rich (Waitrose) *serving 90g/3oz* 14
Chocolate Cake with Butter Icing *serving 90g/3oz* 27
Chocolate Cake with Chocolate Frosting *serving 90g/3oz* 15
Chocolate Chip Cake Bars (Mr Kipling) *serving 90g/3oz* 24
Chocolate Chip Cake (Waitrose) *serving 90g/3oz* 16
Chocolate Corner House Cake (Lyons) *serving 90g/3oz* 19
Chocolate Cream Gateau, Frozen (Marks & Spencer) *serving 90g/3oz* 26
Chocolate Cream Pie, Home Made *serving 90g/3oz* 14
Chocolate Cup Cakes (Somerfield) *serving 90g/3oz* 19
Chocolate Enrobed Roll (Lyons) *serving 90g/3oz* 20
Chocolate Family Roll (Lyons) *serving 90g/3oz* 15
Chocolate Fancies (Lyons) *serving 90g/3oz* 28
Chocolate Fudge Brownies (Tesco) *serving 90g/3oz* 22
Chocolate Fudge Cake (Marks & Spencer) *serving 90g/3oz* 17
Chocolate Fudge Cake (Somerfield) *serving 90g/3oz* 17
Chocolate Fudge Cake (Waitrose) *serving 90g/3oz* 16
Chocolate Fudge Gateau (Waitrose) *serving 90g/3oz* 14
Chocolate Fudge Sponge Cake (Tesco) *serving 90g/3oz* 20
Chocolate Gateau, Mini Eggs (Cadbury's) *serving 90g/3oz* 17
Chocolate Gateau, Rich, Frozen (Marks & Spencer) *serving 90g/3oz* 18
Chocolate Layer Cake (Somerfield) *serving 90g/3oz* 19
Chocolate Layer Gateau, Frozen (Marks & Spencer) *serving 90g/3oz* 16
Chocolate & Mandarin Gateau, Frozen (Iceland) *serving 90g/3oz* 12
Chocolate Marble Cake (Tesco) *serving 90g/3oz* 18
Chocolate Meringue Gateau, Frozen (Tesco) *serving 90g/3oz* 18
Chocolate Mini Roll, Kingsize (Tesco) *serving 90g/3oz* 24
Chocolate Mini Rolls (Cadbury's) *serving 90g/3oz* 19
Chocolate Mini Rolls with Vanilla Filling (Asda) *serving 90g/3oz* 11
Chocolate Mousse Pie, Prepared from mix, no Bake Type *serving 90g/3oz* 14

Chocolate & Orange Cake (Somerfield) *serving 90g/3oz* 23
Chocolate & Orange Gateau (Somerfield) *serving 90g/3oz* 8
Chocolate & Orange Whirls (Lyons) *serving 90g/3oz* 28
Chocolate Overload Gateau, Frozen (Iceland) *serving 90g/3oz* 15
Chocolate Roll (Cadbury's) *serving 90g/3oz* 16
Chocolate Sandwich (Lyons) *serving 90g/3oz* 15
Chocolate Sponge Mix (Somerfield) *serving 90g/3oz* 14
Chocolate Sponge Sandwich (Asda) *serving 90g/3oz* 23
Chocolate Sponge Sandwich with Chocolate Flavour Filling (Asda) *serving 90g/3oz* 16
Chocolate Tart (Waitrose) *serving 90g/3oz* 29
Chocolate Truffle Gateau, Frozen (Marks & Spencer) *serving 90g/3oz* 31
Chocolate & Vanilla Swiss Roll (Lyons) *serving 90g/3oz* 14
Chocolate Victoria Sponge (Waitrose) *serving 90g/3oz* 21
Chorley Cakes (Marks & Spencer) *serving 90g/3oz* 16
Christmas Cake (Mr Kipling) *serving 90g/3oz* 7
Christmas Cake, Violin (Waitrose) *serving 90g/3oz* 7
Christmas Cake Portions (Waitrose) *serving 90g/3oz* 9
Christmas Chocolate Gateau (Cadbury's) *serving 90g/3oz* 18
Christmas Log (Cadbury's) *serving 90g/3oz* 18
Christmas Slices (Mr Kipling) *serving 90g/3oz* 6
Christmas Stollen (Waitrose) *serving 90g/3oz* 20
Classic Chocolate Cake (Lyons) *serving 90g/3oz* 24
Classic Chocolate Rolls (Lyons) *serving 90g/3oz* 20
Coconut Cake *serving 90g/3oz* 21
Coconut Cake (Marks & Spencer) *serving 90g/3oz* 18
Coconut Cake (Somerfield) *serving 90g/3oz* 22
Coconut Chocolate Fudge Cake (Waitrose) *serving 90g/3oz* 23
Coconut Cream Pie, Home Made *serving 90g/3oz* 14
Coconut Crunch Cakes (Lyons) *serving 90g/3oz* 29
Coconut Decorated Sponge Sandwich (Tesco) *serving 90g/3oz* 19
Coconut Layer Cake (Somerfield) *serving 90g/3oz* 17
Coconut Macaroons (Mr Kipling) *serving 90g/3oz* 16
Coconut Macaroons (Tesco) *serving 90g/3oz* 16
Coconut Sponge Sandwich with Coconut, Jam & Buttercream (Asda) *serving 90g/3oz* 16

Coffee Cake (Marks & Spencer) *serving 90g/3oz*	23
Coffee Cake, Cinnamon with Crumb Topping *serving 90g/3oz*	21
Coffee & Cream Gateau, Frozen (Iceland) *serving 90g/3oz*	15
Coffee Fudge Brownies (Tesco) *serving 90g/3oz*	23
Coffee Iced Sponge Bar (Marks & Spencer) *serving 90g/3oz*	20
Coffee & Walnut Cake (Waitrose) *serving 90g/3oz*	19
Coffee & Walnut Sponge Sandwich (Asda) *serving 90g/3oz*	20
Cointreau Gateau, Frozen (Marks & Spencer) *serving 90g/3oz*	16
Computer Cake (Waitrose) *serving 90g/3oz*	15
Cornbread, Dry Mix, Prepared *serving 90g/3oz*	9
Country Cake (Marks & Spencer) *serving 90g/3oz*	17
Country Slices (Mr Kipling) *serving 90g/3oz*	14
Cream Doughnut (Tesco) *serving 90g/3oz*	20
Cream Doughnut, Fresh as Sold (Iceland) *serving 90g/3oz*	26
Cream Puffs, Prepared from Recipe, Shell (includes Eclair) *serving 90g/3oz*	23
Crispie Cakes *serving 90g/3oz*	17
Cup Cakes, Assorted (Lyons) *serving 90g/3oz*	5
Cup Cakes, Chocolate (Lyons) *serving 90g/3oz*	4
Danish Pastry *serving 90g/3oz*	16
Danish Pastry, Cinnamon, Unenriched *serving 90g/3oz*	20
Danish Pastry, Fruit *serving 90g/3oz*	15
Danish Pastry, Lemon Unenriched *serving 90g/3oz*	17
Danish Pastry, Nut (includes Almond, Raisin, Cinnamon, Nut) *serving 90g/3oz*	23
Danish Pastry, Raspberry, Unenriched *serving 90g/3oz*	17
Date & Walnut Cake (Marks & Spencer) *serving 90g/3oz*	12
Devil's Food Cake (Betty Crocker) *serving 90g/3oz*	13
Dinosaur Sponge Cake (Waitrose) *serving 90g/3oz*	14
Dolcetta Double Chocolate Icecream Gateau (Heinz Weight Watchers) *serving 90g/3oz*	7
Dolcetta Vanilla & Chocolate Chip Icecream Gateau (Heinz Weight Watchers) *serving 90g/3oz*	7
Double Chocolate Cake Bites (Mr Kipling) *serving 90g/3oz*	18
Double Chocolate Gateau (Sara Lee) *serving 90g/3oz*	16
Double Lemon Gateau (Sara Lee) *serving 90g/3oz*	13
Doughnut American Style Ring (Tesco) *serving 90g/3oz*	21

Doughnut, Apple (Waitrose) *serving 90g/3oz* 6
Doughnut, Apple & Cinnamon (Waitrose) *serving 90g/3oz* 14
Doughnut, Apple & Custard (Somerfield) *serving 90g/3oz* 20
Doughnut, Banana (Somerfield) *serving 90g/3oz* 11
Doughnut, Cake-Type, Chocolate, Sugared or Glazed *serving 90g/3oz* 18
Doughnut, Cake-Type, Plain Chocolate Coated or Frosted *serving 90g/3oz* 28
Doughnut, Cake-Type, Plain, Sugared or Glazed *serving 90g/3oz* 21
Doughnut, Cake-Type, Wheat, Sugared or Glazed *serving 90g/3oz* 17
Doughnut Caramel (Somerfield) *serving 90g/3oz* 15
Doughnut, Cherry Filled (Waitrose) *serving 90g/3oz* 8
Doughnut, Chocolate (Somerfield) *serving 90g/3oz* 17
Doughnut, Chocolate (Waitrose) *serving 90g/3oz* 11
Doughnut, Chocolate Flavour, Filled (Somerfield) *serving 90g/3oz* 17
Doughnut, Chocolate Ring (Waitrose) *serving 90g/3oz* 22
Doughnut, Cream Chocolate (Waitrose) *serving 90g/3oz* 24
Doughnut, Custard (Tesco) *serving 90g/3oz* 7
Doughnut, Custard Filled *serving 90g/3oz* 17
Doughnut, Dairy Cream (Marks & Spencer) *serving 90g/3oz* 17
Doughnut Faces (Waitrose) *serving 90g/3oz* 14
Doughnut, French, Crullers Glazed *serving 90g/3oz* 16
Doughnut, Fresh Cream Lemon (Waitrose) *serving 90g/3oz* 24
Doughnut, Fresh Cream Ring (Waitrose) *serving 90g/3oz* 20
Doughnut, Jam *serving 90g/3oz* 13
Doughnut, Jam (Somerfield) *serving 90g/3oz* 16
Doughnut, Jam (Tesco) *serving 90g/3oz* 13
Doughnut, Jam (Waitrose) *serving 90g/3oz* 11
Doughnut, Jam (6) (Waitrose) *serving 90g/3oz* 23
Doughnut, Lemon (Waitrose) *serving 90g/3oz* 11
Doughnut, Lemon Curd (Somerfield) *serving 90g/3oz* 10
Doughnut Men (Waitrose) *serving 90g/3oz* 23
Doughnut, Mini Jam (Somerfield) *serving 90g/3oz* 16
Doughnut, Mini Jam (Waitrose) *serving 90g/3oz* 23

Doughnut, Mini Jam Ball (Somerfield) *serving 90g/3oz* 17
Doughnut, Mini Ring, Banana (Somerfield) *serving 90g/3oz* 17
Doughnut, Mini Ring, Blueberry (Somerfield) *serving 90g/3oz* 17
Doughnut, Mini Ring, Cinnamon (Somerfield) *serving 90g/3oz* 15
Doughnut, Mini Ring, Vanilla (Somerfield) *serving 90g/3oz* 18
Doughnut, Raspberry (Waitrose) *serving 90g/3oz* 19
Doughnut, Ring *serving 90g/3oz* 20
Doughnut, Ring (Somerfield) *serving 90g/3oz* 16
Doughnut, Ring (Waitrose) *serving 90g/3oz* 26
Doughnut, Ring, Iced *serving 90g/3oz* 16
Doughnut, Ring, Sugar Glazed (Somerfield) *serving 90g/3oz* 18
Doughnut Snowmen (Waitrose) *serving 90g/3oz* 23
Doughnut, Mini Ring, Vanilla (Somerfield) *serving 90g/3oz* 18
Doughnut Xmas Trees (Waitrose) *serving 90g/3oz* 20
Dundee Cake (Waitrose) *serving 90g/3oz* 9
Dundee Cake, Luxury (Somerfield) *serving 90g/3oz* 10
Dundee Cake, Standard (Somerfield) *serving 90g/3oz* 10
Easter Bakewells (Mr Kipling) *serving 90g/3oz* 16
Easter Cake (Waitrose) *serving 90g/3oz* 18
Easter Cake, Mini Eggs (Cadbury's) *serving 90g/3oz* 24
Easter Cake, Oval (Waitrose) *serving 90g/3oz* 7
Easter Cake, Sponge (Waitrose) *serving 90g/3oz* 14
Easter Cake with Mini Creme Eggs (Cadbury's) *serving 90g/3oz* 22
Easter Egg Cakes (Cadbury's) *serving 90g/3oz* 18
Easter Mini Sponge (Waitrose) *serving 90g/3oz* 12
Easter Nests, Mini Eggs (Cadbury's) *serving 90g/3oz* 21
Eccles Cake *serving 90g/3oz* 24
Eccles Cake (Marks & Spencer) *serving 90g/3oz* 16
Eccles Cake, Butter (Waitrose) *serving 90g/3oz* 16
Eccles Cake, Traditional (Tesco) *serving 90g/3oz* 16
Eclair (Waitrose) *serving 90g/3oz* 32
Eclair, Chocolate (Tesco) *serving 90g/3oz* 26
Eclair, Chocolate (Waitrose) *serving 90g/3oz* 18
Eclair, Chocolate, Grocery (Iceland) *serving 90g/3oz* 18
Eclair, Cream Chocolate Fudge (Waitrose) *serving 90g/3oz* 26
Eclair, Custard Filled, with Chocolate Glaze, Prepared from Recipe *serving 90g/3oz* 14

Eclair, Dairy Cream (Somerfield) *serving 90g/3oz*	24
Eclair, Dairy Cream, White Chocolate (Somerfield) *serving 90g/3oz*	26
Eclair, Fresh *serving 90g/3oz*	21
Eclair, Fresh Cream Chocolate (Waitrose) *serving 90g/3oz*	31
Eclair, Large Chocolate (Marks & Spencer) *serving 90g/3oz*	29
Eclair, Mega Dairy Cream (Somerfield) *serving 90g/3oz*	26
Eclair, Mega Jumbo, White Chocolate (Tesco) *serving 90g/3oz*	16
Eclair, Milk Chocolate (Marks & Spencer) *serving 90g/3oz*	29
Eclair, Mini Chocolate (Tesco) *serving 90g/3oz*	26
Eclair, Mini Chocolate (Waitrose) *serving 90g/3oz*	16
Eclair, White Chocolate (Tesco) *serving 90g/3oz*	16
Egg Custard Pie, Home Made *serving 90g/3oz*	8
Fancy Iced Cakes, Individual *serving 90g/3oz*	13
Father's Day Cake (Somerfield) *serving 90g/3oz*	12
Festive Cakes, 10 Cake Selection, Christmas (Cadbury's) *serving 90g/3oz*	19
Flake Cakes (Cadbury's) *serving 90g/3oz*	22
Flan Case, Giant (Tesco) *serving 90g/3oz*	3
Flan Case, Medium (Tesco) *serving 90g/3oz*	3
Flan Case, Medium, Luxury (Waitrose) *serving 90g/3oz*	9
Flapjack with Raisins, Traditional (Tesco) *serving 90g/3oz*	18
Fondant Fancies (Asda) *serving 90g/3oz*	9
Fondant Fancies (Tesco) *serving 90g/3oz*	8
Fondant Parcels, Mini (Marks & Spencer) *serving 90g/3oz*	9
Football Cake, Chocolate (Marks & Spencer) *serving 90g/3oz*	20
Football Pitch Cake (Waitrose) *serving 90g/3oz*	14
Frangipans, Continental Style (Tesco) *serving 90g/3oz*	17
French Fancies (Mr Kipling) *serving 90g/3oz*	9
French Sandwich (Lyons) *serving 90g/3oz*	13
Fried Fruit Pie, Apple, Cherry or Lemon *serving 90g/3oz*	15
Fruit Bar, Rich (Marks & Spencer) *serving 90g/3oz*	8
Fruit Base, Rich, Luxury (Tesco) *serving 90g/3oz*	9
Fruit Cake *serving 90g/3oz*	12
Fruit Cake 8in. Square (Marks & Spencer) *serving 90g/3oz*	8
Fruit Cake, Family Size, Light (Tesco) *serving 90g/3oz*	9
Fruit Cake, Home Made *serving 90g/3oz*	10
Fruit Cake, Large, Rich (Marks & Spencer) *serving 90g/3oz*	9

Fruit Cake, Light (Tesco) *serving 90g/3oz*	9
Fruit Cake, Luxury Rich (Somerfield) *serving 90g/3oz*	10
Fruit Cake, Luxury Rich (Waitrose) *serving 90g/3oz*	8
Fruit Cake, Medium Rich (Marks & Spencer) *serving 90g/3oz*	9
Fruit Cake, Rich *serving 90g/3oz*	10
Fruit Cake, Rich (Waitrose) *serving 90g/3oz*	10
Fruit Cake, Rich Iced *serving 90g/3oz*	10
Fruit Cake, Rich Small (Marks & Spencer) *serving 90g/3oz*	8
Fruit Cake, Round Rich (2 lb) (Tesco) *serving 90g/3oz*	8
Fruit Cake, Square Rich (Tesco) *serving 90g/3oz*	8
Fruit Cake, Rich, Standard (Tesco) *serving 90g/3oz*	8
Fruit Cake, Standard, Rich (Waitrose) *serving 90g/3oz*	9
Fruit Cake, Wholemeal *serving 90g/3oz*	14
Fruit Cake Slices, Luxury (Waitrose) *serving 90g/3oz*	14
Fruit & Cinnamon Marble Bar (Marks & Spencer) *serving 90g/3oz*	13
Fruit Pie, Large (Waitrose) *serving 90g/3oz*	10
Fruit Pies, Small (Waitrose) *serving 90g/3oz*	12
Fruit Slab Cake, Light (Tesco) *serving 90g/3oz*	10
Fruit Slice (Somerfield) *serving 90g/3oz*	10
Fruit Slices, Rich (Marks & Spencer) *serving 90g/3oz*	9
Fudge Teddy Cake (Marks & Spencer) *serving 90g/3oz*	15
Gateau *serving 90g/3oz*	15
Genoa Cake (Tesco) *serving 90g/3oz*	7
Genoa Cake, Luxury (Somerfield) *serving 90g/3oz*	10
Ginger Buttercream Cut Cake (Tesco) *serving 90g/3oz*	14
Ginger Cake, Iced (Marks & Spencer) *serving 90g/3oz*	13
Ginger Cake, Stem (Waitrose) *serving 90g/3oz*	11
Golden Crisp Cake Bars (Cadbury's) *serving 90g/3oz*	27
Graduation Cake, Fruit (Marks & Spencer) *serving 90g/3oz*	8
Graduation Cake, Madeira (Marks & Spencer) *serving 90g/3oz*	15
Grannies Cake (Lyons) *serving 90g/3oz*	20
Halloween Cake (Waitrose) *serving 90g/3oz*	13
Halloween Pumpkin Sponge (Waitrose) *serving 90g/3oz*	14
Heart Cake, Large (Waitrose) *serving 90g/3oz*	16
Heart Cake, Small (Waitrose) *serving 90g/3oz*	15
Horoscope Cake (Waitrose) *serving 90g/3oz*	13

Ice Cream Gateau, Chocolate & Vanilla, Frozen, Defrosted (Iceland) *serving 90g/3oz* 4
Iced Cake, Luxury (Waitrose) *serving 90g/3oz* 8
Iced Gateaux Torrone, Frozen (Marks & Spencer) *serving 90g/3oz* 19
Iced Strawberry Delights (Mr Kipling) *serving 90g/3oz* 13
Iced Toffee Tart (Mr Kipling) *serving 90g/3oz* 17
Iced Top Cake Bar, Luxury (Waitrose) *serving 90g/3oz* 9
Iced Topped Soft Cake (Waitrose) *serving 90g/3oz* 9
Icing, Chocolate Creamy, Dry Mix, Prepared with Butter *serving 90g/3oz* 12
Icing, Chocolate Creamy, Dry Mix, Prepared with Margarine *serving 90g/3oz* 12
Icing, Chocolate Creamy, Prepared from Recipe with Butter *serving 90g/3oz* 10
Icing, Chocolate Creamy, Prepared from Recipe with Margarine *serving 90g/3oz* 10
Icing, Chocolate Creamy, Ready to Eat *serving 90g/3oz* 16
Icing, Coconut Nut, Ready to Eat *serving 90g/3oz* 22
Icing, Cream Cheese Flavour, Ready to Eat *serving 90g/3oz* 16
Icing, Glaze, Prepared from Recipe *serving 90g/3oz* 7
Icing, Seven Minute, Prepared from Recipe *serving 90g/3oz* 0
Icing, Sour Cream Flavour, Ready to Eat *serving 90g/3oz* 15
Icing, Vanilla Creamy, Dry Mix, Prepared with Butter *serving 90g/3oz* 15
Icing, Vanilla Creamy, Dry Mix, Prepared with Margarine *serving 90g/3oz* 15
Icing, Vanilla Creamy, Ready to Eat *serving 90g/3oz* 15
Icing, White Fluffy, Dry Mix, Prepared with Water *serving 90g/3oz* 0
Irish Cream Liqueur Cake (Waitrose) *serving 90g/3oz* 14
Jaffa Fingers (Asda) *serving 90g/3oz* 10
Jaffa Fingers (Mr Kipling) *serving 90g/3oz* 23
Jam Family Roll (Lyons) *serving 90g/3oz* 11
Key Lime Pie (Waitrose) *serving 90g/3oz* 19
Kunzle Cake, Cherry (Waitrose) *serving 90g/3oz* 21
Kunzle Cake, Orange (Waitrose) *serving 90g/3oz* 24

Lardy Cake *serving 90g/3oz*	15
Lardy Cake (Waitrose) *serving 90g/3oz*	22
Lemon Corner House Cake (Lyons) *serving 90g/3oz*	19
Lemon Drizzle Cake (Asda) *serving 90g/3oz*	23
Lemon Drizzle Cake (4) (Marks & Spencer) *serving 90g/3oz*	13
Lemon & Lime Cake Bars (Mr Kipling) *serving 90g/3oz*	16
Lemon Meringue Pie *serving 90g/3oz*	13
Lemon Meringue Pie, Frozen (Marks & Spencer) *serving 90g/3oz*	9
Lemon Meringue Pie, Frozen (Sara Lee) *serving 90g/3oz*	8
Lemon Meringue Pie, Home Made *serving 90g/3oz*	12
Lemon Meringue Pies (Asda) *serving 90g/3oz*	10
Lemon Slices (Asda) *serving 90g/3oz*	12
Lemon Slices (Lyons) *serving 90g/3oz*	12
Lemon Slices (Mr Kipling) *serving 90g/3oz*	15
Lime & Lemon Loaf (Marks & Spencer) *serving 90g/3oz*	17
Madeira Bar (Marks & Spencer) *serving 90g/3oz*	17
Madeira Cake *serving 90g/3oz*	15
Madeira Cake (Somerfield) *serving 90g/3oz*	17
Madeira Cake, 8in. Square (Marks & Spencer) *serving 90g/3oz*	15
Madeira Cake, Apricot & Orange (Somerfield) *serving 90g/3oz*	17
Madeira Cake, Chocolate (Asda) *serving 90g/3oz*	15
Madeira Cake, Cherry (Somerfield) *serving 90g/3oz*	11
Madeira Car Cake (Marks & Spencer) *serving 90g/3oz*	15
Madeira Cut Cake (Tesco) *serving 90g/3oz*	13
Madeira Cut Piece, Cherry (Tesco) *serving 90g/3oz*	13
Madeira Cake, Lemon Iced (Tesco) *serving 90g/3oz*	15
Madeira Cake, Lemon Iced (Waitrose) *serving 90g/3oz*	18
Madeira Slice (Waitrose) *serving 90g/3oz*	18
Madeira Teddy Cake (Marks & Spencer) *serving 90g/3oz*	15
Malt Loaf, Family (Somerfield) *serving 90g/3oz*	2
Mandarin Cake (Lyons) *serving 90g/3oz*	19
Mandarin Chocolate Enrobed Roll (Lyons) *serving 90g/3oz*	16
Manor House Cake (Mr Kipling) *serving 90g/3oz*	19
Marble Chocolate & Vanilla Slices (Mr Kipling) *serving 90g/3oz*	22
Meringue Nests (Tesco) *serving 90g/3oz*	0

Milk Chocolate Cake Bars (Cadbury's) *serving 90g/3oz*	19
Milk Chocolate Gateau (Asda) *serving 90g/3oz*	23
Milk Chocolate Mini Rolls (Tesco) *serving 90g/3oz*	20
Milk Chocolate Snowballs (Tesco) *serving 90g/3oz*	23
Milk Chocolate Whips (5) (Asda) *serving 90g/3oz*	27
Mince Pie, Cake Filled (Marks & Spencer) *serving 90g/3oz*	14
Mince Pie, Family Almond (Waitrose) *serving 90g/3oz*	12
Mince Pie, Traditionally Made (Tesco) *serving 90g/3oz*	13
Mince Pie Creams (Frozen) (Marks & Spencer) *serving 90g/3oz*	17
Mince Pies (Somerfield) *serving 90g/3oz*	13
Mince Pies (2) Grocery (Iceland) *serving 90g/3oz*	13
Mince Pies (6) (Tesco) *serving 90g/3oz*	13
Mince Pies (12) (Waitrose) *serving 90g/3oz*	13
Mince Pies, Almond (Waitrose) *serving 90g/3oz*	14
Mince Pies, Christmas (Mr Kipling) *serving 90g/3oz*	13
Mince Pies, Cream Almond (Waitrose) *serving 90g/3oz*	20
Mince Pies, Iced, Grocery, Oven Baked (Iceland) *serving 90g/3oz*	11
Mince Pies, Luxury (Mr Kipling) *serving 90g/3oz*	13
Mince Pies, Luxury (Somerfield) *serving 90g/3oz*	14
Mince Pies, Luxury (Tesco) *serving 90g/3oz*	14
Mince Pies, Luxury (Waitrose) *serving 90g/3oz*	14
Mince Pies, Luxury Mini (Waitrose) *serving 90g/3oz*	13
Mince Pies, Mini (Waitrose) *serving 90g/3oz*	14
Mince Pies, Puff Pastry (Waitrose) *serving 90g/3oz*	17
Mince Pies, Select (Waitrose) *serving 90g/3oz*	17
Mince Pies, Shortcrust (Waitrose) *serving 90g/3oz*	13
Mince Pies, Vegetarian (Holland & Barrett) *serving 90g/3oz*	15
Mince Slices (Mr Kipling) *serving 90g/3oz*	13
Mince Tartlets, Glazed (Mr Kipling) *serving 90g/3oz*	13
Mincemeat & Apple Pie (Waitrose) *serving 90g/3oz*	10
Mincemeat Tart, One Crust *serving 90g/3oz*	14
Mini Logs (Cadbury's) *serving 90g/3oz*	18
Mini Roll with Jam & Vanilla Flavoured Filling (6) (Asda) *serving 90g/3oz*	9
Mini Rolls (Marks & Spencer) *serving 90g/3oz*	21
Mini Rolls (Tesco) *serving 90g/3oz*	19

Mini Rolls with Strawberry Jam (Cadbury's) *serving 90g/3oz* 15
Mother's Day Cake, Small (Waitrose) *serving 90g/3oz* 12
Mother's Day Sponge (Waitrose) *serving 90g/3oz* 12
Orange & Carrot Cake (Marks & Spencer) *serving 90g/3oz* 13
Orange Cream Gateau, Frozen (Marks & Spencer) *serving 90g/3oz* 14
Orange & Lemon Gateau, Frozen (Iceland) *serving 90g/3oz* 8
Orchard Fruit Pie, Deep Filled, Chilled (Tesco) *serving 90g/3oz* 7
Paradise Cake (Waitrose) *serving 90g/3oz* 14
Party Cake, Large (Marks & Spencer) *serving 90g/3oz* 14
Passion Cake (Tesco) *serving 90g/3oz* 15
Pastry Case, Plain (Tesco) *serving 90g/3oz* 25
Pecan Pie (Waitrose) *serving 90g/3oz* 17
Pecan Pie, Home Made *serving 90g/3oz* 20
Pie Crust, Cookie-Type, Prepared from Recipe, with Chocolate Wafer, Baked *serving 90g/3oz* 29
Pie Crust, Cookie-Type, Prepared from Recipe, with Chocolate Wafer, Chilled *serving 90g/3oz* 28
Pie Crust, Cookie-Type, Prepared from Recipe, with Graham Cracker, Baked *serving 90g/3oz* 22
Pie Crust, Cookie-Type, Prepared from Recipe, Chilled *serving 90g/3oz* 22
Pie Crust, Cookie-Type, Prepared from Recipe, with Vanilla Wafer, Baked *serving 90g/3oz* 33
Pie Crust, Cookie-Type, Prepared from Recipe, with Vanilla Wafer, Chilled *serving 90g/3oz* 33
Piemonte Gateaux, Frozen (Marks & Spencer) *serving 90g/3oz* 17
Pineapple Upside Down Cake, Home Made *serving 90g/3oz* 11
Pop Tarts, Apple (Kellogg's) *serving 90g/3oz* 12
Pop Tarts, Frosted Blueberry (Kellogg's) *serving 90g/3oz* 11
Pop Tarts, Frosted Chocolate (Kellogg's) *serving 90g/3oz* 9
Pop Tarts, Frosted Strawberry (Kellogg's) *serving 90g/3oz* 11
Pop Tarts, Strawberry (Kellogg's) *serving 90g/3oz* 12
Poppy & Daisy Cake (Waitrose) *serving 90g/3oz* 6
Pound Cake, Home Made *serving 90g/3oz* 22
Pumpkin Pie, Home Made *serving 90g/3oz* 8

Redcurrant & Strawberry Pies (2, 6) (Lyons) *serving 90g/3oz*	12
Rembrandt Cake (Waitrose) *serving 90g/3oz*	16
Rock Cakes *serving 90g/3oz*	15
Rum Baba, Dairy Cream (Tesco) *serving 90g/3oz*	5
Scottish Pineapple Fancies (Marks & Spencer) *serving 90g/3oz*	14
Sherry Trifle Gateau, Frozen (Marks & Spencer) *serving 90g/3oz*	12
Simnel Cake, Large (Waitrose) *serving 90g/3oz*	10
Simnel Cake, Small (Waitrose) *serving 90g/3oz*	10
Simnel Slab Portions (Waitrose) *serving 90g/3oz*	10
Snowballs (Marks & Spencer) *serving 90g/3oz*	12
Sponge, Dairy Cream (Somerfield) *serving 90g/3oz*	9
Sponge, Dairy Cream, Luxury, Frozen (Iceland) *serving 90g/3oz*	9
Sponge Burger Cake (Waitrose) *serving 90g/3oz*	14
Sponge Cake *serving 90g/3oz*	24
Sponge Cake, Frozen *serving 90g/3oz*	15
Sponge Cake, Iced (Marks & Spencer) *serving 90g/3oz*	14
Sponge Cake, Mini Chocolate (Mr Kipling) *serving 90g/3oz*	21
Sponge Cake, Mini Lemon (Mr Kipling) *serving 90g/3oz*	19
Sponge Cake, Mini Victoria (Mr Kipling) *serving 90g/3oz*	19
Sponge Cake with Butter Icing *serving 90g/3oz*	28
Sponge Fingers (Tesco) *serving 90g/3oz*	3
Sponge Mix, Luxury (Somerfield) *serving 90g/3oz*	14
Sponge Roll, Chocolate (Marks & Spencer) *serving 90g/3oz*	19
Sponge Roll, Strawberry (Marks & Spencer) *serving 90g/3oz*	9
Sponge Sandwich, Raspberry (Hales) *serving 90g/3oz*	14
Sponge Sandwich, Raspberry with Raspberry Jam & Vanilla Fill (Asda) *serving 90g/3oz*	14
Sponge Sunbathing Bear (Waitrose) *serving 90g/3oz*	14
Sponge Valentine Cake (Waitrose) *serving 90g/3oz*	14
Sticky Toffee Gateau (Somerfield) *serving 90g/3oz*	14
Stollen (Somerfield) *serving 90g/3oz*	17
Stollen (Tesco) *serving 90g/3oz*	20
Stollen, Mini (Tesco) *serving 90g/3oz*	20
Stollen Slices (Mr Kipling) *serving 90g/3oz*	15
Strawberry Cake Bar, Chocolate Coated (Asda) *serving 90g/3oz*	19

Strawberry Gateau (Somerfield) *serving 90g/3oz*	14
Stawberry Gateau (Waitrose) *serving 90g/3oz*	14
Strawberry Gateau, Frozen (Iceland) *serving 90g/3oz*	11
Strawberry Gateau, Frozen (Marks & Spencer) *serving 90g/3oz*	16
Strawberry Gateau, Frozen (Tesco) *serving 90g/3oz*	14
Strawberry Sundae (Marks & Spencer) *serving 90g/3oz*	16
Strawberry Sundae (Mr Kipling) *serving 90g/3oz*	14
Strawberry Sundaes (Asda) *serving 90g/3oz*	13
Sultana & Cherry Cake (Marks & Spencer) *serving 90g/3oz*	10
Sultana & Cherry Cake (Somerfield) *serving 90g/3oz*	11
Sultana Cherry Slab (Tesco) *serving 90g/3oz*	7
Sultana & Currant Cake (Somerfield) *serving 90g/3oz*	14
Sultana Slab (Marks & Spencer) *serving 90g/3oz*	10
Summer Fruit Pie, Deep Filled, Chilled (Asda) *serving 90g/3oz*	13
Summer Fruit Tart (Waitrose) *serving 90g/3oz*	9
Summer Fruits Dessert (Mr Kipling) *serving 90g/3oz*	15
Summer Fruits, Lattice Pie, Frozen (Tesco) *serving 90g/3oz*	11
Swiss Bun (Tesco) *serving 90g/3oz*	12
Swiss Gateau (Cadbury's) *serving 90g/3oz*	17
Swiss Roll, Chocolate (Asda) *serving 90g/3oz*	10
Swiss Roll, Chocolate (Marks & Spencer) *serving 90g/3oz*	15
Swiss Roll, Chocolate (Mr Kipling) *serving 90g/3oz*	14
Swiss Roll, Chocolate (Somerfield) *serving 90g/3oz*	15
Swiss Roll, Chocolate, Large (Hales) *serving 90g/3oz*	16
Swiss Roll, Raspberry, Large (Hales) *serving 90g/3oz*	8
Swiss Roll, Economy Chocolate (Hales) *serving 90g/3oz*	16
Swiss Roll, Economy Raspberry (Hales) *serving 90g/3oz*	2
Swiss Roll Chocolate, Individual *serving 90g/3oz*	10
Swiss Roll, Jam (Marks & Spencer) *serving 90g/3oz*	2
Swiss Roll, Milk Chocolate (Tesco) *serving 90g/3oz*	21
Swiss Roll, Raspberry (Asda) *serving 90g/3oz*	2
Swiss Roll, Raspberry (Lyons) *serving 90g/3oz*	2
Swiss Roll, Raspberry (Mr Kipling) *serving 90g/3oz*	2
Swiss Roll, Raspberry & Vanilla (Asda) *serving 90g/3oz*	9
Swiss Roll, Raspberry & Vanilla (Lyons) *serving 90g/3oz*	7
Tart, Apple & Blackcurrant Lattice (Tesco) *serving 90g/3oz*	9
Tart, Apple with Dairy Cream (Tesco) *serving 90g/3oz*	9

Tart, Apricot & Peach (Marks & Spencer) *serving 90g/3oz*	10
Tart au Citron (Waitrose) *serving 90g/3oz*	17
Tart, Blackcurrant (Tesco) *serving 90g/3oz*	12
Tart, Bramley Apple (Marks & Spencer) *serving 90g/3oz*	9
Tart, Cherry (Marks & Spencer) *serving 90g/3oz*	14
Tart, Coconut (Marks & Spencer) *serving 90g/3oz*	18
Tart, Coconut (Tesco) *serving 90g/3oz*	25
Tart, Coconut, Chilled (Asda) *serving 90g/3oz*	20
Tart, Custard (4) (Tesco) *serving 90g/3oz*	9
Tart, Custard, Individual *serving 90g/3oz*	13
Tart, Custard, Large *serving 90g/3oz*	15
Tart, Custard, Large (Tesco) *serving 90g/3oz*	9
Tart, Custard, Large (Waitrose) *serving 90g/3oz*	12
Tart, Egg Custard (Marks & Spencer) *serving 90g/3oz*	13
Tart, Egg Custard, Large (Marks & Spencer) *serving 90g/3oz*	10
Tart, Free Range Egg Custard (Large) (Tesco) *serving 90g/3oz*	9
Tart, Fruits of the Forest with Dairy Cream (Tesco) *serving 90g/3oz*	12
Tart, Jam, Assorted (Tesco) *serving 90g/3oz*	13
Tart, Jam (Hales) *serving 90g/3oz*	14
Tart, Jam, (Lyons) *serving 90g/3oz*	14
Tart, Jam, Home Made *serving 90g/3oz*	13
Tart, Jam, Retail *serving 90g/3oz*	12
Tart, Jam, Selection (Mr Kipling) *serving 90g/3oz*	13
Tart, Jam, Wholemeal *serving 90g/3oz*	14
Tart, Lemon Curd (Asda) *serving 90g/3oz*	13
Tart, Lemon Curd (Lyons) *serving 90g/3oz*	15
Tart, Lemon Curd (Tesco) *serving 90g/3oz*	15
Tart, Manchester (Marks & Spencer) *serving 90g/3oz*	21
Tart, Mini Creme Pat (Waitrose) *serving 90g/3oz*	11
Tart, Mixed Fruit (Peach & Kiwi, Mandarin & Cherry) (Somerfield) *serving 90g/3oz*	11
Tart, Normandy Apple (Waitrose) *serving 90g/3oz*	16
Tart, Raspberry & Redcurrant with Dairy Cream (Tesco) *serving 90g/3oz*	14
Tart, Strawberry (Somerfield) *serving 90g/3oz*	15
Tart, Strawberry (Tesco) *serving 90g/3oz*	16

Tart, Strawberry & Rhubarb (Marks & Spencer) *serving 90g/3oz*	9
Tart, Summerfruit (Marks & Spencer) *serving 90g/3oz*	14
Tart, Toffee Apple (Mr Kipling) *serving 90g/3oz*	13
Tart, Toffee & Pecan (Marks & Spencer) *serving 90g/3oz*	21
Tart, Treacle (Marks & Spencer) *serving 90g/3oz*	4
Tart, Treacle (Waitrose) *serving 90g/3oz*	10
Tart, Treacle, Frozen (Iceland) *serving 90g/3oz*	11
Tart, Treacle Lattice (Mr Kipling) *serving 90g/3oz*	11
Tart, Treacle Lattice, Frozen (Tesco) *serving 90g/3oz*	10
Tarte au Chocolat (Marks & Spencer) *serving 90g/3oz*	23
Tarte aux Abricots (Marks & Spencer) *serving 90g/3oz*	13
Tarte aux Cerises (Marks & Spencer) *serving 90g/3oz*	17
Tarte aux Framboises (Marks & Spencer) *serving 90g/3oz*	21
Tarte, Provencale (8) Flute (Waitrose) *serving 90g/3oz*	15
Tartlet, Almond (Waitrose) *serving 90g/3oz*	19
Tartlet, Banana (Waitrose) *serving 90g/3oz*	8
Tartlet, Blackcurrant (Waitrose) *serving 90g/3oz*	8
Tartlet, Blueberry (Waitrose) *serving 90g/3oz*	14
Tartlet, Exotic Fruit (Waitrose) *serving 90g/3oz*	8
Tartlet, Peach (Waitrose) *serving 90g/3oz*	8
Tartlet, Strawberry *serving 90g/3oz*	10
Tartlets, Pecan (8) (Waitrose) *serving 90g/3oz*	17
Teacake (Waitrose) *serving 90g/3oz*	6
Teacake, Basics (Somerfield) *serving 90g/3oz*	4
Teacake, Large Fruited (Tesco) *serving 90g/3oz*	7
Tiramisu Gateau, Frozen (Marks & Spencer) *serving 90g/3oz*	20
Toadstool Cake (Waitrose) *serving 90g/3oz*	20
Toffee & Almond Loaf (Marks & Spencer) *serving 90g/3oz*	17
Toffee Apple Pie, Deep Fill, Chilled (Asda) *serving 90g/3oz*	15
Toffee Cake (Somerfield) *serving 90g/3oz*	18
Toffee Flavour Layer Cake (Somerfield) *serving 90g/3oz*	17
Toffee Layer Cake (Waitrose) *serving 90g/3oz*	17
Toffee Pecan Dream Pie, Frozen (Marks & Spencer) *serving 90g/3oz*	23
Toffee Pecan Tibakes (Marks & Spencer) *serving 90g/3oz*	27

Toffee Sandwich (Lyons) *serving 90g/3oz*	16
Toffee Sponge Sandwich (Tesco) *serving 90g/3oz*	15
Treacle & Walnut Tart (Waitrose) *serving 90g/3oz*	19
Trifle Sponges (Lyons) *serving 90g/3oz*	2
Trifle Sponges (Tesco) *serving 90g/3oz*	2
Tunis Cake (Waitrose) *serving 90g/3oz*	25
Valentine Heart Cake (Waitrose) *serving 90g/3oz*	18
Vanilla Cream, Pie Home Made *serving 90g/3oz*	13
Vanilla Lion Sponge (Waitrose) *serving 90g/3oz*	21
Vanilla Slices *serving 90g/3oz*	16
Victoria Sandwich (Asda) *serving 90g/3oz*	21
Victoria Sandwich (Marks & Spencer) *serving 90g/3oz*	19
Victoria Sponge, Grocery (Iceland) *serving 90g/3oz*	15
Victoria Sponge, Raspberry (Waitrose) *serving 90g/3oz*	17
Viennese Sandwich (Marks & Spencer) *serving 90g/3oz*	28
Viennese Slices (Lyons) *serving 90g/3oz*	21
Viennese Whirls (Lyons) *serving 90g/3oz*	27
Waffles *serving 90g/3oz*	15
Walnut Buttercream Layer (Tesco) *serving 90g/3oz*	18
Walnut Cake (Somerfield) *serving 90g/3oz*	19
Walnut Layer Cake (Waitrose) *serving 90g/3oz*	18
Walnut Layer Cake (Somerfield) *serving 90g/3oz*	20
Walnut Slab Cake (Marks & Spencer) *serving 90g/3oz*	21
Wedding Cake (Waitrose) *serving 90g/3oz*	12
Wedding Cake, 3 Tier (Waitrose) *serving 90g/3oz*	12
Wedding Cake, Iced, Large (Waitrose) *serving 90g/3oz*	13
Wedding Cake, Iced, Small (Waitrose) *serving 90g/3oz*	13
Wedding Cake, Ivory (Waitrose) *serving 90g/3oz*	10
Wedding Cake, Peach (Waitrose) *serving 90g/3oz*	12
Wedding Cake, Peach, Iced (Waitrose) *serving 90g/3oz*	12
Wedding Cake, Soft Iced (Waitrose) *serving 90g/3oz*	13
Welsh Cakes *serving 90g/3oz*	18
White Cake (Betty Crocker) *serving 90g/3oz*	12
White Chocolate Gateau (Sara Lee) *serving 90g/3oz*	15
Yule Log (Tesco) *serving 90g/3oz*	19
Yule Log, Milk Chocolate Luxury Fudge (Tesco) *serving 90g/3oz*	20

Cereals

NOTE: The standard serving size in this section is 30g/1oz. If you wish to consume more or less than this amount (e.g. if you are going to consume a pack of food whose weight differs from the standard serving size) use the conversion tables on page 386 to calculate the new amount of fat in the food.

Food	Fat
All Bran Plus (Kellogg's) *serving 30g/1oz*	1
Apple & Blueberry Crisp (Somerfield) *serving 30g/1oz*	5
Apple & Spice Hot Oat Cereal (Holland & Barrett) *serving 30g/1oz*	2
Apple Wheats (Kellogg's) *serving 30g/1oz*	1
Apricot Crunchies (Tesco) *serving 30g/1oz*	1
Apricot Hot Oat Cereal (Holland & Barrett) *serving 30g/1oz*	1
Bran (Holland & Barrett) *serving 30g/1oz*	1
Bran Breakfast Cereal (Tesco) *serving 30g/1oz*	1
Bran Buds (Kellogg's) *serving 30g/1oz*	1
Bran Flakes (Kellogg's) *serving 30g/1oz*	1
Bran Flakes (Somerfield) *serving 30g/1oz*	1
Bran Flakes (Tesco) *serving 30g/1oz*	1
Bran Flakes, Healthy Eating (Tesco) *serving 30g/1oz*	1
Branflakes (Waitrose) *serving 30g/1oz*	1
Breakfast Boulders (Tesco) *serving 30g/1oz*	0
Breakfast Bran (Somerfield) *serving 30g/1oz*	1
Chocco Crunchies (Tesco) *serving 30g/1oz*	2
Choco Flakes (Kellogg's) *serving 30g/1oz*	1
Chocolate Cereal (Marks & Spencer) *serving 30g/1oz*	5
Chocolate & Hazelnut Crunch (Waitrose) *serving 30g/1oz*	7
Chocolate Toffee Banana (Waitrose) *serving 30g/1oz*	5
Cinnamon Toast Crunch *serving 30g/1oz*	3
Clusters *serving 30g/1oz*	2
Coco Pops (Kellogg's) *serving 30g/1oz*	1
Cocoa Corn Flakes (Tesco) *serving 30g/1oz*	0
Cocoa Puffs (Tesco) *serving 30g/1oz*	0
Common Sense Oat Bran Flakes (Kellogg's) *serving 30g/1oz*	2
Corn Crisp (Somerfield) *serving 30g/1oz*	6
Corn Flakes (Kellogg's) *serving 30g/1oz*	0

Corn Flakes (Somerfield) *serving 30g/1oz*	0
Corn Flakes (Tesco) *serving 30g/1oz*	0
Corn Flakes (Waitrose) *serving 30g/1oz*	0
Corn Flakes, Basics (Somerfield) *serving 30g/1oz*	0
Corn Flakes, Crunchy Nut (Kellogg's) *serving 30g/1oz*	1
Cornflakes, Honey Nut (Iceland) *serving 30g/1oz*	1
Corn Flakes, Honey Nut (Somerfield) *serving 30g/1oz*	1
Corn Flakes, Honey Nut (Tesco) *serving 30g/1oz*	1
Corn Flakes, Honey Nut (Waitrose) *serving 30g/1oz*	1
Corn Pops (Kellogg's) *serving 30g/1oz*	0
Country Store (Kellogg's) *serving 30g/1oz*	1
Crisp Puffed Rice (Tesco) *serving 30g/1oz*	0
Crisp Rice (Tesco) *serving 30g/1oz*	0
Crisp Rice (Waitrose) *serving 30g/1oz*	0
Crunchy Flakes (Tesco) *serving 30g/1oz*	1
Crunchy Oat Cereal (Somerfield) *serving 30g/1oz*	5
Frosted Flakes (Iceland) *serving 30g/1oz*	1
Frosted Flakes (Somerfield) *serving 30g/1oz*	0
Frosted Flakes (Tesco) *serving 30g/1oz*	0
Frosted Flakes (Waitrose) *serving 30g/1oz*	0
Frosted Shreddies (Nestlé) *serving 30g/1oz*	0
Frosted Wheats (Kellogg's) *serving 30g/1oz*	0
Frosties (Kellogg's) *serving 30g/1oz*	0
Fruit & Fibre (Somerfield) *serving 30g/1oz*	2
Fruit & Fibre (Tesco) *serving 30g/1oz*	1
Fruit 'n' Fibre (Kellogg's) *serving 30g/1oz*	2
Fruit & Fibre Flakes (Waitrose) *serving 30g/1oz*	2
Golden Grahams (Nestlé) *serving 30g/1oz*	1
Honey Nut Cheerios (Nestlé) *serving 30g/1oz*	1
Honey Nut Loops (Kellogg's) *serving 30g/1oz*	1
Instant Hot Oat Cereal (Somerfield) *serving 30g/1oz*	2
Instant Hot Oat Cereal (Tesco) *serving 30g/1oz*	2
Krumbly (Kellogg's) *serving 30g/1oz*	6
Lucky Charms (Nestlé) *serving 30g/1oz*	1
Muesli, Apricot (Holland & Barrett) *serving 30g/1oz*	1
Muesli, Basics (Somerfield) *serving 30g/1oz*	2
Muesli, Bran (Tesco) *serving 30g/1oz*	2

Muesli, Bran (Waitrose) *serving 30g/1oz* 2
Muesli, Cereal Bran Fibre (Somerfield) *serving 30g/1oz* 1
Muesli, Deluxe (Dorset Cereals) *serving 30g/1oz* 3
Muesli, Deluxe, Whole Wheat (Tesco) *serving 30g/1oz* 3
Muesli, Dorset (Dorset Cereals) *serving 30g/1oz* 3
Muesli, Fruit (Holland & Barrett) *serving 30g/1oz* 2
Muesli, Fruit (Marks & Spencer) *serving 30g/1oz* 2
Muesli, Fruit & Fibre (Holland & Barrett) *serving 30g/1oz* 1
Muesli, Fruit & Fibre (Waitrose) *serving 30g/1oz* 1
Muesli, Fruit & Fibre, No Added Salt or Sugar (Asda) *serving 30g/1oz* 1
Muesli, Fruit & Nut (Holland & Barrett) *serving 30g/1oz* 2
Muesli, Fruit/Nut (Waitrose) *serving 30g/1oz* 3
Muesli, Fruit, Nut & Seeds (Holland & Barrett) *serving 30g/1oz* 3
Muesli, Gluten Free (Holland & Barrett) *serving 30g/1oz* 3
Muesli, Healthy Eating, Swiss Style (Tesco) *serving 30g/1oz* 2
Muesli, High Fibre (Holland & Barrett) *serving 30g/1oz* 1
Muesli, Luxury (Dorset Cereals) (Somerfield) *serving 30g/1oz* 2
Muesli, Luxury (Marks & Spencer) *serving 30g/1oz* 3
Muesli, Luxury (Somerfield) *serving 30g/1oz* 3
Muesli, Luxury (Waitrose) *serving 30g/1oz* 2
Muesli, Luxury 45% (Waitrose) *serving 30g/1oz* 2
Muesli, Luxury Fruit (Holland & Barrett) *serving 30g/1oz* 1
Muesli, Luxury Fruit & Nut (Holland & Barrett) *serving 30g/1oz* 2
Muesli, Luxury Fruit (Tesco) *serving 30g/1oz* 1
Muesli, Neal's Yard Base (Holland & Barrett) *serving 30g/1oz* 3
Muesli, Neal's Yard Crunchy Bran (Holland & Barrett) *serving 30g/1oz* 2
Muesli, Neal's Yard Gluten Free (Holland & Barrett) *serving 30g/1oz* 2
Muesli, Neal's Yard Organic (Holland & Barrett) *serving 30g/1oz* 4
Muesli, Neal's Yard Rich (Holland & Barrett) *serving 30g/1oz* 4
Muesli, No Added Sugar (Waitrose) *serving 30g/1oz* 2
Muesli, Nut (Holland & Barrett) *serving 30g/1oz* 3
Muesli, Original (Holland & Barrett) *serving 30g/1oz* 3
Muesli, Swiss Style *serving 30g/1oz* 2
Muesli, Swiss Style (Somerfield) *serving 30g/1oz* 2

Muesli, Swiss Style (Waitrose) *serving 30g/1oz* 2
Muesli, Swiss Style, No Added Sugar or Salt (Asda) *serving 30g/1oz* 2
Muesli, Whole Wheat (Somerfield) *serving 30g/1oz* 2
Multi Cheerios *serving 30g/1oz* 1
Multi Flake Cereal (Marks & Spencer) *serving 30g/1oz* 1
Multi Grain Start (Kellogg's) *serving 30g/1oz* 1
Neal's Yard Fruit & Nut Crunch (Holland & Barrett) *serving 30g/1oz* 3
Neal's Yard Tropical Nut Breakfast (Holland & Barrett) *serving 30g/1oz* 2
Noughts & Crosses Cereal (Marks & Spencer) *serving 30g/1oz* 0
Nut Feast (Kellogg's) *serving 30g/1oz* 2
Oat & Cinnamon Cereal (Marks & Spencer) *serving 30g/1oz* 5
Oat Crunchy, Almonds (Waitrose) *serving 30g/1oz* 4
Oat Crunchy, Fruits (Waitrose) *serving 30g/1oz* 4
Oats, Instant, Plain, Made with Water *serving 30g/1oz* 0
Oats, Instant, with Apples & Cinnamon, Made with Water *serving 30g/1oz* 0
Oats, Instant, with Bran & Raisins, Made with Water *serving 30g/1oz* 0
Oats, Instant, with Cinnamon & Spice, Made with Water *serving 30g/1oz* 0
Oats, Instant, with Maple & Brown Sugar, Made with Water *serving 30g/1oz* 0
Oats, Instant, with Raisins & Spice, Made with Water *serving 30g/1oz* 0
Oats, Reg & Quick & Instant, Made with Water *serving 30g/1oz* 0
Porridge, Quick (Marks & Spencer) *serving 30g/1oz* 3
Puffed Rice *serving 30g/1oz* 0
Puffed Wheat (Somerfield) *serving 30g/1oz* 1
Raisin Wheats (Kellogg's) *serving 30g/1oz* 0
Ralston, Cooked with Water *serving 30g/1oz* 0
Raspberry Country Crunch (Waitrose) *serving 30g/1oz* 5
Raspberry Crisp Cereal (Somerfield) *serving 30g/1oz* 5
Rice Krispies (Kellogg's) *serving 30g/1oz* 0
Ricicles (Kellogg's) *serving 30g/1oz* 0

Scotch Porridge Oats (Tesco) *serving 30g/1oz* 2
Scottish Porridge Oats (Waitrose) *serving 30g/1oz* 2
Scotch Porridge Oats with 20% Bran (Tesco) *serving 30g/1oz* 2
Shredded Malt Wheats (Tesco) *serving 30g/1oz* 1
Shedded Wheat (Nestlé) *serving 30g/1oz* 1
Shreddies (Nestlé) *serving 30g/1oz* 1
Special K (Kellogg's) *serving 30g/1oz* 0
Strawberry Cereal (Marks & Spencer) *serving 30g/1oz* 6
Strike! (Kellogg's) *serving 30g/1oz* 0
Sugar Frosted Flakes (Tesco) *serving 30g/1oz* 0
Sultana Bran (Kellogg's) *serving 30g/1oz* 1
Sultana Bran, Healthy Eating (Tesco) *serving 30g/1oz* 1
Sunny Jim Force Flakes (Nestlé) *serving 30g/1oz* 1
Super High Fibre Cereal (Dorset Cereals) *serving 30g/1oz* 3
Sustain (Kellogg's) *serving 30g/1oz* 1
Toffee & Pecan Cereal (Marks & Spencer) *serving 30g/1oz* 6
Tropical Crunch Cereal (Waitrose) *serving 30g/1oz* 5
Wheat Flakes (Waitrose) *serving 30g/1oz* 1
Whole Wheat Cereal Biscuit (Waitrose) *serving 30g/1oz* 1
Whole Wheat Cereal Biscuit, Healthy Eating (Tesco) *serving 30g/1oz* 1
Whole Wheat Flakes, Healthy Eating (Tesco) *serving 30g/1oz* 1

CHEESE

NOTE: The standard serving size in this section is 60g/2oz. If you wish to consume more or less than this amount (e.g. if you are going to consume a pack of food whose weight differs from the standard serving size) use the conversion tables on page 386 to calculate the new amount of fat in the food.

Bavarian Smoked, Processed (Somerfield) *serving 60g/2oz* 14
Bavarian Smoked, Processed, with Ham (Somerfield) *serving 60g/2oz* 12
Bavarian Smoked, Slices (Marks & Spencer) *serving 60g/2oz* 14
Bleu d'Auvergne (Waitrose) *serving 60g/2oz* 16
Blue Cheese *serving 60g/2oz* 17

Blue Shropshire (Safeway) *serving 60g/2oz*	21
Blue Shropshire (Waitrose) *serving 60g/2oz*	20
Boursin, Ail & Fines Herbes (Van Den Bergh) *serving 60g/2oz*	25
Boursin, en Habit de Ciboulette (Van Den Bergh) *serving 60g/2oz*	25
Boursin, en Habit de Noix (Van Den Bergh) *serving 60g/2oz*	27
Boursin, en Habit de Poivre (Van Den Bergh) *serving 60g/2oz*	24
Boursin, Léger (Van Den Bergh) *serving 60g/2oz*	6
Boursin, Naturel (Van Den Bergh) *serving 60g/2oz*	26
Boursin, Poivre (Van Den Bergh) *serving 60g/2oz*	25
Bresse Blue, Pick & Mix (Marks & Spencer) *serving 60g/2oz*	19
Brie *serving 60g/2oz*	17
Brie (Marks & Spencer) *serving 60g/2oz*	16
Brie (Somerfield) *serving 60g/2oz*	15
Brie, Bavarian Blue (Somerfield) *serving 60g/2oz*	25
Brie, Bavarian, with Garlic & Chives (Somerfield) *serving 60g/2oz*	25
Brie, Bavarian, with Green Peppers (Somerfield) *serving 60g/2oz*	25
Brie, Cambozola Blue (Somerfield) *serving 60g/2oz*	25
Brie, Coeur de Lion (Safeway) *serving 60g/2oz*	19
Brie, French (Safeway) *serving 60g/2oz*	19
Brie, French (Somerfield) *serving 60g/2oz*	15
Brie, French (Waitrose) *serving 60g/2oz*	15
Brie, French, with Peppers (Safeway) *serving 60g/2oz*	16
Brie, French, Ripe (Waitrose) *serving 60g/2oz*	15
Brie, German, Blue Vein (Waitrose) *serving 60g/2oz*	25
Brie, German, with Herbs (Waitrose) *serving 60g/2oz*	23
Brie, Howgate Scottish (Safeway) *serving 60g/2oz*	16
Brie, Medium Mature (Waitrose) *serving 60g/2oz*	15
Brie, President, Whole (Somerfield) *serving 60g/2oz*	15
Brie, Ready to Eat (Waitrose) *serving 60g/2oz*	15
Brie, Somerset (Safeway) *serving 60g/2oz*	16
Brie, Somerset (Somerfield) *serving 60g/2oz*	14
Brie, Somerset (Waitrose) *serving 60g/2oz*	14
Brie, Somerset, Ripe (Waitrose) *serving 60g/2oz*	14
Brie, Supreme (Waitrose) *serving 60g/2oz*	19
Brie, Traditional (Waitrose) *serving 60g/2oz*	13

Buxton Blue (Waitrose) *serving 60g/2oz* 21
Caerphilly *serving 60g/2oz* 19
Caerphilly (Somerfield) *serving 60g/2oz* 19
Caerphilly (Waitrose) *serving 60g/2oz* 19
Caerphilly, Prepacked (Asda) *serving 60g/2oz* 19
Caerphilly, Welsh, Traditional (Safeway) *serving 60g/2oz* 19
Cambozola (Marks & Spencer) *serving 60g/2oz* 25
Cambozola (Safeway) *serving 60g/2oz* 19
Camembert *serving 60g/2oz* 14
Camembert (Marks & Spencer) *serving 60g/2oz* 14
Camembert (Somerfield) *serving 60g/2oz* 14
Camembert, French (Safeway) *serving 60g/2oz* 13
Caraway Cheese *serving 60g/2oz* 18
Cashel Blue (Marks & Spencer) *serving 60g/2oz* 17
Cashel Irish Blue Cheese (Waitrose) *serving 60g/2oz* 17
Chaumes (Marks & Spencer) *serving 60g/2oz* 16
Chaumes (Waitrose) *serving 60g/2oz* 15
Chaumes, French (Safeway) *serving 60g/2oz* 15
Cheddar, American *serving 60g/2oz* 20
Cheddar, Anchor Vintage (Waitrose) *serving 60g/2oz* 21
Cheddar, Applewood Smoke Flavour (Safeway) *serving 60g/2oz* 21
Cheddar, Australian Mature (Waitrose) *serving 60g/2oz* 21
Cheddar, Australian Mature, Prepacked (Asda) *serving 60g/2oz* 21
Cheddar, Australian Medium (Waitrose) *serving 60g/2oz* 21
Cheddar, Canadian (Marks & Spencer) *serving 60g/2oz* 21
Cheddar, Canadian Mature Prepacked (Asda) *serving 60g/2oz* 21
Cheddar, Canadian (Waitrose) *serving 60g/2oz* 21
Cheddar, Canadian Mature (Safeway) *serving 60g/2oz* 21
Cheddar, Canadian, White (Somerfield) *serving 60g/2oz* 21
Cheddar, Cathedral City (Waitrose) *serving 60g/2oz* 21
Cheddar, Cathedral City Mature (Safeway) *serving 60g/2oz* 21
Cheddar, with Chives & Onions (Safeway) *serving 60g/2oz* 20
Cheddar, with Claret (Somerfield) *serving 60g/2oz* 21
Cheddar, Dairy Crest Mild (Waitrose) *serving 60g/2oz* 21
Cheddar, Davidstow Matured (Waitrose) *serving 60g/2oz* 21
Cheddar, Davidstow Extra Matured (Waitrose) *serving 60g/2oz* 21

Cheddar, English Mature (Safeway) *serving 60g/2oz*	21
Cheddar, English, White, Chilled (Iceland) *serving 60g/2oz*	21
Cheddar, English Mature, White, Prepacked (Asda) *serving 60g/2oz*	21
Cheddar, English Mild (Safeway) *serving 60g/2oz*	21
Cheddar, English Mild (Waitrose) *serving 60g/2oz*	21
Cheddar, English Mild, Coloured (Safeway) *serving 60g/2oz*	21
Cheddar, English Mild, Coloured, Prepacked (Asda) *serving 60g/2oz*	21
Cheddar, English Mild, White, Prepacked (Asda) *serving 60g/2oz*	21
Cheddar, English Red (Waitrose) *serving 60g/2oz*	21
Cheddar, Extra Mature, Chilled (Iceland) *serving 60g/2oz*	21
Cheddar, Farmhouse (Marks & Spencer) *serving 60g/2oz*	21
Cheddar, Farmhouse (Somerfield) *serving 60g/2oz*	21
Cheddar, Farmhouse (Waitrose) *serving 60g/2oz*	21
Cheddar, Farmhouse, Prepacked (Asda) *serving 60g/2oz*	21
Cheddar, Farmhouse Extra Mature (Marks & Spencer) *serving 60g/2oz*	21
Cheddar, Farmhouse Mature (Somerfield) *serving 60g/2oz*	20
Cheddar, Farmhouse Mature (Waitrose) *serving 60g/2oz*	21
Cheddar, Full Flavour, Chilled (Iceland) *serving 60g/2oz*	20
Cheddar, Full Flavour, White (Somerfield) *serving 60g/2oz*	21
Cheddar, Grated, 14% Fat White (Somerfield) *serving 60g/2oz*	9
Cheddar, Grated, Chilled (Iceland) *serving 60g/2oz*	21
Cheddar, Grated, Half Fat (Waitrose) *serving 60g/2oz*	8
Cheddar, Grated, Mature, Prepacked (Asda) *serving 60g/2oz*	21
Cheddar, Grated, Mature White (Somerfield) *serving 60g/2oz*	21
Cheddar, Grated, Mature White (Waitrose) *serving 60g/2oz*	20
Cheddar, Grated, Matured (Marks & Spencer) *serving 60g/2oz*	20
Cheddar, Grated, Medium Red (Marks & Spencer) *serving 60g/2oz*	20
Cheddar, Grated, Medium White (Marks & Spencer) *serving 60g/2oz*	20
Cheddar, Grated, Mild Coloured (Somerfield) *serving 60g/2oz*	21
Cheddar, Grated, Mild, Prepacked (Asda) *serving 60g/2oz*	21
Cheddar, Grated, Mild White (Somerfield) *serving 60g/2oz*	21

Cheddar, Grated, Reduced Fat (Marks & Spencer) *serving 60g/2oz* 14
Cheddar, Grated, White (Waitrose) *serving 60g/2oz* 20
Cheddar, Green Label Mature (Marks & Spencer) *serving 60g/2oz* 21
Cheddar, Half Fat Mature (Somerfield) *serving 60g/2oz* 9
Cheddar, Half Fat Mild (Somerfield) *serving 60g/2oz* 10
Cheddar, Healthy Choice Mature (Asda) *serving 60g/2oz* 14
Cheddar, Home Produced (Waitrose) *serving 60g/2oz* 21
Cheddar, Imported (Waitrose) *serving 60g/2oz* 21
Cheddar, Irish *serving 60g/2oz* 20
Cheddar, Irish (Waitrose) *serving 60g/2oz* 21
Cheddar, Irish Mature (Waitrose) *serving 60g/2oz* 21
Cheddar, Irish Mature, Wexford (Safeway) *serving 60g/2oz* 21
Cheddar, Irish Medium (Safeway) *serving 60g/2oz* 21
Cheddar, Keenes Farmhouse (Marks & Spencer) *serving 60g/2oz* 21
Cheddar, Low Fat (Somerfield) *serving 60g/2oz* 10
Cheddar, Mature, Chilled (Iceland) *serving 60g/2oz* 21
Cheddar, Mature, Pick & Mix (Marks & Spencer) *serving 60g/2oz* 21
Cheddar, Mature White (Somerfield) *serving 60g/2oz* 20
Cheddar, Mature White, Cheese Sticks (Somerfield) *serving 60g/2oz* 21
Cheddar, Mature White, Chilled (Iceland) *serving 60g/2oz* 21
Cheddar, Matured Red (Marks & Spencer) *serving 60g/2oz* 21
Cheddar, Matured White (Marks & Spencer) *serving 60g/2oz* 21
Cheddar, Medium, Reduced Fat (Marks & Spencer) *serving 60g/2oz* 14
Cheddar, Medium Red (Marks & Spencer) *serving 60g/2oz* 21
Cheddar, Medium White (Marks & Spencer) *serving 60g/2oz* 21
Cheddar, Medium with Full Fat Soft Cheese & Pineapple (Somerfield) *serving 60g/2oz* 20
Cheddar, Mild (Marks & Spencer) *serving 60g/2oz* 21
Cheddar, Mild (Safeway) *serving 60g/2oz* 21
Cheddar, Mild, Pick & Mix (Marks & Spencer) *serving 60g/2oz* 21
Cheddar, Mild Coloured (Safeway) *serving 60g/2oz* 21

Cheddar, Mild Coloured, Chilled (Iceland) *serving 60g/2oz* 21
Cheddar, Mild Red, Chilled (Iceland) *serving 60g/2oz* 21
Cheddar, Mild Red (Marks & Spencer) *serving 60g/2oz* 21
Cheddar, Mild White (Marks & Spencer) *serving 60g/2oz* 21
Cheddar, Mild White, Chilled (Iceland) *serving 60g/2oz* 21
Cheddar, Nanny's Goat (Waitrose) *serving 60g/2oz* 21
Cheddar, New Zealand *serving 60g/2oz* 21
Cheddar, Oak Smoked Ring (Waitrose) *serving 60g/2oz* 21
Cheddar, Old (Holland & Barrett) *serving 60g/2oz* 21
Cheddar, Old Shire Special Reserve Vintage (Safeway) *serving 60g/2oz* 21
Cheddar, Onion & Chive (Marks & Spencer) *serving 60g/2oz* 19
Cheddar, Orkney Mature (Safeway) *serving 60g/2oz* 21
Cheddar, Quickes, Traditional Mature (Safeway) *serving 60g/2oz* 21
Cheddar, Real Slices, White, Chilled (Iceland) *serving 60g/2oz* 21
Cheddar, Reduced Fat *serving 60g/2oz* 9
Cheddar, Reduced Fat (Sainsbury's) *serving 60g/2oz* 14
Cheddar, Scottish, Chilled (Iceland) *serving 60g/2oz* 21
Cheddar, Scottish, White, Chilled (Iceland) *serving 60g/2oz* 14
Cheddar, Scottish Mature, White, Prepacked (Asda) *serving 60g/2oz* 21
Cheddar, Scottish Mild, Coloured (Safeway) *serving 60g/2oz* 21
Cheddar, Scottish Mature (Safeway) *serving 60g/2oz* 21
Cheddar, Scottish Mature (Somerfield) *serving 60g/2oz* 21
Cheddar, Scottish Mature, Coloured (Safeway) *serving 60g/2oz* 21
Cheddar, Scottish Mature, Coloured, Prepacked (Asda) *serving 60g/2oz* 21
Cheddar, Scottish Mild, Coloured, Prepacked (Asda) *serving 60g/2oz* 21
Cheddar, Shape Alternative to Farmhouse Cheddar *serving 60g/2oz* 9
Cheddar, Shape Alternative to Mature Cheddar (St Ivel) *serving 60g/2oz* 10

Cheddar, Shape Alternative to Mild Cheddar *serving 60g/2oz*	10
Cheddar, Slices, Matured (Marks & Spencer) *serving 60g/2oz*	21
Cheddar, Slices, Mild (Marks & Spencer) *serving 60g/2oz*	21
Cheddar, Smoked (Marks & Spencer) *serving 60g/2oz*	21
Cheddar, Somerset Farmhouse (Waitrose) *serving 60g/2oz*	21
Cheddar, Spread (Somerfield) *serving 60g/2oz*	14
Cheddar Spread, Mature, Prepacked (Asda) *serving 60g/2oz*	12
Cheddar, with Spring Onion (Somerfield) *serving 60g/2oz*	20
Cheddar, St Illtyd Welsh Farmhouse (Safeway) *serving 60g/2oz*	20
Cheddar Style Cheese Spread, Healthy Choice (Asda) *serving 60g/2oz*	5
Cheddar, Taw Valley, White (Waitrose) *serving 60g/2oz*	21
Cheddar, Taw Valley Medium, White (Waitrose) *serving 60g/2oz*	21
Cheddar, Traditional Farmhouse Mature with Rind on (Somerfield) *serving 60g/2oz*	21
Cheddar, Traditional West Country Mature (Safeway) *serving 60g/2oz*	21
Cheddar, Traditional White Mature (Waitrose) *serving 60g/2oz*	21
Cheddar, Vegetarian *serving 60g/2oz*	21
Cheddar, Vegetarian Farmhouse (Tesco) *serving 60g/2oz*	21
Cheddar, Vegetarian Full Flavour (Tesco) *serving 60g/2oz*	21
Cheddar, Vegetarian Mature (Waitrose) *serving 60g/2oz*	21
Cheddar, Vegetarian Medium (Safeway) (Somerfield) *serving 60g/2oz*	21
Cheddar, Vegetarian Medium Mature (Tesco) *serving 60g/2oz*	21
Cheddar, Vegetarian (Waitrose) *serving 60g/2oz*	21
Cheddar, Vegetarian Mild (Tesco) *serving 60g/2oz*	21
Cheddar, Vintage (Marks & Spencer) *serving 60g/2oz*	21
Cheddar, Vintage, Large (Marks & Spencer) *serving 60g/2oz*	21
Cheddar, Vintage Mature (Somerfield) *serving 60g/2oz*	21
Cheddar, Vintage Pick & Mix (Marks & Spencer) *serving 60g/2oz*	21
Cheddar, Welsh (Marks & Spencer) *serving 60g/2oz*	21
Cheddar, Welsh Medium Matured (Safeway) *serving 60g/2oz*	21
Cheddar, Welsh, Smoked (Marks & Spencer) *serving 60g/2oz*	21
Cheddarie (Kraft Jacobs Suchard) *serving 60g/2oz*	13
Cheddarie Light (Kraft Jacobs Suchard) *serving 60g/2oz*	9

Cheese Enchiladas, Chilled Ready Meal (Tesco) *serving 60g/2oz* 5
Cheese & Ham Grills, Grocery (Iceland) *serving 60g/2oz* 15
Cheese & Ham Nibbles Grocery (Iceland) *serving 60g/2oz* 15
Cheese & Ham Nibbles (Waitrose) *serving 60g/2oz* 16
Cheese, Onion & Chive Pick & Mix (Marks & Spencer) *serving 60g/2oz* 19
Cheese & Onion Cocktail Rolls, Chilled (Iceland) *serving 60g/2oz* 12
Cheese & Onion Crispbake, Frozen (Tesco) *serving 60g/2oz* 7
Cheese & Onion Slice, Frozen (Tesco) *serving 60g/2oz* 9
Cheese Platter (Waitrose) *serving 60g/2oz* 19
Cheese Savouries: *See under* Nuts & Savoury Snacks
Cheese Savoyard (Birds Eye) *serving 60g/2oz* 9
Cheese Selection Pack (Waitrose) *serving 60g/2oz* 10
Cheese Selection Tray (Somerfield) *serving 60g/2oz* 19
Cheese Shapes, Grocery (Iceland) *serving 60g/2oz* 17
Cheese Singles, Lite (Somerfield) *serving 60g/2oz* 6
Cheese Slice, Original (Kraft Jacobs Suchard) *serving 60g/2oz* 15
Cheese Slices, Reduced Fat (Marks & Spencer) *serving 60g/2oz* 14
Cheese Spread, Plain *serving 60g/2oz* 14
Cheese Spread, Prepacked (Asda) *serving 60g/2oz* 13
Cheshire *serving 60g/2oz* 19
Cheshire, Bourne's Original Farmhouse (Safeway) *serving 60g/2oz* 17
Cheshire, Coloured (Somerfield) *serving 60g/2oz* 19
Cheshire, Coloured, Prepacked (Asda) *serving 60g/2oz* 19
Cheshire, Farmhouse (Safeway) *serving 60g/2oz* 19
Cheshire, Red (Marks & Spencer) *serving 60g/2oz* 19
Cheshire Type, Reduced Fat *serving 60g/2oz* 9
Cheshire, White (Marks & Spencer) *serving 60g/2oz* 19
Cheshire, White (Somerfield) *serving 60g/2oz* 19
Cheshire, White (Waitrose) *serving 60g/2oz* 19
Cheshire, White, Chilled (Iceland) *serving 60g/2oz* 19
Cheshire, White, Prepacked (Asda) *serving 60g/2oz* 19
Cheshire, White Farmhouse, Prepacked (Asda) *serving 60g/2oz* 19
Cheshire Wheel, Red (Waitrose) *serving 60g/2oz* 19

Chevre Blanc (Waitrose) *serving 60g/2oz* 15
Chevre du Berry (Marks & Spencer) *serving 60g/2oz* 9
Colby *serving 60g/2oz* 19
Cottage Cheese *serving 60g/2oz* 2
Cottage Cheese (Safeway) *serving 60g/2oz* 2
Cottage Cheese (Waitrose) *serving 60g/2oz* 1
Cottage Cheese, Apricot & Mango (Waitrose) *serving 60g/2oz* 2
Cottage Cheese, Chive (Marks & Spencer) *serving 60g/2oz* 1
Cottage Cheese, with Cheddar Cheese & Onion (Somerfield) *serving 60g/2oz* 5
Cottage Cheese, with Chives (Somerfield) *serving 60g/2oz* 2
Cottage Cheese, Chive & Onion, Chilled (Iceland) *serving 60g/2oz* 2
Cottage Cheese, Creamed, Large or Small Curd *serving 60g/2oz* 3
Cottage Cheese, Creamed with Fruit *serving 60g/2oz* 2
Cottage Cheese, Diet (Waitrose) *serving 60g/2oz* 1
Cottage Cheese, Half Fat (Sainsbury's) *serving 60g/2oz* 1
Cottage Cheese, Healthy Choice, Natural (Asda) *serving 60g/2oz* 2
Cottage Cheese, Healthy Eating, Very Low Fat (Tesco) *serving 60g/2oz* 1
Cottage Cheese, Healthy Eating, with Apple (Tesco) *serving 60g/2oz* 1
Cottage Cheese, Healthy Eating, with Coleslaw (Tesco) *serving 60g/2oz* 1
Cottage Cheese, Healthy Eating, with Herbs (Tesco) *serving 60g/2oz* 1
Cottage Cheese, Healthy Eating, with Onion (Tesco) *serving 60g/2oz* 1
Cottage Cheese, Healthy Eating, with Pineapple (Tesco) *serving 60g/2oz* 1
Cottage Cheese, Lemon Chicken (Marks & Spencer) *serving 60g/2oz* 3
Cottage Cheese, Light, Natural, Very Low Fat (Asda) *serving 60g/2oz* 1
Cottage Cheese, Light, with Cheddar & Onion (Asda) *serving 60g/2oz* 2

Cottage Cheese, Light, with Pineapple, Very Low Fat (Asda) *serving 60g/2oz* 1
Cottage Cheese, Lite, (Marks & Spencer) *serving 60g/2oz* 1
Cottage Cheese, Lite (Somerfield) *serving 60g/2oz* 1
Cottage Cheese, Lite, Natural (Marks & Spencer) *serving 60g/2oz* 1
Cottage Cheese, Lite, with Chives (Somerfield) *serving 60g/2oz* 1
Cottage Cheese, Lite, with Pineapple (Somerfield) *serving 60g/2oz* 1
Cottage Cheese, Low Fat (Waitrose) *serving 60g/2oz* 2
Cottage Cheese, Low Fat, with Lemon Prawns (Asda) *serving 60g/2oz* 4
Cottage Cheese, Low Fat, with Prawn Cocktail (Asda) *serving 60g/2oz* 5
Cottage Cheese, Low Fat, 1% Fat *serving 60g/2oz* 1
Cottage Cheese, Low Fat, 2% *serving 60g/2oz* 1
Cottage Cheese, Natural (Asda) *serving 60g/2oz* 2
Cottage Cheese, Natural (Marks & Spencer) *serving 60g/2oz* 2
Cottage Cheese, Natural (Somerfield) *serving 60g/2oz* 2
Cottage Cheese, Natural, Chilled (Iceland) *serving 60g/2oz* 2
Cottage Cheese, Natural, & Onion & Chives (Eden Vale) *serving 60g/2oz* 0
Cottage Cheese, with Onion & Chives (Safeway) *serving 60g/2oz* 2
Cottage Cheese, Onion & Chives (Waitrose) *serving 60g/2oz* 2
Cottage Cheese, Pineapple (Eden Vale) *serving 60g/2oz* 0
Cottage Cheese, Pineapple (Marks & Spencer) *serving 60g/2oz* 0
Cottage Cheese, with Pineapple (Somerfield) *serving 60g/2oz* 2
Cottage Cheese, Pineapple, Chilled (Iceland) *serving 60g/2oz* 2
Cottage Cheese, Prawn (Marks & Spencer) *serving 60g/2oz* 3
Cottage Cheese, with Prawns (Somerfield) *serving 60g/2oz* 6
Cottage Cheese, Prawns (6oz) (Waitrose) *serving 60g/2oz* 6
Cottage Cheese, Prawn & Cucumber (Marks & Spencer) *serving 60g/2oz* 1
Cottage Cheese, Prawn & Lime (Marks & Spencer) *serving 60g/2oz* 2
Cottage Cheese, Prawn & Seafood (Marks & Spencer) *serving 60g/2oz* 8
Cottage Cheese, Salmon & Cucumber (Marks & Spencer) *serving 60g/2oz* 1

Cottage Cheese, Salmon & Cucumber (Waitrose) *serving 60g/2oz*	9
Cottage Cheese, Shape (St Ivel) *serving 60g/2oz*	0
Cottage Cheese, Shape Pineapple (St Ivel) *serving 60g/2oz*	0
Cottage Cheese, Tomato & Basil (Marks & Spencer) *serving 60g/2oz*	1
Cottage Cheese, with Tuna & Sweetcorn (Somerfield) *serving 60g/2oz*	6
County Carnival (Safeway) *serving 60g/2oz*	19
Cream Cheese, Howgate (Safeway) *serving 60g/2oz*	17
Curd Cheese (Safeway) *serving 60g/2oz*	7
Curd Cheese (Waitrose) *serving 60g/2oz*	7
Dairylea Light Slices (Kraft Jacobs Suchard) *serving 60g/2oz*	8
Dairylea Light Triangles (Kraft Jacobs Suchard) *serving 60g/2oz*	7
Dairylea Light Tub (Kraft Jacobs Suchard) *serving 60g/2oz*	7
Dairylea Portions (Kraft Jacobs Suchard) *serving 60g/2oz*	14
Dairylea Slices (Kraft Jacobs Suchard) *serving 60g/2oz*	15
Dairylea Tub (Kraft Jacobs Suchard) *serving 60g/2oz*	14
Danish Blue *serving 60g/2oz*	18
Danish Blue (Safeway) *serving 60g/2oz*	17
Danish Blue (Waitrose) *serving 60g/2oz*	17
Danish Blue, Prepacked (Asda) *serving 60g/2oz*	17
Danish Blue, Extra Matured (Waitrose) *serving 60g/2oz*	17
Danish Blue, Matured (Waitrose) *serving 60g/2oz*	17
Danish Blue, Mild (Waitrose) *serving 60g/2oz*	17
Derby *serving 60g/2oz*	20
Dolcelatte (Marks & Spencer) *serving 60g/2oz*	16
Dolcelatte (Safeway) *serving 60g/2oz*	24
Dolcelatte (Somerfield) *serving 60g/2oz*	22
Dolcelatte (Waitrose) *serving 60g/2oz*	22
Doolin (Marks & Spencer) *serving 60g/2oz*	19
Double Gloucester *serving 60g/2oz*	20
Double Gloucester (Marks & Spencer) *serving 60g/2oz*	20
Double Gloucester (Somerfield) *serving 60g/2oz*	20
Double Gloucester (Waitrose) *serving 60g/2oz*	20
Double Gloucester, Prepacked (Asda) *serving 60g/2oz*	20
Double Gloucester, Old (Holland & Barrett) *serving 60g/2oz*	20

Double Gloucester, Onion & Chive (Waitrose) *serving 60g/2oz* 20
Double Gloucester, Traditional (Safeway) *serving 60g/2oz* 20
Double Gloucester, with Onion & Chives (Safeway) *serving 60g/2oz* 20
Dunlop (Marks & Spencer) *serving 60g/2oz* 20
Edam *serving 60g/2oz* 17
Edam, (Marks & Spencer) *serving 60g/2oz* 15
Edam (Safeway) *serving 60g/2oz* 15
Edam (Somerfield) *serving 60g/2oz* 14
Edam, Baby (Somerfield) *serving 60g/2oz* 15
Edam, Dutch (Waitrose) *serving 60g/2oz* 15
Edam, Dutch Cheese Ball (Waitrose) *serving 60g/2oz* 14
Edam, Dutch with Garlic & Herbs, Prepacked (Asda) *serving 60g/2oz* 14
Edam, Dutch Pick & Mix (Marks & Spencer) *serving 60g/2oz* 15
Edam, Dutch, Vegetarian, Prepacked (Asda) *serving 60g/2oz* 14
Edam, Prepacked (Asda) *serving 60g/2oz* 14
Edam, Reduced Fat (Sainsbury's) *serving 60g/2oz* 8
Edam, Vegetarian (Tesco) *serving 60g/2oz* 15
Edam Type, Healthy Eating, Half Fat Cheese (Tesco) *serving 60g/2oz* 7
Edam Type, Reduced Fat *serving 60g/2oz* 7
Edam with Herbs (Somerfield) *serving 60g/2oz* 14
Edam Wedges (Somerfield) *serving 60g/2oz* 14
Emmental *serving 60g/2oz* 18
Emmental (Marks & Spencer) *serving 60g/2oz* 19
Emmental (Somerfield) *serving 60g/2oz* 18
Emmental, Swiss Extra Mature (Waitrose) *serving 60g/2oz* 18
Emmental, Swiss (Safeway) *serving 60g/2oz* 18
Emmental, Swiss (Waitrose) *serving 60g/2oz* 19
Emmental Cuts (Waitrose) *serving 60g/2oz* 17
Emmental Pick & Mix (Marks & Spencer) *serving 60g/2oz* 19
Emmental & Salami Filling (Waitrose) *serving 60g/2oz* 14
Farmhouse Cheese Pâté with Garlic & Chives, Prepacked (Asda) *serving 60g/2oz* 21
Feta *serving 60g/2oz* 13
Feta (Marks & Spencer) *serving 60g/2oz* 15

Feta (Safeway) *serving 60g/2oz*	15
Feta Cheese, Pepper Knot (Waitrose) *serving 60g/2oz*	8
Five Counties Cheese (Safeway) *serving 60g/2oz*	20
Five Counties Cheese (Somerfield) *serving 60g/2oz*	20
Flora Alternative to Cheddar *serving 60g/2oz*	21
Fontina *serving 60g/2oz*	19
German Smoked Cheese, (Safeway) *serving 60g/2oz*	14
Gjetost *serving 60g/2oz*	18
Goat, Hard *serving 60g/2oz*	21
Goat, Semisoft *serving 60g/2oz*	18
Goat, Soft *serving 60g/2oz*	13
Goats, French (Safeway) *serving 60g/2oz*	11
Goats, Somerset (Waitrose) *serving 60g/2oz*	17
Goats Milk, Soft *serving 60g/2oz*	9
Gorgonzola (Somerfield) *serving 60g/2oz*	20
Gorgonzola (Waitrose) *serving 60g/2oz*	20
Gouda *serving 60g/2oz*	16
Gouda (Safeway) *serving 60g/2oz*	19
Gouda (Somerfield) *serving 60g/2oz*	19
Gouda, Dutch (Waitrose) *serving 60g/2oz*	14
Gouda, Dutch, Prepacked (Asda) *serving 60g/2oz*	18
Gouda, Frico Brand (Waitrose) *serving 60g/2oz*	19
Gouda, Matured (Waitrose) *serving 60g/2oz*	19
Gougères (Waitrose) *serving 60g/2oz*	13
Grated Cheese, Chilled (Iceland) *serving 60g/2oz*	21
Grated Pizza Mix Cheese (Waitrose) *serving 60g/2oz*	17
Gruyère *serving 60g/2oz*	20
Gruyère (Marks & Spencer) *serving 60g/2oz*	19
Gruyère (Somerfield) *serving 60g/2oz*	19
Gruyère, Swiss (Somerfield) *serving 60g/2oz*	19
Gruyère, Swiss (Waitrose) *serving 60g/2oz*	19
Gruyère Wheel Cuts (Waitrose) *serving 60g/2oz*	19
Gubeen (Marks & Spencer) *serving 60g/2oz*	15
Half Fat (16%) Cheese (Waitrose) *serving 60g/2oz*	10
Half Shropshire Blue Cheese (Somerfield) *serving 60g/2oz*	21
Hereford Hop Cheese (Safeway) *serving 60g/2oz*	19
Hereford Hop Cheese (Waitrose) *serving 60g/2oz*	19

Jarlsberg (Waitrose) *serving 60g/2oz* 18
Jarlsberg, Norwegian (Safeway) *serving 60g/2oz* 18
Jarlsberg, Norwegian (Somerfield) *serving 60g/2oz* 18
Kraft Singles (Kraft Jacobs Suchard) *serving 60g/2oz* 14
Lancashire *serving 60g/2oz* 19
Lancashire (Somerfield) *serving 60g/2oz* 19
Lancashire (Waitrose) *serving 60g/2oz* 19
Lancashire, Creamy Wedge, Prepacked (Asda) *serving 60g/2oz* 19
Lancashire, Dewlay Crumbly (Safeway) *serving 60g/2oz* 19
Lancashire, Dewlay Tasty (Safeway) *serving 60g/2oz* 19
Lancashire, Farmhouse (Marks & Spencer) *serving 60g/2oz* 19
Lancashire, Farmhouse, Prepacked (Asda) *serving 60g/2oz* 19
Lancashire, Garlic & Chive Wedges Prepacked (Asda) *serving 60g/2oz* 19
Lancashire, Tasty Wedge, Prepacked (Asda) *serving 60g/2oz* 19
Layered Salmon & Cottage Cheese (Marks & Spencer) *serving 60g/2oz* 3
Le Brin d'Affinois (Marks & Spencer) *serving 60g/2oz* 14
Le Roulé with Garlic & Herbs (Safeway) *serving 60g/2oz* 19
Le Roulé Light with Garlic & Herbs (Safeway) *serving 60g/2oz* 7
Leicester *serving 60g/2oz* 20
Leicester (Marks & Spencer) *serving 60g/2oz* 20
Leicester (Somerfield) *serving 60g/2oz* 20
Leicester, Farmhouse, Prepacked (Asda) *serving 60g/2oz* 20
Leicester, Old (Holland & Barrett) *serving 60g/2oz* 20
Leicester, Pick & Mix (Marks & Spencer) *serving 60g/2oz* 20
Leicester, Red (Somerfield) *serving 60g/2oz* 20
Leicester, Red (Waitrose) *serving 60g/2oz* 20
Leicester, Red Grated, Prepacked (Asda) *serving 60g/2oz* 20
Leicester, Red, Shape Alternative to Red Leicester (St Ivel) *serving 60g/2oz* 10
Leicester, Red Traditional (Safeway) *serving 60g/2oz* 20
Leicester, Traditional (Marks & Spencer) *serving 60g/2oz* 20
Light Singles (Kraft Jacobs Suchard) *serving 60g/2oz* 6
Limburger *serving 60g/2oz* 16

Lockerbie (Safeway) *serving 60g/2oz* 21
Maasdam, Dutch (Waitrose) *serving 60g/2oz* 17
Malvern Cheese (Waitrose) *serving 60g/2oz* 20
Mascarpone (Marks & Spencer) *serving 60g/2oz* 28
Mascarpone (Somerfield) *serving 60g/2oz* 27
Mexican Selection Cheese Wedge, Frozen (Iceland) *serving 60g/2oz* 8
Mexicana (Safeway) *serving 60g/2oz* 20
Mild Coloured Cheese (Somerfield) *serving 60g/2oz* 21
Mini Smoked Cheese with Ham (Somerfield) *serving 60g/2oz* 14
Monterey (Somerfield) *serving 60g/2oz* 18
Mozzarella *serving 60g/2oz* 13
Mozzarella, Danish (Asda) *serving 60g/2oz* 13
Mozzarella (Marks & Spencer) *serving 60g/2oz* 12
Mozzarella, Danish (Safeway) *serving 60g/2oz* 13
Mozzarella, Danish (Waitrose) *serving 60g/2oz* 13
Mozzarella, Grated (Marks & Spencer) *serving 60g/2oz* 14
Mozzarella, Grated (Somerfield) *serving 60g/2oz* 13
Mozzarella, Grated (Waitrose) *serving 60g/2oz* 14
Mozzarella Substitute *serving 60g/2oz* 7
Muenster *serving 60g/2oz* 18
Neufchâtel *serving 60g/2oz* 14
Parmesan *serving 60g/2oz* 20
Parmesan (Marks & Spencer) *serving 60g/2oz* 15
Parmesan, Napolina (CPC) *serving 60g/2oz* 20
Parmesan (Somerfield) *serving 60g/2oz* 22
Parmesan, Grana Padano (Somerfield) *serving 60g/2oz* 20
Parmesan, Grated (Marks & Spencer) *serving 60g/2oz* 18
Parmesan, Italian (Waitrose) *serving 60g/2oz* 15
Parmesan Wedge (Marks & Spencer) *serving 60g/2oz* 9
Parmigiano Reggiano (Safeway) *serving 60g/2oz* 17
Philadelphia (Kraft Jacobs Suchard) *serving 60g/2oz* 18
Philadelphia Light (Kraft Jacobs Suchard) *serving 60g/2oz* 10
Philadelphia Light with Chives (Kraft Jacobs Suchard) *serving 60g/2oz* 9
Philadelphia Light with Garlic & Herbs (Kraft Jacobs Suchard) *serving 60g/2oz* 9

Philadelphia Light with Ham (Kraft Jacobs Suchard) *serving 60g/2oz*	9
Pimiento Pasteurized, Processed *serving 60g/2oz*	19
Port Salut *serving 60g/2oz*	17
Port Salut (Marks & Spencer) *serving 60g/2oz*	16
Port Salut, Affine (Waitrose) *serving 60g/2oz*	16
Port Salut, French (Safeway) *serving 60g/2oz*	16
Port & Stilton (Waitrose) *serving 60g/2oz*	21
Processed Cheese Slices, Chilled (Iceland) *serving 60g/2oz*	14
Processed Cheese Slices, for Cheeseburger Prepacked (Asda) *serving 60g/2oz*	14
Processed Cheese Slices, Low Fat, Chilled (Iceland) *serving 60g/2oz*	6
Processed Cheese Slices, Prepacked (Asda) *serving 60g/2oz*	14
Processed Plain *serving 60g/2oz*	16
Provolone *serving 60g/2oz*	16
Quark *serving 60g/2oz*	0
Raclette, French (Waitrose) *serving 60g/2oz*	16
Rambol Walnut (Safeway) *serving 60g/2oz*	20
Reduced Fat Mature (Heinz Weight Watchers) *serving 60g/2oz*	13
Reduced Fat Mild (Heinz Weight Watchers) *serving 60g/2oz*	13
Ricotta *serving 60g/2oz*	7
Romano *serving 60g/2oz*	16
Roquefort *serving 60g/2oz*	20
Roquefort (Marks & Spencer) *serving 60g/2oz*	19
Roquefort (Safeway) *serving 60g/2oz*	20
Roquefort Société (Waitrose) *serving 60g/2oz*	19
Roulade, Mini (Marks & Spencer) *serving 60g/2oz*	19
Sage Derby *serving 60g/2oz*	20
Sage Derby (Waitrose) *serving 60g/2oz*	20
Saint Agur (Safeway) *serving 60g/2oz*	20
Shape Spread with Low Fat Soft Cheese (St Ivel) *serving 60g/2oz*	3
Shape Spread with Low Fat Soft Cheese, with Smoked Ham (St Ivel) *serving 60g/2oz*	2
Shropshire Blue (Somerfield) *serving 60g/2oz*	21
Shropshire Blue Wedges (Waitrose) *serving 60g/2oz*	20

Smoked Cheese *serving 60g/2oz* 15
Smoked Cheese (Waitrose) *serving 60g/2oz* 15
Soft Cheese (Somerfield) *serving 60g/2oz* 10
Soft Cheese, Extra Creamy, Prepacked (Asda) *serving 60g/2oz* 16
Soft Cheese, Extra Creamy, with Chives, Prepacked (Asda) *serving 60g/2oz* 16
Soft Cheese, Extra Creamy, with Salmon, Prepacked (Asda) *serving 60g/2oz* 16
Soft Cheese, Full Fat *serving 60g/2oz* 19
Soft Cheese, Full Fat (Safeway) *serving 60g/2oz* 17
Soft Cheese, Full Fat (Somerfield) *serving 60g/2oz* 19
Soft Cheese, Full Fat (Waitrose) *serving 60g/2oz* 18
Soft Cheese, Healthy Eating, Half Fat (Tesco) *serving 60g/2oz* 9
Soft Cheese, Low Fat (Safeway) *serving 60g/2oz* 3
Soft Cheese, Low Fat (Somerfield) *serving 60g/2oz* 1
Soft Cheese, Low Fat (Waitrose) *serving 60g/2oz* 4
Soft Cheese, Low Fat, Delicatessen (Asda) *serving 60g/2oz* 3
Soft Cheese, Medium Fat (Waitrose) *serving 60g/2oz* 7
Soft Cheese, Reduced Fat (Marks & Spencer) *serving 60g/2oz* 10
Soft Cheese with Garlic & Herbs (Marks & Spencer) *serving 60g/2oz* 18
Soft Cheese with Garlic & Herbs (Somerfield) *serving 60g/2oz* 9
Soya Cheese *serving 60g/2oz* 16
St Agur (Marks & Spencer) *serving 60g/2oz* 20
St Julien (Walnut) (Marks & Spencer) *serving 60g/2oz* 15
Stilton (Marks & Spencer) *serving 60g/2oz* 21
Stilton, Best Blue (Somerfield) *serving 60g/2oz* 21
Stilton, Blue (Safeway) *serving 60g/2oz* 21
Stilton, Blue (Somerfield) *serving 60g/2oz* 21
Stilton, Blue (Waitrose) *serving 60g/2oz* 21
Stilton, Blue, Chilled (Iceland) *serving 60g/2oz* 21
Stilton, Blue, Deli (Asda) *serving 60g/2oz* 22
Stilton, Blue Wedge, Prepacked (Asda) *serving 60g/2oz* 21
Stilton, Blue Wedges (Somerfield) *serving 60g/2oz* 21
Stilton, Blue Wedges (Waitrose) *serving 60g/2oz* 21
Stilton, Extra Matured (Marks & Spencer) *serving 60g/2oz* 21
Stilton, Half Baby (Somerfield) *serving 60g/2oz* 21

Stilton, Mature Blue (Waitrose) *serving 60g/2oz*	21
Stilton, Mature Cheese Wedges (Somerfield) *serving 60g/2oz*	21
Stilton, Miniature Blue (Waitrose) *serving 60g/2oz*	21
Stilton, Standard Half Moon (Somerfield) *serving 60g/2oz*	21
Stilton, Vegetarian (Tesco) *serving 60g/2oz*	21
Stilton, Vintage Blue (Safeway) *serving 60g/2oz*	21
Stilton, Vintage Blue (Waitrose) *serving 60g/2oz*	21
Stilton, White *serving 60g/2oz*	19
Stilton, White (Safeway) *serving 60g/2oz*	18
Stilton, White (Waitrose) *serving 60g/2oz*	18
Stilton, White, Deli (Asda) *serving 60g/2oz*	22
Stilton, White, Prepacked (Asda) *serving 60g/2oz*	20
Stilton, White, with Apricot (Safeway) *serving 60g/2oz*	19
Stilton, White, & Apricot (Waitrose) *serving 60g/2oz*	19
Stilton, White, & Citrus Peel (Somerfield) *serving 60g/2oz*	16
Stilton, White, & Stem Ginger (Waitrose) *serving 60g/2oz*	18
Stilton, Whole Blue (Somerfield) *serving 60g/2oz*	21
Stilton, Whole Mature, Deli (Asda) *serving 60g/2oz*	21
Swaledale (Waitrose) *serving 60g/2oz*	20
Swiss Pasteurized, Processed *serving 60g/2oz*	14
Taymere (Marks & Spencer) *serving 60g/2oz*	18
Tilsit, Whole Milk *serving 60g/2oz*	16
Torta di Dolcellate (Safeway) *serving 60g/2oz*	24
Vegetarian Cheese Spread (Holland & Barrett) *serving 60g/2oz*	13
Welsh Rarebit *serving 60g/2oz*	16
Welsh Rarebit on Wholemeal Bread *serving 60g/2oz*	15
Wensleydale *serving 60g/2oz*	19
Wensleydale (Marks & Spencer) *serving 60g/2oz*	19
Wensleydale (Somerfield) *serving 60g/2oz*	19
Wensleydale, (Waitrose) *serving 60g/2oz*	19
Wensleydale & Ginger (Somerfield) *serving 60g/2oz*	16
Wensleydale, Prepacked (Asda) *serving 60g/2oz*	19
Wensleydale, Tall (Safeway) *serving 60g/2oz*	20
Wensleydale, Traditional (Marks & Spencer) *serving 60g/2oz*	19
Wensleydale, Traditional (Safeway) *serving 60g/2oz*	19
Windsor, Red *serving 60g/2oz*	20
Worcester Gold (Safeway) *serving 60g/2oz*	21

Chicken

NOTE: The standard serving size in this section is 110g/4oz. If you wish to consume more or less than this amount (e.g. if you are going to consume a pack of food whose weight differs from the standard serving size) use the conversion tables on page 386 to calculate the new amount of fat in the food.

Balti Chicken Curry, Bulk (Safeway) *serving 110g/4oz*	28
Balti Chicken Masala, Bulk (Safeway) *serving 110g/4oz*	18
Basted Oven Ready Chicken, Frozen, Roast (Iceland) *serving 110g/4oz*	8
BBQ Dusted Drumsticks (Waitrose) *serving 110g/4oz*	6
BBQ Style Roast Chicken Wings, Frozen, Microwaved (Iceland) *serving 110g/4oz*	20
Biryani Chicken Tikka Bit (Waitrose) *serving 110g/4oz*	9
Boneless Breast, Free Range (Waitrose) *serving 110g/4oz*	14
Boneless Chicken Breasts, Frozen, Roast (Iceland) *serving 110g/4oz*	19
Breaded Chicken Portions (Waitrose) *serving 110g/4oz*	14
Breaded Chicken Portions, Fresh (Iceland) *serving 110g/4oz*	13
Breaded Chicken Steak (Somerfield) *serving 110g/4oz*	11
Breast Fillets, Fresh (Iceland) *serving 110g/4oz*	19
Breast Fillets, Kashmiri (Waitrose) *serving 110g/4oz*	4
Breast of Chicken Roll (Waitrose) *serving 110g/4oz*	3
Breast Roll, 70% (Somerfield) *serving 110g/4oz*	8
Breast Roll, 80% (Somerfield) *serving 110g/4oz*	2
Breast Roll, Cured (Somerfield) *serving 110g/4oz*	8
Breasts, Part Boned, with Garlic & Herb Butter (Somerfield) *serving 110g/4oz*	21
Butter Tandoori Breast (Waitrose) *serving 110g/4oz*	2
Capon, Meat & Skin, Roasted *serving 110g/4oz*	13
Casserole (Somerfield) *serving 110g/4oz*	5
Chicken Tikka Makhani (Waitrose) *serving 110g/4oz*	9
Chicken (1.2 kg, 1.3 kg, 1.8 kg, 2.0 kg), Frozen, Roasted (Iceland) *serving 110g/4oz*	19
Chicken à l'Orange (Findus Lean Cuisine) *serving 110g/4oz*	1
Chicken à la Sauce Creamy Garlic (Birds Eye) *serving 110g/4oz*	11

Chicken à la Sauce Curry Sauce (Birds Eye) *serving 110g/4oz* 10
Chicken à la Sauce Provencale (Birds Eye) *serving 110g/4oz* 6
Chicken à la Sauce Texas Griddlers (Birds Eye) *serving 110g/4oz* 19
Chicken Achari (Waitrose) *serving 110g/4oz* 12
Chicken & Asparagus, Main Meals (Marks & Spencer) *serving 110g/4oz* 5
Chicken & Bacon Filling (Waitrose) *serving 110g/4oz* 28
Chicken, Bacon & Mushroom, Main Meals (Marks & Spencer) *serving 110g/4oz* 17
Chicken Balti (Marks & Spencer) *serving 110g/4oz* 7
Chicken Balti Satay, Mini (Asda) *serving 110g/4oz* 6
Chicken Basilico (Marks & Spencer) *serving 110g/4oz* 6
Chicken Biryani (Asda) *serving 110g/4oz* 6
Chicken Biryani, Chilled, Ready Meal (Safeway) *serving 110g/4oz* 40
Chicken Biryani, (Waitrose) *serving 110g/4oz* 8
Chicken Bites (Marks & Spencer) *serving 110g/4oz* 18
Chicken Bites (Waitrose) *serving 110g/4oz* 15
Chicken, Breaded & Fried, Boneless Pieces *serving 110g/4oz* 19
Chicken, Breaded & Fried, Breast or Wing *serving 110g/4oz* 20
Chicken, Breaded & Fried, Drumstick or Thigh *serving 110g/4oz* 20
Chicken Breast, Boneless, Roast (Asda) *serving 110g/4oz* 9
Chicken Breast, Cooked (Waitrose) *serving 110g/4oz* 2
Chicken Breast Fillet, Frozen, Roasted (Iceland) *serving 110g/4oz* 5
Chicken Breast, Fillet, Roast (Somerfield) *serving 110g/4oz* 9
Chicken Breast Fillet, Skinless, Delicatessen (Marks & Spencer) *serving 110g/4oz* 2
Chicken Breast Fillets, Skin on, Fresh (Iceland) *serving 110g/4oz* 19
Chicken Breast Fillets, Skinless, Fresh (Iceland) *serving 110g/4oz* 4
Chicken Breast Fillets, Skinless (2) Fresh, Roast (Iceland) *serving 110g/4oz* 4
Chicken Breast Golden Roasted (Bernard Matthews) *serving 110g/4oz* 2
Chicken Breast in Gravy (Birds Eye) *serving 110g/4oz* 4
Chicken Breast Joint (Marks & Spencer) *serving 110g/4oz* 6
Chicken Breast & Leg, Free Range (Waitrose) *serving 110g/4oz* 15

Chicken Breast Platter, Frozen (Iceland) *serving 110g/4oz* 3
Chicken Breast, Roast, Boneless (Waitrose) *serving 110g/4oz* 10
Chicken Breast Slices, Premium, Cooked, Norfolk (Bernard Matthews) *serving 110g/4oz* 3
Chicken Breast Steaks (Marks & Spencer) *serving 110g/4oz* 12
Chicken Breast Steaks, Wholemeal, Fresh, Conventional Oven (Iceland) *serving 110g/4oz* 11
Chicken Breast, Wafer Thin, American Fried (Bernard Matthews) *serving 110g/4oz* 3
Chicken Breasts, Fresh (Waitrose) *serving 110g/4oz* 5
Chicken Breasts, Part Boned, Fresh (Iceland) *serving 110g/4oz* 12
Chicken Breasts, Part Boned, Roast (Iceland) *serving 110g/4oz* 19
Chicken Breasts, Seasoned (Marks & Spencer) *serving 110g/4oz* 4
Chicken Breasts (Waitrose) *serving 110g/4oz* 9
Chicken Breasteaks, Low Fat, Frozen (Iceland) *serving 110g/4oz* 4
Chicken & Broccoli (Waitrose) *serving 110g/4oz* 6
Chicken & Broccoli, Main Meals, Lite (Marks & Spencer) *serving 110g/4oz* 3
Chicken, Broccoli & Pasta Bake (Asda) *serving 110g/4oz* 3
Chicken Burgers (Birds Eye) *serving 110g/4oz* 18
Chicken Cacciatoria (Waitrose) *serving 110g/4oz* 7
Chicken & Cashew Nuts, Chilled, Ready Meal (Safeway) *serving 110g/4oz* 11
Chicken & Cashew Nuts (Marks & Spencer) *serving 110g/4oz* 6
Chicken Casserole (Marks & Spencer) *serving 110g/4oz* 3
Chicken Casserole (Waitrose) *serving 110g/4oz* 3
Chicken Casserole, Chilled, Ready Meal (Safeway) *serving 110g/4oz* 5
Chicken Casserole, Grocery (Iceland) *serving 110g/4oz* 4
Chicken Casserole, Healthy Eating (Tesco) *serving 110g/4oz* 1
Chicken Casserole with Herb Dumplings (Sainsbury's) *serving 110g/4oz* 7
Chicken Casserole & Mash (Asda) *serving 110g/4oz* 2
Chicken Casserole & Vegetable Filled Yorkshire Pudding, Frozen Filling, Pan Boil (Iceland) *serving 110g/4oz* 4
Chicken Chasseur (Waitrose) *serving 110g/4oz* 4
Chicken Chasseur, Healthy Options (Birds Eye) *serving 110g/4oz* 2

Chicken Chilli (Marks & Spencer) *serving 110g/4oz* 3
Chicken Chow Mein, Bulk (Safeway) *serving 110g/4oz* 11
Chicken Chow Mein, Chilled, Ready Meal (Safeway) *serving 110g/4oz* 10
Chicken Chunks in Gravy (Princes) *serving 110g/4oz* 6
Chicken Chunks in White Sauce (Princes) *serving 110g/4oz* 8
Chicken Cordon Bleu (Somerfield) *serving 110g/4oz* 12
Chicken Cordon Bleu 2s (Waitrose) *serving 110g/4oz* 9
Chicken Cordon Bleu, Main Meals (Marks & Spencer) *serving 110g/4oz* 11
Chicken, Corn Fed, Free Range (Waitrose) *serving 110g/4oz* 16
Chicken Curry (Asda) *serving 110g/4oz* 4
Chicken Curry (Crosse & Blackwell) *serving 110g/4oz* 24
Chicken Curry (Findus Dinner Supreme) *serving 110g/4oz* 3
Chicken Curry, Hot, Grocery (Iceland) *serving 110g/4oz* 7
Chicken Curry, Hot (Tesco) *serving 110g/4oz* 7
Chicken Curry, Individual, Main Meals (Marks & Spencer) *serving 110g/4oz* 5
Chicken Curry, Kashmiri (Findus Lean Cuisine) *serving 110g/4oz* 3
Chicken Curry, Mild, Tinned (Tesco) *serving 110g/4oz* 6
Chicken Curry, Pot Rice (CPC) *serving 110g/4oz* 3
Chicken Curry with Rice (Birds Eye) *serving 110g/4oz* 3
Chicken Curry & Rice (Marks & Spencer) *serving 110g/4oz* 10
Chicken Curry with Rice, Chilled, Ready Meal (Safeway) *serving 110g/4oz* 8
Chicken Curry & Rice, Frozen, Pan Boil (Iceland) *serving 110g/4oz* 5
Chicken Curry with Rice, Frozen, Ready Meal (Heinz Weight Watchers) *serving 110g/4oz* 2
Chicken Curry with Rice, Frozen, Ready Meal (Safeway) *serving 110g/4oz* 4
Chicken Curry with Rice, Lunch Bowl, Ready Meal (Heinz) *serving 110g/4oz* 2
Chicken Curry, Sri Lankan (Marks & Spencer) *serving 110g/4oz* 11
Chicken, Dark Meat & Skin, Roasted *serving 110g/4oz* 17
Chicken Dhansak, Bulk (Safeway) *serving 110g/4oz* 33

Chicken Dhansak, Chilled, Ready Meal (Safeway) *serving 110g/4oz* 34
Chicken Dhansak Curry Pot (Asda) *serving 110g/4oz* 8
Chicken Dippers (Birds Eye) *serving 110g/4oz* 18
Chicken Dippers, Frozen (Iceland) *serving 110g/4oz* 21
Chicken Dopiaza, Chilled, Ready Meal (Tesco) *serving 110g/4oz* 8
Chicken Drumsticks, Chilled, Roast (Iceland) *serving 110g/4oz* 8
Chicken Drumsticks, Crumb (Waitrose) *serving 110g/4oz* 9
Chicken Drumsticks, Free Range (Waitrose) *serving 110g/4oz* 15
Chicken Drumsticks, Fresh (Iceland) *serving 110g/4oz* 19
Chicken Drumsticks, Pouch Pack (Waitrose) *serving 110g/4oz* 19
Chicken Drumsticks, Roast (Somerfield) *serving 110g/4oz* 10
Chicken Drumstick & Thigh, Free Range (Waitrose) *serving 110g/4oz* 15
Chicken en Croute, Cheddar Cheese & Broccoli (Birds Eye) *serving 110g/4oz* 13
Chicken en Croute, Italian Tomato & Mozzarella (Birds Eye) *serving 110g/4oz* 13
Chicken en Croute, Normandy Mushroom (Birds Eye) *serving 110g/4oz* 16
Chicken Fillet Roast (Marks & Spencer) *serving 110g/4oz* 9
Chicken Fillets, Crumb (Waitrose) *serving 110g/4oz* 10
Chicken Giblets, Simmered *serving 110g/4oz* 6
Chicken Goujons (Waitrose) *serving 110g/4oz* 10
Chicken Goujons, Fresh (Waitrose) *serving 110g/4oz* 4
Chicken Goujons, Poultry (Marks & Spencer) *serving 110g/4oz* 17
Chicken, Grade A, Frozen (Waitrose) *serving 110g/4oz* 19
Chicken Herb, Chargrilled (Marks & Spencer) *serving 110g/4oz* 10
Chicken Hot Dogs (Princes) *serving 110g/4oz* 15
Chicken in Peppercorn Sauce, Frozen, Ready Meal (Heinz Weight Watchers) *serving 110g/4oz* 2
Chicken in Red Wine Casserole, Main Meals (Marks & Spencer) *serving 110g/4oz* 5
Chicken in White Sauce, Grocery (Iceland) *serving 110g/4oz* 14
Chicken in White Sauce, Tinned (Tesco) *serving 110g/4oz* 11
Chicken in White Wine (Marks & Spencer) *serving 110g/4oz* 10
Chicken Italienne (Safeway) *serving 110g/4oz* 0

Chicken Jalfrezi (Asda) *serving 110g/4oz* 10
Chicken Jalfrezi (Marks & Spencer) *serving 110g/4oz* 6
Chicken Jalfrezi, Chilled, Ready Meal (Tesco) *serving 110g/4oz* 9
Chicken Jalfrezi with Rice, Frozen, Ready Meal (Safeway) *serving 110g/4oz* 6
Chicken Jalfrezi Balti (Asda) *serving 110g/4oz* 14
Chicken Jardinière (Birds Eye) *serving 110g/4oz* 3
Chicken Jeera, Bulk (Safeway) *serving 110g/4oz* 23
Chicken Joint, Seasoned/Basted, Poultry (Marks & Spencer) *serving 110g/4oz* 4
Chicken Joint with Mushroom & Garlic Butter, Poultry (Marks & Spencer) *serving 110g/4oz* 8
Chicken Joint with Sage & Onion, Delicatessen (Marks & Spencer) *serving 110g/4oz* 9
Chicken Joint with Sage & Onion, Poultry (Marks & Spencer) *serving 110g/4oz* 10
Chicken Kashmir (Birds Eye) *serving 110g/4oz* 6
Chicken Kiev (Marks & Spencer) *serving 110g/4oz* 17
Chicken Kiev (Waitrose) *serving 110g/4oz* 16
Chicken Kiev, Cordon Bleu, Chilled, Ready Meal (Tesco) *serving 110g/4oz* 13
Chicken Kiev, Creamy (Somerfield) *serving 110g/4oz* 12
Chicken Kiev, Main Meals (6) (Marks & Spencer) *serving 110g/4oz* 18
Chicken Kiev, Mini, Frozen (Waitrose) *serving 110g/4oz* 16
Chicken Kievs, Low Fat, Frozen (Iceland) *serving 110g/4oz* 3
Chicken Kiev Steaks, Fresh, Cooked (Iceland) *serving 110g/4oz* 17
Chicken Kiev Tikka Masala, Chilled, Ready Meal (Tesco) *serving 110g/4oz* 11
Chicken Korma (Asda) *serving 110g/4oz* 12
Chicken Korma (Marks & Spencer) *serving 110g/4oz* 11
Chicken Korma (Waitrose) *serving 110g/4oz* 15
Chicken Korma, Chilled, Ready Meal (Safeway) *serving 110g/4oz* 29
Chicken Korma Curry Pot (Asda) *serving 110g/4oz* 12
Chicken Korma, Frozen (Iceland) *serving 110g/4oz* 11

Chicken Korma with Cumin Rice, Frozen, Ready Meal (Tesco) *serving 110g/4oz* 6
Chicken Korma with Pilau Rice (Asda) *serving 110g/4oz* 12
Chicken Korma with Pilau Rice (Somerfield) *serving 110g/4oz* 14
Chicken Korma with Rice, Frozen Ready Meal (Safeway) *serving 110g/4oz* 8
Chicken Korma with Rice, Microwave Ready Meal (Safeway) *serving 110g/4oz* 11
Chicken Korma with Rice, Frozen Ready Meal (Heinz Weight Watchers) *serving 110g/4oz* 2
Chicken Korma with Rice (Somerfield) *serving 110g/4oz* 8
Chicken, Leek & Bacon, Main Meals (Marks & Spencer) *serving 110g/4oz* 12
Chicken Leg Quarters, Fresh (Iceland) *serving 110g/4oz* 19
Chicken Legs, Fresh (Waitrose) *serving 110g/4oz* 4
Chicken Legs, Roast (Marks & Spencer) *serving 110g/4oz* 18
Chicken with Lemon Mayonnaise, Reduced Fat (Marks & Spencer) *serving 110g/4oz* 8
Chicken, Light Meat & Skin, Roasted *serving 110g/4oz* 11
Chicken Liver, Simmered *serving 110g/4oz* 6
Chicken Livers (Waitrose) *serving 110g/4oz* 6
Chicken Madras (Waitrose) *serving 110g/4oz* 12
Chicken Madras, Chilled, Ready Meal (340g) Pack (Safeway) *serving 110g/4oz* 9
Chicken Madras Curry Pot (Asda) *serving 110g/4oz* 14
Chicken Madras with Pilau Rice (Somerfield) *serving 110g/4oz* 12
Chicken Madras with Pilau Rice, Frozen, Ready Meal (Tesco) *serving 110g/4oz* 4
Chicken, Mango & Pineapple (Marks & Spencer) *serving 110g/4oz* 7
Chicken Masala (Waitrose) *serving 110g/4oz* 3
Chicken Masala, Tinned, Ready Meal (Tesco) *serving 110g/4oz* 5
Chicken Masala Balti (Asda) *serving 110g/4oz* 6
Chicken, Meat Only, Roasted *serving 110g/4oz* 8
Chicken Mini Fillets (Marks & Spencer) *serving 110g/4oz* 2
Chicken Moneybags (Safeway) *serving 110g/4oz* 3
Chicken & Mushroom (Crosse & Blackwell) *serving 110g/4oz* 20

Chicken & Mushroom Casserole (Birds Eye) *serving 110g/4oz* 5
Chicken & Mushroom Fun Pots (CPC) *serving 110g/4oz* 16
Chicken, Mushroom & Garlic Filled (Marks & Spencer) *serving 110g/4oz* 9
Chicken & Mushroom Pot, Light (CPC) *serving 110g/4oz* 2
Chicken & Mushroom Slice, Chilled (Iceland) *serving 110g/4oz* 25
Chicken & Mushroom Slices (Waitrose) *serving 110g/4oz* 21
Chicken & Mushroom Slices, Frozen, Baked (Iceland) *serving 110g/4oz* 18
Chicken Nuggets (Somerfield) *serving 110g/4oz* 16
Chicken Nuggets, Battered (Somerfield) *serving 110g/4oz* 14
Chicken Nuggets, Battered, with Sweet & Sour Dip (Somerfield) *serving 110g/4oz* 10
Chicken Olives (Waitrose) *serving 110g/4oz* 22
Chicken, Orange Glazed Breast (Marks & Spencer) *serving 110g/4oz* 6
Chicken Pappardelle (Marks & Spencer) *serving 110g/4oz* 6
Chicken Pasanda (Asda) *serving 110g/4oz* 8
Chicken Pasanda (Waitrose) *serving 110g/4oz* 14
Chicken Pasanda, Bulk (Safeway) *serving 110g/4oz* 27
Chicken Pasta Dishes: *see under* Pasta & Noodles
Chicken Paste: *see under* Dips, Dressings, Savoury Spreads, Pickles & Pâté
Chicken Piccante (Marks & Spencer) *serving 110g/4oz* 3
Chicken Piccata (Marks & Spencer) *serving 110g/4oz* 16
Chicken Pies: *see under* Pies, Pasties, Flans & Quiches
Chicken Piri Piri (Marks & Spencer) *serving 110g/4oz* 5
Chicken & Pork Loaf (Somerfield) *serving 110g/4oz* 9
Chicken & Prawn Creole (Findus Lean Cuisine Snackpots) *serving 110g/4oz* 1
Chicken Provencale (Birds Eye) *serving 110g/4oz* 2
Chicken Provencale (Crosse & Blackwell) *serving 110g/4oz* 12
Chicken Quarter Pounders (Birds Eye) *serving 110g/4oz* 15
Chicken Quarterpounders, Frozen (Iceland) *serving 110g/4oz* 17
Chicken, Rice & Apricot Breast (Marks & Spencer) *serving 110g/4oz* 11

Chicken Rice Bowl, Low Fat, International (Marks & Spencer) *serving 110g/4oz* 1
Chicken, Rich Pastry Pie, Hot (Marks & Spencer) *serving 110g/4oz* 20
Chicken Risotto (Marks & Spencer) *serving 110g/4oz* 6
Chicken Roast, Large (Marks & Spencer) *serving 110g/4oz* 16
Chicken Roast, Medium (Marks & Spencer) *serving 110g/4oz* 16
Chicken Roast, Small (Marks & Spencer) *serving 110g/4oz* 16
Chicken, Roasting, Dark Meat, Meat Only Roasted *serving 110g/4oz* 10
Chicken, Roasting, Giblets Simmered *serving 110g/4oz* 6
Chicken, Roasting, Light Meat, Meat Only Roasted *serving 110g/4oz* 4
Chicken, Roasting, Meat Only, Roasted *serving 110g/4oz* 7
Chicken, Roasting, Meat & Skin, Roasted *serving 110g/4oz* 15
Chicken Rogan Josh with Pilau Rice (Somerfield) *serving 110g/4oz* 9
Chicken Roll, Cold Meats (Tesco) *serving 110g/4oz* 8
Chicken Roll with Apricot Stuffing (Waitrose) *serving 110g/4oz* 18
Chicken Rustica (Marks & Spencer) *serving 110g/4oz* 3
Chicken Saag, Chilled, Ready Meal (Safeway) *serving 110g/4oz* 18
Chicken, Sage & Onion, Poultry (Marks & Spencer) *serving 110g/4oz* 15
Chicken Samosas, Frozen (Iceland) *serving 110g/4oz* 13
Chicken Satay (Waitrose) *serving 110g/4oz* 6
Chicken Savoury Rice (Somerfield) *serving 110g/4oz* 2
Chicken, Seasoned & Basted, Poultry (Marks & Spencer) *serving 110g/4oz* 5
Chicken, Seasoned Garlic & Herb, Poultry (Marks & Spencer) *serving 110g/4oz* 11
Chicken Slices in Gravy (Princes) *serving 110g/4oz* 1
Chicken Spring Rolls, Chilled (Tesco) *serving 110g/4oz* 16
Chicken Steak, Battered (Somerfield) *serving 110g/4oz* 12
Chicken Steaks, Wholemeal (Somerfield) *serving 110g/4oz* 11
Chicken Steak, Garlic & Herb (Somerfield) *serving 110g/4oz* 8

Chicken Stew & Herb Dumplings, Tinned, Ready Meal (Tesco) *serving 110g/4oz* 6
Chicken, Stewing, Meat Only, Stewed *serving 110g/4oz* 13
Chicken, Stewing, Meat & Skin, Stewed *serving 110g/4oz* 21
Chicken on a Stick, Satay (Safeway) *serving 110g/4oz* 9
Chicken Stock Cube *serving 110g/4oz* 17
Chicken Stock Cubes (Waitrose) *serving 110g/4oz* 12
Chicken Supreme, Healthy Eating, Frozen, Ready Meal (Tesco) *serving 110g/4oz* 3
Chicken Supreme with Rice (Birds Eye) *serving 110g/4oz* 5
Chicken Supreme with Rice, Frozen, Ready Meal (Heinz Weight Watchers) *serving 110g/4oz* 2
Chicken, Sweet & Sour (Marks & Spencer) *serving 110g/4oz* 4
Chicken & Sweetcorn (Marks & Spencer) *serving 110g/4oz* 16
Chicken & Sweetcorn Pot Rice (CPC) *serving 110g/4oz* 5
Chicken Tandoori Fillets, Delicatessen (Marks & Spencer) *serving 110g/4oz* 1
Chicken Thigh/Drumstick Mix, Chilled (Iceland) *serving 110g/4oz* 6
Chicken Thigh Fillet, Fresh (Waitrose) *serving 110g/4oz* 6
Chicken Thighs, Fresh (Iceland) *serving 110g/4oz* 19
Chicken Thighs, Fresh, Roasted (Iceland) *serving 110g/4oz* 19
Chicken Thighs, Pouch Pack (Waitrose) *serving 110g/4oz* 19
Chicken Thighs, Raw, Balti (Waitrose) *serving 110g/4oz* 19
Chicken Thighs, Roast (Marks & Spencer) *serving 110g/4oz* 21
Chicken Tikka (Marks & Spencer) *serving 110g/4oz* 6
Chicken Tikka, Mini Fillets, Delicatessen (Marks & Spencer) *serving 110g/4oz* 3
Chicken Tikka, Wafer Thin (Asda) *serving 110g/4oz* 6
Chicken Tikka, Wafer Thin (Somerfield) *serving 110g/4oz* 2
Chicken Tikka Bites (Somerfield) *serving 110g/4oz* 8
Chicken Tikka Bites, Party Food (Marks & Spencer) *serving 110g/4oz* 13
Chicken Tikka Breast Chunks, Delicatessen (Marks & Spencer) *serving 110g/4oz* 3
Chicken Tikka Lattice (Somerfield) *serving 110g/4oz* 22
Chicken Tikka Makhani (Waitrose) *serving 110g/4oz* 12

Chicken Tikka Masala (Somerfield) *serving 110g/4oz* 16
Chicken Tikka Masala, Chilled, Ready Meal (Safeway) *serving 110g/4oz* 27
Chicken Tikka Masala, Chilled Ready Meal (Tesco) *serving 110g/4oz* 12
Chicken Tikka Masala Curry Pot (Asda) *serving 110g/4oz* 11
Chicken Tikka Masala, Frozen (Iceland) *serving 110g/4oz* 9
Chicken Tikka Masala, Frozen, Oven Baked (Iceland) *serving 110g/4oz* 9
Chicken Tikka Masala Filled Naan Bread, Chilled, Ready Meal (Tesco) *serving 110g/4oz* 6
Chicken Tikka Masala with Rice, Frozen Ready Meal (Safeway) *serving 110g/4oz* 7
Chicken Tikka Masala with Rice, Microwave Ready Meal (Safeway) *serving 110g/4oz* 9
Chicken Tikka Masala Spring Rolls Frozen (Tesco) *serving 110g/4oz* 7
Chicken Tikka Pakora, Chilled (Tesco) *serving 110g/4oz* 19
Chicken Tikka Platter, Healthy Options (Birds Eye) *serving 110g/4oz* 3
Chicken Tikka & Rice (Birds Eye) *serving 110g/4oz* 7
Chicken Tikka with Rice (Somerfield) *serving 110g/4oz* 6
Chicken Tikka Samosa, Chilled (Tesco) *serving 110g/4oz* 18
Chicken Tikka Style Roast Chicken Bites (Safeway) *serving 110g/4oz* 16
Chicken Tikka Wings (Somerfield) *serving 110g/4oz* 16
Chicken, Tomato & Couscous (Marks & Spencer) *serving 110g/4oz* 6
Chicken & Tripe & Green Vegetable (Waitrose) *serving 110g/4oz* 6
Chicken Vartha (Waitrose) *serving 110g/4oz* 15
Chicken & Vegetable Casserole (Waitrose) *serving 110g/4oz* 17
Chicken & Vegetable Roll, Frozen, Oven Baked (Iceland) *serving 110g/4oz* 15
Chicken & Vegetables Puff, Hot (Marks & Spencer) *serving 110g/4oz* 19
Chicken Vindaloo (Waitrose) *serving 110g/4oz* 6

Chicken Wafer, Breast of Chicken (Marks & Spencer) *serving 110g/4oz* 4
Chicken Wafer, Roast Chicken (Marks & Spencer) *serving 110g/4oz* 7
Chicken Wafer, Tikka Chicken (Marks & Spencer) *serving 110g/4oz* 2
Chicken Wedges, Party Fayre, Frozen (Iceland) *serving 110g/4oz* 22
Chicken Whole, Fresh (Iceland) *serving 110g/4oz* 19
Chicken, Whole, Fresh, Roasted (Iceland) *serving 110g/4oz* 19
Chicken, Bacon & Dumplings, Main Meals (Marks & Spencer) *serving 110g/4oz* 11
Chicken with Creamy Cheese & Ham (Somerfield) *serving 110g/4oz* 14
Chicken with Creamy Mushroom & Cheese (Somerfield) *serving 110g/4oz* 12
Chicken with Lemon Mayo (Waitrose) *serving 110g/4oz* 17
Chicken, Wine & Grape, Poultry (Marks & Spencer) *serving 110g/4oz* 10
Chicken & White Wine & Herbs (Waitrose) *serving 110g/4oz* 4
Chicken, Yoghurt & Mint, Main Meals (Marks & Spencer) *serving 110g/4oz* 5
Chicksticks (Birds Eye) *serving 110g/4oz* 16
Chilli Chicken & Rice, Main Meals (Marks & Spencer) *serving 110g/4oz* 1
Chinese Breast Portion, Delicatessen (Marks & Spencer) *serving 110g/4oz* 11
Chinese Chicken Spring Roll, Bulk (Safeway) *serving 110g/4oz* 8
Chinese Chicken Wings, Frozen (Iceland) *serving 110g/4oz* 22
Chinese Drums & Wings, Fresh, Oven Baked (Iceland) *serving 110g/4oz* 6
Chinese Drumsticks, Roast (Asda) *serving 110g/4oz* 9
Chinese Style Chicken Wings, Frozen (Iceland) *serving 110g/4oz* 11
Chinese Style Chicken with Egg Fried Rice, Chilled Ready Meal (Safeway) *serving 110g/4oz* 11
Chinese Style Roast Chicken Wings (Safeway) *serving 110g/4oz* 26
Chinese Wings, Large Pack, Delicatessen (Marks & Spencer) *serving 110g/4oz* 19

Chow Mein Mix, Frozen, Stir Fried (Iceland) *serving 110g/4oz*	1
Chunky Chicken, Premium (Marks & Spencer) *serving 110g/4oz*	13
Chunky Chicken & Ham, Tinned (Tesco) *serving 110g/4oz*	11
Coq au Vin, Tinned Ready Meal (Tesco) *serving 110g/4oz*	5
Coronation Chicken (Waitrose) *serving 110g/4oz*	24
Creamy Garlic Chicken (Birds Eye) *serving 110g/4oz*	5
Creamy Kiev Steaks, Fresh, Conventional, Oven Baked (Iceland) *serving 110g/4oz*	13
Crispy Chicken (Birds Eye) *serving 110g/4oz*	15
Crunchy Chicken Steaks (Somerfield) *serving 110g/4oz*	15
Crunchy Garlic Chicken (Birds Eye) *serving 110g/4oz*	13
Crunchy Garlic Chicken Dippers (Birds Eye) *serving 110g/4oz*	18
Cured Chicken Breast (Marks & Spencer) *serving 110g/4oz*	2
Cured Chicken Breast (Princes) *serving 110g/4oz*	5
Curry Chicken with Bone *serving 110g/4oz*	14
Curry Chicken without Bone *serving 110g/4oz*	19
Drumsticks, Roast (Waitrose) *serving 110g/4oz*	10
Farmhouse Chicken (Waitrose) *serving 110g/4oz*	18
Filled Yorkshire Chicken & Vegetables (Waitrose) *serving 110g/4oz*	8
French Garlic & Herb Chicken Marinade (Birds Eye) *serving 110g/4oz*	8
Fresh Chicken (5) Legs (Waitrose) *serving 110g/4oz*	26
Fresh Chicken, Grade A (Waitrose) *serving 110g/4oz*	19
Garlic Basted Chicken (Waitrose) *serving 110g/4oz*	15
Glazed Chicken (Findus Lean Cuisine) *serving 110g/4oz*	2
Glazed Chicken Platter, Healthy Options (Birds Eye) *serving 110g/4oz*	3
Honey & Mustard Chicken (Marks & Spencer) *serving 110g/4oz*	13
Honey Roast Chicken (Waitrose) *serving 110g/4oz*	10
Hot & Spicy Chicken Nibbles, Frozen, Oven Baked (Iceland) *serving 110g/4oz*	19
Hot & Spicy Chinese Chicken (Birds Eye) *serving 110g/4oz*	3
Hot 'n' spicy Drumsticks (Waitrose) *serving 110g/4oz*	10
Hot & Spicy Wings, Delicatessen (Marks & Spencer) *serving 110g/4oz*	17

International Cantonese Chicken Bowl (Marks & Spencer) *serving 110g/4oz* 3
Jumbo Chicken Spring Roll Curry Pot (Asda) *serving 110g/4oz* 8
Jumbo Chicken Tikka Satay (Asda) *serving 110g/4oz* 7
Lemon Chicken (Marks & Spencer) *serving 110g/4oz* 4
Lemon & Pepper Chicken (Waitrose) *serving 110g/4oz* 11
Lemon Pepper Chicken Grill (Birds Eye) *serving 110g/4oz* 14
Low Fat Sweet and Sour Chicken (Marks & Spencer) *serving 110g/4oz* 1
Mexican Chicken (Birds Eye) *serving 110g/4oz* 13
Mexican Chicken Bites (Somerfield) *serving 110g/4oz* 7
Chicken Tikka Satay, Mini (Asda) *serving 110g/4oz* 7
Mozzarella Chicken in Tomato Sauce, Main Meals (Marks & Spencer) *serving 110g/4oz* 6
Peppered Sandwich Chicken, Chilled (Iceland) *serving 110g/4oz* 5
Potted Chicken (Princes) *serving 110g/4oz* 10
Poussin, Boned & Stuffed (Waitrose) *serving 110g/4oz* 19
Poussin, Fresh (Waitrose) *serving 110g/4oz* 18
Roast Breast of Chicken (Marks & Spencer) *serving 110g/4oz* 6
Roast Chicken Half, Browned with Sugars (Asda) *serving 110g/4oz* 15
Roast Chicken Leg Portion (Somerfield) *serving 110g/4oz* 13
Roast Chicken Legs, Chilled (Iceland) *serving 110g/4oz* 15
Roast Chicken Platter (Birds Eye) *serving 110g/4oz* 6
Roast Chicken Portions, Frozen, Roast (Iceland) *serving 110g/4oz* 14
Roast Chicken Portions, Frozen, Thawed (Iceland) *serving 110g/4oz* 17
Roast Chicken & Smoked Ham (Waitrose) *serving 110g/4oz* 6
Roast Chicken Thighs (Somerfield) *serving 110g/4oz* 21
Roast Chicken Thighs, Chilled (Iceland) *serving 110g/4oz* 18
Roast Chicken Tikka Bites (Asda) *serving 110g/4oz* 11
Roast Chicken, Wafer Thin, Cold Meats (Tesco) *serving 110g/4oz* 4
Roast Chicken, Whole, Browned with Sugars (Asda) *serving 110g/4oz* 16

Roast Thighs (Waitrose) *serving 110g/4oz*	21
Roast Chicken, Small, Chilled Roasted (Iceland) *serving 110g/4oz*	15
Roast Chicken, Whole (Somerfield) *serving 110g/4oz*	15
Roasted Chicken Breast with Garlic (Asda) *serving 110g/4oz*	2
Sage & Onion Chicken, Wafer Thin (Asda) *serving 110g/4oz*	7
Self-Basting Fresh Chicken (Waitrose) *serving 110g/4oz*	22
Southern Chicken Fries, Savoury Snacks (Marks & Spencer) *serving 110g/4oz*	31
Southern Fried Chicken (Birds Eye) *serving 110g/4oz*	18
Southern Fried Chicken & Fries, Hot (Marks & Spencer) *serving 110g/4oz*	10
Southern Fried Chicken Nibbles, Frozen, Oven Baked (Iceland) *serving 110g/4oz*	17
Southern Fried Chicken Nuggets (Birds Eye) *serving 110g/4oz*	15
Southern Fried Chicken Portions, Frozen, Oven Baked (Iceland) *serving 110g/4oz*	17
Southern Fried Chicken Steak (Somerfield) *serving 110g/4oz*	10
Southern Fried Chicken Steaks, Frozen, Oven Baked (Iceland) *serving 110g/4oz*	19
Spanish Chicken & Rice (Birds Eye) *serving 110g/4oz*	3
Spicy Cajun Chicken Marinade (Birds Eye) *serving 110g/4oz*	7
Sweet & Sour Chicken (Marks & Spencer) *serving 110g/4oz*	11
Sweet & Sour Chicken, Microwave Ready Meal (Safeway) *serving 110g/4oz*	1
Sweet & Sour Chicken, Tinned Ready Meal (Tesco) *serving 110g/4oz*	2
Sweet & Sour Chicken & Rice (Birds Eye) *serving 110g/4oz*	1
Sweet & Sour Chicken with Rice, Frozen Ready Meal (Safeway) *serving 110g/4oz*	2
Sweet & Spicy Chicken Stir Fry (Somerfield) *serving 110g/4oz*	5
Tandoori Bhuna Chicken (Waitrose) *serving 110g/4oz*	11
Tandoori Chicken Marinade (Birds Eye) *serving 110g/4oz*	10
Tandoori Chicken Masala (Asda) *serving 110g/4oz*	8
Thai Green Chicken Curry (Waitrose) *serving 110g/4oz*	17
Thai Red Chicken Curry with Fried Onion, Frozen Ready Meal (Tesco) *serving 110g/4oz*	6

CHIPS

NOTE: The standard serving size in this section is 60g/2oz. If you wish to consume more or less than this amount (e.g. if you are going to consume a pack of food whose weight differs from the standard serving size) use the conversion tables on page 386 to calculate the new amount of fat in the food.

American Fries, (Asda) *serving 60g/2oz*	6
American Fries (Somerfield) *serving 60g/2oz*	3
American Fries (Tesco) *serving 60g/2oz*	10
American Slim Fries, Frozen, Oven Baked (Iceland) *serving 60g/2oz*	4
American Style Fries (Marks & Spencer) *serving 60g/2oz*	3
Chipped Old Potatoes, Crinkle Cut, Frozen, Fried in Corn Oil *serving 60g/2oz*	10
Chipped Old Potatoes, Fine Cut, Frozen, Fried in Corn Oil *serving 60g/2oz*	13
Chipped Old Potatoes, French Fries, Retail *serving 60g/2oz*	9
Chipped Old Potatoes, Microwave Chips, Cooked *serving 60g/2oz*	6
Chipped Old Potatoes, Oven Chips, Frozen, Baked *serving 60g/2oz*	3
Chipped Old Potatoes, Oven Chips, Thick Cut, Frozen, Baked *serving 60g/2oz*	3
Chipped Old Potatoes, Retail, Fried in Vegetable Oil *serving 60g/2oz*	7
Chipped Old Potatoes, Straight Cut, Frozen, Fried in Corn Oil *serving 60g/2oz*	8
Chipped Old Potatoes, Thick Cut, Frozen, Fried in Corn Oil *serving 60g/2oz*	6
Crinkle Cut Chips (Birds Eye) *serving 60g/2oz*	3
Crisps: *see under* Nuts & Savoury Snacks	
Everyday Supervalue Chips, Frozen (Iceland) *serving 60g/2oz*	4
Frying Chips, Thin Cut (Waitrose) *serving 60g/2oz*	3
Low Fat Just Bake Chips (Marks & Spencer) *serving 60g/2oz*	2
Microwave Chips (Marks & Spencer) *serving 60g/2oz*	5
New Potatoes, Chipped Fried in Corn Oil *serving 60g/2oz*	3

Oven Chips (Birds Eye) *serving 60g/2oz*	3
Oven Chips, Frozen (Asda) *serving 60g/2oz*	3
Oven Chips, Sunflower Oil (Waitrose) *serving 60g/2oz*	3
Oven Steak House Chips (Tesco) *serving 60g/2oz*	2
Southern Fried Chips, Frozen, Oven Baked (Iceland) *serving 60g/2oz*	5
Steak Cut Oven Chips (Somerfield) *serving 60g/2oz*	3
Steak Cut Oven Chips, Frozen, Oven Baked (Iceland) *serving 60g/2oz*	2
Steakhouse Chips, Cooked (Tesco) *serving 60g/2oz*	7
Steakhouse Chips, Raw (Tesco) *serving 60g/2oz*	2
Twister Fries, Frozen, Oven Baked (Iceland) *serving 60g/2oz*	4

Confectionery

NOTE: The standard serving size in this section is 30g/1oz. If you wish to consume more or less than this amount (e.g. if you are going to consume a pack of food whose weight differs from the standard serving size) use the conversion tables on page 386 to calculate the new amount of fat in the food.

Acid Drops (Tesco) *serving 30g/1oz*	0
After Dinner Mints (Marks & Spencer) *serving 30g/1oz*	6
After Dinner Mints (Tesco) *serving 30g/1oz*	7
After Dinner Mints (Waitrose) *serving 30g/1oz*	7
Almonds with Milk Chocolate *serving 30g/1oz*	10
Amaretto Bar (Marks & Spencer) *serving 30g/1oz*	9
American Hard Gums (Somerfield) *serving 30g/1oz*	0
American Hard Gums (Tesco) *serving 30g/1oz*	0
American Hard Gums (Waitrose) *serving 30g/1oz*	0
Apple Danish Bar (Sara Lee) *serving 30g/1oz*	3
Banana Chips *serving 30g/1oz*	10
Barley Sugar with Honey (Tesco) *serving 30g/1oz*	0
Beanies Bar (Iceland) *serving 30g/1oz*	9
Belgian Chocolate (Tesco) *serving 30g/1oz*	10
Belgian White Chocolate Assortment (Tesco) *serving 30g/1oz*	9
Belgium Chocolate Selection (Waitrose) *serving 30g/1oz*	8

Belgium Chocolate Shells (Waitrose) *serving 30g/1oz*	9
Bitter Chocolate (Waitrose) *serving 30g/1oz*	13
Bounty Dark, Twin (Mars) *serving 30g/1oz*	8
Bounty Milk, Twin (Mars) *serving 30g/1oz*	8
Brazil Nut Selection (Tesco) *serving 30g/1oz*	13
Breaktime, Plain (Waitrose) *serving 30g/1oz*	8
Bubbly Bar, Chunky (Marks & Spencer) *serving 30g/1oz*	3
Butter Drops (Tesco) *serving 30g/1oz*	1
Butter Mintoes (Waitrose) *serving 30g/1oz*	3
Butter Mints (Tesco) *serving 30g/1oz*	3
Buttermints (Marks & Spencer) *serving 30g/1oz*	3
Butterscotch *serving 30g/1oz*	1
Butterscotch Traditional Style (Somerfield) *serving 30g/1oz*	1
Butterscotch (Waitrose) *serving 30g/1oz*	2
Butterscotch with Lemon (Tesco) *serving 30g/1oz*	2
Button Easter Egg (Iceland) *serving 30g/1oz*	9
Buttons & Beanies Twin Pack (Iceland) *serving 30g/1oz*	10
Cappuccino Bar, Chunky Chocolate (Marks & Spencer) *serving 30g/1oz*	10
Cappuccino Bar, Miniature (Marks & Spencer) *serving 30g/1oz*	5
Cappuccino Coll Bar (Marks & Spencer) *serving 30g/1oz*	11
Cappuccino Mountain Bar (Marks & Spencer) *serving 30g/1oz*	10
Cappuccino Whips (Marks & Spencer) *serving 30g/1oz*	8
Caramel Chocolate Bar, Chunky (Marks & Spencer) *serving 30g/1oz*	7
Caramels *serving 30g/1oz*	2
Cereal Bar, Chewy *serving 30g/1oz*	5
Cereal Bar, Crunchy *serving 30g/1oz*	7
Cheeky Monkey Bag (Marks & Spencer) *serving 30g/1oz*	12
Cheeky Monkey Box (Marks & Spencer) *serving 30g/1oz*	0
Cheeky Monkey Fabric Bag (Marks & Spencer) *serving 30g/1oz*	10
Cheeky Monkey Lolly (Marks & Spencer) *serving 30g/1oz*	10
Cheeky Monkey Mini Figs (Marks & Spencer) *serving 30g/1oz*	10
Chewing Gum *serving 30g/1oz*	0
Chocolate, Baking, Unsweetened Squares *serving 30g/1oz*	17
Chocolate, Cooking *serving 30g/1oz*	10
Chocolate, Diabetic *serving 30g/1oz*	9

Chocolate, Fancy & Filled *serving 30g/1oz*	6
Chocolate Assortment, Luxury (Waitrose) *serving 30g/1oz*	9
Chocolate Assortment Egg (Iceland) *serving 30g/1oz*	10
Chocolate Bar, Chunky Layered (Marks & Spencer) *serving 30g/1oz*	10
Chocolate Bar, Mint Fill (Waitrose) *serving 30g/1oz*	6
Chocolate Bar, Strawberry (Waitrose) *serving 30g/1oz*	6
Chocolate Buttercream Roll (Somerfield) *serving 30g/1oz*	4
Chocolate Caramel Bar (Waitrose) *serving 30g/1oz*	8
Chocolate Coffee Assortment (Waitrose) *serving 30g/1oz*	10
Chocolate Covered Bar with Fruit/Nuts & Wafer Biscuit *serving 30g/1oz*	8
Chocolate Covered Caramels *serving 30g/1oz*	7
Chocolate Crisp Pieces (Marks & Spencer) *serving 30g/1oz*	8
Chocolate Digestive Balls (Marks & Spencer) *serving 30g/1oz*	6
Chocolate Eclairs (Marks & Spencer) *serving 30g/1oz*	6
Chocolate Limes (Iceland) *serving 30g/1oz*	2
Chocolate Limes (Waitrose) *serving 30g/1oz*	1
Chocolate Lolly Pack (Marks & Spencer) *serving 30g/1oz*	10
Chocolate Nut Assortment (Tesco) *serving 30g/1oz*	11
Chocolate Orange Creams (Waitrose) *serving 30g/1oz*	4
Chocolate Peanut Clusters (Safeway) *serving 30g/1oz*	2
Chocolate Peanuts (Marks & Spencer) *serving 30g/1oz*	9
Chocolate Peppermint Creme (Waitrose) *serving 30g/1oz*	4
Chocolate Raisins (Marks & Spencer) *serving 30g/1oz*	3
Chocolate Roll Log (Waitrose) *serving 30g/1oz*	6
Chocolate Stem Ginger (Waitrose) *serving 30g/1oz*	4
Christmas Cream Selection (Somerfield) *serving 30g/1oz*	12
Clear Fruits (Waitrose) *serving 30g/1oz*	0
Clear Mints (Waitrose) *serving 30g/1oz*	0
Cocoa, Dry Powder *serving 30g/1oz*	4
Coconut Bars (Iceland) *serving 30g/1oz*	9
Coconut Grove Chocolate Bar (Marks & Spencer) *serving 30g/1oz*	7
Coconut Grove Miniature (Marks & Spencer) *serving 30g/1oz*	7
Coconut Ice *serving 30g/1oz*	4
Coffee & Walnut Delights (Marks & Spencer) *serving 30g/1oz*	11

Coin, Large Gold Chocolate (Marks & Spencer) *serving 30g/1oz*	10
Conservation Chocolate Game (Tesco) *serving 30g/1oz*	9
Crisped Rice Bar, Almond *serving 30g/1oz*	6
Crisped Rice Bar, Chocolate Chip *serving 30g/1oz*	4
Crunchy Honey Clusters (Marks & Spencer) *serving 30g/1oz*	2
Dark Chocolate Coffee Bean (Waitrose) *serving 30g/1oz*	10
Dewdrops (Tesco) *serving 30g/1oz*	0
Dolly Mixtures (Marks & Spencer) *serving 30g/1oz*	0
Dolly Mixtures (Somerfield) *serving 30g/1oz*	0
Dolly Mixtures (Tesco) *serving 30g/1oz*	0
Dolly Mixtures (Waitrose) *serving 30g/1oz*	1
Double Chocolate Delights (Marks & Spencer) *serving 30g/1oz*	9
Easter Egg Nests (Waitrose) *serving 30g/1oz*	5
Fizzy Fish (Marks & Spencer) *serving 30g/1oz*	0
Flyte (Mars) *serving 30g/1oz*	4
Foam Sweets *serving 30g/1oz*	1
Fondant *serving 30g/1oz*	0
Fruit Gums (Marks & Spencer) *serving 30g/1oz*	0
Fruit Gums/Jellies *serving 30g/1oz*	0
Fruit Humbugs (Tesco) *serving 30g/1oz*	0
Fruit Humbugs (Waitrose) *serving 30g/1oz*	0
Fruit Jellies (Waitrose) *serving 30g/1oz*	0
Fruit Leather Bars *serving 30g/1oz*	2
Fruit Leather Bars with Cream *serving 30g/1oz*	2
Fruit Leather Pieces *serving 30g/1oz*	2
Fruit Leather Rolls *serving 30g/1oz*	1
Fruit & Nut Chocolate (Tesco) *serving 30g/1oz*	9
Fruit & Nut Chocolate Bar (Iceland) *serving 30g/1oz*	8
Fruit Pastilles *serving 30g/1oz*	0
Fruit Pastilles (Iceland) *serving 30g/1oz*	0
Fruit Pastilles (Marks & Spencer) *serving 30g/1oz*	0
Fruit Pastilles (Tesco) *serving 30g/1oz*	0
Fruit Quenchers, Assorted (Marks & Spencer) *serving 30g/1oz*	0
Fruit Rocks, Assorted (Marks & Spencer) *serving 30g/1oz*	6
Fruit Wine Gums (Iceland) *serving 30g/1oz*	0
Fudge *serving 30g/1oz*	4

Fudge, Brown Sugar with Nuts *serving 30g/1oz* 3
Fudge, Chocolate *serving 30g/1oz* 3
Fudge, Chocolate with Nuts *serving 30g/1oz* 5
Fudge, Dairy (Waitrose) *serving 30g/1oz* 3
Fudge, Devon (Somerfield) *serving 30g/1oz* 3
Fudge, Peanut Butter *serving 30g/1oz* 2
Fudge, Vanilla (Marks & Spencer) *serving 30g/1oz* 6
Fudge, Vanilla (Tesco) *serving 30g/1oz* 4
Fudge, Yule Log with Chocolate Filling (Somerfield) *serving 30g/1oz* 7
Galaxy Block (Mars) *serving 30g/1oz* 9
Galaxy Caramel (Mars) *serving 30g/1oz* 8
Galaxy Double Nut/Raisin (Mars) *serving 30g/1oz* 9
Galaxy Hazelnut (Mars) *serving 30g/1oz* 12
Galaxy Mini Egg (Mars) *serving 30g/1oz* 11
Galaxy Minstrels (Mars) *serving 30g/1oz* 6
Galaxy Ripple (Mars) *serving 30g/1oz* 9
Galaxy Smooth & Creamy Chocolate Drink (Mars) *serving 30g/1oz* 1
Galaxy Truffle Egg (Mars) *serving 30g/1oz* 12
Golden Marzipan (Somerfield) *serving 30g/1oz* 5
Golden Marzipan (Waitrose) *serving 30g/1oz* 4
Gum Bears, Children's Assortment (Tesco) *serving 30g/1oz* 0
Halva, Asian *serving 30g/1oz* 4
Halva, Carrot *serving 30g/1oz* 6
Halva, Greek *serving 30g/1oz* 10
Halva, Semolina *serving 30g/1oz* 5
Hazelnut Chocolate Bar (Iceland) *serving 30g/1oz* 10
Here Bar (Marks & Spencer) *serving 30g/1oz* 4
Humbugs (Iceland) *serving 30g/1oz* 2
Italian Tiramisu Bar (Marks & Spencer) *serving 30g/1oz* 10
Japonais (Chocolate) (Waitrose) *serving 30g/1oz* 9
Jelly Babies (Iceland) *serving 30g/1oz* 0
Jelly Babies (Marks & Spencer) *serving 30g/1oz* 0
Jelly Babies (Waitrose) *serving 30g/1oz* 0
Jelly Beans (Tesco) *serving 30g/1oz* 0
Jelly Beans (Waitrose) *serving 30g/1oz* 0

Jelly Belly Beans (Marks & Spencer) *serving 30g/1oz*	0
Liquorice Allsorts (Marks & Spencer) *serving 30g/1oz*	1
Liquorice Allsorts (Somerfield) *serving 30g/1oz*	1
Liquorice Allsorts (Tesco) *serving 30g/1oz*	1
Liquorice Allsorts (Waitrose) *serving 30g/1oz*	1
Liquorice Comfits, Children's Assortment (Tesco) *serving 30g/1oz*	0
Liquorice Twists (Tesco) *serving 30g/1oz*	0
Lockets (Mars) *serving 30g/1oz*	0
M&M's, Chocolate (Mars) *serving 30g/1oz*	6
M&M's, Peanut (Mars) *serving 30g/1oz*	8
Mallows, Assorted (Iceland) *serving 30g/1oz*	0
Maltesers (Mars) *serving 30g/1oz*	7
Mars (Mars) *serving 30g/1oz*	5
Mars Filled Egg (Mars) *serving 30g/1oz*	9
Mars Light (Mars) *serving 30g/1oz*	4
Marshmallows *serving 30g/1oz*	0
Marshmallows (Tesco) *serving 30g/1oz*	0
Marzipan, Home Made *serving 30g/1oz*	8
Marzipan Characters (Waitrose) *serving 30g/1oz*	8
Marzipan Fruits, Loose (Waitrose) *serving 30g/1oz*	3
Milk Chocolate *serving 30g/1oz*	9
Milk Chocolate (Iceland) *serving 30g/1oz*	8
Milk Chocolate (Waitrose) *serving 30g/1oz*	9
Milk Chocolate, Multipack (Iceland) *serving 30g/1oz*	8
Milk Chocolate, Smooth (Somerfield) *serving 30g/1oz*	10
Milk Chocolate Balls (Tesco) *serving 30g/1oz*	8
Milk Chocolate Bar (Iceland) *serving 30g/1oz*	8
Milk Chocolate Bar (Tesco) *serving 30g/1oz*	10
Milk Chocolate Bar with Crisp Rice (Iceland) *serving 30g/1oz*	8
Milk Chocolate Bar, Fruit & Nuts (Waitrose) *serving 30g/1oz*	8
Milk Chocolate Bar & Hazelnuts (Waitrose) *serving 30g/1oz*	10
Milk Chocolate Beanies Egg (Iceland) *serving 30g/1oz*	9
Milk Chocolate Brazils (Somerfield) *serving 30g/1oz*	12
Milk Chocolate Buttercream Roll (Waitrose) *serving 30g/1oz*	7
Milk Chocolate Buttons (Marks & Spencer) *serving 30g/1oz*	10
Milk Chocolate Buttons (Somerfield) *serving 30g/1oz*	8
Milk Chocolate Buttons (Waitrose) *serving 30g/1oz*	7

Milk Chocolate Caramel Shortcake Bars (Somerfield) *serving 30g/1oz* 36
Milk Chocolate Coated Brazils (Iceland) *serving 30g/1oz* 12
Milk Chocolate Coated Peanuts *serving 30g/1oz* 10
Milk Chocolate Coated Raisins *serving 30g/1oz* 4
Milk Chocolate Coins (Marks & Spencer) *serving 30g/1oz* 10
Milk Chocolate Cornflakes (Marks & Spencer) *serving 30g/1oz* 8
Milk Chocolate Covered Raisins (Tesco) *serving 30g/1oz* 4
Milk Chocolate Crunch Bars, Chunky (Somerfield) *serving 30g/1oz* 8
Milk Chocolate Digestive Bars (Somerfield) *serving 30g/1oz* 8
Milk Chocolate Easter Bunny (Iceland) *serving 30g/1oz* 9
Milk Chocolate Eclairs (Somerfield) *serving 30g/1oz* 6
Milk Chocolate with Hazelnuts (Waitrose) *serving 30g/1oz* 10
Milk Chocolate Mini Eggs (Waitrose) *serving 30g/1oz* 7
Milk Chocolate Orange Bar (Iceland) *serving 30g/1oz* 8
Milk Chocolate Orange Sandwich Bars (Somerfield) *serving 30g/1oz* 7
Milk Chocolate Orange Wafer Fingers (Somerfield) *serving 30g/1oz* 9
Milk Chocolate Peanuts (Iceland) *serving 30g/1oz* 12
Milk Chocolate Peanuts (Somerfield) *serving 30g/1oz* 12
Milk Chocolate Peanuts (Waitrose) *serving 30g/1oz* 12
Milk Chocolate Peanuts & Raisins (Tesco) *serving 30g/1oz* 7
Milk Chocolate Raisins (Iceland) *serving 30g/1oz* 5
Milk Chocolate Raisins (Somerfield) *serving 30g/1oz* 4
Milk Chocolate Raisins (Waitrose) *serving 30g/1oz* 4
Milk Chocolate Sandwich (Waitrose) *serving 30g/1oz* 2
Milk Chocolate Sandwich Bars (Somerfield) *serving 30g/1oz* 7
Milk Chocolate Shortbread Rings (Somerfield) *serving 30g/1oz* 9
Milk Chocolate Shortcake Bars (Somerfield) *serving 30g/1oz* 8
Milk Chocolate Shortcake Biscuits (Somerfield) *serving 30g/1oz* 7
Milk Chocolate Teacakes (Somerfield) *serving 30g/1oz* 4
Milk Chocolate Vanilla Crunch Bars (Somerfield) *serving 30g/1oz* 7
Milk Chocolate Wafers (Iceland) *serving 30g/1oz* 9
Milk Chocolate Whip (Iceland) *serving 30g/1oz* 4
Milk & White Chocolate Crispies (Safeway) *serving 30g/1oz* 1

Milky Way (Mars) *serving 30g/1oz*	5
Milky Way Crispy Rolls (Mars) *serving 30g/1oz*	9
Milky Way Magic Stars (Mars) *serving 30g/1oz*	11
Mini Allsorts (Somerfield) *serving 30g/1oz*	13
Mini Allsorts, Children's Assortment (Tesco) *serving 30g/1oz*	2
Mini Bears (Tesco) *serving 30g/1oz*	0
Mini Jelly Babies (Somerfield) *serving 30g/1oz*	0
Mini Jelly Babies (Tesco) *serving 30g/1oz*	0
Mini Liquorice Allsorts (Tesco) *serving 30g/1oz*	1
Mini Liquorice Allsorts (Waitrose) *serving 30g/1oz*	1
Mini Wine Gums (Waitrose) *serving 30g/1oz*	0
Mint Assortment (Tesco) *serving 30g/1oz*	1
Mint Assortment (Waitrose) *serving 30g/1oz*	3
Mint Caramel (Tesco) *serving 30g/1oz*	9
Mint Chocolate Assortment (Iceland) *serving 30g/1oz*	7
Mint Chocolate Selection (Somerfield) *serving 30g/1oz*	7
Mint Collection Bar (Marks & Spencer) *serving 30g/1oz*	10
Mint Crisp (Tesco) *serving 30g/1oz*	7
Mint Crisps (Waitrose) *serving 30g/1oz*	7
Mint Crumbles (Marks & Spencer) *serving 30g/1oz*	6
Mint Filled Sticks (Tesco) *serving 30g/1oz*	9
Mint Humbugs (Marks & Spencer) *serving 30g/1oz*	1
Mint Humbugs (Tesco) *serving 30g/1oz*	2
Mint Humbugs (Waitrose) *serving 30g/1oz*	2
Mint Imperials (Tesco) *serving 30g/1oz*	0
Mint Imperials (Waitrose) *serving 30g/1oz*	0
Mint Jelly (Tesco) *serving 30g/1oz*	0
Mint Selection (Marks & Spencer) *serving 30g/1oz*	6
Mint Selection (Waitrose) *serving 30g/1oz*	7
Mint Sticks (Marks & Spencer) *serving 30g/1oz*	8
Mint Sticks (Somerfield) *serving 30g/1oz*	9
Mintoes (Iceland) *serving 30g/1oz*	3
Mintoes (Somerfield) *serving 30g/1oz*	3
Mints, Curiously Strong (Marks & Spencer) *serving 30g/1oz*	0
Muesli Bars, Hard *serving 30g/1oz*	6
Muesli Bars, Soft, Coated, Milk Chocolate Coating, Chocolate Chip *serving 30g/1oz*	7

Muesli Bars, Soft, Coated, Milk Chocolate Coating, Peanut Butter *serving 30g/1oz*	9
Muesli Bars, Soft, Uncoated *serving 30g/1oz*	5
Muesli Bars, Soft, Uncoated, Chocolate Chip *serving 30g/1oz*	5
Muesli Bars, Soft, Uncoated, Chocolate Chip Graham & Marshmallow *serving 30g/1oz*	5
Muesli Bars, Soft, Uncoated, Nut & Raisin *serving 30g/1oz*	6
Muesli Bars, Soft, Uncoated, Peanut Butter *serving 30g/1oz*	5
Muesli Bars, Soft, Uncoated, Peanut Butter & Chocolate Chip *serving 30g/1oz*	6
Muesli Bars, Soft, Uncoated, Raisin *serving 30g/1oz*	5
Nougat *serving 30g/1oz*	3
Nougat, Traditional Cherry (Marks & Spencer) *serving 30g/1oz*	2
Nut & Popcorn Mix, Premium (Tesco) *serving 30g/1oz*	8
Opal Fruits (Mars) *serving 30g/1oz*	2
Orange Crisps (Tesco) *serving 30g/1oz*	7
Orange & Lemon Creams (Waitrose) *serving 30g/1oz*	3
Orange & Lemon Slices (Tesco) *serving 30g/1oz*	0
Peanut Brittle *serving 30g/1oz*	6
Peanut Brittle (Marks & Spencer) *serving 30g/1oz*	9
Peanuts, Raisins & Choc Chips (Somerfield) *serving 30g/1oz*	8
Pear Drops (Tesco) *serving 30g/1oz*	0
Peppermint Creams (Marks & Spencer) *serving 30g/1oz*	3
Peppermints *serving 30g/1oz*	0
Percy Pigs (Marks & Spencer) *serving 30g/1oz*	0
Plain Chocolate *serving 30g/1oz*	8
Plain Chocolate, Rich Dark (Somerfield) *serving 30g/1oz*	9
Plain Chocolate Bar (Tesco) *serving 30g/1oz*	9
Plain Chocolate Bar (Waitrose) *serving 30g/1oz*	9
Plain Chocolate Bar, Fruit/Nuts (Waitrose) *serving 30g/1oz*	9
Plain Chocolate Bar with Hazelnuts (Waitrose) *serving 30g/1oz*	11
Plain Chocolate Brazil Nuts (Waitrose) *serving 30g/1oz*	14
Plain Chocolate Digestives (Iceland) *serving 30g/1oz*	7
Plain Chocolate Mint Sandwich Bars (Somerfield) *serving 30g/1oz*	7

Plain Wholenut Bar (Tesco) *serving 30g/1oz*	11
Popcorn, Air Popped *serving 30g/1oz*	1
Popcorn, Candied *serving 30g/1oz*	6
Popcorn, Caramel Coated with Peanuts *serving 30g/1oz*	2
Popcorn, Cheese Flavour *serving 30g/1oz*	10
Popcorn, Oil Popped *serving 30g/1oz*	8
Popcorn Cakes *serving 30g/1oz*	1
Praline *serving 30g/1oz*	7
Revels (Mars) *serving 30g/1oz*	7
Rhapsody Bars (Asda) *serving 30g/1oz*	8
Roasted Nut Chewy Bars (Asda) *serving 30g/1oz*	7
Rose & Violet Cremes (Waitrose) *serving 30g/1oz*	4
Sherbert Sweets *serving 30g/1oz*	0
Sherberts, Assorted Fruit (Marks & Spencer) *serving 30g/1oz*	2
Skittles (Mars) *serving 30g/1oz*	1
Snickers (Mars) *serving 30g/1oz*	8
Soft Caramel Eggs, (Iceland) *serving 30g/1oz*	8
Sparkling Fruits (Tesco) *serving 30g/1oz*	0
Sparkling Mints (Tesco) *serving 30g/1oz*	0
Sparks Chocolate Bar (Marks & Spencer) *serving 30g/1oz*	6
Sparks Chocolate Bar, Miniature (Marks & Spencer) *serving 30g/1oz*	6
Splits, Assorted (Waitrose) *serving 30g/1oz*	1
Sprint Peanut Bars (Iceland) *serving 30g/1oz*	9
Strawberry Shakes (Marks & Spencer) *serving 30g/1oz*	0
Strike Caramel Bars (Iceland) *serving 30g/1oz*	5
Sugar, Brown *serving 30g/1oz*	0
Sugar, Granulated *serving 30g/1oz*	0
Sugar, Icing *serving 30g/1oz*	0
Sugar, Maple *serving 30g/1oz*	0
Sugar, White *serving 30g/1oz*	0
Sugar Coated Chocolate Eggs (Tesco) *serving 30g/1oz*	6
Sugar Free Delight Chocolate (Asda) *serving 30g/1oz*	5
Sweets, Boiled *serving 30g/1oz*	0
Sweets, Chewy *serving 30g/1oz*	2
Sweets Now Chocolate Bar (Marks & Spencer) *serving 30g/1oz*	8

Swiss Milk Chocolate Bar (Marks & Spencer) *serving 30g/1oz* 9
Swiss Milk Chocolate Discs (Marks & Spencer) *serving 30g/1oz* 11
Swiss Milk & Hazelnut Chocolate (Marks & Spencer) *serving 30g/1oz* 11
Swiss Plain Chocolate & Ginger (Waitrose) *serving 30g/1oz* 9
Swiss Plain Chocolate & Orange (Waitrose) *serving 30g/1oz* 8
Swiss White Chocolate Tablet (Waitrose) *serving 30g/1oz* 9
Teddy Lollipop (Marks & Spencer) *serving 30g/1oz* 10
Toffee, Assorted (Iceland) *serving 30g/1oz* 6
Toffee, Assorted (Waitrose) *serving 30g/1oz* 5
Toffee, Blackcurrant & Liquorice (Tesco) *serving 30g/1oz* 2
Toffee, Brazil Nut (Tesco) *serving 30g/1oz* 7
Toffee, Butter Popcorn (Tesco) *serving 30g/1oz* 3
Toffee, Chocolate & Toffee Assortment (Somerfield) *serving 30g/1oz* 6
Toffee, Chocolate Toffee Bites (Waitrose) *serving 30g/1oz* 6
Toffee, Cream (Tesco) *serving 30g/1oz* 6
Toffee, Cream Assortment (Tesco) *serving 30g/1oz* 5
Toffee, Dairy (Iceland) *serving 30g/1oz* 6
Toffee, Dairy (Waitrose) *serving 30g/1oz* 6
Toffee, Double Devon Toffees (Marks & Spencer) *serving 30g/1oz* 6
Toffee, Malt & Butter (Tesco) *serving 30g/1oz* 5
Toffee, Mixed *serving 30g/1oz* 6
Toffee Pecan Whips (Marks & Spencer) *serving 30g/1oz* 9
Toffee, Plain Chocolate with Toffee (Waitrose) *serving 30g/1oz* 9
Toffee, Popcorn (Marks & Spencer) *serving 30g/1oz* 4
Toffee, Sticky Toffee Bars (Waitrose) *serving 30g/1oz* 6
Toffee, Treacle (Tesco) *serving 30g/1oz* 4
Topic (Mars) *serving 30g/1oz* 8
Tracker, Chocolate Chip (Mars) *serving 30g/1oz* 9
Tracker, Roast Nut (Mars) *serving 30g/1oz* 9
Truffle *serving 30g/1oz* 10
Truffle, Apricot Brandy (Waitrose) *serving 30g/1oz* 8
Truffle, Belgian Chocolate (Waitrose) *serving 30g/1oz* 12

Truffle, Belgian White Chocolate (Waitrose) *serving 30g/1oz* 11
Truffle, Cappuccino (Waitrose) *serving 30g/1oz* 11
Truffle, Champagne (Waitrose) *serving 30g/1oz* 11
Truffle, Champagne Belgian (Waitrose) *serving 30g/1oz* 11
Truffle, Champagne Truffle Bar (Marks & Spencer) *serving 30g/1oz* 9
Truffle, Coffee & Tia Maria (Waitrose) *serving 30g/1oz* 9
Truffle, Grand Marnier Chocolate (Waitrose) *serving 30g/1oz* 5
Truffle, Mint Selection (Tesco) *serving 30g/1oz* 12
Truffle, Mint Truffle Bar (Marks & Spencer) *serving 30g/1oz* 8
Truffle, Mocha *serving 30g/1oz* 7
Truffle, Orange Truffle Bar (Marks & Spencer) *serving 30g/1oz* 12
Truffle, Rum *serving 30g/1oz* 10
Truffle, Tipsy Fudge (Waitrose) *serving 30g/1oz* 7
Tunes (Mars) *serving 30g/1oz* 1
Turkish Delight Chocolate Bar (Marks & Spencer) *serving 30g/1oz* 3
Turkish Delight *serving 30g/1oz* 0
Turkish Delight with Nuts *serving 30g/1oz* 1
Twix (Mars) *serving 30g/1oz* 7
Walnut Whips (Marks & Spencer) *serving 30g/1oz* 8
White Chocolate *serving 30g/1oz* 9
White Chocolate Bar (Iceland) *serving 30g/1oz* 10
White Chocolate Bar (Tesco) *serving 30g/1oz* 9
White Chocolate Bar (Waitrose) *serving 30g/1oz* 10
White Chocolate Bar with Crisp Rice (Iceland) *serving 30g/1oz* 9
White Chocolate Buttons (Marks & Spencer) *serving 30g/1oz* 10
White Chocolate Buttons (Somerfield) *serving 30g/1oz* 8
White Chocolate Coins (Tesco) *serving 30g/1oz* 9
White Mints (Marks & Spencer) *serving 30g/1oz* 10
White Mountain Bar (Marks & Spencer) *serving 30g/1oz* 11
Whole Nut Milk Chocolate, (Tesco) *serving 30g/1oz* 11
Wine Gums (Marks & Spencer) *serving 30g/1oz* 0
Wine Gums (Somerfield) *serving 30g/1oz* 0

Wine Gums (Tesco) *serving 30g/1oz*	0
Wine Gums (Waitrose) *serving 30g/1oz*	0

Cream

NOTE: The standard serving size in this section is 30g/1oz. If you wish to consume more or less than this amount (e.g. if you are going to consume a pack of food whose weight differs from the standard serving size) use the conversion tables on page 386 to calculate the new amount of fat in the food.

Aerosol Cream (Asda) *serving 30g/1oz*	9
Aerosol Cream, Chilled (Iceland) *serving 30g/1oz*	9
Aerosol Cream (Marks & Spencer) *serving 30g/1oz*	11
Brandy Cream (Waitrose) *serving 30g/1oz*	12
Clotted Cream (Asda) *serving 30g/1oz*	19
Clotted Cream (Marks & Spencer) *serving 30g/1oz*	19
Clotted Cream (Safeway) *serving 30g/1oz*	19
Clotted Cream (Somerfield) *serving 30g/1oz*	19
Coffee Whitener, Reduced Fat (Asda) *serving 30g/1oz*	5
Coffeemate Creamer (Carnation) *serving 30g/1oz*	10
Coffeemate Lite Creamer (Carnation) *serving 30g/1oz*	4
Cream Chantilly (Marks & Spencer) *serving 30g/1oz*	11
Creme Fraiche (Marks & Spencer) *serving 30g/1oz*	12
Creme Fraiche (Somerfield) *serving 30g/1oz*	12
Creme Fraiche (Waitrose) *serving 30g/1oz*	12
Creme Fraiche, Half Fat (Marks & Spencer) *serving 30g/1oz*	6
Creme Fraiche, Half Fat (Waitrose) *serving 30g/1oz*	5
Creme Fraiche, Reduced Fat (Sainsbury's) *serving 30g/1oz*	6
Delight Double Cream Alternative *serving 30g/1oz*	7
Delight Single Cream Alternative *serving 30g/1oz*	3
Delight Whipping Cream Alternative *serving 30g/1oz*	5
Double Cream (Asda) *serving 30g/1oz*	14
Double Cream (Eden Vale) *serving 30g/1oz*	7
Double Cream (Somerfield) *serving 30g/1oz*	14
Double Cream (Waitrose) *serving 30g/1oz*	14
Double Cream, Chilled (Iceland) *serving 30g/1oz*	14

Double Cream, Extra Thick (Asda) *serving 30g/1oz*	14
Double Cream, Extra Thick (Waitrose) *serving 30g/1oz*	14
Double Cream, Extra Thick, Sweetened, with Brandy (Somerfield) *serving 30g/1oz*	12
Double Cream, Extra Thick, Sweetened, with Rum (Somerfield) *serving 30g/1oz*	12
Double Cream, Fresh, Pasteurized (St Ivel) *serving 30g/1oz*	14
Double Cream, Half 24% (Waitrose) *serving 30g/1oz*	7
Double Cream, Thick, Half Fat (Marks & Spencer) *serving 30g/1oz*	7
Double Cream & Cointreau (Waitrose) *serving 30g/1oz*	12
Double Dairy Cream (Marks & Spencer) *serving 30g/1oz*	14
Double Dairy Cream, Extra Thick (Marks & Spencer) *serving 30g/1oz*	14
Elmlea Aerosol Cream Alternative *serving 30g/1oz*	7
Elmlea Double Cream Alternative *serving 30g/1oz*	11
Elmlea Single Cream Alternative *serving 30g/1oz*	4
Elmlea Whipping Cream Alternative *serving 30g/1oz*	9
Fussell's Golden (Nestlé) *serving 30g/1oz*	7
Half Cream (Waitrose) *serving 30g/1oz*	4
Malt Whisky Cream *serving 30g/1oz*	11
Pouring Cream (Waitrose) *serving 30g/1oz*	14
Pouring Double Cream (Waitrose) *serving 30g/1oz*	14
Pouring Single Cream (Waitrose) *serving 30g/1oz*	5
Single Cream (Asda) *serving 30g/1oz*	5
Single Cream (Eden Vale) *serving 30g/1oz*	3
Single Cream (Somerfield) *serving 30g/1oz*	5
Single Cream (Waitrose) *serving 30g/1oz*	5
Single Cream, Chilled (Iceland) *serving 30g/1oz*	5
Single Cream, Extra Thick (Asda) *serving 30g/1oz*	5
Single Cream, Fresh, Pasteurized (St Ivel) *serving 30g/1oz*	5
Single Dairy Cream (Marks & Spencer) *serving 30g/1oz*	5
Soured Cream (Somerfield) *serving 30g/1oz*	6
Soured Cream (Waitrose) *serving 30g/1oz*	5
Soya Dream Non Dairy Alternative to Single Cream (Provamel) *serving 30g/1oz*	5

Sterilized Cream (Somerfield) *serving 30g/1oz* 7
Tea Mate Creamer (Nestlé) *serving 30g/1oz* 5
Thick Creamy Cream (Marks & Spencer) *serving 30g/1oz* 16
UHT Cream, Double (Asda) *serving 30g/1oz* 14
UHT Cream, Single (Asda) *serving 30g/1oz* 5
UHT Cream, Whipping (Asda) *serving 30g/1oz* 12
Whipping Cream (Asda) *serving 30g/1oz* 12
Whipping Cream (Eden Vale) *serving 30g/1oz* 6
Whipping Cream (Somerfield) *serving 30g/1oz* 11
Whipping Cream (Waitrose) *serving 30g/1oz* 12
Whipping Cream, Chilled (Iceland) *serving 30g/1oz* 12
Whipping Cream, Fresh, Pasteurized (St Ivel) *serving 30g/1oz* 12
Whipping Dairy Cream (Marks & Spencer) *serving 30g/1oz* 12

Desserts

NOTE: The standard serving size in this section is 110g/4oz. If you wish to consume more or less than this amount (e.g. if you are going to consume a pack of food whose weight differs from the standard serving size) use the conversion tables on page 386 to calculate the new amount of fat in the food.

Almond Custard Danish Bar, Frozen (Tesco) *serving 110g/4oz* 16
Ambrosia Dessert Pot (CPC), Banana Flavour *serving 110g/4oz* 3
Ambrosia Dessert Pot (CPC), Devon Fudge Flavour *serving 110g/4oz* 3
Ambrosia Dessert Pot (CPC), Milk Chocolate Flavour *serving 110g/4oz* 2
Ambrosia Dessert Pot (CPC), Strawberry Flavour *serving 110g/4oz* 3
Ambrosia Dessert Pot (CPC), White Chocolate Flavour *serving 110g/4oz* 3
Ambrosia Macaroni Pudding, Creamed (CPC) *serving 110g/4oz* 2
Ambrosia Milk Chocolate Flavour Pot (CPC) *serving 110g/4oz* 2
Appenzell (Waitrose) *serving 110g/4oz* 34
Apple & Blackberry Crumble (Marks & Spencer) *serving 110g/4oz* 9

Apple Crisp, Home Made *serving 110g/4oz*	4
Apple Pie (Sara Lee) *serving 110g/4oz*	11
Apple Puffs (Marks & Spencer) *serving 110g/4oz*	20
Apple Strudel *serving 110g/4oz*	12
Apple Strudel (Marks & Spencer) *serving 110g/4oz*	17
Apple Torta (Marks & Spencer) *serving 110g/4oz*	16
Apple Turnovers, Dairy Cream (Somerfield) *serving 110g/4oz*	30
Apricot Fool, Chilled (Tesco) *serving 110g/4oz*	10
Asian Pastries *serving 110g/4oz*	43
Banana, Custard Style (Waitrose) *serving 110g/4oz*	1
Banana Delight (Somerfield) *serving 110g/4oz*	17
Banana Delight, Sugar Free (Asda) *serving 110g/4oz*	19
Banana Pudding, Dry Mix, Instant, Made with Low-fat Milk *serving 110g/4oz*	2
Banana Pudding, Dry Mix, Instant, Made with Whole Milk *serving 110g/4oz*	3
Banana Pudding, Ready to Eat *serving 110g/4oz*	4
Banana Smoothy Pot Dessert (Marks & Spencer) *serving 110g/4oz*	0
Banoffee Dessert, Chilled (Asda) *serving 110g/4oz*	4
Blackcurrant Delice (Marks & Spencer) *serving 110g/4oz*	11
Blackcurrant Jelly (Somerfield) *serving 110g/4oz*	1
Blancmange, Chocolate, Duplex Pack Only (Brown & Polson) *serving 110g/4oz*	2
Blancmange, Strawberry, Duplex Pack Only (Brown & Polson) *serving 110g/4oz*	1
Bramley Apple Turnover, Fresh (Iceland) *serving 110g/4oz*	31
Bread & Butter Pudding (Somerfield) *serving 110g/4oz*	21
Bread & Butter Pudding (Waitrose) *serving 110g/4oz*	14
Bread & Butter Pudding, Frozen (Tesco) *serving 110g/4oz*	19
Bread & Butter Pudding, Small (Marks & Spencer) *serving 110g/4oz*	19
Bread Pudding (Somerfield) *serving 110g/4oz*	6
Bread Puding, Home Made *serving 110g/4oz*	6
Burfi *serving 110g/4oz*	22
Butterscotch Delight (Somerfield) *serving 110g/4oz*	17
Butterscotch Delight, Sugar Free (Asda) *serving 110g/4oz*	19
Cadbury's Caramel Dessert (St Ivel) *serving 110g/4oz*	9

Cadbury's Chocolate Orange Dessert (St Ivel) *serving 110g/4oz* 13
Cadbury's Dairy Milk Dessert (St Ivel) *serving 110g/4oz* 19
Cadbury's Flake Dessert (St Ivel) *serving 110g/4oz* 16
Cadbury's Turkish Delight Dessert (St Ivel) *serving 110g/4oz* 7
Cakes: *see under* Cakes, Gateaux, Sweet Pies & Tarts
Cappuccino Log, Frozen (Marks & Spencer) *serving 110g/4oz* 13
Caramel Dessert, Pot Dessert (Marks & Spencer) *serving 110g/4oz* 5
Caramel Surprise (Waitrose) *serving 110g/4oz* 5
Cheesecake *serving 110g/4oz* 25
Cheesecake, Apricot (Somerfield) *serving 110g/4oz* 16
Cheesecake, Blackcurrant (Heinz Weight Watchers) *serving 110g/4oz* 5
Cheesecake, Blackcurrant (Safeway) *serving 110g/4oz* 15
Cheesecake, Blackcurrant (Somerfield) *serving 110g/4oz* 16
Cheesecake, Blackcurrant Frozen (Asda) *serving 110g/4oz* 21
Cheesecake, Blackcurrant, Frozen (Iceland) *serving 110g/4oz* 17
Cheesecake, Blackcurrant, Frozen (Marks & Spencer) *serving 110g/4oz* 9
Cheesecake, Blackcurrant, Frozen (Tesco) *serving 110g/4oz* 16
Cheesecake, Choc Chip (Marks & Spencer) *serving 110g/4oz* 22
Cheesecake, Chocolate (Marks & Spencer) *serving 110g/4oz* 23
Cheesecake, Chocolate (Safeway) *serving 110g/4oz* 17
Cheesecake, Chocolate (Somerfield) *serving 110g/4oz* 16
Cheesecake, Chocolate & Cream, Frozen (Tesco) *serving 110g/4oz* 26
Cheesecake, Chocolate Marble, Slices (Somerfield) *serving 110g/4oz* 24
Cheesecake, Chocolate Sensations (Heinz Weight Watchers) *serving 110g/4oz* 5
Cheesecake, Devonshire Blackcurrant (St Ivel) *serving 110g/4oz* 16
Cheesecake, Devonshire Strawberry (St Ivel) *serving 110g/4oz* 16
Cheesecake, Exotic Fruit (Marks & Spencer) *serving 110g/4oz* 13
Cheesecake, Healthy Eating, Strawberry, Frozen (Tesco) *serving 110g/4oz* 7
Cheesecake, Home Made *serving 110g/4oz* 29
Cheesecake, Lemon (Marks & Spencer) *serving 110g/4oz* 17

Cheesecake, Lemon & Cream, Frozen (Tesco) *serving 110g/4oz* 19
Cheesecake, Lemon & Cream (Marks & Spencer) *serving 110g/4oz* 26
Cheesecake, Lemon Pot (Marks & Spencer) *serving 110g/4oz* 29
Cheesecake, Lemon & Sultana Slices (Somerfield) *serving 110g/4oz* 18
Cheesecake, Luxury Banana, Frozen (Tesco) *serving 110g/4oz* 25
Cheesecake, Orange & Lemon, Frozen (Asda) *serving 110g/4oz* 22
Cheesecake, Prepared from Mix *serving 110g/4oz* 14
Cheesecake, Raspberry (Marks & Spencer) *serving 110g/4oz* 17
Cheesecake, Really Rich Chocolate (Sara Lee) *serving 110g/4oz* 21
Cheesecake, Really Rich Lemon (Sara Lee) *serving 110g/4oz* 16
Cheesecake, Rich Caramel (Marks & Spencer) *serving 110g/4oz* 22
Cheesecake, Strawberry (Heinz Weight Watchers) *serving 110g/4oz* 5
Cheesecake, Strawberry (Safeway) *serving 110g/4oz* 15
Cheesecake, Strawberry (Somerfield) *serving 110g/4oz* 15
Cheesecake, Strawberry (Waitrose) *serving 110g/4oz* 23
Cheesecake, Strawberry, Frozen (Iceland) *serving 110g/4oz* 16
Cheesecake, Strawberry, Frozen (Tesco) *serving 110g/4oz* 16
Cheesecake, Strawberry Twin Pack, Chilled (Asda) *serving 110g/4oz* 15
Cherry & Almond Lattice (Waitrose) *serving 110g/4oz* 32
Cherry & Custard Strudel, Frozen (Asda) *serving 110g/4oz* 16
Cherry Danish, Frozen (Marks & Spencer) *serving 110g/4oz* 8
Cherry Lattice (Waitrose) *serving 110g/4oz* 11
Cherry Puffs, Frozen (Marks & Spencer) *serving 110g/4oz* 10
Choc Buttercream Log (Waitrose) *serving 110g/4oz* 23
Choc Fudgenut Florentine (Waitrose) *serving 110g/4oz* 28
Chocolate Brownie Dessert, Chilled (Asda) *serving 110g/4oz* 11
Chocolate & Cream Dessert, Chilled (Iceland) *serving 110g/4oz* 7
Chocolate Creme Dessert (Somerfield) *serving 110g/4oz* 5
Chocolate Dairy Cream Sponge, Frozen (Asda) *serving 110g/4oz* 17
Chocolate Danish Dessert (Sara Lee) *serving 110g/4oz* 25
Chocolate Delice (Marks & Spencer) *serving 110g/4oz* 28
Chocolate Delight (Somerfield) *serving 110g/4oz* 17

Chocolate Delight, Pot Desserts (Marks & Spencer) *serving 110g/4oz* 7
Chocolate Delight, Sugar Free (Somerfield) *serving 110g/4oz* 18
Chocolate Dream Desserts, Chilled (Iceland) *serving 110g/4oz* 17
Chocolate Fudge Cake Portion (Marks & Spencer) *serving 110g/4oz* 24
Chocolate Pudding (Marks & Spencer) *serving 110g/4oz* 20
Chocolate Pudding, Dry Mix, Instant, Made with Low-fat Milk *serving 110g/4oz* 2
Chocolate Pudding, Dry Mix, Instant, Made with Whole Milk *serving 110g/4oz* 3
Chocolate Pudding, Ready to Eat *serving 110g/4oz* 4
Chocolate Pudding with Custard (Somerfield) *serving 110g/4oz* 9
Chocolate Sensations, Chocolate Cherry (Heinz Weight Watchers) *serving 110g/4oz* 5
Chocolate Sensations, Chocolate Orange (Heinz Weight Watchers) *serving 110g/4oz* 5
Chocolate Soufflé, Chilled (Tesco) *serving 110g/4oz* 17
Chocolate Sponge Pudding (Tesco) *serving 110g/4oz* 14
Chocolate Sponge Pudding (Waitrose) *serving 110g/4oz* 22
Chocolate Sponge Pudding, Chilled (Asda) *serving 110g/4oz* 15
Chocolate Surprise (Waitrose) *serving 110g/4oz* 5
Chocolate Surprise Dessert (Safeway) *serving 110g/4oz* 11
Choux Buns *serving 110g/4oz* 36
Choux Buns (Marks & Spencer) *serving 110g/4oz* 24
Choux Buns, Dairy Cram (Somerfield) *serving 110g/4oz* 36
Choux Buns, Frozen (Iceland) *serving 110g/4oz* 39
Choux Pastry, Cooked *serving 110g/4oz* 22
Christmas Puddings (4) (Somerfield) *serving 110g/4oz* 6
Christmas Pudding, Luxury (Somerfield) *serving 110g/4oz* 6
Christmas Pudding, Luxury (Tesco) *serving 110g/4oz* 9
Christmas Pudding, Luxury (Waitrose) *serving 110g/4oz* 7
Christmas Pudding, Luxury, with Brandy (Holland & Barrett) *serving 110g/4oz* 7
Christmas Pudding, Mini (Holland & Barrett) *serving 110g/4oz* 10
Christmas Pudding, Rich Fruit (Somerfield) *serving 110g/4oz* 7

Christmas Pudding, Rich Fruit (Tesco) *serving 110g/4oz* 6
Christmas Pudding Round (Waitrose) *serving 110g/4oz* 10
Christmas Pudding, Select (Waitrose) *serving 110g/4oz* 11
Christmas Pudding, Standard (Somerfield) *serving 110g/4oz* 8
Christmas Pudding, Traditional (Holland & Barrett) *serving 110g/4oz* 10
Cinnamon Danish Bar, Frozen (Tesco) *serving 110g/4oz* 37
Cinnamon Danish Whirl (Waitrose) *serving 110g/4oz* 30
Coconut Cream Pudding, Dry Mix, Instant, Made with Low-fat Milk *serving 110g/4oz* 3
Coconut Cream Pudding, Dry Mix, Instant, Made with Whole Milk *serving 110g/4oz* 4
Coffee Brownies (Waitrose) *serving 110g/4oz* 28
Coffee Delice (Marks & Spencer) *serving 110g/4oz* 27
Compote, Summerfruits (Marks & Spencer) *serving 110g/4oz* 0
Cream Horns *serving 110g/4oz* 39
Cream Horns, Dairy (Somerfield) *serving 110g/4oz* 37
Cream Puffs, Prepared from Recipe, Shell with Custard Filling *serving 110g/4oz* 17
Cream Slices (Marks & Spencer) *serving 110g/4oz* 25
Cream Slices, Mini Frozen (Iceland) *serving 110g/4oz* 22
Creamed Rice (Libby's) *serving 110g/4oz* 2
Creamed Rice Pudding (Tesco) *serving 110g/4oz* 2
Crème Brulée, Pot Dessert (Marks & Spencer) *serving 110g/4oz* 32
Creme Caramel (Marks & Spencer) *serving 110g/4oz* 12
Creme Caramel (Safeway) *serving 110g/4oz* 1
Creme Caramel (Somerfield) *serving 110g/4oz* 1
Creme Caramel, Chilled (Tesco) *serving 110g/4oz* 1
Crumble Mix (Somerfield) *serving 110g/4oz* 18
Custard, 2 Egg, Fresh (Iceland) *serving 110g/4oz* 14
Custard, Tinned *serving 110g/4oz* 3
Custard Cluster Pots (Waitrose) *serving 110g/4oz* 6
Custard, Confectioners' *serving 110g/4oz* 6
Custard Devon (Ambrosia) (CPC) *serving 110g/4oz* 3
Custard, Devon, Low Fat (Ambrosia) (CPC) *serving 110g/4oz* 1
Custard, Devon, Ready to Serve Pot (Ambrosia) (CPC) *serving 110g/4oz* 3

Flan Case Sponge *serving 110g/4oz*	7
Flan Lemon Cream, Frozen (Marks & Spencer) *serving 110g/4oz*	31
Flan Pastry with Fruit *serving 110g/4oz*	5
Flan Sponge with Fruit *serving 110g/4oz*	2
Florentines, Mini (Waitrose) *serving 110g/4oz*	32
Fools, Low Fat (Sainsbury's) *serving 110g/4oz*	4
Fromage Frais Lite, Pot Dessert (Marks & Spencer) *serving 110g/4oz*	0
Fruit Cocktail, Luxury, Sherry (St Ivel) *serving 110g/4oz*	9
Fruit Finger Danish (Waitrose) *serving 110g/4oz*	17
Fruit Fool, Real (Safeway) *serving 110g/4oz*	12
Fruit Fool, Rhubarb (Somerfield) *serving 110g/4oz*	7
Fruit Fool, Strawberry (Somerfield) *serving 110g/4oz*	6
Fruit Jelly, Ready to Eat (Rowntree) *serving 110g/4oz*	0
Fruit Jelly, Tropical, Pot Dessert (Marks & Spencer) *serving 110g/4oz*	5
Fruit Pudding, Mixed Grill (Somerfield) *serving 110g/4oz*	12
Fruit Strudel, Woodland, Frozen (Tesco) *serving 110g/4oz*	14
Gateaux: *see under* Cakes, Gateaux, Sweet Pies & Tarts	
Golden Puffs (Somerfield) *serving 110g/4oz*	12
Gooseberry Crumble (Waitrose) *serving 110g/4oz*	10
Gooseberry Fool (Waitrose) *serving 110g/4oz*	12
Gooseberry Fool Lite, Pot Dessert (Marks & Spencer) *serving 110g/4oz*	5
Gooseberry Fruit Fool (Safeway) *serving 110g/4oz*	12
Gooseberry Fruit Fool (4 Pack), Chilled (Tesco) *serving 110g/4oz*	9
Greek Pastries *serving 110g/4oz*	19
Iced Bar, Luxury (Somerfield) *serving 110g/4oz*	11
Iced Dessert, Raspberry Swirl (Heinz Weight Watchers) *serving 110g/4oz*	3
Iced Dessert, Vanilla Flavour (Heinz Weight Watchers) *serving 110g/4oz*	5
Instant Dessert, Made with Semi-Skimmed Milk *serving 110g/4oz*	5
Instant Dessert, Made with Skimmed Milk *serving 110g/4oz*	4
Instant Dessert, Made with Whole Milk *serving 110g/4oz*	7

Lemon Meringue Pot Dessert (Marks & Spencer) *serving 110g/4oz* 16
Lemon Meringue Roulade, Frozen (Marks & Spencer) *serving 110g/4oz* 14
Lemon Pot Dessert (Marks & Spencer) *serving 110g/4oz* 18
Lemon Pudding, Dry Mix, Instant, Made with Low-fat Milk *serving 110g/4oz* 2
Lemon Pudding, Dry Mix, Instant, Made with Whole Milk *serving 110g/4oz* 3
Lemon Pudding, Ready to Eat *serving 110g/4oz* 3
Lemon Sorbet, Frozen (Tesco) *serving 110g/4oz* 0
Lemon Syllabub, Chilled (Tesco) *serving 110g/4oz* 16
Mango Smoothy Pot Dessert (Marks & Spencer) *serving 110g/4oz* 0
Marzipan, White (Somerfield) *serving 110g/4oz* 17
Meringue *serving 110g/4oz* 0
Meringue, Choc & Nut, Frozen (Marks & Spencer) *serving 110g/4oz* 26
Meringue with Cream *serving 110g/4oz* 26
Meringue Dessert, Hazelnut, Frozen (Tesco) *serving 110g/4oz* 26
Meringue, Fresh Cream (Waitrose) *serving 110g/4oz* 17
Meringue Nests (Somerfield) *serving 110g/4oz* 1
Meringues (Marks & Spencer) *serving 110g/4oz* 32
Meringues, Dairy Cream (Somerfield) *serving 110g/4oz* 25
Meringues Pack (Marks & Spencer) *serving 110g/4oz* 0
Milk Puddings (e.g. Sago, Rice, Semolina, Tapioca) Made with Semi-Skimmed Milk *serving 110g/4oz* 2
Milk Puddings (e.g. Sago, Rice, Semolina, Tapioca), Made with Skimmed Milk *serving 110g/4oz* 0
Milk Puddings (e.g. Sago, Rice, Semolina, Tapioca) Made with Whole Milk *serving 110g/4oz* 5
Milk & White Chocolate Bavarois, Chilled (Tesco) *serving 110g/4oz* 13
Mille Feuille Slice (Somerfield) *serving 110g/4oz* 0
Mincemeat *serving 110g/4oz* 5
Mincemeat, Luxury (Somerfield) *serving 110g/4oz* 3
Mincemeat, Traditional (Somerfield) *serving 110g/4oz* 3

Mousse, Dairy Milk (Cadbury's) *serving 110g/4oz* 10
Mousse, Low Fat Chocolate (Cadbury's) *serving 110g/4oz* 5
Mousse, Children's Chocolate, Chilled (Tesco) *serving 110g/4oz* 8
Mousse, Chocolate *serving 110g/4oz* 6
Mousse, Chocolate (Heinz Weight Watchers) *serving 110g/4oz* 4
Mousse, Chocolate (Safeway) *serving 110g/4oz* 11
Mousse, Chocolate (Somerfield) *serving 110g/4oz* 8
Mousse, Chocolate, Chilled (Iceland) *serving 110g/4oz* 8
Mousse, Chocolate, Chilled (Tesco) *serving 110g/4oz* 8
Mousse, Chocolate, Roll (Somerfield) *serving 110g/4oz* 21
Mousse, Chocolate Flavoured, Frozen (Iceland) *serving 110g/4oz* 8
Mousse, Chocolate Sensations, Chocolate Mousse Dessert (Heinz Weight Watchers) *serving 110g/4oz* 3
Mousse, Frozen *serving 110g/4oz* 8
Mousse, Fruit *serving 110g/4oz* 6
Mousse, Milk Chocolate, Chilled (Tesco) *serving 110g/4oz* 8
Mousse, Monster (Safeway) *serving 110g/4oz* 9
Mousse, Pot Desserts, Chocolate Cream (Marks & Spencer) *serving 110g/4oz* 29
Mousse, Pot Desserts, Lemon Mousse (Marks & Spencer) *serving 110g/4oz* 20
Mousse, Pot Desserts, Strawberry Mousse (Marks & Spencer) *serving 110g/4oz* 19
Mousse, Pot Desserts Lite, Chocolate Mousse (Marks & Spencer) *serving 110g/4oz* 3
Mousse, Pot Desserts Lite, Citrus Lay Mousse (Marks & Spencer) *serving 110g/4oz* 2
Mousse, Pot Desserts Lite, Coffee Mousse (Marks & Spencer) *serving 110g/4oz* 5
Mousse, Pot Desserts Lite, Lemon Mousse (Marks & Spencer) *serving 110g/4oz* 4
Mousse, Pot Desserts Lite, Raspberry Mousse (Marks & Spencer) *serving 110g/4oz* 4
Mousse, Pot Desserts Lite, Strawberry Mousse (Marks & Spencer) *serving 110g/4oz* 4
Mousse, Raspberry Ripple, Basics (Somerfield) *serving 110g/4oz* 6

Mousse, Raspberry Ripple, Frozen (Asda) *serving 110g/4oz* 6
Mousse, Raspberry Ripple Flavour, Frozen (Iceland) *serving 110g/4oz* 6
Mousse, Savers Chocolate (Safeway) *serving 110g/4oz* 8
Mousse, Shape Mousse, Strawberry *serving 110g/4oz* 3
Mousse, Strawberry, Frozen (Iceland) *serving 110g/4oz* 7
Mousse, Strawberry Flavoured Dessert, Frozen (Iceland) *serving 110g/4oz* 7
Mousse, Suchard Rich Chocolate Flavour Mousse Mix, Made with Whole Milk (Kraft) *serving 110g/4oz* 7
Mousse, Suchard Rich Chocolate Flavour Mousse Mix, Made with Skimmed Milk (Kraft) *serving 110g/4oz* 5
Mousse, Terry's Chocolate Orange Flavour Mousse Mix, Made with Skimmed Milk (Kraft) *serving 110g/4oz* 5
Mousse, Terry's Chocolate Orange Flavour Mousse Mix, Made with Whole Milk (Kraft) *serving 110g/4oz* 7
Mousse, White Chocolate, Chilled (Iceland) *serving 110g/4oz* 11
Pancakes, American Chocolate (Waitrose) *serving 110g/4oz* 14
Pancakes, Blueberry, Prepared from Recipe *serving 110g/4oz* 10
Pancakes, Bread, Maple & Raisin (Marks & Spencer) *serving 110g/4oz* 6
Pancakes, Buttermilk, Prepared from Recipe *serving 110g/4oz* 10
Pancakes, Maple (Waitrose) *serving 110g/4oz* 6
Pancakes, Plain, Frozen, Ready to Heat (includes Buttermilk) *serving 110g/4oz* 4
Pancakes, Plain, Prepared from Recipe *serving 110g/4oz* 11
Pancakes, Raisin & Lemon (Waitrose) *serving 110g/4oz* 3
Pancakes, Savoury, *see under* Pies, Pastries, Flans & Quiches
Pancakes, Sultana & Syrup (Waitrose) *serving 110g/4oz* 11
Pancakes, Sweet *serving 110g/4oz* 18
Pancakes, Sweet, Made with Skimmed Milk *serving 110g/4oz* 15
Pancakes, Syrup & Sultana (Somerfield) *serving 110g/4oz* 7
Pannacotta, Pot Dessert (Marks & Spencer) *serving 110g/4oz* 26
Pavlovas, Mini, Chocolate, Frozen (Iceland) *serving 110g/4oz* 5
Peach with Creme Fraiche, Pot Dessert (Marks & Spencer) *serving 110g/4oz* 15
Pineapple Sponge Pudding (Waitrose) *serving 110g/4oz* 15

Pineapple Upside Down Pudding, Chilled (Asda) *serving 110g/4oz* 12
Pineapple Upside Down Pudding, Frozen (Tesco) *serving 110g/4oz* 16
Plum Pudding, Original (Waitrose) *serving 110g/4oz* 9
Pommes Noisettes, Frozen, Oven Baked (Iceland) *serving 110g/4oz* 11
Pot au Chocolate, Pot Dessert (Marks & Spencer) *serving 110g/4oz* 40
Pot Dessert, Greek with Honey (Marks & Spencer) *serving 110g/4oz* 8
Praline Crunch, Frozen (Marks & Spencer) *serving 110g/4oz* 16
Profiteroles, Chocolate (Tesco) *serving 110g/4oz* 17
Profiteroles (Somerfield) *serving 110g/4oz* 30
Profiteroles (Waitrose) *serving 110g/4oz* 27
Profiteroles, Chocolate, Chilled (Asda) *serving 110g/4oz* 20
Profiteroles, Chocolate Dessert (Sara Lee) *serving 110g/4oz* 28
Profiteroles, Dairy Cream (Somerfield) *serving 110g/4oz* 32
Profiteroles, Dessert, Large (Marks & Spencer) *serving 110g/4oz* 24
Profiteroles, Family, Chilled (Asda) *serving 110g/4oz* 14
Profiteroles, Frozen (Somerfield) *serving 110g/4oz* 30
Profiteroles, Frozen (Waitrose) *serving 110g/4oz* 29
Profiteroles, Mini (Waitrose) *serving 110g/4oz* 39
Profiteroles, with Chocolate Sauce *serving 110g/4oz* 30
Profiteroles with Chocolate Sauce (Somerfield) *serving 110g/4oz* 40
Profiteroles with Chocolate Sauce, Fresh (Iceland) *serving 110g/4oz* 40
Queen of Puddings *serving 110g/4oz* 9
Raspberry, Luxury (St Ivel) *serving 110g/4oz* 7
Raspberry, Standard (St Ivel) *serving 110g/4oz* 6
Raspberry & Apple Turnovers, Dairy Cream (Somerfield) *serving 110g/4oz* 30
Raspberry & Drambuie Meringue (Waitrose) *serving 110g/4oz* 18
Raspberry Fruit Flip (Safeway) *serving 110g/4oz* 6
Raspberry Hearts, Small (Waitrose) *serving 110g/4oz* 20

Raspberry Meringue Pot Dessert (Marks & Spencer) *serving 110g/4oz*	17
Raspberry Pavlova (Somerfield) *serving 110g/4oz*	13
Raspberry Pavlova, Frozen (Asda) *serving 110g/4oz*	13
Raspberry Pavlova, Frozen (Iceland) *serving 110g/4oz*	11
Raspberry Pavlova, Frozen (Marks & Spencer) *serving 110g/4oz*	15
Raspberry Pavlova, Frozen (Tesco) *serving 110g/4oz*	13
Raspberry Pavlova, Party Size, Frozen (Tesco) *serving 110g/4oz*	15
Raspberry Roulade, Large, Frozen (Marks & Spencer) *serving 110g/4oz*	12
Raspberry Royale Pot Dessert (Marks & Spencer) *serving 110g/4oz*	7
Rhubarb Crumble (Marks & Spencer) *serving 110g/4oz*	9
Rhubarb Crumble (Somerfield) *serving 110g/4oz*	7
Rhubarb Crumble (Waitrose) *serving 110g/4oz*	8
Rhubarb Crumble, Chilled (Asda) *serving 110g/4oz*	10
Rhubarb Crumble, Chilled (Tesco) *serving 110g/4oz*	9
Rhubarb Crumble, Frozen (Tesco) *serving 110g/4oz*	12
Rhubarb Crumble, Frozen, Oven Baked (Iceland) *serving 110g/4oz*	9
Rhubarb Fruit Fool, Chilled (Tesco) *serving 110g/4oz*	7
Rhubarb Pot Dessert, Fat Free, (Marks & Spencer) *serving 110g/4oz*	0
Rice, Creamed, Peach Flavour, Ring Pull (Ambrosia) *serving 110g/4oz*	3
Rice, Creamed, Vanilla Flavour, Ring Pull (Ambrosia) *serving 110g/4oz*	3
Rice Dessert, Apple & Strawberry, Creamed, Chilled (Iceland) *serving 110g/4oz*	3
Rice, Mullerice, Caramel, Strawberry & Apple (Muller) *serving 110g/4oz*	3
Rice, Mullerice, Peach & Pineapple (Muller) *serving 110g/4oz*	2
Rice, Mullerice, Raspberry & Raisin & Nutmeg (Muller) *serving 110g/4oz*	3
Rice Pudding, Tinned *serving 110g/4oz*	3
Rice Pudding, Clotted Cream (Marks & Spencer) *serving 110g/4oz*	18

Rice Pudding, Creamed, Ambrosia (CPC) *serving 110g/4oz* 2
Rice Pudding, Creamed, Ready to Serve, Pot, Ambrosia (CPC) *serving 110g/4oz* 3
Rice Pudding, Creamed (Somerfield) *serving 110g/4oz* 2
Rice Pudding, Creamed, with Apple (Ambrosia) *serving 110g/4oz* 3
Rice Pudding, Creamed, with Apricot (Ambrosia) *serving 110g/4oz* 3
Rice Pudding, Healthy Eating, Low Fat (Tesco) *serving 110g/4oz* 1
Rice Pudding, Low Fat, Ambrosia (CPC) *serving 110g/4oz* 1
Rice Pudding, Low Fat, Tinned (Asda) *serving 110g/4oz* 1
Rice Pudding, (Waitrose) *serving 110g/4oz* 15
Rice Pudding, Low Fat (Somerfield) *serving 110g/4oz* 2
Rice Pudding, Low Fat, Ready to Serve Pot, Ambrosia (CPC) *serving 110g/4oz* 1
Rice Pudding, No Added Sugar, Low Fat (Heinz Weight Watchers) *serving 110g/4oz* 2
Rice Pudding, Traditional, with Sultanas & Nutmeg, Ambrosia (CPC) *serving 110g/4oz* 3
Rum Baba *serving 110g/4oz* 9
Rum Baba, Dairy Cream (Somerfield) *serving 110g/4oz* 8
Sago Pudding, Creamed, Ambrosia (CPC) *serving 110g/4oz* 2
Semolina Pudding, Creamed, Ambrosia (CPC) *serving 110g/4oz* 2
Shape Citrus Promise (St Ivel) *serving 110g/4oz* 2
Shape Strawberry Heaven (St Ivel) *serving 110g/4oz* 2
Shape Trialto (St Ivel) *serving 110g/4oz* 2
Soya Dessert, Chocolate Pots (Provamel) *serving 110g/4oz* 3
Soya Dessert, Vanilla Pots (Provamel) *serving 110g/4oz* 2
Sponge, Dairy Cream, Frozen (Asda) *serving 110g/4oz* 17
Sponge, Dairy Cream, Frozen (Tesco) *serving 110g/4oz* 10
Sponge Dessert, Golden Syrup, Chilled (Tesco) *serving 110g/4oz* 10
Sponge Dessert, Lemon Syrup (St Ivel) *serving 110g/4oz* 10
Sponge Dessert, Syrup (St Ivel) *serving 110g/4oz* 10
Sponge Pudding, Apricot with Custard (Somerfield) *serving 110g/4oz* 8
Sponge Pudding, Banana with Toffee Sauce (Heinz) *serving 110g/4oz* 11

Toffee Pecan Crunch, Frozen (Marks & Spencer) *serving 110g/4oz* 10
Toffee Pecan Pavlova, Frozen (Iceland) *serving 110g/4oz* 18
Toffee Surprise Dessert (Safeway) *serving 110g/4oz* 9
Torte, Blackcurrant (Heinz Weight Watchers) *serving 110g/4oz* 3
Torte, Cappucino (Somerfield) *serving 110g/4oz* 25
Torte, Chocolate, Frozen (Tesco) *serving 110g/4oz* 20
Torte, Chocolate Truffle (Waitrose) *serving 110g/4oz* 32
Torte, Fruit Fromage Frais (Waitrose) *serving 110g/4oz* 15
Torte, Lemon (Heinz Weight Watchers) *serving 110g/4oz* 5
Torte, Lemon (Sara Lee) *serving 110g/4oz* 20
Torte, Lemon, Frozen (Tesco) *serving 110g/4oz* 16
Torte, Passion Fruit (Waitrose) *serving 110g/4oz* 14
Torte, Raspberry (Somerfield) *serving 110g/4oz* 13
Torte, Raspberry, Frozen (Tesco) *serving 110g/4oz* 17
Trifle, Caramel (Cadbury's) *serving 110g/4oz* 15
Trifle, Milk Chocolate (Cadbury's) *serving 110g/4oz* 20
Trifle, Cherry (Safeway) *serving 110g/4oz* 11
Trifle, Cherry, Frozen (Tesco) *serving 110g/4oz* 11
Trifle, Chocolate (Safeway) *serving 110g/4oz* 16
Trifle, Chocolate (Somerfield) *serving 110g/4oz* 18
Trifle with Creamy Type Topping *serving 110g/4oz* 5
Trifle with Fresh Cream *serving 110g/4oz* 10
Trifle, Fresh Cream Fruit Cocktail, Chilled (Tesco) *serving 110g/4oz* 9
Trifle, Fresh Cream Fruit, Chilled (Asda) *serving 110g/4oz* 9
Trifle, Fresh Cream Raspberry, Chilled (Tesco) *serving 110g/4oz* 9
Trifle, Fresh Cream Strawberry, Chilled (Asda) *serving 110g/4oz* 9
Trifle, Fruit (Marks & Spencer) *serving 110g/4oz* 10
Trifle, Fruit (Mr Kipling) *serving 110g/4oz* 10
Trifle, Fruit Cocktail (Waitrose) *serving 110g/4oz* 10
Trifle, Fruit Cocktail, Chilled (Iceland) *serving 110g/4oz* 1
Trifle, Fruit Cocktail, Individual, Chilled (Tesco) *serving 110g/4oz* 10
Trifle, Fruit Cocktail Cream, Chilled (Iceland) *serving 110g/4oz* 9
Trifle, Luxury Fruit Cocktail (St Ivel) *serving 110g/4oz* 7
Trifle, Luxury Raspberry (St Ivel) *serving 110g/4oz* 7
Trifle, Luxury Sherry Fruit Cocktail (St Ivel) *serving 110g/4oz* 9

Trifle, Luxury Strawberry (St Ivel) *serving 110g/4oz* 7
Trifle, Pot Desserts, Premium Chocolate (Marks & Spencer) *serving 110g/4oz* 26
Trifle, Pot Desserts, Premium Raspberry (Marks & Spencer) *serving 110g/4oz* 18
Trifle, Pot Desserts, Premium Sherry (Marks & Spencer) *serving 110g/4oz* 17
Trifle, Pot Desserts, Sherry (Marks & Spencer) *serving 110g/4oz* 12
Trifle, Pot Desserts, Strawberry (Marks & Spencer) *serving 110g/4oz* 10
Trifle, Raspberry (Waitrose) *serving 110g/4oz* 9
Trifle, Raspberry, Chilled (Tesco) *serving 110g/4oz* 10
Trifle, Sherry, Chilled (Asda) *serving 110g/4oz* 9
Trifle, Sherry, Frozen (St Ivel) *serving 110g/4oz* 8
Trifle, Sherry Frozen (Tesco) *serving 110g/4oz* 11
Trifle Sponge (Somerfield) *serving 110g/4oz* 2
Trifle Sponge (Waitrose) *serving 110g/4oz* 2
Trifle, Standard Peach (St Ivel) *serving 110g/4oz* 6
Trifle, Standard Raspberry (St Ivel) *serving 110g/4oz* 6
Trifle, Standard Strawberry (St Ivel) *serving 110g/4oz* 6
Trifle, Strawberry (Waitrose) *serving 110g/4oz* 10
Trifle, Strawberry, Chilled (Iceland) *serving 110g/4oz* 11
Trifle, Strawberry, Chilled (Tesco) *serving 110g/4oz* 9
Trifle, Strawberry, Fresh Cream, Chilled (Iceland) *serving 110g/4oz* 9
Trifle, Traditional, Chilled (Tesco) *serving 110g/4oz* 12
Upside Down Pudding, Apricot, Frozen (Tesco) *serving 110g/4oz* 14
Vanilla Danish Bar (Sara Lee) *serving 110g/4oz* 13
Vanilla Pudding, Dry Mix, Instant, Made with Low-fat Milk *serving 110g/4oz* 2
Vanilla Pudding, Dry Mix, Instant, Made with Whole Milk *serving 110g/4oz* 3
Vanilla Pudding, Ready to Eat *serving 110g/4oz* 4
Vanilla Slices (Marks & Spencer) *serving 110g/4oz* 20
Vanilla Smoothy, Pot Dessert (Marks & Spencer) *serving 110g/4oz* 0

White Chocolate Flavour Pot, Ambrosia (CPC) *serving 110g/4oz* 3
Yule Log (Iceland) *serving 110g/4oz* 22
Yule Log (Somerfield) *serving 110g/4oz* 22
Yule Log, Mini Chocolate (Waitrose) *serving 110g/4oz* 18

Dips, Dressings, Savoury Spreads, Pickles & Pâté

NOTE: The standard serving size in this section is 30g/1oz. If you wish to consume more or less than this amount (e.g. if you are going to consume a pack of food whose weight differs from the standard serving size) use the conversion tables on page 386 to calculate the new amount of fat in the food.

Chutney, Apple, Home Made *serving 30g/1oz* 0
Chutney, Apple & Walnut (Waitrose) *serving 30g/1oz* 1
Chutney, Fruit, Mixed *serving 30g/1oz* 0
Chutney, Fruit, Traditional (Marks & Spencer) *serving 30g/1oz* 0
Chutney, Mango (Marks & Spencer) *serving 30g/1oz* 0
Chutney, Mango, Neal's Yard (Holland & Barrett) *serving 30g/1oz* 0
Chutney, Mango, Oily *serving 30g/1oz* 3
Chutney, Mango, Sweet *serving 30g/1oz* 0
Chutney, Tomato *serving 30g/1oz* 0
Chutney, Tomato, Home Made *serving 30g/1oz* 0
Dip, Blue Cheese (Tesco) *serving 30g/1oz* 13
Dip, Cheese & Chive (Somerfield) *serving 30g/1oz* 20
Dip, Cheese & Chive (Tesco) *serving 30g/1oz* 15
Dip, Cheese & Chive, Chilled (Iceland) *serving 30g/1oz* 7
Dip, Cheese & Chive, Fresh (Waitrose) *serving 30g/1oz* 14
Dip, Cheese & Chive, Fresh, Multipack (Somerfield) *serving 30g/1oz* 17
Dip, Cheese & Chive, Standard Multipack (Somerfield) *serving 30g/1oz* 20
Dip, Garlic & Herb (Tesco) *serving 30g/1oz* 12
Dip, Garlic, Onion & Herb (Tesco) *serving 30g/1oz* 14
Dip, Greek Dip Selection Chilled (Iceland) *serving 30g/1oz* 17

Dip, Guacomole (Asda) *serving 30g/1oz* 4
Dip, Guacamole (Marks & Spencer) *serving 30g/1oz* 4
Dip, Guacamole (Tesco) *serving 30g/1oz* 7
Dip, Guacamole (Waitrose) *serving 30g/1oz* 7
Dip, Healthy Eating, Cheese & Chive (Tesco) *serving 30g/1oz* 5
Dip, Healthy Eating, Cucumber & Mint (Tesco) *serving 30g/1oz* 4
Dip, Healthy Eating, Ham & Mustard (Tesco) *serving 30g/1oz* 4
Dip, Healthy Eating, Onion & Garlic (Tesco) *serving 30g/1oz* 5
Dip, Herb & Onion, Fresh Multipack (Somerfield) *serving 30g/1oz* 11
Dip, Hot Spicy & Cool Tomato Salsa (Walkers) *serving 30g/1oz* 0
Dip, Light Fromage Frais, Cheese & Chive (Asda) *serving 30g/1oz* 7
Dip, Light Fromage Frais, Onion & Herb (Asda) *serving 30g/1oz* 0
Dip, Light Fromage Frais, Spicy Chilli (Asda) *serving 30g/1oz* 7
Dip, Light Fromage Frais, Spicy Tikka (Asda) *serving 30g/1oz* 5
Dip, Luxury Selection Pack (Tesco) *serving 30g/1oz* 16
Dip, Luxury Selection Pack, Tropical (Tesco) *serving 30g/1oz* 14
Dip, Mexican (Asda) *serving 30g/1oz* 8
Dip, Mexican (Tesco) *serving 30g/1oz* 4
Dip, Mexican (4), Frijoles Con Crema (St Ivel) *serving 30g/1oz* 3
Dip, Mexican (4), Guacamole (St Ivel) *serving 30g/1oz* 9
Dip, Mexican (4), Salsa (St Ivel) *serving 30g/1oz* 1
Dip, Mexican (4), Soured Cream (St Ivel) *serving 30g/1oz* 7
Dip, Mexican, Round the World Multipack (Somerfield) *serving 30g/1oz* 12
Dip, Onion & Garlic (Somerfield) *serving 30g/1oz* 19
Dip, Onion & Garlic (Tesco) *serving 30g/1oz* 14
Dip, Onion & Garlic, Chilled (Iceland) *serving 30g/1oz* 9
Dip, Onion, Garlic & Herb (Asda) *serving 30g/1oz* 15
Dip, Onion, Garlic & Herb, Standard Multipack (Somerfield) *serving 30g/1oz* 19
Dip, Onion & Herb (Marks & Spencer) *serving 30g/1oz* 10
Dip, Salsa (Asda) *serving 30g/1oz* 1
Dip, Shape 95% Fat Free, Ham & Pineapple *serving 30g/1oz* 1
Dip, Shape 95% Fat Free, Onion & Garlic *serving 30g/1oz* 1
Dip, Shape 95% Fat Free, Tikka *serving 30g/1oz* 1
Dip, Shape 95% Fat Free, Tuna & Sweetcorn *serving 30g/1oz* 1

Dip, Shape Mexican Dips, Frijoles Con Crema *serving 30g/1oz* 3
Dip, Shape Mexican Dips, Guacamole *serving 30g/1oz* 9
Dip, Shape Mexican Dips, Salsa *serving 30g/1oz* 1
Dip, Shape Mexican Dips, Soured Cream *serving 30g/1oz* 7
Dip, Smoked Salmon (Tesco) *serving 30g/1oz* 14
Dip, Sour Cream Based *serving 30g/1oz* 11
Dip, Sour Cream & Chive (Marks & Spencer) *serving 30g/1oz* 8
Dip, Sour Cream & Chive (Somerfield) *serving 30g/1oz* 18
Dip, Soured Cream, Cheese & Chive (St Ivel) *serving 30g/1oz* 12
Dip, Soured Cream & Chives, Standard Multipack (Somerfield) *serving 30g/1oz* 18
Dip, Soured Cream, Onion, Garlic & Herb (St Ivel) *serving 30g/1oz* 13
Dip, Soured Cream, Blue Cheese (St Ivel) *serving 30g/1oz* 13
Dip, Soured Cream, Cheese & Chive (St Ivel) *serving 30g/1oz* 12
Dip, Soured Cream, Onion & Garlic (St Ivel) *serving 30g/1oz* 13
Dip, Soured Cream, Onion, Garlic & Herb *serving 30g/1oz* 13
Dip, Soured Cream, Tikka (St Ivel) *serving 30g/1oz* 12
Dip, Standard Selection Pack, Cheese (Tesco) *serving 30g/1oz* 15
Dip, Standard Selection Pack, Mexican (Tesco) *serving 30g/1oz* 4
Dip, Sweetcorn & Tuna, Fresh, Multipack (Somerfield) *serving 30g/1oz* 14
Dip, Tangy Cheese (Walkers) *serving 30g/1oz* 3
Dip, Thousand Island, Fresh, Multipack (Somerfield) *serving 30g/1oz* 15
Dip, Tikka, Chilled (Iceland) *serving 30g/1oz* 10
Dip, Tikka, Round the World Multipack (Somerfield) *serving 30g/1oz* 18
Dip, Tomato & Basil, Round the World Multipack (Somerfield) *serving 30g/1oz* 16
Dip, Tomato & Herb, Standard Multipack (Somerfield) *serving 30g/1oz* 14
Dip, Tsatsiki, Round the World Multipack (Somerfield) *serving 30g/1oz* 2
Dip, Tuna (Tesco) *serving 30g/1oz* 15
Dressing, Blue Cheese *serving 30g/1oz* 14
Dressing, Blue Cheese (Waitrose) *serving 30g/1oz* 17

Dressing, Blue Cheese Flavoured, Low Fat (Heinz Weight Watchers) *serving 30g/1oz*	1
Dressing, Blue Cheese Light (Crosse & Blackwell) *serving 30g/1oz*	4
Dressing, Blue & Roquefort Cheese *serving 30g/1oz*	16
Dressing, Caesar & Anchovy (Waitrose) *serving 30g/1oz*	7
Dressing, Caesar Style, Low Fat (Heinz Weight Watchers) *serving 30g/1oz*	1
Dressing 'Fat Free' *serving 30g/1oz*	0
Dressing, Four Cheese for Pasta Salads (Crosse & Blackwell) *serving 30g/1oz*	6
Dressing, French *serving 30g/1oz*	15
Dressing, French (Marks & Spencer) *serving 30g/1oz*	19
Dressing, French (Somerfield) *serving 30g/1oz*	19
Dressing, French (Waitrose) *serving 30g/1oz*	12
Dressing, French, Chilled (Tesco) *serving 30g/1oz*	20
Dressing, French, Common Regular with Salt *serving 30g/1oz*	12
Dressing, French, Diet Lo Fat 5 Cal/Tsp *serving 30g/1oz*	2
Dressing, French, Home Made *serving 30g/1oz*	21
Dressing, French, Lite (Marks & Spencer) *serving 30g/1oz*	12
Dressing, French, Oil Free (Waistline) *serving 30g/1oz*	0
Dressing, Fromage Frais Light (Crosse & Blackwell) *serving 30g/1oz*	3
Dressing, Fromage Frais Lite (Marks & Spencer) *serving 30g/1oz*	0
Dressing, Garlic & Herb Light (Crosse & Blackwell) *serving 30g/1oz*	4
Dressing, Garlic Vinaigrette (Tesco) *serving 30g/1oz*	12
Dressing, Honey & Mustard (Somerfield) *serving 30g/1oz*	14
Dressing, Honey & Mustard (Waitrose) *serving 30g/1oz*	4
Dressing, Honey & Mustard Light (Crosse & Blackwell) *serving 30g/1oz*	5
Dressing, Home Made, Vinegar & Oil *serving 30g/1oz*	15
Dressing, Italian *serving 30g/1oz*	14
Dressing, Italian (Waitrose) *serving 30g/1oz*	14
Dressing, Italian, Chilled (Tesco) *serving 30g/1oz*	17
Dressing, Italian Common Diet 2 Cal/Tsp *serving 30g/1oz*	3
Dressing, Italian, Common Regular with Salt *serving 30g/1oz*	14
Dressing, Italian, Diet *serving 30g/1oz*	3

Dressing, Italian, Low Fat (Waistline) *serving 30g/1oz*	0
Dressing, Lemon, Garlic & Chive (Waitrose) *serving 30g/1oz*	5
Dressing, Lime & Coriander (Marks & Spencer) *serving 30g/1oz*	12
Dressing, Low Fat *serving 30g/1oz*	1
Dressing, Low Fat (Heinz Weight Watchers) *serving 30g/1oz*	1
Dressing, Mediterranean Tomato for Pasta Salads (Crosse & Blackwell) *serving 30g/1oz*	1
Dressing, Mild Mustard, Low Fat (Heinz Weight Watchers) *serving 30g/1oz*	1
Dressing, Oil Free (Somerfield) *serving 30g/1oz*	0
Dressing, Oil Free, Chilled (Tesco) *serving 30g/1oz*	0
Dressing, Oil & Lemon *serving 30g/1oz*	21
Dressing, Pesto for Pasta Salads (Crosse & Blackwell) *serving 30g/1oz*	2
Dressing, Pesto Salad (Waitrose) *serving 30g/1oz*	4
Dressing, Reduced Calorie (Tesco) *serving 30g/1oz*	3
Dressing, Reduced Calorie (Waistline) *serving 30g/1oz*	2
Dressing, Reduced Calorie, Healthy Selection (Somerfield) *serving 30g/1oz*	3
Dressing, Roast Red Pepper (Marks & Spencer) *serving 30g/1oz*	12
Dressing, Roasted Red Pepper for Pasta Salads (Crosse & Blackwell) *serving 30g/1oz*	1
Dressing, Russian *serving 30g/1oz*	15
Dressing, Russian, Low Calorie *serving 30g/1oz*	1
Dressing, Salsa, Low Fat (Waistline) *serving 30g/1oz*	0
Dressing, Seafood (Marks & Spencer) *serving 30g/1oz*	17
Dressing, Sesame Seed *serving 30g/1oz*	14
Dressing, Sherry Vinaigrette (Waitrose) *serving 30g/1oz*	14
Dressing, Sun Dried Tomato (Waitrose) *serving 30g/1oz*	13
Dressing, Thousand Island *serving 30g/1oz*	11
Dressing, Thousand Island (Somerfield) *serving 30g/1oz*	10
Dressing, Thousand Island (Tesco) *serving 30g/1oz*	13
Dressing, Thousand Island (Waitrose) *serving 30g/1oz*	5
Dressing, Thousand Island, Diet Lo Cal, *serving 30g/1oz*	3
Dressing, Thousand Island, Low Fat (Heinz Weight Watchers) *serving 30g/1oz*	1
Dressing, Thousand Island, Reduced Calorie *serving 30g/1oz*	5

Dressing, Tomato & Basil, Fat Free (Marks & Spencer) *serving 30g/1oz*	0
Dressing, Vinaigrette, French Herbs (Lesieur) *serving 30g/1oz*	8
Dressing, Vinaigrette, Garlic & Herbs (Lesieur) *serving 30g/1oz*	8
Dressing, Vinaigrette, Oil Free (Waistline) *serving 30g/1oz*	0
Dressing, Vinaigrette, Original Fat Free (Lesieur) *serving 30g/1oz*	0
Dressing, Vinaigrette, Traditional Mustard (Lesieur) *serving 30g/1oz*	8
Dressing, Virtually Oil Free, Healthy Selection (Somerfield) *serving 30g/1oz*	0
Hollandaise Sauce, Home Made *serving 30g/1oz*	23
Houmous (Asda) *serving 30g/1oz*	8
Houmous (Safeway) *serving 30g/1oz*	13
Houmous, Greek Dip Selection, Chilled (Tesco) *serving 30g/1oz*	8
Houmous, Reduced Fat (Safeway) *serving 30g/1oz*	5
Houmous, Reduced Fat (Marks & Spencer) *serving 30g/1oz*	6
Houmous, Reduced Fat (Sainsbury's) *serving 30g/1oz*	5
Ketchup, Mushroom (Burgess Food Frontiers) *serving 30g/1oz*	0
Ketchup, Tomato *serving 30g/1oz*	0
Ketchup, Tomato (Heinz) *serving 30g/1oz*	0
Ketchup, Tomato (Marks & Spencer) *serving 30g/1oz*	0
Ketchup, Tomato (Somerfield) *serving 30g/1oz*	0
Ketchup, Tomato (Tesco) *serving 30g/1oz*	0
Ketchup, Tomato Basics (Somerfield) *serving 30g/1oz*	0
Ketchup, Tomato, Healthy Selection (Somerfield) *serving 30g/1oz*	0
Ketchup, Tomato, Low Sugar & Salt (Asda) *serving 30g/1oz*	0
Ketchup, Tomato, Reduced Calorie (Waitrose) *serving 30g/1oz*	0
Marinade, Honey & Mustard (Marks & Spencer) *serving 30g/1oz*	5
Mayonnaise *serving 30g/1oz*	23
Mayonnaise (Marks & Spencer) *serving 30g/1oz*	25
Mayonnaise (Tesco) *serving 30g/1oz*	24
Mayonnaise (Waitrose) *serving 30g/1oz*	23
Mayonnaise, Basics (Somerfield) *serving 30g/1oz*	24

Mayonnaise, Classic Continental (Heinz) *serving 30g/1oz* 24
Mayonnaise, French Style (Marks & Spencer) *serving 30g/1oz* 24
Mayonnaise, Garlic (Waitrose) *serving 30g/1oz* 23
Mayonnaise, Grocery (Iceland) *serving 30g/1oz* 24
Mayonnaise, Dijonnaise (Hellmann's) *serving 30g/1oz* 6
Mayonnaise, Garlic (Hellmann's) *serving 30g/1oz* 9
Mayonnaise, Light (Hellmann's) *serving 30g/1oz* 9
Mayonnaise, Real (Hellmann's) *serving 30g/1oz* 24
Mayonnaise, Home Made *serving 30g/1oz* 26
Mayonnaise, Lemon (Waitrose) *serving 30g/1oz* 23
Mayonnaise, Light (Heinz) *serving 30g/1oz* 9
Mayonnaise, Lite (Marks & Spencer) *serving 30g/1oz* 9
Mayonnaise, Mustard (Waitrose) *serving 30g/1oz* 23
Mayonnaise, Real (Burgess Food Frontiers) *serving 30g/1oz* 23
Mayonnaise, Reduced Calorie *serving 30g/1oz* 8
Mayonnaise, Reduced Calorie, Grocery (Iceland) *serving 30g/1oz* 9
Mayonnaise, Reduced Calorie (Tesco) *serving 30g/1oz* 8
Mayonnaise, Reduced Calorie (Waitrose) *serving 30g/1oz* 9
Mayonnaise, Reduced Calorie, Healthy Selection (Somerfield) *serving 30g/1oz* 10
Mayonnaise Style Dressing, 90% Fat Free (Heinz Weight Watchers) *serving 30g/1oz* 3
Mustard, Dijon (Marks & Spencer) *serving 30g/1oz* 3
Mustard, Dijon (Tesco) *serving 30g/1oz* 3
Mustard, Dijon (Waitrose) *serving 30g/1oz* 3
Mustard, English (Marks & Spencer) *serving 30g/1oz* 5
Mustard, English (Tesco) *serving 30g/1oz* 2
Mustard, French (Waitrose) *serving 30g/1oz* 1
Mustard & Honey (Heinz) *serving 30g/1oz* 10
Mustard Piccalilli (Tesco) *serving 30g/1oz* 1
Mustard Piccalilli (Waitrose) *serving 30g/1oz* 0
Mustard, Powder, Made Up *serving 30g/1oz* 4
Mustard, Smooth *serving 30g/1oz* 2
Mustard, Strong English (Waitrose) *serving 30g/1oz* 5
Mustard & Tarragon (Tesco) *serving 30g/1oz* 12
Mustard, Wholegrain *serving 30g/1oz* 3

Mustard, Wholegrain (Tesco) *serving 30g/1oz*	3
Mustard, Wholegrain (Waitrose) *serving 30g/1oz*	1
Paste, Beef (Princes) *serving 30g/1oz*	4
Paste, Beef (Somerfield) *serving 30g/1oz*	6
Paste, Beef (Tesco) *serving 30g/1oz*	4
Paste, Beef & Ham (Somerfield) *serving 30g/1oz*	5
Paste, Beef & Onion (Tesco) *serving 30g/1oz*	3
Paste, Chicken (Princes) *serving 30g/1oz*	3
Paste, Chicken (Somerfield) *serving 30g/1oz*	5
Paste, Chicken (Tesco) *serving 30g/1oz*	5
Paste, Chicken & Ham (Princes) *serving 30g/1oz*	5
Paste, Chicken & Ham (Tesco) *serving 30g/1oz*	6
Paste, Chicken & Stuffing (Princes) *serving 30g/1oz*	5
Paste, Corned Beef (Princes) *serving 30g/1oz*	4
Paste, Crab (Princes) *serving 30g/1oz*	1
Paste, Crab (Somerfield) *serving 30g/1oz*	3
Paste, Crab (Tesco) *serving 30g/1oz*	2
Paste, Fish *serving 30g/1oz*	3
Paste, Salmon & Shrimp (Somerfield) *serving 30g/1oz*	12
Paste, Sardine & Tomato (Princes) *serving 30g/1oz*	1
Paste, Sardine & Tomato (Somerfield) *serving 30g/1oz*	4
Paste, Sardine & Tomato (Tesco) *serving 30g/1oz*	2
Paste, Tomato Basil (Waitrose) *serving 30g/1oz*	0
Paste, Tuna & Mayonnaise (Princes) *serving 30g/1oz*	4
Paste, Tuna & Mayonnaise (Somerfield) *serving 30g/1oz*	13
Paste, Tuna & Mayonnaise (Tesco) *serving 30g/1oz*	5
Pâté, Ardennes (Somerfield) *serving 30g/1oz*	9
Pâté, Broccoli & Stilton (Cauldron Foods) *serving 30g/1oz*	8
Pâté, Brussels (Somerfield) *serving 30g/1oz*	9
Pâté, Brussels Fat Reduced (Somerfield) *serving 30g/1oz*	4
Pâté, Chicken (Somerfield) *serving 30g/1oz*	6
Pâté, Chicken Liver (Marks & Spencer) *serving 30g/1oz*	6
Pâté, Chicken Liver, Tinned *serving 30g/1oz*	4
Pâté, Crab (Marks & Spencer) *serving 30g/1oz*	5
Pâté de Campagne (Somerfield) *serving 30g/1oz*	11
Pâté de Foie Gras, Tinned (Goose Liver Pate) Smoked *serving 30g/1oz*	13

Pâté de Forestier (Somerfield) *serving 30g/1oz*	9
Pâté, Duck & Orange (Marks & Spencer) *serving 30g/1oz*	6
Pâté, Duck & Orange (Somerfield) *serving 30g/1oz*	9
Pâté, Duck with Port Wine (Somerfield) *serving 30g/1oz*	10
Pâté, Farmhouse (Marks & Spencer) *serving 30g/1oz*	5
Pâté, Farmhouse with Fresh Mushrooms (Somerfield) *serving 30g/1oz*	8
Pâté Forestiere (Marks & Spencer) *serving 30g/1oz*	8
Pâté, Garlic (Somerfield) *serving 30g/1oz*	9
Pâté, Garlic & Liver (Somerfield) *serving 30g/1oz*	8
Pâté, Goose Liver, Smoked, Tinned *serving 30g/1oz*	13
Pâté, Healthy Selection, Reduced Fat, Ardennes (Somerfield) *serving 30g/1oz*	4
Pâté, Healthy Selection, Reduced Fat, Brussels (Somerfield) *serving 30g/1oz*	4
Pâté, Liver & Bacon, Spreading (Somerfield) *serving 30g/1oz*	6
Pâté, Liver, Spreading (Somerfield) *serving 30g/1oz*	7
Pâté, Liver with Garlic, Spreading (Somerfield) *serving 30g/1oz*	7
Pâté, Mackerel (Somerfield) *serving 30g/1oz*	6
Pâté, Mackerel Smoked *serving 30g/1oz*	10
Pâté, Mackerel Smoked (Marks & Spencer) *serving 30g/1oz*	10
Pâté, Mushroom (Somerfield) *serving 30g/1oz*	4
Pâté, Provencal (Somerfield) *serving 30g/1oz*	9
Pâté, Red Pepper (Cauldron Foods) *serving 30g/1oz*	4
Pâté, Salmon, Spreading (Somerfield) *serving 30g/1oz*	5
Pâté, Smoked Salmon (Somerfield) *serving 30g/1oz*	6
Pâté, Tuna *serving 30g/1oz*	6
Pâté, Tuna (Marks & Spencer) *serving 30g/1oz*	11
Pâté, Tuna (Somerfield) *serving 30g/1oz*	7
Pâté, Tuna & Tomato (Marks & Spencer) *serving 30g/1oz*	1
Pâté, Turkey with Double Cream & Brandy (Bernard Matthews) *serving 30g/1oz*	8
Pâté, Vegetarian, Herb & Pepper (Holland & Barrett) *serving 30g/1oz*	3
Pâté, Vegetarian, Mushroom (Holland & Barrett) *serving 30g/1oz*	3

Pâté, Vegetarian, Retail (Soya, Cereal & Vegetable Based) *serving 30g/1oz*	4
Pâté, Venison with Armagnac (Somerfield) *serving 30g/1oz*	7
Piccalilli *serving 30g/1oz*	0
Piccalilli (Marks & Spencer) *serving 30g/1oz*	0
Piccalilli (Somerfield) *serving 30g/1oz*	0
Piccalilli, Sweet (Tesco) *serving 30g/1oz*	0
Piccalilli, Sweet (Waitrose) *serving 30g/1oz*	0
Pickle, Branston (Nestlé) *serving 30g/1oz*	0
Pickle, Branston Chilli (Nestlé) *serving 30g/1oz*	0
Pickle, Branston Sandwich (Nestlé) *serving 30g/1oz*	0
Pickle, Branston Tomato (Nestlé) *serving 30g/1oz*	0
Pickle, Chilli, Oily *serving 30g/1oz*	7
Pickle, Cucumber Dill *serving 30g/1oz*	0
Pickle, Cucumber Sour *serving 30g/1oz*	0
Pickle, Cucumber Sweet *serving 30g/1oz*	0
Pickle, Lime, Oily *serving 30g/1oz*	5
Pickle, Mango, Oily *serving 30g/1oz*	5
Pickle, Mixed Vegetable *serving 30g/1oz*	0
Pickle, Piccalilli (Heinz) *serving 30g/1oz*	0
Pickle, Ploughman's (Heinz) *serving 30g/1oz*	0
Pickle, Sandwich (Tesco) *serving 30g/1oz*	0
Pickle, Sweet *serving 30g/1oz*	0
Pickle, Sweet (Somerfield) *serving 30g/1oz*	0
Pickle, Sweet (Tesco) *serving 30g/1oz*	0
Pickle, Sweet (Waitrose) *serving 30g/1oz*	0
Pickle, Tangy Sandwich (Heinz) *serving 30g/1oz*	0
Pickle, Tangy Tomato (Heinz) *serving 30g/1oz*	0
Pickled Onions: *see* Onions, Pickled *under* Vegetables & Vegetable Dishes	
Potted Beef, Traditional Yorkshire, Chilled (Tesco) *serving 30g/1oz*	4
Relish, Barbecue Smoke (Heinz) *serving 30g/1oz*	0
Relish, Chilli (Heinz) *serving 30g/1oz*	0
Relish, Corn (Tesco) *serving 30g/1oz*	0
Relish, Corn, Cucumber or Onion *serving 30g/1oz*	0
Relish, Hamburger *serving 30g/1oz*	0

Relish, Hamburger (Burgess Food Frontiers) *serving 30g/1oz*	0
Relish, Hamburger (Heinz) *serving 30g/1oz*	0
Relish, Honey & Mustard (Heinz) *serving 30g/1oz*	0
Relish, Hot Dog *serving 30g/1oz*	0
Relish, Pepper, Olive & Herb (Waitrose) *serving 30g/1oz*	0
Relish, Provencal Style (Heinz) *serving 30g/1oz*	0
Relish, Sweet *serving 30g/1oz*	0
Relish, Sweetcorn (Heinz) *serving 30g/1oz*	0
Relish, Tomato (Tesco) *serving 30g/1oz*	0
Relish, Tomato & Chilli (Tesco) *serving 30g/1oz*	0
Salad Cream *serving 30g/1oz*	9
Salad Cream (Burgess Food Frontiers) *serving 30g/1oz*	8
Salad Cream (Iceland) *serving 30g/1oz*	9
Salad Cream (Heinz) *serving 30g/1oz*	8
Salad Cream, Light (Heinz) *serving 30g/1oz*	6
Salad Cream (Marks & Spencer) *serving 30g/1oz*	11
Salad Cream (Somerfield) *serving 30g/1oz*	9
Salad Cream (Waitrose) *serving 30g/1oz*	8
Salad Cream, Premium (Tesco) *serving 30g/1oz*	8
Salad Cream, Reduced Calorie *serving 30g/1oz*	5
Salad Cream, Sunflower (Somerfield) *serving 30g/1oz*	9
Sandwich Fillers, Bacon & Tomato (Heinz) *serving 30g/1oz*	4
Sandwich Fillers, Chicken in Light Mayonnaise (Heinz) *serving 30g/1oz*	5
Sandwich Fillers, Curried Chicken (Heinz) *serving 30g/1oz*	4
Sandwich Fillers, Ham (Heinz) *serving 30g/1oz*	5
Sandwich Fillers, Ham & Cheese (Heinz) *serving 30g/1oz*	4
Sandwich Fillers, Pink Salmon & Cucumber (Heinz) *serving 30g/1oz*	4
Sandwich Fillers, Prawn & Salad Vegetables (Heinz) *serving 30g/1oz*	2
Sandwich Fillers, Tuna (Heinz) *serving 30g/1oz*	4
Sandwich Filling, Tuna Nicoise (Waitrose) *serving 30g/1oz*	4
Seafood Sauce, Reduced Calorie (Tesco) *serving 30g/1oz*	5
Spread, Beef (Somerfield) *serving 30g/1oz*	3
Spread, Beef (Tesco) *serving 30g/1oz*	3
Spread, Chicken (Tesco) *serving 30g/1oz*	4

Spread, Chicken, Tinned *serving 30g/1oz*	4
Spread, Chicken, Potted (Marks & Spencer) *serving 30g/1oz*	3
Spread, Chicken Salad Sandwich *serving 30g/1oz*	4
Spread, Chicken Tikka (Tesco) *serving 30g/1oz*	6
Spread, Garlic & Herb Cheese, Prepacked (Asda) *serving 30g/1oz*	6
Spread, Healthy Eating, Low Fat with Cheese (Tesco) *serving 30g/1oz*	3
Spread, Mackerel, Smoked (Tesco) *serving 30g/1oz*	8
Spread, Pork Cured Ham & Cheese *serving 30g/1oz*	6
Spread, Pork Cured Ham Salad *serving 30g/1oz*	5
Spread, Sandwich *serving 30g/1oz*	3
Spread, Sandwich (Tesco) *serving 30g/1oz*	3
Spread, Sandwich, Cucumber (Heinz) *serving 30g/1oz*	3
Spread, Sandwich, Mild (Heinz) *serving 30g/1oz*	6
Spread, Sandwich, Original (Heinz) *serving 30g/1oz*	4
Spread, Sandwich, Pork & Beef *serving 30g/1oz*	5
Spread, Sardine & Tomato (Tesco) *serving 30g/1oz*	3
Spread, Tofu *serving 30g/1oz*	6
Taramasalata *serving 30g/1oz*	16
Taramasalata (Safeway) *serving 30g/1oz*	23
Taramasalata (Marks & Spencer) *serving 30g/1oz*	15
Taramasalata (Waitrose) *serving 30g/1oz*	15
Taramasalata, Chilled, (Tesco) *serving 30g/1oz*	14
Taramasalata, Greek Dip Selection, Chilled (Tesco) *serving 30g/1oz*	15
Taramasalata (Greek Style Starter) (Asda) *serving 30g/1oz*	15
Taramasalata, Premium, Chilled (Tesco) *serving 30g/1oz*	14
Taramasalata, Reduced Fat (Sainsbury's) *serving 30g/1oz*	10
Taramasalata, Reduced Fat (Waitrose) *serving 30g/1oz*	10
Taramasalata, Supreme (Waitrose) *serving 30g/1oz*	12
Toast Toppers, Chicken & Mushroom (Heinz) *serving 30g/1oz*	0
Toast Toppers, Ham & Cheese (Heinz) *serving 30g/1oz*	1
Toast Toppers, Mushrooom & Bacon (Heinz) *serving 30g/1oz*	1
Yeast Extract (Tesco) *serving 30g/1oz*	0

Yoghurts: *see under* Yoghurt & Fromage Frais

Eggs

NOTE: The standard serving size in this section is 110g/4oz. If you wish to consume more or less than this amount (e.g. if you are going to consume a pack of food whose weight differs from the standard serving size) use the conversion tables on page 386 to calculate the new amount of fat in the food.

Colombian Blacktail Eggs (Waitrose) *serving 110g/4oz*	11
Duck Egg, Whole, Fresh, Raw *serving 110g/4oz*	15
Egg Fu Yung *serving 110g/4oz*	23
Egg Mayonnaise (Marks & Spencer) *serving 110g/4oz*	22
Egg & Mayonnaise Savoury Bites, Chilled (Tesco) *serving 110g/4oz*	19
Egg Nests with Spinach (Waitrose) *serving 110g/4oz*	3
Egg & Onion (Marks & Spencer) *serving 110g/4oz*	21
Egg Substitute, Frozen *serving 110g/4oz*	12
Egg Substitute, Powder *serving 110g/4oz*	14
Goose Egg, Whole, Fresh, Raw *serving 110g/4oz*	15
Omelette *serving 110g/4oz*	18
Omelette, Cheese *serving 110g/4oz*	25
Omelette, Cheese & Ham, Hot (Marks & Spencer) *serving 110g/4oz*	30
Omelette, Curried Omelette/Egg Masala *serving 110g/4oz*	40
Omelette, Spanish *serving 110g/4oz*	9
Picnic Eggs (Asda) *serving 110g/4oz*	19
Quail Egg, Whole, Fresh, Raw *serving 110g/4oz*	12
Savoury Egg (Asda) *serving 110g/4oz*	21
Omelette *serving 110g/4oz*	18
Savoury Egg, Mini (Asda) *serving 110g/4oz*	23
Scotch Egg (Asda) *serving 110g/4oz*	18
Scotch Egg, (Marks & Spencer) *serving 110g/4oz*	21
Scotch Egg (Waitrose) *serving 110g/4oz*	22
Scotch Egg, Chilled (Iceland) *serving 110g/4oz*	19
Scotch Egg, Chilled (Tesco) *serving 110g/4oz*	19
Scotch Egg, Home Made *serving 110g/4oz*	23
Scotch Egg, Vegetarian (Holland & Barrett) *serving 110g/4oz*	5
Scrambled Eggs *serving 110g/4oz*	18

Soufflé *serving 110g/4oz*	16
Soufflé, Cheese *serving 110g/4oz*	21
Soufflé, Triple Cheese (Waitrose) *serving 110g/4oz*	15
Stuffed Eggs (Waitrose) *serving 110g/4oz*	10
Turkey Egg, Whole, Fresh, Raw *serving 110g/4oz*	13

Fish & Seafood

NOTE: The standard serving size in this section is 110g/4oz. If you wish to consume more or less than this amount (e.g. if you are going to consume a pack of food whose weight differs from the standard serving size) use the conversion tables on page 386 to calculate the new amount of fat in the food.

Abalone, Mixed Species, Fried *serving 110g/4oz*	7
Anchovy, Raw *serving 110g/4oz*	5
Anchovy, Tinned, in Oil *serving 110g/4oz*	11
Anchovy Fillets (Princes) *serving 110g/4oz*	14
Anchovy Fillets (Waitrose) *serving 110g/4oz*	50
Anchovy Fillets & Capers (Princes) *serving 110g/4oz*	15
Arbroath Smokies (Waitrose) *serving 110g/4oz*	1
Bass, Freshwater, Cooked *serving 110g/4oz*	5
Bass, Sea, Cooked *serving 110g/4oz*	3
Bass, Sea, Fresh (Marks & Spencer) *serving 110g/4oz*	9
Blue Marlin, Loin Fillet (Waitrose) *serving 110g/4oz*	0
Bluefish, Raw *serving 110g/4oz*	5
Bluefish, Cooked *serving 110g/4oz*	6
Bream, Red Sea (Waitrose) *serving 110g/4oz*	2
Brill (Waitrose) *serving 110g/4oz*	2
Burbot, Raw *serving 110g/4oz*	1
Burbot, Cooked *serving 110g/4oz*	1
Butterfish, Raw *serving 110g/4oz*	9
Butterfish, Cooked *serving 110g/4oz*	11
Caledonian Fillets, Fresh (Marks & Spencer) *serving 110g/4oz*	13
Carp, Raw *serving 110g/4oz*	6
Carp, Cooked *serving 110g/4oz*	8
Carp, Freshwater (Waitrose) *serving 110g/4oz*	5

Catfish, Raw *serving 110g/4oz* 8
Catfish, Breaded & Fried *serving 110g/4oz* 15
Catfish, Cooked, Dry Heat *serving 110g/4oz* 9
Caviar, Black & Red *serving 110g/4oz* 20
Caviar, Sevruga (Marks & Spencer) *serving 110g/4oz* 31
Cisco, Raw *serving 110g/4oz* 2
Cisco, Smoked *serving 110g/4oz* 13
Clams, Breaded & Fried *serving 110g/4oz* 25
Clam, Meats (Waitrose) *serving 110g/4oz* 1
Clam, Mixed Species, Raw *serving 110g/4oz* 1
Clam, Mixed Species, Tinned, Drained, Solids *serving 110g/4oz* 2
Clam, Mixed Species, Cooked, Moist Heat *serving 110g/4oz* 2
Cockles, Meat (Waitrose) *serving 110g/4oz* 0
Cod, Atlantic, Raw *serving 110g/4oz* 1
Cod, Atlantic, Cooked, Dry Heat *serving 110g/4oz* 1
Cod, Batter, Fresh (Marks & Spencer) *serving 110g/4oz* 16
Cod Bites, Frozen, Oven Baked (Iceland) *serving 110g/4oz* 13
Cod Bites with Cheddar Cheese (Waitrose) *serving 110g/4oz* 15
Cod, Breaded Chunky Fillets (Somerfield) *serving 110g/4oz* 8
Cod, Breaded Fillets, Prepacked (Asda) *serving 110g/4oz* 12
Cod, Breaded Fillets (Waitrose) *serving 110g/4oz* 10
Cod, Breaded Formed Portions (Somerfield) *serving 110g/4oz* 8
Cod, Breaded, Skinless, Boneless Fillets, Frozen, Oven Baked (Iceland) *serving 110g/4oz* 13
Cod in Broccoli Sauce, Frozen (Marks & Spencer) *serving 110g/4oz* 3
Cod Burgers in Breadcrumbs, Prepacked (Asda) *serving 110g/4oz* 15
Cod in Butter Sauce, Frozen (Tesco) *serving 110g/4oz* 5
Cod, Captain's Pie (Birds Eye) *serving 110g/4oz* 5
Cod & Chips, Fresh (Marks & Spencer) *serving 110g/4oz* 6
Cod & Chips, Frozen (Marks & Spencer) *serving 110g/4oz* 6
Cod, Chunky, & Batter, Frozen (Marks & Spencer) *serving 110g/4oz* 9
Cod, Chunky, Breaded (Waitrose) *serving 110g/4oz* 10
Cod, Chunky, in Country Grain Crumb, Frozen, Coated (Tesco) *serving 110g/4oz* 6

Cod, Chunky Fillets (Somerfield) *serving 110g/4oz* 1
Cod, Chunky, in Parsley (Waitrose) *serving 110g/4oz* 19
Cod, Chunky, Skinless in a Light Crispy Breadcrumb Coat, Prepacked (Asda) *serving 110g/4oz* 10
Cod, Chunky Steaks, Crisp Crunch Crumb (Birds Eye) *serving 110g/4oz* 9
Cod, Chunky Steaks, Oven Crispy Batter (Birds Eye) *serving 110g/4oz* 10
Cod in Creamy Tomato Sauce, Prepacked (Asda) *serving 110g/4oz* 7
Cod, Crisp Crunch Crumb Steaks (Birds Eye) *serving 110g/4oz* 15
Cod in Crispy Crumb (Waitrose) *serving 110g/4oz* 8
Cod Fillets (Somerfield) *serving 110g/4oz* 1
Cod Fillets (Waitrose) *serving 110g/4oz* 1
Cod Fillets & Butter, Frozen (Marks & Spencer) *serving 110g/4oz* 6
Cod Fillets, Counter (Asda) *serving 110g/4oz* 1
Cod Fillets, Deep Sea (Waitrose) *serving 110g/4oz* 1
Cod Fillets, Fish Cakes in Crisp Crunch Crumb (Birds Eye) *serving 110g/4oz* 8
Cod Fillets, Fish Fingers, Best Ever (Birds Eye) *serving 110g/4oz* 9
Cod Fillets, Fish Fingers, Frozen (Asda) *serving 110g/4oz* 9
Cod Fillets, Fish Fingers, Frozen, Coated (Tesco) *serving 110g/4oz* 10
Cod Fillets, Fresh (Marks & Spencer) *serving 110g/4oz* 1
Cod Fillets in Crispy Breadcrumbs (Somerfield) *serving 110g/4oz* 14
Cod Fillets in Crispy Breadcrumbs, Healthy Selection, Premium, Skinless & Boneless, Low Fat (Somerfield) *serving 110g/4oz* 5
Cod Fillets, Frozen, Lower Fat (Iceland) *serving 110g/4oz* 7
Cod Fillets in a Light Crispy Bread Coating, Prepacked (Asda) *serving 110g/4oz* 12
Cod Fillets in Ovencrisp Batter, Frozen, Coated (Tesco) *serving 110g/4oz* 17
Cod Fillets in Ovencrisp Breadcrumbs, Frozen, Coated (Tesco) *serving 110g/4oz* 21
Cod Fillets in Ovencrisp Breadcrumbs, Frozen, Oven Baked (Iceland) *serving 110g/4oz* 11

Cod Fillets, Large, Frozen (Marks & Spencer) *serving 110g/4oz* 0
Cod Fillets, Portions, Frozen, Oven Baked (Iceland) *serving 110g/4oz* 1
Cod Fillets, Premium (Waitrose) *serving 110g/4oz* 1
Cod Fillets, Premium, in Fresh Breadcrumbs, Frozen, Coated (Tesco) *serving 110g/4oz* 12
Cod Fillets, Premium, in Litecrisp Batter, Frozen, Oven Baked (Iceland) *serving 110g/4oz* 12
Cod Fillets, Prepacked (Asda) *serving 110g/4oz* 1
Cod Fillets Skinless (Waitrose) *serving 110g/4oz* 1
Cod Fillets, Skinless & Boneless, in Crispy Breadcrumbs (Somerfield) *serving 110g/4oz* 14
Cod Fillets, Skinless, Chunky, Chilled, Coated (Tesco) *serving 110g/4oz* 1
Cod Fillets, Smoked, Chilled (Tesco) *serving 110g/4oz* 0
Cod Fillets, Smoked, Dyed (Waitrose) *serving 110g/4oz* 1
Cod Fillets, Smoked, Prepacked (Asda) *serving 110g/4oz* 1
Cod Fillets, Smoked, Undyed (Waitrose) *serving 110g/4oz* 1
Cod Fillets, Value, Breaded (Waitrose) *serving 110g/4oz* 11
Cod Fish Cakes, Fresh (Marks & Spencer) *serving 110g/4oz* 11
Cod Fish Cakes, Frozen (Asda) *serving 110g/4oz* 8
Cod Fish Cakes, Frozen (Tesco) *serving 110g/4oz* 10
Cod Fish Cakes, Frozen, Grilled (Iceland) *serving 110g/4oz* 8
Cod Fish Cakes, Home Made *serving 110g/4oz* 18
Cod Fish Fingers (Somerfield) *serving 110g/4oz* 9
Cod Fish Fingers (Waitrose) *serving 110g/4oz* 7
Cod Fish Fingers, Fried in Sunflower Oil *serving 110g/4oz* 16
Cod Fish Fingers, Frozen (Marks & Spencer) *serving 110g/4oz* 10
Cod Fish Fingers, Frozen, Grilled (Iceland) *serving 110g/4oz* 8
Cod Fish Fingers, Grilled *serving 110g/4oz* 10
Cod Fish (Frozen) Cod Steak & Chips (Marks & Spencer) *serving 110g/4oz* 7
Cod, Formed, Breaded (Somerfield) *serving 110g/4oz* 8
Cod, Fresh (Marks & Spencer) *serving 110g/4oz* 7
Cod Kiev, Frozen, Oven Bake (Iceland) *serving 110g/4oz* 11
Cod Kiev, Frozen (Tesco) *serving 110g/4oz* 11
Cod Kievs, Frozen (Asda) *serving 110g/4oz* 7

Cod Meal, Main Meal (Marks & Spencer) *serving 110g/4oz*	4
Cod Mornay (Birds Eye) *serving 110g/4oz*	9
Cod & Mushroom in Cheese Sauce, Frozen (Marks & Spencer) *serving 110g/4oz*	3
Cod, Normandy, Frozen, Oven Baked (Iceland) *serving 110g/4oz*	10
Cod Nuggets, Frozen, Coated (Tesco) *serving 110g/4oz*	15
Cod & Parsley in Crumb, Frozen (Marks & Spencer) *serving 110g/4oz*	14
Cod & Parsley Sauce, Frozen (Marks & Spencer) *serving 110g/4oz*	4
Cod in Parsley Sauce, Frozen (Tesco) *serving 110g/4oz*	4
Cod Portions, Crumb, Large, Frozen (Marks & Spencer) *serving 110g/4oz*	12
Cod Portions, Frozen (Asda) *serving 110g/4oz*	0
Cod Portions & Batter, Frozen (Marks & Spencer) *serving 110g/4oz*	11
Cod Portions in Crispy Batter (Somerfield) *serving 110g/4oz*	12
Cod Portions in Crispy Breadcrumbs (Somerfield) *serving 110g/4oz*	12
Cod Portions in Crumb (Waitrose) *serving 110g/4oz*	8
Cod Portions in Parsley Sauce, Frozen (Asda) *serving 110g/4oz*	4
Cod, Premium, in Ovencrisp Crumb, Frozen, Coated (Tesco) *serving 110g/4oz*	8
Cod Roe (Waitrose) *serving 110g/4oz*	2
Cod Roe, Coated in Batter, Fried *serving 110g/4oz*	13
Cod Roe, Fried in Blended Oil *serving 110g/4oz*	13
Cod Roe, Pressed (Princes) *serving 110g/4oz*	3
Cod, Shaped, Skinless, Boned, Portions in Crispy Batter (Somerfield) *serving 110g/4oz*	11
Cod, Skinless, Frozen, Poached (Iceland) *serving 110g/4oz*	1
Cod, Skinless, in Ovencrisp Batter, Frozen, Oven Baked (Iceland) *serving 110g/4oz*	10
Cod Steaks (Birds Eye) *serving 110g/4oz*	0
Cod Steaks (Waitrose) *serving 110g/4oz*	1
Cod Steaks, Crumb, Frozen (Marks & Spencer) *serving 110g/4oz*	9

Cod Steaks in Breadcrumbs, Frozen (Asda) *serving 110g/4oz* 11
Cod Steaks in Breadcrumbs, Frozen, Oven Baked (Iceland) *serving 110g/4oz* 8
Cod Steaks in Butter Sauce (Birds Eye) *serving 110g/4oz* 6
Cod Steaks in Cheese Sauce (Birds Eye) *serving 110g/4oz* 4
Cod Steaks in Crispy Batter, Frozen, Oven Baked (Iceland) *serving 110g/4oz* 12
Cod Steaks in Mushroom Sauce (Birds Eye) *serving 110g/4oz* 5
Cod Steaks in Ovencrisp Batter, Frozen, Coated (Tesco) *serving 110g/4oz* 14
Cod Steaks in Ovencrisp Breadcrumbs, Frozen, Coated (Tesco) *serving 110g/4oz* 8
Cod Steaks, Oven Crispy (Birds Eye) *serving 110g/4oz* 14
Cod Steaks in Parsley Sauce (Birds Eye) *serving 110g/4oz* 4
Cod Steaks in Waferlite Batter, Frozen (Asda) *serving 110g/4oz* 12
Cod, Whole (Waitrose) *serving 110g/4oz* 1
Cod, Whole, Fresh (Marks & Spencer) *serving 110g/4oz* 7
Coley Fillets (Somerfield) *serving 110g/4oz* 1
Coley Fillets (Waitrose) *serving 110g/4oz* 1
Coley Fillets, Bulk (Waitrose) *serving 110g/4oz* 1
Coley Fillets, Chunky (Somerfield) *serving 110g/4oz* 1
Coley Fillets, Frozen (Asda) *serving 110g/4oz* 1
Coley Fillets, Portions, Frozen, Poached in Water (Iceland) *serving 110g/4oz* 0
Coley Portions (Somerfield) *serving 110g/4oz* 1
Coley Portions, Frozen (Asda) *serving 110g/4oz* 0
Coley Steaks (Waitrose) *serving 110g/4oz* 1
Crab, Alaska, King, Cooked, Moist Heat *serving 110g/4oz* 2
Crab, Alaska, King, Imitation, Made from Surimi *serving 110g/4oz* 1
Crab, Baked *serving 110g/4oz* 2
Crab, Blue, Tinned *serving 110g/4oz* 1
Crab, in Brine (Princes) *serving 110g/4oz* 0
Crab Cake *serving 110g/4oz* 19
Crab, Dressed (Princes) *serving 110g/4oz* 6
Crab, Dressed, Fresh (Waitrose) *serving 110g/4oz* 7
Crab, Dressed, in Shell (Waitrose) *serving 110g/4oz* 7

Crab, Dungeness, Cooked, Moist Heat *serving 110g/4oz* 1
Crab, Meat, in Brine (Princes) *serving 110g/4oz* 0
Crab, Seafood Sticks (Waitrose) *serving 110g/4oz* 1
Crab, White Meat, in Brine, Grocery (Iceland) *serving 110g/4oz* 1
Crab, Whole, Cooked (Waitrose) *serving 110g/4oz* 6
Crabsticks *serving 110g/4oz* 0
Crayfish, Mixed Species, Farmed, Cooked, Moist Heat *serving 110g/4oz* 1
Croaker, Atlantic, Cooked, Breaded & Fried *serving 110g/4oz* 14
Cusk, Raw *serving 110g/4oz* 1
Cusk, Cooked, Dry Heat *serving 110g/4oz* 1
Cuttlefish, Mixed Species, Cooked, Moist Heat *serving 110g/4oz* 2
Eel, Mixed Species, Cooked, Dry Heat *serving 110g/4oz* 16
Fish Bake, Crunchy (Birds Eye) *serving 110g/4oz* 7
Fish Balls, Steamed *serving 110g/4oz* 1
Fish Bites (Somerfield) *serving 110g/4oz* 13
Fish Bites, Breaded, Prepacked (Asda) *serving 110g/4oz* 11
Fish Cakes, Breaded, Frozen, Coated (Tesco) *serving 110g/4oz* 5
Fish Cakes, Captain's Coins (Birds Eye) *serving 110g/4oz* 9
Fish Cakes, Fried in Sunflower Oil *serving 110g/4oz* 15
Fish Cakes, Grilled *serving 110g/4oz* 5
Fish Cakes, Value (Birds Eye) *serving 110g/4oz* 8
Fish & Chips for Two, Frozen, Oven Baked (Iceland) *serving 110g/4oz* 10
Fish Curry, Bangladeshi *serving 110g/4oz* 9
Fish Curry & Vegetable, Bangladeshi *serving 110g/4oz* 9
Fish Fillet, Battered or Breaded, Fried *serving 110g/4oz* 14
Fish Fingers (Birds Eye) *serving 110g/4oz* 8
Fish Fingers, Basics (Somerfield) *serving 110g/4oz* 9
Fish Fingers, Oven Crispy (Birds Eye) *serving 110g/4oz* 14
Fish Goujons, Breaded, (Somerfield) *serving 110g/4oz* 19
Fish Goujons, Breaded, Prepacked (Asda) *serving 110g/4oz* 19
Fish Grill, Italian Herb (Birds Eye) *serving 110g/4oz* 9
Fish Grill, Original (Birds Eye) *serving 110g/4oz* 6
Fish Nuggets, Breaded, Salt & Vinegar, Frozen, Oven Baked (Iceland) *serving 110g/4oz* 11

Fish Portions in Breadcrumbs, Frozen (Iceland) *serving 110g/4oz* 9
Fish Portions in Breadcrumbs, Frozen, Oven Baked (Iceland) *serving 110g/4oz* 12
Fish Selection, Gourmet (Waitrose) *serving 110g/4oz* 17
Fish Steaks in Butter Sauce, Frozen, Boil in the Bag (Iceland) *serving 110g/4oz* 8
Fish Steaks in Parsley Sauce, Frozen, Boil in the Bag (Iceland) *serving 110g/4oz* 5
Fish Steaks in Traditional Batter (Birds Eye) *serving 110g/4oz* 10
Fish Sticks, Frozen, Reheated *serving 110g/4oz* 13
Flatfish (Flounder & Sole Species), Cooked, Dry Heat *serving 110g/4oz* 2
Garlic Bordelaise Crumb (Birds Eye) *serving 110g/4oz* 14
Gelfilte Fish, Commercial, Sweet Recipe *serving 110g/4oz* 2
Golden Fishies, Frozen (Bernard Matthews) *serving 110g/4oz* 13
Gravadlax, Fresh (Marks & Spencer) *serving 110g/4oz* 19
Gravlax (Waitrose) *serving 110g/4oz* 13
Grey Mullet (Waitrose) *serving 110g/4oz* 4
Grouper, Mixed Species, Cooked, Dry Heat *serving 110g/4oz* 1
Haddock, in Batter, Fresh (Marks & Spencer) *serving 110g/4oz* 18
Haddock, Batter, Large, Frozen (Marks & Spencer) *serving 110g/4oz* 16
Haddock, Breaded (Waitrose) *serving 110g/4oz* 9
Haddock, Breaded Formed Portions (Somerfield) *serving 110g/4oz* 8
Haddock, Smoked Buttered, (Birds Eye) *serving 110g/4oz* 2
Haddock & Cauliflower, Frozen (Marks & Spencer) *serving 110g/4oz* 7
Haddock & Cauliflower, Main Meal Lite (Marks & Spencer) *serving 110g/4oz* 2
Haddock, Cauliflower & Cheese Bake Prepacked (Asda) *serving 110g/4oz* 6
Haddock & Chips, Fresh (Marks & Spencer) *serving 110g/4oz* 7
Haddock & Chips, Frozen (Marks & Spencer) *serving 110g/4oz* 7
Haddock, Chunky & Batter, Frozen (Marks & Spencer) *serving 110g/4oz* 9

Haddock, Chunky, Crumb, Frozen (Marks & Spencer) *serving 110g/4oz* 12
Haddock, Chunky, Skinless, Crispy Breadcrumb Coating, Prepacked (Asda) *serving 110g/4oz* 10
Haddock, Cooked, Dry Heat *serving 110g/4oz* 1
Haddock, Cordon Bleu, Frozen, Coated (Tesco) *serving 110g/4oz* 10
Haddock, Cutlets, Fresh (Marks & Spencer) *serving 110g/4oz* 1
Haddock Fillets (Somerfield) *serving 110g/4oz* 1
Haddock Fillets, Breaded (Asda) *serving 110g/4oz* 13
Haddock Fillets, Breaded (Waitrose) *serving 110g/4oz* 13
Haddock Fillets, Chilled (Tesco) *serving 110g/4oz* 1
Haddock Fillets, Breaded, Chilled, Coated (Tesco) *serving 110g/4oz* 8
Haddock Fillets, Breaded, Chunky (Somerfield) *serving 110g/4oz* 8
Haddock Fillets, Counter (Asda) *serving 110g/4oz* 1
Haddock Fillets, Healthy Eating, in Ovencrisp, Frozen, Coated (Tesco) *serving 110g/4oz* 6
Haddock Fillet, Prepacked (Asda) *serving 110g/4oz* 1
Haddock Fillet Fish Fingers (Birds Eye) *serving 110g/4oz* 8
Hadock Fillets, Large, Frozen (Marks & Spencer) *serving 110g/4oz* 0
Haddock Fillets in Crispy Breadcrumbs (Somerfield) *serving 110g/4oz* 14
Haddock Fillets in Ovencrisp Breadcrumbs, Frozen, Coated (Tesco) *serving 110g/4oz* 12
Haddock Fillets in Ovencrisp Breadcrumbs, Frozen, Oven Baked (Iceland) *serving 110g/4oz* 12
Haddock Fillets in Ovencrisp Crumb, Frozen (Asda) *serving 110g/4oz* 16
Haddock, Finnan (Waitrose) *serving 110g/4oz* 1
Haddock, Fish 'N' Chips Prepacked (Asda) *serving 110g/4oz* 14
Haddock Fishcake, Fresh (Marks & Spencer) *serving 110g/4oz* 10
Haddock, Formed Breaded (Somerfield) *serving 110g/4oz* 8
Haddock, Fresh (Marks & Spencer) *serving 110g/4oz* 10
Haddock, Goujons (4), Frozen (Asda) *serving 110g/4oz* 13
Haddock Mornay, Frozen (Marks & Spencer) *serving 110g/4oz* 7
Haddock Mornay, Main Meal (Marks & Spencer) *serving 110g/4oz* 8

Haddock Mornay in Crumb, Frozen (Marks & Spencer) *serving 110g/4oz*	13
Haddock & Parsley Bake, Frozen (Marks & Spencer) *serving 110g/4oz*	4
Haddock Portions in Crispy Batter (Somerfield) *serving 110g/4oz*	14
Haddock Portions in Crispy Breadcrumbs (Somerfield) *serving 110g/4oz*	14
Haddock Portions in Crumb (Waitrose) *serving 110g/4oz*	8
Haddock, Premium Breaded Fillets (Waitrose) *serving 110g/4oz*	8
Haddock, Premium Fillets (Waitrose) *serving 110g/4oz*	1
Haddock, Prime Fillets (Waitrose) *serving 110g/4oz*	1
Haddock, Scottish Smoked Fillets, Chilled, Coated (Tesco) *serving 110g/4oz*	3
Haddock, Skinless & Boneless Fillets in Crispy Breadcrumbs (Somerfield) *serving 110g/4oz*	14
Haddock, Skinless Cutlets (Waitrose) *serving 110g/4oz*	0
Haddock, Skinless, Golden (Waitrose) *serving 110g/4oz*	1
Haddock, Small, Frozen (Marks & Spencer) *serving 110g/4oz*	0
Haddock, Smoked *serving 110g/4oz*	1
Haddock, Smoked, & Broccoli (Waitrose) *serving 110g/4oz*	15
Haddock, Smoked, & Egg & Cheese (Waitrose) *serving 110g/4oz*	22
Haddock, Smoked Fillets (Waitrose) *serving 110g/4oz*	1
Haddock, Smoked Fillets, Chilled (Tesco) *serving 110g/4oz*	1
Haddock, Smoked Fillets, Chilled, Coated (Tesco) *serving 110g/4oz*	1
Haddock, Smoked Fillet, Prepacked (Asda) *serving 110g/4oz*	1
Haddock, Smoked Fishcakes (Waitrose) *serving 110g/4oz*	11
Haddock, Smoked, Fresh (Marks & Spencer) *serving 110g/4oz*	1
Haddock, Smoked, Large, Frozen (Marks & Spencer) *serving 110g/4oz*	0
Haddock & Spinach Pie, Frozen (Marks & Spencer) *serving 110g/4oz*	2
Haddock Steaks, Crumb, Frozen (Marks & Spencer) *serving 110g/4oz*	10
Haddock Steaks, Frozen, Poached (Iceland) *serving 110g/4oz*	0

Haddock Steaks in Breadcrumbs, Frozen (Asda) *serving 110g/4oz* 11
Haddock Steaks in Crispy Batter, Frozen, Oven Baked (Iceland) *serving 110g/4oz* 12
Haddock Steaks, Crisp Crunch Crumb (Birds Eye) *serving 110g/4oz* 15
Haddock Steaks in Golden Breadcrumbs, Frozen, Oven Baked (Iceland) *serving 110g/4oz* 9
Haddock Steaks, Oven Crispy (Birds Eye) *serving 110g/4oz* 16
Haddock Steaks in Waferlite Batter, Frozen (Asda) *serving 110g/4oz* 18
Haddock, Whole, Fresh (Marks & Spencer) *serving 110g/4oz* 10
Hake Fillets, Frozen Poached in Water (Iceland) *serving 110g/4oz* 1
Hake Fillets in Crispy Breadcrumbs (Somerfield) *serving 110g/4oz* 12
Hake, Fresh (Marks & Spencer) *serving 110g/4oz* 14
Hake Goujons, Fresh (Marks & Spencer) *serving 110g/4oz* 14
Hake Portions, Breaded, Formed (Somerfield) *serving 110g/4oz* 9
Hake, Whole, Gutted (Waitrose) *serving 110g/4oz* 2
Halibut, Atlantic & Pacific, Cooked, Dry Heat *serving 110g/4oz* 3
Halibut, Fresh (Marks & Spencer) *serving 110g/4oz* 3
Halibut, Greenland Fillets, Chilled (Tesco) *serving 110g/4oz* 2
Halibut Steaks (Waitrose) *serving 110g/4oz* 2
Halibut, Whole (Waitrose) *serving 110g/4oz* 2
Herring, Atlantic, Cooked, Dry Heat *serving 110g/4oz* 13
Herring, Atlantic, Pickled *serving 110g/4oz* 20
Herring, Gutted, Chilled (Tesco) *serving 110g/4oz* 15
Herring, Marina Spiced (Waitrose) *serving 110g/4oz* 15
Herring, Marinated (Princes) *serving 110g/4oz* 12
Herring, Marinated, & Onions (Waitrose) *serving 110g/4oz* 9
Herring Milts (Waitrose) *serving 110g/4oz* 3
Herring, Whole (Waitrose) *serving 110g/4oz* 20
Herring in Crème Fraiche with Herb (Waitrose) *serving 110g/4oz* 32
Herring in Soured Cream, Fresh (Marks & Spencer) *serving 110g/4oz* 14

Herring in Tomato Sauce (Princes) *serving 110g/4oz* 18
Hoki, Breaded, Formed Portions (Somerfield) *serving 110g/4oz* 9
Hoki, Breaded Portions (Waitrose) *serving 110g/4oz* 8
Hoki Fillets, Skinless (Waitrose) *serving 110g/4oz* 1
Hoki in Breadcrumbs, Prepacked (Asda) *serving 110g/4oz* 11
Italiano Bake (Birds Eye) *serving 110g/4oz* 3
Kedgeree *serving 110g/4oz* 10
Kippers, Boned with Butter, Chilled (Tesco) *serving 110g/4oz* 21
Kippers, Boned, Frozen, Grilled (Iceland) *serving 110g/4oz* 17
Kipper Fillets, Butter (Birds Eye) *serving 110g/4oz* 18
Kipper Fillets, Chilled, Ready to Eat, Chilled (Tesco) *serving 110g/4oz* 18
Kipper Fillet, Prepacked (Asda) *serving 110g/4oz* 19
Kippers, Frozen, Boiled (Iceland) *serving 110g/4oz* 17
Kippers, Fried with Butter (Marks & Spencer) *serving 110g/4oz* 17
Kippers, Herring Atlantic *serving 110g/4oz* 14
Kippered Mackerel Fillets, Chilled (Tesco) *serving 110g/4oz* 33
Kippers, Mackerel Fillets (Waitrose) *serving 110g/4oz* 34
Kippers, Manx Kippers (Waitrose) *serving 110g/4oz* 19
Kippers, Oak Smoked, Bag (Waitrose) *serving 110g/4oz* 30
Kippers, Traditionally Oak Smoked, Whole, Chilled (Tesco) *serving 110g/4oz* 17
Langoustines (Waitrose) *serving 110g/4oz* 0
Ling, Raw *serving 110g/4oz* 1
Ling, Cooked, Dry Heat *serving 110g/4oz* 1
Lobster, Dressed, Fresh (Marks & Spencer) *serving 110g/4oz* 26
Lobster, Meat (Waitrose) *serving 110g/4oz* 2
Lobster, Rock, Tails, Raw (Waitrose) *serving 110g/4oz* 1
Lobster, Spiny, Mixed Species, Raw *serving 110g/4oz* 2
Lobster, Spiny, Mixed Species, Cooked, Moist Heat *serving 110g/4oz* 2
Lobster, Whole, cooked (Waitrose) *serving 110g/4oz* 2
Mackerel, Atlantic, Raw *serving 110g/4oz* 15
Mackerel, Atlantic, Cooked, Dry Heat *serving 110g/4oz* 20
Mackerel, Breaded Fillets (Somerfield) *serving 110g/4oz* 31
Mackerel in Curry Sauce (Princes) *serving 110g/4oz* 16

Mackerel Fillets in Brine (Princes) *serving 110g/4oz* 18
Mackerel Fillets in Brine (Waitrose) *serving 110g/4oz* 18
Mackerel Fillets in Oil (Princes) *serving 110g/4oz* 23
Mackerel Fillets in Oil (Waitrose) *serving 110g/4oz* 24
Mackerel Fillets in Sauce (Waitrose) *serving 110g/4oz* 23
Mackerel Fillets in Spicy Tomato (Princes) *serving 110g/4oz* 17
Mackerel Fillets in Tomato (Princes) *serving 110g/4oz* 19
Mackerel in Hot Chilli (Princes) *serving 110g/4oz* 22
Mackerel, Hot Smoked Fillet (Waitrose) *serving 110g/4oz* 33
Mackerel, Hot Smoked Fillets, Frozen, Microwaved (Iceland) *serving 110g/4oz* 26
Mackerel, Jack, Canned, Drained, Solids *serving 110g/4oz* 7
Mackerel in Mustard Sauce (Princes) *serving 110g/4oz* 15
Mackerel, Pacific & Jack, Mixed Species, Cooked, Dry Heat *serving 110g/4oz* 11
Mackerel, Peppered Fillet (Waitrose) *serving 110g/4oz* 32
Mackerel, Smoked Fillets (Waitrose) *serving 110g/4oz* 33
Mackerel, Smoked Fillets, Chilled (Tesco) *serving 110g/4oz* 33
Mackerel, Smoked Fillet, Fresh (Marks & Spencer) *serving 110g/4oz* 36
Mackerel, Smoked, with Peppercorns, Chilled (Tesco) *serving 110g/4oz* 31
Mackerel, Spanish, Cooked, Dry Heat *serving 110g/4oz* 7
Mackerel, Whole (Waitrose) *serving 110g/4oz* 18
Mahi Mahi Fillets (Waitrose) *serving 110g/4oz* 0
Monkfish, Raw *serving 110g/4oz* 2
Monkfish, Cooked, Dry Heat *serving 110g/4oz* 2
Monkfish, Fresh (Marks & Spencer) *serving 110g/4oz* 0
Monkfish, Whole (Waitrose) *serving 110g/4oz* 2
Mullet, Striped, Raw *serving 110g/4oz* 4
Mullet, Striped, Cooked, Dry Heat *serving 110g/4oz* 5
Mussels, Blue, Raw *serving 110g/4oz* 2
Mussels, Blue,Cooked, Moist Heat *serving 110g/4oz* 5
Mussels, Green, Lip (Waitrose) *serving 110g/4oz* 3
Mussels, Live (Waitrose) *serving 110g/4oz* 2
Mussels, Meat (Waitrose) *serving 110g/4oz* 2
Mussels, Moules Bonne Femme (Waitrose) *serving 110g/4oz* 5

Mussels, Moules Bonne Femme, Main Meal (Marks & Spencer) *serving 110g/4oz* 4
Ocean Perch, Atlantic, Raw *serving 110g/4oz* 2
Ocean Perch, Atlantic, Cooked, Dry Heat *serving 110g/4oz* 2
Octopus, Common, Raw *serving 110g/4oz* 1
Octopus, Common, Cooked, Moist Heat *serving 110g/4oz* 2
Oysters, Battered or Breaded, Fried *serving 110g/4oz* 14
Oysters, Fresh/Live (Waitrose) *serving 110g/4oz* 1
Oysters, Native Scottish (Waitrose) *serving 110g/4oz* 1
Perch, Mixed Species, Raw *serving 110g/4oz* 1
Perch, Mixed Species, Cooked, Dry Heat *serving 110g/4oz* 1
Pike, Raw *serving 110g/4oz* 1
Pike, Cooked, Dry Heat *serving 110g/4oz* 1
Pilchards in Brine (Princes) *serving 110g/4oz* 12
Pilchards in Tomato (Princes) *serving 110g/4oz* 8
Plaice, Breadcrumb, Frozen (Marks & Spencer) *serving 110g/4oz* 12
Plaice, Breaded, Chunky (Somerfield) *serving 110g/4oz* 11
Plaice, Breaded Goujons (Somerfield) *serving 110g/4oz* 17
Plaice, Broccoli & Cheese (Waitrose) *serving 110g/4oz* 14
Plaice, & Chips, Frozen (Marks & Spencer) *serving 110g/4oz* 7
Plaice, Chunky, Breaded, Prepacked (Asda) *serving 110g/4oz* 16
Plaice, Chunky in a Light Crispy Breadcrumb Coating, Prepacked (Asda) *serving 110g/4oz* 16
Plaice Filled with Mushroom (Somerfield) *serving 110g/4oz* 7
Plaice Filled with Prawns & Garlic (Somerfield) *serving 110g/4oz* 10
Plaice Fillets (Somerfield) *serving 110g/4oz* 2
Plaice Fillets (Waitrose) *serving 110g/4oz* 2
Plaice Fillets, Chilled (Tesco) *serving 110g/4oz* 2
Plaice Fillets, Filled, Frozen (Marks & Spencer) *serving 110g/4oz* 4
Plaice Fillets, Fresh (Marks & Spencer) *serving 110g/4oz* 2
Plaice Fillets, Frozen (Marks & Spencer) *serving 110g/4oz* 2
Plaice Fillets, Healthy Choice, Frozen (Asda) *serving 110g/4oz* 3
Plaice Fillets in Breadcrumbs, Frozen, Oven Baked (Iceland) *serving 110g/4oz* 19

Plaice Fillets in Crispy Breadcrumbs (Somerfield) *serving 110g/4oz* 17
Plaice Fillets in Crumb (Waitrose) *serving 110g/4oz* 19
Plaice Fillets, Oven Bake (Waitrose) *serving 110g/4oz* 10
Plaice Fillets in Ovencrisp Crumb (4), Frozen (Asda) *serving 110g/4oz* 14
Plaice Fillets, Premium, Whole, Boneless, in Crispy Breadcrumbs (Somerfield) *serving 110g/4oz* 12
Plaice Fillets, Prepacked (Asda) *serving 110g/4oz* 2
Plaice Goujons (Waitrose) *serving 110g/4oz* 12
Plaice in Home baked Breadcrumbs, Frozen, Coated (Tesco) *serving 110g/4oz* 15
Plaice, Large, Breadcrumb, Frozen (Marks & Spencer) *serving 110g/4oz* 14
Plaice Mornay, Main Meal (Marks & Spencer) *serving 110g/4oz* 7
Plaice in Ovencrisp Breadcrumbs, Frozen, Coated (Tesco) *serving 110g/4oz* 14
Plaice in Ovencrisp Crumb (Waitrose) *serving 110g/4oz* 12
Plaice, Premium, Skinless, Boneless, Chunky, Chilled, Coated (Tesco) *serving 110g/4oz* 11
Plaice, Seasoned, Fresh (Marks & Spencer) *serving 110g/4oz* 8
Plaice, Whole (Waitrose) *serving 110g/4oz* 2
Plaice, Whole, Boned, with Lemon Sauce & Prawns in Crumb, Frozen (Asda) *serving 110g/4oz* 5
Plaice, Whole Boned, in Ovencrisp Crumb, Frozen (Asda) *serving 110g/4oz* 10
Plaice, Whole, Boneless, in Breadcrumbs, Frozen, Oven Baked (Iceland) *serving 110g/4oz* 14
Plaice, Whole, Boneless, in Lemon & Parsley, Frozen, Coated (Tesco) *serving 110g/4oz* 11
Plaice, Whole, Chilled (Tesco) *serving 110g/4oz* 2
Plaice, Whole in Ovencrisp Crumb, Frozen, Coated (Tesco) *serving 110g/4oz* 12
Plaice, Whole, Seasoned (Waitrose) *serving 110g/4oz* 11
Pollock, Atlantic, Raw *serving 110g/4oz* 1
Pollock, Atlantic, Cooked, Dry Heat *serving 110g/4oz* 1

Pout, Ocean, Raw *serving 110g/4oz* 1
Pout, Ocean, Cooked, Dry Heat *serving 110g/4oz* 1
Prawn Cocktail (Somerfield) *serving 110g/4oz* 44
Prawn Cocktail, Chilled (Tesco) *serving 110g/4oz* 44
Prawn Cocktail, Fresh (Marks & Spencer) *serving 110g/4oz* 40
Prawn Cocktail, Prepacked (Asda) *serving 110g/4oz* 40
Prawn Cocktail, Reduced Fat (Marks & Spencer) *serving 110g/4oz* 12
Prawn Curry, Frozen (Asda) *serving 110g/4oz* 4
Prawn Curry & Mushroom *serving 110g/4oz* 16
Prawn Curry with Rice (Birds Eye) *serving 110g/4oz* 4
Prawn Curry & Rice, Frozen, Pan Boil (Iceland) *serving 110g/4oz* 10
Prawn Fried Rice (Asda) *serving 110g/4oz* 5
Prawn Linguini (Marks & Spencer) *serving 110g/4oz* 11
Prawn & Mushroom Provencale, Fresh (Marks & Spencer) *serving 110g/4oz* 3
Prawn Rogan Josh (Marks & Spencer) *serving 110g/4oz* 5
Prawn Sweet & Sour (Marks & Spencer) *serving 110g/4oz* 0
Prawns, Balchao (Waitrose) *serving 110g/4oz* 3
Prawns, Black Tiger, Raw (Waitrose) *serving 110g/4oz* 1
Prawns in Breadcrumb, Frozen (Marks & Spencer) *serving 110g/4oz* 14
Prawns & Broccoli & Basil, Main Meal (Marks & Spencer) *serving 110g/4oz* 8
Prawns, & Broccoli Lattice, Frozen Ovenbake (Iceland) *serving 110g/4oz* 15
Prawns, Canadian, Peeled (Waitrose) *serving 110g/4oz* 2
Prawns, Chinese Stir Fry, Frozen, Stir Fried (Iceland) *serving 110g/4oz* 0
Prawns, Cocktail, Chilled (Tesco) *serving 110g/4oz* 1
Prawns, Cocktail, Frozen (Marks & Spencer) *serving 110g/4oz* 2
Prawns, Cocktail, Frozen, Defrosted (Iceland) *serving 110g/4oz* 1
Prawns, Cold Water, Cooked & Peeled, Frozen (Tesco) *serving 110g/4oz* 2
Prawns, Coleslaw (Asda) *serving 110g/4oz* 15
Prawns, Cooked, Fan Tail (Waitrose) *serving 110g/4oz* 2

Prawns, Cooked, King, Fresh (Marks & Spencer) *serving 110g/4oz* 1
Prawns, Cooked, Tiger, Counter (Asda) *serving 110g/4oz* 1
Prawns, Cooked & Peeled (Waitrose) *serving 110g/4oz* 1
Prawns, Cooked & Peeled, Tiger King (Somerfield) *serving 110g/4oz* 1
Prawns, Cooking, Frozen (Tesco) *serving 110g/4oz* 1
Prawns, Extra Large, Frozen (Iceland) *serving 110g/4oz* 1
Prawns, Fjord (Waitrose) *serving 110g/4oz* 1
Prawns, Freshwater, King (Waitrose) *serving 110g/4oz* 2
Prawns, Garlic & Herb Kebab (Waitrose) *serving 110g/4oz* 2
Prawns with Garlic Mayonnaise, Chilled (Tesco) *serving 110g/4oz* 46
Prawns, Giant Tiger (Waitrose) *serving 110g/4oz* 1
Prawns, Hot/Spicy, Frozen (Marks & Spencer) *serving 110g/4oz* 19
Prawns, Kashmiri Spicy (Waitrose) *serving 110g/4oz* 4
Prawns, King, Frozen (Marks & Spencer) *serving 110g/4oz* 1
Prawns, King, Masala (Waitrose) *serving 110g/4oz* 10
Prawns, Large (Somerfield) *serving 110g/4oz* 1
Prawns & Mayonnaise, Delicatessen (Marks & Spencer) *serving 110g/4oz* 35
Prawns, Medium (Somerfield) *serving 110g/4oz* 1
Prawns, North Atlantic, Frozen, Defrosted & Drained (Iceland) *serving 110g/4oz* 1
Prawns, Party Platter (Waitrose) *serving 110g/4oz* 1
Prawns, Peeled (Somerfield) *serving 110g/4oz* 1
Prawns, Peeled, Frozen (Marks & Spencer) *serving 110g/4oz* 2
Prawns, Peeled, Large, Fresh (Marks & Spencer) *serving 110g/4oz* 2
Prawns, Pilau *serving 110g/4oz* 4
Prawns, Pilau (Waitrose) *serving 110g/4oz* 2
Prawns, Plaice & Mushroom Sauce (Waitrose) *serving 110g/4oz* 14
Prawns & Scallops, Fresh (Marks & Spencer) *serving 110g/4oz* 9
Prawns & Sesame Wontons (Asda) *serving 110g/4oz* 21
Prawns, Stir Crazy Style, Frozen, Stir Fried (Iceland) *serving 110g/4oz* 0
Prawns, Terrine, Fresh (Marks & Spencer) *serving 110g/4oz* 4

Prawns, Thai & Noodles, Delicatessen (Marks & Spencer) *serving 110g/4oz* 4
Prawns, Tiger, Kebab (Waitrose) *serving 110g/4oz* 2
Prawns, Tiger, Korma (Waitrose) *serving 110g/4oz* 6
Prawns, Whole, Frozen (Marks & Spencer) *serving 110g/4oz* 1
Prawns, Whole, Giant Tiger (Waitrose) *serving 110g/4oz* 1
Red Mullet, Whole (Waitrose) *serving 110g/4oz* 4
Rollmop Herrings, Ready to Eat, with Sweetener, Prepacked (Asda) *serving 110g/4oz* 12
Rollmops, Fresh (Marks & Spencer) *serving 110g/4oz* 7
Rollmops, Marinated (Waitrose) *serving 110g/4oz* 13
Salmon & Asparagus Pâté, Fresh (Marks & Spencer) *serving 110g/4oz* 33
Salmon & Asparagus Terrine (Marks & Spencer) *serving 110g/4oz* 29
Salmon, Atlantic (Waitrose) *serving 110g/4oz* 12
Salmon, Atlantic, Farmed, Raw *serving 110g/4oz* 12
Salmon, Atlantic, Farmed, Cooked, Dry Heat *serving 110g/4oz* 14
Salmon, Atlantic, Wild, Cooked, Dry Heat *serving 110g/4oz* 9
Salmon, Boneless, Skinless (Marks & Spencer) *serving 110g/4oz* 10
Salmon & Broccoli, Premium, Frozen, Oven Baked (Iceland) *serving 110g/4oz* 21
Salmon, Chargrilled, Fresh (Marks & Spencer) *serving 110g/4oz* 20
Salmon, Chinook, Cooked, Dry Heat *serving 110g/4oz* 15
Salmon, Chinook, Smoked *serving 110g/4oz* 5
Salmon, Chinook, Smoked (Lox), Regular *serving 110g/4oz* 5
Salmon, Chum, Tinned, without Salt, Drained Solids, with Bone *serving 110g/4oz* 6
Salmon, Chum, Cooked, Dry Heat *serving 110g/4oz* 5
Salmon, Chum, Drained Solids, with Bone *serving 110g/4oz* 6
Salmon, Coho, Farmed, Cooked, Dry Heat *serving 110g/4oz* 9
Salmon, Coho, Wild, Cooked, Dry Heat *serving 110g/4oz* 5
Salmon, Coho, Wild, Cooked, Moist Heat *serving 110g/4oz* 8
Salmon in Cream, Main Meals (Marks & Spencer) *serving 110g/4oz* 10
Salmon, Eggs, Fresh (Marks & Spencer) *serving 110g/4oz* 18
Salmon en Croute *serving 110g/4oz* 21

Salmon en Croute (Waitrose) *serving 110g/4oz* 15
Salmon en Croute, Chilled (Tesco) *serving 110g/4oz* 27
Salmon en Croute, Frozen (Asda) *serving 110g/4oz* 19
Salmon en Croute, Main Meals (Marks & Spencer) *serving 110g/4oz* 23
Salmon en Croute, Main Meals, Large (Marks & Spencer) *serving 110g/4oz* 19
Salmon Escalope & Butter (Marks & Spencer) *serving 110g/4oz* 20
Salmon, Farmed (Somerfield) *serving 110g/4oz* 9
Salmon, Fillets, Fresh (Marks & Spencer) *serving 110g/4oz* 7
Salmon, Fillets, Frozen (Marks & Spencer) *serving 110g/4oz* 5
Salmon Fillets, Poached, Fresh (Marks & Spencer) *serving 110g/4oz* 9
Salmon, Fillets, Prepacked (Asda) *serving 110g/4oz* 13
Salmon Fish Cakes, Fresh (Marks & Spencer) *serving 110g/4oz* 14
Salmon Fish Cakes, Frozen (Tesco) *serving 110g/4oz* 14
Salmon Fish Cakes, Frozen, Grilled (Iceland) *serving 110g/4oz*
Salmon Fish Cakes, Home Made *serving 110g/4oz* 22
Salmon Fish Cakes in Wholemeal Breadcrumbs (Birds Eye) *serving 110g/4oz* 10
Salmon, Fresh, Whole (Waitrose) *serving 110g/4oz* 12
Salmon & Guacamole Terrine (Waitrose) *serving 110g/4oz* 18
Salmon, Heads (Waitrose) *serving 110g/4oz* 12
Salmon, Herby Lemon (Waitrose) *serving 110g/4oz* 6
Salmon, Honey Roasted, Fresh (Marks & Spencer) *serving 110g/4oz* 13
Salmon, Irish Smoked, Fresh (Marks & Spencer) *serving 110g/4oz* 5
Salmon in Lemon Sauce, Main Meals (Marks & Spencer) *serving 110g/4oz* 8
Salmon, Maple Syrup Smoked (Waitrose) *serving 110g/4oz* 11
Salmon, Medium Red (Princes) *serving 110g/4oz* 8
Salmon Mornay with Broccoli, Frozen Ready Meal (Heinz Weight Watchers) *serving 110g/4oz* 3
Salmon Mousse, Fresh (Waitrose) *serving 110g/4oz* 19
Salmon, Orkney Slices, Fresh (Marks & Spencer) *serving 110g/4oz* 11

Salmon, Parcels, Fresh (Marks & Spencer) *serving 110g/4oz*	23
Salmon Paste (Princes) *serving 110g/4oz*	15
Salmon Pie, Frozen (Marks & Spencer) *serving 110g/4oz*	9
Salmon, Pink (Princes) *serving 110g/4oz*	6
Salmon, Pink, Raw *serving 110g/4oz*	4
Salmon, Poached Fillets (Waitrose) *serving 110g/4oz*	14
Salmon, Pink, Tinned, Solids, with Bone & Liquid *serving 110g/4oz*	7
Salmon, Pink, Tinned, without Salt, Solids, with Bone & Liquid *serving 110g/4oz*	7
Salmon, Pink, Cooked, Dry Heat *serving 110g/4oz*	5
Salmon, Poached Fillets (Waitrose) *serving 110g/4oz*	14
Salmon, Poached, & Prawn Knot (Waitrose) *serving 110g/4oz*	12
Salmon, Poached Scottish (Waitrose) *serving 110g/4oz*	14
Salmon, Poached Terrine, Fresh (Marks & Spencer) *serving 110g/4oz*	33
Salmon, Poached Vol au Vent (Waitrose) *serving 110g/4oz*	30
Salmon, Potted (Marks & Spencer) *serving 110g/4oz*	12
Salmon, Potted (Princes) *serving 110g/4oz*	17
Salmon, Red (Marks & Spencer) *serving 110g/4oz*	9
Salmon, Red (Princes) *serving 110g/4oz*	14
Salmon, Red (Waitrose) *serving 110g/4oz*	11
Salmon, Red Sockeye (Marks & Spencer) *serving 110g/4oz*	9
Salmon, Rosti (Waitrose) *serving 110g/4oz*	13
Salmon, Scottish (Waitrose) *serving 110g/4oz*	14
Salmon, Scottish Assortment (Waitrose) *serving 110g/4oz*	14
Salmon, Scottish Fillets, Chilled (Tesco) *serving 110g/4oz*	12
Salmon, Scottish Smoked Slices (Waitrose) *serving 110g/4oz*	14
Salmon, Scottish Smoked Slices (Waitrose) *serving 110g/4oz*	14
Salmon, Seagrown (Waitrose) *serving 110g/4oz*	12
Salmon, Seagrown, Portions (Waitrose) *serving 110g/4oz*	6
Salmon, Seagrown, Steaks (Waitrose) *serving 110g/4oz*	12
Salmon & Shrimp Paste (Tesco) *serving 110g/4oz*	3
Salmon, Skinless, Boneless, Pink, Tinned (Tesco) *serving 110g/4oz*	8
Salmon, Skinless & Boneless, Red, Tinned (Tesco) *serving 110g/4oz*	8

Salmon, Smoked, Fresh (Marks & Spencer) *serving 110g/4oz* 12
Salmon, Smoked, Frozen, Thawed (Iceland) *serving 110g/4oz* 5
Salmon, Smoked Parcel, Deli (Waitrose) *serving 110g/4oz* 15
Salmon, Smoked Pâté, Fresh (Marks & Spencer) *serving 110g/4oz* 32
Salmon, Smoked, Platter (Waitrose) *serving 110g/4oz* 14
Salmon, Smoked Scotch (Waitrose) *serving 110g/4oz* 14
Salmon, Smoked Scottish (Somerfield) *serving 110g/4oz* 9
Salmon, Smoked Scottish, Frozen, Thawed (Iceland) *serving 110g/4oz* 14
Salmon, Smoked Strip, Fresh (Marks & Spencer) *serving 110g/4oz* 12
Salmon, Smoked Trimmings (Waitrose) *serving 110g/4oz* 14
Salmon, Sockeye, Raw *serving 110g/4oz* 9
Salmon, Sockeye, Tinned, Drained, Solids with Bone *serving 110g/4oz* 8
Salmon, Sockeye, Tinned, without Salt, Drained, Solids, with Bone *serving 110g/4oz* 8
Salmon, Sockeye, Cooked, Dry Heat *serving 110g/4oz* 12
Salmon, Spicy Tomato (Waitrose) *serving 110g/4oz* 4
Salmon Spread (Tesco) *serving 110g/4oz* 8
Salmon Steaks (Waitrose) *serving 110g/4oz* 12
Salmon Steaks, Fresh (Marks & Spencer) *serving 110g/4oz* 7
Salmon Steaks, Frozen, Poached (Iceland) *serving 110g/4oz* 12
Salmon Steaks, Prepacked (Asda) *serving 110g/4oz* 13
Salmon Steaks, with Dill Butter, Chilled (Tesco) *serving 110g/4oz* 21
Salmon, Tail Fillets (Waitrose) *serving 110g/4oz* 12
Salmon, Tails (Waitrose) *serving 110g/4oz* 12
Salmon Terrine (Waitrose) *serving 110g/4oz* 18
Salmon with Tarragon Sauce (Waitrose) *serving 110g/4oz* 17
Salmon, Thai Fillet (Waitrose) *serving 110g/4oz* 13
Salmon & Tomato & Basil, Main Meals (Marks & Spencer) *serving 110g/4oz* 13
Salmon & Watercress Sauce, Main Meals (Marks & Spencer) *serving 110g/4oz* 13
Salmon Wee Poached (Waitrose) *serving 110g/4oz* 14
Salmon, Whole, Farmed (Waitrose) *serving 110g/4oz* 12

Salmon, Whole, Fresh (Waitrose) *serving 110g/4oz* 12
Salmon, Whole, Wild (Waitrose) *serving 110g/4oz* 9
Salmon, Wild, Slices (Waitrose) *serving 110g/4oz* 14
Sardines (Somerfield) *serving 110g/4oz* 14
Sardines (Waitrose) *serving 110g/4oz* 10
Sardines, Atlantic, Tinned, in Oil, Drained, Solids with Bone *serving 110g/4oz* 13
Sardines in Brine (Princes) *serving 110g/4oz* 14
Sardines in Brine (Waitrose) *serving 110g/4oz* 7
Sardines with Hot Pepper (Waitrose) *serving 110g/4oz* 28
Sardines with Lemon (Waitrose) *serving 110g/4oz* 28
Sardines in Olive Oil (Marks & Spencer) *serving 110g/4oz* 13
Sardines in Olive Oil (Waitrose) *serving 110g/4oz* 37
Sardines in Soya Oil (Waitrose) *serving 110g/4oz* 37
Sardines in Tomato (Princes) *serving 110g/4oz* 24
Sardines in Tomato (Waitrose) *serving 110g/4oz* 16
Sardines in Vegetable & Olive Oil (Princes) *serving 110g/4oz* 24
Sardines, Skinless, Boneless, in Brine, Tinned (Tesco) *serving 110g/4oz* 6
Sardines, Skinless, Boneless, in Oil, Tinned (Tesco) *serving 110g/4oz* 18
Sardines, Skinless, Boneless, in Tomato Sauce, Tinned (Tesco) *serving 110g/4oz* 8
Scallops à la Crème (Waitrose) *serving 110g/4oz* 6
Scallops, Breaded & Fried *serving 110g/4oz* 15
Scallops on Half Shell (Waitrose) *serving 110g/4oz* 2
Scallops, King (Waitrose) *serving 110g/4oz* 0
Scallops, King, Fresh (Marks & Spencer) *serving 110g/4oz* 1
Scallops, Mixed Species, Raw, *serving 110g/4oz* 1
Scallops, Mixed Species, Cooked, Breaded & Fried *serving 110g/4oz* 12
Scallops, Mixed Species, Imitation, Made from Surimi *serving 110g/4oz* 0
Scallops, Queen (Waitrose) *serving 110g/4oz* 0
Scallops without Roe (Waitrose) *serving 110g/4oz* 1
Scampi, Breaded, (Somerfield) *serving 110g/4oz* 11
Scampi, Breaded, Frozen, Deep Fried (Iceland) *serving 110g/4oz* 1

Scampi, Breaded, Wholetail, Chilled, Coated (Tesco) *serving 110g/4oz* 14
Scampi & Chips, Frozen Ready Meal (Tesco) *serving 110g/4oz* 7
Scampi in Crispy Crumb (Waitrose) *serving 110g/4oz* 11
Scampi in Ovencrisp Breadcrumbs, Frozen, Coated (Tesco) *serving 110g/4oz* 8
Scampi Provencale (Waitrose) *serving 110g/4oz* 4
Scampi, Re-Formed, Golden, in Ovencrisp Breadcrumbs, Frozen, Coated (Tesco) *serving 110g/4oz* 13
Scampi, Whole, Fresh (Marks & Spencer) *serving 110g/4oz* 16
Scampi, Whole, in a Light Crispy Breadcrumb Coating, Prepacked (Asda) *serving 110g/4oz* 16
Scampi, Whole, in Crumb, Frozen (Marks & Spencer) *serving 110g/4oz* 11
Scup, Cooked, Dry Heat *serving 110g/4oz* 4
Sea Bass, Portion, Skin On (Waitrose) *serving 110g/4oz* 3
Sea Bass, Whole (Waitrose) *serving 110g/4oz* 3
Sea Treasures, Frozen (Marks & Spencer) *serving 110g/4oz* 13
Seafood Casserole with Potato Gratin, Frozen Ready Meal (Tesco) *serving 110g/4oz* 6
Seafood Cocktail *serving 110g/4oz* 2
Seafood Cocktail (Waitrose) *serving 110g/4oz* 2
Seafood Cocktail, Chilled (Tesco) *serving 110g/4oz* 1
Seafood Cocktail, Frozen, Microwaved (Iceland) *serving 110g/4oz* 1
Seafood Medley, Main Meal (Marks & Spencer) *serving 110g/4oz* 14
Seafood Selection, Premium, Chilled (Tesco) *serving 110g/4oz* 1
Seafood Selection, Premium, Chilled Coated (Tesco) *serving 110g/4oz* 1
Seafood Sticks (Somerfield) *serving 110g/4oz* 1
Seafood Sticks, Chilled (Tesco) *serving 110g/4oz* 0
Shark, Fresh Mako Loin (Waitrose) *serving 110g/4oz* 0
Shark, Mixed Species, Raw *serving 110g/4oz* 5
Shark, Mixed Species, Cooked, Batter, Dipped & Fried *serving 110g/4oz* 15
Shark Steaks, Mesquite (Waitrose) *serving 110g/4oz* 4
Sheepshead, Cooked, Dry Heat *serving 110g/4oz* 2

Shrimps, Raw *serving 110g/4oz* 2
Shrimps, Breaded & Fried *serving 110g/4oz* 17
Shrimps in Brine (Princes) *serving 110g/4oz* 1
Shrimps, Tinned *serving 110g/4oz* 2
Shrimps, Cooked, Moist Heat *serving 110g/4oz* 1
Shrimps, Imitation, Made from Surimi *serving 110g/4oz* 2
Silk Snapper (Waitrose) *serving 110g/4oz* 2
Skate, Fresh (Marks & Spencer) *serving 110g/4oz* 0
Skate Wings (Waitrose) *serving 110g/4oz* 0
Smelt, Rainbow, Raw *serving 110g/4oz* 3
Smelt, Rainbow, Cooked, Dry Heat *serving 110g/4oz* 3
Snapper, Mixed Species, Raw *serving 110g/4oz* 1
Snapper, Mixed Species, Cooked, Dry Heat *serving 110g/4oz* 2
Sole, Dover, Fresh (Marks & Spencer) *serving 110g/4oz* 0
Sole, Dover, & Lemon (Waitrose) *serving 110g/4oz* 2
Sole, Dover, Whole, Chilled (Tesco) *serving 110g/4oz* 2
Sole, Lemon, Breadcrumbs, Frozen (Marks & Spencer) *serving 110g/4oz* 14
Sole, Lemon, Butter, Fresh (Marks & Spencer) *serving 110g/4oz* 10
Sole, Lemon, Crumb, Fresh (Marks & Spencer) *serving 110g/4oz* 13
Sole, Lemon Fillets (Somerfield) *serving 110g/4oz* 2
Sole, Lemon Fillets (Waitrose) *serving 110g/4oz* 2
Sole, Lemon Fillets, Fresh (Marks & Spencer) *serving 110g/4oz* 2
Sole, Lemon Fillets, Frozen (Marks & Spencer) *serving 110g/4oz* 2
Sole, Lemon Fillets in Breadcrumbs, Frozen Oven Bake (Iceland) *serving 110g/4oz* 18
Sole, Lemon, Fresh (Marks & Spencer) *serving 110g/4oz* 2
Sole, Lemon Goujons (Waitrose) *serving 110g/4oz* 12
Sole, Lemon Goujons, Fresh (Marks & Spencer) *serving 110g/4oz* 12
Sole, Lemon Goujons, Frozen (Marks & Spencer) *serving 110g/4oz* 13
Sole, Seasoned Lemon, Fresh (Marks & Spencer) *serving 110g/4oz* 6
Sole, Seasoned Lemon, Frozen (Marks & Spencer) *serving 110g/4oz* 8
Sole, Lemon, Whole (Waitrose) *serving 110g/4oz* 2

Sprats (Waitrose) *serving 110g/4oz* 12
Squid (Calamari), Chilled, Coated (Tesco) *serving 110g/4oz* 19
Squid (Calamari), Fresh (Marks & Spencer) *serving 110g/4oz* 16
Squid (Calamari), Mixed Species, Raw *serving 110g/4oz* 2
Squid (Calamari), Mixed Species, Cooked, Fried *serving 110g/4oz* 8
Squid (Calamari), Rings (Waitrose) *serving 110g/4oz* 2
Squid (Calamari), Stuffed with Head (Waitrose) *serving 110g/4oz* 2
Sturgeon, Cooked, Dry Heat *serving 110g/4oz* 6
Sturgeon, Raw *serving 110g/4oz* 4
Sturgeon, Smoked *serving 110g/4oz* 5
Surimi *serving 110g/4oz* 1
Swordfish, Raw *serving 110g/4oz* 4
Swordfish, Cooked, Dry Heat *serving 110g/4oz* 6
Swordfish Loins/Fillets (Waitrose) *serving 110g/4oz* 5
Swordfish Steaks (Waitrose) *serving 110g/4oz* 5
Trout, Caledonian Fillets, Fresh (Marks & Spencer) *serving 110g/4oz* 12
Trout, Golden Rainbow (Waitrose) *serving 110g/4oz* 6
Trout, Hot Smoked (Waitrose) *serving 110g/4oz* 8
Trout & Lemon, Main Meal (Marks & Spencer) *serving 110g/4oz* 9
Trout, Lemon/Pepper Portions (Waitrose) *serving 110g/4oz* 17
Trout in Lemon Sauce, Frozen (Marks & Spencer) *serving 110g/4oz* 11
Trout, Mixed Species, Raw *serving 110g/4oz* 7
Trout, Mixed Species, Cooked, Dry Heat *serving 110g/4oz* 9
Trout, Rainbow (Waitrose) *serving 110g/4oz* 6
Trout, Rainbow, Chilled, Coated (Tesco) *serving 110g/4oz* 6
Trout, Rainbow, Farmed, Raw *serving 110g/4oz* 6
Trout, Rainbow, Farmed, Cooked, Dry Heat *serving 110g/4oz* 8
Trout, Rainbow Fillets (Waitrose) *serving 110g/4oz* 6
Trout, Rainbow Fillets, Fresh, Chilled (Tesco) *serving 110g/4oz* 6
Trout, Rainbow, Fresh (Marks & Spencer) *serving 110g/4oz* 5
Trout, Rainbow, Fresh (Waitrose) *serving 110g/4oz* 6
Trout, Rainbow, Whole, Chilled (Tesco) *serving 110g/4oz* 6
Trout, Rainbow, Wild, Raw *serving 110g/4oz* 4

Trout, Rainbow, Wild, Cooked, Dry Heat *serving 110g/4oz* 6
Trout, Scottish Smoked (Waitrose) *serving 110g/4oz* 10
Trout, Smoked, Fresh (Marks & Spencer) *serving 110g/4oz* 9
Trout, Smoked Rainbow (Somerfield) *serving 110g/4oz* 4
Trout, Whole (Somerfield) *serving 110g/4oz* 6
Trout, Whole, Prepacked (Asda) *serving 110g/4oz* 6
Trout, Whole, Sea (Wild) (Waitrose) *serving 110g/4oz* 2
Tuna & Brine (Waitrose) *serving 110g/4oz* 1
Tuna, Tinned, Drained, Solids, White Meat, Tinned in Oil *serving 110g/4oz* 9
Tuna, Tinned, Drained, Solids, White Meat, Tinned in Water *serving 110g/4oz* 3
Tuna, Chargrilled, Fresh (Marks & Spencer) *serving 110g/4oz* 3
Tuna Chunks, Tinned in Brine (Heinz) *serving 110g/4oz* 1
Tuna Chunks, Tinned in Vegetable Oil (Heinz) *serving 110g/4oz* 10
Tuna Chunks in Brine (Princes) *serving 110g/4oz* 1
Tuna Chunks in Brine (Somerfield) *serving 110g/4oz* 1
Tuna Chunks in Brine (Waitrose) *serving 110g/4oz* 1
Tuna Chunks in Oil (Somerfield) *serving 110g/4oz* 10
Tuna Chunks in Oil (Waitrose) *serving 110g/4oz* 12
Tuna Chunks in Vegetable Oil (Princes) *serving 110g/4oz* 12
Tuna Crispbreak (Somerfield) *serving 110g/4oz* 11
Tuna Fish Cakes, Fresh (Marks & Spencer) *serving 110g/4oz* 11
Tuna, Flaked, in Brine (Princes) *serving 110g/4oz* 1
Tuna, Flaked, in Oil (Princes) *serving 110g/4oz* 16
Tuna, Fresh, Bluefin, Raw *serving 110g/4oz* 5
Tuna, Fresh, Bluefin, Cooked, Dry Heat *serving 110g/4oz* 7
Tuna, Fresh, Loins (Waitrose) *serving 110g/4oz* 4
Tuna, Fresh, Skipjack, Raw *serving 110g/4oz* 1
Tuna, Fresh, Yellowfin, Raw *serving 110g/4oz* 1
Tuna in Oil (Waitrose) *serving 110g/4oz* 12
Tuna in Olive Oil (Waitrose) *serving 110g/4oz* 14
Tuna in Spring Water (Marks & Spencer) *serving 110g/4oz* 1
Tuna in Vegetable Oil (Marks & Spencer) *serving 110g/4oz* 23
Tuna in Vegetable Oil & Lemon (Princes) *serving 110g/4oz* 16
Tuna, Light Meat, Tinned in Oil, without Salt, Drained Solids *serving 110g/4oz* 9

Tuna, Light Meat, Tinned in Water, without Salt, Drained Solids *serving 110g/4oz* 1
Tuna Nicoise Turnover Roll (Waitrose) *serving 110g/4oz* 11
Tuna Provencale Steaks (Waitrose) *serving 110g/4oz* 8
Tuna & Red Pepper Fish Cake (Waitrose) *serving 110g/4oz* 13
Tuna Salad *serving 110g/4oz* 10
Tuna, Skipjack, Fresh, Cooked, Dry Heat *serving 110g/4oz* 1
Tuna, Skipjack, in Brine (Waitrose) *serving 110g/4oz* 1
Tuna Steak, Tinned in Brine (Heinz) *serving 110g/4oz* 1
Tuna Steak, Tinned in Vegetable Oil (Heinz) *serving 110g/4oz* 10
Tuna Steaks in Brine (Princes) *serving 110g/4oz* 1
Tuna Steaks in Brine (Somerfield) *serving 110g/4oz* 1
Tuna Steaks in Oil (Princes) *serving 110g/4oz* 8
Tuna Steaks in Oil (Somerfield) *serving 110g/4oz* 10
Tuna Steak in Oil (Waitrose) *serving 110g/4oz* 12
Tuna, White Meat, Tinned in Oil, without Salt, Drained Solids *serving 110g/4oz* 9
Tuna, White Meat, Tinned in Water, without Salt, Drained Solids *serving 110g/4oz* 3
Tuna, Yellowfin, Fresh, Cooked, Dry Heat *serving 110g/4oz* 1
Tuna, Yellowfin, Loin Steak (Waitrose) *serving 110g/4oz* 5
Turbot, Raw *serving 110g/4oz* 3
Turbot, Cooked, Dry Heat *serving 110g/4oz* 4
Turbot, Whole (Waitrose) *serving 110g/4oz* 3
Whelk, Raw *serving 110g/4oz* 0
Whelk, Cooked, Moist Heat *serving 110g/4oz* 1
White Minced Fish (Waitrose) *serving 110g/4oz* 1
Whitebait (Waitrose) *serving 110g/4oz* 3
Whitefish, Mixed Species, Cooked, Dry Heat *serving 110g/4oz* 8
Whiting, Raw *serving 110g/4oz* 1
Whiting, Breadcrumbs, Large (Marks & Spencer) *serving 110g/4oz* 16
Whiting, Chunky Fillets, Chilled, Coated (Tesco) *serving 110g/4oz* 9
Whiting, Cooked, Dry Heat *serving 110g/4oz* 2
Whiting Fillets, Frozen, Poached (Iceland) *serving 110g/4oz* 1
Willy Whales, Frozen (Bernard Matthews) *serving 110g/4oz* 14
Winkles (Waitrose) *serving 110g/4oz* 1

Flours & Grains

NOTE: The standard serving size in this section is 110g/4oz. If you wish to consume more or less than this amount (e.g. if you are going to consume a pack of food whose weight differs from the standard serving size) use the conversion tables on page 386 to calculate the new amount of fat in the food.

Amaranth Grain, Raw *serving 110g/4oz*	0
Arrowroot Flour *serving 110g/4oz*	0
Barley, Pearled, Cooked *serving 110g/4oz*	0
Besan Flour *serving 110g/4oz*	6
Buckwheat/Buckwheat Flour *serving 110g/4oz*	4
Bulghur, Cooked *serving 110g/4oz*	0
Bulghur Wheat (Waitrose) *serving 110g/4oz*	2
Carob Flour *serving 110g/4oz*	1
Chick Pea Flour *serving 110g/4oz*	6
Corn, Yellow *serving 110g/4oz*	5
Cornflour (Brown & Polson Patent) *serving 110g/4oz*	1
Corn Flour, Whole Grain, Yellow *serving 110g/4oz*	4
Cornmeal, Degermed, Enriched Yellow *serving 110g/4oz*	2
Cornstarch *serving 110g/4oz*	0
Couscous, Cooked *serving 110g/4oz*	0
Flour, Plain (Somerfield) *serving 110g/4oz*	2
Flour, Plain (Waitrose) *serving 110g/4oz*	1
Flour, Plain, Super Fine (Waitrose) *serving 110g/4oz*	1
Flour, Self Raising (Somerfield) *serving 110g/4oz*	2
Flour, Self Raising (Waitrose) *serving 110g/4oz*	1
Flour, Self Raising, Organic (Waitrose) *serving 110g/4oz*	1
Flour, Self Raising, Wholemeal (Somerfield) *serving 110g/4oz*	2
Flour, Self Raising, Wholemeal (Waitrose) *serving 110g/4oz*	2
Flour, Strong Canadian (Waitrose) *serving 110g/4oz*	2
Flour, Strong Organic, Wholemeal (Doves Farm) *serving 110g/4oz*	2
Flour, Strong White Bread (Somerfield) *serving 110g/4oz*	1
Flour, Strong White, Plain (Waitrose) *serving 110g/4oz*	2
Flour, White All-Purpose *serving 110g/4oz*	1
Flour, White Bread *serving 110g/4oz*	2
Flour, White Cake *serving 110g/4oz*	1

Flour, White Organic (Waitrose) *serving 110g/4oz*	1
Flour, White Tortilla Mix *serving 110g/4oz*	12
Flour, Whole Grain *serving 110g/4oz*	2
Flour, Wholemeal (Waitrose) *serving 110g/4oz*	2
Flour, Wholemeal Organic (Waitrose) *serving 110g/4oz*	2
Millet, Cooked *serving 110g/4oz*	1
Oat Bran, Cooked *serving 110g/4oz*	1
Oat Bran, Raw *serving 110g/4oz*	8
Oats *serving 110g/4oz*	8
Oats Porridge, Basics (Somerfield) *serving 110g/4oz*	8
Peanut Flour, Defatted *serving 110g/4oz*	1
Peanut Flour, Defatted, with Salt Added *serving 110g/4oz*	1
Pearl Barley (Waitrose) *serving 110g/4oz*	2
Pecan Flour *serving 110g/4oz*	2
Quinoa *serving 110g/4oz*	6
Rice Flour, Brown *serving 110g/4oz*	3
Rice Flour, White *serving 110g/4oz*	2
Rye *serving 110g/4oz*	3
Rye Flour, Dark *serving 110g/4oz*	3
Rye Flour, Light *serving 110g/4oz*	1
Rye Flour, Medium *serving 110g/4oz*	2
Semolina (Waitrose) *serving 110g/4oz*	2
Semolina, Enriched *serving 110g/4oz*	1
Sorghum *serving 110g/4oz*	4
Soy Flour, Defatted *serving 110g/4oz*	1
Soy Flour, Defatted, Crude Protein Basis *serving 110g/4oz*	1
Soy Flour, Full Fat, Roasted *serving 110g/4oz*	24
Soy Flour, Full Fat, Roasted, Crude Protein Basis *serving 110g/4oz*	24
Soy Flour, Low Fat, Crude Protein Basis *serving 110g/4oz*	7
Stoneground Organic Wholemeal (Waitrose) *serving 110g/4oz*	2
Sunflower Seed Flour, Partially Defatted *serving 110g/4oz*	2
Triticale *serving 110g/4oz*	2
Triticale Flour, Whole Grain *serving 110g/4oz*	2
Wheat, Sprouted *serving 110g/4oz*	1
Wheat Bran, Crude *serving 110g/4oz*	5
Wheat, Durum *serving 110g/4oz*	3
Wheat Germ, Crude *serving 110g/4oz*	11

FRUIT

Apple *serving 110g/4oz* 0
Apple, baked with Sugar, Flesh & Skin *serving 110g/4oz* 0
Apple & Blackberry Fruit Filling (Waitrose) *serving 110g/4oz* 0
Apple, Dehydrated *serving 110g/4oz* 1
Apple, Dried & Stewed *serving 110g/4oz* 0
Apple Juice, Canned or Bottled *serving 110g/4oz* 0
Apple & Pear Fruit Stir Fry (Waitrose) *serving 110g/4oz* 0
Apple & Raspberry Fruit Filling (Waitrose) *serving 110g/4oz* 0
Apple Sauce, Tinned *serving 110g/4oz* 0
Apple, Tinned *serving 110g/4oz* 0
Apricot *serving 110g/4oz* 0
Apricot, Dehydrated *serving 110g/4oz* 1
Apricot, Dehydrated & Stewed *serving 110g/4oz* 0
Apricot, Frozen *serving 110g/4oz* 0
Apricot Fruit Filling (Waitrose) *serving 110g/4oz* 0
Apricot Juice, Tinned *serving 110g/4oz* 0
Apricot Nectar *serving 110g/4oz* 0
Apricot, Tinned *serving 110g/4oz* 0
Autumn Fruit Compote (Waitrose) *serving 110g/4oz* 0
Avocado *serving 110g/4oz* 17
Avocado, California *serving 110g/4oz* 19
Avocado, Florida *serving 110g/4oz* 10
Banana *serving 110g/4oz* 1
Banana Chips *serving 110g/4oz* 35
Banana, Dehydrated or Powder *serving 110g/4oz* 2
Banana, Red *serving 110g/4oz* 0
Banana, Small *serving 110g/4oz* 0
Blackberry *serving 110g/4oz* 0
Blackberry & Apple, Stewed *serving 110g/4oz* 0
Blackberry, Frozen *serving 110g/4oz* 0
Blackberry, Tinned *serving 110g/4oz* 0
Blackcurrant *serving 110g/4oz* 0
Blackcurrant, Stewed *serving 110g/4oz* 0
Blueberry *serving 110g/4oz* 0
Blueberry, Frozen *serving 110g/4oz* 0

Blueberry, Tinned *serving 110g/4oz* 0
Boysenberry, Frozen *serving 110g/4oz* 0
Boysenberry, Tinned *serving 110g/4oz* 0
Breadfruit *serving 110g/4oz* 0
Bullock's Heart: *see* Custard Apple
Cape Gooseberry: *see* Groundcherry
Carissa *serving 110g/4oz* 1
Chayote Fruit *serving 110g/4oz* 0
Cherimoya *serving 110g/4oz* 0
Cherry, Black, Fruit Filling (Waitrose) *serving 110g/4oz* 0
Cherry Cocktail (Waitrose) *serving 110g/4oz* 0
Cherry Glacé *serving 110g/4oz* 0
Cherry Pie Filling *serving 110g/4oz* 0
Cherry, Red, Fruit Filling (Waitrose) *serving 110g/4oz* 0
Cherry, Sour Red *serving 110g/4oz* 0
Cherry, White *serving 110g/4oz* 0
Chinese Date: *see* Jujube
Clear Fruits, Grocery (Iceland) *serving 110g/4oz* 0
Clementine, Whole *serving 110g/4oz* 0
Crabapple *serving 110g/4oz* 0
Cranberry *serving 110g/4oz* 0
Cranberry Juice Cocktail, Bottled *serving 110g/4oz* 0
Cranberry Sauce, Tinned, Sweetened *serving 110g/4oz* 0
Currant Zante, Dried *serving 110g/4oz* 0
Custard Apple *serving 110g/4oz* 1
Date, Domestic, Natural & Dry *serving 110g/4oz* 0
Date, Hadrawi (Waitrose) *serving 110g/4oz* 1
Date & Walnuts (Waitrose) *serving 110g/4oz* 15
Dates, Muscovado, Sugared (Waitrose) *serving 110g/4oz* 0
Elderberry *serving 110g/4oz* 1
Feijoa *serving 110g/4oz* 1
Fig *serving 110g/4oz* 0
Fig, Dried, Stewed *serving 110g/4oz* 1
Fig, Dried, Uncooked *serving 110g/4oz* 1
Fruit Cocktail in Juice (Asda) *serving 110g/4oz* 0
Fruit Cocktail in Light Syrup (Somerfield) *serving 110g/4oz* 0
Fruit Cocktail in Syrup (Somerfield) *serving 110g/4oz* 0

Fruit Cocktail, Luxury (St Ivel) *serving 110g/4oz*	7
Fruit Cocktail in Syrup (Waitrose) *serving 110g/4oz*	0
Fruit, Dried Mixed *serving 110g/4oz*	0
Fruit, Exotic Dried (Waitrose) *serving 110g/4oz*	0
Fruit, Luxury Mixed (Waitrose) *serving 110g/4oz*	1
Fruit & Nut Rice Salad (Somerfield) *serving 110g/4oz*	12
Fruit Salad, Dried (Waitrose) *serving 110g/4oz*	1
Fruit Salad, Exotic (Marks & Spencer) *serving 110g/4oz*	0
Fruit Salad, Fresh, Mixed (Marks & Spencer) *serving 110g/4oz*	0
Fruit Salad, Home Made *serving 110g/4oz*	0
Fruit Salad, Luxury, Large (Marks & Spencer) *serving 110g/4oz*	0
Fruits of the Forest (Waitrose) *serving 110g/4oz*	0
Gooseberry *serving 110g/4oz*	0
Gooseberry, Tinned *serving 110g/4oz*	0
Gooseberry, Stewed *serving 110g/4oz*	0
Granadilla: *see* Passion Fruit	
Grape *serving 110g/4oz*	0
Grape Juice *serving 110g/4oz*	0
Grapefruit *serving 110g/4oz*	0
Grapefruit Juice *serving 110g/4oz*	0
Grapefruit Sections, Tinned *serving 110g/4oz*	0
Greengage *serving 110g/4oz*	0
Groundcherry *serving 110g/4oz*	1
Guava *serving 110g/4oz*	1
Guava, Tinned *serving 110g/4oz*	0
Guava Sauce, Cooked *serving 110g/4oz*	0
Japonica: *see* Loquat	
Java Plum *serving 110g/4oz*	0
Jambolan: *see* Java Plum	
Jujube *serving 110g/4oz*	0
Kiwifruit *serving 110g/4oz*	0
Kumquat *serving 110g/4oz*	0
Lemon with Peel *serving 110g/4oz*	0
Lemon Peel *serving 110g/4oz*	0
Lemon Juice, Frozen *serving 110g/4oz*	0

Lemon Slices in Lemon Juice (Waitrose) *serving 110g/4oz*	0
Lime *serving 110g/4oz*	0
Limequat *serving 110g/4oz*	0
Loganberry *serving 110g/4oz*	0
Longan *serving 110g/4oz*	0
Longan, Dried *serving 110g/4oz*	0
Loquat *serving 110g/4oz*	0
Lychee *serving 110g/4oz*	0
Lychee, Tinned *serving 110g/4oz*	0
Lychee, Dried *serving 110g/4oz*	1
Mandarin *serving 110g/4oz*	0
Mandarins in Juice (Waitrose) *serving 110g/4oz*	0
Mandoras (Waitrose) *serving 110g/4oz*	0
Mango *serving 110g/4oz*	0
Mango, Semi Dried (Waitrose) *serving 110g/4oz*	1
Melon, Cantaloup *serving 110g/4oz*	0
Melon, Casaba *serving 110g/4oz*	0
Melon, Galia *serving 110g/4oz*	0
Melon, Honeydew *serving 110g/4oz*	0
Mulberry *serving 110g/4oz*	0
Natal Plum: *see* Carissa	
Nectarine *serving 110g/4oz*	1
Nectarine, White Flesh (Waitrose) *serving 110g/4oz*	0
Olive, Ripe, Tinned (Jumbo Super Colossal) *serving 110g/4oz*	8
Olive, Ripe, Tinned (Small – Extra Large) *serving 110g/4oz*	12
Orange *serving 110g/4oz*	0
Orange with Peel *serving 110g/4oz*	0
Orange Juice *serving 110g/4oz*	0
Orange Peel *serving 110g/4oz*	0
Papaya *serving 110g/4oz*	0
Papaya Nectar, Tinned *serving 110g/4oz*	0
Passion Fruit, Purple *serving 110g/4oz*	1
Passion Fruit Juice *serving 110g/4oz*	0
Paw Paw *serving 110g/4oz*	0
Paw Paw, Semi Dried (Waitrose) *serving 110g/4oz*	0
Peach *serving 110g/4oz*	0

Peach, Tinned, Heavy Syrup *serving 110g/4oz*	0
Peach, Tinned, Light Syrup *serving 110g/4oz*	0
Peach Dehydrated, Stewed *serving 110g/4oz*	0
Peach Dehydrated, Uncooked *serving 110g/4oz*	1
Peach Juice, Tinned *serving 110g/4oz*	0
Pear *serving 110g/4oz*	0
Pear, Asian (Chinese) *serving 110g/4oz*	0
Pear, Tinned, Heavy Syrup *serving 110g/4oz*	0
Pear, Tinned, Light Syrup *serving 110g/4oz*	0
Pear, Dried, Stewed *serving 110g/4oz*	0
Pear, Dried, Uncooked *serving 110g/4oz*	1
Pear Juice, Tinned *serving 110g/4oz*	0
Pear Nectar *serving 110g/4oz*	0
Peel, Mixed *serving 110g/4oz*	1
Persimmon, Japanese *serving 110g/4oz*	0
Persimmon, Japanese, Dried *serving 110g/4oz*	1
Physalis *serving 110g/4oz*	0
Pineapple *serving 110g/4oz*	0
Pineapple, Tinned, Heavy Syrup *serving 110g/4oz*	0
Pineapple, Tinned, Light Syrup *serving 110g/4oz*	0
Pineapple, Dwarf (Waitrose) *serving 110g/4oz*	0
Pineapple, Frozen Chunks *serving 110g/4oz*	0
Pineapple Juice *serving 110g/4oz*	0
Pineapple, Semi Dried (Waitrose) *serving 110g/4oz*	0
Pitanga *serving 110g/4oz*	0
Plantain *serving 110g/4oz*	0
Plantain, Cooked *serving 110g/4oz*	0
Plum, Damson *serving 110g/4oz*	0
Plum, Stewed *serving 110g/4oz*	0
Plum, Purple, Tinned, Heavy Syrup *serving 110g/4oz*	0
Plum, Purple, Tinned, Light Syrup *serving 110g/4oz*	0
Plum Juice, Purple, Tinned *serving 110g/4oz*	0
Poha: *see* Groundcherry	
Pomegranate *serving 110g/4oz*	0
Pricklypear *serving 110g/4oz*	1
Prune, Tinned, Heavy Syrup *serving 110g/4oz*	0
Prune, Dehydrated, Stewed *serving 110g/4oz*	0

Prune, Dehydrated, Uncooked *serving 110g/4oz*	1
Prune, Honeyed (Waitrose) *serving 110g/4oz*	0
Prune Juice, Tinned *serving 110g/4oz*	0
Prune, Pitted *serving 110g/4oz*	1
Pummelo *serving 110g/4oz*	0
Quince *serving 110g/4oz*	0
Raisin, Seeded *serving 110g/4oz*	1
Raisin, Seedless *serving 110g/4oz*	1
Rambutans *serving 110g/4oz*	0
Raspberry *serving 110g/4oz*	1
Raspberries, Frozen, Thawed (Iceland) *serving 110g/4oz*	0
Raspberry, Tinned, Heavy Syrup *serving 110g/4oz*	0
Raspberry, Stewed *serving 110g/4oz*	0
Rhubarb *serving 110g/4oz*	0
Rhubarb, Frozen, Cooked *serving 110g/4oz*	0
Rhbarb in Light Syrup (Somerfield) *serving 110g/4oz*	1
Roselle *serving 110g/4oz*	1
Sapodilla *serving 110g/4oz*	1
Sharon Fruit *serving 110g/4oz*	0
Soursop *serving 110g/4oz*	0
Starfruit Carambola *serving 110g/4oz*	0
Strawberry *serving 110g/4oz*	0
Strawberry, Tinned, Heavy Syrup *serving 110g/4oz*	0
Strawberry, Frozen *serving 110g/4oz*	0
Sugar Apple *serving 110g/4oz*	0
Sultanas *serving 110g/4oz*	0
Summer Fruits in Syrup (Waitrose) *serving 110g/4oz*	0
SummerfruitMix, Frozen, Thawed (Iceland) *serving 110g/4oz*	0
Surinam Cherry *see* Pitanga	
Sweetsop: *see* Sugar Apple	
Tamarind *serving 110g/4oz*	1
Tangerine *serving 110g/4oz*	1
Tangering Juice *serving 110g/4oz*	0
Tangerine Juice, Tinned *serving 110g/4oz*	0
Tangerine, Tinned, Light Syrup *serving 110g/4oz*	0
Watermelon *serving 110g/4oz*	0
Whitecurrant *serving 110g/4oz*	0

HAM

NOTE: The standard serving size in this section is 90g/3oz. If you wish to consume more or less than this amount (e.g. if you are going to consume a pack of food whose weight differs from the standard serving size) use the conversion tables on page 386 to calculate the new amount of fat in the food.

Apricot Ham (Somerfield) *serving 90g/3oz*	9
Bayonne Ham (Waitrose) *serving 90g/3oz*	12
BBQ Flavoured Ham (Somerfield) *serving 90g/3oz*	6
Belgium Ham, Sliced, Dry Cure (Waitrose) *serving 90g/3oz*	4
Blackforest Ham, Sliced (Waitrose) *serving 90g/3oz*	16
Boiled Dry Cured Ham (Waitrose) *serving 90g/3oz*	9
Boiled Ham (Somerfield) *serving 90g/3oz*	4
Breaded Ham, Delicatessen (Marks & Spencer) *serving 90g/3oz*	2
British Ham (Somerfield) *serving 90g/3oz*	3
British Cooked Ham (Somerfield) *serving 90g/3oz*	4
British Honey Roast Ham (Somerfield) *serving 90g/3oz*	4
Cerrano Ham, Cold Meats (Tesco) *serving 90g/3oz*	12
Cheese & Chive Ham, Chilled (Iceland) *serving 90g/3oz*	4
Cheese Hamwich, Frozen (Bernard Matthews) *serving 90g/3oz*	14
Chopped Ham (Marks & Spencer) *serving 90g/3oz*	18
Chopped Ham, Delicatessen (Marks & Spencer) *serving 90g/3oz*	12
Chopped Ham & Pork (Princes) *serving 90g/3oz*	27
Cider Cured Ham (Waitrose) *serving 90g/3oz*	4
Continental Honey Ham (Waitrose) *serving 90g/3oz*	7
Cooked Ham (Somerfield) *serving 90g/3oz*	6
Cooked Ham, Delicatessen (Marks & Spencer) *serving 90g/3oz*	2
Cooked Ham on the Bone, Deli (Asda) *serving 90g/3oz*	6
Cooked & Roasted Ham, Deli (Asda) *serving 90g/3oz*	6
Crumbed Carving Ham (Waitrose) *serving 90g/3oz*	9
Crumbed Carving Ham Knuckle (Waitrose) *serving 90g/3oz*	9
Cured Ham, Boneless, Extra Lean (approx. 5% Fat), Roasted *serving 90g/3oz*	5
Cured Ham, Boneless, Regular (approx. 11% Fat), Roasted *serving 90g/3oz*	8

Cured Ham, Tinned, Extra Lean (approx. 4% Fat), Roasted *serving 90g/3oz* 4
Cured Ham, Tinned, Regular (approx. 13% Fat), Roasted *serving 90g/3oz* 14
Cured Ham, Chopped, Tinned *serving 90g/3oz* 17
Cured Ham, Chopped, not Tinned *serving 90g/3oz* 16
Cured Ham, Minced *serving 90g/3oz* 19
Cured Ham, Premium (Princes) *serving 90g/3oz* 5
Cured Ham, Whole, Lean & Fat, Roasted *serving 90g/3oz* 15
Cured Ham Patties, Grilled *serving 90g/3oz* 28
Danish Breaded Ham, Delicatessen (Marks & Spencer) *serving 90g/3oz* 5
Danish Ham, Delicatessen (Marks & Spencer) *serving 90g/3oz* 2
Danish Ham, Groceries (Marks & Spencer) *serving 90g/3oz* 3
Danish Ham, Wafer, Delicatessen (Marks & Spencer) *serving 90g/3oz* 3
Danish Roast Ham, Delicatessen (Marks & Spencer) *serving 90g/3oz* 5
English Ham (Waitrose) *serving 90g/3oz* 3
Free Range Ham, Cold Meats (Tesco) *serving 90g/3oz* 5
French Country Ham, Sliced (Waitrose) *serving 90g/3oz* 4
French Mustard Ham with Sugar (Somerfield) *serving 90g/3oz* 6
Gammon, British, Boiled, Delicatessen (Marks & Spencer) *serving 90g/3oz* 4
Gammon, British, Delicatessen (Marks & Spencer) *serving 90g/3oz* 4
Gammon, Cooked, no Added Water (Somerfield) *serving 90g/3oz* 6
Gammon, Danish Bacon Joint (Waitrose) *serving 90g/3oz* 8
Gammon, Free Range Joint, Main Meal (Marks & Spencer) *serving 90g/3oz* 2
Gammon, Free Range Steak, Main Meal (Marks & Spencer) *serving 90g/3oz* 2
Gammon, Half Holiday (Waitrose) *serving 90g/3oz* 14
Gammon, Herb, Delicatessen (Marks & Spencer) *serving 90g/3oz* 4
Gammon, Holiday, Unsmoked (Waitrose) *serving 90g/3oz* 14
Gammon, Honey Cured Steaks, Main Meal (Marks & Spencer) *serving 90g/3oz* 1

Gammon Joint, Chilled (Iceland) *serving 90g/3oz* 11
Gammon, Marinaded Steak, Main Meal (Marks & Spencer) *serving 90g/3oz* 3
Gammon, Premium, Cold Meats (Tesco) *serving 90g/3oz* 6
Gammon, Prepared Honey Gammon Joint, Main Meal (Marks & Spencer) *serving 90g/3oz* 4
Gammon, Prepared Joint, Main Meal (Marks & Spencer) *serving 90g/3oz* 4
Gammon, Scottish Roll (Somerfield) *serving 90g/3oz* 2
Gammon, Smoked Danish (Waitrose) *serving 90g/3oz* 8
Gammon, Smoked Joint (Somerfield) *serving 90g/3oz* 7
Gammon, Smoked Joint, Chilled (Iceland) *serving 90g/3oz* 8
Gammon, Smoked Slices, Delicatessen (Marks & Spencer) *serving 90g/3oz* 5
Gammon, Somerset, Delicatessen (Marks & Spencer) *serving 90g/3oz* 3
Gammon, Steaks, Chilled, Grilled (Iceland) *serving 90g/3oz* 6
Gammon Style Steaks (Bernard Matthews) *serving 90g/3oz* 8
Gammon, Topped Steak, Main Meal (Marks & Spencer) *serving 90g/3oz* 10
Gammon, Traditional Steaks (2), Main Meal (Marks & Spencer) *serving 90g/3oz* 4
Gammon, Unsmoked Joint (Somerfield) *serving 90g/3oz* 7
Gammon, Unsmoked Joint, Chilled (Iceland) *serving 90g/3oz* 2
Golden Jubilee Ham (Somerfield) *serving 90g/3oz* 6
Ham (Princes) *serving 90g/3oz* 8
Ham, Premium, Prepacked (Asda) *serving 90g/3oz* 4
Ham, Thin Sliced (Waitrose) *serving 90g/3oz* 2
Ham, Wafer, Standard, Delicatessen (Marks & Spencer) *serving 90g/3oz* 3
Ham & Broccoli Pappardelle (Asda) *serving 90g/3oz* 4
Ham & Cheese Savoury Slices, Frozen, Baked (Iceland) *serving 90g/3oz* 16
Ham & Egg Roll (Princes) *serving 90g/3oz* 16
Ham & Mustard, Delicatessen (Marks & Spencer) *serving 90g/3oz* 24
Hand Carved Ham (Waitrose) *serving 90g/3oz* 4

Honey Baked Ham (Somerfield) *serving 90g/3oz* 6
Honey Cured Ham, Groceries (Marks & Spencer) *serving 90g/3oz* 2
Honey Glazed Ham, Premium (Somerfield) *serving 90g/3oz* 2
Honey Roast Ham (Waitrose) *serving 90g/3oz* 5
Honey Roast Ham, British, Cold Meats (Tesco) *serving 90g/3oz* 2
Honeyroast Ham, Delicatessen (Marks & Spencer) *serving 90g/3oz* 2
Honey Roast Ham, Premium (Waitrose) *serving 90g/3oz* 4
Honey Roast Ham, Premium, Cold Meats (Tesco) *serving 90g/3oz* 4
Honey Roast Ham, Premium, Prepacked (Asda) *serving 90g/3oz* 5
Honey Roast Ham, Thin Sliced (Somerfield) *serving 90g/3oz* 4
Honeyroast Ham Wafer, Large, Delicatessen (Marks & Spencer) *serving 90g/3oz* 2
Honeyroast Ham, Wafer Thin (Somerfield) *serving 90g/3oz* 3
Honey Roast Ham, Wafer Thin (Waitrose) *serving 90g/3oz* 3
Honeyroast Ham, Wafer Thin, Cold Meats (Tesco) *serving 90g/3oz* 2
Honey Roast Ham off the Bone, Deli (Asda) *serving 90g/3oz* 4
Roasted Ham, Wafer Thin, Delicatessen (Marks & Spencer) *serving 90g/3oz* 3
Honey Roast Ham, Wafer Thin, (Prepacked) (Asda) *serving 90g/3oz* 2
Honeyroast Ham Joint, Delicatessen (Marks & Spencer) *serving 90g/3oz* 2
Honey Roast Yorkshire Ham, Cold Meats (Tesco) *serving 90g/3oz* 5
Honey/Mustard Ham, Delicatessen (Marks & Spencer) *serving 90g/3oz* 4
Italian Roast Ham (Waitrose) *serving 90g/3oz* 8
Jambon Parisien, Sliced (Waitrose) *serving 90g/3oz* 2
Leicester Easy Carve Ham (Waitrose) *serving 90g/3oz* 9
Luncheon Meat Ham, Chopped, Spiced, Tinned *serving 90g/3oz* 17
Luncheon Meat Ham, Extra Lean (approx. 5% Fat), Sliced *serving 90g/3oz* 4
Luncheon Meat Ham, Minced *serving 90g/3oz* 19

Luncheon Meat Ham (approx. 11% Fat), Sliced *serving 90g/3oz* 10
Marmalade Ham (Somerfield) *serving 90g/3oz* 6
Mild Cure Ham (Somerfield) *serving 90g/3oz* 2
Mild Cure Ham (Waitrose) *serving 90g/3oz* 5
Mild Cured Ham, Prepacked, Cold Meats (Tesco) *serving 90g/3oz* 4
Mini Breaded Ham, Delicatessen (Marks & Spencer) *serving 90g/3oz* 3
Mixed Pepper Ham, Deli (Asda) *serving 90g/3oz* 6
Pan Baked Ham & Pineapple (Waitrose) *serving 90g/3oz* 6
Parma Ham (Somerfield) *serving 90g/3oz* 16
Parma Ham (Waitrose) *serving 90g/3oz* 17
Parma Ham, Continental Selection, Cold Meats (Tesco) *serving 90g/3oz* 9
Parma Ham, Deli (Asda) *serving 90g/3oz* 14
Parma Ham, Delicatessen (Marks & Spencer) *serving 90g/3oz* 8
Parma Ham, Sliced, Cold Meats (Tesco) *serving 90g/3oz* 16
Parmigiano Reggiano (Waitrose) *serving 90g/3oz* 26
Peppered Ham (Somerfield) *serving 90g/3oz* 6
Peppered Ham (Waitrose) *serving 90g/3oz* 8
Peppered Ham, Prepacked (Asda) *serving 90g/3oz* 4
Prosciutto, Continental Selection, Cold Meats (Tesco) *serving 90g/3oz* 12
Prosciutto, Parma Kern (Waitrose) *serving 90g/3oz* 17
Roast Danish Ham, Delicatessen (Marks & Spencer) *serving 90g/3oz* 5
Roast Ham, Premium, Cold Meats (Tesco) *serving 90g/3oz* 6
Roast Ham, Prepacked (Asda) *serving 90g/3oz* 5
Serrano Ham (Waitrose) *serving 90g/3oz* 8
Smoked Ham, Beech Smoked Yorkshire, Cold Meats (Tesco) *serving 90g/3oz* 5
Smoked Ham, Beechwood, Deli (Asda) *serving 90g/3oz* 7
Smoked Ham, British, Cold Meats (Tesco) *serving 90g/3oz* 3
Smoked Ham, Brunswick (Waitrose) *serving 90g/3oz* 8
Smoked Ham, Continental (Waitrose) *serving 90g/3oz* 5
Smoked Ham, Cooked (Somerfield) *serving 90g/3oz* 2
Smoked Ham, Hickory (Somerfield) *serving 90g/3oz* 6

Smoked Ham, Norfolk (Bernard Matthews) *serving 90g/3oz* 1
Smoked Ham, Oak English (Waitrose) *serving 90g/3oz* 6
Smoked Ham, Oak Mini (Waitrose) *serving 90g/3oz* 3
Smoked Ham, Oven, Sliced (Waitrose) *serving'90g/3oz* 8
Smoked Ham, Premium, Cold Meats (Tesco) *serving 90g/3oz* 5
Smiked Ham, Premium, Oak (Waitrose) *serving 90g/3oz* 6
Smoked Ham, Premium, Prepacked (Asda) *serving 90g/3oz* 4
Smoked Ham, Slices, Chilled (Iceland) *serving 90g/3oz* 5
Smoked Ham, Spiced, Delicatessen (Marks & Spencer) *serving 90g/3oz* 4
Smoked Ham, Thin Sliced (Somerfield) *serving 90g/3oz* 3
Smoked Ham, Thin Sliced (Waitrose) *serving 90g/3oz* 2
Smoked Ham, Wafer, Delicatessen (Marks & Spencer) *serving 90g/3oz* 2
Smoked Ham, Wafer, Spiced, Delicatessen (Marks & Spencer) *serving 90g/3oz* 4
Smoked Ham, Wafer, Standard, Delicatessen (Marks & Spencer) *serving 90g/3oz* 2
Smoked Ham, Wafer Thin (Somerfield) *serving 90g/3oz* 2
Smoked Ham, Wafer Thin (Waitrose) *serving 90g/3oz* 3
Smoked Ham, Wafer Thin, Chilled (Iceland) *serving 90g/3oz* 2
Smoked Ham, Wafer Thin, Cold Meats (Tesco) *serving 90g/3oz* 2
Smoked Ham, Wafer Thin, Deli (Asda) *serving 90g/3oz* 3
Smoked Ham, Wafer Thin, Prepacked (Asda) *serving 90g/3oz* 3
Smoked Ham, Welsh (Waitrose) *serving 90g/3oz* 11
Smoked Ham & Cheese Slice, Chilled (Iceland) *serving 90g/3oz* 19
Smoked Ham & Mushroom (Findus Lean Cuisine Snackpots) *serving 90g/3oz* 1
Unsmoked Ham, Premium, Sliced Chilled (Iceland) *serving 90g/3oz* 2
Westphalian Ham (Waitrose) *serving 90g/3oz* 3
Wiltshire-Cured Ham (Somerfield) *serving 90g/3oz* 6
Wiltshire Ham, Sliced (Somerfield) *serving 90g/3oz* 6
Yorkshire Carver Ham, Deli (Asda) *serving 90g/3oz* 6
Yorkshire Ham, Sliced, Cold Meats (Tesco) *serving 90g/3oz* 5

ICES & LOLLIES

NOTE: The standard serving size in this section is 90g/3oz. If you wish to consume more or less than this amount (e.g. if you are going to consume a pack of food whose weight differs from the standard serving size) use the conversion tables on page 386 to calculate the new amount of fat in the food.

95% Fat Free Ice Cream Dessert (Sainsbury's) *serving 90g/3oz*	5
Almond Choc Bar, Magnum (Walls) *serving 90g/3oz*	22
Banana Dairy Ice Cream (Tesco) *serving 90g/3oz*	9
Banana & Toffee Cones Frozen (Iceland) *serving 90g/3oz*	11
Banoffee Dairy Ice Cream (Waitrose) *serving 90g/3oz*	9
Belgian Milk Chocolate Ice Cream (Waitrose) *serving 90g/3oz*	10
Big Bang (Walls) *serving 90g/3oz*	18
Blackberry & Apple Crumble Ice Cream, Exquisite (Somerfield) *serving 90g/3oz*	11
Blueberry Cheesecake Ice Cream (Waitrose) *serving 90g/3oz*	7
Bounty Chocolate Stick, Frozen (Mars) *serving 90g/3oz*	23
Butter/Toffee Soft Ice Cream (Waitrose) *serving 90g/3oz*	10
Cadbury Caramel Choc Bar (Walls) *serving 90g/3oz*	18
Cadbury Crunchie Choc Bar (Walls) *serving 90g/3oz*	18
Cappuccino Chunk Dessert, Frozen, Healthy Choice (Iceland) *serving 90g/3oz*	2
Cappuccino Ice Cream, Frozen (Marks & Spencer) *serving 90g/3oz*	10
Caramel Crispy Bar, Frozen (Tesco) *serving 90g/3oz*	25
Choc Chip, Gino Ginelli (Walls) *serving 90g/3oz*	10
Choc Hazelnut Dairy Cone (Waitrose) *serving 90g/3oz*	14
Choc Ices, Dark (Tesco) *serving 90g/3oz*	16
Choc Ices, Light (Tesco) *serving 90g/3oz*	17
Choc 'n' Nut Cones, Frozen, as Sold (Iceland) *serving 90g/3oz*	14
Choc & Nut Cornetto (Walls) *serving 90g/3oz*	15
Choc & Nut Ice Cream, Gino Ginelli (Walls) *serving 90g/3oz*	11
Choc & Nut Ice Cream Cones (Asda) *serving 90g/3oz*	15
Choc Nut Ice Cream Cones (Tesco) *serving 90g/3oz*	14
Choc & Nut Slice, Gino Ginelli (Walls) *serving 90g/3oz*	10
Choc 'n' Nut Supermousse (Walls) *serving 90g/3oz*	11

Chocolate Soft Ice Cream, Dairy (Waitrose) *serving 90g/3oz*	6
Chocolate Truffle Ice Cream (Waitrose) *serving 90g/3oz*	10
Chocolate & Banana Flavour Ice Cream Dessert (Asda) *serving 90g/3oz*	7
Chocolate Cherry Crunch Ice Cream (Asda) *serving 90g/3oz*	12
Chocolate Classics (4) (Asda) *serving 90g/3oz*	21
Chocolate Covered Ice Cream Bar *serving 90g/3oz*	21
Chocolate Fudge & Nut Ice (Waitrose) *serving 90g/3oz*	11
Chocolate Ice Cream *serving 90g/3oz*	10
Chocolate Ice Cream (Waitrose) *serving 90g/3oz*	13
Chocolate Ice Cream, Soft Scoop (Asda) *serving 90g/3oz*	8
Chocolate Ice Cream, Soft Scoop (Somerfield) *serving 90g/3oz*	7
Chocolate Ice Cream, Soft Scoop (Tesco) *serving 90g/3oz*	7
Chocolate Ice Cream, Soft Scoop (Walls) *serving 90g/3oz*	7
Chocolate Real Dairy Ice Cream (Somerfield) *serving 90g/3oz*	9
Chunky Choc Bar (Walls) *serving 90g/3oz*	20
Clotted Cream Fudge Ice Cream (Waitrose) *serving 90g/3oz*	8
Clotted Cream Ice Cream, Luxury (Waitrose) *serving 90g/3oz*	15
Clotted Cream/Raspberry Ice (Waitrose) *serving 90g/3oz*	7
Coffee Dairy Ice Cream (Waitrose) *serving 90g/3oz*	8
Cone, Sugar Rolled Type *serving 90g/3oz*	3
Cones, Cake or Wafer Type *serving 90g/3oz*	6
Cookies & Cream Ice Cream (Tesco) *serving 90g/3oz*	16
Cookies & Cream Ice Cream (Waitrose) *serving 90g/3oz*	8
Cool Bits (Walls) *serving 90g/3oz*	14
Cornet d'Or (Waitrose) *serving 90g/3oz*	40
Cornish Dairy Ice Cream (Waitrose) *serving 90g/3oz*	10
Cornish Raspberry Ripple, Frozen (Marks & Spencer) *serving 90g/3oz*	8
Cornish Raspberry Splits (Tesco) *serving 90g/3oz*	4
Cornish Vanilla Ice Cream, Frozen (Iceland) *serving 90g/3oz*	8
Cornish Vanilla Ice Cream, Soft Scoop, Frozen (Marks & Spencer) *serving 90g/3oz*	11
Country Cream Liqueur Ice Cream (Asda) *serving 90g/3oz*	14
Cream of Cornish Vanilla Ice Cream (Walls) *serving 90g/3oz*	8
Creamy Butterscotch Fudge Ice Cream (Asda) *serving 90g/3oz*	17
Dark Choc Bar, Blue Ribbon (Walls) *serving 90g/3oz*	18

Dark Choc Ices (Asda) *serving 90g/3oz*	19
Dark Choc Ices, (Iceland) *serving 90g/3oz*	18
Dark Choc Ices (Somerfield) *serving 90g/3oz*	11
Dark Choc Ices (Tesco) *serving 90g/3oz*	16
Dark Choc Ices (Waitrose) *serving 90g/3oz*	19
Dark Chocolate Choc Bar, Magnum (Walls) *serving 90g/3oz*	19
Double Choc Cones (4), Frozen, as Sold (Iceland) *serving 90g/3oz*	12
Double Choc Crunch, Gino Ginelli (Walls) *serving 90g/3oz*	11
Double Chocolate Choc Bar, Magnum (Walls) *serving 90g/3oz*	20
Double Chocolate Crisp Ice Cream (Asda) *serving 90g/3oz*	16
Dove Milk, Frozen (Mars) *serving 90g/3oz*	19
Exoticas, Mini, Frozen (Iceland) *serving 90g/3oz*	5
Feast, Big (Walls) *serving 90g/3oz*	25
Feast, Toffee (Walls) *serving 90g/3oz*	24
Fruit & Juice Bars *serving 90g/3oz*	0
Galaxy Milk/Petite (Mars) *serving 90g/3oz*	19
Golden Vanilla Ice Cream, Sliceable (Walls) *serving 90g/3oz*	8
Ice Lollies, Low Sugar, Frozen (Iceland) *serving 90g/3oz*	0
Ice Snaps, Orange & Lemon Flavour (Asda) *serving 90g/3oz*	0
Iced Bar, Standard (Somerfield) *serving 90g/3oz*	9
Knickerbocker Glory, Frozen (Marks & Spencer) *serving 90g/3oz*	10
Lemon Juice Bar, Frozen (Marks & Spencer) *serving 90g/3oz*	0
Light Choc Bar, Blue Ribbon (Walls) *serving 90g/3oz*	18
Light Choc Ices (Asda) *serving 90g/3oz*	19
Light Choc Ices (Iceland) *serving 90g/3oz*	16
Light Choc Ices (Somerfield) *serving 90g/3oz*	11
Light Choc Ices (Tesco) *serving 90g/3oz*	17
Mango/Passion Fruit Ice Cream (Waitrose) *serving 90g/3oz*	7
Maple & Almond Ice Cream (Waitrose) *serving 90g/3oz*	13
Mars, Frozen *serving 90g/3oz*	18
Mars, Dark, Frozen *serving 90g/3oz*	18
Mars, Mini, Frozen *serving 90g/3oz*	19
Mars, Stick, Frozen *serving 90g/3oz*	16
Milk Choc Ices (Marks & Spencer) *serving 90g/3oz*	14
Milk Choc Ices (Waitrose) *serving 90g/3oz*	18
Milk Chocolate Choc Bar, Blue Ribbon (Walls) *serving 90g/3oz*	18
Milk Chocolate, Real, Choc Ices (Somerfield) *serving 90g/3oz*	21

Milky Way (Mars) *serving 90g/3oz* 20
Milky Way Abracadabra (Mars) *serving 90g/3oz* 5
Mint Choc Chip, Gino Ginelli (Walls) *serving 90g/3oz* 11
Mint Choc Bar, Magnum (Walls) *serving 90g/3oz* 18
Mint Choc Chip, Cornetto (Walls) *serving 90g/3oz* 13
Mint Choc Chip Ice Cream, Gino Ginelli (Walls) *serving 90g/3oz* 9
Mint Choc Chip Dessert, Healthy Choice, Frozen (Iceland) *serving 90g/3oz* 2
Mint Ice Cream, Soft Scoop (Walls) *serving 90g/3oz* 9
Mountain Bar, Frozen (Marks & Spencer) *serving 90g/3oz* 23
Mousses, Sweet: *see under* Desserts
Mousses, Savoury: *see under* main ingredient
Neapolitan Brick (Tesco) *serving 90g/3oz* 6
Neopolitan Cones, Frozen (Iceland) *serving 90g/3oz* 14
Neopolitan Ice Cream (Iceland) *serving 90g/3oz* 7
Neapolitan Ice Cream (Waitrose) *serving 90g/3oz* 7
Neapolitan Ice Cream, Gino Ginelli (Walls) *serving 90g/3oz* 7
Neopolitan Ice Cream, Soft Scoop (Marks & Spencer) *serving 90g/3oz* 7
Neapolitan Ice Cream, Soft Scoop (Somerfield) *serving 90g/3oz* 7
Neapolitan Ice Cream, Soft Scoop (Tesco) *serving 90g/3oz* 8
Now Bar, Frozen (Marks & Spencer) *serving 90g/3oz* 20
Opal Fruits, Blackcurrant (Mars) *serving 90g/3oz* 1
Opal Fruits, Orange & Lemon (Mars) *serving 90g/3oz* 1
Opal Fruits, Strawberry (Mars) *serving 90g/3oz* 1
Orange & Blackcurrant Ice Breakers, Frozen (Iceland) *serving 90g/3oz* 0
Orange Flavour Ice Lolly (Waitrose) *serving 90g/3oz* 0
Orange Frutie (Walls) *serving 90g/3oz* 0
Orange Juice Bar, Frozen (Marks & Spencer) *serving 90g/3oz* 0
Orange Juice Lollies, Frozen (Iceland) *serving 90g/3oz* 0
Orange Lollies (Somerfield) *serving 90g/3oz* 1
Peanut Butter Ice Cream (Waitrose) *serving 90g/3oz* 9
Peanut Clusters, Gino Ginelli (Walls) *serving 90g/3oz* 10
Raspberry Ripple Ice Cream (Iceland) *serving 90g/3oz* 3
Raspberry Ripple Ice Cream (Tesco) *serving 90g/3oz* 6
Raspberry Ripple Ice Cream (Waitrose) *serving 90g/3oz* 9

Raspberry Ripple Ice Cream, Soft Scoop (Somerfield) *serving 90g/3oz* 6
Raspberry Ripple Ice Cream, Soft Scoop (Tesco) *serving 90g/3oz* 6
Raspberry Ripple Ice Cream, Soft Scoop (Walls) *serving 90g/3oz* 6
Raspberry Ripple Slice, Gino Ginelli (Walls) *serving 90g/3oz* 7
Raspberry Splits (Asda) *serving 90g/3oz* 3
Rocket Lollies (Iceland) *serving 90g/3oz* 0
Rocket Lollies (Somerfield) *serving 90g/3oz* 0
Rocky Road Iced Dessert, Healthy Choice, Frozen (Iceland) *serving 90g/3oz* 4
Rum & Raisin Ice Cream (Waitrose) *serving 90g/3oz* 6
Rum & Raisin Ice Cream, Gino Ginelli (Walls) *serving 90g/3oz* 7
Rum & Raisin Ice Cream, Soft Scoop (Walls) *serving 90g/3oz* 7
Skittles, Frozen (Mars) *serving 90g/3oz* 0
Snickers, Frozen (Mars) *serving 90g/3oz* 22
Solero, Forest Fruits (Walls) *serving 90g/3oz* 5
Sorbet, Blackcurrant (Tesco) *serving 90g/3oz* 0
Sorbet, Passion Fruit (Tesco) *serving 90g/3oz* 0
Sorbet, Tropical Fruit (Waitrose) *serving 90g/3oz* 0
Splits, Fruit, Assorted (Tesco) *serving 90g/3oz* 3
Splits, Ice Lollies, Assorted (Iceland) *serving 90g/3oz* 4
Splits, Raspberry (Asda) *serving 90g/3oz* 3
Splits, Strawberry (Iceland) *serving 90g/3oz* 4
Strawberry Champagne Swirl Ice Cream (Asda) *serving 90g/3oz* 17
Strawberries & Cream Ice Cream (Tesco) *serving 90g/3oz* 10
Strawberry & Cream Ice Cream (Waitrose) *serving 90g/3oz* 9
Strawberry, Cornetto (Walls) *serving 90g/3oz* 9
Strawberry Ice Cream *serving 90g/3oz* 8
Strawberry Ice Cream, Dairy (Waitrose) *serving 90g/3oz* 9
Strawberry Ice Cream, Soft Scoop (Somerfield) *serving 90g/3oz* 7
Strawberry Ice Cream, Soft Scoop (Tesco) *serving 90g/3oz* 7
Strawberry Ice Cream, Soft Scoop (Walls) *serving 90g/3oz* 7
Strawberry Light Ice Cream, Soft Scoop (Walls) *serving 90g/3oz* 6
Strawberry Pavlova Ice Cream, Exquisite (Somerfield) *serving 90g/3oz* 7
Strawberry, Real Dairy Ice Cream (Somerfield) *serving 90g/3oz* 7
Strawberry Splits (Iceland) *serving 90g/3oz* 4

Strawberry Splits (Walls) *serving 90g/3oz* 4
Strawberry Supermousse (Walls) *serving 90g/3oz* 4
Strawberry Swirl Dairy Ice Cream (Tesco) *serving 90g/3oz* 10
Strawberry & Vanilla Cone, Frozen (Marks & Spencer) *serving 90g/3oz* 14
Sundae, Ice Cream, Caramel *serving 90g/3oz* 5
Sundae, Ice Cream, Hot Fudge *serving 90g/3oz* 5
Sundae, Ice Cream, Strawberry *serving 90g/3oz* 5
Super Mario (Walls) *serving 90g/3oz* 8
Tangle Twister (Walls) *serving 90g/3oz* 2
Tartufo Ice Cream (Marks & Spencer) *serving 90g/3oz* 17
Tiramisu Ice Cream (Marks & Spencer) *serving 90g/3oz* 12
Toffee Choc Bar, Blue Ribbon (Walls) *serving 90g/3oz* 18
Toffee Crunch Ice Cream (Iceland) *serving 90g/3oz* 8
Toffee Crunch Ice Cream (Tesco) *serving 90g/3oz* 7
Toffee Fudge, Gino Ginelli (Walls) *serving 90g/3oz* 9
Toffee Fudge & Hazelnut Surprise Ice Cream, Exquisite (Somerfield) *serving 90g/3oz* 12
Toffee Fudge Supermousse (Walls) *serving 90g/3oz* 6
Toffee Ice Cream, Soft Scoop (Walls) *serving 90g/3oz* 9
Toffee Real Dairy Ice Cream (Somerfield) *serving 90g/3oz* 9
Toffee Ripple Dairy Ice Cream (Tesco) *serving 90g/3oz* 10
Toffee Sundae, Chilled (Iceland) *serving 90g/3oz* 16
Topic (Mars) *serving 90g/3oz* 21
Triple Choc Ice Cream, Gino Ginelli (Walls) *serving 90g/3oz* 9
Triple Chocolate Ice Cream, Exquisite (Somerfield) *serving 90g/3oz* 11
Turkish Delight Ice Cream (Waitrose) *serving 90g/3oz* 7
Tutti Frutti Ice Cream (Waitrose) *serving 90g/3oz* 6
Tutti Frutti Ice Cream, Gino Ginelli (Walls) *serving 90g/3oz* 7
Twix, Frozen (Mars) *serving 90g/3oz* 22
Vanilla Cream of Cornish (Walls) *serving 90g/3oz* 7
Vanilla Flavour, Basics (Somerfield) *serving 90g/3oz* 5
Vanilla Flavour Ice Cream, Cutting Brick (Tesco) *serving 90g/3oz* 6
Vanilla Flavour Ice Cream, Soft Scoop (Asda) *serving 90g/3oz* 6
Vanilla Flavour Ice Cream, Soft Scoop (Tesco) *serving 90g/3oz* 7
Vanilla, French, Ice Cream Soft Serve *serving 90g/3oz* 12

Vanilla Golden Ice Cream (Walls) *serving 90g/3oz*	8
Vanilla Ice Cream *serving 90g/3oz*	10
Vanilla Ice Cream (Waitrose) *serving 90g/3oz*	8
Vanilla Ice Cream, Cutting Block (Somerfield) *serving 90g/3oz*	6
Vanilla Ice Cream, Dairy (Waitrose) *serving 90g/3oz*	10
Vanilla Ice Cream, Hard (Tesco) *serving 90g/3oz*	5
Vanilla Ice Cream, Original Economy, Frozen (Iceland) *serving 90g/3oz*	2
Vanilla Ice Cream, Rich *serving 90g/3oz*	15
Vanilla Ice Cream, Soft (Waitrose) *serving 90g/3oz*	8
Vanilla Ice Cream, Soft Scoop (Asda) *serving 90g/3oz*	8
Vanilla Ice Cream, Soft Scoop (Marks & Spencer) *serving 90g/3oz*	7
Vanilla Ice Cream, Soft Scoop (Somerfield) *serving 90g/3oz*	7
Vanilla Ice Cream, Soft Scoop (Tesco) *serving 90g/3oz*	7
Vanilla Ice Cream, Soft Scoop, Blue Ribbon (Walls) *serving 90g/3oz*	9
Vanilla Ice Cream, Super Value (Iceland) *serving 90g/3oz*	2
Vanilla Ice Milk, Soft Serve *serving 90g/3oz*	2
Vanilla, Jersey, Frozen (Marks & Spencer) *serving 90g/3oz*	15
Vanilla Light Ice Cream, Soft Scoop, Blue Ribbon (Walls) *serving 90g/3oz*	6
Vanilla Real Dairy Ice Cream (Somerfield) *serving 90g/3oz*	9
Vanilla Slice (Somerfield) *serving 90g/3oz*	27
Vanilla/Strawberry Ripple (Walls) *serving 90g/3oz*	1
Vanilla Traditional Dairy Ice Cream (Tesco) *serving 90g/3oz*	16
Vanilla Ice Cream, Yellow (Iceland) *serving 90g/3oz*	7
Walnut Whirl Ice Creams (Iceland) *serving 90g/3oz*	15
Whippy Ice Cream in Medium Cone (Walls) *serving 90g/3oz*	6
White Choc Ices (Iceland) *serving 90g/3oz*	12
White Chocolate Choc Bar, Magnum (Walls) *serving 90g/3oz*	20
White Chocolate Crisp Ice Cream (Asda) *serving 90g/3oz*	14
White Chocolate Ice Cream (Waitrose) *serving 90g/3oz*	11
White Chocolate, Real, Choc Ices (Somerfield) *serving 90g/3oz*	22
Wild Strawberries & Cream, Frozen (Marks & Spencer) *serving 90g/3oz*	6
Yule Log, Christmas, Ice Cream (Marks & Spencer) *serving 90g/3oz*	8
Yule Logs, Mini Ice Cream (Iceland) *serving 90g/3oz*	9

Jam, Toppings & Preserves

NOTE: The standard serving size in this section is 30g/1oz. If you wish to consume more or less than this amount (e.g. if you are going to consume a pack of food whose weight differs from the standard serving size) use the conversion tables on page 386 to calculate the new amount of fat in the food.

Apricot Conserve (Marks & Spencer) *serving 30g/1oz*	0
Blackcherry Conserve (Waitrose) *serving 30g/1oz*	0
Blackcurrant Conserve (Marks & Spencer) *serving 30g/1oz*	0
Brandy Butter (Waitrose) *serving 30g/1oz*	11
Brandy Sauce, Fresh (Somerfield) *serving 30g/1oz*	2
Chocolate Hazelnut Spread (Waitrose) *serving 30g/1oz*	11
Chocolate Nut Spread *serving 30g/1oz*	10
Chocolate Sauce (Asda) *serving 30g/1oz*	9
Chocolate Sauce, Groceries (Marks & Spencer) *serving 30g/1oz*	2
Chocolate Spread *serving 30g/1oz*	11
Chocolate Syrup *serving 30g/1oz*	0
Cranberry/Port Wine Mince (Waitrose) *serving 30g/1oz*	1
Creamed Horseradish (Waitrose) *serving 30g/1oz*	3
Dessert Sauce (Ambrosia) (CPC) *serving 30g/1oz*	1
Fruit Butters, Apple *serving 30g/1oz*	0
Fruit Spread *serving 30g/1oz*	0
Ginger, Stem, in Syrup (Waitrose) *serving 30g/1oz*	0
Honey *serving 30g/1oz*	0
Honey, Comb *serving 30g/1oz*	1
Ice Cream Sauce Topping *serving 30g/1oz*	0
Icing Fondant *serving 30g/1oz*	0
Icing Glacé *serving 30g/1oz*	0
Icing Royal *serving 30g/1oz*	0
Jam, Apple & Strawberry, Basics (Somerfield) *serving 30g/1oz*	0
Jam, Apricot (Somerfield) *serving 30g/1oz*	0
Jam, Blackcurrant (Iceland) *serving 30g/1oz*	0
Jam, Blackcurrant (Somerfield) *serving 30g/1oz*	0
Jam, Diabetic *serving 30g/1oz*	0
Jam, Fruit with Edible Seeds *serving 30g/1oz*	0
Jam, Ginger, Extra (Waitrose) *serving 30g/1oz*	0

Jam, Mixed Fruit, Basics (Somerfield) *serving 30g/1oz*	0
Jam, Morello Cherry (Waitrose) *serving 30g/1oz*	0
Jam, Raspberry (Iceland) *serving 30g/1oz*	0
Jam, Raspberry (Somerfield) *serving 30g/1oz*	0
Jam, Reduced Sugar *serving 30g/1oz*	0
Jam, Stone Fruit *serving 30g/1oz*	0
Jam, Strawberry (Iceland) *serving 30g/1oz*	0
Jam, Strawberry (Somerfield) *serving 30g/1oz*	0
Jellies *serving 30g/1oz*	0
Lemon Curd *serving 30g/1oz*	2
Lemon Curd (Waitrose) *serving 30g/1oz*	3
Lemon Curd, Home Made *serving 30g/1oz*	5
Maple Syrup (Marks & Spencer) *serving 30g/1oz*	0
Marmalade, Frank Cooper's (CPC) *serving 30g/1oz*	0
Marmalade, Fresh Lemon (Waitrose) *serving 30g/1oz*	0
Marmalade, Lemon Jelly (Waitrose) *serving 30g/1oz*	0
Marmalade, Lemon & Lime (Marks & Spencer) *serving 30g/1oz*	0
Marmalade, Lemon Shred (Somerfield) *serving 30g/1oz*	0
Marmalade, Mandarin (Marks & Spencer) *serving 30g/1oz*	0
Marmalade, Medium Cut (Somerfield) *serving 30g/1oz*	0
Marmalade, Medium Cut Orange (Marks & Spencer) *serving 30g/1oz*	0
Marmalade, Orange *serving 30g/1oz*	0
Marmalade, Orange Shred (Somerfield) *serving 30g/1oz*	0
Marmalade, Thick Cut (Iceland) *serving 30g/1oz*	0
Marmalade, Thin Cut (Marks & Spencer) *serving 30g/1oz*	0
Marmalade, Thin Cut (Somerfield) *serving 30g/1oz*	0
Marmalade, Three Fruits (Waitrose) *serving 30g/1oz*	0
Mincemeat, Special (Waitrose) *serving 30g/1oz*	2
Mincemeat, Traditional (Waitrose) *serving 30g/1oz*	1
Miso *serving 30g/1oz*	2
Molasses *serving 30g/1oz*	0
Molasses, Blackstrap *serving 30g/1oz*	0
Molasses, Cane (Waitrose) *serving 30g/1oz*	0
Orange Curd, Luxury (Waitrose) *serving 30g/1oz*	3
Plum, Victoria Conserve (Waitrose) *serving 30g/1oz*	0
Raspberry Curd (Waitrose) *serving 30g/1oz*	2

Raspberry Conserve (Marks & Spencer) *serving 30g/1oz*	0
Red Cherry Conserve (Marks & Spencer) *serving 30g/1oz*	0
Rum Flavour Sauce (Kraft) *serving 30g/1oz*	2
Rum Sauce (Somerfield) *serving 30g/1oz*	2
Strawberry Conserve (Marks & Spencer) *serving 30g/1oz*	0
Strawberry Conserve (Waitrose) *serving 30g/1oz*	0
Sugar, Brown *serving 30g/1oz*	0
Sugar, Demerara *serving 30g/1oz*	0
Sugar, Icing *serving 30g/1oz*	0
Syrup, Chocolate Fudge Type *serving 30g/1oz*	4
Syrup, Corn, Dark *serving 30g/1oz*	0
Syrup, Corn, High Fructose *serving 30g/1oz*	0
Syrup, Corn, Light *serving 30g/1oz*	0
Syrup, Golden *serving 30g/1oz*	0
Syrup, Malt *serving 30g/1oz*	0
Syrup, Maple *serving 30g/1oz*	0
Syrup, Pouring *serving 30g/1oz*	0
Syrup, Sorghum *serving 30g/1oz*	0
Syrup, Table Blends, Cane & 15% Maple *serving 30g/1oz*	0
Syrup, Table Blends, Pancake *serving 30g/1oz*	0
Syrup, Table Blends, Pancake, Reduced Calorie *serving 30g/1oz*	0
Syrup, Table Blends, Pancake, with 2% Maple *serving 30g/1oz*	0
Toffee Sauce, Groceries (Marks & Spencer) *serving 30g/1oz*	1
Tomato, Apple/Tarragon Relish (Waitrose) *serving 30g/1oz*	0
Tomato, Onion/Garlic Relish (Waitrose) *serving 30g/1oz*	0
Toppings, Butterscotch or Caramel *serving 30g/1oz*	0
Toppings, Marshmallow Cream *serving 30g/1oz*	0
Toppings, Nuts in Syrup *serving 30g/1oz*	7
Toppings, Pineapple *serving 30g/1oz*	0
Toppings, Strawberry *serving 30g/1oz*	0
Treacle, Black *serving 30g/1oz*	0

Lamb

NOTE: The standard serving size in this section is 110g/4oz. If you wish to consume more or less than this amount (e.g. if you are going to consume a pack of food whose weight differs from the standard serving size) use the conversion tables on page 386 to calculate the new amount of fat in the food.

Blade (Waitrose) *serving 110g/4oz*	31
Brain, Braised *serving 110g/4oz*	11
Chops, British Butterfly (Waitrose) *serving 110g/4oz*	39
Chops, British Leg (Waitrose) *serving 110g/4oz*	21
Chops, & Cutlets (Waitrose) *serving 110g/4oz*	39
Chops, Kashmiri (Waitrose) *serving 110g/4oz*	19
Chops, Loin (Waitrose) *serving 110g/4oz*	39
Chops, Loin, Fresh, Grilled (Iceland) *serving 110g/4oz*	40
Chops, New Zealand, Chilled (Waitrose) *serving 110g/4oz*	28
Chops, New Zealand, Chump (Waitrose) *serving 110g/4oz*	11
Chops, New Zealand, Frozen (Iceland) *serving 110g/4oz*	18
Chops, Salsa Flavoured (Waitrose) *serving 110g/4oz*	16
Chops, Select Choice (Somerfield) *serving 110g/4oz*	25
Chops, Select Choice, Chump (Somerfield) *serving 110g/4oz*	14
Chops, Welsh (Waitrose) *serving 110g/4oz*	11
Crown of Lamb (Waitrose) *serving 110g/4oz*	22
Curry, Lamb & Tomato (Marks & Spencer) *serving 110g/4oz*	7
Curry, Mutton *serving 110g/4oz*	37
Cutlets (Waitrose) *serving 110g/4oz*	39
Cutlets, New Zealand, Chilled (Waitrose) *serving 110g/4oz*	28
Cutlets, New Zealand, Frozen, Grilled (Iceland) *serving 110g/4oz*	40
Diced, Chilled, Healthy Eating (Tesco) *serving 110g/4oz*	5
Diced, Chilled, New Zealand (Waitrose) *serving 110g/4oz*	11
Diced, Farmhouse (Waitrose) *serving 110g/4oz*	14
Dopiaza (Waitrose) *serving 110g/4oz*	10
Glazed Boneless Lamb, Fresh (Marks & Spencer) *serving 110g/4oz*	6
Grillsteaks (Birds Eye) *serving 110g/4oz*	23
Grillsteaks (Somerfield) *serving 110g/4oz*	22
Grillsteaks, Frozen, Grilled (Iceland) *serving 110g/4oz*	33
Grillsteaks, Main Meal (Marks & Spencer) *serving 110g/4oz*	18
Ground Lamb (Waitrose) *serving 110g/4oz*	20

Ground, New Zealand, Chilled (Waitrose) *serving 110g/4oz*	17
Half Knuckles of Lamb (Waitrose) *serving 110g/4oz*	21
Heart, Braised *serving 110g/4oz*	9
Jalfrezi, Lamb, with Rice, Microwave Ready Meal (Safeway) *serving 110g/4oz*	8
Kebabs, Fresh (Marks & Spencer) *serving 110g/4oz*	8
Kebab Selection, Frozen (Iceland) *serving 110g/4oz*	14
Kheema *serving 110g/4oz*	32
Kidney (Somerfield) *serving 110g/4oz*	3
Kidneys, Braised *serving 110g/4oz*	4
Kofta al Fresco, Lamb (Waitrose) *serving 110g/4oz*	11
Lamb Casserole, Main Meal (Marks & Spencer) *serving 110g/4oz*	6
Lamb Chop, Pieces, Frozen, Grill (Iceland) *serving 110g/4oz*	9
Lamb Garlic Marinade, Fresh (Marks & Spencer) *serving 110g/4oz*	9
Lamb Joint, Prepared, Fresh (Marks & Spencer) *serving 110g/4oz*	15
Lamb & Mint Dumplings, Large, Main Meal (Marks & Spencer) *serving 110g/4oz*	11
Lamb Pasanda (Marks & Spencer) *serving 110g/4oz*	5
Lamb Roast (Bernard Matthews) *serving 110g/4oz*	13
Lamb Roast, Main Meal (Marks & Spencer) *serving 110g/4oz*	38
Lamb with Garden Vegetables (Waitrose) *serving 110g/4oz*	4
Lamb & Vegetable Casserole, Lunch Bowl, Ready Meal (Heinz) *serving 110g/4oz*	3
Lancashire Hot Pot, Frozen (Asda) *serving 110g/4oz*	6
Leg, Boneless, Half (Waitrose) *serving 110g/4oz*	25
Leg, British, Whole of (Waitrose) *serving 110g/4oz*	22
Leg, Carvery of (Waitrose) *serving 110g/4oz*	22
Leg, Choice, Whole, Untrimmed (Separable Lean & Fat) Roasted *serving 110g/4oz*	18
Leg, County (Waitrose) *serving 110g/4oz*	21
Leg, Farmhouse, Boneless (Waitrose) *serving 110g/4oz*	21
Leg, Farmhouse, Whole (Waitrose) *serving 110g/4oz*	21
Leg, Half, Fresh Roast (Iceland) *serving 110g/4oz*	21
Leg, Knuckle (Marks & Spencer) *serving 110g/4oz*	4
Leg, Marinated (Waitrose) *serving 110g/4oz*	4

Leg, New Zealand, 1/2 Fillet, Frozen, Roasted (Iceland) *serving 110g/4oz*	21
Leg, New Zealand, 1/2 Knuckle, Frozen, Roasted (Iceland) *serving 110g/4oz*	21
Leg, New Zealand, Frozen, Whole, Untrimmed (Separable Lean & Fat), Roasted *serving 110g/4oz*	17
Leg, New Zealand, Whole, Frozen (Iceland) *serving 110g/4oz*	21
Leg, New Zealand, Whole, Frozen, Roasted (Iceland) *serving 110g/4oz*	21
Leg, Select Choice (Somerfield) *serving 110g/4oz*	14
Leg, Whole (Waitrose) *serving 110g/4oz*	21
Leg, Whole, Frozen, Roast (Iceland) *serving 110g/4oz*	21
Liver, Braised *serving 110g/4oz*	10
Liver, Fresh, Fried (Iceland) *serving 110g/4oz*	11
Liver, Pan Fried *serving 110g/4oz*	14
Loin, English County (Waitrose) *serving 110g/4oz*	39
Loin, Stuffed (Waitrose) *serving 110g/4oz*	15
Lungs, Braised *serving 110g/4oz*	3
Madras, Lamb (Safeway) *serving 110g/4oz*	50
Minced Lamb (Marks & Spencer) *serving 110g/4oz*	6
Minced Lamb, Extra Fill (Marks & Spencer) *serving 110g/4oz*	6
Minced Lamb, Frozen (Waitrose) *serving 110g/4oz*	21
Minced Lamb & Mint Dumplings (Marks & Spencer) *serving 110g/4oz*	9
Moussaka *serving 110g/4oz*	15
Moussaka, Lamb, Frozen Ready Meal (Heinz Weight Watchers) *serving 110g/4oz*	2
Mutton Biriani *serving 110g/4oz*	19
Neck Fillets, Farmhouse (Waitrose) *serving 110g/4oz*	31
Neck Fillets (Waitrose) *serving 110g/4oz*	31
Neck Fillets, New Zealand (Waitrose) *serving 110g/4oz*	11
Pancreas, Braised *serving 110g/4oz*	17
Quarter Pounders, Lamb (Somerfield) *serving 110g/4oz*	22
Rogan Josh, Lamb (Waitrose) *serving 110g/4oz*	14
Rogan Goshi, Lamb, Chilled Ready Meal (Tesco) *serving 110g/4oz*	9
Rosemary, Lamb (Waitrose) *serving 110g/4oz*	7
Saddle of Lamb (Waitrose) *serving 110g/4oz*	22

Samosa Curry Pot, Jumbo (Asda) *serving 110g/4oz*	15
Samosa Curry Pot, Mini (Asda) *serving 110g/4oz*	9
Samosa, Lamb (Safeway) *serving 110g/4oz*	12
Samosa, Lamb (Somerfield) *serving 110g/4oz*	15
Samosa, Lamb (Waitrose) *serving 110g/4oz*	13
Shepherd's Pie *serving 110g/4oz*	7
Shoulder (Waitrose) *serving 110g/4oz*	22
Shoulder, Boneless (Waitrose) *serving 110g/4oz*	22
Shoulder, Boneless, Fresh, Roasted (Iceland) *serving 110g/4oz*	31
Shoulder, British (Waitrose) *serving 110g/4oz*	22
Shoulder, Choice, Untrimmed (Separable Lean & Fat), Roasted *serving 110g/4oz*	22
Shoulder, Farmhouse, Boneless (Waitrose) *serving 110g/4oz*	31
Shoulder, Farmhouse, Half (Waitrose) *serving 110g/4oz*	31
Shoulder, Half Knuckle (Waitrose) *serving 110g/4oz*	31
Shoulder, with Mint (Waitrose) *serving 110g/4oz*	22
Shoulder, New Zealand, Chops (Waitrose) *serving 110g/4oz*	22
Shoulder, New Zealand, Frozen, Whole (Arm & Blade), Untrimmed (Separable Lean & Fat), Braised *serving 110g/4oz*	29
Shoulder, New Zealand, Half (Waitrose) *serving 110g/4oz*	22
Shoulder, New Zealand, Stuffed, Fresh (Marks & Spencer) *serving 110g/4oz*	13
Shoulder, Select Choice, Boneless, Rolled (Somerfield) *serving 110g/4oz*	29
Shoulder, Select Choice of (Somerfield) *serving 110g/4oz*	29
Shoulder, Steaks, Fresh, Roast (Iceland) *serving 110g/4oz*	31
Shoulder, Stuffed (Waitrose) *serving 110g/4oz*	21
Shoulder, Welsh Chops (Waitrose) *serving 110g/4oz*	22
Sliced Lamb, Quick Cook (Waitrose) *serving 110g/4oz*	21
Spleen, Braised *serving 110g/4oz*	5
Steaks, Farmhouse, Chump (Waitrose) *serving 110g/4oz*	39
Stewing Lamb (Waitrose) *serving 110g/4oz*	31
Stewing Lamb, Frozen, Stewed (Iceland) *serving 110g/4oz*	31
Stir Fry Lamb, Quick Cook (Waitrose) *serving 110g/4oz*	21
Stuffed Lamb Joint, Fresh (Marks & Spencer) *serving 110g/4oz*	20
Thai Flavoured Lamb (Waitrose) *serving 110g/4oz*	23
Tongue, Braised *serving 110g/4oz*	22

Welsh Lamb Cutlets (Waitrose) *serving 110g/4oz* 39

Welsh Lamb, Whole (Waitrose) *serving 110g/4oz* 22

Welsh Lamb, Whole & $^1/_2$ (Waitrose) *serving 110g/4oz* 22

Whole Lamb Loin (Waitrose) *serving 110g/4oz* 39

Whole Lamb, New Zealand, Chilled (Waitrose) *serving 110g/4oz* 22

Milk

NOTE: The standard serving size in this section is 1 cup/250g. If you wish to consume more or less than this amount (e.g. if you are going to consume a carton of milk whose weight differs from the standard serving size) use the conversion tables on page 386 to calculate the new amount of fat in the food.

Ayrshires Semi Skimmed Milk (Waitrose) *1 cup/250g* 4

Ayrshires Whole Milk (Waitrose) *1 cup/250g* 10

Banana Flavoured Milk, Chilled (Tesco) *1 cup/250g* 4

Banana Milk (Marks & Spencer) *1 cup/250g* 4

Buttermilk *1 cup/250g* 2

Carnation (Nestlé) *1 cup/250g* 23

Carnation Light (Nestlé) *1 cup/250g* 10

Channel Isle Milk (Waitrose) *1 cup/250g* 13

Chocolate Beverage, Hot Cocoa, Home Made *1 cup/250g* 9

Chocolate Drink, Made with Low Fat 1% Fat Milk *1 cup/250g* 3

Chocolate Drink, Made with Whole Milk *1 cup/250g* 8

Chocolate Flavoured Milk, Chilled (Tesco) *1 cup/250g* 9

Chocolate Milk Drink, Made with Low Fat 2% Fat Milk *1 cup/250g* 5

Chocolate, Milkshake, Milk (Marks & Spencer) *1 cup/250g* 5

Chocolate Milkshake, Extra Thick, American Style, Chilled (Tesco) *serving 1 cup/250g* 7

Condensed Milk, Sweetened, Tinned *1 cup/250g* 22

Evaporated Milk, (Somerfield) *1 cup/250g* 23

Evaporated Milk (Waitrose) *1 cup/250g* 23

Evapotated Milk, Full Cream (Tesco) *1 cup/250g* 23

Evaporated Milk, Low Fat (Somerfield) *1 cup/250g* 10

Evaporated Milk, Skimmed, Tinned *1 cup/250g* 1

Fresh Milk (Asda) *1 cup/250g* 10
Full Cream Milk (Waitrose) *1 cup/250g* 10
Full Cream Milk, UHT (Waitrose) *1 cup/250g* 10
Full Cream Whole Milk, Longlife (Tesco) *1 cup/250g* 10
Goat's Milk *1 cup/250g* 10
Half Fat Milk (Marks & Spencer) *1 cup/250g* 4
Half Fat Milk, Vitamin Enriched (Somerfield) *1 cup/250g* 4
Kool Forest Fruit Mix (Marks & Spencer) *1 cup/250g* 4
Low Fat Milk, 1% Fat *1 cup/250g* 3
Malted Milk, Instant (Waitrose) *1 cup/250g* 10
Malted Milk Beverage *1 cup/250g* 9
Semi Skimmed Milk *1 cup/250g* 4
Semi Skimmed Milk, Healthy Choice (Asda) *1 cup/250g* 4
Semi Skimmed Milk, Healthy Eating, Half Fat, Fresh (Tesco) *1 cup/250g* 4
Sheep's Milk, Whole *1 cup/250g* 18
Skimmed Milk *1 cup/250g* 0
Skimmed Milk, Dried *1 cup/250g* 3
Skimmed Milk, Dried, Basics (Somerfield) *1 cup/250g* 3
Skimmed Milk, Dried (Tesco) *1 cup/250g* 2
Soya Alternative to Milk – No Sugar, No Salt (Organic) (Provamel) *1 cup/250g* 5
Soya Alternative to Milk – Sweetened (Provamel) *1 cup/250g* 5
Soya Milk (Asda) *1 cup/250g* 5
Soya Milk, Calcium Enriched (Holland & Barrett) *1 cup/250g* 5
Soya Milk, Calcium Enriched (Tesco) *1 cup/250g* 5
Soya Milk, Calcium Enriched (Waitrose) *1 cup/250g* 5
Soya Milk, Unsweetened (Holland & Barrett) *1 cup/250g* 5
Strawberry Milk (Marks & Spencer) *1 cup/250g* 4
Strawberry Milkshake, Extra, Thick, American Style *1 cup/250g* 5
UHT Milk (Asda) *1 cup/250g* 10
Vanilla Milkshake, Thick *1 cup/250g* 8
Virtually Fat Free Milk (Marks & Spencer) *1 cup/250g* 0
Virtually Fat Free Milk, Fresh Somerfield *1 cup/250g* 0
Virtually Fat Free Milk, Healthy Eating Fresh (Tesco) *1 cup/250g* 0
Virtually Fat Free Milk, Healthy Eating, Longlife (Tesco) *1 cup/250g* 0

Virtually Fat Free Milk, Sterilized (Somerfield) *1 cup/250g* 0
Virtually Fat Free Milk, UHT (Somerfield) *1 cup/250g* 0
Vitamin Enriched Milk (Marks & Spencer) *1 cup/250g* 4
Whole Milk *1 cup/250g* 10
Whole Milk, Dried *1 cup/250g* 67
Whole Milk, Sterilized (Somerfield) *1 cup/250g* 10
Whole Milk, UHT (Somerfield) *1 cup/250g* 10

Meats & Game – Miscellaneous

NOTE: The standard serving size in this section is 110g/4oz. If you wish to consume more or less than this amount (e.g. if you are going to consume a pack of food whose weight differs from the standard serving size) use the conversion tables on page 386 to calculate the new amount of fat in the food.

Beefalo, Roasted *serving 110g/4oz* 7
Bison, Roasted *serving 110g/4oz* 3
Black Pudding, Main Meal (Marks & Spencer) *serving 110g/4oz* 27
Black Pudding, Mixed Grill (Somerfield) *serving 110g/4oz* 18
Boar, Wild, Roasted *serving 110g/4oz* 5
Caribou, Roasted *serving 110g/4oz* 5
Curried Meat *serving 110g/4oz* 12
Deer: *see also* Venison
Deer, Roasted *serving 110g/4oz* 4
Duck, Breast Joint (Marks & Spencer) *serving 110g/4oz* 28
Duck, in Cherry Sauce, Frozen, Oven Baked (Iceland) *serving 110g/4oz* 1
Duck, Crispy (Marks & Spencer) *serving 110g/4oz* 16
Duck, Crispy Peking (Waitrose) *serving 110g/4oz* 9
Duck, Farmed Mallard (Waitrose) *serving 110g/4oz* 47
Duck, Farmhouse (Waitrose) *serving 110g/4oz* 47
Duck, Farmhouse Large (Waitrose) *serving 110g/4oz* 47
Duck Fat *serving 110g/4oz* 110
Duck, Fresh Liver (Waitrose) *serving 110g/4oz* 3
Duck, Meat Only, Roasted *serving 110g/4oz* 12
Duck, Meat & Skin, Roasted *serving 110g/4oz* 31

Duck, Mousse de Canard (Waitrose) *serving 110g/4oz* 51
Duck, in Orange Sauce, Frozen *serving 110g/4oz* 6
Duck, Peking with Noodles (Waitrose) *serving 110g/4oz* 6
Duck, Peking in Plum Sauce (Marks & Spencer) *serving 110g/4oz* 6
Duck, Peppercorn, Main Meal (Marks & Spencer) *serving 110g/4oz* 11
Duck, Stuffed Breast (Waitrose) *serving 110g/4oz* 19
Duckling, Easy Carve (Waitrose) *serving 110g/4oz* 15
Duckling, Portions (Somerfield) *serving 110g/4oz* 47
Duckling, Portions, Fresh (Waitrose) *serving 110g/4oz* 47
Duckling, Ra Peking (Waitrose) *serving 110g/4oz* 16
Duckling, Whole (Somerfield) *serving 110g/4oz* 35
Elk, Roasted *serving 110g/4oz* 2
Faggots, Frozen (Iceland) *serving 110g/4oz* 7
Faggots in Tomato Sauce, Mini, Frozen (Iceland) *serving 110g/4oz* 3
Game Casserole, Fresh (Waitrose) *serving 110g/4oz* 5
Gelatine *serving 110g/4oz* 0
Goat, Roasted *serving 110g/4oz* 3
Goose Fat *serving 110g/4oz* 110
Goose, Fresh, Free Range (Waitrose) *serving 110g/4oz* 25
Goose with Giblets (Waitrose) *serving 110g/4oz* 36
Goose, Meat Only, Roasted, Domesticated *serving 110g/4oz* 14
Goose, Meat & Skin, Roasted, Domesticated *serving 110g/4oz* 24
Goujon, Breaded Selection (Waitrose) *serving 110g/4oz* 23
Grouse, Fresh (Waitrose) *serving 110g/4oz* 5
Guinea Hen, Meat & Skin, (Waitrose) *serving 110g/4oz* 7
Haggis, Main Meal (Marks & Spencer) *serving 110g/4oz* 13
Horse, Roasted *serving 110g/4oz* 7
Hotpot *serving 110g/4oz* 5
Liver & Bacon, Chilled Ready Meal (Safeway) *serving 110g/4oz* 7
Liver & Onion Dumplings, Main Meal (Marks & Spencer) *serving 110g/4oz* 7
Lunch Tongue (Somerfield) *serving 110g/4oz* 6
Meatballs in Gravy (Princes) *serving 110g/4oz* 6
Meatballs in Onion Gravy (Princes) *serving 110g/4oz* 6
Meatloaf with Gravy, Main Meal (Marks & Spencer) *serving 110g/4oz* 6

Meat Balls in Sauce (Waitrose) *serving 110g/4oz* 6
Meat Extract *serving 110g/4oz* 1
Meat Loaf (Somerfield) *serving 110g/4oz* 15
Meat Loaf & Gravy, Frozen Ready Meal (Tesco) *serving 110g/4oz* 10
Mince & Tatties, Chilled Ready Meal (Safeway) *serving 110g/4oz* 21
Mixed Grill, Fresh (Iceland) *serving 110g/4oz* 14
Moose, Roasted *serving 110g/4oz* 1
Offal, Kidney, Chilled (Waitrose) *serving 110g/4oz* 3
Offal, Liver, Chilled (Waitrose) *serving 110g/4oz* 11
Opossum, Roasted *serving 110g/4oz* 11
Partridge, Fresh (Waitrose) *serving 110g/4oz* 5
Pheasant Breast, Meat Only, Raw *serving 110g/4oz* 4
Pheasant, Fresh Brace of (Waitrose) *serving 110g/4oz* 5
Pheasant, Fresh, Hen (Waitrose) *serving 110g/4oz* 5
Pheasant, Leg, Meat Only, Raw *serving 110g/4oz* 5
Pheasant, Meat & Skin, Raw *serving 110g/4oz* 10
Pigeon, Fresh (Waitrose) *serving 110g/4oz* 6
Poultry, Chargrilled Escalopes (Marks & Spencer) *serving 110g/4oz* 12
Poultry, Southern Fried Escalopes (Marks & Spencer) *serving 110g/4oz* 8
Quail, Boned & Stuffed (Marks & Spencer) *serving 110g/4oz* 11
Quail, Breast, Meat Only, Raw *serving 110g/4oz* 3
Quail, Meat Only, Raw *serving 110g/4oz* 5
Quail, Meat & Skin, Raw *serving 110g/4oz* 13
Rabbit, Domesticated, Composite of Cuts *serving 110g/4oz* 9
Rabbit, Domesticated, Stewed *serving 110g/4oz* 9
Rabbit, English Legs, Fresh (Waitrose) *serving 110g/4oz* 4
Rabbit, English Loins (Waitrose) *serving 110g/4oz* 4
Rabbit, English Shoulders (Waitrose) *serving 110g/4oz* 4
Rabbit & Game & Vegetable Casserole (Waitrose) *serving 110g/4oz* 5
Rabbit, Goujons (Waitrose) *serving 110g/4oz* 4
Rabbit, Wild, Stewed *serving 110g/4oz* 4
Samosa, Meat, Chilled (Tesco) *serving 110g/4oz* 15
Squirrel, Roasted *serving 110g/4oz* 5
Tikka Meatballs (Waitrose) *serving 110g/4oz* 14
Venison, Saddle, with Port Fat (Waitrose) *serving 110g/4oz* 7
Venison, Topside, Counter (Waitrose) *serving 110g/4oz* 5

Venison, Wild, in a Cream & Whisky Sauce, Chilled Ready Meal (Safeway) *serving 110g/4oz* 12
Venison & Mushroom in Cranberry Sauce (Waitrose) *serving 110g/4oz* 3
Water Buffalo, Roasted *serving 110g/4oz* 2

NUTS & SAVOURY SNACKS

NOTE: The standard serving size in this section is 30g/1oz. If you wish to consume more or less than this amount (e.g. if you are going to consume a pack of food whose weight differs from the standard serving size) use the conversion tables on page 386 to calculate the new amount of fat in the food.

Almond Paste *serving 30g/1oz* 8
Almonds, Blanched *serving 30g/1oz* 16
Almonds, Dry Roasted, Unblanched *serving 30g/1oz* 15
Almonds, Flaked (Waitrose) *serving 30g/1oz* 17
Almonds, Ground, Partially Defatted *serving 30g/1oz* 5
Almonds, Honey Roasted, Unblanched *serving 30g/1oz* 15
Almonds, Oil Roasted, Blanched *serving 30g/1oz* 17
Almonds, Oil Roasted, Unblanched *serving 30g/1oz* 17
Almonds, Powdered *serving 30g/1oz* 16
Almonds, Powdered, Partially Defatted *serving 30g/1oz* 5
Almonds, Slivered (Waitrose) *serving 30g/1oz* 17
Almonds, Sugared (Waitrose) *serving 30g/1oz* 5
Almonds & Sultanas (Waitrose) *serving 30g/1oz* 8
Almonds, Toasted, Unblanched *serving 30g/1oz* 15
Almonds, Unblanched *serving 30g/1oz* 16
Bacon Crunchies (Iceland) *serving 90g/3oz* 23
BBQ Coated Nuts (Marks & Spencer) *serving 30g/1oz* 12
Beechnuts, Dried *serving 30g/1oz* 15
Bombay Mix *serving 30g/1oz* 10
Brazil Nuts, Dried, Unblanched *serving 30g/1oz* 20
Butternuts, Dried *serving 30g/1oz* 17
Cashew Nuts (Somerfield) *serving 30g/1oz* 14
Cashew Nuts, Dry Roasted *serving 30g/1oz* 14

Cashew Nuts, Honey Roast (Waitrose) *serving 30g/1oz* 13
Cashew Nuts, Oil Roasted *serving 30g/1oz* 14
Cashew & Raisins (Waitrose) *serving 30g/1oz* 7
Cereal & Potato Flour Snacks *serving 30g/1oz* 7
Cheese Buttons (Tesco) *serving 30g/1oz* 7
Cheese & Garlic Bites, Party Food (Marks & Spencer) *serving 30g/1oz* 7
Cheese & Ham Nibbles (Somerfield) *serving 30g/1oz* 24
Cheese Puffs, Grocery (Iceland) *serving 30g/1oz* 9
Cheese Savouries (Tesco) *serving 30g/1oz* 9
Cheese Savouries (Waitrose) *serving 30g/1oz* 9
Cheese & Sesame Crumbles (Marks & Spencer) *serving 30g/1oz* 12
Cheese Squares (Marks & Spencer) *serving 30g/1oz* 13
Cheese Straws (Marks & Spencer) *serving 30g/1oz* 13
Cheese Triangles (Tesco) *serving 30g/1oz* 7
Cheese Twists (Marks & Spencer) *serving 30g/1oz* 7
Chestnuts, Chinese, Boiled & Steamed *serving 30g/1oz* 0
Chestnuts, European, Boiled & Steamed *serving 30g/1oz* 0
Chestnuts, European, Roasted *serving 30g/1oz* 1
Chestnuts, Japanese, Boiled & Steamed *serving 30g/1oz* 0
Coconut Cream, Tinned (Liquid Expressed from Grated Meat) *serving 30g/1oz* 5
Coconut, Dessicated (Waitrose) *serving 30g/1oz* 19
Coconut Meat, Dried (Desiccated) Creamed *serving 30g/1oz* 21
Coconut Meat, Dried (Desiccated), Sweetened, Flaked, Packaged *serving 30g/1oz* 10
Coconut Milk, Tinned (Liquid Expressed from Grated Meat & Wafer) *serving 30g/1oz* 6
Coconut Milk, Raw (Liquid Expressed from Grated Meat & Wafer) *serving 30g/1oz* 7
Cordon Bleu Crunchies (Somerfield) *serving 30g/1oz* 5
Corn Based, Chips, Extruded *serving 30g/1oz* 10
Corn Based Packet Snacks *serving 30g/1oz* 10
Corn Based Puffs or Twists, Extruded Snacks *serving 30g/1oz* 10
Corn Cakes *serving 30g/1oz* 1
Corn Chips (Waitrose) *serving 30g/1oz* 11
Corn Curls, Reduced Fat (Sainsbury's) *serving 30g/1oz* 5

Crinkles, Lower Fat (Waitrose) *serving 30g/1oz*	7
Crisps, All Flavours (Walkers) *serving 30g/1oz*	11
Crisps, Apple (Marks & Spencer) *serving 30g/1oz*	6
Crisps, Assorted Flavour (Iceland) *serving 30g/1oz*	11
Crisps, Assorted Meat Flavour (Iceland) *serving 30g/1oz*	10
Crisps, Assorted (Waitrose) *serving 30g/1oz*	11
Crisps, Bacon Fries (Walkers) *serving 30g/1oz*	9
Crisps, Barbeque (Marks & Spencer) *serving 30g/1oz*	10
Crisps, Beef (Iceland) *serving 30g/1oz*	10
Crisps, Beef & Onion (Marks & Spencer) *serving 30g/1oz*	11
Crisps, Cheese Curls (Marks & Spencer) *serving 30g/1oz*	10
Crisps, Cheese Moments (Walkers) *serving 30g/1oz*	10
Crisps, Cheese & Onion (Marks & Spencer) *serving 30g/1oz*	10
Crisps, Cheese & Onion (Somerfield) *serving 30g/1oz*	10
Crisps, Cheese & Onion (Tesco) *serving 30g/1oz*	10
Crisps, Cheese & Onion Standard (Waitrose) *serving 30g/1oz*	11
Crisps, Cheese Puffs (Somerfield) *serving 30g/1oz*	12
Crisps, Cheese Savouries (Somerfield) *serving 30g/1oz*	9
Crisps, Cheese Tasters (Marks & Spencer) *serving 30g/1oz*	10
Crisps, Chipsticks (Walkers) *serving 30g/1oz*	7
Crisps, Crinkle Cut *serving 30g/1oz*	11
Crisps, Frazzles (Walkers) *serving 30g/1oz*	7
Crisps, French Fries, All-Flavours (Walkers) *serving 30g/1oz*	5
Crisps, Garlic Butter and Herbs (Tesco) *serving 30g/1oz*	9
Crisps, Honey Roast Ham (Marks & Spencer) *serving 30g/1oz*	10
Crisps, Lightly Salted (Waitrose) *serving 30g/1oz*	9
Crisps, Lites (Walkers) *serving 30g/1oz*	9
Crisps, Low Fat *serving 30g/1oz*	6
Crisps, Low Fat Crinkle (Waitrose) *serving 30g/1oz*	7
Crisps, Low Salt, 35% Low Fat (Waitrose) *serving 30g/1oz*	7
Crisps, Monster Munch (Walkers) *serving 30g/1oz*	8
Crisps, *serving 30g/1oz*	11
Crisps, Potato Jacket *serving 30g/1oz*	10
Crisps, Square *serving 30g/1oz*	6
Crisps, Prawn Cocktail (Tesco) *serving 30g/1oz*	10
Crisps, Quavers (Walkers) *serving 30g/1oz*	11
Crisps, Ready Salted (Iceland) *serving 30g/1oz*	11

Crisps, Ready Salted (Marks & Spencer) *serving 30g/1oz*	11
Crisps, Ready Salted (Somerfield) *serving 30g/1oz*	10
Crisps, Ready Salted (Tesco) *serving 30g/1oz*	11
Crisps, Ready Salted (Waitrose) *serving 30g/1oz*	11
Crisps, Reduced Fat (Sainsbury's) *serving 30g/1oz*	7
Crisps, Roast Chicken (Marks & Spencer) *serving 30g/1oz*	10
Crisps, Salt & Vinegar (Iceland) *serving 30g/1oz*	10
Crisps, Salt & Vinegar (Marks & Spencer) *serving 30g/1oz*	10
Crisps, Salt & Vinegar (Somerfield) *serving 30g/1oz*	10
Crisps, Salt & Vinegar (Waitrose) *serving 30g/1oz*	11
Crisps, Scampi Fries (Walkers) *serving 30g/1oz*	8
Crisps, Snaps (Walkers) *serving 30g/1oz*	8
Crisps, Sour Cream & Sweet Onion (Tesco) *serving 30g/1oz*	9
Crisps, Spring Onion (Marks & Spencer) *serving 30g/1oz*	10
Crisps, Spring Onion (Tesco) *serving 30g/1oz*	10
Crisps, Square (Walkers) *serving 30g/1oz*	7
Crisps, Thick Crinkle Cut *serving 30g/1oz*	9
Crisps, Thick Cut *serving 30g/1oz*	8
Crisps, Variety Flavour (Iceland) *serving 30g/1oz*	11
Crunchy Sticks, Ready Salted (Tesco) *serving 30g/1oz*	6
Crunchy Sticks, Salt & Vinegar (Somerfield) *serving 30g/1oz*	7
Crunchy Sticks, Salt & Vinegar (Tesco) *serving 30g/1oz*	6
Doritos (Walkers) *serving 30g/1oz*	8
Enchilada Chips (Waitrose) *serving 30g/1oz*	7
Fruit & Nuts, Exotic (Waitrose) *serving 30g/1oz*	7
Fruit, Seeds & Nuts (Waitrose) *serving 30g/1oz*	9
Garlic Bread Snacks (Tesco) *serving 30g/1oz*	8
Ginkgo Nuts, Tinned *serving 30g/1oz*	0
Ginkgo Nuts, Dried *serving 30g/1oz*	1
Grissini Sticks (Marks & Spencer) *serving 30g/1oz*	6
Hazelnuts (Somerfield) *serving 30g/1oz*	11
Hazelnuts or Filberts, Dried, Blanched *serving 30g/1oz*	20
Hazelnuts or Filberts, Dried, Unblanched *serving 30g/1oz*	19
Hazelnuts or Filberts, Dry Roasted, Unblanched, no Salt Added *serving 30g/1oz*	20
Hazelnuts or Filberts, Oil Roasted, Unblanched, no Salt Added *serving 30g/1oz*	19

Hazelnuts, Sunpat Hazelnut Chocolate Spread (Nestlé) *serving 30g/1oz*	9
Hickorynuts, Dried *serving 30g/1oz*	19
Hickory Peanuts & Almonds (Marks & Spencer) *serving 30g/1oz*	16
Linseed, Organic Golden (Holland & Barrett) *serving 30g/1oz*	11
Macadamia Nuts, Dried *serving 30g/1oz*	22
Macadamia Nuts, Oil Roasted, with Salt Added *serving 30g/1oz*	23
Maize & Rice Flour Snacks *serving 30g/1oz*	6
Mexican Corn Chips (Tesco) *serving 30g/1oz*	10
Mini Teddies (Waitrose) *serving 30g/1oz*	0
Mixed Nut Kernels (Waitrose) *serving 30g/1oz*	18
Mixed Nut Kernels, Luxury (Waitrose) *serving 30g/1oz*	18
Mixed Nuts, Chopped (Somerfield) *serving 30g/1oz*	16
Mixed Nuts, Chopped (Waitrose) *serving 30g/1oz*	12
Mixed Nuts, Luxury (Waitrose) *serving 30g/1oz*	19
Mixed Nuts with Peanuts, Dry Roasted *serving 30g/1oz*	15
Mixed Nuts with Peanuts, Oil Roasted *serving 30g/1oz*	17
Mixed Nuts without Peanuts, Oil Roasted *serving 30g/1oz*	17
Mixed Nuts & Raisins *serving 30g/1oz*	10
Mixed Nuts & Raisins (Iceland) *serving 30g/1oz*	11
Mixed Nuts & Raisins, (Somerfield) *serving 30g/1oz*	12
Mixed Nuts & Raisins (Waitrose) *serving 30g/1oz*	7
Nut Croquettes, Fried in Sunflower Oil *serving 30g/1oz*	8
Nut Croquettes, Fried in Vegetable Oil *serving 30g/1oz*	8
Nut Cutlets, Fried in Sunflower Oil *serving 30g/1oz*	7
Nut Cutlets, Fried in Vegetable Oil *serving 30g/1oz*	7
Nut Cutlets, Grilled *serving 30g/1oz*	4
Nut Roast *serving 30g/1oz*	8
Nut Roast with Egg *serving 30g/1oz*	7
Nut, Mushroom & Rice Nut Roast *serving 30g/1oz*	5
Nut & Rice Nut Roast *serving 30g/1oz*	7
Nut & Rice Nut Roast with Egg *serving 30g/1oz*	7
Nut & Seed Nut Roast *serving 30g/1oz*	7
Nut & Seed Nut Roast with Egg *serving 30g/1oz*	7
Nut & Vegetable Nut Roast *serving 30g/1oz*	7
Nut & Vegetable with Egg Nut Roast *serving 30g/1oz*	6
Nuts & Raisins, Yoghurt Coated (Waitrose) *serving 30g/1oz*	12

Oriental Mix, Rice Based *serving 30g/1oz*	12
Peanut Butter, Chunk Style with Salt *serving 30g/1oz*	15
Peanut Butter, Chunk Style without Salt *serving 30g/1oz*	15
Peanut Butter, Crunchy (Holland & Barrett) *serving 30g/1oz*	15
Peanut Butter, Crunchy (Somerfield) *serving 30g/1oz*	15
Peanut Butter, Crunchy (Waitrose) *serving 30g/1oz*	15
Peanut Butter, Neal's Yard (Holland & Barrett) *serving 30g/1oz*	15
Peanut Butter, Smooth (Holland & Barrett) *serving 30g/1oz*	15
Peanut Butter, Smooth (Somerfield) *serving 30g/1oz*	15
Peanut Butter, Smooth Style with Salt *serving 30g/1oz*	15
Peanut Butter, Smooth Style without Salt *serving 30g/1oz*	15
Peanut Butter, Sunpat, & Chocolate Spread, Stripey Range (Nestlé) *serving 30g/1oz*	13
Peanut Butter, Sunpat, Crunchy (Nestlé) *serving 30g/1oz*	16
Peanut Butter, Wholenut (Waitrose) *serving 30g/1oz*	15
Peanuts, Boiled *serving 30g/1oz*	7
Peanuts, Dry Roasted *serving 30g/1oz*	15
Peanuts, Honey Roast (Waitrose) *serving 30g/1oz*	13
Peanuts, Oil Roasted *serving 30g/1oz*	15
Peanuts & Raisins *serving 30g/1oz*	8
Peanuts, Roasted in Shell (Percy Dalton's) *serving 30g/1oz*	15
Pecans, Dried *serving 30g/1oz*	20
Pecans, Dry Roasted *serving 30g/1oz*	19
Pecans, Oil Roasted *serving 30g/1oz*	21
Pilinuts, Canarytree, Dried *serving 30g/1oz*	24
Pine Nuts, Pignolia, Dried *serving 30g/1oz*	15
Pine Nuts, Pinyon, Dried *serving 30g/1oz*	18
Pinenut Kernels (Waitrose) *serving 30g/1oz*	21
Pistachio Nuts, Dried *serving 30g/1oz*	15
Pistachio Nuts, Dry Roasted *serving 30g/1oz*	16
Pistachio Savoury Snacks (Marks & Spencer) *serving 30g/1oz*	17
Pizza Croutons (Tesco) *serving 30g/1oz*	8
Poppadums, Savoury Snack (Marks & Spencer) *serving 30g/1oz*	10
Poppadums, Spicy (Marks & Spencer) *serving 30g/1oz*	10
Poppadums, Spicy Mini (Tesco) *serving 30g/1oz*	11
Potato & Corn Sticks *serving 30g/1oz*	7
Potato Hoops (Iceland) *serving 30g/1oz*	10

Potato Rings (Snack) *serving 30g/1oz*	10
Potato Rings (Somerfield) *serving 110g/4oz*	36
Potato Rings (Marks & Spencer) *serving 30g/1oz*	10
Potato Sticks *serving 30g/1oz*	10
Potato & Tapioca Snacks *serving 30g/1oz*	7
Potato Twists, Salt & Vinegar (Tesco) *serving 30g/1oz*	6
Potato Waffles (Snack) (Sainsbury's) *serving 30g/1oz*	1
Prawn Cocktail Shells (Tesco) *serving 30g/1oz*	9
Prawn Cocktail Snacks (Marks & Spencer) *serving 30g/1oz*	9
Prawn Cocktail Snacks (Tesco) *serving 30g/1oz*	9
Prawn Crackers (Marks & Spencer) *serving 30g/1oz*	8
Prawn Crackers (Somerfield) *serving 30g/1oz*	11
Prawn Crackers (Tesco) *serving 30g/1oz*	10
Prawn Crackers (Waitrose) *serving 30g/1oz*	11
Pretzels *serving 30g/1oz*	1
Pretzels, Hard, Confectioner's Coating, Chocolate Flavour *serving 30g/1oz*	5
Pretzels, Hard, Plain, Salted *serving 30g/1oz*	1
Pretzels, Honey & Mustard (Marks & Spencer) *serving 30g/1oz*	6
Puffed Potato Products *serving 30g/1oz*	10
Pumpkin & Squash Seed Kernels, Dried *serving 30g/1oz*	14
Pumpkin & Squash Seed Kernels, Roasted *serving 30g/1oz*	13
Pumpkin & Squash Seeds, Whole, Roasted *serving 30g/1oz*	6
Rhaita Puri Chips (Waitrose) *serving 30g/1oz*	10
Safflower Seed Kernels, Dried *serving 30g/1oz*	12
Salt & Vinegar Sticks (Iceland) *serving 30g/1oz*	8
Salted Tort, Savoury Snacks (Marks & Spencer) *serving 30g/1oz*	8
Sesame Butter Paste *serving 30g/1oz*	15
Sesame Seed Kernels, Dried *serving 30g/1oz*	16
Sesame Seed Kernels, Toasted *serving 30g/1oz*	14
Sesame Seeds, Whole Dried *serving 30g/1oz*	15
Sesame Seeds, Whole, Roasted *serving 30g/1oz*	14
Sesame Sticks (Marks & Spencer) *serving 30g/1oz*	8
Sesame Sticks, Wheat Based, Salted *serving 30g/1oz*	11
Sev/Ganthia (Extruded Chick Pea Flour Snack) *serving 30g/1oz*	8
Steak, Oven Baked Chargrill, Savoury Snack (Marks & Spencer) *serving 30g/1oz*	2
Sunflower Seed Butter *serving 30g/1oz*	14

Sunflower Seed Kernels, Dried *serving 30g/1oz* 15
Sunflower Seed Kernels, Dry Roasted *serving 30g/1oz* 15
Sunflower Seed Kernels, Oil Roasted *serving 30g/1oz* 17
Sunflower Seed Kernels, Toasted *serving 30g/1oz* 17
Sunpat, Smooth (Nestlé) *serving 30g/1oz* 15
Sunpat, Wholenut (Nestlé) *serving 30g/1oz* 16
Tahini from Raw & Stone Ground Sesame Kernels *serving 30g/1oz* 14
Tahini from Roasted & Toasted Sesame Kernels (most common type) *serving 30g/1oz* 16
Tahini from Unroasted Sesame Kernels (non-chemical removal of seed coat) *serving 30g/1oz* 17
Tortilla Chips *serving 30g/1oz* 7
Tortilla Chips (Marks & Spencer) *serving 30g/1oz* 7
Tortilla Chips (Tesco) *serving 30g/1oz* 8
Tortilla Chips, Chilli Flavour (Somerfield) *serving 30g/1oz* 6
Tortilla Chips, Lightly Salted (Somerfield) *serving 30g/1oz* 5
Tortilla Chips, Lightly Salted (Waitrose) *serving 30g/1oz* 7
Tortilla Chips, Nacho Cheese Flavour (Somerfield) *serving 30g/1oz* 5
Tortilla Chips, Nacho Flavour *serving 30g/1oz* 8
Tortilla Chips, Nacho Flavour Light *serving 30g/1oz* 5
Tortilla Chips, Ranch Flavour *serving 30g/1oz* 7
Tortilla Chips, Salsa Flavour (Somerfield) *serving 30g/1oz* 6
Tortilla Chips, Salsa Flavour (Tesco) *serving 30g/1oz* 8
Tortilla Chips, Taco Flavour *serving 30g/1oz* 7
Tortilla Nacho (Marks & Spencer) *serving 30g/1oz* 8
Trail Mix, Regular *serving 30g/1oz* 9
Trail Mix, Tropical *serving 30g/1oz* 5
Waffles (Marks & Spencer) *serving 30g/1oz* 7
Walnuts, Black, Dried *serving 30g/1oz* 17
Walnuts, English or Persian, Dried *serving 30g/1oz* 19
Walnuts, French or Chilean (Waitrose) *serving 30g/1oz* 21
Watermelon Seed Kernels, Dried *serving 30g/1oz* 14
Weaver's Potato Snacks, Salt & Vinegar Flavour (Heinz Weight Watchers) *serving 30g/1oz* 0
Weaver's Potato Snacks, Smoky Bacon Flavour (Heinz Weight Watchers) *serving 30g/1oz* 0
Western Barbeque Corn Strips (Tesco) *serving 30g/1oz* 9

Oils & Cooking Fats

Almond Oil *serving 30g/1oz*	30
Apricot Kernel Oil *serving 30g/1oz*	30
Avocado Oil *serving 30g/1oz*	30
Babassu Oil *serving 30g/1oz*	30
Canola Oil *serving 30g/1oz*	30
Chicken Fat *serving 30g/1oz*	30
Cocoa Butter Oil *serving 30g/1oz*	30
Coconut Oil *serving 30g/1oz*	30
Cod Liver Oil *serving 30g/1oz*	30
Cookeen (Van Den Bergh) *serving 30g/1oz*	30
Corn Oil *serving 30g/1oz*	30
Cottonseed Oil *serving 30g/1oz*	30
Cupu Assu Oil *serving 30g/1oz*	30
Flora, White (Van Den Bergh) *serving 30g/1oz*	30
Grapeseed Oil *serving 30g/1oz*	30
Groundnut Oil *serving 30g/1oz*	27
Hazelnut Oil *serving 30g/1oz*	30
Herring Oil *serving 30g/1oz*	30
Lard *serving 30g/1oz*	30
Lard, Pork *serving 30g/1oz*	30
Menhaden Oil *serving 30g/1oz*	30
Nutmeg Butter *serving 30g/1oz*	30
Oat Oil *serving 30g/1oz*	30
Olive Oil *serving 30g/1oz*	30
Palm Kernel Oil *serving 30g/1oz*	30
Palm Oil *serving 30g/1oz*	30
Peanut Oil *serving 30g/1oz*	30
Poppyseed Oil *serving 30g/1oz*	30
Rice Bran Oil *serving 30g/1oz*	30
Safflower Oil *serving 30g/1oz*	30
Safflowerseed Oil *serving 30g/1oz*	28
Salmon Oil *serving 30g/1oz*	30
Sesame Oil *serving 30g/1oz*	30
Sheanut Oil *serving 30g/1oz*	30

Shortening, Frying (Regular), Soyabean (Hydrogenated) & Cottonseed (Hydrogenated) *serving 30g/1oz* 30
Shortening, Household, Soyabean (Hydrogenated) & Palm *serving 30g/1oz* 30
Soya Bean Lecithin *serving 30g/1oz* 30
Soya Bean Oil *serving 30g/1oz* 30
Spry Crisp 'n' Dry (Van Den Bergh) *serving 30g/1oz* 30
Suet, Beef, Shredded *serving 30g/1oz* 26
Sunflower Oil *serving 30g/1oz* 30
Teaseed Oil *serving 30g/1oz* 30
Tomato Seed Oil *serving 30g/1oz* 30
Ucuhuba Butter *serving 30g/1oz* 30
Vegetable Oil *serving 30g/1oz* 30
Vegetable Suet *serving 30g/1oz* 27
Walnut Oil *serving 30g/1oz* 30
Wheat Germ Oil *serving 30g/1oz* 30

Pasta & Noodles

NOTE: The standard serving size in this section is 280g/10oz. If you wish to consume more or less than this amount (e.g. if you are going to consume a pack of food whose weight differs from the standard serving size) use the conversion tables on page 386 to calculate the new amount of fat in the food.

Agnolotti Pasta with Mushroom (Somerfield) *serving 280g/10oz* 15
Agnolotti Pasta with Mushrooms (Safeway) *serving 280g/10oz* 27
Agnolotti Pasta with Spicy Vegetables (Safeway) *serving 280g/10oz* 18
Anoloni Pasta Napoletana (Safeway) *serving 280g/10oz* 31
Arrabbiata (Findus Lean Cuisine Snackpots) *serving 280g/10oz* 4
Arrabbiata Pasta, Tinned (Tesco) *serving 280g/10oz* 3
Bolognese Pasta, Tinned (Tesco) *serving 280g/10oz* 6
Cannelloni (Marks & Spencer) *serving 280g/10oz* 19
Cannelloni (Somerfield) *serving 280g/10oz* 17
Cannelloni, Frozen (Asda) *serving 280g/10oz* 13
Cannelloni, Beef (Asda) *serving 280g/10oz* 18

Cannelloni, Beef, Chilled Ready Meal (Tesco) *serving 280g/10oz* 24
Cannelloni, Beef, Frozen Oven Baked (Iceland) *serving 280g/10oz* 20
Cannelloni, Cheese (Marks & Spencer) *serving 280g/10oz* 22
Cannelloni, Cheesey Vegetable Filling *serving 280g/10oz* 25
Cannelloni, Meat, Chilled Ready Meal (Safeway) *serving 280g/10oz* 58
Cannelloni, Spinach & Ricotta *serving 280g/10oz* 21
Cannelloni, Spinach Ricotta (Marks & Spencer) *serving 280g/10oz* 22
Cannelloni, Vegetable (Marks & Spencer) *serving 280g/10oz* 11
Cannelloni, Vegetable, Chilled Ready Meal (Tesco) *serving 280g/10oz* 15
Capellini (Waitrose) *serving 280g/10oz* 5
Cappelletti, Cheese & Smoked Ham (Somerfield) *serving 280g/10oz* 15
Cappelletti with Chicken & Smoked Ham (Safeway) *serving 280g/10oz* 20
Cappelletto Con Proscuito Crudo, Fresco (Buitoni) *serving 280g/10oz* 29
Chicken & Pasta Bake (Marks & Spencer) *serving 280g/10oz* 20
Chicken & Pasta Bake (Waitrose) *serving 280g/10oz* 14
Chicken & Broccoli Pasta (Findus Lean Cuisine Snackpots) *serving 280g/10oz* 5
Chicken & Broccoli Pasta Bake, Frozen Ready Meal (Heinz Weight Watchers) *serving 280g/10oz* 6
Chicken & Broccoli Pasta Bake, Frozen Ready Meal (Safeway) *serving 280g/10oz* 16
Chicken, Mushroom & Sweetcorn Pasta (Somerfield) *serving 280g/10oz* 13
Conchiglie Pasta (Safeway) *serving 280g/10oz* 4
Conchiglie Pasta, Healthy Selection (Somerfield) *serving 280g/10oz* 6
Egg Pasta (Buitoni) *serving 280g/10oz* 4
Egg Pasta Dried (Tesco) *serving 280g/10oz* 10
Egg Pasta, Garlic/Herb (Waitrose) *serving 280g/10oz* 4
Egg Pasta Penne (Somerfield) *serving 280g/10oz* 7

Egg Pasta Shells (Somerfield) *serving 280g/10oz* 7
Egg Pasta Shells, Fresh (Waitrose) *serving 280g/10oz* 5
Egg Pasta Spirals, Fresh (Waitrose) *serving 280g/10oz* 5
Egg Pasta Tubes, Fresh (Waitrose) *serving 280g/10oz* 5
Egg Pasta Twists, Fresh (Asda) *serving 280g/10oz* 4
Egg Pasta Twists, Fresh (Waitrose) *serving 280g/10oz* 5
Egg Tortellini with Cheese & Tomato Filling, Frozen, Boiled (Iceland) *serving 280g/10oz* 22
Egg Vermicelli, Dried (Tesco) *serving 280g/10oz* 10
Farfalle, Pasta Bows (Waitrose) *serving 280g/10oz* 5
Farfalle, Pasta Bows, Dried (Tesco) *serving 280g/10oz* 6
Farfalle Pasta, Healthy Selection (Somerfield) *serving 280g/10oz* 6
Fettucine Verdi Fresco (Buitoni) *serving 280g/10oz* 11
Fiorelli Pasta (Marks & Spencer) *serving 280g/10oz* 8
Fusilli Lunghi (Waitrose) *serving 280g/10oz* 5
Fusilli Pasta (Marks & Spencer) *serving 280g/10oz* 8
Fusilli Pasta (Safeway) *serving 280g/10oz* 4
Fusilli Pasta, Healthy Selection (Somerfield) *serving 280g/10oz* 6
Fusilli Pasta (Waitrose) *serving 280g/10oz* 5
Fusilli Tricolore Pasta (Waitrose) *serving 280g/10oz* 5
Fusilli Tricolore Pasta, Healthy Selection (Somerfield) *serving 280g/10oz* 6
Giglio Riccio Pasta (Safeway) *serving 280g/10oz* 4
Gnocchi Pasta Shells (Waitrose) *serving 280g/10oz* 5
Lasagne (Birds Eye) *serving 280g/10oz* 16
Lasagne (Marks & Spencer) *serving 280g/10oz* 15
Lasagne (Princes) *serving 280g/10oz* 3
Lasagne (Somerfield) *serving 280g/10oz* 15
Lasagne, Beef (Somerfield) *serving 280g/10oz* 17
Lasagne, Beef, Frozen Ready Meal (Heinz Weight Watchers) *serving 280g/10oz* 9
Lasagne, Beef, Lean (Findus Lean Cuisine) *serving 280g/10oz* 6
Lasagne, Beef, Savers, Frozen Ready Meal (Safeway) *serving 280g/10oz* 10
Lasagne, Cheese, Onion & Tomato (Birds Eye) *serving 280g/10oz* 17
Lasagne, Chicken (Waitrose) *serving 280g/10oz* 10

Lasagne, Chicken, Chilled Ready Meal (Tesco) *serving 280g/10oz* 13
Lasagne, Chicken Tikka, Frozen Oven Baked (Iceland) *serving 280g/10oz* 17
Lasagne, Chilled Ready Meal (Safeway) *serving 280g/10oz* 40
Lasagne, De Lusso, Meat (Waitrose) *serving 280g/10oz* 14
Lasagne, De Lusso, Vegetable (Waitrose) *serving 280g/10oz* 14
Lasagne, Deep Dish (Waitrose) *serving 280g/10oz* 13
Lasagne, Deep Fill, Chilled Ready Meal (Tesco) *serving 280g/10oz* 23
Lasagne, Deep Filled (Asda) *serving 280g/10oz* 20
Lasagne, Dried (Tesco) *serving 280g/10oz* 8
Lasagne, Egg Verdi, Quick Cook, Dried (Tesco) *serving 280g/10oz* 8
Lasagne, Family (Marks & Spencer) *serving 280g/10oz* 15
Lasagne, Family, Frozen Ready Meal (Tesco) *serving 280g/10oz* 17
Lasagne, Family, Meat, Chilled Ready Meal (Tesco) *serving 280g/10oz* 14
Lasagne, Fish (Waitrose) *serving 280g/10oz* 19
Lasagne, Frozen (Asda) *serving 280g/10oz* 21
Lasagne, Frozen (Tesco) *serving 280g/10oz* 11
Lasagne, Frozen, Cooked *serving 280g/10oz* 11
Lasagne, Frozen, Healthy Choice (Asda) *serving 280g/10oz* 6
Lasagne, Frozen, Oven Baked (Iceland) *serving 280g/10oz* 5
Lasagne, Frozen Ready Meal (Safeway) *serving 280g/10oz* 15
Lasagne, Homestyle (Marks & Spencer) *serving 280g/10oz* 20
Lasagne, Low Fat (Marks & Spencer) *serving 280g/10oz* 5
Lasagne, Meat (Waitrose) *serving 280g/10oz* 17
Lasagne, Meat Al Forno (Waitrose) *serving 280g/10oz* 17
Lasagne, Meat, Chilled Ready Meal (Tesco) *serving 280g/10oz* 17
Lasagne, Meat, Frozen (Tesco) *serving 280g/10oz* 17
Lasagne, Microwave Ready Meal (Safeway) *serving 280g/10oz* 18
Lasagne, Pasta, 'No Cook' (Waitrose) *serving 280g/10oz* 11
Lasagne, Plain (Waitrose) *serving 280g/10oz* 4
Lasagne, Roast Vegetable Al Forno (Waitrose) *serving 280g/10oz* 20

Lasagne, Seafood, Frozen Ready Meal (Tesco) *serving 280g/10oz* 15
Lasagne, Twin Pack (Marks & Spencer) *serving 280g/10oz* 15
Lasagne, Vegetable *serving 110g/4oz* 5
Lasagne, Vegetable (Somerfield) *serving 280g/10oz* 15
Lasagne, Vegetable (Waitrose) *serving 280g/10oz* 16
Lasagne, Vegetable, Chilled Ready Meal (Tesco) *serving 280g/10oz* 14
Lasagne, Vegetable, Frozen (Asda) *serving 280g/10oz* 27
Lasagne, Vegetable, Frozen Ready Meal (Heinz Weight Watchers) *serving 280g/10oz* 8
Lasagne, Verdi (Princes) *serving 280g/10oz* 3
Lasagne, Wholewheat, Dried (Tesco) *serving 280g/10oz* 8
Leek & Bacon Pasta Bake, Main Meal (Marks & Spencer) *serving 280g/10oz* 29
Linguine, Dried (Tesco) *serving 280g/10oz* 6
Macaroni (Waitrose) *serving 280g/10oz* 5
Macaroni Cheese (Asda) *serving 280g/10oz* 24
Macaroni Cheese (Findus Dinner Supreme) *serving 280g/10oz* 22
Macaroni Cheese (Somerfield) *serving 280g/10oz* 17
Macaroni Cheese, Chefs Specials (Heinz) *serving 280g/10oz* 13
Macaroni Cheese, Chilled Ready Meal (Safeway) *serving 280g/10oz* 32
Macaroni Cheese, Frozen (Asda) *serving 280g/10oz* 27
Macaroni, Cheese, Home Made *serving 280g/10oz* 30
Macaroni, Cheese & Ham (Birds Eye) *serving 280g/10oz* 3
Macaroni Cheese with Ham, Tinned (Tesco) *serving 280g/10oz* 14
Macaroni, Chicken/Bacon (Findus Dinner Supreme) *serving 280g/10oz* 23
Macaroni, Healthy Selection (Somerfield) *serving 280g/10oz* 6
Macaroni, Pasta (Safeway) *serving 280g/10oz* 4
Macaroni, Pasta Cheese (Marks & Spencer) *serving 280g/10oz* 29
Macaroni, Pastichio (Greek Macaroni Lentils & Vegetables with White Sauce) *serving 280g/10oz* 20
Macaroni, Plain, Cooked *serving 280g/10oz* 2
Macaroni, Quick (Princes) *serving 280g/10oz* 3
Macaroni Short Cut, Dried (Tesco) *serving 280g/10oz* 6

Macaroni, Vegetarian Cheese (Birds Eye) *serving 280g/10oz* 3
Macaroni, Whole Wheat, Cooked *serving 280g/10oz* 2
Meatballs with Pasta (Marks & Spencer) *serving 280g/10oz* 10
Medaglioni, with Cheese & Broccoli *serving 280g/10oz* 25
Medaglioni with Cheese & Herbs Pack (Safeway) *serving 280g/10oz* 29
Medaglioni, Cheese & Spinach (Waitrose) *serving 280g/10oz* 19
Mediterranean Pasta & Vegetable (Waitrose) *serving 280g/10oz* 17
Mushroom, Garlic & White Wine Pasta (Somerfield) *serving 280g/10oz* 13
Nidi Fettuccine all'Uovo (Waitrose) *serving 280g/10oz* 7
Noodles, Beef & Tomato, Pot Noodle (CPC) *serving 280g/10oz* 41
Noodles, Burger, Fun Pot (CPC) *serving 280g/10oz* 41
Noodles, Chicken, 3 Minute Noodles (Crosse & Blackwell) *serving 280g/10oz* 4
Noodles, Chicken Micro Noodle (CPC) *serving 280g/10oz* 67
Noodles, Chicken & Mushroom, Fun Pot (CPC) *serving 280g/10oz* 41
Noodles, Chicken & Mushroom, Pot Noodle (CPC) *serving 280g/10oz* 41
Noodles, Chicken & Mushroom, Pot Noodle Light (CPC) *serving 280g/10oz* 6
Noodles, Chinese Chicken, Pot Noodle Light (CPC) *serving 280g/10oz* 7
Noodles, Chow Mein, Pot Noodle (CPC) *serving 280g/10oz* 42
Noodles, Curry, 3 Minute Noodles (Crosse & Blackwell) *serving 280g/10oz* 7
Noodles, Egg, Cooked *serving 280g/10oz* 4
Noodles, Egg Spinach, Cooked *serving 280g/10oz* 4
Noodles, Italian Chicken Pasta, Pot Noodle Light (CPC) *serving 280g/10oz* 5
Noodles, Japanese Soba, Cooked *serving 280g/10oz* 0
Noodles, Japanese Somen, Cooked *serving 280g/10oz* 1
Noodles, Mild Curry, Micro Noodles (CPC) *serving 280g/10oz* 67
Noodles, Nice 'n' spicy, Fun Pot (CPC) *serving 280g/10oz* 47
Noodles, Nice 'n' spicy, Pot Noodle (CPC) *serving 280g/10oz* 47

Noodles, Oriental Beef, 3 Minute Noodles (Crosse & Blackwell) *serving 280g/10oz* 6
Noodles, Rice or Chilli, Instant Pot Savouries, Made Up *serving 280g/10oz* 9
Noodles, Rice & Noodles, International Duet (Marks & Spencer) *serving 280g/10oz* 9
Noodles, Sausage & Tomato, Pot Noodle (CPC) *serving 280g/10oz* 42
Noodles, Savoury Tomato, Micro Noodle (CPC) *serving 280g/10oz* 67
Noodles, Singapore Noodles (Marks & Spencer) *serving 280g/10oz* 21
Noodles, Singapore Noodles (Waitrose) *serving 280g/10oz* 4
Noodles, Spicy Curry, Pot Noodle (CPC) *serving 280g/10oz* 44
Noodles, Spicy Prawn, 3 Minute Noodles (Crosse & Blackwell) *serving 280g/10oz* 4
Noodles, Spicy Tomato Salsa, Pot Noodle (CPC) *serving 280g/10oz* 43
Noodles, Sweet & Sour, Pot Noodle (CPC) *serving 280g/10oz* 48
Noodles, Vermicelli Nests (Waitrose) *serving 280g/10oz* 5
Pagli El Fieno Pasta (Safeway) *serving 280g/10oz* 2
Panzerotti Pasta with Smoked Salmon (Somerfield) *serving 280g/10oz* 3
Panzotti Pasta with Smoked Salmon (Safeway) *serving 280g/10oz* 38
Pappardelle Pasta (Marks & Spencer) *serving 280g/10oz* 7
Pasta à la Grécque (Waitrose) *serving 280g/10oz* 43
Pasta & Chicken, Low Fat (Marks & Spencer) *serving 280g/10oz* 2
Pasta, Dried Napolina (CPC) *serving 280g/10oz* 3
Pasta, Dried Tricolore Napolina (CPC) *serving 280g/10oz* 3
Pasta, Fresh, Refrigerated, Plain, Cooked *serving 280g/10oz* 3
Pasta, Fresh, Refrigerated, Spinach, Cooked *serving 280g/10oz* 3
Pasta, Home Made, Made with Egg, Cooked *serving 280g/10oz* 5
Pasta, Home Made, Made without Egg, Cooked *serving 280g/10oz* 3
Pasta Knots (Waitrose) *serving 280g/10oz* 5

Pasta Nests, Gold & Green, Dried (Tesco) *serving 280g/10oz* 6
Pasta & Nut Medley Pack (Safeway) *serving 280g/10oz* 47
Pasta & Prawn Bowl (Asda) *serving 280g/10oz* 25
Pasta & Prawn, Low Fat (Marks & Spencer) *serving 280g/10oz* 4
Pasta Quills (Waitrose) *serving 280g/10oz* 5
Pasta Quills, Dried (Tesco) *serving 280g/10oz* 6
Pasta Salad (Pasta, Vegetables & Mayonnaise) *serving 280g/10oz* 21
Pasta Salad with Vegetables, Reduced Calorie, Chilled (Iceland) *serving 280g/10oz* 24
Pasta Shells, Dried (Tesco) *serving 280g/10oz* 6
Pasta Shells, Fresh (Asda) *serving 280g/10oz* 4
Pasta Shells in Spicy Tomato Sauce (Princes) *serving 280g/10oz* 3
Pasta Shells in Tuna (Princes) *serving 280g/10oz* 3
Pasta Shells (Princes) *serving 280g/10oz* 3
Pasta Shells, Wholewheat, Dried (Tesco) *serving 280g/10oz* 8
Pasta Shells, Wholewheat, Healthy Selection (Somerfield) *serving 280g/10oz* 8
Pasta & Tomato, Lightly Dressed (Safeway) *serving 280g/10oz* 3
Pasta Tubes (Waitrose) *serving 280g/10oz* 5
Pasta & Tuna Bake (Marks & Spencer) *serving 280g/10oz* 19
Pasta & Tuna, Low Fat (Marks & Spencer) *serving 280g/10oz* 3
Pasta & Tuna Snack Salad (Somerfield) *serving 280g/10oz* 32
Pasta Twists (Princes) *serving 280g/10oz* 3
Pasta Twists, Coloured, Dried (Tesco) *serving 280g/10oz* 6
Pasta Twists, Dried (Tesco) *serving 280g/10oz* 6
Pasta Twists in Bolognaise (Princes) *serving 280g/10oz* 3
Pasta Twists in Tomato & Cream Sauce (Princes) *serving 280g/10oz* 3
Pasta Twists, Wholewheat, Dried (Tesco) *serving 280g/10oz* 8
Pasta & Vegetable Bake (Marks & Spencer) *serving 280g/10oz* 16
Pasta & Vegetable Bake (Somerfield) *serving 280g/10oz* 11
Pasta Verdi (Buitoni) *serving 280g/10oz* 2
Pasta Whirls (Princes) *serving 280g/10oz* 3
Pasta, White, All Types Dried (Tesco) *serving 280g/10oz* 6
Pasta with Ham & Mushroom, Main Meal (Marks & Spencer) *serving 280g/10oz* 21

Pasta with Sweetcorn & Tuna Salad (Safeway) *serving 280g/10oz* 27
Penne Rigate Pasta (Marks & Spencer) *serving 280g/10oz* 8
Penne Rigate Pasta, Healthy Selection (Somerfield) *serving 280g/10oz* 6
Pot Light Italian Chicken Pasta (CPC) *serving 280g/10oz* 5
Prawn & Pasta Salad (Safeway) *serving 280g/10oz* 44
Ravioli (Marks & Spencer) *serving 280g/10oz* 19
Ravioli (Princes) *serving 280g/10oz* 6
Ravioli (Waitrose) *serving 280g/10oz* 4
Ravioli, Al Brasato Fresco (Buitoni) *serving 280g/10oz* 28
Ravioli, Asparagus & Cheese (Waitrose) *serving 280g/10oz* 9
Ravioli, Beef Bolognese, Chilled (Tesco) *serving 280g/10oz* 11
Ravioli, Beef in Tomato Sauce, Tinned (Tesco) *serving 280g/10oz* 7
Ravioli, Cheddar & Garlic, Fresh (Tesco) *serving 280g/10oz* 18
Ravioli, Cheese in Tomato Sauce, Tinned (Tesco) *serving 280g/10oz* 4
Ravioli, Cheese, Tomato & Basil, Fresh (Asda) *serving 280g/10oz* 5
Ravioli, Cheese & Tomato Sauce (Marks & Spencer) *serving 280g/10oz* 15
Ravioli, Cheese & Tomato (Waitrose) *serving 280g/10oz* 28
Ravioli, Pasta Chicken & Mushroom, Fresh (Asda) *serving 280g/10oz* 9
Ravioli, Chicken & Spinach (Waitrose) *serving 280g/10oz* 25
Ravioli, Chicken Tikka, Complete Pasta Meal (Heinz) *serving 280g/10oz* 16
Ravioli, Con Quatro Formaggio, Fresco (Buitoni) *serving 280g/10oz* 36
Ravioli, Garlic & Herb with Chicken & Bacon, Frozen, Boiled (Iceland) *serving 280g/10oz* 15
Ravioli, International Spinach (Marks & Spencer) *serving 280g/10oz* 16
Ravioli, Meat (Somerfield) *serving 280g/10oz* 24
Ravioli, Meat-Free, in Tomato Sauce (Heinz) *serving 280g/10oz* 2
Ravioli, Mushroom, Fresh (Tesco) *serving 280g/10oz* 13
Ravioli, Spicy Bolognese (Waitrose) *serving 280g/10oz* 17

Ravioli with Spicy Pork Frozen Boiled (Iceland) *serving 280g/10oz* 20
Ravioli in Tomato Sauce, Tinned (Tesco) *serving 280g/10oz* 4
Ravioli in Tomato Sauce, Chefs Specials (Heinz) *serving 280g/10oz* 3
Ravioli, Tuna in Tomato Sauce, Tinned (Tesco) *serving 280g/10oz* 7
Ravioli, Vegetable, Tinned (Tesco) *serving 280g/10oz* 2
Ravioli, Vegetable in Tomato Sauce Italiana (Heinz Weight Watchers) *serving 280g/10oz* 6
Ricotta & Spinach Tortelloni Pasta (Somerfield) *serving 280g/10oz* 14
Rigatoni, Dried (Tesco) *serving 280g/10oz* 6
Rigatoni, Healthy Selection (Somerfield) *serving 280g/10oz* 6
Rigatoni Carbonara, Tinned (Tesco) *serving 280g/10oz* 16
Salmon & Prawn Tagliatelle (Waitrose) *serving 280g/10oz* 14
Seafood Pasta, Retail *serving 280g/10oz* 13
Smoked Salmon Panzerotti Pasta (Somerfield) *serving 280g/10oz* 25
Spaghetti (Buitoni) *serving 280g/10oz* 2
Spaghetti (Marks & Spencer) *serving 280g/10oz* 8
Spaghetti (Safeway) *serving 280g/10oz* 4
Spaghetti (Somerfield) *serving 280g/10oz* 5
Spaghetti (Waitrose) *serving 280g/10oz* 5
Spaghetti, Basics (Somerfield) *serving 280g/10oz* 6
Spaghetti, Tinned (Waitrose) *serving 280g/10oz* 1
Spaghetti, Cooked, without Added Salt *serving 280g/10oz* 2
Spaghetti, Egg (Somerfield) *serving 280g/10oz* 6
Spaghetti, Fresh (Asda) *serving 280g/10oz* 5
Spaghetti, Fresh (Tesco) *serving 280g/10oz* 10
Spaghetti, Fresh (Waitrose) *serving 280g/10oz* 5
Spaghetti, Healthy Selection, Quick Cook (Somerfield) *serving 280g/10oz* 6
Spaghetti, Healthy Selection, Wholewheat (Somerfield) *serving 280g/10oz* 8
Spaghetti, Italian (Waitrose) *serving 280g/10oz* 5
Spaghetti, Long (Princes) *serving 280g/10oz* 3
Spaghetti, Protein Fortified, Cooked, Enriched *serving 280g/10oz* 1
Spaghetti, Quick to Cook (Marks & Spencer) *serving 280g/10oz* 7
Spaghetti, Quick Cook, Dried (Tesco) *serving 280g/10oz* 6

Spaghetti, Reduced Sugar & Salt, in Tomato, Tinned (Tesco) *serving 280g/10oz* 1
Spaghetti, Short (Princes) *serving 280g/10oz* 1
Spaghetti, Short, in Tomato Sauce (Princes) *serving 280g/10oz* 1
Spaghetti, Tricolour (Waitrose) *serving 280g/10oz* 5
Spaghetti, Verdi Dried (Tesco) *serving 280g/10oz* 6
Spaghetti, Wholewheat (Waitrose) *serving 280g/10oz* 4
Spaghetti, Wholewheat, Cooked *serving 280g/10oz* 2
Spaghetti, Wholewheat, Dried (Tesco) *serving 280g/10oz* 8
Spaghetti, Wholewheat, in Tomato Sauce (Somerfield) *serving 280g/10oz* 1
Spaghetti Bolognaise (Marks & Spencer) *serving 280g/10oz* 8
Spaghetti Bolognaise (Somerfield) *serving 280g/10oz* 9
Spaghetti Bolognese (Asda) *serving 280g/10oz* 11
Spaghetti Bolognese (Birds Eye) *serving 280g/10oz* 11
Spaghetti Bolognese (Somerfield) *serving 280g/10oz* 12
Spaghetti Bolognese, Tinned (Tesco) *serving 280g/10oz* 9
Spaghetti Bolognese, Chefs Specials (Heinz) *serving 280g/10oz* 7
Spaghetti Bolognese, Chilled Ready Meal (Safeway) *serving 280g/10oz* 14
Spaghetti Bolognese, Frozen, Boil/Microwave (Iceland) *serving 280g/10oz* 13
Spaghetti Bolognese, Lunch Bowl, Ready Meal (Heinz) *serving 280g/10oz* 12
Spaghetti Bolognese, Meat Free (Heinz) *serving 280g/10oz* 7
Spaghetti Carbonara (Marks & Spencer) *serving 280g/10oz* 14
Spaghetti Hoops with Hotdogs (Heinz) *serving 280g/10oz* 9
Spaghetti Hoops in Tomato Sauce (Heinz) *serving 280g/10oz* 1
Spaghetti Letters in Tomato Sauce, Tinned (Tesco) *serving 280g/10oz* 1
Spaghetti Rings (Waitrose) *serving 280g/10oz* 1
Spaghetti Rings with Sausages in Tomato, Tinned (Tesco) *serving 280g/10oz* 9
Spaghetti Rings in Tomato Sauce (Somerfield) *serving 280g/10oz* 1
Spaghetti Rings in Tomato Sauce, Tinned (Tesco) *serving 280g/10oz* 1

Spaghetti with Sausages (Heinz) *serving 280g/10oz* 13
Spaghetti in Tomato Sauce (Heinz) *serving 280g/10oz* 1
Spaghetti in Tomato Sauce (Iceland) *serving 280g/10oz* 2
Spaghetti in Tomato Sauce (Somerfield) *serving 280g/10oz* 1
Spaghetti in Tomato Sauce, 50% Less Salt, Tinned (Tesco) *serving 280g/10oz* 1
Spaghetti in Tomato Sauce, Tinned (Tesco) *serving 280g/10oz* 1
Spaghetti in Tomato Sauce with Parsley (Heinz Weight Watchers) *serving 280g/10oz* 1
Spicy Pasta Bake, Vegetable Meal (Marks & Spencer) *serving 280g/10oz* 17
Spicy Pepperoni Pasta, Complete Pasta Meal (Heinz) *serving 280g/10oz* 11
Spicy Salsa Twists, Complete Pasta Meal (Heinz) *serving 280g/10oz* 6
Spinach Pasta, Fresh (Waitrose) *serving 280g/10oz* 4
Spirali Pasta, Healthy Selection (Somerfield) *serving 280g/10oz* 6
Tagliatelle, Dried (Marks & Spencer) *serving 280g/10oz* 8
Tagliatelle (Marks & Spencer) *serving 280g/10oz* 18
Tagliatelle, Chilled (Somerfield) *serving 280g/10oz* 5
Tagliatele, Dry (Somerfield) *serving 280g/10oz* 2
Tagliatelle (Waitrose) *serving 280g/10oz* 5
Tagliatelle, Bianche (Safeway) *serving 280g/10oz* 3
Tagliatelle, Blanche (Waitrose) *serving 280g/10oz* 7
Tagliatelle, Egg Dried (Tesco) *serving 280g/10oz* 10
Tagliatelle, Fresco (Buitoni) *serving 280g/10oz* 11
Tagliatelle, Fresh (Asda) *serving 280g/10oz* 4
Tagliatelle, Fresh, Garlic & Herb (Asda) *serving 280g/10oz* 8
Tagliatelle, Fresh, Garlic & Herb, Chilled Ready Meal (Tesco) *serving 280g/10oz* 12
Tagliatelle, Frozen, Microwaved (Iceland) *serving 280g/10oz* 9
Tagliatelle, with Garlic & Herbs (Safeway) *serving 280g/10oz* 3
Tagliatelle, Garlic & Herb (Somerfield) *serving 280g/10oz* 6
Tagliatelle, Nests (Waitrose) *serving 280g/10oz* 5
Tagliatelle, Rosemary (Safeway) *serving 280g/10oz* 7
Tagliatelle, Straight (Princes) *serving 280g/10oz* 3
Tagliatelle, Sun Dried Tomato Pasta (Somerfield) *serving280g/10oz* 4
Tagliatelle, Tricolore (Waitrose) *serving 280g/10oz* 9

Tagliatelle, Verdi (Safeway) *serving 280g/10oz* 1
Tagliatelle, Verdi, Fresh (Asda) *serving 280g/10oz* 4
Tagliatelle, Verdi, Fresh (Tesco) *serving 280g/10oz* 10
Tagliatelle Carbonara (Somerfield) *serving 280g/10oz* 16
Tagliatelle Carbonara, Frozen (Asda) *serving 280g/10oz* 4
Tagliatelle Carbonara, Frozen Ready Meal (Heinz Weight Watchers) *serving 280g/10oz* 7
Tagliatelle Carbonara, Microwave Ready Meal (Safeway) *serving 280g/10oz* 21
Tagliatelle, Ham & Mushroom (Marks & Spencer) *serving 280g/10oz* 17
Tagliatelle, Ham & Mushroom (Somerfield) *serving 280g/10oz* 11
Tagliatelle, Ham & Mushroom, Chilled Ready Meal (Tesco) *serving 280g/10oz* 19
Tagliatelle Nicoise (Waitrose) *serving 280g/10oz* 29
Tagliatelle, Salmon, Frozen Ready Meal (Tesco) *serving 280g/10oz* 18
Tagliatelle, Seafood (Somerfield) *serving 280g/10oz* 16
Tagliatelle, Seafood, Frozen (Marks & Spencer) *serving 280g/10oz* 11
Tagliatelle with Vegetables, Retail *serving 280g/10oz* 8
Taglioni Fresco (Buitoni) *serving 280g/10oz* 11
Tomato, Vegetable & Olive Pasta Sauce (Marks & Spencer) *serving 280g/10oz* 6
Tomato Pepper & Herb Pasta (Somerfield) *serving 280g/10oz* 9
Tortelli Al Funghi Fresco (Buitoni) *serving 280g/10oz* 31
Tortellini, Amatriciana, Tinned (Tesco) *serving 280g/10oz* 8
Tortellini, Arrabbiata (Safeway) *serving 280g/10oz* 34
Tortellini, Four Cheese, Fresh (Asda) *serving 280g/10oz* 15
Tortellini, Four Cheese & Basil, Chilled Ready Meal (Tesco) *serving 280g/10oz* 21
Tortellini Smoked Ham & Cheese, Fresh (Asda) *serving 280g/10oz* 16
Tortellini, Garlic & Herb with Spicy Pork, Frozen, Boiled (Iceland) *serving 280g/10oz* 19
Tortellini, Garlic Mushroom, Fresh *serving 280g/10oz* 5
Tortelini, Ricotta & Spinach, Fresh (Asda) *serving 280g/10oz* 6

Tortellini, Ricotta & Spinach, Fresh (Tesco) *serving 280g/10oz* 15
Tortellini, Smoked Ham & Cheese (Waitrose) *serving 280g/10oz* 17
Tortelloni, Cheese & Garlic Pasta (Somerfield) *serving 280g/10oz* 18
Tortelloni with Cheese & Sundried Tomatoes (Safeway) *serving 280g/10oz* 32
Tortelloni, Five Cheese (Waitrose) *serving 280g/10oz* 29
Tortelloni with Five Cheeses (Safeway) *serving 280g/10oz* 42
Tortelloni with Garlic & Herbs (Safeway) *serving 280g/10oz* 25
Tortelloni, Ricotta (Waitrose) *serving 280g/10oz* 24
Tortelloni, Ricotta e Spinaci (Buitoni) Fresco *serving 280g/10oz* 26
Tricolour Pasta Nests (Waitrose) *serving 280g/10oz* 5
Tuna & Pasta Bake Fresh (Asda) *serving 280g/10oz* 17
Tuna & Pasta Bake (Somerfield) *serving 280g/10oz* 23
Tuna & Pasta Bake, Frozen (Asda) *serving 280g/10oz* 20
Tuna & Pineapple Pasta Bake, Frozen Ready Meal (Heinz Weight Watchers) *serving 280g/10oz* 4
Vegetable Pasta Bake, Frozen Ready Meal (Safeway) *serving 280g/10oz* 13
Vegetable & Pasta Bake, Frozen Ready Meal (Tesco) *serving 280g/10oz* 12
Vegetable Pasta Bows in Creamy Mushroom Sauce, Frozen (Iceland) *serving 280g/10oz* 25
Vegetable Pasta Medley (Birds Eye) *serving 280g/10oz* 4
Vegetable & Pasta Medley, Frozen Ready Meal (Heinz Weight Watchers) *serving 280g/10oz* 8
Vegetable Pasta Twists in Spicy Tomato Sauce, Frozen (Iceland) *serving 280g/10oz* 4

Pies, Pasties, Flans & Quiches

NOTE: The standard serving size in this section is 170g/6oz. If you wish to consume more or less than this amount (e.g. if you are going to consume a pack of food whose weight differs from the standard serving size) use the conversion tables on page 386 to calculate the new amount of fat in the food.

Bacon Toppers/Cheese, Hot (Marks & Spencer) *serving 170g/6oz* 36
Beef, Corned, Crispbakes, Hot (Marks & Spencer) *serving 170g/6oz* 21
Beef, Minced, Onion Pastry (Waitrose) *serving 170g/6oz* 28
Broccoli, Ham & Cheese Pastry Nests, Frozen (Asda) *serving 170g/6oz* 34
Cheese & Chive Lattice Slices, Frozen (Asda) *serving 170g/6oz* 31
Cheese & Onion Crispbake, Hot (Marks & Spencer) *serving 170g/6oz* 23
Chicken & Bacon Baked Suet Pastry Pudding, Prepacked (Asda) *serving 170g/6oz* 25
Chicken Breast & Leek Plate, Hot (Marks & Spencer) *serving 170g/6oz* 29
Chicken & Broccoli Crispbake, Hot (Marks & Spencer) *serving 170g/6oz* 19
Chicken & Broccoli, Reduced Fat, Hot (Marks & Spencer) *serving 170g/6oz* 9
Chicken Fajitas, Hot (Marks & Spencer) *serving 170g/6oz* 13
Chicken & Fries, Hot (Marks & Spencer) *serving 170g/6oz* 25
Chicken & Gravy, Reduced Fat, Hot (Marks & Spencer) *serving 170g/6oz* 4
Chicken & Leek Pastry Nests, Frozen (Asda) *serving 170g/6oz* 31
Chicken & Mushroom Lattice Slices, Frozen (Asda) *serving 170g/6oz* 27
Chicken & Red Pepper Tourte (Waitrose) *serving 170g/6oz* 21
Chicken & Tarragon Tourte (Waitrose) *serving 170g/6oz* 36
Chicken Tourte, Coronation (Waitrose) *serving 170g/6oz* 20
Creamy Mushroom Lattice Slices, Frozen *serving 170g/6oz* 27
Flaky Pastry, Cooked *serving 170g/6oz* 69
Flans, Bacon, Onion & Watercress (Waitrose) *serving 170g/6oz* 38
Flans, Bolognese (Somerfield) *serving 170g/6oz* 21
Flans, Broccoli *serving 170g/6oz* 26
Flans, Case, Medium (Somerfield) *serving 170g/6oz* 4
Flans, Case, Pastry *serving 170g/6oz* 57
Flans, Cauliflower & Broccoli (Somerfield) *serving 170g/6oz* 27
Flans, Cauliflower & Cheese *serving 170g/6oz* 21
Flans, Cheese, Egg & Bacon, Frozen (Asda) *serving 170g/6oz* 38

Flans, Cheese, Egg & Bacon, Frozen, Oven Baked (Iceland) *serving 170g/6oz*	33
Flans, Cheese & Mushroom, Wholemeal *serving 170g/6oz*	32
Flans, Cheese & Onion, Frozen (Iceland) *serving 170g/6oz*	32
Flans, Cheese, Onion & Potato Wholemeal *serving 170g/6oz*	41
Flans, Cheese & Tomato, Frozen Oven Baked (Iceland) *serving 170g/6oz*	34
Flans, Chicken & Almond (Waitrose) *serving 170g/6oz*	34
Flans, Chicken, Bacon & Onion (Waitrose) *serving 170g/6oz*	35
Flans, Chicken, Mushroom & Leek (Somerfield) *serving 170g/6oz*	22
Flans, Goat's Cheese & Tomato (Waitrose) *serving 170g/6oz*	23
Flans, Ham, Cheese & Mushroom (Waitrose) *serving 170g/6oz*	44
Flans, Mushroom & Broccoli, Chilled (Tesco) *serving 170g/6oz*	25
Flans, Salmon & Broccoli (Waitrose) *serving 170g/6oz*	27
Flans, Salmon & Broccoli, Chilled (Tesco) *serving 170g/6oz*	23
Flans, Sausage Lattice, Chilled (Tesco) *serving 170g/6oz*	34
Flans, Spinach *serving 170g/6oz*	22
Flans, Spinach & Cream Cheese (Waitrose) *serving 170g/6oz*	29
Flans, Triple Cheese & Tomato, Frozen (Asda) *serving 170g/6oz*	38
Flans, Triple Pack Frozen (Iceland) *serving 170g/6oz*	30
Flans, Vegetable *serving 170g/6oz*	22
Haggis & Neeps & Tatties, Hot (Marks & Spencer) *serving 170g/6oz*	11
Ham & Mushroom Lattice, Hot (Marks & Spencer) *serving 170g/6oz*	52
Lamb & Pea Mash, Home Style, Hot (Marks & Spencer) *serving 170g/6oz*	9
Lancashire Hot Pot Filled Yorkshire Pudding, Frozen Filling, Pan Boil (Iceland) *serving 170g/6oz*	7
Leek & Mushroom Crispbake, Hot (Marks & Spencer) *serving 170g/6oz*	16
Mince Beef Round, Made in Scotland, Prepacked (Asda) *serving 170g/6oz*	26
Pancakes, Barbecue Chicken, Crispy (Findus) *serving 170g/6oz*	8
Pancakes, Bread Scotch (Marks & Spencer) *serving 170g/6oz*	20

Pancakes, Cheddar Cheese, Crispy (Findus) *serving 170g/6oz* 13
Pancakes, Cheese & Onion, Frozen, Grilled (Iceland) *serving 170g/6oz* 9
Pancakes, Chicken & Bacon, Crispy (Findus) *serving 170g/6oz* 9
Pancakes, Chicken & Bacon, Frozen, Grilled (Iceland) *serving 170g/6oz* 14
Pancakes, Chicken Curry, Crispy (Findus) *serving 170g/6oz* 11
Pancakes, Chicken & Mushroom, Crispy (Findus) *serving 170g/6oz* 10
Pancakes, Country Vegetable, Crispy (Findus) *serving 170g/6oz* 13
Pancakes, Minced Beef, Crispy (Findus) *serving 170g/6oz* 9
Pancakes, Minced Beef, Frozen, Deep Fried (Iceland) *serving 170g/6oz* 12
Pancakes, Pizza Style, Crispy, Frozen, Grilled (Iceland) *serving 170g/6oz* 15
Pancakes, Potato, Home Made *serving 170g/6oz* 26
Pancakes, Roll (Meat Vegetable & Beansprout Filling) *serving 170g/6oz* 21
Pancakes Roll, Vegetable (from Chinese Take Away) *serving 170g/6oz* 21
Pancakes, Scotch *serving 170g/6oz* 20
Pancakes, Stuffed with Vegetables *serving 170g/6oz* 14
Pancakes, Sweet: *see under* Desserts
Pancakes, White Scotch (Waitrose) *serving 170g/6oz* 5
Pastry, Puff, Frozen, Ready to Bake *serving 170g/6oz* 65
Pastry, Shortcrust, Cooked *serving 170g/6oz* 55
Pastry, Wholemeal, Cooked *serving 170g/6oz* 56
Pasty, Beef & Onion (Marks & Spencer) *serving 170g/6oz* 33
Pasty, Cheese & Onion (Somerfield) *serving 170g/6oz* 31
Pasty, Cheese & Onion, Buffet (Somerfield) *serving 170g/6oz* 31
Pasty, Cheese & Onion, Chilled (Iceland) *serving 170g/6oz* 30
Pasty, Cheese & Onion, Individual, Prepacked (Asda) *serving 170g/6oz* 23
Pasty, Chicken & Leek (Marks & Spencer) *serving 170g/6oz* 34
Pasty, Chicken & Mushroom Chilled (Iceland) *serving 170g/6oz* 38
Pasty, Chicken & Mushroom (Marks & Spencer) *serving 170g/6oz* 31

Pasty, Cornish, D-shape, Individual, Prepacked (Asda) *serving 170g/6oz*	24
Pasty, Cornish, Basics (Somerfield) *serving 170g/6oz*	31
Pasty, Cornish, Buffet (Somerfield) *serving 170g/6oz*	25
Pasty, Cornish, Frozen, Baked (Iceland) *serving 170g/6oz*	28
Pasty, Cornish, Giant, Frozen, Reheated (Iceland) *serving 170g/6oz*	35
Pasty, Cornish Puff (Marks & Spencer) *serving 170g/6oz*	37
Pasty, Cornish, Puff Pastry, Prepacked (Asda) *serving 170g/6oz*	34
Pasty, Cornish, Traditional (Waitrose) *serving 170g/6oz*	24
Pasty, Cornish, Vegemince (Holland & Barrett) *serving 170g/6oz*	9
Pasty, Potato, Cheese & Onion (Holland & Barrett) *serving 170g/6oz*	11
Pasty, Shepherd's, Hot (Marks & Spencer) *serving 170g/6oz*	35
Pasty, Spicy Chicken (Somerfield) *serving 170g/6oz*	34
Pasty, Top, Crimp (Waitrose) *serving 170g/6oz*	24
Pasty, Traditional (Somerfield) *serving 170g/6oz*	24
Pasty, Turkey & Ham (Marks & Spencer) *serving 170g/6oz*	33
Pasty, Vegemince Chilli (Holland & Barrett) *serving 170g/6oz*	10
Pasty, Vegetable *serving 170g/6oz*	25
Pasty, Vegetable Tandoori (Holland & Barrett) *serving 170g/6oz*	10
Pasty, Vegetable & Tomato (Somerfield) *serving 170g/6oz*	23
Pie, Balti Vegetable (Holland & Barrett) *serving 170g/6oz*	12
Pie, Beef, Aberdeen Angus, Mini, Hot (Marks & Spencer) *serving 170g/6oz*	29
Pie, Beef (Corned) Plate, Hot (Marks & Spencer) *serving 170g/6oz*	30
Pie, Beef (Corned) & Potato, Mighty, Prepacked (Asda) *serving 170g/6oz*	24
Pie, Beef (Minced) & Onion (Waitrose) *serving 170g/6oz*	29
Pie, Beef (Minced) & Onion Chilled (Tesco) *serving 170g/6oz*	30
Pie, Beef (Minced) & Onion, Family (Somerfield) *serving 170g/6oz*	27
Pie, Beef (Minced) & Onion, Frozen (Asda) *serving 170g/6oz*	29
Pie, Beef (Minced) & Onion (4), Small, Prepacked (Asda) *serving 170g/6oz*	35

Pie, Beef (Minced) & Onion, Individual, Chilled (Tesco) *serving 170g/6oz* 34
Pie, Beef (Minced) & Onion, Large, Prepacked (Asda) *serving 170g/6oz* 31
Pie, Beef (Minced) & Vegetable, Frozen, Oven Baked (Iceland) *serving 170g/6oz* 28
Pie, Beef & Mushroom (Somerfield) *serving 170g/6oz* 23
Pie, Beef, Mushroom & Beer, Oval (Waitrose) *serving 170g/6oz* 25
Pie, Beef Plate, Mini, Hot (Marks & Spencer) *serving 170g/6oz* 27
Pie, Breakfast Topcrust, Small, Hot (Marks & Spencer) *serving 170g/6oz* 26
Pie, Cheese & Onion Plate, Hot (Marks & Spencer) *serving 170g/6oz* 38
Pie, Chicken (4) (Somerfield) *serving 170g/6oz* 21
Pie, Chicken & Gravy, Small (Marks & Spencer) *serving 170g/6oz* 30
Pie, Chicken Home Style, Hot (Marks & Spencer) *serving 170g/6oz* 7
Pie, Chicken & Ham, Frozen, Oven Baked (Iceland) *serving 170g/6oz* 29
Pie, Chicken & Leek Puff, Hot (Marks & Spencer) *serving 170g/6oz* 32
Pie, Chicken & Mushroom (Somerfield) *serving 170g/6oz* 26
Pie, Chicken & Mushroom (4) (Somerfield) *serving 170g/6oz* 42
Pie, Chicken & Mushroom (Waitrose) *serving 170g/6oz* 27
Pie, Chicken & Mushroom, Cumberland (Somerfield) *serving 170g/6oz* 12
Pie, Chicken & Mushroom, Family (Somerfield) *serving 170g/6oz* 25
Pie, Chicken & Mushroom, Frozen, Family (Iceland) *serving 170g/6oz* 29
Pie, Chicken & Mushroom, Frozen (Iceland) *serving 170g/6oz* 28
Pie, Chicken & Mushroom, Frozen, Oven Baked (Iceland) *serving 170g/6oz* 28
Pie, Chicken & Mushroom (Waitrose) *serving 170g/6oz* 27
Pie, Chicken, Mushroom & Bacon, Deepfill (Somerfield) *serving 170g/6oz* 26

Pie, Chicken, Mushroom & Bacon (Waitrose) *serving 170g/6oz* 29
Pie, Chicken & Vegetable (Somerfield) *serving 170g/6oz* 23
Pie, Chicken & Vegetable, Frozen (Asda) *serving 170g/6oz* 27
Pie, Chicken & Vegetable (4), Frozen (Asda) *serving 170g/6oz* 26
Pie, Chicken & Vegetable, Family, Frozen (Iceland) *serving 170g/6oz* 30
Pie, Chicken & Vegetable, Lattice Top, Prepacked (Asda) *serving 170g/6oz* 27
Pie, Cod, Savoury (Waitrose) *serving 170g/6oz* 13
Pie, Cod & Leek, Family, Hot (Marks & Spencer) *serving 170g/6oz* 6
Pie, Cod & Prawn, Frozen Ready Meal (Tesco) *serving 170g/6oz* 23
Pie, Cod, Prawn & Broccoli, Deepfill (Somerfield) *serving 170g/6oz* 26
Pie, Cornish Plate, Hot (Marks & Spencer) *serving 170g/6oz* 37
Pie, Cottage (Somerfield) *serving 170g/6oz* 5
Pie, Cottage, Chilled Ready Meal (Tesco) *serving 170g/6oz* 14
Pie, Cottage, Deep Dish (Waitrose) *serving 170g/6oz* 11
Pie, Cottage, Family, Frozen (Asda) *serving 170g/6oz* 12
Pie, Cottage, Family, Hot (Marks & Spencer) *serving 170g/6oz* 12
Pie, Cottage, Frozen (Asda) *serving 170g/6oz* 12
Pie, Cottage, Frozen (Waitrose) *serving 170g/6oz* 11
Pie, Cottage, Home Style, Hot (Marks & Spencer) *serving 170g/6oz* 12
Pie, Cottage, Main Meals (Marks & Spencer) *serving 170g/6oz* 10
Pie, Cottage, Meat Free (Birds Eye) *serving 170g/6oz* 4
Pie, Cottage, Reduced Fat (Sainsbury's) *serving 170g/6oz* 3
Pie, Cottage, Small, Hot (Marks & Spencer) *serving 170g/6oz* 9
Pie, Crust, Standard Type, Dry Mix, Prepared, Baked *serving 170g/6oz* 52
Pie, Crust, Standard Type, Frozen, Ready to Bake, Baked *serving 170g/6oz* 56
Pie, Crust, Standard Type, Prepared from Recipe, Baked *serving 170g/6oz* 59
Pie, Cumberland (Somerfield) *serving 170g/6oz* 9
Pie, Cumberland (Waitrose) *serving 170g/6oz* 10

Pie, Cumberland, Chilled Ready Meal (Safeway) *serving 170g/6oz* 39
Pie, Cumberland, Chilled Ready Meal (Tesco) *serving 170g/6oz* 12
Pie, Cumberland, Frozen (Waitrose) *serving 170g/6oz* 13
Pie, Cumberland, Medium, Hot (Marks & Spencer) *serving 170g/6oz* 12
Pie, Cumberland, Small, Hot (Marks & Spencer) *serving 170g/6oz* 12
Pie, Duck & Orange (Waitrose) *serving 170g/6oz* 32
Pie, Fish *serving 170g/6oz* 9
Pie, Fish, Cumberland (Waitrose) *serving 170g/6oz* 12
Pie, Fisherman's *serving 170g/6oz* 9
Pie, Fisherman's (Somerfield) *serving 170g/6oz* 4
Pie, Fisherman's (Waitrose) *serving 170g/6oz* 8
Pie, Fisherman's Family, Frozen (Marks & Spencer) *serving 170g/6oz* 14
Pie, Fisherman's, Frozen (Marks & Spencer) *serving 170g/6oz* 14
Pie, Haddock & Veg, Family, Hot (Marks & Spencer) *serving 170g/6oz* 8
Pie, Ham & Chicken (Waitrose) *serving 170g/6oz* 32
Pie, Leek, Potato & Cheese (Waitrose) *serving 170g/6oz* 33
Pie, Lincoln Lattice, Large, Party Food (Marks & Spencer) *serving 170g/6oz* 40
Pie, Lincolnshire, Mini, Party Food (Marks & Spencer) *serving 170g/6oz* 53
Pie, Macaroni (2), Made in Scotland, Prepacked (Asda) *serving 170g/6oz* 20
Pie, Macaroni Cheese, Mini, Deli (Asda) *serving 170g/6oz* 23
Pie, Meat & Potato (4), Prepacked (Asda) *serving 170g/6oz* 28
Pie, Meat & Potato (4) Frozen (Iceland) *serving 170g/6oz* 31
Pie, Melton Mowbray, Mini, Deli (Asda) *serving 170g/6oz* 42
Pie, Melton Mowbray, Party Food (Marks & Spencer) *serving 170g/6oz* 43
Pie, Ocean, Frozen (Marks & Spencer) *serving 170g/6oz* 9
Pie, Ocean, Family, Frozen (Marks & Spencer) *serving 170g/6oz* 10
Pie, Ocean with Haddock, Frozen Ready Meal (Heinz Weight Watchers) *serving 170g/6oz* 5
Pie, Ploughman's, Deli (Asda) *serving 170g/6oz* 32

Pie, Pork: *see* Pork Pie
Pie, Roast Chicken Plate, Hot (Marks & Spencer) *serving 170g/6oz* 30
Pie, Roast Chicken & Mushroom, Shortcrust, Prepacked (Asda) *serving 170g/6oz* 31
Pie, Roast Chicken, Mushroom & Bacon (Waitrose) *serving 170g/6oz* 26
Pie, Round Lamb & Gravy, Small, Hot (Marks & Spencer) *serving 170g/6oz* 29
Pie, Salmon & Broccoli, Light/Crisp, Hot (Marks & Spencer) *serving 170g/6oz* 26
Pie, Salmon, Cumberland, Hot (Marks & Spencer) *serving 170g/6oz* 10
Pie, Salmon, Home Style, Hot (Marks & Spencer) *serving 170g/6oz* 6
Pie, Salmon & Broccoli (Waitrose) *serving 170g/6oz* 33
Pie, Salmon & Asparagus, Lattice Top, Prepacked (Asda) *serving 170g/6oz* 36
Pie, Sausage & Onion, Mini (Somerfield) *serving 170g/6oz* 36
Pie, Savoury, Frozen, Oven Baked (Iceland) *serving 170g/6oz* 23
Pie, Shepherds: *see* Shepherd's Pie
Pie, Steak & Kidney: *see* Steak & Kidney Pie
Pie, Turkey & Ham Plate, Hot (Marks & Spencer) *serving 170g/6oz* 25
Pie, Turkey, Ham & Asparagus (Waitrose) *serving 170g/6oz* 27
Pie, Turkey, Pork & Cranberry (Waitrose) *serving 170g/6oz* 33
Pie, Vegetable (Somerfield) *serving 170g/6oz* 28
Pie, Vegetable (Waitrose) *serving 170g/6oz* 27
Pie, Vegetable Casserole, Chunky (Waitrose) *serving 170g/6oz* 32
Pie, Vegetable, Cumberland, Chilled Ready Meal (Tesco) *serving 170g/6oz* 14
Pie, Vegetable, Frozen (Iceland) *serving 170g/6oz* 31
Pie, Vegetable, Layered, Deli (Asda) *serving 170g/6oz* 22
Pie, Vegetable & Cheese (Somerfield) *serving 170g/6oz* 27
Pie, Vegetable & Cheese (Waitrose) *serving 170g/6oz* 30
Pie, Vegetable & Cheese, Deepfill (Somerfield) *serving 170g/6oz* 28
Pie, Vegetable & Cheese, Frozen (Asda) *serving 170g/6oz* 32

Pie, Vegetable & Cheese Oval (Waitrose) *serving 170g/6oz* 35
Pork Pie (Somerfield) *serving 170g/6oz* 36
Pork Pie (Waitrose) *serving 170g/6oz* 47
Pork Pie, Buffet (4) (Waitrose) *serving 170g/6oz* 52
Pork Pie, Cheese Crust, Melton Mowbray Mini, Deli (Asda) *serving 170g/6oz* 48
Pork Pie, Chicken & Pork & Garlic Pie (Waitrose) *serving 170g/6oz* 40
Pork Pie, Chicken & Pork Pies, Mini *serving 170g/6oz* 40
Pork Pie, Crispy Bake, Buffet, Chilled, Eaten Cold (Iceland) *serving 170g/6oz* 28
Pork Pie, Crispy, with Egg (Somerfield) *serving 170g/6oz* 38
Pork Pie, Farmhouse (Waitrose) *serving 170g/6oz* 30
Pork Pie, Gala (Waitrose) *serving 170g/6oz* 34
Pork Pie, Gala, Deli (Asda) *serving 170g/6oz* 45
Pork Pie, Individual (Waitrose) *serving 170g/6oz* 46
Pork Pie, Individual, Made in Scotland, Prepacked (Asda) *serving 170g/6oz* 48
Pork Pie, Melton Mowbray (Somerfield) *serving 170g/6oz* 48
Pork Pie, Melton Mowbray (Waitrose) *serving 170g/6oz* 46
Pork Pie, Melton Mowbray, Buffet (Somerfield) *serving 170g/6oz* 44
Pork Pie, Melton Mowbray, Deli (Asda) *serving 170g/6oz* 46
Pork Pie, Melton Mowbray, Mini (Somerfield) *serving 170g/6oz* 49
Pork Pie, Melton Mowbray, Mini (Waitrose) *serving 170g/6oz* 42
Pork Pie, Melton Mowbray, Mini, Prepacked (Asda) *serving 170g/6oz* 42
Pork Pie, Melton Mowbray, Traditional, Prepacked (Asda) *serving 170g/6oz* 46
Pork Pie, Party Food (Marks & Spencer) *serving 170g/6oz* 49
Pork Pie, Pork, Bacon & Apricot, Lattice (Waitrose) *serving 170g/6oz* 25
Pork Pie, Pork, Cheese & Pickle Pie (Somerfield) *serving 170g/6oz* 47
Pork Pie, Pork, Cheese & Pickle Pie (Waitrose) *serving 170g/6oz* 53
Pork Pie, Pork, Chicken & Apricot Pie (Waitrose) *serving 170g/6oz* 29

Pork Pie, Pork, Chicken & Apricot Pie, Deli (Asda) *serving 170g/6oz* 29
Pork Pie, Pork, Chicken & Ham Slicing Pie, Deli (Asda) *serving 170g/6oz* 32
Pork Pie, Pork & Egg Pie, Gala, Deli (Asda) *serving 170g/6oz* 37
Pork Pie, Pork & Egg Pie, Party Food (Marks & Spencer) *serving 170g/6oz* 41
Pork Pie, Pork Turkey & Gammon Pie (Waitrose) *serving 170g/6oz* 22
Pork Pie & Turkey & Stuffing (Waitrose) *serving 170g/6oz* 24
Puff Pastry, Assorted (Waitrose) *serving 170g/6oz* 38
Quiche, Asparagus, Party Food (Marks & Spencer) *serving 170g/6oz* 31
Quiche, Bacon & Leek, Party Food (Marks & Spencer) *serving 170g/6oz* 34
Quiche, Broccoli, Individual, Party Food (Marks & Spencer) *serving 170g/6oz* 28
Quiche, Broccoli, Medium, Party Food (Marks & Spencer) *serving 170g/6oz* 26
Quiche, Broccoli & Cheese (Waitrose) *serving 170g/6oz* 22
Quiche, Cheese & Egg *serving 170g/6oz* 38
Quiche, Cheese & Egg, Wholemeal *serving 170g/6oz* 38
Quiche, Cheese & Mushroom *serving 170g/6oz* 32
Quiche, Cheese & Onion (Waitrose) *serving 170g/6oz* 28
Quiche, Cheese & Onion, Prepacked (Asda) *serving 170g/6oz* 24
Quiche, Cheese & Onion, Chilled, Baked (Iceland) *serving 170g/6oz* 28
Quiche, Cheese & Onion, Deli (Asda) *serving 170g/6oz* 23
Quiche, Cheese & Onion, Family, Chilled (Tesco) *serving 170g/6oz* 34
Quiche, Cheese & Onion, Frozen (Iceland) *serving 170g/6oz* 30
Quiche, Cheese & Onion, Individual, Chilled (Tesco) *serving 170g/6oz* 32
Quiche, Cheese & Onion, Individual, Party Food (Marks & Spencer) *serving 170g/6oz* 36
Quiche, Cheese & Onion, Medium, Party Food (Marks & Spencer) *serving 170g/6oz* 33

Quiche, Cheese & Onion, Mini, Chilled (Iceland) *serving 170g/6oz* 28
Quiche, Cheese, Onion & Potato *serving 170g/6oz* 41
Quiche, Chicken & Spring Onion (Waitrose) *serving 170g/6oz* 24
Quiche, Chilled Brunch, Chilled (Tesco) *serving 170g/6oz* 29
Quiche, Country Vegetable, Chilled (Tesco) *serving 170g/6oz* 31
Quiche, Country Vegetable, Family, Chilled (Tesco) *serving 170g/6oz* 25
Quiche, Deep Dish (Waitrose) *serving 170g/6oz* 44
Quiche, Egg, Cheese & Bacon, Family, Chilled (Tesco) *serving 170g/6oz* 27
Quiche, Egg, Cheese & Bacon, Individual, Chilled (Tesco) *serving 170g/6oz* 26
Quiche, Fish, Mini (Waitrose) *serving 170g/6oz* 34
Quiche, Ham & Cheese, Prepacked (Asda) *serving 170g/6oz* 24
Quiche, Leek & Bacon (Waitrose) *serving 170g/6oz* 27
Quiche, Leek & Stilton (Waitrose) *serving 170g/6oz* 28
Quiche, Lorraine *serving 170g/6oz* 48
Quiche, Lorraine, Chilled (Tesco) *serving 170g/6oz* 34
Quiche, Lorraine, Deli (Asda) *serving 170g/6oz* 22
Quiche, Lorraine, Family (Waitrose) *serving 170g/6oz* 37
Quiche, Lorraine, Frozen, Baked (Iceland) *serving 170g/6oz* 31
Quiche, Lorraine, Medium, Party Food (Marks & Spencer) *serving 170g/6oz* 35
Quiche, Lorraine, Mini, Chilled (Iceland) *serving 170g/6oz* 31
Quiche, Lorraine, Mini, Chilled, Baked (Iceland) *serving 170g/6oz* 21
Quiche, Lorraine, Tartlet (Waitrose) *serving 170g/6oz* 37
Quiche, Lorraine, Wholemeal *serving 170g/6oz* 48
Quiche, Mini (Waitrose) *serving 170g/6oz* 38
Quiche, Mushroom *serving 170g/6oz* 33
Quiche, Mushroom (Waitrose) *serving 170g/6oz* 34
Quiche, Mushroom & Ham, Party (Waitrose) *serving 170g/6oz* 27
Quiche, Mushroom, Wholemeal *serving 170g/6oz* 33
Quiche, Party Foods Selection (Marks & Spencer) *serving 170g/6oz* 32
Quiche, Reduced Fat (Sainsbury's) *serving 170g/6oz* 31

Quiche, Salmon & Dill (Waitrose) *serving 170g/6oz* 25
Quiche, Sausage, Bacon & Egg, Chilled (Iceland) *serving 170g/6oz* 13
Quiche, Sausage & Bacon & Mushroom (Waitrose) *serving 170g/6oz* 33
Quiche, Sausage, Tomato & Bacon, Deli (Asda) *serving 170g/6oz* 25
Quiche, Smoked Ham & Gruyere, Deli (Asda) *serving 170g/6oz* 21
Quiche, Smoked Salmon/Dill (Waitrose) *serving 170g/6oz* 26
Quiche, Salmon & Watercress (Waitrose) *serving 170g/6oz* 28
Quiche, Three Cheese & Tomato, Prepacked (Asda) *serving 170g/6oz* 33
Quiche, Tomato & Broccoli (Waitrose) *serving 170g/6oz* 24
Quiche, Tomato & Cheese, Medium, Party Food (Marks & Spencer) *serving 170g/6oz* 31
Quiche, Tomato, Ham & Cheese, Chilled (Tesco) *serving 170g/6oz* 25
Quiche, Variety Cocktail, Frozen (Iceland) *serving 170g/6oz* 37
Salmon & Spinach Lattice (Waitrose) *serving 170g/6oz* 40
Savoury Puffs (Waitrose) *serving 170g/6oz* 49
Scotch Pie, Hot (Marks & Spencer) *serving 170g/6oz* 31
Scotch Pie, Individual, Prepacked (Asda) *serving 170g/6oz* 28
Scotch Pie, Twin Pack, Prepacked (Asda) *serving 170g/6oz* 28
Shepherd's Pie (Birds Eye) *serving 170g/6oz* 6
Shepherd's Pie (Crosse & Blackwell) *serving 170g/6oz* 11
Shepherd's Pie (Somerfield) *serving 170g/6oz* 7
Shepherd's Pie (Waitrose) *serving 170g/6oz* 11
Shepherd's Pie, Basics (Somerfield) *serving 170g/6oz* 6
Shepherd's Pie, Family, Hot (Marks & Spencer) *serving 170g/6oz* 6
Shepherd's Pie, Frozen (Asda) *serving 170g/6oz* 12
Shepherd's Pie, Frozen Ready Meal (Tesco) *serving 170g/6oz* 5
Shepherd's Pie, Home Style, Hot (Marks & Spencer) *serving 170g/6oz* 9
Shepherd's Pie, Individual, Frozen, Oven Baked (Iceland) *serving 170g/6oz* 8

Shepherd's Pie, Medium, Hot (Marks & Spencer) *serving 170g/6oz* 10
Shepherd's Pie, Reduced Fat, Hot (Marks & Spencer) *serving 170g/6oz* 4
Shepherd's Pie with Lamb, Frozen Ready Meal (Heinz Weight Watchers) *serving 170g/6oz* 5
Smoked Bacon & Leek Tourte (Waitrose) *serving 170g/6oz* 26
Southern Fried Chicken Sandwich, Hot (Marks & Spencer) *serving 170g/6oz* 13
Steak & Ale Baked Suet Pastry Pudding, Prepacked (Asda) *serving 170g/6oz* 23
Steak Pie (Somerfield) *serving 170g/6oz* 27
Steak Pie, Chunky (Waitrose) *serving 170g/6oz* 34
Steak Pie, Deep Filled, Prepacked (Asda) *serving 170g/6oz* 28
Steak Pie, Frozen, Oven Baked (Iceland) *serving 170g/6oz* 29
Steak Plate Pie, Hot (Marks & Spencer) *serving 170g/6oz* 27
Steak Pie, Scottish, Hot (Marks & Spencer) *serving 170g/6oz* 25
Steak Pie, Shortcrust, Prepacked (Asda) *serving 170g/6oz* 31
Steak Pie, Small, Hot (Marks & Spencer) *serving 170g/6oz* 32
Steak Pie, Top Crust (Waitrose) *serving 170g/6oz* 16
Steak & Ale Pie, Premium, Frozen Oven Baked (Iceland) *serving 170g/6oz* 30
Steak & Kidney Pie (Somerfield) *serving 170g/6oz* 27
Steak & Kidney Pie (Waitrose) *serving 170g/6oz* 24
Steak & Kidney Pie, Chunky (Waitrose) *serving 170g/6oz* 30
Steak & Kidney Pie, Deep Filled, Prepacked (Asda) *serving 170g/6oz* 29
Steak & Kidney Pie, Deepfill (Somerfield) *serving 170g/6oz* 21
Steak & Kidney Pie, Family (Somerfield) *serving 170g/6oz* 26
Steak & Kidney Pie, Frozen, Oven Baked (Iceland) *serving 170g/6oz* 27
Steak & Kidney Plate Pie, Hot (Marks & Spencer) *serving 170g/6oz* 22
Steak & Kidney Pudding, Small, Hot (Marks & Spencer) *serving 170g/6oz* 16
Steak & Kidney Puff Pie, Hot (Marks & Spencer) *serving 170g/6oz* 30

Steak & Mushroom Pie (Somerfield) *serving 170g/6oz* 31
Steak & Mushroom Pie, Frozen (Asda) *serving 170g/6oz* 30
Steak & Mushroom Pie, in Red Wine (Waitrose) *serving 170g/6oz* 28
Steak, Kidney & Onion (4) Prepacked (Asda) *serving 170g/6oz* 23
Steak, Mushroom & Onion Suet Pudding (Waitrose) *serving 170g/6oz* 23
Steak Pie (Minced), & Onion (Waitrose) *serving 170g/6oz* 28
Steak Pie, & Onion, Family, Frozen (Iceland) *serving 170g/6oz* 29
Steak, Small, Round, Hot (Marks & Spencer) *serving 170g/6oz* 29
Steak, Small, Scottish, Hot (Marks & Spencer) *serving 170g/6oz* 33
Stonebake Garlic Bread, Hot (Marks & Spencer) *serving 170g/6oz* 20
Stonebake Supreme, Hot (Marks & Spencer) *serving 170g/6oz* 14
Stuffed Crust, Meat, Hot (Marks & Spencer) *serving 170g/6oz* 11
Stuffed Crust, Vegetable, Hot (Marks & Spencer) *serving 170g/6oz* 9
Tart, Bean & Sausage & Bacon (Waitrose) *serving 170g/6oz* 24
Tart, Onion, Continental (Waitrose) *serving 170g/6oz* 24
Tart, Prawn/Courgette (Waitrose) *serving 170g/6oz* 32
Tart Am Tomat, Continental (Waitrose) *serving 170g/6oz* 22
Tarte à l'Oignon (Waitrose) *serving 170g/6oz* 30
Tarte, Haddock & Spinach (Waitrose) *serving 170g/6oz* 27
Tartlet, Haddock & Chips (Waitrose) *serving 170g/6oz* 22
Tartlet, Roast Vegetable (Waitrose) *serving 170g/6oz* 26
Torta di Dolcelatte (Waitrose) *serving 170g/6oz* 68
Turkey/Herb & Pork Plait (Waitrose) *serving 170g/6oz* 14
Vegetable Crispbake, Hot (Marks & Spencer) *serving 170g/6oz* 13
Vol au Vents, Mini, Party Food (Marks & Spencer) *serving 170g/6oz* 41
Wontons, Crispy (Marks & Spencer) *serving 170g/6oz* 47

Pizza

NOTE: The standard serving size in this section is 110g/4oz. If you wish to consume more or less than this amount (e.g. if you are going to consume a pack of food whose weight differs from the standard serving size) use the conversion tables on page 386 to calculate the new amount of fat in the food.

Bacon & Mushroom (Waitrose) *serving 110g/4oz* 9
Bacon & Mushroom, Deep Pan, Fresh, Chilled (Tesco) *serving 110g/4oz* 10
Bacon & Mushroom, Mighty Pizza, Prepacked (Asda) *serving 110g/4oz* 7
Bacon & Mushroom, Thin & Crispy (Somerfield) *serving 110g/4oz* 12
Bacon & Mushroom, Thin & Crispy, Chilled (Tesco) *serving 110g/4oz* 11
Baked Beans & Sausage, Frozen, Oven Baked (Iceland) *serving 110g/4oz* 8
Barbecue Chicken French Bread Pizza (Nestlé) *serving 110g/4oz* 6
Beef, Spicy, Deep & Crispy, Chilled (Tesco) *serving 110g/4oz* 6
Big 'n' Meaty, Frozen (Asda) *serving 110g/4oz* 9
Cheese, American Pan Pizza, Pizza Feast (Somerfield) *serving 110g/4oz* 13
Cheese, Three & Tomato (Somerfield) *serving 110g/4oz* 7
Cheese, Three & Tomato, Pizzeria (Marks & Spencer) *serving 110g/4oz* 6
Cheese, Three & Tomato with Ham (Somerfield) *serving 110g/4oz* 6
Cheese, Four (Waitrose) *serving 110g/4oz* 16
Cheese, Four, Authentic Italian, Prepacked (Asda) *serving 110g/4oz* 8
Cheese, Four, New (Somerfield) *serving 110g/4oz* 7
Cheese, Five, Italian (Waitrose) *serving 110g/4oz* 11
Cheese, Italian (Waitrose) *serving 110g/4oz* 8
Cheese with Meat & Vegetables *serving 110g/4oz* 7
Cheese & Onion, Frozen (Asda) *serving 110g/4oz* 9
Cheese & Tomato *serving 110g/4oz* 13
Cheese & Tomato (Somerfield) *serving 110g/4oz* 10
Cheese & Tomato (Waitrose) *serving 110g/4oz* 9
Cheese & Tomato Basil (Waitrose) *serving 110g/4oz* 13

Cheese & Tomato, Chilled (Tesco) *serving 110g/4oz* 10
Cheese & Tomato, Deep & Crispy, Chilled (Tesco) *serving 110g/4oz* 6
Cheese & Tomato, Deep & Crispy, Frozen (Tesco) *serving 110g/4oz* 6
Cheese & Tomato, Deep & Crispy (Somerfield) *serving 110g/4oz* 8
Cheese & Tomato, Deep Pan, Chilled (Tesco) *serving 110g/4oz* 5
Cheese & Tomato Flavour, Basics (Somerfield) *serving 110g/4oz* 6
Cheese & Tomato French Bread Pizza (Nestlé) *serving 110g/4oz* 8
Cheese & Tomato French Bread Pizzas, Frozen, Oven Baked (Iceland) *serving 110g/4oz* 9
Cheese & Tomato, Frozen (Somerfield) *serving 110g/4oz* 8
Cheese & Tomato, Frozen (Tesco) *serving 110g/4oz* 10
Cheese & Tomato (4), Frozen (Asda) *serving 110g/4oz* 10
Cheese & Tomato, Frozen, Oven Baked (Iceland) *serving 110g/4oz* 8
Cheese & Tomato, Italian Style, Twin Pack, Frozen (Iceland) *serving 110g/4oz* 9
Cheese & Tomato Mighty Pizza, Prepacked (Asda) *serving 110g/4oz* 6
Cheese & Tomato, Prepacked (Asda) *serving 110g/4oz* 5
Cheese & Tomato, Thin & Crispy, Chilled (Tesco) *serving 110g/4oz* 9
Cheese & Tomato, Thin & Crispy (Waitrose) *serving 110g/4oz* 5
Cheese & Tomato, Triple Pack, Frozen, Oven Baked (Iceland) *serving 110g/4oz* 7
Cheese & Tomato Christmas Shaped Pizzas, Frozen, Oven Baked (Iceland) *serving 110g/4oz* 7
Chicken, 95% Fat Free (Marks & Spencer) *serving 110g/4oz* 3
Chicken, Spicy, Thin & Crispy, Chilled (Tesco) *serving 110g/4oz* 8
Chicken Feast, Spicy, Frozen (Asda) *serving 110g/4oz* 8
Chicken Tikka, Deep & Crispy, Frozen (Tesco) *serving 110g/4oz* 5
Chicken Tikka, Deep Fill, Chilled (Tesco) *serving 110g/4oz* 11
Chilli Beef French Bread Pizza (Nestlé) *serving 110g/4oz* 8
Four Season Meat Pizza (Waitrose) *serving 110g/4oz* 9
Garlic Ciabatta, Chilled (Tesco) *serving 110g/4oz* 20

Garlic Pizza Bread, Chilled (Tesco) *serving 110g/4oz*	20
Garlic Pizza Bread, Frozen (Iceland) *serving 110g/4oz*	19
Garlic & Mushroom (Waitrose) *serving 110g/4oz*	10
Garlic Mushroom Authentic Italian Pizza, Prepacked (Asda) *serving 110g/4oz*	5
Garlic & Mushroom, Deep & Crispy, Chilled (Tesco) *serving 110g/4oz*	7
Garlic & Mushroom, Thin & Crispy, Chilled (Tesco) *serving 110g/4oz*	8
Gigantica, Italian Style, Frozen, Oven Baked (Iceland) *serving 110g/4oz*	11
Ham & Mushroom (Somerfield) *serving 110g/4oz*	10
Ham & Mushroom, Deep & Crispy (Somerfield) *serving 110g/4oz*	5
Ham & Mushroom French Bread Pizza (Nestlé) *serving 110g/4oz*	6
Ham & Mushroom (4), Frozen (Asda) *serving 110g/4oz*	10
Ham & Mushroom (4), Frozen (Tesco) *serving 110g/4oz*	9
Ham & Mushroom, Healthy Choice, Frozen, Oven Baked (Iceland) *serving 110g/4oz*	4
Ham & Mushroom, Thin & Crispy (Somerfield) *serving 110g/4oz*	5
Ham & Mushroom, Thin & Crispy Frozen (Asda) *serving 110g/4oz*	4
Ham & Mushroom, Thin & Crispy, Frozen (Tesco) *serving 110g/4oz*	8
Ham & Pepperoni, Pizzeria (Marks & Spencer) *serving 110g/4oz*	7
Ham & Pineapple (Waitrose) *serving 110g/4oz*	7
Ham & Pineapple, Deep & Crispy (Somerfield) *serving 110g/4oz*	5
Ham & Pineapple French Bread Pizza (Nestlé) *serving 110g/4oz*	5
Ham & Pineapple French Bread Pizza, Frozen, Oven Baked (Iceland) *serving 110g/4oz*	9
Ham & Pineapple Stonebake Pizza, Frozen, Oven Baked (Iceland) *serving 110g/4oz*	9
Ham, Smoked, & Mushroom, Frozen, Oven Baked (Iceland) *serving 110g/4oz*	8
Ham, Smoked, & Pineapple, Thin & Crispy (Somerfield) *serving 110g/4oz*	9

Ham & Vegetable Mighty Pizza, Prepacked (Asda) *serving 110g/4oz* 4
Hawaiian American Pan Pizza (Somerfield) *serving 110g/4oz* 8
Margherita (Holland & Barrett) *serving 110g/4oz* 7
Margerita, Authentic Italian Style, Chilled (Tesco) *serving 110g/4oz* 9
Margherita, Authentic Italian (Somerfield) *serving 110g/4oz* 7
Margherita, Chilled (Tesco) *serving 110g/4oz* 6
Margherita, Stone Oven Baked (Somerfield) *serving 110g/4oz* 10
Meat Feast, American Pan Pizza (Somerfield) *serving 110g/4oz* 10
Meat Feast, Deep & Crispy (Somerfield) *serving 110g/4oz* 9
Meat Feast, Italian (Waitrose) *serving 110g/4oz* 14
Mini Pizza, Canapé Pack (Waitrose) *serving 110g/4oz* 9
Mushroom & Garlic (Waitrose) *serving 110g/4oz* 13
Mushroom & Garlic, Deep & Crispy, Frozen (Tesco) *serving 110g/4oz* 4
Mushroom & Garlic, Microwave, Frozen (Tesco) *serving 110g/4oz* 7
Pepper, Mixed, & Mushroom (Holland & Barrett) *serving 110g/4oz* 5
Pepperoni (Somerfield) *serving 110g/4oz* 9
Pepperoni, Deep, Pizzeria, Frozen (Tesco) *serving 110g/4oz* 9
Pepperoni, Deep & Crispy (Somerfield) *serving 110g/4oz* 9
Pepperoni, Deep & Crispy, Chilled (Tesco) *serving 110g/4oz* 9
Pepperoni (4), Frozen (Asda) *serving 110g/4oz* 10
Pepperoni, Frozen (Tesco) *serving 110g/4oz* 9
Pepperoni, Frozen, Oven Baked (Iceland) *serving 110g/4oz* 7
Pepperoni Mighty Pizza, Prepacked (Asda) *serving 110g/4oz* 8
Pepperoni, Pan Baked (Waitrose) *serving 110g/4oz* 7
Pepperoni, Ristorante Pizza (Waitrose) *serving 110g/4oz* 14
Pepperoni, Thin & Crispy (Somerfield) *serving 110g/4oz* 11
Pepperoni, Thin & Crispy, Frozen (Asda) *serving 110g/4oz* 5
Pepperoni, Thin & Crispy, Frozen (Tesco) *serving 110g/4oz* 15
Pepperoni, Triple, Deep & Crispy, Frozen (Tesco) *serving 110g/4oz* 16
Pepperoni & Kabanos, Thin & Crispy (Somerfield) *serving 110g/4oz* 14

Pineapple & Ham (Waitrose) *serving 110g/4oz* 10
Pizza Base (Napolina) (CPC) *serving 110g/4oz* 5
Pizza Base, Deep & Crispy (Somerfield) *serving 110g/4oz* 3
Pizza Base, Deep & Crispy, Chilled (Tesco) *serving 110g/4oz* 2
Pizza Base, Thin & Crispy (12 in.) Chilled (Tesco) *serving 110g/4oz* 2
Pizza Squares (Waitrose) *serving 110g/4oz* 15
Pizza Squares, Party Food (Marks & Spencer) *serving 110g/4oz* 12
Pizza Wedge Selection, Chilled (Tesco) *serving 110g/4oz* 10
Proscuitto & Funghi, Authentic, Chilled (Tesco) *serving 110g/4oz* 9
Proscuitto & Fungi, Authentic Italian (Somerfield) *serving 110g/4oz* 6
Proscuitto & Funghi, Chilled (Tesco) *serving 110g/4oz* 8
Proscuitto, Italian (Waitrose) *serving 110g/4oz* 9
Quattro Stagioni, Authentic Italian, Chilled (Tesco) *serving 110g/4oz* 7
Sauce, Tomato DIY Pizzeria, Chilled (Tesco) *serving 110g/4oz* 1
Sausage, Spicy (Waitrose) *serving 110g/4oz* 9
Seafood, Deep & Crispy, Chilled (Tesco) *serving 110g/4oz* 6
Supreme, Deep & Crispy, Chilled (Tesco) *serving 110g/4oz* 10
Three Cheese & Tomato (Somerfield) *serving 110g/4oz* 8
Tomato Pizza *serving 110g/4oz* 12
Topping, Beef Spicy, DIY Pizzeria, Chilled (Tesco) *serving 110g/4oz* 8
Topping, Cheese, Tomato, Onions & Herbs (Napolina) (CPC) *serving 110g/4oz* 4
Topping, Frankfurter, DIY Pizzeria, Chilled (Tesco) *serving 110g/4oz* 30
Topping, Pepperoni, DIY Pizzeria, Chilled (Tesco) *serving 110g/4oz* 21
Topping, Spicy Tomato (Napolina) (CPC) *serving 110g/4oz* 3
Topping, Tomato, Cheese, Onions & Herbs (Napolina) (CPC) *serving 110g/4oz* 4
Topping, Tomato, Herbs & Spices, Traditional (Napolina) *serving 110g/4oz* 3
Tuna & Prawn, Thin & Crispy, Frozen (Tesco) *serving 110g/4oz* 9
Vegetable, Deep & Crispy (Somerfield) *serving 110g/4oz* 6

Vegetable, Deep Fill, Chilled (Tesco) *serving 110g/4oz* 8
Vegetable, Italian (Waitrose) *serving 110g/4oz* 9
Vegetable, Pan Baked (Waitrose) *serving 110g/4oz* 6

Pork

NOTE: The standard serving size in this section is 90g/3oz. If you wish to consume more or less than this amount (e.g. if you are going to consume a pack of food whose weight differs from the standard serving size) use the conversion tables on page 386 to calculate the new amount of fat in the food.

Bacon, Back, Chilled, (Iceland) *serving 90g/3oz* 30
Bacon, Back, Chilled, Grilled (Iceland) *serving 90g/3oz* 37
Bacon, Back Economy, Chilled (Iceland) *serving 90g/3oz* 17
Bacon, Back, Reduced Salt, Chilled (Iceland) *serving 90g/3oz* 15
Bacon, Back, Rindless, Reduced Salt, Chilled (Iceland) *serving 90g/3oz* 37
Bacon, Back, Rindless, Smoked, Chilled (Iceland) *serving 90g/3oz* 13
Bacon, Back, Rindless, Smoked, Thick Sliced, Chilled (Iceland) *serving 90g/3oz* 13
Bacon, Back, Rindless, Unsmoked, Chilled (Iceland) *serving 90g/3oz* 13
Bacon, Back, Rindless, Unsmoked, Thick Sliced, Chilled (Iceland) *serving 90g/3oz* 13
Bacon, Back, Smoked (Waitrose) *serving 90g/3oz* 14
Bacon, Back, Smoked, Chilled, Special Twin Pack (Iceland) *serving 90g/3oz* 16
Bacon, Back, Sweetcure, Chilled (Iceland) *serving 90g/3oz* 14
Bacon, Back, Unsmoked, Dry (Waitrose) *serving 90g/3oz* 16
Bacon Chops, Low Salt, Main Meal (Marks & Spencer) *serving 90g/3oz* 16
Bacon, Creamy Empanada (Waitrose) *serving 90g/3oz* 22
Bacon, Crunchies, Cheese & Leek (Tesco) *serving 90g/3oz* 16
Bacon, Crunchies, Kiev (Tesco) *serving 90g/3oz* 15
Bacon, Crunchies, Mushroom (Tesco) *serving 90g/3oz* 15

Bacon, Crunchies, Mustard (Tesco) *serving 90g/3oz* 16
Bacon, Cured, Canadian Style, Back, Grilled *serving 90g/3oz* 8
Bacon, Cured, Streaky Breakfast Strips *serving 90g/3oz* 33
Bacon, Grill (Princes) *serving 90g/3oz* 20
Bacon, Grillers (Waitrose) *serving 90g/3oz* 15
Bacon, Holiday, British (Waitrose) *serving 90g/3oz* 14
Bacon, Honey Cured, Back, Main Meal (Marks & Spencer) *serving 90g/3oz* 13
Bacon, Joint, Chilled (Iceland) *serving 90g/3oz* 3
Bacon, Middle, Chilled, Grilled (Iceland) *serving 90g/3oz* 27
Bacon, Middle, Unsmoked, Chilled (Iceland) *serving 90g/3oz* 18
Bacon, Pizza Style Slice (Waitrose) *serving 90g/3oz* 12
Bacon, Rashers, Savoury Snacks (Marks & Spencer) *serving 90g/3oz* 20
Bacon, Rashers, Traditional (Waitrose) *serving 90g/3oz* 14
Bacon, Smoked Danish (Waitrose) *serving 90g/3oz* 37
Bacon, Smoked, Rindless, Streaky, Chilled (Iceland) *serving 90g/3oz* 25
Bacon, Smokey Crispy Cutlets (Somerfield) *serving 90g/3oz* 10
Bacon, Snacks (Waitrose) *serving 90g/3oz* 20
Bacon, Steak, Chilled, Grilled (Iceland) *serving 90g/3oz* 4
Bacon, Steak, Sweetcure, Chilled (Iceland) *serving 90g/3oz* 4
Bacon, Streakies (Somerfield) *serving 90g/3oz* 28
Bacon, Streaky, Chilled, Grilled (Iceland) *serving 90g/3oz* 23
Bacon, Thin & Crispy, Main Meal (Marks & Spencer) *serving 90g/3oz* 18
Bacon, Unsmoked Danish (Waitrose) *serving 90g/3oz* 37
Bcon, Unsmoked Streaky (Waitrose) *serving 90g/3oz* 23
Bacon, Unsmoked Streaky, Chilled (Iceland) *serving 90g/3oz* 25
Bacon, Wafer Thin, Delicatessen (Marks & Spencer) *serving 90g/3oz* 29
Barbecue Pack, British (Waitrose) *serving 90g/3oz* 10
Bhuna Pork Stir Fry (Waitrose) *serving 90g/3oz* 3
Boneless Pork, Farmhouse (Waitrose) *serving 90g/3oz* 14
Brains, Braised *serving 90g/3oz* 9
Canadian, Streaky Bacon, Main Meal (Marks & Spencer) *serving 90g/3oz* 18

Cantonese Pork (Marks & Spencer) *serving 90g/3oz* 4
Casserole Pork, Cubed, Chilled, Healthy Eating (Tesco) *serving 90g/3oz* 2
Chitterlings, Simmered *serving 90g/3oz* 26
Chop, Fresh (Iceland) *serving 90g/3oz* 14
Chop, Lean & Fat, Braised *serving 90g/3oz* 14
Chop, Lean & Fat, Broiled *serving 90g/3oz* 14
Chop, Lean & Fat, Pan Fried *serving 90g/3oz* 15
Chop, Lean & Fat, Roasted *serving 90g/3oz* 14
Chop, Lean Only, Braised *serving 90g/3oz* 8
Chop, Lean Only, Broiled *serving 90g/3oz* 9
Chop, Lean Only, Pan Fried *serving 90g/3oz* 10
Chop, Lean Only, Roasted *serving 90g/3oz* 10
Chop, Pieces, Frozen, Grilled (Iceland) *serving 90g/3oz* 27
Chop, Prime Loin, Frozen, Grilled (Iceland) *serving 90g/3oz* 22
Chop, Rindless (Waitrose) *serving 90g/3oz* 14
Chop, Rind on (Waitrose) *serving 90g/3oz* 14
Chop, Shoulder, Frozen (Iceland) *serving 90g/3oz* 20
Chop, Tandoori Flavour (Waitrose) *serving 90g/3oz* 16
Chop, Tray, Frozen (Iceland) *serving 90g/3oz* 27
Chop, Tray, Frozen, Grilled (Iceland) *serving 90g/3oz* 27
Chop, Value (Waitrose) *serving 90g/3oz* 14
Chop with Herb Butter (Marks & Spencer) *serving 90g/3oz* 18
Chopped Ham & Pork (Somerfield) *serving 90g/3oz* 25
Chopped Pork & Ham, Cold Meats (Tesco) *serving 90g/3oz* 18
Chopped Pork, Premium, Cured (Princes) *serving 90g/3oz* 21
Cooked Roast Pork (Somerfield) *serving 90g/3oz* 6
Cooked & Roasted Pork, Deli (Asda) *serving 90g/3oz* 8
Corndog (Hotdog with Corn Flour Coating) *serving 90g/3oz* 10
Cumberland Pork Chipolatas (Waitrose) *serving 90g/3oz* 20
Cured Pork Steak, Chilled (Iceland) *serving 90g/3oz* 8
Cured Pork Tongues/Jelly (Waitrose) *serving 90g/3oz* 9
Cuts (Composite), Lean Only, Roasted *serving 90g/3oz* 9
Danish, Lean, Light Smoked, Delicatessen (Marks & Spencer) *serving 90g/3oz* 1
Diced Pork (Waitrose) *serving 90g/3oz* 3
Diced Pork, Bhuna Flavour (Waitrose) *serving 90g/3oz* 3

Diced Pork, Farmhouse (Waitrose) *serving 90g/3oz*	5
Diced Pork, Lean Fresh (Iceland) *serving 90g/3oz*	6
Ears, Frozen, Simmered *serving 90g/3oz*	10
Escalopes, Chilled, Healthy Eating (Tesco) *serving 90g/3oz*	1
Escalope, Crumbed, Fresh (Marks & Spencer) *serving 90g/3oz*	9
Escalopes (Waitrose) *serving 90g/3oz*	5
Euroloins (Waitrose) *serving 90g/3oz*	14
Feet, Cured, Pickled *serving 90g/3oz*	15
Feet, Simmered *serving 90g/3oz*	11
Fillet (Waitrose) *serving 90g/3oz*	4
Frenched Cutlets (Waitrose) *serving 90g/3oz*	9
Gammon: *see under* Ham	
Ginger & Onion Pork Stirfry (Waitrose) *serving 90g/3oz*	3
Glazed Pork, Fresh (Marks & Spencer) *serving 90g/3oz*	1
Goujons, Frozen (Iceland) *serving 90g/3oz*	16
Grillsteaks (Somerfield) *serving 90g/3oz*	14
Ground Pork *serving 90g/3oz*	19
Ground Pork, British (Waitrose) *serving 90g/3oz*	9
Ground Pork, Farmhouse (Waitrose) *serving 90g/3oz*	9
Ham: *see under* Ham	
Head Cheese, Cured *serving 90g/3oz*	14
Heart, Braised *serving 90g/3oz*	5
Hotdog *serving 90g/3oz*	13
Hotdog with Chilli *serving 90g/3oz*	11
Joint, Fresh (Marks & Spencer) *serving 90g/3oz*	6
Joint, Mini (Waitrose) *serving 90g/3oz*	6
Kebabs in Barbecue Marinade, Chilled (Tesco) *serving 90g/3oz*	3
Kidneys, Braised *serving 90g/3oz*	4
Kofta al Fresco (Waitrose) *serving 90g/3oz*	10
Leg (Waitrose) *serving 90g/3oz*	14
Leg, Bone in (Waitrose) *serving 90g/3oz*	7
Leg, Boneless Roast (Waitrose) *serving 90g/3oz*	8
Leg, British Roast (Waitrose) *serving 90g/3oz*	14
Leg, Cooked (Somerfield) *serving 90g/3oz*	5
Leg Joint, Bone in (Waitrose) *serving 90g/3oz*	14
Leg, Joint, Fresh (Iceland) *serving 90g/3oz*	15
Leg, Joint, Traditional, Frozen (Iceland) *serving 90g/3oz*	20

Leg, Lean Roast (Waitrose) *serving 90g/3oz*	9
Leg, Premium Roast (Somerfield) *serving 90g/3oz*	4
Leg, Roast (Somerfield) *serving 90g/3oz*	5
Leg, Steak (Waitrose) *serving 90g/3oz*	14
Leg, Steak, Fresh (Iceland) *serving 90g/3oz*	10
Leg, Steak, Healthy Eating, Chilled (Tesco) *serving 90g/3oz*	2
Liver, Braised *serving 90g/3oz*	4
Liver Cheese, Cured *serving 90g/3oz*	23
Loin, Boneless (Waitrose) *serving 90g/3oz*	14
Loin Joint, Cured Pork, Main Meal (Marks & Spencer) *serving 90g/3oz*	8
Loin, Lean & Fat, Braised *serving 90g/3oz*	12
Loin, Lean & Fat, Broiled *serving 90g/3oz*	13
Loin, Lean & Fat, Roasted *serving 90g/3oz*	13
Loin, Lean Only, Braised *serving 90g/3oz*	8
Loin, Lean Only, Broiled *serving 90g/3oz*	9
Loin, Lean Only, Roasted *serving 90g/3oz*	9
Loin, Light Smoked, Cured, Delicatessen (Marks & Spencer) *serving 90g/3oz*	5
Loin Roast (Waitrose) *serving 90g/3oz*	14
Loin Roast, Boneless (Waitrose) *serving 90g/3oz*	14
Loin Roast, Delicatessen (Marks & Spencer) *serving 90g/3oz*	9
Loin, Smoked, Cured (Waitrose) *serving 90g/3oz*	6
Loin Steak (Waitrose) *serving 90g/3oz*	14
Loin Steak, Boneless (Waitrose) *serving 90g/3oz*	14
Loin Steak, Fresh (Iceland) *serving 90g/3oz*	14
Loin, Stuffed (Waitrose) *serving 90g/3oz*	16
Loin Stuffing, Roast, Delicatessen (Marks & Spencer) *serving 90g/3oz*	7
Lunch Tongue (Somerfield) *serving 90g/3oz*	9
Luncheon Meat (Princes) *serving 90g/3oz*	14
Luncheon Meat (Somerfield) *serving 90g/3oz*	27
Luncheon Meat, Deli (Asda) *serving 90g/3oz*	21
Luncheon Meat, Prime Quality (Princes) *serving 90g/3oz*	24
Lungs, Braised *serving 90g/3oz*	3
Marinade, Pork & Herb, Fresh (Marks & Spencer) *serving 90g/3oz*	13

Medallions, Chilled, Healthy Eating (Tesco) *serving 90g/3oz*	2
Pancreas, Braised *serving 90g/3oz*	10
Pork, Sage and Onion Stuffing Balls, Frozen, Oven Baked (Iceland) *serving 90g/3oz*	12
Pork Scratchings *serving 90g/3oz*	41
Pork Spatchcock (Waitrose) *serving 90g/3oz*	9
Pork/Stuffing Balls, (Marks & Spencer) *serving 90g/3oz*	3
Pork & Stuffing Roll (Princes) *serving 90g/3oz*	13
Pork Whirls, Spicy, Mini (Waitrose) *serving 90g/3oz*	19
Pork with Dijonnaise Sauce (Waitrose) *serving 90g/3oz*	22
Rack Roast, Farmhouse (Waitrose) *serving 90g/3oz*	14
Ribs, Back, BBQ Range (Waitrose) *serving 90g/3oz*	8
Ribs, BBQ Steaks, Main Meal (Marks & Spencer) *serving 90g/3oz*	11
Ribs, Lean & Fat, Braised *serving 90g/3oz*	14
Ribs, Lean & Fat, Broiled *serving 90g/3oz*	14
Ribs, Lean & Fat, Pan Fried *serving 90g/3oz*	11
Ribs, Lean & Fat, Roasted *serving 90g/3oz*	14
Ribs, Lean Only, Braised *serving 90g/3oz*	9
Ribs, Lean Only, Broiled *serving 90g/3oz*	9
Ribs, Lean Only, Pan Fried *serving 90g/3oz*	11
Ribs, Lean Only, Roasted *serving 90g/3oz*	9
Ribs, Rack of, Barbecue, Chilled Ready Meal (Tesco) *serving 90g/3oz*	10
Ribs, Spare (Somerfield) *serving 90g/3oz*	11
Ribs, Spare (Waitrose) *serving 90g/3oz*	14
Ribs, Spare, Barbecue, Chilled (Tesco) *serving 90g/3oz*	6
Ribs, Spare, British (Waitrose) *serving 90g/3oz*	10
Ribs, Spare, Chinese (Waitrose) *serving 90g/3oz*	9
Ribs, Spare, Hot & Spicy, Frozen, Grilled (Iceland) *serving 90g/3oz*	6
Roast Pork, on the Bone, Deli (Asda) *serving 90g/3oz*	7
Roast Pork, Cold Meats (Tesco) *serving 90g/3oz*	3
Roast Pork, Seasoned (Waitrose) *serving 90g/3oz*	6
Roast Pork, Sliced (Waitrose) *serving 90g/3oz*	3
Savoury Grills, Rindless Pork, Frozen, Grilled (Iceland) *serving 90g/3oz*	27

Shoulder, BBQ Steaks (Waitrose) *serving 90g/3oz*	7
Shoulder, Boneless (Waitrose) *serving 90g/3oz*	23
Shoulder, Boneless, Frozen, Roasted (Iceland) *serving 90g/3oz*	20
Shoulder, Boneless Joint, Fresh (Iceland) *serving 90g/3oz*	15
Shoulder, Boneless Roast (Waitrose) *serving 90g/3oz*	18
Shoulder, Cooked, Cured (Somerfield) *serving 90g/3oz*	2
Shoulder, Cooked, Deli (Asda) *serving 90g/3oz*	2
Shoulder, Fresh (Iceland) *serving 90g/3oz*	18
Shoulder, Holiday Joint (Waitrose) *serving 90g/3oz*	14
Shoulder, Lean & Fat, Braised *serving 90g/3oz*	21
Shoulder, Lean & Fat, Roasted *serving 90g/3oz*	22
Shoulder, Lean Only, Braised *serving 90g/3oz*	11
Shoulder, Lean Only, Roasted *serving 90g/3oz*	11
Shoulder, Sliced, Cooked, Cured, Chilled (Iceland) *serving 90g/3oz*	1
Shoulder, Stuffed Joint, Fresh (Marks & Spencer) *serving 90g/3oz*	15
Shoulder, Wafer Thin, Smoked, Cured (Somerfield) *serving 90g/3oz*	2
Sliced Pork, Quick Cook (Waitrose) *serving 90g/3oz*	6
Spleen, Braised *serving 90g/3oz*	3
Steaks, Frozen, Grilled (Iceland) *serving 90g/3oz*	20
Steaks, Frozen, Shallow Fat Fry (Iceland) *serving 90g/3oz*	20
Stirfry, Chilled (Tesco) *serving 90g/3oz*	1
Stir Fry Pork, Quick Cook (Waitrose) *serving 90g/3oz*	6
Sweet & Sout Pork (Waitrose) *serving 90g/3oz*	6
Sweet & Sour Pork, Tinned Ready Meal (Tesco) *serving 90g/3oz*	3
Sweet & Sour Pork with Rice, Chilled Ready Meal (Safeway) *serving 90g/3oz*	3
Tail, Simmered *serving 90g/3oz*	32
Tenderloins (Waitrose) *serving 90g/3oz*	5
Tongue (Waitrose) *serving 90g/3oz*	9
Tongue, Braised *serving 90g/3oz*	17
Valentine Steaks (Waitrose) *serving 90g/3oz*	9
Wild Boar Apple Burger (Waitrose) *serving 90g/3oz*	4
Yorkshire Pork Forcemeat (Waitrose) *serving 90g/3oz*	23

Ready Meals

NOTE: The standard serving size in this section is 280g/10oz. If you wish to consume more or less than this amount (e.g. if you are going to consume a pack of food whose weight differs from the standard serving size) use the conversion tables on page 386 to calculate the new amount of fat in the food.

Where there is one major ingredient for a ready meal, you will generally find it listed under its main ingredient (e.g. turkey casserole is listed under the turkey section.) This section includes meals in which there is no single, easily identifiable major ingredient.

Burrito with Beans, Fast Food *serving 280g/10oz* 17
Burrito with Beans & Cheese, Fast Food *serving 280g/10oz* 18
Burrito with Beans, Cheese & Chilli Peppers, Fast Food *serving 280g/10oz* 19
Burrito with Beans & Chilli Peppers, Fast Food *serving 280g/10oz* 20
Chinese Banquet for Two, Frozen, Microwaved (Iceland) *serving 280g/10oz* 6
Chinese Meal for One, Fresh (Asda) *serving 280g/10oz* 4
Chinese Stir Fry, Chilled Ready Meal (Tesco) *serving 280g/10oz* 1
Country Casserole, Fresh (Waitrose) *serving 280g/10oz* 14
Country Supper (Waitrose) *serving 280g/10oz* 18
Enchilada with Cheese, Fast Food *serving 280g/10oz* 32
Frijoles with Cheese, Fast Food *serving 280g/10oz* 13
Garlic & Herb Grills, Meat Free (Birds Eye) *serving 280g/10oz* 37
Honey & Ginger Stir Fry (Waitrose) *serving 280g/10oz* 19
Hot Pot (Somerfield) *serving 280g/10oz* 15
Hot Pot, Lancashire, Chilled Ready Meal (Safeway) *serving 280g/10oz* 21
Indian Meal for One, Fresh (Asda) *serving 280g/10oz* 24
Indian Meal for One, Vegetarian, Fresh (Asda) *serving 280g/10oz* 17
Indian Menu (Marks & Spencer) *serving 280g/10oz* 31
Indian Selection Pack, Chilled Ready Meal (Tesco) *serving 280g/10oz* 20

Indian Vegetable Meal, Low Fat (Marks & Spencer) *serving 280g/10oz*	3
Italian Oven Bake (Waitrose) *serving 280g/10oz*	14
Mature Cheddar Edgers (Birds Eye) *serving 280g/10oz*	18
Mexican Barbecue Ribs, Frozen Ready Meal (Tesco) *serving 280g/10oz*	38
Mexican Cutlets (Goodlife Foods) *serving 280g/10oz*	27
Nachos with Cheese, Fast Food *serving 280g/10oz*	47
Nachos with Cheese & Jalapeno Peppers, Fast Food *serving 280g/10oz*	47
Provolone Pepperoni Ravio (Waitrose) *serving 280g/10oz*	32
Sausage Roll, Vegetarian, Soya (Marks & Spencer) *serving 280g/10oz*	67
Sausages, Meat Free (Birds Eye) *serving 280g/10oz*	37
Shepherd's Pie, Vegetable *serving 280g/10oz*	11
Spring Rolls, Frozen Ready Meal (Tesco) *serving 280g/10oz*	21
Sweet & Sour Platter, Healthy Options (Birds Eye) *serving 280g/10oz*	6
Sweet & Sour Stir Fry (Marks & Spencer) *serving 280g/10oz*	0
Taco, Fast Food *serving 280g/10oz*	34
Tandoori Cutlets (Goodlife Foods) *serving 280g/10oz*	17
Taste of China, Microwave Ready Meal (Safeway) *serving 280g/10oz*	10
Thai Menu (2), International (Marks & Spencer) *serving 280g/10oz*	8
Tortilla, Mediterranean, Slicing (Waitrose) *serving 280g/10oz*	21
Tostada with Beans & Cheese, Fast Food *serving 280g/10oz*	19
Tostada with Guacamole, Fast Food *serving 280g/10oz*	25
Vegetable Cutlets (Safeway) *serving 280g/10oz*	22
Vegetarian Drumstick (Tivall) *serving 280g/10oz*	17
Vegetarian Nuggets (Tivall) *serving 280g/10oz*	50
Vegetarian Schnitzels (Tivall) *serving 280g/10oz*	50
Vegetarian Selection Pack (Waitrose) *serving 280g/10oz*	58
Wildbites (Birds Eye) *serving 280g/10oz*	27
Wonton Wrappers (includes Egg Roll Wrappers), Fast Food *serving 280g/10oz*	4
Yorkshire Pudding with Sausage, Frozen, Oven/Boilable Pouch (Iceland) *serving 280g/10oz*	24

Rice

NOTE: The standard serving size in this section is 170g/6oz. If you wish to consume more or less than this amount (e.g. if you are going to consume a pack of food whose weight differs from the standard serving size) use the conversion tables on page 386 to calculate the new amount of fat in the food.

American Boil-in-the-Bag Quick Rice (Waitrose) *serving 170g/6oz* 6
American Boil-in-the-Bag Wild Rice (Waitrose) *serving 170g/6oz* 5
American Easy Cook Rice (Waitrose) *serving 170g/6oz* 6
American Wild Rice (Waitrose) *serving 170g/6oz* 1
Arborio Risotto Rice (Waitrose) *serving 170g/6oz* 2
Basmati Rice (Marks & Spencer) *serving 170g/6oz* 1
Basmati Rice (Somerfield) *serving 170g/6oz* 3
Basmati Rice (Waitrose) *serving 170g/6oz* 1
Basmati & Wild Rice Pilaff, Chilled Ready Meal (Safeway) *serving 170g/6oz* 27
Brown Rice, American Long Grain (Somerfield) *serving 170g/6oz* 5
Brown Rice, Boil-in-the-Bag (Waitrose) *serving 170g/6oz* 5
Brown Rice, Italian (Waitrose) *serving 170g/6oz* 5
Brown Rice, Long Grain (Waitrose) *serving 170g/6oz* 5
Brown Rice, Long Grain, Cooked *serving 170g/6oz* 2
Brown Rice, Medium Grain, Cooked *serving 170g/6oz* 1
Cocoa Rice (Somerfield) *serving 170g/6oz* 3
Country Rice & Vegetable Mix, Frozen, Boiled (Iceland) *serving 170g/6oz* 1
Crisp Rice (Somerfield) *serving 170g/6oz* 2
Curry Rice, Mild (Safeway) *serving 170g/6oz* 13
Easy Cook Rice (Waitrose) *serving 170g/6oz* 6
Easy Cook Rice, American (Somerfield) *serving 170g/6oz* 2
Easy Cook Rice, Grocery, Boiled in Water (Iceland) *serving 170g/6oz* 2
Easy Cook Rice, Grocery, Boiled/Microwaved (Iceland) *serving 170g/6oz* 2
Egg Fried Rice *serving 170g/6oz* 18
Egg Fried Rice (Asda) *serving 170g/6oz* 7
Egg Fried Rice (Marks & Spencer) *serving 170g/6oz* 9

Egg Fried Rice (Waitrose) *serving 170g/6oz*	9
Egg Fried Rice Curry Pot (Asda) *serving 170g/6oz*	7
Flaked Rice (Waitrose) *serving 170g/6oz*	2
Golden Vegetable Savoury Rice (Somerfield) *serving 170g/6oz*	1
Indian Rice, Tinned, Groceries (Marks & Spencer) *serving 170g/6oz*	2
Indian Rice, International (Marks & Spencer) *serving 170g/6oz*	7
Lemon Rice (Waitrose) *serving 170g/6oz*	16
Long Grain Rice (Waitrose) *serving 170g/6oz*	2
Long Grain Rice, American (Somerfield) *serving 170g/6oz*	2
Long Grain Rice, Basics (Somerfield) *serving 170g/6oz*	2
Long Grain Rice, Tinned, Groceries (Marks & Spencer) *serving 170g/6oz*	2
Long Grain Rice, Frozen, Boiling (Iceland) *serving 170g/6oz*	2
Long Grain Rice, Groceries (Marks & Spencer) *serving 170g/6oz*	1
Long Grain Rice, Grocery, Boiled in Water (Iceland) *serving 170g/6oz*	2
Long Grain Rice, Grocery, Boiled/Microwaved (Iceland) *serving 170g/6oz*	2
Long Grain Rice, Parboiled, Cooked *serving 170g/6oz*	0
Long Grain Rice, Precooked or Instant, *serving 170g/6oz*	0
Long Grain Rice, Regular, Cooked *serving 170g/6oz*	0
Long Grain & Wild Rice, Groceries (Marks & Spencer) *serving 170g/6oz*	1
Mediterranean Savoury Rice (Somerfield) *serving 170g/6oz*	2
Medium Grain Rice, Cooked *serving 170g/6oz*	0
Mexican Rice Chilled (Iceland) *serving 170g/6oz*	5
Paella, Main Meal (Marks & Spencer) *serving 170g/6oz*	1
Paella, Spanish Lean Cuisine Snackpots, (Findus) *serving 170g/6oz*	4
Pilau *serving 170g/6oz*	8
Pilau, Egg & Potato *serving 170g/6oz*	7
Pilau, Lemon (Waitrose) *serving 170g/6oz*	16
Pilau Rice (Safeway) *serving 170g/6oz*	26
Pilau Rice (Somerfield) *serving 170g/6oz*	2
Pilau Rice, Chilled Ready Meal (Safeway) *serving 170g/6oz*	36
Pilau Rice, Curry Pot (Asda) *serving 170g/6oz*	4
Pudding Rice (Waitrose) *serving 170g/6oz*	3

Pudding Rice, Italian (Somerfield) *serving 170g/6oz* 1
Rice & Black Eye Beans (West Indian) *serving 170g/6oz* 6
Rice Bran, Crude *serving 170g/6oz* 35
Rice Cakes, Organic, Salted (Holland & Barrett) *serving 170g/6oz* 6
Rice Cakes, Organic, Unsalted (Holland & Barrett) *serving 170g/6oz* 6
Rice & Pigeon Peas (West Indian) *serving 170g/6oz* 6
Rice Pudding: *see under* Desserts
Rice & Red Kidney Beans (West Indian) *serving 170g/6oz* 6
Rice Rissoles, Fried in Sunflower Oil *serving 170g/6oz* 15
Rice Rissoles, Fried in Vegetable Oil *serving 170g/6oz* 15
Rice & Split Peas (West Indian) *serving 170g/6oz* 7
Rice Surprise (Safeway) *serving 170g/6oz* 5
Rice with Spinach Pilaf *serving 170g/6oz* 4
Rice with Tomato Pilaf *serving 170g/6oz* 6
Rice & Vegetable Mix, Frozen Produce (Marks & Spencer) *serving 170g/6oz* 2
Risotto Milanese, Lean Cuisine Snackpots, (Findus) *serving 170g/6oz* 5
Risotto Rice, Italian, Groceries (Marks & Spencer) *serving 170g/6oz* 1
Risotto, Vegetable *serving 170g/6oz* 11
Saffron Pilau (Waitrose) *serving 170g/6oz* 10
Saffron Rice, International (Marks & Spencer) *serving 170g/6oz* 7
Savoury Rice, Mixed Vegetable (Somerfield) *serving 170g/6oz* 2
Savoury Rice, & Vegetables, Mix, Frozen, Boiled (Iceland) *serving 170g/6oz* 1
Short Grain Rice, Cooked *serving 170g/6oz* 0
Southern Fried Rice & Vegetable Mix, Frozen, Pan Cooked (Iceland) *serving 170g/6oz* 1
Special Fried Rice (Safeway) *serving 170g/6oz* 30
Special Fried Rice (Waitrose) *serving 170g/6oz* 11
Special Fried Rice, Chilled Ready Meal (Safeway) *serving 170g/6oz* 30
Special Fried Rice, Frozen, Boil in Bag (Iceland) *serving 170g/6oz* 4
Special Fried Rice, International (Marks & Spencer) *serving 170g/6oz* 7

Spicy Rice (Waitrose) *serving 170g/6oz*	4
Swet & Sour Savoury Rice (Somerfield) *serving 170g/6oz*	20
Tandoori Rice & Vegetable Mix, Frozen, Boiled (Iceland) *serving 170g/6oz*	1
Thai Coconut Rice (Waitrose) *serving 170g/6oz*	16
Thai Fragrant Rice (Waitrose) *serving 170g/6oz*	1
Thai Rice, Groceries (Marks & Spencer) *serving 170g/6oz*	1
Tikka Rice, Low Fat, Vegetable Meal (Marks & Spencer) *serving 170g/6oz*	2
White Rice, Glutinous, Cooked *serving 170g/6oz*	0
Wild Rice, Cooked *serving 170g/6oz*	1
Yellow Rice, Frozen, Boiled (Iceland) *serving 170g/6oz*	2

SALADS

NOTE: The standard serving size in this section is 110g/4oz. If you wish to consume more or less than this amount (e.g. if you are going to consume a pack of food whose weight differs from the standard serving size) use the conversion tables on page 386 to calculate the new amount of fat in the food.

Apple, Celery & Peanut Salad (Somerfield) *serving 110g/4oz*	19
Apple, Peach & Nut Salad, Chilled (Iceland) *serving 110g/4oz*	21
Asparagus & Salmon Salad (Waitrose) *serving 110g/4oz*	8
Baby Leaf Salad (Somerfield) *serving 110g/4oz*	1
Baby Leaves & Watercress Salad (Marks & Spencer) *serving 110g/4oz*	0
Bean Salad *serving 110g/4oz*	10
Bean Salad (Marks & Spencer) *serving 110g/4oz*	9
Bean Salad, Spicy (Asda) *serving 110g/4oz*	5
Bean, Three, Salad (Somerfield) *serving 110g/4oz*	10
Bean & Tuna Salad (Safeway) *serving 110g/4oz*	15
Beetroot Salad *serving 110g/4oz*	7
Beetroot Salad (Marks & Spencer) *serving 110g/4oz*	0
Beetroot Salad (Safeway) *serving 110g/4oz*	0
Bismark Salad (Waitrose) *serving 110g/4oz*	53

Brown Rice Salad with Vegetables & Raisins, Chilled (Tesco) *serving 110g/4oz* 8
Brunch Snack Salad (Safeway) *serving 110g/4oz* 11
Californian Style Salad (Marks & Spencer) *serving 110g/4oz* 0
Caribbean Salad (Waitrose) *serving 110g/4oz* 0
Carrot & Nut Salad (Safeway) *serving 110g/4oz* 14
Carrot & Nut Salad, Chilled (Tesco) *serving 110g/4oz* 13
Carrot & Nut Salad with French Dressing, Retail *serving 110g/4oz* 19
Carrot & Nut Salad with Mayonnaise *serving 110g/4oz* 27
Carrot with Parsnip & Apple, Spicy, Fresh (Safeway) *serving 110g/4oz* 5
Celery, Nut & Sultana Salad (Asda) *serving 110g/4oz* 12
Celery, Nut & Sultana Salad (Safeway) *serving 110g/4oz* 15
Celery, Nut & Sultana Salad (Somerfield) *serving 110g/4oz* 18
Celery, Nut & Sultana Salad, Chilled (Tesco) *serving 110g/4oz* 24
Celery, Nut & Sultana Salad, Chilled, Healthy Eating (Tesco) *serving 110g/4oz* 8
Cheese Salad, Mini (Marks & Spencer) *serving 110g/4oz* 21
Cheese Layer Salad (Marks & Spencer) *serving 110g/4oz* 19
Cheese & Pineapple Salad (Safeway) *serving 110g/4oz* 18
Cherry Tomato Salad (Marks & Spencer) *serving 110g/4oz* 0
Cherry Tomato & Mozzarella Salad (Waitrose) *serving 110g/4oz* 10
Cherry Tomato Pasta Salad (Marks & Spencer) *serving 110g/4oz* 9
Chicken, Blackened, Salad, Snack Pack (Safeway) *serving 110g/4oz* 36
Chicken, Chargrill, Layer Salad (Marks & Spencer) *serving 110g/4oz* 4
Chicken, Chargrill, Meal Salad (Marks & Spencer) *serving 110g/4oz* 10
Chicken, Coronation, Salad (Asda) *serving 110g/4oz* 28
Chicken, Florida, Snack Salad, Chilled, Healthy Eating (Tesco) *serving 110g/4oz* 4
Chicken Tikka & Couscous Salad (Marks & Spencer) *serving 110g/4oz* 9
Chinese Salad, Mini (Marks & Spencer) *serving 110g/4oz* 1
Coleslaw (Asda) *serving 110g/4oz* 13

Coleslaw (Safeway) *serving 110g/4oz* 14
Coleslaw (Waitrose) *serving 110g/4oz* 14
Coleslaw (Somerfield) *serving 110g/4oz* 13
Coleslaw, Chilled (Iceland) *serving 110g/4oz* 13
Coleslaw, Chilled (Tesco) *serving 110g/4oz* 14
Coleslaw, Chunky (Safeway) *serving 110g/4oz* 14
Coleslaw, Classic Salad (Marks & Spencer) *serving 110g/4oz* 17
Coleslaw, Cottage (Waitrose) *serving 110g/4oz* 28
Coleslaw, Extra Creamy (Asda) *serving 110g/4oz* 16
Coleslaw, Healthy Eating, Chilled (Tesco) *serving 110g/4oz* 4
Coleslaw, Lite (Waitrose) *serving 110g/4oz* 5
Coleslaw, Premium (Somerfield) *serving 110g/4oz* 22
Coleslaw, Premium, Chilled (Tesco) *serving 110g/4oz* 23
Coleslaw, Light (Asda) *serving 110g/4oz* 4
Coleslaw, Reduced Calorie (Safeway) *serving 110g/4oz* 9
Coleslaw, Reduced Calorie, Chilled (Iceland) *serving 110g/4oz* 6
Coleslaw, Reduced Calorie, Healthy Selection (Somerfield) *serving 110g/4oz* 6
Coleslaw Salad (Heinz) *serving 110g/4oz* 11
Coleslaw, Salad, Large (Marks & Spencer) *serving 110g/4oz* 16
Coleslaw, Savers (Safeway) *serving 110g/4oz* 11
Coleslaw, Selection Salad, Chilled (Tesco) *serving 110g/4oz* 14
Coleslaw, Cheese (Somerfield) *serving 110g/4oz* 16
Coleslaw with Cheese (Waitrose) *serving 110g/4oz* 19
Coleslaw, Cheese Salad (Marks & Spencer) *serving 110g/4oz* 31
Coleslaw, Cranberry & Orange (Safeway) *serving 110g/4oz* 12
Coleslaw, Curry (Waitrose) *serving 110g/4oz*
Coleslaw, Fruity, Lightly Dressed (Safeway) *serving 110g/4oz* 5
Coleslaw, Fruity, Reduced Calorie (Safeway) *serving 110g/4oz* 9
Coleslaw, Garlic & Herb (Safeway) *serving 110g/4oz* 18
Coleslaw, Garlic & Parsley (Waitrose) *serving 110g/4oz* 13
Coleslaw, Potato Salad & Florida Salad, Salad Selection Pack (Somerfield) *serving 110g/4oz* 13
Coleslaw, Prawn (Somerfield) *serving 110g/4oz* 13
Coleslaw with Prawns (Safeway) *serving 110g/4oz* 16
Coleslaw with Prawns (Waitrose) *serving 110g/4oz* 15
Coleslaw, Prawn, Chilled (Tesco) *serving 110g/4oz* 13

Coleslaw, Prawn, Reduced Calorie, Healthy Selection (Somerfield) *serving 110g/4oz* 3
Coleslaw,Tuna (Asda) *serving 110g/4oz* 16
Continental Salad (Somerfield) *serving 110g/4oz* 0
Coronation Salad, Mini (Marks & Spencer) *serving 110g/4oz* 3
Couscous Salad (Waitrose) *serving 110g/4oz* 6
Couscous & Chargrill Vegetable Salad (Marks & Spencer) *serving 110g/4oz* 3
Couscous & Vegetable Salad (Marks & Spencer) *serving 110g/4oz* 6
Crispy Salad (Somerfield) *serving 110g/4oz* 0
Crispy Salad Mix (Marks & Spencer) *serving 110g/4oz* 1
Croutons Salad, Fresh (Marks & Spencer) *serving 110g/4oz* 60
Crudité with Dip (Marks & Spencer) *serving 110g/4oz* 7
Endive & Radicchio (Somerfield) *serving 110g/4oz* 0
Endive & Radicchio Salad (Waitrose) *serving 110g/4oz* 0
Florida Salad (White Cabbage, Celery & Fruit), *serving 110g/4oz* 23
Florida Salad (Marks & Spencer) *serving 110g/4oz* 21
Florida Salad (Somerfield) *serving 110g/4oz* 13
Florida Salad (Waitrose) *serving 110g/4oz* 8
Garden Salad (Somerfield) *serving 110g/4oz* 0
Greek Salad (Feta Cheese, Olives & Olive Oil) *serving 110g/4oz* 14
Greek Rice Salad (Waitrose) *serving 110g/4oz* 11
Greek Snack Salad (Somerfield) *serving 110g/4oz* 10
Green Salad (Lettuce, Cucumber, Pepper & Celery) *serving 110g/4oz* 0
Green Salad (Marks & Spencer) *serving 110g/4oz* 0
Green Salad, Large (Marks & Spencer) *serving 110g/4oz* 0
Ham Salad Stottie (Somerfield) *serving 110g/4oz* 13
Herring, Chopped, Salad (Waitrose) *serving 110g/4oz* 11
Iceberg Salad & Dressing (Waitrose) *serving 110g/4oz* 11
Italian Salad (Marks & Spencer) *serving 110g/4oz* 1
Italian Style Salad, Chilled (Tesco) *serving 110g/4oz* 0
Layered Salad with Cheese (Waitrose) *serving 110g/4oz* 32
Leaf Salad with Herbs (Waitrose) *serving 110g/4oz* 0
Lettuce, Crispheart, Salad (Marks & Spencer) *serving 110g/4oz* 0
Mediterranean Style Salad with Feta Cheese (Safeway) *serving 110g/4oz* 8

Mixed Bean Salad (Holland & Barrett) *serving 110g/4oz* 1
Mixed Bean Salad (Waitrose) *serving 110g/4oz* 4
Mixed Bean Salad (Safeway) *serving 110g/4oz* 4
Mixed Salad (Marks & Spencer) *serving 110g/4oz* 0
Mixed Salad (Somerfield) *serving 110g/4oz* 0
Mixed Salad with Peppers & Iceberg Lettuce (Somerfield) *serving 110g/4oz* 0
Mixed Salad with Radish & Little Gem Lettuce (Somerfield) *serving 110g/4oz* 0
Mushroom & Pepper Salad, Lightly Dressed (Safeway) *serving 110g/4oz* 1
New Potato Salad, Large (Marks & Spencer) *serving 110g/4oz* 18
New Potato & Egg Salad (Marks & Spencer) *serving 110g/4oz* 2
New Potato & Salmon Salad (Waitrose) *serving 110g/4oz* 6
New Potato & Sweetcorn Salad (Marks & Spencer) *serving 110g/4oz* 1
New Potato & Tomato Salad (Marks & Spencer) *serving 110g/4oz* 0
Olives & Feta Cubes (Waitrose) *serving 110g/4oz* 21
Oriental Salad (Marks & Spencer) *serving 110g/4oz* 0
Pasta Salad, Italian (Asda) *serving 110g/4oz* 7
Pasta Salad, Italian (Safeway) *serving 110g/4oz* 7
Pasta Salad, Italian Style (Safeway) *serving 110g/4oz* 7
Pasta Salad, Healthy Eating, Chilled (Tesco) *serving 110g/4oz* 6
Pasta Snack Salad, Mediterranean (Somerfield) *serving 110g/4oz* 6
Pasta Salad with 1000 Island Dressing (Marks & Spencer) *serving 110g/4oz* 13
Pasta & Blue Cheese Salad *serving 110g/4oz* 23
Pasta & Chilli Bean Salad (Safeway) *serving 110g/4oz* 4
Pasta Salad with Creamy Garlic Dressing, Chilled (Tesco) *serving 110g/4oz* 18
Pasta Salad & Garlic Mayonnaise, Chilled (Iceland) *serving 110g/4oz* 26
Pasta & Ham Salad (Safeway) *serving 110g/4oz* 17
Pasta & Ham Salad (Somerfield) *serving 110g/4oz* 15
Pasta & Prawn Meal Salad (Marks & Spencer) *serving 110g/4oz* 13
Pasta Salad, Mushroom (Marks & Spencer) *serving 110g/4oz* 7
Pasta Salad, Pesto (Safeway) *serving 110g/4oz* 8

Pasta Salad, Pesto (Somerfield) *serving 110g/4oz* 21
Pasta & Tomato Salad (Somerfield) *serving 110g/4oz* 7
Pasta & Vegetable Salad (Waitrose) *serving 110g/4oz* 11
Pasta & Vegetable Salad, Italian (Safeway) *serving 110g/4oz* 16
Pasta & Vegetable Salad, Mediterranean (Somerfield) *serving 110g/4oz* 6
Ploughmans Style Salad (Safeway) *serving 110g/4oz* 20
Potato Salad *serving 110g/4oz* 7
Potato Salad (Asda) *serving 110g/4oz* 10
Potato Salad (Heinz) *serving 110g/4oz* 9
Potato Salad (Safeway) *serving 110g/4oz* 18
Potato Salad, Chilled (Tesco) *serving 110g/4oz* 21
Potato Salad, Chileld, Low Calorie, Healthy Eating (Tesco) *serving 110g/4oz* 4
Potato Salad, Reduced Calorie (Asda) *serving 110g/4oz* 4
Potato Salad, Reduced Calorie (Safeway) *serving 110g/4oz* 4
Potato Salad, Reduced Calorie, Healthy Selection (Somerfield) *serving 110g/4oz* 3
Potato Salad Selection, Chilled, Healthy Eating (Tesco) *serving 110g/4oz* 7
Potato & Bacon Salad (Waitrose) *serving 110g/4oz* 18
Potato & Chive Salad (Asda) *serving 110g/4oz* 12
Potato & Onion Salad (Waitrose) *serving 110g/4oz* 13
Potato Salad & Chives, Chilled (Iceland) *serving 110g/4oz* 14
Potato Salad with French Dressing *serving 110g/4oz* 12
Potato Salad with Mayonnaise *serving 110g/4oz* 23
Potato Salad with Onion & Chives (Waitrose) *serving 110g/4oz* 13
Potato Salad with Reduced Calorie Dressing, Retail *serving 110g/4oz* 5
Potato, Scallop, & Poached Salmon Salad (Safeway) *serving 110g/4oz* 17
Potato Salad & Stuffing (Safeway) *serving 110g/4oz* 16
Prawn, Apple & Celery Salad (Somerfield) *serving 110g/4oz* 9
Prawn Cocktail Salad Meal, Chilled, Healthy Eating (Tesco) *serving 110g/4oz* 4
Prawn Layer Salad (Marks & Spencer) *serving 110g/4oz* 10
Red Cabbage Salad (Safeway) *serving 110g/4oz* 29

Ribbon Salad (Marks & Spencer) *serving 110g/4oz* 0
Rice Salad (Rice, Vegetables, Nuts & Raisins) *serving 110g/4oz* 8
Rice Salad, Brown (Rice, Vegetables, Nuts & Raisins) *serving 110g/4oz* 8
Rice Salad, Greek (Waitrose) *serving 110g/4oz* 11
Rice Salad, Italian (Marks & Spencer) *serving 110g/4oz* 9
Rice Salad, Spicy (Somerfield) *serving 110g/4oz* 10
Salad Bowl (Somerfield) *serving 110g/4oz* 0
Salad Bowl, Large (Marks & Spencer) *serving 110g/4oz* 0
Salad & Coleslaw, Fresh (Marks & Spencer) *serving 110g/4oz* 9
Salad de Calamars (Waitrose) *serving 110g/4oz* 20
Salad, Fresh (Marks & Spencer) *serving 110g/4oz* 0
Salad Selection, Chilled (Iceland) *serving 110g/4oz* 24
Salmon (Warm) & Potato Salad, Main Meal (Marks & Spencer) *serving 110g/4oz* 5
Spinach Pasta Salad (Marks & Spencer) *serving 110g/4oz* 17
Spinach & Watercress Salad (Marks & Spencer) *serving 110g/4oz* 1
Sweet & Sour Noodle Bowl (Asda) *serving 110g/4oz* 4
Sweetcorn Salad (Marks & Spencer) *serving 110g/4oz* 4
Tabbouleh *serving 110g/4oz* 5
Tabbouleh (Safeway) *serving 110g/4oz* 4
Taco Salad, Fast Food *serving 110g/4oz* 8
Taco Salad with Chilli Con Carne *serving 110g/4oz* 6
Tomato & Bacon Pasta Salad (Marks & Spencer) *serving 110g/4oz* 18
Tomato, Cheese & Pasta Snack Salad (Safeway) *serving 110g/4oz* 40
Tomato & Onion Salad *serving 110g/4oz* 7
Tomato Onion Salad (Marks & Spencer) *serving 110g/4oz* 9
Tortellini & Cheese Salad (Safeway) *serving 110g/4oz* 30
Tuna Curried Rice Salad (Princes) *serving 110g/4oz* 14
Tuna Hawaian Rice Salad (Princes) *serving 110g/4oz* 11
Tuna Hot & Spicy Chilli Salad (Princes) *serving 110g/4oz* 9
Tuna, Italian, Pasta Salad Lunch Break (Princes) *serving 110g/4oz* 6
Tuna Mexican Salad Lunch Break (Princes) *serving 110g/4oz* 10
Tuna Nicoise Snack Salad (Safeway) *serving 110g/4oz* 26
Tuna Salad Continental RI (Waitrose) *serving 110g/4oz* 21
Tuna Salad Meal (Marks & Spencer) *serving 110g/4oz* 13

Tuna & Vegetable Mayonase Salad Lunch Break (Princes) *serving 110g/4oz* 25
USA Spring Mix Salad (Marks & Spencer) *serving 110g/4oz* 0
Vegetable Salad (Heinz) *serving 110g/4oz* 9
Vegetable Salad (Safeway) *serving 110g/4oz* 23
Vegetable Salad, Crispy (Safeway) *serving 110g/4oz* 11
Vegetable Salad, Roasted (Waitrose) *serving 110g/4oz* 16
Vegetable Salad, without Dressing *serving 110g/4oz* 0
Vegetable Salad, with Cheese & Egg without Dressing *serving 110g/4oz* 3
Vegetable Salad, with Pasta & Seafood without Dressing, *serving 110g/4oz* 6
Vegetable & Prawn Salad (Safeway) *serving 110g/4oz* 9
Vegetable Salad, with Shrimp Without Dressing, *serving 110g/4oz* 1
Vegetable Salad, Tinned *serving 110g/4oz* 11
Vegetable Salad, with Turkey, Ham & Cheese without Dressing *serving 110g/4oz* 5
Waldorf Salad *serving 110g/4oz* 19
Waldorf Salad (Safeway) *serving 110g/4oz* 34
Waldorf Salad (Waitrose) *serving 110g/4oz* 41
Watercress Salad (Marks & Spencer) *serving 110g/4oz* 1

Sandwiches

NOTE: The standard serving size in this section is 170g/6oz. If you wish to consume more or less than this amount (e.g. if you are going to consume a pack of food whose weight differs from the standard serving size) use the conversion tables on page 386 to calculate the new amount of fat in the food.

Bacon & Avocado (Marks & Spencer) *serving 170g/6oz* 28
Bacon & Cheese Roll (Marks & Spencer) *serving 170g/6oz* 38
Bacon, Lettuce & Tomato (Marks & Spencer) *serving 170g/6oz* 33
Bacon, Lettuce & Tomato (Tesco) *serving 170g/6oz* 31
Bacon, Lettuce & Tomato, Reduced Fat (Marks & Spencer) *serving 170g/6oz* 21

Bacon, Lettuce & Tomato, Reduced Fat (Sainsbury's) *serving 170g/6oz* 17
Bacon, Lettuce & Tomato, White Bread (Asda) *serving 170g/6oz* 20
Bacon, Lettuce & Tomato with Mayonnaise (Somerfield) *serving 170g/6oz* 23
Bacon, Lettuce, Tomato, Prawn & Ham (Marks & Spencer) *serving 170g/6oz* 28
Bacon, Lettuce, Tomato, Prawn & Ham, Reduced Fat (Marks & Spencer) *serving 170g/6oz* 16
Baked Garlic & Herb Roll, Deli (Asda) *serving 170g/6oz* 9
BBQ Chicken (Somerfield) *serving 170g/6oz* 25
Beef Roll, Healthy Selection (Marks & Spencer) *serving 170g/6oz* 20
Beef & Onion Roll, Large (Marks & Spencer) *serving 170g/6oz* 26
Beef, Roast *serving 170g/6oz* 17
Beef, Roast, Medium Rare (Marks & Spencer) *serving 170g/6oz* 17
Beef, Roast, with Cheese *serving 170g/6oz* 17
Beef, Roast, Salad (Tesco) *serving 170g/6oz* 17
Beef & Ham Roll, Wafer Thin, Deli (Asda) *serving 170g/6oz* 23
Brie & Tomato (Waitrose) *serving 170g/6oz* 30
Cheddar Cheese & Branston Pickle (Tesco) *serving 170g/6oz* 25
Cheddar Cheese & Celery with Full Fat Soft Cheese & Mayonnaise (Somerfield) *serving 170g/6oz* 33
Cheese & Apple (Marks & Spencer) *serving 170g/6oz* 39
Cheese with Bacon Bap (Waitrose) *serving 170g/6oz* 24
Cheese & Celery (Marks & Spencer) *serving 170g/6oz* 29
Cheese & Celery (Mature Cheddar & Celery with Mayo & Full Fat Soft Cheese) (Asda) *serving 170g/6oz* 36
Cheese & Chicken Tikka Pitta (Marks & Spencer) *serving 170g/6oz* 15
Cheese & Coleslaw (Marks & Spencer) *serving 170g/6oz* 27
Cheese & Coleslaw (Waitrose) *serving 170g/6oz* 21
Cheese & Onion (Waitrose) *serving 170g/6oz* 36
Cheese & Onion, White Bread (Marks & Spencer) *serving 170g/6oz* 41
Cheese & Pickle (Waitrose) *serving 170g/6oz* 24
Cheese & Pickle Bap (Waitrose) *serving 170g/6oz* 23
Cheese Ploughman's (Marks & Spencer) *serving 170g/6oz* 23

Cheese Ploughman's, Reduced Fat (Sainsbury's) *serving 170g/6oz* 8
Cheese Ploughman's (Waitrose) *serving 170g/6oz* 21
Cheese & Salad Roll (Waitrose) *serving 170g/6oz* 25
Cheese & Salad Stottie (Waitrose) *serving 170g/6oz* 21
Cheese & Spring Onion (Red Leicester & Mature Cheddar With Mayo/Spring Onion) (Asda) *serving 170g/6oz* 44
Cheese & Tomato (Asda) *serving 170g/6oz* 19
Cheese & Tomato, Thick Cut (Somerfield) *serving 170g/6oz* 24
Cheese & Tomato, White Bread (Marks & Spencer) *serving 170g/6oz* 33
Cheese Topped Ham Bap (Waitrose) *serving 170g/6oz* 22
Cheese (Triple), Ham, Tomato & Celery (Waitrose) *serving 170g/6oz* 27
Chicken & Back Bacon (Marks & Spencer) *serving 170g/6oz* 28
Chicken & Bacon Club (Somerfield) *serving 170g/6oz* 21
Chicken & Bacon Roll, Large (Marks & Spencer) *serving 170g/6oz* 32
Chicken & Bacon, Light (Roast with Tomato & Yoghurt) (Asda) *serving 170g/6oz* 11
Chicken, Chargrill (Waitrose) *serving 170g/6oz* 17
Chicken, Chargrilled Roll, (Marks & Spencer) *serving 170g/6oz* 26
Chicken, Chargrill, & Lemon (Marks & Spencer) *serving170g/6oz* 3
Chicken, Chargrill, Pitta (Marks & Spencer) *serving 170g/6oz* 9
Chicken & Coleslaw (Marks & Spencer) *serving 170g/6oz* 20
Chicken Fillet *serving 170g/6oz* 28
Chicken Fillet with Cheese *serving 170g/6oz* 29
Chicken, Ham & Lettuce (Waitrose) *serving 170g/6oz* 19
Chicken, Hickory (Marks & Spencer) *serving 170g/6oz* 17
Chicken & Lemon, Low Calorie (Marks & Spencer) *serving 170g/6oz* 8
Chicken, No Mayo (Marks & Spencer) *serving 170g/6oz* 9
Chicken, Poached, & Grape (Marks & Spencer) *serving 170g/6oz* 14
Chicken, Reduced Fat (Waitrose) *serving 170g/6oz* 11
Chicken, Roast, Wholemeal Bread (Asda) *serving 170g/6oz* 19
Chicken, Roast, Salad Bap (Somerfield) *serving 170g/6oz* 23
Chicken & Salad Roll (Waitrose) *serving 170g/6oz* 18
Chicken & Salad (Marks & Spencer) *serving 170g/6oz* 20

Chicken Salad (Tesco) *serving 170g/6oz*	21
Chicken Salad (Waitrose) *serving 170g/6oz*	20
Chicken Salad, Deep Fill (Somerfield) *serving 170g/6oz*	18
Chicken Salad, Reduced Fat (Marks & Spencer) *serving 170g/6oz*	10
Chicken Salad with Lettuce, Tomato, Cucumber & Mayonnaise (Somerfield) *serving 170g/6oz*	18
Chicken Sandwich, Hot (Marks & Spencer) *serving 170g/6oz*	25
Chicken Selection (Somerfield) *serving 170g/6oz*	23
Chicken & Smoked Ham (Tesco) *serving 170g/6oz*	25
Chicken & Stuffing (Marks & Spencer) *serving 170g/6oz*	15
Chicken & Stuffing, Thick Cut (Somerfield) *serving 170g/6oz*	23
Chicken & Stuffing Roll, Healthy Selection (Marks & Spencer) *serving 170g/6oz*	22
Chicken & Sweetcorn (Marks & Spencer) *serving 170g/6oz*	20
Chicken Tikka (Marks & Spencer) *serving 170g/6oz*	23
Chicken Tikka (Tesco) *serving 170g/6oz*	12
Chicken Tikka with Tomatoes & Lettuce, Wholemeal Bread (Asda) *serving 170g/6oz*	14
Chinese Chicken (Waitrose) *serving 170g/6oz*	30
Chinese Chicken, Wholemeal Bread (Asda) *serving 170g/6oz*	13
Coronation Chicken (Asda) *serving 170g/6oz*	32
Cottage Cheese & Fruit (Waitrose) *serving 170g/6oz*	8
Crab (Marks & Spencer) *serving 170g/6oz*	17
Crème Frais, Salmon & Prawn (Waitrose) *serving 170g/6oz*	11
Double Gloucester & Tomato (Waitrose) *serving 170g/6oz*	31
Egg & Bacon (Marks & Spencer) *serving 170g/6oz*	23
Egg & Bacon (Somerfield) *serving 170g/6oz*	24
Egg & Bacon (Tesco) *serving 170g/6oz*	25
Egg & Bacon, Thick Cut (Somerfield) *serving 170g/6oz*	25
Egg & Bacon Pieces, Extra Thick (Somerfield) *serving 170g/6oz*	25
Egg, Bacon & Cheese, French Bread (Marks & Spencer) *serving 170g/6oz*	30
Egg, Bacon, Chicken & Smoked Ham (Marks & Spencer) *serving 170g/6oz*	18
Egg & Cheese *serving 170g/6oz*	23
Egg & Cress (Marks & Spencer) *serving 170g/6oz*	15
Egg & Cress, Reduced Fat (Marks & Spencer) *serving 170g/6oz*	10

Egg & Cress, Tuna & Sweetcorn, Cheese Coleslaw, Selection Pack (Somerfield) *serving 170g/6oz* 25
Egg Florentine (Waitrose) *serving 170g/6oz* 15
Egg & Mayonnaise Finger Roll (Somerfield) *serving 170g/6oz* 21
Egg Mayo, Reduced Fat (Waitrose) *serving 170g/6oz* 17
Egg Mayonnaise with Bacon (Asda) *serving 170g/6oz* 68
Egg Mayonnaise & Bacon (Waitrose) *serving 170g/6oz* 28
Egg Mayonnaise & Cress (Somerfield) *serving 170g/6oz* 26
Egg Mayonnaise & Cress (Waitrose) *serving 170g/6oz* 24
Egg Mayonnaise & Cress, Wholemeal (Asda) *serving 170g/6oz* 18
Egg Mayonnaise & Cress, Wholemeal (Tesco) *serving 170g/6oz* 17
Egg Salad, Extra Thick (Somerfield) *serving 170g/6oz* 19
Egg Salad, Free Range (Waitrose) *serving 170g/6oz* 29
Egg Salad, Light (Asda) *serving 170g/6oz* 11
Egg Salad, Light, White Bread (Asda) *serving 170g/6oz* 11
Egg & Salad, Low Calorie (Marks & Spencer) *serving 170g/6oz* 8
Egg Salad & Salad Cream, Thick Cut (Somerfield) *serving 170g/6oz* 17
Egg & Tomato, Thick Cut (Somerfield) *serving 170g/6oz* 19
Fish with Tartar Sauce *serving 170g/6oz* 24
Fish with Tartar Sauce & Cheese *serving 170g/6oz* 27
Ham, White Bread (Asda) *serving 170g/6oz* 7
Ham, Bel Paese & Pineapple (Waitrose) *serving 170g/6oz* 12
Ham & Cheese (Waitrose) *serving 170g/6oz* 21
Ham & Cheese Roll, Large (Marks & Spencer) *serving 170g/6oz* 28
Ham, Cheese & Pickle (Marks & Spencer) *serving 170g/6oz* 27
Ham, Cheese & Pickle (Somerfield) *serving 170g/6oz* 20
Ham, Cheese & Pickle, Reduced Fat (Marks & Spencer) *serving 170g/6oz* 13
Ham, Cheese & Pickle, White Bread (Asda) *serving 170g/6oz* 28
Ham & Coleslaw (Somerfield) *serving 170g/6oz* 24
Ham, Danish, & Salad, Low Calorie (Marks & Spencer) *serving 170g/6oz* 6
Ham & Egg Roll, (Marks & Spencer) *serving 170g/6oz* 24
Ham, Roast, & Turkey, Wholemeal Bread (Asda) *serving 170g/6oz* 14
Ham & Salad Bap, (Waitrose) *serving 170g/6oz* 16

Ham Salad Roll, Healthy Selection (Marks & Spencer) *serving 170g/6oz* 17
Ham & Salad Stottie (Waitrose) *serving 170g/6oz* 9
Ham Salad, White Bread (Waitrose) *serving 170g/6oz* 6
Ham Salad with Mayonnaise, Light, White Bread (Asda) *serving 170g/6oz* 6
Ham, Smoked, & Cheddar Cheese with Mayonnaise (Somerfield) *serving 170g/6oz* 29
Ham, Smoked & Egg (Waitrose) *serving 170g/6oz* 12
Ham, Smoked, Mature Cheddar Cheese & Mayo (Tesco) *serving 170g/6oz* 31
Ham & Tomato (Waitrose) *serving 170g/6oz* 16
Ham & Tomato, Thick Cut (Somerfield) *serving 170g/6oz* 9
Ham & Wholegrain Mustard, Extra Thick (Somerfield) *serving 170g/6oz* 21
Houmous, Carrot & Spinach (Waitrose) *serving 170g/6oz* 13
Mediterranean Salad (Waitrose) *serving 170g/6oz* 8
Pastrami in Provencale Bread (Waitrose) *serving 170g/6oz* 14
Pastrami Turnover Roll (Waitrose) *serving 170g/6oz* 16
Pepper, Cheese & Tomato Roll (Waitrose) *serving 170g/6oz* 20
Ploughman's Roll (Marks & Spencer) *serving 170g/6oz* 32
Ploughman's (Cheddar Cheese, Tomatoes, Onion, Mayo & Pickle) (Asda) *serving 170g/6oz* 25
Ploughman's, Cheese & Salad Roll (Somerfield) *serving 170g/6oz* 26
Ploughman's, Chunky (Marks & Spencer) *serving 170g/6oz* 32
Ploughman's, Thick Cut, Thick Malted Wholegrain Bread (Asda) *serving 170g/6oz* 23
Ploughman's Traditional Cheese (Marks & Spencer) *serving 170g/6oz* 27
Pork Ham & Cheese *serving 170g/6oz* 18
Pork Ham, Egg & Cheese *serving 170g/6oz* 19
Prawn & Avocado (Marks & Spencer) *serving 170g/6oz* 20
Prawn, Cheese & Ham (Tesco) *serving 170g/6oz* 30
Prawn, Chicken & Cheese (Marks & Spencer) *serving 170g/6oz* 27
Prawn Cocktail (Tesco) *serving 170g/6oz* 10
Prawn Cocktail, French Bread (Marks & Spencer) *serving 170g/6oz* 17

Prawn Cocktail, Low Calorie (Marks & Spencer) *serving 170g/6oz*	9
Prawns & Crème Fraiche, Low Calorie (Marks & Spencer) *serving 170g/6oz*	7
Prawn & Egg Roll (Marks & Spencer) *serving 170g/6oz*	29
Prawn & Egg (Somerfield) *serving 170g/6oz*	26
Prawn, Ham & Chicken, Low Cal (Marks & Spencer) *serving 170g/6oz*	8
Prawn & Lemon Mayo (Waitrose) *serving 170g/6oz*	23
Prawn Marie Rose (Waitrose) *serving 170g/6oz*	28
Prawn Mayonnaise (Somerfield) *serving 170g/6oz*	37
Prawn & Mayonnaise (Waitrose) *serving 170g/6oz*	39
Prawn Mayo, Reduced Fat (Waitrose) *serving 170g/6oz*	17
Prawn Mayonnaise, Oatmeal Bread (Tesco) *serving 170g/6oz*	38
Prawn & Mayonnaise, Triple (Waitrose) *serving 170g/6oz*	28
Prawn Mayonnaise, Triple, Oatmeal Bread (Asda) *serving 170g/6oz*	26
Prawn & Mayonnaise, Ham & Cheese Coleslaw, Chicken & Smoked Ham, Selection Pack (Somerfield) *serving 170g/6oz*	28
Prawn & Salad Roll (Waitrose) *serving 170g/6oz*	16
Salmon & Cucumber (Marks & Spencer) *serving 170g/6oz*	19
Salmon & Cucumber, Healthy Eating (Tesco) *serving 170g/6oz*	6
Salmon & Lemon/Pepper Fromage (Waitrose) *serving 170g/6oz*	16
Salmon, Poached (Marks & Spencer) *serving 170g/6oz*	20
Salmon, Poached, & Egg (Marks & Spencer) *serving 170g/6oz*	23
Salmon, Smoked, Bagel (Marks & Spencer) *serving 170g/6oz*	23
Salmon, Smoked, Luxury (Marks & Spencer) *serving 170g/6oz*	20
Salmon, Smoked, & Cream Cheese (Marks & Spencer) *serving 170g/6oz*	28
Sausage, Thick Cut (Somerfield) *serving 170g/6oz*	20
Sausage, Egg & Bacon (Waitrose) *serving 170g/6oz*	21
Steak *serving 170g/6oz*	12
Submarine with Coldcuts *serving 170g/6oz*	14
Submarine with Roast Beef *serving 170g/6oz*	10
Submarine, Tuna Salad *serving 170g/6oz*	19
Tomato, Courgettes & Nuts (Waitrose) *serving 170g/6oz*	12
Tuna, Celery & Lemon (Waitrose) *serving 170g/6oz*	27

Tuna & Cucumber Finger Roll, (Somerfield) *serving 170g/6oz*	17
Tuna & Cucumber (Tesco) *serving 170g/6oz*	7
Tuna & Cucumber, Healthy Eating (Tesco) *serving 170g/6oz*	7
Tuna & Cucumber with Mayo & Iceberg, Light (Asda) *serving 170g/6oz*	7
Tuna, Mayonnaise & Cucumber (Somerfield) *serving 170g/6oz*	23
Tuna Nicoise, French Bread (Marks & Spencer) *serving 170g/6oz*	30
Tuna Salad (Sainsbury's) *serving 170g/6oz*	5
Tuna & Salad, Low Calorie (Marks & Spencer) *serving 170g/6oz*	6
Tuna & Salad Continental Roll, (Waitrose) *serving 170g/6oz*	19
Tuna & Sweetcorn (Marks & Spencer) *serving 170g/6oz*	16
Tuna & Sweetcorn with Lettuce, White Bread (Asda) *serving 170g/6oz*	13
Tuna & Sweetcorn, Egg & Cress, Cheddar Cheese & Coleslaw, Selection Pack (Somerfield) *serving 170g/6oz*	25
Turkey & Ham (Marks & Spencer) *serving 170g/6oz*	22
Turkey Relish (Waitrose) *serving 170g/6oz*	15
Turkey Salad, Reduced Fat (Sainsbury's) *serving 170g/6oz*	6
Turkey, Smoked, & Coleslaw, Low Calorie (Marks & Spencer) *serving 170g/6oz*	4
Turkey, Stuffing & Cranberry Sauce, White Bread (Christmas only) (Asda) *serving 170g/6oz*	17
Turkey & Stuffing (Waitrose) *serving 170g/6oz*	25
Vegetables, Grilled (Marks & Spencer) *serving 170g/6oz*	9
Vegetarian Cheddar, Reduced Fat (Waitrose) *serving 170g/6oz*	12
Vegetarian Salad (Waitrose) *serving 170g/6oz*	30
Waldorf Salad (Waitrose) *serving 170g/6oz*	23
Wensleydale & Carrot (Marks & Spencer) *serving 170g/6oz*	26

Sauces

NOTE: The standard serving size for sauces in this section is 110g/4oz, which is appropriate for an average serving of the type of sauce you might eat with pasta. More concentrated sauces, however, will be consumed in smaller quantities; barbeque sauce or salsa might only require a 10ml dessert spoon, weighing about 10g. As always, you can use the conversion tables on page 386 to change the fat values given here to account for smaller portion sizes.

Amatriciana Pasta Sauce, Chilled (Safeway) *serving 110g/4oz*	6
Amatriciana Sauce (Waitrose) *serving 110g/4oz*	4
American BBQ Sauce, Groceries (Marks & Spencer) *serving 110g/4oz*	12
Anchovy Essence (Burgess Food Frontiers) *serving 110g/4oz*	12
Apple Sauce (Heinz) *serving 110g/4oz*	0
Apple Sauce (Somerfield) *serving 110g/4oz*	0
Apple Sauce, Home Made *serving 110g/4oz*	0
Apple Sauce, Groceries (Marks & Spencer) *serving 110g/4oz*	0
Apple & Herb Cooking Sauce (Waitrose) *serving 110g/4oz*	8
Arabbiata Sauce (Marks & Spencer) *serving 110g/4oz*	4
Arabbiata Sauce (Waitrose) *serving 110g/4oz*	3
Balti Indian Sauce, Groceries (Marks & Spencer) *serving 110g/4oz*	6
Barbecue Sauce *serving 110g/4oz*	2
Barbecue Sauce (Tesco) *serving 110g/4oz*	1
Barbecue Sauce, Honey (Heinz) *serving 110g/4oz*	1
Barbecue Sauce, Original (Heinz) *serving 110g/4oz*	0
Barbecue Sauce, Smokey (Heinz)*serving 110g/4oz*	0
Barbecue Sauce, Texas Hot (Heinz) *serving 110g/4oz*	0
Bearnaise Sauce, Dehydrated, Prepared with Milk & Butter *serving 110g/4oz*	29
Beer & Onion Sauce, Groceries (Marks & Spencer) *serving 110g/4oz*	2
Black Bean Sauce *serving 110g/4oz*	2
Bolognese Sauce *serving 110g/4oz*	12
Bolognese Sauce (Somerfield) *serving 110g/4oz*	3
Bolognese Sauce (Waitrose) *serving 110g/4oz*	2
Bolognese Pasta Sauce, Chilled (Safeway) *serving 110g/4oz*	4
Bolognese Pasta Sauce, Tinned (Safeway) *serving 110g/4oz*	2
Bolognese Sauce, Tinned (Tesco) *serving 110g/4oz*	5
Bolognese Sauce, Chilled (Tesco) *serving 110g/4oz*	7
Bolognese Sauce, Groceries (Marks & Spencer) *serving 110g/4oz*	4
Bolognese, Traditional Sauce, Healthy Choice, Lower in Sugar (Asda) *serving 110g/4oz*	0

Bramley Apple Sauce (Tesco) *serving 110g/4oz* 0
Brandy Flavour Sauce (Kraft) *serving 110g/4oz* 2
Brandy Sauce (Waitrose) *serving 110g/4oz* 6
Bread Sauce Mix (Somerfield) *serving 110g/4oz* 9
Brown Sauce (Somerfield) *serving 110g/4oz* 0
Brown Sauce, Basics (Somerfield) *serving 110g/4oz* 0
Brown Sauce Grocery (Iceland) *serving 110g/4oz* 0
Brown Sauce, Hot *serving 110g/4oz* 0
Brown Sauce, Spicy (Tesco) *serving 110g/4oz* 1
Brown Sauce, Sweet *serving 110g/4oz* 0
Carbonara (Somerfield) *serving 110g/4oz* 11
Carbonara Sauce (Waitrose) *serving 110g/4oz* 21
Carbonara, Fresh (Asda) *serving 110g/4oz* 12
Carbonara Pasta Sauce, Chilled (Safeway) *serving 110g/4oz* 19
Carbonara Sauce, Chilled (Tesco) *serving 110g/4oz* 9
Carbonara Sauce, Italian (Waitrose) *serving 110g/4oz* 12
Caribbean Creole Sauce (Waitrose) *serving 110g/4oz* 0
Casserole Sauce, Dry Mix, Made Up *serving 110g/4oz* 0
Cheese Sauce (Waitrose) *serving 110g/4oz* 18
Cheese Sauce, Dehydrated, Prepared with Milk *serving 110g/4oz* 7
Cheese Sauce, Fresh (Asda) *serving 110g/4oz* 14
Chilli Sauce *serving 110g/4oz* 1
Chilli Sauce (Tesco) *serving 110g/4oz* 1
Chilli Sauce (Waitrose) *serving 110g/4oz* 1
Chilli Cook in Sauce, Grocery (Iceland) *serving 110g/4oz* 1
Chinese Szechuan Sauce (Heinz Weight Watchers) *serving 110g/4oz* 2
Coronation Sauce (Heinz) *serving 110g/4oz* 34
Cranberry Sauce *serving 110g/4oz* 0
Cranberry Sauce (Burgess Food Frontiers) *serving 110g/4oz* 0
Cranberry Sauce (Marks & Spencer) *serving 110g/4oz* 0
Cranberry Sauce (Tesco) *serving 110g/4oz* 0
Cream & Mushroom Sauce, Groceries (Marks & Spencer)
serving 110g/4oz 10
Creamy Carbonara Pasta Bake (Napolina) (CPC) *serving 110g/4oz* 6
Creamy Lasagne Pasta Bake (Napolina) (CPC) *serving 110g/4oz* 4
Creamy Tuna Pasta Bake (Napolina) (CPC) *serving 110g/4oz* 4
Creamy Vegetable Pasta Bake (Napolina) (CPC) *serving 110g/4oz* 5

Curry Cook in Sauce, Grocery (Iceland) *serving 110g/4oz* 6
Curry Korma Mild Sauce, Healthy Choice, Low in Fat (Asda) *serving 110g/4oz* 2
Curry Paste *serving 110g/4oz* 23
Curry Sauce (Tesco) *serving 110g/4oz* 1
Curry Sauce, Dry, Prepared with Milk *serving 110g/4oz* 6
Curry Sauce, Tinned *serving 110g/4oz* 6
Curry Sauce, Onion & Butter *serving 110g/4oz* 27
Curry Sauce, Onion & Vegetable Oil *serving 110g/4oz* 33
Curry Sauce, Tomato & Onion *serving 110g/4oz* 21
Curry, Thai Green, Sauce, Groceries (Marks & Spencer) *serving 110g/4oz* 10
Curry Tikka Masala Mild Sauce, Healthy Choice, Low in Fat (Asda) *serving 110g/4oz* 2
Four Cheeses, Pasta Sauce, Chilled (Safeway) *serving 110g/4oz* 22
Four Cheese & Bacon Sauce (Marks & Spencer) *serving 110g/4oz* 13
Fruit Sauce (Somerfield) *serving 110g/4oz* 0
Fruit Sauce (Waitrose) *serving 110g/4oz* 0
Fruity Sauce, Bottled (Tesco) *serving 110g/4oz* 1
Funghi Sauce, Italian Pasta (Waitrose) *serving 110g/4oz* 6
Gravy au Jus, Dehydrated, Prepared with Water *serving 110g/4oz* 1
Gravy, Brown, Dehydrated, Prepared with Water *serving 110g/4oz* 1
Gravy, Chicken, Canned *serving 110g/4oz* 6
Gravy, Chicken, Dehydrated, Prepared with Water *serving 110g/4oz* 1
Gravy, Instant Granules, Made Up *serving 110g/4oz* 3
Gravy, Mushroom, Canned *serving 110g/4oz* 3
Gravy, Mushroom, Dehydrated, Prepared with Water *serving 110g/4oz* 0
Gravy, Onion, Dehydrated, Prepared with Water *serving 110g/4oz* 0
Gravy, Pork, Dehydrated, Prepared with Water *serving 110g/4oz* 1
Ham & Mushroom Sauce, Groceries (Marks & Spencer) *serving 110g/4oz* 11
Horseradish Cream (Tesco) *serving 110g/4oz* 12
Horseradish Hot Sauce (Waitrose) *serving 110g/4oz* 8
Horseradish Sauce *serving 110g/4oz* 9

Horseradish Sauce (Tesco) *serving 110g/4oz* 6
Horseradish Sauce, Creamed (Burgess Food Frontiers) *serving 110g/4oz* 11
Horseradish Sauce, Hot (Burgess Food Frontiers) *serving 110g/4oz* 7
Horseradish Sauce, Hot (Waitrose) *serving 110g/4oz* 8
Hot Pepper Sauce *serving 110g/4oz* 2
Hot & Spicy Onions (Tesco) *serving 110g/4oz* 1
Indian Tikka Masala Sauce (Heinz Weight Watchers) *serving 110g/4oz* 2
Jal Frezi Indian Sauce, Groceries (Marks & Spencer) *serving 110g/4oz* 3
Korma Indian Sauce, Groceries (Marks & Spencer) *serving 110g/4oz* 14
Lemon Sauce with Tarragon (Waitrose) *serving 110g/4oz* 1
Marinade, Cajun (Burgess Food Frontiers) *serving 110g/4oz* 5
Marinade, Chinese (Burgess Food Frontiers) *serving 110g/4oz* 6
Marinade, Garlic/Rosemary, Groceries (Marks & Spencer) *serving 110g/4oz* 24
Marinade, Hot & Spicy, Groceries (Marks & Spencer) *serving 110g/4oz* 13
Marinade, Italian Style, Groceries (Marks & Spencer) *serving 110g/4oz* 11
Marinade, Lime/Coriander, Groceries (Marks & Spencer) *serving 110g/4oz* 21
Marinade, Mexican (Burgess Food Frontiers) *serving 110g/4oz* 18
Marinade, Orange & Herb, Groceries (Marks & Spencer) *serving 110g/4oz* 16
Marinade, Satay (Burgess Food Frontiers) *serving 110g/4oz* 11
Marinade, Shaschlik (Burgess Food Frontiers) *serving 110g/4oz* 16
Marinade, Tikka (Burgess Food Frontiers) *serving 110g/4oz* 16
Marinade, Tikka, Groceries (Marks & Spencer) *serving 110g/4oz* 30
Marinara Sauce, Tinned *serving 110g/4oz* 4
Mexican Chilli Sauce (Heinz Weight Watchers) *serving 110g/4oz* 0
Mexican Salsa, Groceries (Marks & Spencer) *serving 110g/4oz* 1
Mint Jelly (Burgess Food Frontiers) *serving 110g/4oz* 1
Mint Sauce *serving 110g/4oz* 0
Mint Sauce (Somerfield) *serving 110g/4oz* 0

Mint Sauce (Tesco) *serving 110g/4oz*	0
Mint Sauce (Burgess Food Frontiers) *serving 110g/4oz*	0
Mint Sauce, Garden, Fresh (Tesco) *serving 110g/4oz*	0
Mint Sauce, Groceries (Marks & Spencer) *serving 110g/4oz*	0
Mint Sauce, Home Made *serving 110g/4oz*	0
Mint Sauce, Mrs B's (Burgess Food Frontiers) *serving 110g/4oz*	0
Miso *serving 110g/4oz*	7
Mushroom Sauce (Waitrose) *serving 110g/4oz*	8
Mushroom, Creamy Cooking Sauce (Waitrose) *serving 110g/4oz*	6
Mushroom, Creamy Pasta Sauce, Chilled (Safeway) *serving 110g/4oz*	11
Mushroom, Creamy Sauce (Somerfield) *serving 110g/4oz*	9
Mushroom, Creamy Sauce, Fresh (Asda) *serving 110g/4oz*	11
Mushroom, Pasta Sauce (Waitrose) *serving 110g/4oz*	2
Mushroom Sauce, Dehydrated, Prepared with Milk *serving 110g/4oz*	4
Napoletana Pasta Sauce, Chilled (Safeway) *serving 110g/4oz*	2
Napoletana Sauce, Fresh (Waitrose) *serving 110g/4oz*	1
Napoletana Sauce, Italian (Waitrose) *serving 110g/4oz*	4
Onion Relish (Tesco) *serving 110g/4oz*	0
Onion Sauce, Made with Semi-Skimmed Milk *serving 110g/4oz*	6
Onion Sauce, Made with Skimmed Milk *serving 110g/4oz*	4
Onion Sauce, Made with Whole Milk *serving 110g/4oz*	7
Orange Sauce with Ginger (Waitrose) *serving 110g/4oz*	0
Oriental Sweet & Sour Sauce (Heinz Weight Watchers) *serving 110g/4oz*	0
Oyster Sauce *serving 110g/4oz*	0
Passata with Basil (Waitrose) *serving 110g/4oz*	0
Pasta Sauce (Somerfield) *serving 110g/4oz*	1
Pasta Sauce, Bottled, Healthy Eating (Tesco) *serving 110g/4oz*	1
Pasta Sauce with Chunky Vegetables, Bottled (Tesco) *serving 110g/4oz*	2
Pasta Sauce with Chunky Vegetables (Somerfield) *serving 110g/4oz*	12
Pasta Sauce Classico (Waitrose) *serving 110g/4oz*	2
Pasta Sauce with Extra Onion & Garlic, Grocery (Iceland) *serving 110g/4oz*	15

Pasta Sauce, Garlic (Waitrose) *serving 110g/4oz* 1
Pasta Sauce, Italian (Heinz Weight Watchers) *serving 110g/4oz* 0
Pasta Sauce with Mushrooms (Somerfield) *serving 110g/4oz* 1
Pasta Sauce with Mushrooms, Bottled (Tesco) *serving 110g/4oz* 2
Pasta Sauce with Mushrooms, Tinned (Tesco) *serving 110g/4oz* 0
Pasta Sauce with Onion & Garlic (Somerfield) *serving 110g/4oz* 12
Pasta Sauce with Onion and Garlic, Tinned (Tesco) *serving 110g/4oz* 0
Pasta Sauce with Onion & Garlic, Bottled (Tesco) *serving 110g/4oz* 2
Pasta Sauce, Original, Bottled (Tesco) *serving 110g/4oz* 2
Pasta Sauce, Original, Chilled (Tesco) *serving 110g/4oz* 1
Pasta Sauce with Peppers (Somerfield) *serving 110g/4oz* 1
Pasta Sauce with Peppers, Bottled (Tesco) *serving 110g/4oz* 2
Pasta Sauce, Spicy, Bottled (Tesco) *serving 110g/4oz* 2
Pasta Sauce, Spicy, Tinned (Tesco) *serving 110g/4oz* 0
Pasta Sauce, Tomato Based *serving 110g/4oz* 2
Pasta Sauce, Traditional, in a Jar (Safeway) *serving 110g/4oz* 2
Pasta Sauce, White *serving 110g/4oz* 12
Pepper & Basil, Pasta Sauce, Chilled (Safeway) *serving 110g/4oz* 4
Peppercorn Sauce, Groceries (Marks & Spencer) *serving 110g/4oz* 10
Peppers, Pasta Sauce (Waitrose) *serving 110g/4oz* 1
Pesto Medaglioni, Creamy (Waitrose) *serving 110g/4oz* 11
Pesto Sauce *serving 110g/4oz* 52
Pesto Sauce (Waitrose) *serving 110g/4oz* 58
Pesto Sauce, Groceries (Marks & Spencer) *serving 110g/4oz* 44
Pesto Sauce in Olive Oil (Waitrose) *serving 110g/4oz* 42
Pesto, Red, in Olive Oil (Waitrose) *serving 110g/4oz* 30
Pesto, Sun Dried Tomato, Groceries (Marks & Spencer) *serving 110g/4oz* 36
Plum Sauce, Hong Kong Duck (Waitrose) *serving 110g/4oz* 5
Prawn Cocktail Sauce (Burgess Food Frontiers) *serving 110g/4oz* 29
Raspberry Sauce, Groceries (Marks & Spencer) *serving 110g/4oz* 0
Redcurrant Jelly *serving 110g/4oz* 0
Redcurrant Jelly (Burgess Food Frontiers) *serving 110g/4oz* 0
Redcurrant Jelly (Tesco) *serving 110g/4oz* 0

Redcurrant & Port Sauce (Tesco) *serving 110g/4oz* 0
Salsa Cool (Heinz) *serving 110g/4oz* 0
Salsa Empanada (Waitrose) *serving 110g/4oz* 13
Salsa, Hot (Heinz) *serving 110g/4oz* 0
Salsa Relish (Waitrose) *serving 110g/4oz* 0
Salsiccia Napoli Piccante (Waitrose) *serving 110g/4oz* 29
Satay Sauce (Waitrose) *serving 110g/4oz* 15
Sauces from Dry Mix (e.g. Parsley, Onion & Bread), Made Up *serving 110g/4oz* 5
Seafood Sauce (Waitrose) *serving 110g/4oz* 42
Sour Cream Sauce, Dehydrated, Prepared with Milk *serving 110g/4oz* 11
Soy Sauce, Dark (Waitrose) *serving 110g/4oz* 1
Soy Sauce, Japanese (Waitrose) *serving 110g/4oz* 1
Soy Sauce, Light (Waitrose) *serving 110g/4oz* 1
Soy Sauce, Made from Hydrolysed Vegetable Protein *serving 110g/4oz* 0
Soy Sauce, Made from Soya Beans (Tamari) *serving 110g/4oz* 0
Soy Sauce, Made from Soya & Wheat (Shoyu) *serving 110g/4oz* 0
Spaghetti Sauce, Tinned *serving 110g/4oz* 5
Spicy Sauce (Heinz) *serving 110g/4oz* 1
Spicy Sauce (Waitrose) *serving 110g/4oz* 0
Sweet & Sour Chinese Style Sauce, Healthy Choice, Lower in Sugar (Asda) *serving 110g/4oz* 0
Sweet & Sour Cook in Sauce, Grocery (Iceland) *serving 110g/4oz* 0
Sweet & Sour Cooking Sauce (Waitrose) *serving 110g/4oz* 0
Sweet & Sour Sauce, Tinned *serving 110g/4oz* 0
Sweet & Sour Sauce, Dehydrated, Prepared with Water & Vinegar *serving 110g/4oz* 0
Sweet & Sour Sauce, from Take Away *serving 110g/4oz* 4
Tartare Sauce *serving 110g/4oz* 27
Tartare Sauce (Burgess Food Frontiers) *serving 110g/4oz* 22
Tartare Sauce (Marks & Spencer) *serving 110g/4oz* 68
Tartare Sauce (Tesco) *serving 110g/4oz* 27
Tartare Sauce (Waitrose) *serving 110g/4oz* 24
Teriyaki Sauce (Waitrose) *serving 110g/4oz* 1

Teriyaki Sauce, Dehydrated, Prepared with Water *serving 110g/4oz* 0
Teriyaki Sauce, Ready to Serve *serving 110g/4oz* 0
Tikka Masala Indian Sauce, Groceries (Marks & Spencer) *serving 110g/4oz* 10
Tomato Base Sauce *serving 110g/4oz* 6
Tomato Sauce, Italian, Groceries (Marks & Spencer) *serving 110g/4oz* 1
Tomato Sauce, Creamy (Somerfield) *serving 110g/4oz* 6
Tomato & Basil Oregano Sauce, Groceries (Marks & Spencer) *serving 110g/4oz* 3
Tomato Frito Sauce (Heinz) *serving 110g/4oz* 5
Tomato & Herb Fresh Sauce, Healthy Choice, (Asda) *serving 110g/4oz* 1
Tomato & Herb Sauce, Bottled (Tesco) *serving 110g/4oz* 1
Tomato Mascapone Sauce, Groceries (Marks & Spencer) *serving 110g/4oz* 6
Tomato & Mushroom Pasta Sauce, Grocery (Iceland) *serving 110g/4oz* 15
Tomato with Mushrooms, Pasta Sauce in a Jar (Safeway) *serving 110g/4oz* 2
Tomato & Mushroom Sauce *serving 110g/4oz* 4
Tomato & Olive Creamy Pasta Sauce Chilled (Safeway) *serving 110g/4oz* 7
Tomato & Onion Pasta Sauce, Grocery (Iceland) *serving 110g/4oz* 2
Tomato with Onions & Garlic, Pasta Sauce in a Jar (Safeway) *serving 110g/4oz* 2
Tomato Puree, Tinned (Tesco) *serving 110g/4oz* 0
Tomato with Pepper, Pasta Sauce in a Jar (Safeway) *serving 110g/4oz* 2
Tuna & Tomato Sauce (Waitrose) *serving 110g/4oz* 7
Turkey Gravy, Tinned *serving 110g/4oz* 2
Turkey Gravy, Dehydrated, Prepared with Water *serving 110g/4oz* 1
Vegetable, Creamy Sauce, Fresh (Asda) *serving 110g/4oz* 3
Vegetali Sauce (Somerfield) *serving 110g/4oz* 1
Vongole Sauce, Italian (Waitrose) *serving 110g/4oz* 5
White Sauce, Dehydrated, Prepared with Milk *serving 110g/4oz* 6

White Sauce, Packet Mix, Made up with Semi-Skimmed Milk *serving 110g/4oz* 3
White Sauce, Packet Mix, Made Up with Skimmed Milk *serving 110g/4oz* 1
White Sauce, Packet Mix, Made Up with Whole Milk *serving 110g/4oz* 5
White Sauce, Savoury, Made with Semi-Skimmed Milk *serving 110g/4oz* 9
White Sauce, Savoury, Made with Skimmed Milk *serving 110g/4oz* 7
White Sauce, Savoury, Made with Whole Milk *serving 110g/4oz* 11
White Sauce, Sweet, Made with Semi-Skimmed Milk *serving 110g/4oz* 8
White Sauce, Sweet, Made with Skimmed Milk *serving 110g/4oz* 6
White Sauce, Sweet, Made with Whole Milk *serving 110g/4oz* 10
White Wine Cooking Sauce (Waitrose) *serving 110g/4oz* 1
White Wine Sauce (Marks & Spencer) *serving 110g/4oz* 13
Worcestershire Sauce *serving 110g/4oz* 0
Yeast Extract *serving 110g/4oz* 0

SAUSAGES

NOTE: The standard serving size in this section is 60g/2oz. If you wish to consume more or less than this amount (e.g. if you are going to consume a pack of food whose weight differs from the standard serving size) use the conversion tables on page 386 to calculate the new amount of fat in the food.

Aberdeen Angus Lorne Sausage, Deli (Asda) *serving 60g/2oz* 14
Bacon & Leek Sausage Meat (Waitrose) *serving 60g/2oz* 13
Bangers, Beans & Mash, Chilled Ready Meal (Safeway) *serving 60g/2oz* 16
Bangers & Mash (Asda) *serving 60g/2oz* 5
Bangers & Mash (Somerfield) *serving 60g/2oz* 3
Bangers 'n' Mash, Frozen (Asda) *serving 60g/2oz* 5
Bangers & Mash, Main Meal (Marks & Spencer) *serving 60g/2oz* 6
BBQ Selection Sausage (Waitrose) *serving 60g/2oz* 13
Beef, Chilled, Cooked (Tesco) *serving 60g/2oz* 11

Beef, Napolitana (Waitrose) *serving 60g/2oz*	11
Beef, Premium (Somerfield) *serving 60g/2oz*	12
Beef, Slicing, Deli (Asda) *serving 60g/2oz*	15
Beef, Thick, Prepacked (Asda) *serving 60g/2oz*	8
Beef, Thin, Prepacked (Asda) *serving 60g/2oz*	8
Berliner *serving 60g/2oz*	10
Bierwurst, Cold Meats (Tesco) *serving 60g/2oz*	9
Black Pudding (Somerfield) *serving 60g/2oz*	10
Black Pudding, Bury, Deli (Asda) *serving 60g/2oz*	5
Black Pudding, Prepacked (Asda) *serving 60g/2oz*	9
Black Pudding Ring, Deli (Asda) *serving 60g/2oz*	8
Black Pudding Stick, Deli (Asda) *serving 60g/2oz*	10
Blood Sausage or Blood Pudding *serving 60g/2oz*	21
Bockworsten (Princes) *serving 60g/2oz*	8
Bockwurst *serving 60g/2oz*	17
Bologna *serving 60g/2oz*	12
Bologna, Beef *serving 60g/2oz*	17
Bologna Turkey Sausage *serving 60g/2oz*	9
Bratwurst *serving 60g/2oz*	16
Braunschweiger *serving 60g/2oz*	19
Braunschweiger (Liver Sausage), Smoked *serving 60g/2oz*	19
Brotwurst *serving 60g/2oz*	17
Butcher's Cocktail Sausage, Main Meal (Marks & Spencer) *serving 60g/2oz*	12
Butcher's Sausages, Main Meal (Marks & Spencer) *serving 60g/2oz*	18
Butcher's Style Sausages (Marks & Spencer) *serving 60g/2oz*	18
Cambridge Sausage (Waitrose) *serving 60g/2oz*	16
Chicken, Leek & Ginger Sausage (Waitrose) *serving 60g/2oz*	11
Chilli Sausages (Somerfield) *serving 60g/2oz*	15
Chorizo *serving 60g/2oz*	23
Chorizo Sausage (Waitrose) *serving 60g/2oz*	10
Chorizo Tradicion Extra (Waitrose) *serving 60g/2oz*	16
Chorizos (Somerfield) *serving 60g/2oz*	12
Chorizos, Deli (Asda) *serving 60g/2oz*	18
Coarse Cut Sausages (Waitrose) *serving 60g/2oz*	13
Cocktail Roll Selection (Waitrose) *serving 60g/2oz*	1

Cocktail Sausage Selection (Waitrose) *serving 60g/2oz* 13
Cocktail Sausages, Frozen (Iceland) *serving 60g/2oz* 13
Cocktail Sausages, Main Meal (Marks & Spencer) *serving 60g/2oz* 18
Cocktail Sausages, Party Food (Marks & Spencer) *serving 60g/2oz* 20
Cocktail Sausages, Skinless (Asda) *serving 60g/2oz* 8
Cumberland Sausages (Somerfield) *serving 60g/2oz* 16
Farmhouse Sausage (Waitrose) *serving 60g/2oz* 12
Florentine Sausage (Waitrose) *serving 60g/2oz* 14
Frankfurters (Princes) *serving 60g/2oz* 18
Frankfurters (Somerfield) *serving 60g/2oz* 12
Frankfurter, Beef *serving 60g/2oz* 17
Frankfurter, Chicken *serving 60g/2oz* 12
Frankfurters, Delicatessen (Marks & Spencer) *serving 60g/2oz* 17
Frankfurters, Giant (Somerfield) *serving 60g/2oz* 12
Frankfurters, Prepacked (Asda) *serving 60g/2oz* 16
Free Range Sausage, Main Meal (Marks & Spencer) *serving 60g/2oz* 11
Garlic Sausage, Continental, Deli (Asda) *serving 60g/2oz* 10
Garlic Sausage, Delicatessen (Marks & Spencer) *serving 60g/2oz* 11
Garlic Sausage, French, Delicatessen (Marks & Spencer) *serving 60g/2oz* 15
Garlic Sausage, French, Strong, Prepacked (Asda) *serving 60g/2oz* 10
Garlic Sausage, French (Waitrose) *serving 60g/2oz* 15
Garlic Sausage, French Style, Cold Meats (Tesco) *serving 60g/2oz* 10
Garlic Sausage, French Style, Deli (Asda) *serving 60g/2oz* 13
Garlic Sausage, German (Somerfield) *serving 60g/2oz* 13
Garlic Sausage, Low Fat, Cold Meats (Tesco) *serving 60g/2oz* 6
Garlic Sausage, Mild (Somerfield) *serving 60g/2oz* 13
Garlic Sausage, Mild (Waitrose) *serving 60g/2oz* 15
Garlic Sausage, Mild, Cold Meats (Tesco) *serving 60g/2oz* 13
Garlic Sausage, Mild, Prepacked (Asda) *serving 60g/2oz* 8
Garlic Sausage, Strong (Somerfield) *serving 60g/2oz* 13
Garlic Sausage, Strong (Waitrose) *serving 60g/2oz* 6
Garlic Slicing Sausage, Prepacked (Asda) *serving 60g/2oz* 13
Gnasher Dogs (Princes) *serving 60g/2oz* 7

Gourmet Sausage, English (Waitrose) *serving 60g/2oz* 13
Haggis (Somerfield) *serving 60g/2oz* 9
Haggis, Scottish (Waitrose) *serving 60g/2oz* 13
Ham & Pistachio Sausage (Waitrose) *serving 60g/2oz* 10
Hot Dog Sausage, American Style, Cold Meats (Tesco) *serving 60g/2oz* 11
Hot Dog Sausages (Princes) *serving 60g/2oz* 8
Hot Dogs in Jars, Premium (Princes) *serving 60g/2oz* 7
Hot Rod Dogs (Princes) *serving 60g/2oz* 8
Irish Recipe Sausages, Thick, Prepacked (Asda) *serving 60g/2oz* 12
Irish Sausages, Frozen (Iceland) *serving 60g/2oz* 13
Jamaican Hot Sausage (Waitrose) *serving 60g/2oz* 17
Jumbo Sausage, Main Meal (Marks & Spencer) *serving 60g/2oz* 18
Kabanos (Somerfield) *serving 60g/2oz* 16
Kassler (Somerfield) *serving 60g/2oz* 3
Kielbasa Kolbassy *serving 60g/2oz* 16
Knockwurst *serving 60g/2oz* 17
Leicestershire Sausage (Waitrose) *serving 60g/2oz* 13
Lincolnshire, Butcher's Best, Thick Smooth Sausages, Prepacked (Asda) *serving 60g/2oz* 11
Lincolnshire Chipolatas, Butcher's Choice, Chilled, Cooked (Tesco) *serving 60g/2oz* 14
Lincolnshire Sausage (Waitrose) *serving 60g/2oz* 10
Lincolnshire Sausage, Deli (Asda) *serving 60g/2oz* 7
Lincolnshire Sausage, Main Meal (Marks & Spencer) *serving 60g/2oz* 15
Lincolnshire Sausage, Thick, Healthy Choice (Asda) *serving 60g/2oz* 6
Lincolnshire, Thick, Lower Fat, Smooth Sausages, Healthy Choice, Prepacked (Asda) *serving 60g/2oz* 6
Lincolnshire Vegetarian Sausages, Premium (Cauldron Foods) *serving 60g/2oz* 6
Liver Sausage, Cold Meats (Tesco) *serving 60g/2oz* 9
Liver Sausage, Continental (Somerfield) *serving 60g/2oz* 21
Liver Sausage, Continental (Waitrose) *serving 60g/2oz* 20
Liver Sausage, Prepacked (Asda) *serving 60g/2oz* 9
Liver Sausage, Slicing (Somerfield) *serving 60g/2oz* 12

Liverwurst *serving 60g/2oz*	17
Lorne Sausage (Marks & Spencer) *serving 60g/2oz*	13
Lorne Sausage (Somerfield) *serving 60g/2oz*	15
Lorne Sausage, Deli (Asda) *serving 60g/2oz*	15
Luncheon Sausage, Continental (Waitrose) *serving 60g/2oz*	11
Luncheon-type Sausage *serving 60g/2oz*	13
Manchester Sausage (Waitrose) *serving 60g/2oz*	14
Mandolato, Italian (Safeway) *serving 60g/2oz*	7
Meatless Sausage *serving 60g/2oz*	11
Mediterranean Style Sausages (Waitrose) *serving 60g/2oz*	15
Mortadella *serving 60g/2oz*	15
Mortadella, Italian (Waitrose) *serving 60g/2oz*	13
Nature's Choice Sausage, Chilled, Cooked (Tesco) *serving 60g/2oz*	10
Pastrami (Somerfield) *serving 60g/2oz*	4
Pastrami, Cold Meats (Tesco) *serving 60g/2oz*	2
Pastrami, Deli (Asda) *serving 60g/2oz*	4
Pastrami, Delicatessen, Wafer (Marks & Spencer) *serving 60g/2oz*	3
Pastrami, Sliced (Waitrose) *serving 60g/2oz*	2
Pastrami, Wafer Thin (Somerfield) *serving 60g/2oz*	2
Pastrami, Wafer Thin (Waitrose) *serving 60g/2oz*	3
Pastrami, Wafer Thin, Prepacked (Asda) *serving 60g/2oz*	3
Pastrami, Turkey *serving 60g/2oz*	4
Pastrami, Turkey Sausage *serving 60g/2oz*	4
Peperami Cheezie, Cheese Alternative (Van Den Bergh) *serving 60g/2oz*	19
Peperami Gobbler, Meat Snack (Van Den Bergh) *serving 60g/2oz*	26
Peperami Hot, Meat Snack (Van Den Bergh) *serving 60g/2oz*	31
Peperami, Meat Snack, (Van Den Bergh) *serving 60g/2oz*	29
Peperami in a Roll, Meat Snack (Van Den Bergh) *serving 60g/2oz*	19
Pepperoni, Cold Meats (Tesco) *serving 60g/2oz*	12
Pepperoni, German, Sliced (Waitrose) *serving 60g/2oz*	24
Pepperoni, Presliced Deli (Asda) *serving 60g/2oz*	25
Polish Style Sausage *serving 60g/2oz*	17
Polony, Deli (Asda) *serving 60g/2oz*	21
Polony Sausage (Somerfield) *serving 60g/2oz*	9
Polony Slicing Sausage, Prepacked (Asda) *serving 60g/2oz*	8
Pork (Somerfield) *serving 60g/2oz*	11

Pork, ½ Skinless (Marks & Spencer) *serving 60g/2oz* 13
Pork, Asparagus (Waitrose) *serving 60g/2oz* 9
Pork & Beef *serving 60g/2oz* 22
Pork & Beef (Somerfield) *serving 60g/2oz* 12
Pork & Beef (Waitrose) *serving 60g/2oz* 11
Pork & Beef Cappelletti (Waitrose) *serving 60g/2oz* 9
Pork & Beef, Chilled, Cooked (Tesco) *serving 60g/2oz* 12
Pork & Beef Chipolatas (Waitrose) *serving 60g/2oz* 11
Pork & Beef Chipolatas, Chilled, Cooked (Tesco) *serving 60g/2oz* 12
Pork & Beef, Healthy Choice (Asda) *serving 60g/2oz* 8
Pork & Beef, Jumbo, Frozen (Iceland) *serving 60g/2oz* 15
Pork & Beef, Skinless, Chilled, Cooked (Tesco) *serving 60g/2oz* 9
Pork & Beef, Smoked, Link *serving 60g/2oz* 18
Pork & Beef, Thick (Asda) *serving 60g/2oz* 11
Pork & Beef, Thick, Frozen (Iceland) *serving 60g/2oz* 15
Pork & Beef, Thick, Prepacked (Asda) *serving 60g/2oz* 9
Pork & Beef, Thin, Prepacked (Asda) *serving 60g/2oz* 9
Pork, Cajun (Waitrose) *serving 60g/2oz* 15
Pork, Chilled, Cooked (Tesco) *serving 60g/2oz* 14
Pork, Chilled, Cooked, Healthy Eating (Tesco) *serving 60g/2oz* 6
Pork, Chilled, Jumbo (Iceland) *serving 60g/2oz* 18
Pork, Chinese Style, Chilled (Iceland) *serving 60g/2oz* 18
Pork, Chipolata (Waitrose) *serving 60g/2oz* 13
Pork, Chipolata (Somerfield) *serving 60g/2oz* 11
Pork, Chipolata, Chilled, Cooked (Tesco) *serving 60g/2oz* 14
Pork, Chipolata, Chilled, Cooked, Healthy Eating (Tesco)
serving 60g/2oz 6
Pork, Chipolata, Premium (Waitrose) *serving 60g/2oz* 14
Pork, Chipolata, Skinless (Waitrose) *serving 60g/2oz* 13
Pork, Cocktail (Somerfield) *serving 60g/2oz* 15
Pork, Cocktail (Waitrose) *serving 60g/2oz* 13
Pork, Cocktail, Chilled, Cooked (Tesco) *serving 60g/2oz* 14
Pork, Cocktail, Cooked, Prepacked (Asda) *serving 60g/2oz* 15
Pork, Cocktail, Prepacked (Asda) *serving 60g/2oz* 14
Pork, Cotswold (Waitrose) *serving 60g/2oz* 11
Pork, Counter (Waitrose) *serving 60g/2oz* 12
Pork, Cumberland (Waitrose) *serving 60g/2oz* 13

Pork, Cumberland, Chilled, Cooked (Tesco) *serving 60g/2oz* 10
Pork, East India (Waitrose) *serving 60g/2oz* 13
Pork, Frozen (Iceland) *serving 60g/2oz* 15
Pork, Glamorgan & Leek, Butcher's Choice (Somerfield) *serving 60g/2oz* 17
Pork, Haslet (Waitrose) *serving 60g/2oz* 9
Pork & Herb, Premium, Chilled Cooked (Tesco) *serving 60g/2oz* 11
Pork & Herb, Thick, Frozen, Shallow Fry (Iceland) *serving 60g/2oz* 13
Pork, Irish Sausage, Main Meals (Marks & Spencer) *serving 60g/2oz* 16
Pork, Italian *serving 60g/2oz* 15
Pork, Jumbo (Somerfield) *serving 60g/2oz* 11
Pork & Leek (Waitrose) *serving 60g/2oz* 16
Pork & Leek, Main Meals (Marks & Spencer) *serving 60g/2oz* 13
Pork, Lincolnshire (Somerfield) *serving 60g/2oz* 16
Pork, Lincolnshire, Cocktail, Chilled, Cooked (Tesco) *serving 60g/2oz* 13
Pork, Lincolnshire, Premium, Chilled, Cooked (Tesco) *serving 60g/2oz* 10
Pork, Loose (Tesco) *serving 60g/2oz* 14
Pork, Low Fat, Main Meals (Marks & Spencer) *serving 60g/2oz* 2
Pork, Main Meals (Marks & Spencer) *serving 60g/2oz* 18
Pork & Pesto (Waitrose) *serving 60g/2oz* 17
Pork, Premium (Somerfield) *serving 60g/2oz* 15
Pork, Premium, Chilled, Cooked (Tesco) *serving 60g/2oz* 13
Pork & Prune Cognac (Waitrose) *serving 60g/2oz* 14
Pork, Ready Cooked, Cocktail, Frozen (Iceland) *serving 60g/2oz* 15
Pork, Skinless, & Beef (Somerfield) *serving 60g/2oz* 10
Pork, Skinless (Somerfield) *serving 60g/2oz* 15
Pork, Skinless, Prepacked (Asda) *serving 60g/2oz* 14
Pork, Smoked, Link *serving 60g/2oz* 19
Pork, Spiced (Waitrose) *serving 60g/2oz* 14
Pork, Standard (Waitrose) *serving 60g/2oz* 12
Pork, Thick, Deli (Asda) *serving 60g/2oz* 17
Pork, Thick, Lower Fat, Smooth, Prepacked, Healthy Choice (Asda) *serving 60g/2oz* 5
Pork, Thick Prepacked (Asda) *serving 60g/2oz* 17

Pork, Thick, Smooth, Butcher's Best, Prepacked (Asda) *serving 60g/2oz* 12
Pork, Thin, Deli (Asda) *serving 60g/2oz* 13
Pork, Thin, Prepacked (Asda) *serving 60g/2oz* 17
Pork & Tomato, Thick, Prepacked (Asda) *serving 60g/2oz* 11
Pork, Toulouse (Waitrose) *serving 60g/2oz* 13
Pork, Traditional (Waitrose) *serving 60g/2oz* 12
Pork, Traditional Style, Butcher's Choice (Somerfield) *serving 60g/2oz* 15
Pork & Turkey (Bernard Matthews) *serving 60g/2oz* 12
Pork, Yorkshire (Waitrose) *serving 60g/2oz* 11
Powter's Newmarket Sausage (Waitrose) *serving 60g/2oz* 12
Reduced Fat Sausage, Main Meal (Marks & Spencer) *serving 60g/2oz* 7
Salami Milano (Waitrose) *serving 60g/2oz* 18
Salami Napoli (Waitrose) *serving 60g/2oz* 17
Salami, Ardenne Pepperblock (Waitrose) *serving 60g/2oz* 23
Salami, Ardenne Sliced (Waitrose) *serving 60g/2oz* 23
Salami, Beef, Cooked *serving 60g/2oz* 12
Salami, Beef & Pork, Cooked *serving 60g/2oz* 12
Salami, Beerwurst Beer *serving 60g/2oz* 18
Salami & Bel Paese (Waitrose) *serving 60g/2oz* 14
Salami, Chambelle, Sliced (Waitrose) *serving 60g/2oz* 20
Salami, Danish (Somerfield) *serving 60g/2oz* 26
Salami, Danish (Waitrose) *serving 60g/2oz* 28
Salami, Danish, Chilled (Iceland) *serving 60g/2oz* 31
Salami, Danish, Cold Meats (Tesco) *serving 60g/2oz* 29
Salami, Danish, Prepacked (Asda) *serving 60g/2oz* 29
Salami, Delicatessen (Marks & Spencer) *serving 60g/2oz* 20
Salami, Delicatessen, Pepper (Marks & Spencer) *serving 60g/2oz* 22
Salami, Dry or Hard *serving 60g/2oz* 20
Salami, French, Sliced (Waitrose) *serving 60g/2oz* 22
Salami, Garlic Coated, Deli (Asda) *serving 60g/2oz* 21
Salami, German (Somerfield) *serving 60g/2oz* 15
Salami, German (Waitrose) *serving 60g/2oz* 16
Salami, German, Continental Selection, Cold Meats (Tesco) *serving 60g/2oz* 17

Salami, German, Peppered (Somerfield) *serving 60g/2oz* 19
Salami, German, Peppered (Waitrose) *serving 60g/2oz* 15
Salami, German, Peppered, Prepacked (Asda) *serving 60g/2oz* 17
Salami, German, Slices, Prepacked (Asda) *serving 60g/2oz* 17
Salami, German, White (Waitrose) *serving 60g/2oz* 24
Salami, Hungarian (Waitrose) *serving 60g/2oz* 28
Salami, Italian (Waitrose) *serving 60g/2oz* 20
Salami, Milano (Somerfield) *serving 60g/2oz* 20
Salami, Milano, Continental Selection, Cold Meats (Tesco) *serving 60g/2oz* 19
Salami, Milano, Italian (Waitrose) *serving 60g/2oz* 20
Salami, Pepper (Somerfield) *serving 60g/2oz* 24
Salami, Pepper Coated (Waitrose) *serving 60g/2oz* 24
Salami, Peppered, Deli (Asda) *serving 60g/2oz* 24
Salami, Royal (Waitrose) *serving 60g/2oz* 18
Salami, Turkey Sausage *serving 60g/2oz* 8
Saucisson Montagne, Sliced (Waitrose) *serving 60g/2oz* 22
Sausage, Basics (Somerfield) *serving 60g/2oz* 11
Sausage, Traditional (Waitrose) *serving 60g/2oz* 12
Sausage Hot Pot (Somerfield) *serving 60g/2oz* 6
Sausages & Mash (Birds Eye) *serving 60g/2oz* 5
Sausage Meat, Main Meal (Marks & Spencer) *serving 60g/2oz* 15
Sausage Meat Stuffing (Waitrose) *serving 60g/2oz* 13
Sausage & Onion Gravy (Findus Dinner Supreme) *serving 60g/2oz* 4
Sausages in Onion Gravy Filled Yorkshire Pudding, Frozen (Iceland) *serving 60g/2oz* 6
Sausage & Tomato Casserole (Crosse & Blackwell) *serving 60g/2oz* 5
Sausage Roll (Waitrose) *serving 60g/2oz* 16
Sausage Roll & Bacon (Waitrose) *serving 60g/2oz* 16
Sausage Roll & Bacon, Party Food (Marks & Spencer) *serving 60g/2oz* 17
Sausage Roll, Bite Size, Frozen, Oven Baked (Iceland) *serving 60g/2oz* 13
Sausage Roll, Buffet, Prepacked (Asda) *serving 60g/2oz* 15
Sausage Roll, Cocktail (Somerfield) *serving 60g/2oz* 10

Sausage Roll, Jumbo, Chilled (Iceland) *serving 60g/2oz* 22
Sausage Roll, Jumbo, Prepacked (Asda) *serving 60g/2oz* 16
Sausage Roll, King Size, Frozen, Oven Baked (Iceland) *serving 60g/2oz* 13
Sausage Roll, Large (Somerfield) *serving 60g/2oz* 12
Sausage Roll, Large, Chilled (Iceland) *serving 60g/2oz* 22
Sausage Roll, Large, Frozen, Oven Baked (Iceland) *serving 60g/2oz* 9
Sausage Roll, Mini, Prepacked (Asda) *serving 60g/2oz* 16
Sausage Roll, Party (Asda) *serving 60g/2oz* 11
Sausage Roll, Party (Somerfield) *serving 60g/2oz* 11
Sausage Roll, Party Food (Marks & Spencer) *serving 60g/2oz* 17
Sausage Roll, Party Size, Frozen, Oven Baked (Iceland) *serving 60g/2oz* 8
Sausage Roll, Vegetarian (Holland & Barrett) *serving 60g/2oz* 5
Sausage Roll, Vegetarian, Soya (Marks & Spencer) *serving 60g/2oz* 14
Sausage Rolls, Puff Pastry, Party Food (Marks & Spencer) *serving 60g/2oz* 17
Saveloys (Somerfield) *serving 60g/2oz* 15
Saveloys, Deli (Asda) *serving 60g/2oz* 15
Skinless Sausages, Mini (Somerfield) *serving 60g/2oz* 12
Thuringer *serving 60g/2oz* 18
Toad in the Hole (Waitrose) *serving 60g/2oz* 15
Tomato Sausage, Main Meal (Marks & Spencer) *serving 60g/2oz* 13
Top Quality Sausage, Main Meal (Marks & Spencer) *serving 60g/2oz* 17
Turkey Frankfurter *serving 60g/2oz* 11
Turkey Sausages, Thick, Prepacked (Asda) *serving 60g/2oz* 7
Turkey, Lemon & Thyme Sausage (Waitrose) *serving 60g/2oz* 5
Vegetable Sausages, Frozen (Holland & Barrett) *serving 30g/1oz* 5
Vegetarian Cocktail Sausage (Tivall) *serving 60g/2oz* 9
Vegetarian Sausages (Tivall) *serving 60g/2oz* 9
Vegetarian Smoked Sausages (Tivall) *serving 60g/2oz* 10
Vegetarian Soya Sausages (Marks & Spencer) *serving 60g/2oz* 11
Wild Boar Herb Sausage (Waitrose) *serving 60g/2oz* 3
Wild Boar Juniper Sausage (Waitrose) *serving 60g/2oz* 3

Soups

NOTE: The standard serving size in this section is 1 cup/250g. If you wish to consume more or less than this amount (e.g. if you are going to consume a tin or packet of soup whose weight differs from the standard serving size) use the conversion tables on page 386 to calculate the new amount of fat in the food.

American Potato & Leek Chowder (Knorr Soups of the World) *1 cup/250g*	3
Asparagus, Cream of (Heinz) *1 cup/250g*	8
Asparagus, Cream of (Somerfield) *1 cup/250g*	9
Asparagus, Cream of (Waitrose) *1 cup/250g*	9
Asparagus, Cream of, Dehydrated, Prepared with Water *1 cup/250g*	2
Asparagus, Cream of, Tinned *1 cup/250g*	8
Asparagus Cream of, Tinned (Tesco) *1 cup/250g*	11
Asparagus Soup, Main Meal (Marks & Spencer) *1 cup/250g*	12
Austrian, Cream of Herb (Knorr Soups of the World) *1 cup/250g*	7
Bean Soup, Mixed, Fresh (Safeway) *1 cup/250g*	11
Bean Soup, Tuscan (Marks & Spencer) *1 cup/250g*	3
Bean Soup, Tuscan (Waitrose) *1 cup/250g*	6
Bean with Frankfurters, Tinned *1 cup/250g*	7
Bean with Ham, Tinned *1 cup/250g*	9
Beef Soup (Heinz) *1 cup/250g*	5
Beef Broth, Big Soup (Heinz) *1 cup/250g*	2
Beef Broth, Cubed, Mixed with Water *1 cup/250g*	0
Beef Broth, Farmhouse Soup (Heinz) *1 cup/250g*	4
Beef Broth or Bouillon, Powder, Mixed with Water *1 cup/250g*	1
Beef Broth or Boullion, Tinned, Ready to Serve *1 cup/250g*	1
Beef & Country Vegetable Soup, Tinned (Heinz Weight Watchers) *1 cup/250g*	1
Beef, Tinned, Chunky, Ready to Serve *1 cup/250g*	5
Beef & Bacon Hotpot, Big Soup (Heinz) *1 cup/250g*	3
Beef & Mushroom, Tinned *1 cup/250g*	3
Beef & Mushroom, Tinned, Condensed *1 cup/250g*	6
Beef Noodle, Tinned, Mixed with Water *1 cup/250g*	3
Beef Noodle, Dehydrated, Mixed with Water *1 cup/250g*	1

Beef Noodle, Tinned, Condensed *1 cup/250g* 6
Beef, Spicy, & Tomato, Chunky, Canned (Tesco) *1 cup/250g* 5
Beef Stew *1 cup/250g* 18
Beef Stew & Dumpling (Birds Eye) *1 cup/250g* 11
Beef Stew & Dumpling, Microwave Ready Meal (Safeway) *1 cup/250g* 8
Beef Stew & Dumplings, Tinned Ready Meal (Tesco) *1 cup/250g* 8
Beef Stew & Dumplings, Frozen (Asda) *1 cup/250g* 10
Beef Stew & Dumplings, Frozen Ready Meal (Tesco) *1 cup/250g* 13
Beef & Vegetable Soup, Chunky (Waitrose) *1 cup/250g* 5
Beef & Vegetable, Big Soup (Heinz) *1 cup/250g* 2
Beef & Vegetable, Chunky, Tinned (Tesco) *1 cup/250g* 2
Beef & Vegetable, Chunky Soup (Marks & Spencer) *1 cup/250g* 6
Beef & Vegetable, Farmhouse Soup (Heinz) *1 cup/250g* 2
Big Soup, Chicken & Ham (Heinz) *1 cup/250g* 2
Big Soup, Chicken, Leek & Potato (Heinz) *1 cup/250g* 3
Big Soup, Chicken, Pasta & Vegetable (Heinz) *1 cup/250g* 1
Big Soup, Chicken & Vegetable (Heinz) *1 cup/250g* 2
Big Soup, Giant Beef Bolognese (Heinz) *1 cup/250g* 4
Big Soup, Giant Minestrone (Heinz) *1 cup/250g* 1
Big Soup, Lamb & Vegetables (Heinz) *1 cup/250g* 3
Big Soup, Lentil & Bacon with Vegetables (Heinz) *1 cup/250g* 2
Big Soup, Minted Lamb & Potato (Heinz) *1 cup/250g* 3
Big Soup, Pork & Vegetables (Heinz) *1 cup/250g* 1
Big Soup, Spicy Tomato with Beef Pasta Parcels (Heinz) *1 cup/250g* 5
Big Soup, Turkey & Vegetable & Cumberland Sausage (Heinz) *1 cup/250g* 4
Big Soup, Vegetarian Bolognese (Heinz) *1 cup/250g* 4
Black Bean, Tinned *1 cup/250g* 3
Bouillabaisse *1 cup/250g* 24
Broccoli & Cheddar, Fresh (Safeway) *1 cup/250g* 13
Broccoli & Stilton (Somerfield) *1 cup/250g* 11
Broccoli & Stilton (Waitrose) *1 cup/250g* 10
Broccoli & Stilton, Chilled (Tesco) *1 cup/250g* 13
Brunswick Stew, Home Made *1 cup/250g* 6

Carrot & Coriander Soup (Somerfield) *1 cup/250g*	4
Carrot & Coriander Soup, Chilled (Tesco) *1 cup/250g*	8
Carrot & Coriander Soup, Main Meal (Marks & Spencer) *1 cup/250g*	11
Carrot & Ginger Soup (Waitrose) *1 cup/250g*	3
Carrot & Lentil Soup, Tinned (Heinz Weight Watchers) *1 cup/250g*	0
Carrot & Orange *1 cup/250g*	1
Carrot & Orange (Somerfield) *1 cup/250g*	3
Carrot & Orange, Tinned (Tesco) *1 cup/250g*	10
Carrot & Orange, Fresh (Safeway) *1 cup/250g*	4
Carrot & Parsnip Soup (Marks & Spencer) *1 cup/250g*	6
Celery, Cream of (Heinz) *1 cup/250g*	8
Celery, Cream of, Dried, Prepared with Water *1 cup/250g*	2
Celery, Cream of, Tinned *1 cup/250g*	11
Chicken, Tinned (Heinz Weight Watchers) *1 cup/250g*	3
Chicken, Tinned, Chunky, Ready to Serve *1 cup/250g*	7
Chicken, Cup Soup (Knorr) *1 cup/250g*	10
Chicken Broth or Bouillon, Dehydrated, Prepared with Water *1 cup/250g*	1
Chicken Broth, Tinned, Condensed, Commercial *1 cup/250g*	3
Chicken Broth, Tinned, Prepared with an Equal Volume of Water, Commercial *1 cup/250g*	1
Chicken Broth, Cubes, Dehydrated, Prepared with Water *1 cup/250g*	0
Chicken, Cream of (Heinz) *1 cup/250g*	9
Chicken, Cream of (Knorr) *1 cup/250g*	2
Chicken, Cream of (Somerfield) *1 cup/250g*	11
Chicken, Cream of (Waitrose) *1 cup/250g*	9
Chicken, Cream of, Condensed Soup, as Served (Heinz) *1 cup/250g*	7
Chicken, Cream of, Dehydrated, Prepared with Water *1 cup/250g*	5
Chicken, Cream of, Prepared with an Equal Volume of Milk *1 cup/250g*	12
Chicken, Cream of, & Garlic Soup (Somerfield) *1 cup/250g*	8
Chicken, Cream of, & Mushroom Soup (Heinz) *1 cup/250g*	8
Chicken, Cream of, Tinned *1 cup/250g*	10

Chicken, Cream of, Tinned (Tesco) *1 cup/250g* 11
Chicken, Cream of, Tinned, Prepared with an Equal Volume of Water *1 cup/250g* 8
Chicken, Cream of, with Wine (Waitrose) *1 cup/250g* 9
Chicken & Broccoli (Knorr) *1 cup/250g* 1
Chicken & Corn, Reduced Calorie, Quick Soup (Waitrose) *1 cup/250g* 2
Chicken with Dumplings, Tinned, Prepared with an Equal Volume of Water *1 cup/250g* 6
Chicken & Garlic, Tinned (Tesco) *1 cup/250g* 17
Chicken Gumbo, Tinned, Prepared with an Equal Volume of Water *1 cup/250g* 1
Chicken & Leek, Condensed Soup, As Served (Heinz) *1 cup/250g* 5
Chicken & Leek, Cup Soup (Knorr) *1 cup/250g* 10
Chicken & Leek, Farmhouse (Knorr) *1 cup/250g* 3
Chicken & Lemon, Tinned (Tesco) *1 cup/250g* 11
Chicken & Mushroom, Tinned, Prepared with an Equal Volume of Water *1 cup/250g* 9
Chicken & Mushroom, Real Soup in Seconds, (Knorr) *1 cup/250g* 7
Chicken Noodle (Heinz) *1 cup/250g* 1
Chicken Noodle (Somerfield) *1 cup/250g* 10
Chicken Noodle, Tinned (Heinz Weight Watchers) *1 cup/250g* 0
Chicken Noodle, Tinned, Chunky, Ready to Serve *1 cup/250g* 6
Chicken Noodle, Tinned, Prepared with an Equal Volume of Water *1 cup/250g* 3
Chicken Noodle, Dehydrated, Prepared with Water *1 cup/250g* 1
Chicken Noodle, Super (Knorr *1 cup/250g* 1
Chicken Noodle, Super, Cup Soup (Knorr) *1 cup/250g* 1
Chicken Noodle, Super, Low Calorie Soup (Knorr) *1 cup/250g* 0
Chicken Noodle, Super, Real Soup in Seconds (Knorr) *1 cup/250g* 1
Chicken Noodle with Meatballs, Tinned, Chunky, Ready to Serve *1 cup/250g* 4
Chicken Rice, Tinned, Chunky, Ready to Serve *1 cup/250g* 3
Chicken & Sweetcorn, Malaysian (Knorr Soups of the World) *1 cup/250g* 3

Chicken Tikka Masala, Speciality, Tinned (Tesco) *1 cup/250g*	9
Chicken Vegetable, Tinned, Chunky, Ready to Serve *1 cup/250g*	5
Chicken Vegetable, Tinned, Prepared with an Equal Volume of Water *1 cup/250g*	3
Chicken & Vegetable, Chunky (Marks & Spencer) *1 cup/250g*	3
Chicken & Vegetable, Chunky (Waitrose) *1 cup/250g*	1
Chicken & Vegetable, Chunky, Tinned (Tesco) *1 cup/250g*	1
Chicken Vegetable, Dehydrated, Prepared with Water *1 cup/250g*	1
Chicken & Vegetable, Farmhouse (Heinz) *1 cup/250g*	3
Chicken & Vegetable, Grocery (Iceland) *1 cup/250g*	5
Chilli Beef, Tinned, Condensed *1 cup/250g*	13
Chilli Beef, Tinned, Mixed with Water *1 cup/250g*	7
Chinese Chicken (Knorr Soups of the World) *1 cup/250g*	1
Clam Chowder (Waitrose) *1 cup/250g*	6
Consommé *1 cup/250g*	0
Cornish Crab Bisque (Waitrose) *1 cup/250g*	11
Country Vegetable (Somerfield) *1 cup/250g*	2
Country Vegetable, Fresh (Safeway) *1 cup/250g*	2
Country Vegetable, Tinned (Heinz Weight Watchers) *1 cup/250g*	1
Crab, Tinned, Ready to Serve *1 cup/250g*	2
Fish Chowder (Marks & Spencer) *1 cup/250g*	9
Gazpacho *1 cup/250g*	9
Gazpacho, Tinned, Ready to Serve *1 cup/250g*	2
Goulash *1 cup/250g*	18
Irish Stew *1 cup/250g*	19
Irish Stew, Main Meal (Marks & Spencer) *1 cup/250g*	7
Lamb & Vegetable, Farmhouse (Heinz) *1 cup/250g*	1
Leek, Dehydrated, Prepared with Water *1 cup/250g*	2
Leek & Potato (Somerfield) *1 cup/250g*	10
Leek & Potato, Chilled (Tesco) *1 cup/250g*	9
Leek & Potato, Main Meal (Marks & Spencer) *1 cup/250g*	23
Lentil, Home Made *1 cup/250g*	12
Lentil, Tinned *1 cup/250g*	1
Lentil, Wholesoup (Heinz) *1 cup/250g*	1
Lentil & Bacon, (Marks & Spencer) *1 cup/250g*	8
Lentil & Bacon (Somerfield) *1 cup/250g*	2

Lentil & Bacon (Waitrose) *1 cup/250g*	3
Lentil & Bacon, Tinned (Tesco) *1 cup/250g*	2
Lentil & Cashew, Spicy (Waitrose) *1 cup/250g*	9
Lentil with Ham, Tinned, Ready to Serve *1 cup/250g*	3
Lettuce & Watercress Soup (Somerfield) *1 cup/250g*	8
Lobster Bisque (Marks & Spencer) *1 cup/250g*	7
Lobster Bisque (Waitrose) *1 cup/250g*	8
Minestrone (Heinz) *1 cup/250g*	2
Minestrone (Knorr) *1 cup/250g*	1
Minestrone (Marks & Spencer) *1 cup/250g*	2
Minestrone (Somerfield) *1 cup/250g*	2
Minestrone (Waitrose) *1 cup/250g*	2
Minestrone, Chunky, Tinned (Tesco) *1 cup/250g*	2
Minestrone, Dehydrated, Prepared with Water *1 cup/250g*	2
Minestrone, Home Made *1 cup/250g*	8
Minestrone, Tinned *1 cup/250g*	2
Minestrone, Tinned (Heinz Weight Watchers) *1 cup/250g*	1
Minestrone, Tinned (Tesco) *1 cup/250g*	2
Minestrone, Tinned, Chunky, Ready to Serve *1 cup/250g*	3
Minestrone, Tinned, Prepared with an Equal Volume of Water *1 cup/250g*	3
Minestrone, Special Cup Soup (Somerfield) *1 cup/250g*	19
Mulligatawny *1 cup/250g*	17
Mulligatawny (Waitrose) *1 cup/250g*	5
Mulligatawny Beef Curry Soup (Heinz) *1 cup/250g*	7
Mushroom, Tinned (Heinz Weight Watchers) *1 cup/250g*	2
Mushroom, Cream of (Heinz) *1 cup/250g*	7
Mushroom, Cream of (Somerfield) *1 cup/250g*	6
Mushroom, Cream of (Waitrose) *1 cup/250g*	9
Mushroom, Cream of, Tinned (Tesco) *1 cup/250g*	9
Mushroom, Cream of, Tinned, Prepared with an Equal Volume of Milk *1 cup/250g*	14
Mushroom, Cream of, Tinned, Prepared with an Equal Volume of Water *1 cup/250g*	9
Mushroom, Cream of, Condensed Soup, as Served (Heinz) *1 cup/250g*	7
Mushroom, Creamy, Fresh (Safeway) *1 cup/250g*	12

Mushroom & Barley, Tinned, Prepared with an Equal Volume of Water *1 cup/250g* 2

Mushroom with Beef Stock, Tinned *1 cup/250g* 4

Mushroom with Beef Stock, Tinned, Condensed *1 cup/250g* 8

Mushroom & Garlic, Chilled (Tesco) *1 cup/250g* 12

Mushroom & Garlic, French, (Knorr Soups of the World) *1 cup/250g* 3

Mushroom & Ham, Condensed, as Served (Heinz) *1 cup/250g* 6

Onion, Tinned, Prepared with an Equal Volume of Water *1 cup/250g* 2

Onion, Cream of, Tinned, Prepared with an Equal Volume of Milk *1 cup/250g* 9

Onion, Cream of, Tinned, Prepared with an Equal Volume of Water *1 cup/250g* 5

Onion, Dehydragted, Prepared with Water *1 cup/250g* 1

Onion, French *1 cup/250g* 5

Onion, French (Knorr) *1 cup/250g* 1

Onion, French (Waitrose) *1 cup/250g* 1

Onion, French, Tinned (Heinz Weight Watchers *1 cup/250g* 1

Onion, French, with Cider (Waitrose) *1 cup/250g* 1

Onion, Fresh (Waitrose) *1 cup/250g* 3

Oxtail (Knorr) *1 cup/250g* 1

Oxtail (Somerfield) *1 cup/250g* 3

Oxtail (Waitrose) *1 cup/250g* 2

Oxtail, Tinned *1 cup/250g* 4

Oxtail, Tinned (Heinz) *1 cup/250g* 3

Oxtail, Tinned (Tesco) *1 cup/250g* 2

Oxtail, Dehydrated, Prepared with Water *1 cup/250g* 3

Oxtail & Onion, Condensed, as Served (Heinz) *1 cup/250g* 2

Parsnip, Spicy (Somerfield) *1 cup/250g* 5

Parsnip & Almond (Waitrose) *1 cup/250g* 13

Pasta e Fagioli, Home Prepared *1 cup/250g* 5

Pea, Green, Tinned, Prepared with an Equal Volume of Milk *1 cup/250g* 7

Pea, Green, Tinned, Prepared with an Equal Volume of Water *1 cup/250g* 3

Pea, Green, Mix, Dehydrated, Prepared with Water *1 cup/250g* 1

Pea & Ham *1 cup/250g* 5
Pea with Ham, Cup Soup (Knorr) *1 cup/250g* 7
Pea & Ham (Marks & Spencer) *1 cup/250g* 4
Pea & Ham (Somerfield) *1 cup/250g* 6
Pea & Ham (Waitrose) *1 cup/250g* 2
Pea & Ham, Farmhouse (Heinz) *1 cup/250g* 1
Pea & Ham, Tinned (Tesco) *1 cup/250g* 2
Pea with Ham Flavour (Knorr) *1 cup/250g* 1
Pea & Mint, Main Meal (Marks & Spencer) *1 cup/250g* 0
Pepperpot, Tinned, Condensed, Commercial *1 cup/250g* 9
Potato & Leek *1 cup/250g* 7
Potato & Leek, Farmhouse (Heinz) *1 cup/250g* 2
Quicksoup, Low Calorie (Waitrose) *1 cup/250g* 1
Scotch Broth *1 cup/250g* 9
Scotch Broth (Waitrose) *1 cup/250g* 6
Scotch Broth, Farmhouse (Heinz) *1 cup/250g* 2
Scotch Broth, Tinned (Tesco) *1 cup/250g* 2
Scotch Broth, Tinned, Prepared with an Equal Volume of Water *1 cup/250g* 3
Shrimp, Cream of, Tinned, Prepared with an Equal Volume of Milk *1 cup/250g* 9
Shrimp, Cream of, Tinned, Prepared with an Equal Volume of Water *1 cup/250g* 5
Soupe Paysanne, French (Knorr Soups of the World) *1 cup/250g* 1
Split Pea & Lentil Soup, Tinned (Heinz) *1 cup/250g* 1
Split Pea with Ham, Tinned, Chunky, Ready to Serve *1 cup/250g* 4
Split Pea with Ham, Tinned, Prepared with an Equal Volume of Water *1 cup/250g* 4
Stockpot, Tinned, Condensed *1 cup/250g* 8
Stockpot, Tinned, Prepared with an Equal Volume of Water *1 cup/250g* 4
Tomato, Tinned (Heinz Weight Watchers) *1 cup/250g* 1
Tomato, Tinned, Prepared with an Equal Volume of Milk *1 cup/250g* 6
Tomato, Tinned, Prepared with an Equal Volume of Water *1 cup/250g* 2
Tomato, Country Soup (Waitrose) *1 cup/250g* 3

Tomato, Cream of (Heinz) *1 cup/250g*	9
Tomato, Cream of (Knorr) *1 cup/250g*	3
Tomato, Cream of (Waitrose) *1 cup/250g*	9
Tomato, Cream of, Tinned *1 cup/250g*	8
Tomato, Cream of, Tinned (Tesco) *1 cup/250g*	10
Tomato, Cream of, Condensed *1 cup/250g*	9
Tomato, Cream of, & Basil (Somerfield) *1 cup/250g*	13
Tomato, Cream of, & Peppers (Waitrose) *1 cup/250g*	7
Tomato, Cup Soup (Knorr) *1 cup/250g*	4
Tomato, Dehydrated, Prepared with Water *1 cup/250g*	2
Tomato, Dried *1 cup/250g*	3
Tomato, Italian Style, Fresh (Safeway) *1 cup/250g*	16
Tomato, Mediterranean, Reduced Calorie, Quick Soup (Waitrose) *1 cup/250g*	2
Tomato & Basil, Chilled (Tesco) *1 cup/250g*	5
Tomato with Basil, Condensed, as Served (Heinz) *1 cup/250g*	6
Tomato & Basil, Main Meal (Marks & Spencer) *1 cup/250g*	2
Tomato & Beef with Noodle, Tinned *1 cup/250g*	4
Tomato & Coconut, Chilled (Tesco) *1 cup/250g*	15
Tomato & Herb (Marks & Spencer) *1 cup/250g*	10
Tomato & Lentil (Marks & Spencer) *1 cup/250g*	1
Tomato & Lentil, Wholesoup (Heinz) *1 cup/250g*	1
Tomato & Pasta, Italian, Chunky, Tinned (Tesco) *1 cup/250g*	2
Tomato & Rice, Tinned, Condensed, Commercial *1 cup/250g*	5
Tomato & Vegetable (Somerfield) *1 cup/250g*	11
Tomato & Vegetable, Dehydrated, Prepared with Water *1 cup/250g*	1
Tomato & Vegetable, Mediterranean, Tinned (Heinz Weight Watchers) *1 cup/250g*	1
Tuna & Sweetcorn (Somerfield) *1 cup/250g*	2
Turkey, Chunky, Ready to Serve *1 cup/250g*	5
Vegetable (Heinz) *1 cup/250g*	2
Vegetable (Somerfield) *1 cup/250g*	2
Vegetable (Waitrose) *1 cup/250g*	0
Vegetable, Tinned *1 cup/250g*	2
Vegetable, Tinned (Heinz Weight Watchers) *1 cup/250g*	1
Vegetable, Tinned (Tesco) *1 cup/250g*	2

Vegetable, Tinned, Chunky, Ready to Serve *1 cup/250g*	4
Vegetable, Cream of, Dehydrated, Prepared with Water *1 cup/250g*	5
Vegetable, Cream of, Real Soup in Seconds (Knorr) *1 cup/250g*	7
Vegetable, Crofter's Thick (Knorr) *1 cup/250g*	1
Vegetable, Extra Thick, Tinned (Tesco) *1 cup/250g*	2
Vegetable, Florida Spring (Knorr) *1 cup/250g*	1
Vegetable, Golden (Knorr) *1 cup/250g*	2
Vegetable, Golden, Cup Soup (Knorr) *1 cup/250g*	9
Vegetable, Golden, (Low Calorie Knorr) *1 cup/250g*	0
Vegetables, Golden, Reduced Calorie, Quick Soup (Waitrose) *1 cup/250g*	2
Vegetable, Grocery (Iceland) *1 cup/250g*	3
Vegetable, Home Made *1 cup/250g*	10
Vegetable Korma, Indian, Tinned (Tesco) *1 cup/250g*	12
Vegetable, Spring (Heinz) *1 cup/250g*	1
Vegetable, Spring (Somerfield) *1 cup/250g*	8
Vegetable, Spring, Low Calorie, (Knorr) *1 cup/250g*	0
Vegetable, Thick (Somerfield) *1 cup/250g*	6
Vegetable, Thick Country, with Ham, Big Soup (Heinz) *1 cup/250g*	1
Vegetable, Wholesoup, Country (Heinz) *1 cup/250g*	1
Vegetable, Wholesoup, Winter (Heinz) *1 cup/250g*	1
Vegetable, Winter (Marks & Spencer) *1 cup/250g*	6
Vegetable, Winter, Tinned (Heinz Weight Watchers) *1 cup/250g*	0
Vegetable & Beef Broth, Tinned *1 cup/250g*	2
Vegetable & Beef, Dehydrated, Mixed with Water *1 cup/250g*	1
Vegetable with Lentils & Beef, Scottish (Heinz) *1 cup/250g*	2
Watercress, Cream of (Waitrose) *1 cup/250g*	6

TURKEY

NOTE: The standard serving size in this section is 110g/4oz. If you wish to consume more or less than this amount (e.g. if you are going to consume a pack of food whose weight differs from the standard

serving size) use the conversion tables on page 386 to calculate the new amount of fat in the food.

Breast, Basted (Somerfield) *serving 110g/4oz*	5
Breast, Boned & Rolled (Waitrose) *serving 110g/4oz*	2
Breast, Cold Meats (Tesco) *serving 110g/4oz*	4
Breast, Cooked 80% (Somerfield) *serving 110g/4oz*	3
Breast, Cooked, Norfolk, Roll, Slices (Bernard Matthews) *serving 110g/4oz*	1
Breast, Cooked, Norfolk, Smoked, Slices (Bernard Matthews) *serving 110g/4oz*	1
Breast, Cooked, Wafer Thin, Smoked (Bernard Matthews) *serving 110g/4oz*	1
Breast, Cooked with Black Pepper (Somerfield) *serving 110g/4oz*	2
Breast, Cooked with Stuffing, Deli (Asda) *serving 110g/4oz*	2
Breast, Cured, Cold Meats (Tesco) *serving 110g/4oz*	1
Breast, Cured, Delicatessen (Marks & Spencer) *serving 110g/4oz*	3
Breast, Deli (Asda) *serving 110g/4oz*	2
Breast, Fillets (Bernard Matthews) *serving 110g/4oz*	2
Breast, For Pies (Waitrose) *serving 110g/4oz*	1
Breast, Golden, Roasted (Bernard Matthews) *serving 110g/4oz*	2
Breast, Honey Roast (Somerfield) *serving 110g/4oz*	4
Breast, Honey Roast, Norfolk, Slices (Bernard Matthews) *serving 110g/4oz*	1
Breast, Honey Roasted, Prepacked (Asda) *serving 110g/4oz*	1
Breast, Italian Style, Cooked, Deli (Asda) *serving 110g/4oz*	2
Breast, Lemon Pepper (Waitrose) *serving 110g/4oz*	1
Breast, Meat *serving 110g/4oz*	2
Breast, Meat & Skin, Roasted *serving 110g/4oz*	8
Breast, Oak Smoked, Deli (Asda) *serving 110g/4oz*	4
Breast, Prebasted, Meat & Skin, Roasted *serving 110g/4oz*	4
Breast, Premium, Cooked, Norfolk, Slices (Bernard Matthews) *serving 110g/4oz*	1
Breast, Premium, Cooked, Norfolk, Garlic & Herb Slices (Bernard Matthews) *serving 110g/4oz*	1
Breast, Premium, Cooked, Norfolk Sage & Onion Slices (Bernard Matthews) *serving 110g/4oz*	2

Breast, Premium, Deli (Asda) *serving 110g/4oz*	2
Breast, Premium Roast (Somerfield) *serving 110g/4oz*	1
Breast, Roast (Waitrose) *serving 110g/4oz*	1
Breast, Roast (Bernard Matthews) *serving 110g/4oz*	4
Breast, Roast Joint, Cold Meats (Tesco) *serving 110g/4oz*	2
Breast, Roast, Sliced, Cold Meats (Tesco) *serving 110g/4oz*	2
Breast, Roasted, Prepacked (Asda) *serving 110g/4oz*	1
Breast, Roll (Somerfield) *serving 110g/4oz*	1
Breast, Sage & Onion Stuffing, Deli (Asda) *serving 110g/4oz*	0
Breast, Smoked (Waitrose) *serving 110g/4oz*	1
Breast, Smoked, Deli (Asda) *serving 110g/4oz*	2
Breast, Smoked, Prepacked (Asda) *serving 110g/4oz*	1
Breast, Steaks (Marks & Spencer) *serving 110g/4oz*	2
Breast, Steaks (Waitrose) *serving 110g/4oz*	1
Breast, Steaks, in Crispy Crumb, Frozen (Bernard Matthews) *serving 110g/4oz*	14
Breast, Stuffed, Delicatessen (Marks & Spencer) *serving 110g/4oz*	5
Breast, Tandoori Style, Slices (Bernard Matthews) *serving 110g/4oz*	2
Breast, Wafer Thin, Chinese Style (Bernard Matthews) *serving 110g/4oz*	2
Breast, with Wings (Waitrose) *serving 110g/4oz*	7
Burgers in Crispy Crumb, Frozen (Bernard Matthews) *serving 110g/4oz*	24
Butter Basted (Waitrose) *serving 110g/4oz*	10
Butter Basted, Fresh (Waitrose) *serving 110g/4oz*	10
Butter Basted, Frozen (Waitrose) *serving 110g/4oz*	4
Butter Basted, Stuffed (Waitrose) *serving 110g/4oz*	9
Butter Basted, Whole (Tesco) *serving 110g/4oz*	10
Casserole (Crosse & Blackwell) *serving 110g/4oz*	10
Cheeseburgers in Crispy Breadcrumbs (Somerfield) *serving 110g/4oz*	18
Dark Meat, Meat & Skin, Roasted *serving 110g/4oz*	13
Dinner, Sliced, Frozen, Oven Baked (Iceland) *serving 110g/4oz*	1
Dino Eggs, Frozen (Bernard Matthews) *serving 110g/4oz*	17
Escalopes (Somerfield) *serving 110g/4oz*	10

Escalopes, Breaded (Somerfield) *serving 110g/4oz* 11
Escalopes, Chinese, Fresh (Iceland) *serving 110g/4oz* 1
Escalopes & Garlic Mushroom Sauce (Somerfield) *serving 110g/4oz* 3
Escalopes & Korma Sauce (Somerfield) *serving 110g/4oz* 11
Free Range, Frozen (Waitrose) *serving 110g/4oz* 10
Fresh Farmhouse (Waitrose) *serving 110g/4oz* 10
Giblets, Simmered, with some Giblet Fat *serving 110g/4oz* 6
Golden Drummers, Frozen (Bernard Matthews) *serving 110g/4oz* 20
Grills, Frozen (Iceland) *serving 110g/4oz* 15
Grillsteaks, Frozen, Grilled (Iceland) *serving 110g/4oz* 11
Ham, Cooked, Norfolk, Wafer Thin (Bernard Matthews) *serving 110g/4oz* 4
Ham, Cooked, Norfolk, with Honey, Slices (Bernard Matthews) *serving 110g/4oz* 4
Ham, Cooked, Wafer Thin, Bar B Que (Bernard Matthews) *serving 110g/4oz* 7
Ham, Cooked, Wafer Thin, Indian Style (Bernard Matthews) *serving 110g/4oz* 6
Ham Pies (Bernard Matthews) *serving 110g/4oz* 30
Hand Carved, Cooked & Roasted, on the Bone, Deli (Asda) *serving 110g/4oz* 6
Honey Roast, on the Bone (Somerfield) *serving 110g/4oz* 6
Joint, Butter Basted (Marks & Spencer) *serving 110g/4oz* 4
Joint, Sage & Onion (Marks & Spencer) *serving 110g/4oz* 5
Kebabs (Waitrose) *serving 110g/4oz* 3
Kebabs in Marinade (Waitrose) *serving 110g/4oz* 7
Kievs, Jumbo, Frozen (Iceland) *serving 110g/4oz* 23
Lasagne (Marks & Spencer) *serving 110g/4oz* 5
Leg, Meat & Skin, Roasted *serving 110g/4oz* 11
Leg Roast (Bernard Matthews *serving 110g/4oz* 8
Light Meat, Meat & Skin, Roasted *serving 110g/4oz* 9
Liver, Simmered *serving 110g/4oz* 7
Meat Only, Roasted *serving 110g/4oz* 5
Meat & Skin, Roasted *serving 110g/4oz* 11
Mignon Steaks (Waitrose) *serving 110g/4oz* 1

Mince, Extra Lean, Frozen, Roast (Iceland) *serving 110g/4oz* 4
Minced, Frozen (Iceland) *serving 110g/4oz* 4
Neck Meat Only, Simmered *serving 110g/4oz* 8
Patties, Breaded, Battered, Fried *serving 110g/4oz* 20
Peppered (Waitrose) *serving 110g/4oz* 2
Pie with Herbs, Large, Family Sized (Bernard Matthews) *serving 110g/4oz* 25
Platter, Luxury, Frozen, Microwaved (Iceland) *serving 110g/4oz* 4
Platter, Roast (Birds Eye) *serving 110g/4oz* 3
Roll, Cooked, Dinosaur Slices (Bernard Matthews) *serving 110g/4oz* 11
Saddle, Cooked (Waitrose) *serving 110g/4oz* 2
Salami (Bernard Matthews) *serving 110g/4oz* 11
Skin Only, Roasted *serving 110g/4oz* 44
Smoked, Premium (Waitrose) *serving 110g/4oz* 4
Spiced, Cooked, Norfolk, Wafer Thin (Bernard Matthews) *serving 110g/4oz* 6
Standard, Frozen (Waitrose) *serving 110g/4oz* 4
Stir Fry (Waitrose) *serving 110g/4oz* 1
Stir Fry in Marinade (Waitrose) *serving 110g/4oz* 1
Stroganoff, Main Meal (Marks & Spencer) *serving 110g/4oz* 6
Thigh Chops, Fresh (Iceland) *serving 110g/4oz* 5
Thigh Joint (Somerfield) *serving 110g/4oz* 11
Thigh, Mince (Waitrose) *serving 110g/4oz* 4
Thigh, Prebasted, Meat & Skin, Roasted *serving 110g/4oz* 9
Thigh Steaks (Waitrose) *serving 110g/4oz* 14
Thigh, Tenderised (Waitrose) *serving 110g/4oz* 5
Tikka Masala, Wafer Thin (Bernard Matthews) *serving 110g/4oz* 1
Tripledeckers, Frozen (Bernard Matthews) *serving 110g/4oz* 18
Turkey & Bacon Loaf (Somerfield) *serving 110g/4oz* 10
Turkey & Bacon Loaf, Chilled, Oven Baked (Iceland) *serving 110g/4oz* 10
Turkey & Bacon Loaf, Main Meal (Marks & Spencer) *serving 110g/4oz* 8
Turkey & Creamy Mushroom au Gratin (Somerfield) *serving 110g/4oz* 5

Turkey Fat *serving 110g/4oz* 110
Turkey & Ham, Main Meal (Marks & Spencer) *serving 110g/4oz* 3
Turkey Jetters, Frozen (Bernard Matthews) *serving 110g/4oz* 19
Turkey, Leek & Ham au Gratins (Somerfield) *serving 110g/4oz* 5
Turkey Sticks, Breaded, Battered, Fried *serving 110g/4oz* 19
Turkistix, Frozen (Bernard Matthews) *serving 110g/4oz* 17
Wafer, Chargrilled, Delicatessen (Marks & Spencer) *serving 110g/4oz* 2
Wafer Thin, Cooked (Bernard Matthews) *serving 110g/4oz* 7
Wafer Thin, Delicatessen (Marks & Spencer) *serving 110g/4oz* 2
Wafer Thin, Oak Smoked, Deli (Asda) *serving 110g/4oz* 2
Wafer Thin, Smoked (Waitrose) *serving 110g/4oz* 1
Wafer Thin, Smoked, Chilled (Iceland) *serving 110g/4oz* 1
Wafer Thin, Smoked, Cold Meats (Tesco) *serving 110g/4oz* 1
Wafer Thin Turkey & Ham, Deli (Asda) *serving 110g/4oz* 3
Whole, Fresh (Waitrose) *serving 110g/4oz* 6
Whole, Standard Frozen (Waitrose) *serving 110g/4oz* 6
Wing, Meat & Skin, Roasted *serving 110g/4oz* 14

VEGETABLES & VEGETABLE DISHES

NOTE: The standard serving size in this section is 110g/4oz. If you wish to consume more or less than this amount (e.g. if you are going to consume a pack of food whose weight differs from the standard serving size) use the conversion tables on page 386 to calculate the new amount of fat in the food.

Herbs and Spices are included in this section for the sake of completeness, but you should note that the standard serving size in this section (110g/4oz) is considerably larger than the usual amount included in recipes. As a rough guide, one tablespoon of seeds, such as dill or cumin, weighs approximately 6g, and the fat content of this serving is minimal.

Ackee, Tinned *serving 110g/4oz* 17
Agar, Soaked & Drained *serving 110g/4oz* 0

Alfalfa Sprouts, Raw *serving 110g/4oz*	1
Allspice, Ground *serving 110g/4oz*	10
Almond Curry *serving 110g/4oz*	37
Aloo Tikkis (Waitrose) *serving 110g/4oz*	14
Alphabites (Birds Eye) *serving 110g/4oz*	7
Amaranth Leaves, Raw *serving 110g/4oz*	0
Anise Seed *serving 110g/4oz*	17
Artichoke Hearts (Waitrose) *serving 110g/4oz*	0
Artichoke, Jerusalem *serving 110g/4oz*	0
Artichokes, Globe or French, Boiled *serving 110g/4oz*	1
Asparagus, Boiled *serving 110g/4oz*	1
Asparagus, Canadian, Green (Waitrose) *serving 110g/4oz*	0
Asparagus, Cuts & Tips (Waitrose) *serving 110g/4oz*	1
Asparagus, Large Spears (Waitrose) *serving 110g/4oz*	0
Aubergine, Raw *serving 110g/4oz*	0
Aubergine, Baked, Vegetable Meal (Marks & Spencer) *serving 110g/4oz*	13
Aubergine, Boiled *serving 110g/4oz*	0
Aubergine Curry *serving 110g/4oz*	11
Aubergine, Fried in Corn Oil *serving 110g/4oz*	35
Aubergine Pakora Bhaji *serving 110g/4oz*	25
Aubergine, Pea, Potato & Cauliflower Bhaji *serving 110g/4oz*	3
Aubergine & Potato Bhaji *serving 110g/4oz*	10
Aubergine, Ricotta & Filo, Vegetable Meal (Marks & Spencer) *serving 110g/4oz*	15
Aubergine, Roasted (Waitrose) *serving 110g/4oz*	28
Aubergine Stuffed with Lentils & Vegetables *serving 110g/4oz*	5
Aubergine Stuffed with Rice *serving 110g/4oz*	3
Aubergine Stuffed with Vegetables & Cheese Topping *serving 110g/4oz*	11
Avocado (Waitrose) *serving 110g/4oz*	24
Balti Vegetable Masala Curry Pot (Asda) *serving 110g/4oz*	5
Bamboo Shoots, Boiled *serving 110g/4oz*	0
Bamboo Shoots, Tinned *serving 110g/4oz*	0
Basil, Fresh *serving 110g/4oz*	1
Basil, Ground *serving 110g/4oz*	4
Bay Leaf, Dried *serving 110g/4oz*	9

Bean & Mixed Vegetable Casserole *serving 110g/4oz*	1
Bean & Root Vegetable Casserole *serving 110g/4oz*	1
Bean Tostada, Chilled Ready Meal (Tesco) *serving 110g/4oz*	11
Beans: *see under* Beans & Lentils	
Beet Greens, Boiled *serving 110g/4oz*	0
Beetroot, Baby, Pickled (Waitrose) *serving 110g/4oz*	0
Beetroot, Boiled *serving 110g/4oz*	0
Beetroot, Crinkle Cut (Tesco) *serving 110g/4oz*	0
Beetroot, Raw or Pickled *serving 110g/4oz*	0
Beetroot, Sweet, Pickled, Crinkle Cut, Healthy Selection (Somerfield) *serving 110g/4oz*	0
Beetroot, Sweet, Pickled, Sliced, Healthy Selection (Somerfield) *serving 110g/4oz*	0
Beetroot, Sweet, Pickled, Whole Baby, Healthy Selection (Somerfield) *serving 110g/4oz*	0
Beetroot, Tinned *serving 110g/4oz*	0
Black Eye Bean Curry *serving 110g/4oz*	5
Borage *serving 110g/4oz*	1
Broccoli, Raw *serving 110g/4oz*	0
Broccoli, Boiled *serving 110g/4oz*	0
Broccoli, Courgette & Peppers, Vegetable Meal (Marks & Spencer) *serving 110g/4oz*	5
Broccoli Flower Clusters, Raw *serving 110g/4oz*	0
Broccoli & Garlic Potato Bake (Safeway) *serving 110g/4oz*	12
Broccoli in Cheese Sauce, Made with Semi-Skimmed Milk *serving 110g/4oz*	8
Broccoli in Cheese Sauce, Made with Skimmed Milk *serving 110g/4oz*	8
Broccoli in Cheese Sauce, Made with Whole Milk *serving 110g/4oz*	9
Broccoli in Cream Sauce, Vegetable Meal (Marks & Spencer) *serving 110g/4oz*	7
Broccoli Mornay (Somerfield) *serving 110g/4oz*	4
Broccoli Mornay, Chilled Ready Meal (Safeway) *serving 110g/4oz*	21
Broccoli, Purple, Sprouting, Raw *serving 110g/4oz*	1
Broccoli, Purple, Sprouting, Boiled *serving 110g/4oz*	1

Broccoli, Select, Vegetable Meal (Marks & Spencer) *serving 110g/4oz* 5
Brussels Sprouts, Raw *serving 110g/4oz* 0
Brussels Sprouts, Boiled *serving 110g/4oz* 1
Bubble & Squeak, Tinned Ready Meal (Tesco) *serving 110g/4oz* 5
Bubble & Squeak, Fried *serving 110g/4oz* 10
Bubble & Squeak, Frozen (Iceland) *serving 110g/4oz* 5
Burdock Root, Raw *serving 110g/4oz* 0
Burdock Root, Boiled *serving 110g/4oz* 0
Butterbur, Boiled *serving 110g/4oz* 0
Cabbage, Raw *serving 110g/4oz* 0
Cabbage Bhaji *serving 110g/4oz* 5
Cabbage, Boiled *serving 110g/4oz* 0
Cabbage & Caraway, Crunchy (Waitrose) *serving 110g/4oz* 5
Cabbage, Chopped (Somerfield) *serving 110g/4oz* 1
Cabbage Curry *serving 110g/4oz* 6
Cabbage, Cut Green, Frozen (Asda) *serving 110g/4oz* 1
Cabbage Greens, Vegetable Meal (Marks & Spencer) *serving 110g/4oz* 14
Cabbage & Pea Bhaji *serving 110g/4oz* 16
Cabbage, Pickled Red, in Vinegar, Healthy Selection (Somerfield) *serving 110g/4oz* 0
Cabbage, Red Cooked with Apple *serving 110g/4oz* 3
Cabbage & Spinach Bhaji *serving 110g/4oz* 19
Cantonese Vegetables with Noodle(Waitrose) *serving 110g/4oz* 4
Caraway Seed *serving 110g/4oz* 16
Cardamon, Ground *serving 110g/4oz* 7
Cardoon, Raw or Cooked *serving 110g/4oz* 0
Carrot, Raw *serving 110g/4oz* 0
Carrot, Baby, Raw *serving 110g/4oz* 1
Carrots, Baby, in Water (Waitrose) *serving 110g/4oz* 0
Carrots, Chocolate Flavoured Frozen (Iceland) *serving 110g/4oz* 0
Carrot, Cooked *serving 110g/4oz* 0
Carrot, Frozen *serving 110g/4oz* 0
Carrot Juice *serving 110g/4oz* 0
Carrot Juice, Tinned *serving 110g/4oz* 0
Carrots, Julienne (Somerfield) *serving 110g/4oz* 0

Carrot & Parsnip Slices, Savoury Snack (Marks & Spencer) *serving 110g/4oz* 20
Carrot, Potato & Pea Bhaji *serving 110g/4oz* 7
Carrot & Swede Baton Mix (Somerfield) *serving 110g/4oz* 0
Carrot, Tinned *serving 110g/4oz* 0
Cassava, Baked & Steamed *serving 110g/4oz* 0
Cauliflower, Raw *serving 110g/4oz* 0
Cauliflower Bhaji *serving 110g/4oz* 23
Cauliflower, Boiled in Salted Water *serving 110g/4oz* 1
Cauliflower & Broccoli Floret Mix (Somerfield) *serving 110g/4oz* 1
Cauliflower, Broccoli & Gruyere Bake, Chilled Ready Meal (Safeway) *serving 110g/4oz* 37
Cauliflower Cheese (Birds Eye) *serving 110g/4oz* 8
Cauliflower Cheese (Somerfield) *serving 110g/4oz* 5
Cauliflower Cheese, 95% Fat Free, Vegetable Meal (Marks & Spencer) *serving 110g/4oz* 1
Cauliflower Cheese, Chilled Ready Meal (Safeway) *serving 110g/4oz* 6
Cauliflower Cheese, Chilled Ready Meal (Tesco) *serving 110g/4oz* 9
Cauliflower Cheese, Large, Vegetable Meal (Marks & Spencer) *serving 110g/4oz* 7
Cauliflower Cheese, Made with Whole Milk *serving 110g/4oz* 8
Cauliflower, Cheese & Onion Flavoured, Frozen (Iceland) *serving 110g/4oz* 1
Cauliflower Cheese Quarter Pounders, Country Club Cuisine (Birds Eye) *serving 110g/4oz* 14
Cauliflower Cheese with Semi-Skimmed/Skimmed Milk *serving 110g/4oz* 7
Cauliflower Curry, Gobi Aloo Sag *serving 110g/4oz* 8
Cauliflower Florets, Frozen (Asda) *serving 110g/4oz* 1
Cauliflower Florets, Frozen (Iceland) *serving 110g/4oz* 1
Cauliflower Florets (Waitrose) *serving 110g/4oz* 1
Cauliflower with Onions & Chilli Pepper *serving 110g/4oz* 4
Cauliflower & Potato Bhaji *serving 110g/4oz* 8
Cauliflower & Potato Curry *serving 110g/4oz* 3

Cauliflower Potato & Pea Bhaji with Vegetable Oil *serving 110g/4oz* 15
Cauliflower in White Sauce, Made with Semi-Skimmed Milk *serving 110g/4oz* 4
Cauliflower in White Sauce, Made with Whole Milk *serving 110g/4oz* 4
Celeriac, Raw *serving 110g/4oz* 0
Celery, Raw *serving 110g/4oz* 0
Celery Hearts (Waitrose) *serving 110g/4oz* 0
Celery Seed *serving 110g/4oz* 28
Celtuce, Raw *serving 110g/4oz* 0
Chard, Swiss, Raw *serving 110g/4oz* 0
Chard, Swiss, Boiled *serving 110g/4oz* 0
Chayote Fruit, Boiled *serving 110g/4oz* 1
Chervil, Dried *serving 110g/4oz* 4
Chicory, Raw *serving 110g/4oz* 1
Chilli Powder *serving 110g/4oz* 18
Chips: *see under* Chips
Chives, Freeze Dried *serving 110g/4oz* 4
Chives, Raw *serving 110g/4oz* 1
Cinnamon, Ground *serving 110g/4oz* 4
Cloves, Ground *serving 110g/4oz* 22
Collards, Raw *serving 110g/4oz* 0
Collards, Cooked, Boiled, Drained, with Salt *serving 110g/4oz* 0
Coriander, Raw *serving 110g/4oz* 1
Coriander Leaf, Dried *serving 110g/4oz* 5
Coriander Seed *serving 110g/4oz* 20
Corn on the Cob (Somerfield) *serving 110g/4oz* 2
Corn Cobs (Waitrose) *serving 110g/4oz* 1
Corn on the Cob with Butter *serving 110g/4oz* 3
Corn Cobs, Baby (Waitrose) *serving 110g/4oz* 1
Corn, Cream Style (Waitrose) *serving 110g/4oz* 1
Corn Fritters, Fried in Vegetable Oil *serving 110g/4oz* 17
Corn with Red & Green Peppers, Tinned *serving 110g/4oz* 1
Corn, Sweet, Crisp/Natural (Waitrose) *serving 110g/4oz* 1
Corn, Sweet, White, Tinned in Brine, Drained, Solids *serving 110g/4oz* 1

Corn, Sweet, Yellow, Boiled *serving 110g/4oz* 1
Corn, Sweet, Yellow, Frozen, Kernels, Cut of Cob, Boiled *serving 110g/4oz* 0
Corn, Sweet, Yellow, Tinned *serving 110g/4oz* 1
Corn, Sweet, Yellow, Tinned, Cream Style *serving 110g/4oz* 0
Cornichons in Brine (Waitrose) *serving 110g/4oz* 0
Cornsalad, Raw *serving 110g/4oz* 0
Country Vegetable Casserole, Lunch Bowl, Ready Meal (Heinz) *serving 110g/4oz* 0
Country Vegetable Slice, Chilled (Iceland) *serving 110g/4oz* 21
Courgette, Raw *serving 110g/4oz* 0
Courgette, Boiled in Unsalted Water *serving 110g/4oz* 0
Courgette, Fried in Corn Oil *serving 110g/4oz* 5
Courgette & Potato Curry, *serving 110g/4oz* 9
Couscous & Roasted Vegetables, Delicatessen (Marks & Spencer) *serving 110g/4oz* 11
Couscous Savoury (Holland & Barrett) *serving 110g/4oz* 2
Cress, Garden, Raw *serving 110g/4oz* 1
Cress, Garden, Boiled *serving 110g/4oz* 1
Crisps: *see under* Nuts & Savoury Snacks
Cucumber, Raw *serving 110g/4oz* 0
Cucumber, Pickled, Groceries (Marks & Spencer) *serving 110g/4oz* 0
Cucumbers in Brine (Waitrose) *serving 110g/4oz* 0
Cumin Seed *serving 110g/4oz* 24
Curry Powder *serving 110g/4oz* 15
Dandelion Greens, Raw *serving 110g/4oz* 1
Dandelion Greens, Boiled *serving 110g/4oz* 1
Dill Seed *serving 110g/4oz* 16
Dill Weed, Fresh *serving 110g/4oz* 1
Dock, Raw *serving 110g/4oz* 1
Dock, Boiled *serving 110g/4oz* 1
Dosa, Plain *serving 110g/4oz* 9
Dosa & Vegetable Filling *serving 110g/4oz* 7
Endive, Raw *serving 110g/4oz* 0
Falafel, Fried in Vegetable Oil *serving 110g/4oz* 12
Fennel Bulb, Raw *serving 110g/4oz* 0

Fennel, Florence, Boiled *serving 110g/4oz*	0
Fennel Seed *serving 110g/4oz*	16
Fenugreek Leaves, Raw *serving 110g/4oz*	0
Fenugreek Seed *serving 110g/4oz*	7
Fu Fu, Sweet Potato *serving 110g/4oz*	0
Fu Fu, Yam *serving 110g/4oz*	0
Garlic, Raw *serving 110g/4oz*	1
Garlic & Herb Edgers (Birds Eye) *serving 110g/4oz*	7
Garlic Powder *serving 110g/4oz*	1
Garlic Purée *serving 110g/4oz*	37
Gherkins, Raw *serving 110g/4oz*	0
Gherkins in Brine (Waitrose) *serving 110g/4oz*	0
Gherkins, Cocktail (Waitrose) *serving 110g/4oz*	0
Gherkins, Crinkle Cut (Waitrose) *serving 110g/4oz*	0
Gherkins, Pickled, Drained *serving 110g/4oz*	0
Gherkins, Sour, Pickled (Tesco) *serving 110g/4oz*	0
Gherkin Spears in Brine (Waitrose) *serving 110g/4oz*	0
Ginger, Ground *serving 110g/4oz*	7
Ginger Root, Raw *serving 110g/4oz*	1
Gram Black Dahl *serving 110g/4oz*	4
Green Bean Bhajia *serving 110g/4oz*	8
Green Bean Curry *serving 110g/4oz*	14
Green Beans, Boiled *serving 110g/4oz*	0
Green Beans, Tinned, Drained *serving 110g/4oz*	0
Green Beans, Cut (Somerfield) *serving 110g/4oz*	1
Green Beans, Frozen, Boiled *serving 110g/4oz*	0
Green Beans in Water, Cut (Somerfield) *serving 110g/4oz*	0
Hash Browns, Frozen (Iceland) *serving 110g/4oz*	11
Hominy, White, Tinned *serving 110g/4oz*	1
Hungry Joes (Birds Eye) *serving 110g/4oz*	9
Jackfruit, Raw *serving 110g/4oz*	0
Jackfruit, Tinned, Drained *serving 110g/4oz*	0
Jerusalem Artichokes, Raw *serving 110g/4oz*	0
Jute Potherb, Boiled *serving 110g/4oz*	0
Kale, Raw *serving 110g/4oz*	1
Kale, Boiled *serving 110g/4oz*	0
Kale, Curly, Raw *serving 110g/4oz*	2

Kale, Curly, Boiled *serving 110g/4oz*	1
Kohl Rabi, Raw *serving 110g/4oz*	0
Kohl Rabi, Boiled in Salted Water *serving 110g/4oz*	0
Leek & Cheese Crunchies (Somerfield) *serving 110g/4oz*	18
Leek & Stilton Quiche (Waitrose) *serving 110g/4oz*	18
Leeks Boiled *serving 110g/4oz*	1
Leeks in Cheese Sauce, Made with Semi-Skimmed Milk *serving 110g/4oz*	7
Leeks in Cheese Sauce, Made with Skimmed Milk *serving 110g/4oz*	6
Leeks in Cheese Sauce, Made with Whole Milk *serving 110g/4oz*	8
Lentil & Cheese Pie *serving 110g/4oz*	10
Lentil Cutlets, Fried in Vegetable Oil *serving 110g/4oz*	9
Lentil Dhal, Indian Cuisine (Holland & Barrett) *serving 110g/4oz*	4
Lentil & Nut Roast *serving 110g/4oz*	13
Lentil & Nut Roast with Egg *serving 110g/4oz*	13
Lentil Pie *serving 110g/4oz*	5
Lentil & Potato Pie *serving 110g/4oz*	2
Lentil & Rice Roast *serving 110g/4oz*	2
Lentil & Rice Roast with Egg *serving 110g/4oz*	3
Lentil Rissoles, Fried in Sunflower Oil *serving 110g/4oz*	12
Lentil Roast *serving 110g/4oz*	3
Lentil Roast with Egg *serving 110g/4oz*	4
Lentil & Tomato Flan *serving 110g/4oz*	7
Lettuce, Average, Raw *serving 110g/4oz*	1
Lettuce, Iceberg & Webb, Raw *serving 110g/4oz*	0
Lotus Root, Raw *serving 110g/4oz*	0
Lotus Root, Boiled *serving 110g/4oz*	0
Lotus Tubers, Raw *serving 110g/4oz*	0
Lotus Tubers, Tinned, Whole *serving 110g/4oz*	0
Mace, Ground *serving 110g/4oz*	36
Mange Tout Peas, Raw *serving 110g/4oz*	0
Mange Tout Peas, Boiled *serving 110g/4oz*	0
Mange Tout Peas, Stir Fried in Blended Oil *serving 110g/4oz*	5
Marjoram, Dried *serving 110g/4oz*	8
Marrow, Boiled *serving 110g/4oz*	0

Masala Dal (Waitrose) *serving 110g/4oz*	5
Masala Dal with Rajma (Waitrose) *serving 110g/4oz*	5
Matoki, Raw *serving 110g/4oz*	0
Matoki, Boiled *serving 110g/4oz*	0
Mchicha (West Indian Steamed Spinach with Onion & Tomato) *serving 110g/4oz*	5
Mushroom, Raw *serving 110g/4oz*	0
Mushroom à la Grècque (Safeway) *serving 110g/4oz*	11
Mushroom à la Grèque (Waitrose) *serving 110g/4oz*	9
Mushroom Bhaji *serving 110g/4oz*	18
Mushroom, Boiled *serving 110g/4oz*	1
Mushrooms, Button, Frozen (Asda) *serving 110g/4oz*	0
Mushrooms, Button, Frozen, Boiled (Iceland) *serving 110g/4oz*	1
Mushrooms, Button in Breadcrumbs, Frozen, Fried (Iceland) *serving 110g/4oz*	12
Mushroom, Tinned *serving 110g/4oz*	0
Mushroom Chantelle (Birds Eye) *serving 110g/4oz*	16
Mushroom & Cheese Crunchies (Somerfield) *serving 110g/4oz*	18
Mushroom, Chinese, Dried, Raw *serving 110g/4oz*	2
Mushroom Dopiaza, Chilled Ready Meal (Tesco) *serving 110g/4oz*	7
Mushroom, Enoki, Raw *serving 110g/4oz*	0
Mushroom, Fried in Corn Oil *serving 110g/4oz*	18
Mushrooms, Fresh Button, Vegetable Meal (Marks & Spencer) *serving 110g/4oz*	6
Mushrooms, Garlic *serving 110g/4oz*	16
Mushroom, Jew's Ear, Dried, Raw *serving 110g/4oz*	1
Mushrooms, Mixed (Waitrose) *serving 110g/4oz*	0
Mushrooms, Oyster, Raw *serving 110g/4oz*	0
Mushroom Parisienne (Birds Eye) *serving 110g/4oz*	5
Mushroom Pilau *serving 110g/4oz*	5
Mushroom & Quorn Stroganoff, Frozen Ready Meal (Tesco) *serving 110g/4oz*	6
Mushroom, Shiitake, Cooked *serving 110g/4oz*	0
Mushroom, Shiitake, Dried *serving 110g/4oz*	1
Mushroom, Sliced (Waitrose) *serving 110g/4oz*	1
Mushrooms, Straw, Tinned *serving 110g/4oz*	0

Mushroom Vol au Vent (Waitrose) *serving 110g/4oz* 26
Mustard & Cress, Raw *serving 110g/4oz* 1
Mustard & Dill Stir Fry (Waitrose) *serving 110g/4oz* 8
Mustard Greens, Raw *serving 110g/4oz* 0
Mustard Greens, Boiled *serving 110g/4oz* 0
Mustard Leaves, Raw *serving 110g/4oz* 0
Mustard Leaves, Boiled *serving 110g/4oz* 0
Mustard Leaves Bhaji *serving 110g/4oz* 7
Mustard Leaves & Spinach Bhaji *serving 110g/4oz* 7
Mustard Seed, Yellow *serving 110g/4oz* 32
Nutmeg, Ground *serving 110g/4oz* 40
Okra, Raw *serving 110g/4oz* 0
Okra Bhaji Bangladeshi with Butter Ghee *serving 110g/4oz* 7
Okra Bhaji Bangladeshi with Vegetable Oil *serving 110g/4oz* 7
Okra Bhaji Islami *serving 110g/4oz* 18
Okra, Boiled *serving 110g/4oz* 0
Okra, Tinned *serving 110g/4oz* 1
Okra Curry *serving 110g/4oz* 10
Okra, Stir Fried in Corn Oil *serving 110g/4oz* 29
Okra with Tomatoes & Onion, Greek *serving 110g/4oz* 18
Okra with Tomatoes & Onion, West Indian *serving 110g/4oz* 8
Olive Twist, Savoury Snack (Marks & Spencer) *serving 110g/4oz* 34
Olives à la Grèque (Waitrose) *serving 110g/4oz* 13
Olives, Almond Stuffed (Waitrose) *serving 110g/4oz* 30
Olives, Black, Kalamata (Waitrose) *serving 110g/4oz* 10
Olives, Black, Marinated (Waitrose) *serving 110g/4oz* 13
Olives, Black, with Orange (Waitrose) *serving 110g/4oz* 50
Olives, Black, Pitted, in Brine (Waitrose) *serving 110g/4oz* 17
Olives, Black, Smoked, & Chilli (Waitrose) *serving 110g/4oz* 11
Olives with Garlic/Chilli (Waitrose) *serving 110g/4oz* 59
Olives, Green, Anchovy Stuffed (Waitrose) *serving 110g/4oz* 16
Olives, Green, in Brine (Waitrose) *serving 110g/4oz* 23
Olives, Green, Large (Waitrose) *serving 110g/4oz* 10
Olives, Green, Pitted, in Brine (Waitrose) *serving 110g/4oz* 23
Olives, Green, Queen Party Food (Marks & Spencer) *serving 110g/4oz* 5

Olives, Green, Stuffed with Pimento (Waitrose) *serving 110g/4oz* 18
Olives, Kalamata, & Anchovy (Waitrose) *serving 110g/4oz* 61
Olives, Mediterranean (Safeway) *serving 110g/4oz* 33
Olives, Mixed, Stuffed, in Brine (Waitrose) *serving 110g/4oz* 18
Olives, Nostraline (Waitrose) *serving 110g/4oz* 24
Olives with Oregano (Waitrose) *serving 110g/4oz* 72
Olives & Peppers, Marinated (Safeway) *serving 110g/4oz* 20
Olives, Queen, Stuffed with Pimento (Waitrose) *serving 110g/4oz* 18
Olives, Spicy (Safeway) *serving 110g/4oz* 29
Onion, Raw *serving 110g/4oz* 0
Onion, Baked *serving 110g/4oz* 1
Onion Bhajia (Holland & Barrett) *serving 110g/4oz* 3
Onion Bhaji (Safeway) *serving 110g/4oz* 10
Onion Bhaji (Somerfield) *serving 110g/4oz* 9
Onion Bhaji (Waitrose) *serving 110g/4oz* 13
Onion Bhaji, Frittery (Waitrose) *serving 110g/4oz* 27
Onion Bhaji, Jumbo, Curry Pot (Asda) *serving 110g/4oz* 13
Onion Bhaji, Mini (Safeway) *serving 110g/4oz* 3
Onion Bhaji, Mini, Chilled (Tesco) *serving 110g/4oz* 15
Onion Bhaji, Mini, Curry Pot (Asda) *serving 110g/4oz* 22
Onion Bhaji Tandoori (Safeway) *serving 110g/4oz* 9
Onion, Boiled *serving 110g/4oz* 0
Onion, Tinned *serving 110g/4oz* 0
Onion, Cocktail (Waitrose) *serving 110g/4oz* 0
Onion, Cocktail/Silverskin, Drained *serving 110g/4oz* 0
Onion, Dehydrated Flakes *serving 110g/4oz* 1
Onion, Dried *serving 110g/4oz* 2
Onion, Fried in Corn Oil *serving 110g/4oz* 12
Onion, Large, Pickled, in Dark Vinegar (Tesco) *serving 110g/4oz* 0
Onion Pakora (Somerfield) *serving 110g/4oz* 21
Onion Pakora with Chilli Sauce (Safeway) *serving 110g/4oz* 43
Onion Pakora/Bhajia, Fried in Vegetable Oil *serving 110g/4oz* 16
Onion, Pickled *serving 110g/4oz* 0
Onion, Pickled, Groceries (Marks & Spencer) *serving 110g/4oz* 0

Onion, Pickled in Light Vinegar, Healthy Selection (Somerfield) *serving 110g/4oz* 0
Onion, Pickled in Light Vinegar, Mixed (Tesco) *serving 110g/4oz* 0
Onion, Pickled Silverskin, Healthy Selection (Somerfield) *serving 110g/4oz* 1
Onion Powder *serving 110g/4oz* 1
Onion, Red, Salad (Waitrose) *serving 110g/4oz* 1
Onion Rings (Somerfield) *serving 110g/4oz* 27
Onion Rings (Waitrose) *serving 110g/4oz* 29
Onion Rings, Battered (Asda) *serving 110g/4oz* 11
Onion Rings, Battered, Frozen, Oven Baked (Iceland) *serving 110g/4oz* 12
Onion Rings, Breaded & Fried *serving 110g/4oz* 21
Onion Rings, Breaded, Frozen, Baked (Iceland) *serving 110g/4oz* 10
Onion Rings, Breaded, Par Fried, Frozen, Prepared, Heated in Oven *serving 110g/4oz* 29
Onion Rings, Breaded, Par Fried, Frozen, Unprepared *serving 110g/4oz* 16
Onion Rings in Crispy Breadcrumbs (Somerfield) *serving 110g/4oz* 11
Onion Rings, Grocery (Iceland) *serving 110g/4oz* 29
Onion Rings, Sliced (Waitrose) *serving 110g/4oz* 0
Onion, Roast with Herbs (Waitrose) *serving 110g/4oz* 4
Onion, Silverskin, Groceries (Marks & Spencer) *serving 110g/4oz* 0
Onion Slices, Crispy, Savoury Snacks (Marks & Spencer) *serving 110g/4oz* 32
Onion, Spring (includes Tops & Bulb) Raw *serving 110g/4oz* 0
Onion, Sweet, Pickled, Healthy Selection (Somerfield) *serving 110g/4oz* 0
Onion, Welsh, Raw *serving 110g/4oz* 0
Oregano, Ground *serving 110g/4oz* 11
Pakora (Somerfield) *serving 110g/4oz* 21
Pakora Vegetable (Waitrose) *serving 110g/4oz* 18
Palum Pakora (Safeway) *serving 110g/4oz* 4
Paprika *serving 110g/4oz* 14
Parsley, Raw *serving 110g/4oz* 1

Parsley, Dried *serving 110g/4oz* 5
Parsley, Freeze Dried *serving 110g/4oz* 6
Parsnip, Boiled *serving 110g/4oz* 1
Patra Leaves, Raw *serving 110g/4oz* 2
Pea, Asparagus & Sugar Snap, Vegetable Meal (Marks & Spencer) *serving 110g/4oz* 4
Peas Bhaji *serving 110g/4oz* 37
Peas, Boiled *serving 110g/4oz* 2
Peas, Canned, Drained *serving 110g/4oz* 1
Peas & Carrots, Frozen, Boiled *serving 110g/4oz* 0
Peas & Carrots, Tinned *serving 110g/4oz* 0
Peas, Dried, Boiled *serving 110g/4oz* 1
Peas, Frozen, Boiled *serving 110g/4oz* 1
Peas, Frozen, Raw *serving 110g/4oz* 1
Peas, Green, Raw *serving 110g/4oz* 0
Peas, Garden (Somerfield) *serving 110g/4oz* 1
Peas, Garden (Waitrose) *serving 110g/4oz* 0
Peas, Garden, Frozen (Asda) *serving 110g/4oz* 1
Peas, Garden, in Water (Somerfield) *serving 110g/4oz* 0
Peas, Garden, in Water (no Colour) Healthy Choice (Asda) *serving 110g/4oz* 0
Peas, Garden, in Water, Sugar, Salt & Mint Flavour Added (Somerfield) *serving 110g/4oz* 1
Peas, Green, Boiled *serving 110g/4oz* 0
Peas, Green, Frozen, Boiled *serving 110g/4oz* 0
Peas, Green, Frozen, Unprepared *serving 110g/4oz* 0
Peas, Green, Tinned *serving 110g/4oz* 0
Peas, Marrowfat (Waitrose) *serving 110g/4oz* 1
Peas, Marrowfat, Tinned, Drained *serving 110g/4oz* 1
Peas, Marrowfat, in Water (Somerfield) *serving 110g/4oz* 0
Peas, Marrowfat, Processed, in Water, Sugar, Salt & Mint Flavour Added (Somerfield) *serving 110g/4oz* 1
Peas, Marrowfat, Processed, Healthy Choice (Asda) *serving 110g/4oz* 0
Peas, Mint (Waitrose) *serving 110g/4oz* 0
Peas & Mushroom Bhajee (Safeway) *serving 110g/4oz* 31
Peas, Mushy, Tinned *serving 110g/4oz* 1

Peas, Mushy, in Water (Somerfield) *serving 110g/4oz* 0
Peas & Onions, Frozen, Boiled *serving 110g/4oz* 0
Peas & Onions, Tinned *serving 110g/4oz* 0
Peas & Potato Curry *serving 110g/4oz* 12
Peas, Processed, Tinned, Reheated, Drained *serving 110g/4oz* 1
Peas, Split, Boiled *serving 110g/4oz* 1
Peas, Sprouted, Raw *serving 110g/4oz* 1
Peas, Sprouted, Boiled *serving 110g/4oz* 1
Peas, Sugar Snap, Boiled *serving 110g/4oz* 0
Pease Pudding, Tinned, Reheated, Drained *serving 110g/4oz* 1
Peppers, Chilli, Red, Raw *serving 110g/4oz* 0
Peppers, Filled, Vegetable Meal (Marks & Spencer) *serving 110g/4oz* 4
Peppers, Green, Raw *serving 110g/4oz* 1
Pepers, Green, Boiled *serving 110g/4oz* 1
Peppers, Hot Chilli, Green, Raw *serving 110g/4oz* 0
Peppers, Hot Chilli, Green, Tinned *serving 110g/4oz* 0
Peppers, Hot Chilli, Red, Raw *serving 110g/4oz* 0
Peppers, Hot Chilli, Red, Tinned *serving 110g/4oz* 0
Peppers, Jalapeno, Tinned *serving 110g/4oz* 1
Peppers, Red, Raw *serving 110g/4oz* 0
Peppers, Red, Boiled *serving 110g/4oz* 0
Peppers, Red, Stuffed, Chilled Ready Meal (Tesco) *serving 110g/4oz* 7
Peppers, Red, Tinned *serving 110g/4oz* 0
Peppers, Red & Yellow, Grilled (Waitrose) *serving 110g/4oz* 3
Peppers, Sliced, Mixed (Waitrose) *serving 110g/4oz* 0
Peppers Stuffed with Rice *serving 110g/4oz* 3
Peppers Stuffed with Vegetables with Cheese Topping *serving 110g/4oz* 7
Peppers, Yellow, Raw *serving 110g/4oz* 0
Petits Pois (Waitrose) *serving 110g/4oz* 1
Petits Pois & Baby Carrot (Waitrose) *serving 110g/4oz* 0
Petits Pois, Frozen (Asda) *serving 110g/4oz* 1
Petits Pois, Frozen, Boiled *serving 110g/4oz* 1
Petit Pois, Vegetable Meal (Marks & Spencer) *serving 110g/4oz* 5
Pimiento, Tinned *serving 110g/4oz* 0

Pineapple & Coconut Stir Fry (Waitrose) *serving 110g/4oz*	4
Plantain, Raw *serving 110g/4oz*	0
Plantain, Boiled *serving 110g/4oz*	0
Plantain, Fried in Oil *serving 110g/4oz*	10
Poi *serving 110g/4oz*	0
Poppy Seed *serving 110g/4oz*	49
Potato au Gratin, Dry Mix, Prepared with Water, Whole Milk & Butter *serving 110g/4oz*	5
Potato au Gratin, Home Made Using Butter *serving 110g/4oz*	8
Potato au Gratin, Home Made Using Margarine *serving 110g/4oz*	8
Potato & Bacon (Waitrose) *serving 110g/4oz*	12
Potato, Baked Flesh *serving 110g/4oz*	0
Potato, Baked Flesh & Skin *serving 110g/4oz*	0
Potato, Baked Flesh & Skin, Main Crop, Old *serving 110g/4oz*	0
Potato, Baked Skin Only *serving 110g/4oz*	0
Potato, Baked & Topped with Cheese Sauce *serving 110g/4oz*	11
Potato, Baked & Topped with Cheese Sauce & Bacon *serving 110g/4oz*	10
Potato, Baked & Topped with Cheese Sauce & Broccoli *serving 110g/4oz*	7
Potato, Baked & Topped with Cheese Sauce & Chilli, *serving 110g/4oz*	6
Potato, Baked & Topped with Sour Cream & Chives *serving 110g/4oz*	8
Potato, Baked, Vegetable Meal (Marks & Spencer) *serving 110g/4oz*	4
Potato Bhaji *serving 110g/4oz*	11
Potato, Boiled, Main Crop, Old *serving 110g/4oz*	0
Potato, Boiled in Skin *serving 110g/4oz*	0
Potato, Bombay (Safeway) *serving 110g/4oz*	7
Potato, Bombay (Somerfield) *serving 110g/4oz*	3
Potato, Bombay (Waitrose) *serving 110g/4oz*	6
Potato, Bombay, Curry *serving 110g/4oz*	7
Potato, Bombay, Frozen Microwave (Iceland) *serving 110g/4oz*	6
Potato Cakes, Fried in Lard *serving 110g/4oz*	9
Potato Cakes, Fried in Vegetable Oil *serving 110g/4oz*	9

Potato, Tinned, Drained, Solids *serving 110g/4oz* 0
Potato, Cauliflower & Broccoli Bake, Vegetable Meal (Marks & Spencer) *serving 110g/4oz* 6
Potato, Cheese & Bacon Bowl (Asda) *serving 110g/4oz* 18
Potato, Cheese & Onion Bake, Vegetable Meal (Marks & Spencer) *serving 110g/4oz* 8
Potato, Chips: *see under* Chips
Potato & Corned Beef Bake (Waitrose) *serving 110g/4oz* 4
Potato Croquettes (Birds Eye) *serving 110g/4oz* 6
Potato Croquettes (Somerfield) *serving 110g/4oz* 7
Potato Croquettes (Tesco) *serving 110g/4oz* 6
Potato Croquettes, Fried in Blended Oil *serving 110g/4oz* 14
Potato Croquettes, Frozen, Oven Baked (Iceland) *serving 110g/4oz* 6
Potato Croquettes, Southern Fried, Frozen, Oven Baked (Iceland) *serving 110g/4oz* 19
Potato Croquettes, Vegetable Meal (Marks & Spencer) *serving 110g/4oz* 7
Potato Crunches (Tesco) *serving 110g/4oz* 9
Potato, Duchesse *serving 110g/4oz* 6
Potato, Farmyard Shapes (Somerfield) *serving 110g/4oz* 7
Potato Flour *serving 110g/4oz* 1
Potato Fritters (Somerfield) *serving 110g/4oz* 11
Potato Fritters, Cooked (Tesco) *serving 110g/4oz* 14
Potato Fritters, Crispy (Birds Eye) *serving 110g/4oz* 10
Potato Fritters, Frozen, Oven Baked (Iceland) *serving 110g/4oz* 11
Potato Gratin (Marks & Spencer) *serving 110g/4oz* 9
Potato Gratin, Creamy, Chilled Ready Meal (Tesco) *serving 110g/4oz* 16
Potato Gratin, Dauphinoise (HeroRosh) *serving 110g/4oz* 3
Potato & Green Pepper Bhaji *serving 110g/4oz* 10
Potato Grills (Somerfield) *serving 110g/4oz* 7
Potato, Gujerati Curry *serving 110g/4oz* 6
Potato & Ham Gratin (Findus Dinner Supreme) *serving 110g/4oz* 9
Potato, Hashed Brown *serving 110g/4oz* 14

Potato, Instant Powder, Made Up with Semi-Skimmed Milk *serving 110g/4oz* 1
Potato, Instant Powder, Made Up with Skimmed Milk *serving 110g/4oz* 0
Potato, Instant Powder, Made Up with Water *serving 110g/4oz* 0
Potato, Instant Powder, Made Up with Whole Milk *serving 110g/4oz* 1
Potato, Jacket & Cauliflower Cheese, Country Club Cuisine (Birds Eye) *serving 110g/4oz* 4
Potato, Jacket, & Cheddar Cheese, Frozen Ovenbaked (Iceland) *serving 110g/4oz* 7
Potato, Jacket, Cheese & Onion (Birds Eye) *serving 110g/4oz* 4
Potato, Jacket, Mini (Waitrose) *serving 110g/4oz* 9
Potato, Leek & Celery Bake *serving 110g/4oz* 7
Potato, Lyonnaise Style (Somerfield) *serving 110g/4oz* 3
Potato, Mashed *serving 110g/4oz* 1
Potato, Mashed (Waitrose) *serving 110g/4oz* 1
Potato, Mashed, Home Made, Whole Milk Added *serving 110g/4oz* 1
Potato, Mashed, Home Made, Whole Milk & Butter Added *serving 110g/4oz* 5
Potato, Mashed, Home Made, Whole Milk & Margarine Added *serving 110g/4oz* 5
Potato, Mashed, Made from Flakes, Whole Milk & Butter Added *serving 110g/4oz* 6
Potato, Mashed, Made from Granules, Milk, Water & Margarine Added *serving 110g/4oz* 2
Potato, Mashed, Main Crop, Old *serving 110g/4oz* 5
Potato, Microwaved, Flesh Only *serving 110g/4oz* 0
Potato, Microwaved, Flesh & Skin *serving 110g/4oz* 0
Potato, Microwaved, Skin Only *serving 110g/4oz* 0
Potato & Mushroom Bake, Creamy (Safeway) *serving 110g/4oz* 12
Potato & Mustard with Cheese (Safeway) *serving 110g/4oz* 14
Potato, New, Boiled in Salted Water *serving 110g/4oz* 0
Potato, New, Tinned, Drained *serving 110g/4oz* 0
Potato Nuggets, Southern Fried (Birds Eye) *serving 110g/4oz* 12

Potato & Onion Bhaji *serving 110g/4oz*	11
Potato, Onion & Mushroom Bhaji *serving 110g/4oz*	19
Potato & Pea Curry *serving 110g/4oz*	4
Potato, Pommes Fines Herbes (Herorosti) *serving 110g/4oz*	5
Potato, Pommes Noisettes (Tesco) *serving 110g/4oz*	9
Potato, Pommes Parmentier Herbs (Waitrose) *serving 110g/4oz*	6
Potato Puffs, Frozen, Prepared *serving 110g/4oz*	12
Potato, Punjabi Curry *serving 110g/4oz*	4
Potato, Roast (Somerfield) *serving 110g/4oz*	3
Potato, Roast, in Corn Oil, Main Crop, Old *serving 110g/4oz*	5
Potato, Roast, Frozen (Iceland) *serving 110g/4oz*	2
Potato, Roast, Traditional, Frozen, Oven Baked (Iceland) *serving 110g/4oz*	3
Potato, Roast, Vegetable Meals (Marks & Spencer) *serving 110g/4oz*	6
Potato, Röschti (HeroRosti) *serving 110g/4oz*	6
Potato Salad *serving 110g/4oz*	9
Potato, Scallop, Groceries (Marks & Spencer) *serving 110g/4oz*	5
Potato, Scalloped, Dry Mix, Prepared with Water, Whole Milk & Butter *serving 110g/4oz*	5
Potato, Scalloped, Home Made with Butter *serving 110g/4oz*	4
Potato, Scalloped, Home Made with Margarine *serving 110g/4oz*	4
Potato, Scallops (Tesco) *serving 110g/4oz*	4
Potato, Spinach & Cauliflower Bhaji *serving 110g/4oz*	17
Potato, Sweet: *see* Sweet Potato	
Potato, Tasty Tatties (Birds Eye) *serving 110g/4oz*	5
Potato, Sliced, Tomato & Basil, Vegetable Meal (Marks & Spencer) *serving 110g/4oz*	2
Potato, Tomato & Courgette, Vegetable Meal (Marks & Spencer) *serving 110g/4oz*	4
Potato, Vegetable Mix, Frozen, Oven Baked (Iceland) *serving 110g/4oz*	6
Potato & Vegetables, Chargrilled (Marks & Spencer) *serving 110g/4oz*	4
Potato & Vegetables, Lyonnaise (Marks & Spencer) *serving 110g/4oz*	10

Potato & Vegetables, Seasoned Wedges (Marks & Spencer) *serving 110g/4oz* 4
Potato Waffles (Birds Eye) *serving 110g/4oz* 10
Potato Waffles (Somerfield) *serving 110g/4oz* 15
Potato Waffles, Frozen (Asda) *serving 110g/4oz* 7
Potato Waffles, Frozen, Baked (Iceland) *serving 110g/4oz* 7
Potato Waffles, Frozen, Cooked *serving 110g/4oz* 9
Potato Waffles, Mini (Somerfield) *serving 110g/4oz* 1
Potato Waffles, Mini, Frozen, Oven Baked (Iceland) *serving 110g/4oz* 7
Potato Waffles, Southern Fried, Frozen, Oven Baked (Iceland) *serving 110g/4oz* 9
Potato Wedges (Somerfield) *serving 110g/4oz* 3
Potato Wedges with Sour Cream (Waitrose) *serving 110g/4oz* 22
Poultry Seasoning *serving 110g/4oz* 8
Pumpkin, Raw *serving 110g/4oz* 0
Pumpkin, Boiled *serving 110g/4oz* 0
Pumpkin, Tinned *serving 110g/4oz* 0
Pumpkin Pie Mix, Tinned *serving 110g/4oz* 0
Purslane, Raw *serving 110g/4oz* 0
Purslane, Boiled *serving 110g/4oz* 0
Raddiccio, Raw *serving 110g/4oz* 0
Radish, Oriental, Raw *serving 110g/4oz* 0
Radish, Oriental, Boiled *serving 110g/4oz* 0
Radish, Oriental, Dried *serving 110g/4oz* 1
Radish, Raw *serving 110g/4oz* 1
Radish Seeds, Sprouted, Raw *serving 110g/4oz* 3
Radish, White/Icicle, Raw *serving 110g/4oz* 0
Radish, White/Mooli, Raw *serving 110g/4oz* 0
Ratatouille *serving 110g/4oz* 8
Ratatouille, (Waitrose) *serving 110g/4oz* 2
Ratatouille Calzone (Waitrose) *serving 110g/4oz* 7
Ratatouille, Chilled Ready Meal (Tesco) *serving 110g/4oz* 4
Ratatouille, Home Prepared *serving 110g/4oz* 13
Ratatouille, Vegetable Meal (Marks & Spencer) *serving 110g/4oz* 5
Red Cabbage, Pickled (Tesco) *serving 110g/4oz* 0

Red Cabbage with Cranberry Glaze (Somerfield) *serving 110g/4oz* 0
Red Pea Loaf (West Indian, Made with Kidney Beans) *serving 110g/4oz* 4
Rosemary, Dried *serving 110g/4oz* 4
Rosti, Baby, Frozen Produce (Marks & Spencer) *serving 110g/4oz* 7
Rosti, Vegetable Meal (Marks & Spencer) *serving 110g/4oz* 17
Rosti (Waitrose) *serving 110g/4oz* 7
Saffron *serving 110g/4oz* 6
Sage, Ground *serving 110g/4oz* 14
Salsify, Raw *serving 110g/4oz* 0
Salsify, Boiled *serving 110g/4oz* 0
Samosa, Vegetable, Curry Pot, Jumbo (Asda) *serving 110g/4oz* 14
Samosa, Vegetable, Curry Pot, Mini (Asda) *serving 110g/4oz* 5
Samosa, Vegetable, Mini (Safeway) *serving 110g/4oz* 2
Samosa, Vegetable, Selection Pack, Mini (Safeway) *serving 110g/4oz* 2
Sauerkraut *serving 110g/4oz* 0
Sauerkraut, Tinned *serving 110g/4oz* 0
Savory, Ground *serving 110g/4oz* 6
Seakale, Boiled *serving 110g/4oz* 0
Seaweed, Agar, Raw *serving 110g/4oz* 0
Seaweed, Agar, Dried *serving 110g/4oz* 0
Seaweed, Irish Moss, Raw *serving 110g/4oz* 0
Seaweed, Kelp, Raw *serving 110g/4oz* 1
Seaweed, Kombu, Dried, Raw *serving 110g/4oz* 2
Seaweed, Laver, Raw *serving 110g/4oz* 0
Seaweed, Nori, Dried, Raw *serving 110g/4oz* 2
Seaweed, Spirulina, Dried *serving 110g/4oz* 8
Seaweed, Wakame, Raw *serving 110g/4oz* 1
Seaweed, Wakame, Dried, Raw *serving 110g/4oz* 3
Shallots, Raw *serving 110g/4oz* 0
Shallots, Freeze Dried *serving 110g/4oz* 1
Shallots, Pickled (Waitrose) *serving 110g/4oz* 0
Shallots, Pickled, Traditional (Tesco) *serving 110g/4oz* 0
Spinach, Raw *serving 110g/4oz* 0

Spinach Bhaji *serving 110g/4oz* 7
Spinach, Boiled *serving 110g/4oz* 0
Spinach, Tinned, Drained *serving 110g/4oz* 1
Spinach & Carrot Pilau (Waitrose) *serving 110g/4oz* 6
Spinach, Chopped (Waitrose) *serving 110g/4oz* 1
Spinach Curry *serving 110g/4oz* 10
Spinach, Frozen, Boiled *serving 110g/4oz* 1
Spinach, Frozen, Chopped or Leaf, Boiled *serving 110g/4oz* 0
Spinach, Gobi Aloo Saag (Safeway) *serving 110g/4oz* 20
Spinach, Gobi Aloo Saag, Chilled Ready Meal (Tesco) *serving 110g/4oz* 5
Spinach, Lasagne *serving 110g/4oz* 3
Spinach Pakora/Bhajia, Fried in Vegetable Oil *serving 110g/4oz* 24
Spinach Pie *serving 110g/4oz* 15
Spinach & Potato Bhaji *serving 110g/4oz* 16
Spinach & Potato Curry *serving 110g/4oz* 9
Spinach Roulade *serving 110g/4oz* 15
Spinach Soufflé *serving 110g/4oz* 15
Spring Greens, Raw *serving 110g/4oz* 1
Spring Greens, Boiled *serving 110g/4oz* 1
Spring Roll, Chinese (Safeway) *serving 110g/4oz* 8
Spring Roll, Mini (Asda) *serving 110g/4oz* 8
Spring Roll, Oriental Vegetable, Frozen Ready Meal (Tesco) *serving 110g/4oz* 15
Spring Roll, Sweet & Sour Vegetable, Frozen (Tesco) *serving 110g/4oz* 6
Spring Roll, Vegetable (Marks & Spencer) *serving 110g/4oz* 9
Spring Roll, Vegetable (Safeway) *serving 110g/4oz* 8
Spring Roll, Vegetable (Somerfield) *serving 110g/4oz* 7
Spring Roll, Vegetable, Chilled (Tesco) *serving 110g/4oz* 9
Spring Roll, Vegetable, Curry Pot, Jumbo (Asda) *serving 110g/4oz* 7
Spring Roll, Vegetable, Curry Pot, Mini (Asda) *serving 110g/4oz* 11
Spring Roll, Vegetable, Jumbo (Waitrose) *serving 110g/4oz* 7
Spring Roll, Vegetable, Mini (Waitrose) *serving 110g/4oz* 22
Stir Fry, Peking (Holland & Barrett) *serving 110g/4oz* 10

Swede, Raw *serving 110g/4oz*	0
Swede, Boiled *serving 110g/4oz*	0
Sweetcorn, Baby, Fresh & Frozen, Boiled *serving 110g/4oz*	0
Sweetcorn, Tinned (Waitrose) *serving 110g/4oz*	1
Sweetcorn Cobs, Mini (Waitrose) *serving 110g/4oz*	1
Sweetcorn, Frozen (Asda) *serving 110g/4oz*	3
Sweetcorn Kernels, Raw *serving 110g/4oz*	2
Sweetcorn Kernels (Waitrose) *serving 110g/4oz*	2
Sweetcorn Kernels, Frozen (Waitrose) *serving 110g/4oz*	2
Sweetcorn with Peppers (Waitrose) *serving 110g/4oz*	1
Sweetcorn, Pizza Flavoured, Frozen (Iceland) *serving 110g/4oz*	2
Sweetcorn, Whole, Boiled *serving 110g/4oz*	2
Sweet Potato, Raw *serving 110g/4oz*	0
Sweet Potato, Baked in Skin *serving 110g/4oz*	0
Sweet Potato, Boiled *serving 110g/4oz*	0
Sweet Potato, Cooked, Candied *serving 110g/4oz*	4
Sweet Potato, Frozen, Baked *serving 110g/4oz*	0
Sweet Potato, Steamed *serving 110g/4oz*	0
Sweet Potato, Tinned, Mashed *serving 110g/4oz*	0
Sweet Potato & Green Banana Casserole *serving 110g/4oz*	7
Taro, Baked *serving 110g/4oz*	0
Taro, Boiled *serving 110g/4oz*	0
Taro, Cooked *serving 110g/4oz*	0
Taro, Steamed *serving 110g/4oz*	0
Taro Shoots, Cooked *serving 110g/4oz*	0
Tarragon, Ground *serving 110g/4oz*	8
Thyme, Ground *serving 110g/4oz*	8
Tofu *see under* Beans & Lentils	
Tomato, Aubergine & Mozzarella Layer, Delicatessen (Marks & Spencer) *serving 110g/4oz*	19
Tomato, Tinned, Whole *serving 110g/4oz*	0
Tomato, Cherry, Raw *serving 110g/4oz*	0
Tomato, Chopped & Garlic (Waitrose) *serving 110g/4oz*	1
Tomato, Chopped, with Garlic (Somerfield) *serving 110g/4oz*	0
Tomato, Chopped, with Herbs (Somerfield) *serving 110g/4oz*	0
Tomato, Chopped, with Peppers (Somerfield) *serving 110g/4oz*	0
Tomato, Crushed (Waitrose) *serving 110g/4oz*	0

Tomato, Diced, with Herbs (Waitrose) *serving 110g/4oz*	0
Tomato, Fried in Corn Oil *serving 110g/4oz*	8
Tomato, Green, Raw *serving 110g/4oz*	0
Tomatoes, Grilled *serving 110g/4oz*	1
Tomato Juice *serving 110g/4oz*	0
Tomato Juice, Tinned *serving 110g/4oz*	0
Tomato Paste, Tinned *serving 110g/4oz*	1
Tomato Powder *serving 110g/4oz*	0
Tomato Purée *serving 110g/4oz*	0
Tomato, Red, Ripe, Raw *serving 110g/4oz*	0
Tomato, Red, Ripe, Boiled *serving 110g/4oz*	0
Tomato, Red, Ripe, Stewed *serving 110g/4oz*	3
Tomato, Red, Ripe, Tinned, Stewed *serving 110g/4oz*	0
Tomato, Red, Ripe, Tinned, Wedges in Tomato Juice *serving 110g/4oz*	0
Tomato, Red, Ripe, Tinned, Whole *serving 110g/4oz*	0
Tomato, Red, Ripe, Tinned, with Green Chillies *serving 110g/4oz*	0
Tomato Sauce, Tinned *serving 110g/4oz*	0
Tomato Sauce, Tinned, Spanish Style *serving 110g/4oz*	0
Tomato Sauce, Tinned, with Herbs & Cheese *serving 110g/4oz*	2
Tomato Sauce, Tinned with Mushrooms *serving 110g/4oz*	0
Tomato Sauce, Tinned, with Onions *serving 110g/4oz*	0
Tomato Sauce, Tinned, with Onions, Green Peppers & Celery *serving 110g/4oz*	1
Tomato Sauce, Tinned, with Tomato Tidbits *serving 110g/4oz*	0
Tomatoes Stuffed with Rice *serving 110g/4oz*	15
Tomatoes Stuffed with Vegetables *serving 110g/4oz*	7
Tomato, Sun Dried *serving 110g/4oz*	3
Tomatoes, Sundried, Packed in Oil, Drained *serving 110g/4oz*	15
Tomatoes, Grilled *serving 110g/4oz*	1
Tree Fern, Cooked *serving 110g/4oz*	0
Turmeric, Ground *serving 110g/4oz*	11
Turnip Bhaji, Made with Butter *serving 110g/4oz*	18
Turnip, Boiled *serving 110g/4oz*	0
Turnip Greens, Boiled *serving 110g/4oz*	0
Turnip Greens, Raw *serving 110g/4oz*	0

Turnip Greens, Tinned *serving 110g/4oz* 0
Turnip & Onion Bhaji *serving 110g/4oz* 12
Turnip, Raw *serving 110g/4oz* 0
Vegebanger, Made Up with Water *serving 110g/4oz* 6
Vegebanger, Made Up with Water & Egg *serving 110g/4oz* 9
Vegebanger, Made Up with Water & Egg, Fried in Sunflower Oil *serving 110g/4oz* 20
Vegebanger, Made Up with Water & Egg, Fried in Vegetable Oil *serving 110g/4oz* 20
Vegebanger, Made Up with Water, Fried in Sunflower Oil *serving 110g/4oz* 17
Vegebanger, Made Up with Water, Fried in Vegetable Oil *serving 110g/4oz* 17
Vegeburger, Grilled *serving 110g/4oz* 12
Vegeburger, Retail, Fried in Vegetable Oil *serving 110g/4oz* 19
Vegetable Aloo Tikka, Mini (Waitrose) *serving 110g/4oz* 8
Vegetable Bake (Mixed Vegetables Topped with Cheese Sauce & Breadcrumbs) *serving 110g/4oz* 8
Vegetable Bake, Chilled Ready Meal (Tesco) *serving 110g/4oz* 7
Vegetable Bake, Frozen Ready Meal (Tesco) *serving 110g/4oz* 3
Vegetable Bake, Large, Vegetable Meal (Marks & Spencer) *serving 110g/4oz* 6
Vegetable Bake, Small, Vegetable Meal (Marks & Spencer) *serving 110g/4oz* 6
Vegetable Bhaji with Butter *serving 110g/4oz* 17
Vegetable Balti & 2 Paratha (Waitrose) *serving 110g/4oz* 9
Vegetable Bhaji, Mini, Mixed Curry Pot (Asda) *serving 110g/4oz* 20
Vegetable Bhaji with Vegetable Oil *serving 110g/4oz* 20
Vegetable Biryani (Waitrose) *serving 110g/4oz* 6
Vegetable Bites, Spicy, Frozen, Oven Baked (Iceland) *serving 110g/4oz* 21
Vegetable Casserole (Sainsbury's) *serving 110g/4oz* 6
Vegetable Casserole (Waitrose) *serving 110g/4oz* 6
Vegetable Casserole Mix, Frozen (Asda) *serving 110g/4oz* 0
Vegetable Casserole, Mixed (Somerfield) *serving 110g/4oz* 1
Vegetable & Cheese Slices (Waitrose) *serving 110g/4oz* 22

Vegetable Chilli *serving 110g/4oz* 1
Vegetable Chilli (Holland & Barrett) *serving 110g/4oz* 0
Vegetable Chilli, Chilled Ready Meal (Safeway) *serving 110g/4oz* 2
Vegetable Chilli, Low Fat, Vegetable Meal (Marks & Spencer) *serving 110g/4oz* 2
Vegetable Country Slice, Frozen, Baking (Iceland) *serving 110g/4oz* 19
Vegetable Crispbreak (Somerfield) *serving 110g/4oz* 8
Vegetable Crostini (Waitrose) *serving 110g/4oz* 21
Vegetable Crumble in Milk Base *serving 110g/4oz* 10
Vegetable Crunch, Chinese, Frozen, Grilled (Iceland) *serving 110g/4oz* 14
Vegetable Curry (Marks & Spencer) *serving 110g/4oz* 7
Vegetable Curry (Safeway) *serving 110g/4oz* 21
Vegetable Curry (Somerfield) *serving 110g/4oz* 4
Vegetable Curry (Waitrose) *serving 110g/4oz* 3
Vegetable Curry, Chilled Ready Meal (Safeway) *serving 110g/4oz* 22
Vegetable Curry, Made with Frozen Mixed Vegetables *serving 110g/4oz* 7
Vegetable Curry, Madras, Indian Cuisine (Holland & Barrett) *serving 110g/4oz* 5
Vegetable Curry, Mild, Indian Cuisine (Holland & Barrett) *serving 110g/4oz* 6
Vegetable Curry, Take Away *serving 110g/4oz* 8
Vegetable Curry, Thai, Tinned Ready Meal (Tesco) *serving 110g/4oz* 1
Vegetable Curry, Thai Style (Waitrose) *serving 110g/4oz* 5
Vegetable Curry, West Indian *serving 110g/4oz* 4
Vegetable Curry with Rice (Birds Eye) *serving 110g/4oz* 4
Vegetable Curry with Rice, Frozen Ready Meal (Safeway) *serving 110g/4oz* 3
Vegetable Fingers, Crispy, Country Club Cuisine (Birds Eye) *serving 110g/4oz* 9
Vegetable Goulash (Holland & Barrett) *serving 110g/4oz* 1
Vegetable Hot Pot, Frozen Ready Meal (Heinz Weight Watchers) *serving 110g/4oz* 3
Vegetable Hot Pot & Yorkshire Pudding (Waitrose) *serving 110g/4oz* 6

Vegetable Juice Cocktail, Tinned *serving 110g/4oz*	0
Vegetable Kievs, Country Club Cuisine (Birds Eye) *serving 110g/4oz*	8
Vegetable Masala with Mustard Seed Rice, Frozen Ready Meal (Tesco) *serving 110g/4oz*	7
Vegetable Medley Bake, Frozen, Oven Baked (Iceland) *serving 110g/4oz*	9
Vegetable Moussaka *serving 110g/4oz*	10
Vegetable Moussaka (Waitrose) *serving 110g/4oz*	12
Vegetable Pakora/Bhajia, Retail *serving 110g/4oz*	16
Vegetable Pilau *serving 110g/4oz*	5
Vegetable Purée *serving 110g/4oz*	5
Vegetable Rissoles, Fried in Sunflower Oil *serving 110g/4oz*	8
Vegetable Rissoles, Fried in Vegetable Oil *serving 110g/4oz*	8
Vegetable Rogan Josh (Asda) *serving 110g/4oz*	6
Vegetable Rogan Josh (Safeway) *serving 110g/4oz*	24
Vegetable Rolls, King Size, Frozen, Oven Baked (Iceland) *serving 110g/4oz*	14
Vegetable Samosa (Holland & Barrett) *serving 110g/4oz*	3
Vegetable Samosa (Safeway) *serving 110g/4oz*	4
Vegetable Samosa (Somerfield) *serving 110g/4oz*	9
Vegetable Samosa (Waitrose) *serving 110g/4oz*	6
Vegetable Samosa, Chilled (Tesco) *serving 110g/4oz*	15
Vegetable Samosa, Retail *serving 110g/4oz*	10
Vegetable Shepherd's Pie (Waitrose) *serving 110g/4oz*	4
Vegetable Spicy Bake (Holland & Barrett) *serving 110g/4oz*	26
Vegetable Stir Fry, Mixed (Somerfield) *serving 110g/4oz*	0
Vegetable Stir Fry, Mix, Fried in Corn Oil *serving 110g/4oz*	4
Vegetable Stir Fry, Mix, Fried in Sunflower Oil *serving 110g/4oz*	4
Vegetable Stir Fry, Mix, Fried in Vegetable Oil *serving 110g/4oz*	4
Vegetable Stroganoff, Frozen Ready Meal (Heinz Weight Watchers) *serving 110g/4oz*	2
Vegetable, Sweet & Sour (Holland & Barrett) *serving 110g/4oz*	0
Vegetable, Sweet & Sour (Waitrose) *serving 110g/4oz*	1
Vegetable Tikka, Frozen (Iceland) *serving 110g/4oz*	6
Vegetable Tikka Crispbakes, Frozen (Tesco) *serving 110g/4oz*	16
Vegetable Tikka Masala (Waitrose) *serving 110g/4oz*	8

Vegetable Tikka Masala, Tinned Ready Meal (Tesco) *serving 110g/4oz* 12
Vegetable Tikka Masala, Chilled Ready Meal (Tesco) *serving 110g/4oz* 6
Vegetable Tuscany (Birds Eye) *serving 110g/4oz* 5
Vegetable Tuscany Toppers, Country Club Cuisine (Birds Eye) *serving 110g/4oz* 6
Vegetables, Farmhouse, Mixed (Somerfield) *serving 110g/4oz* 1
Vegetables, Layered, with Seasoned Butter (Somerfield) *serving 110g/4oz* 3
Vegetables, Mixed (Waitrose) *serving 110g/4oz* 0
Vegetables, Mixed, Tinned *serving 110g/4oz* 1
Vegetables, Mixed, Frozen, Boiled *serving 110g/4oz* 1
Vegetables & Yorkshire Pudding, Vegetable Meal (Marks & Spencer) *serving 110g/4oz* 26
Vine Leaves, Preserved in Brine *serving 110g/4oz* 0
Vine Leaves, Stuffed, Party Food (Marks & Spencer) *serving 110g/4oz* 4
Vine Leaves, Stuffed with Rice *serving 110g/4oz* 20
Water Chestnuts, Raw *serving 110g/4oz* 0
Water Chestnuts, Tinned *serving 110g/4oz* 0
Water Chestnuts, Chinese (Matai), Raw *serving 110g/4oz* 0
Water Chestnuts, Chinese, Tinned *serving 110g/4oz* 0
Watercress, Raw *serving 110g/4oz* 0
Yam, Raw *serving 110g/4oz* 0
Yam, Baked *serving 110g/4oz* 0
Yam, Boiled *serving 110g/4oz* 0
Yam, Steamed *serving 110g/4oz* 0
Yeast, Baker's, Compressed *serving 110g/4oz* 0
Yeast, Dried *serving 110g/4oz* 2

Yoghurt & Fromage Frais

NOTE: The standard serving size in this section is 110g/4oz. If you wish to consume more or less than this amount (e.g. if you are going to consume a pack of food whose weight differs from the standard

serving size) use the conversion tables on page 386 to calculate the new amount of fat in the food.

Fromage Frais *serving 110g/4oz*	8
Fromage Frais (Somerfield) *serving 110g/4oz*	9
Fromage Frais, All Flavours (Müller) *serving 110g/4oz*	7
Fromage Frais, All Flavours (Somerfield) *serving 110g/4oz*	3
Fromage Frais, Chocolate, Chilled (Tesco) *serving 110g/4oz*	11
Fromage Frais, Creamy, Natural, Chilled (Tesco) *serving 110g/4oz*	9
Fromage Frais, Flavoured, Low Fat (Sainsbury's) *serving 110g/4oz*	2
Fromage Frais, Flavoured, Virtually Fat Free (Sainsbury's) *serving 110g/4oz*	0
Fromage Frais, Fruit *serving 110g/4oz*	6
Fromage Frais, Fruit on the Bottom, Light (Asda) *serving 110g/4oz*	0
Fromage Frais & Fruit (Somerfield) *serving 110g/4oz*	5
Fromage Frais & Fruit, Peach (Heinz Weight Watchers) *serving 110g/4oz*	0
Fromage Frais & Fruit, Raspberry & Strawberry (Heinz Weight Watchers) *serving 110g/4oz*	0
Fromage Frais & Fruit, Strawberry (Heinz Weight Watchers) *serving 110g/4oz*	0
Fromage Frais & Fruit, Summer Fruits (Heinz Weight Watchers) *serving 110g/4oz*	0
Fromage Frais, Light, with Fruit, Chilled (Iceland) *serving 110g/4oz*	0
Fromage Frais, Lite (Somerfield) *serving 110g/4oz*	0
Fromage Frais, Lite, with Real Fruit (Somerfield) *serving 110g/4oz*	0
Fromage Frais, Low Fat (Waitrose) *serving 110g/4oz*	4
Fromage Frais, Monster Pots (Safeway) *serving 110g/4oz*	5
Fromage Frais, Natural, 10% Fat (Asda) *serving 110g/4oz*	11
Fromage Frais, Petit (Safeway) *serving 110g/4oz*	5
Fromage Frais, Rich & Creamy, Strawberry, Chilled (Tesco) *serving 110g/4oz*	7

Fromage Frais, Shape, Banana (St Ivel) *serving 110g/4oz* 1
Fromage Frais, Shape, Blackberry (St Ivel) *serving 110g/4oz* 1
Fromage Frais, Shape, Cherry (St Ivel) *serving 110g/4oz* 1
Fromage Frais, Shape, Mango (St Ivel) *serving 110g/4oz* 1
Fromage Frais, Shape, Peach & Passionfruit (St Ivel) *serving 110g/4oz* 1
Fromage Frais, Shape, Pineapple & Coconut (St Ivel) *serving 110g/4oz* 3
Fromage Frais, Shape, Raspberry (St Ivel) *serving 110g/4oz* 1
Fromage Frais, Shape, Strawberry (St Ivel) *serving 110g/4oz* 1
Fromage Frais, Shape, Fruit on the Bottom, Apricot & Vanilla (St Ivel) *serving 110g/4oz* 1
Fromage Frais, Shape, Fruit on the Bottom, Double Strawberry (St Ivel) *serving 110g/4oz* 1
Fromage Frais, Shape, Fruit on the Bottom, Raspberry & Blueberry (St Ivel) *serving 110g/4oz* 1
Fromage Frais, Shape, Fruit on the Bottom, Strawberry & Vanilla (St Ivel) *serving 110g/4oz* 1
Fromage Frais, Tikka Dip (Asda) *serving 110g/4oz* 11
Fromage Frais, Vanilla, Chilled (Tesco) *serving 110g/4oz* 7
Fromage Frais, Vanilla, Chilled, Healthy Eating (Tesco) *serving 110g/4oz* 0
Fromage Frais, Very Low Fat *serving 110g/4oz* 0
Fromage Frais, Very Low Fat, Natural (Asda) *serving 110g/4oz* 0
Fromage Frais, Very Low Fat, Natural, Chilled (Tesco) *serving 110g/4oz* 0
Raita (Safeway) *serving 110g/4oz* 1
Tzatziki *serving 110g/4oz* 5
Tzatziki (Marks & Spencer) *serving 110g/4oz* 8
Tzatziki (Safeway) *serving 110g/4oz* 1
Tzatziki (Waitrose) *serving 110g/4oz* 7
Tzatzik, Chilled (Tesco) *serving 110g/4oz* 7
Tzatsiki, Greek Dip Selection, Chilled (Tesco) *serving 110g/4oz* 6
Tzatziki, Greek Style Starter (Asda) *serving 110g/4oz* 7
Yoghurt, Blackcurrant, Fat Free, Pot Dessert (Marks & Spencer) *serving 110g/4oz* 0

Yoghurt, Greek Style, Natural, Pot Dessert (Marks & Spencer) *serving 110g/4oz*	12
Yoghurt, Lite, Orange, Pot Dessert (Marks & Spencer) *serving 110g/4oz*	0
Yoghurt, Lite, Purple, Pot Dessert (Marks & Spencer) *serving 110g/4oz*	0
Yoghurt, Lite, Rhubarb, Pot Dessert (Marks & Spencer) *serving 110g/4oz*	0
Yoghurt, Low Fat Bio Yoghurt Toffee, Pot Dessert (Marks & Spencer) *serving 110g/4oz*	2
Yoghurt, Low Fat, Natural, Large, Pot Dessert (Marks & Spencer) *serving 110g/4oz*	1
Yoghurt, Peach & Apricot, Fat Free Pot Dessert (Marks & Spencer) *serving 110g/4oz*	0
Yoghurt, Plum, Fat Free, Pot Dessert (Marks & Spencer) *serving 110g/4oz*	0
Yoghurt, Pot Dessert (Marks & Spencer) *serving 110g/4oz*	4
Yoghurt, Rhubarb, Fat Free, Pot Dessert (Marks & Spencer) *serving 110g/4oz*	0
Yoghurt, Thick & Creamy, Strawberry & Vanilla, Chilled (Iceland) *serving 110g/4oz*	3
Yoghurt, Whisp, Fruits of the Forest, Pot Dessert (Marks & Spencer) *serving 110g/4oz*	5
Yoghurt, Whisp, Lemon & Lime, Pot Dessert (Marks & Spencer) *serving 110g/4oz*	5

APPENDIX

CONVERSION TABLES

What happens if you want to eat a different portion size to the one listed under your chosen food in the Counter? Easy! Simply use the following conversion tables to work out quickly the amount of fat in your new serving size. Follow these steps:

1 Go to the conversion table which refers to the existing serving size (example: all beans and lentils are measured in a serving of 170g/6oz, so go to that table).

2 Look down the left hand column until you find the serving size you want to eat (example: you want to eat 280g/10oz, so look at the last row in the table).

3 Read across the top of the table until you find the amount of fat in the OLD serving (example: Baked Beans Hot Pot: 5 grams).

4 Now look down that column to find the amount of fat in your new serving size (example: Baked Beans Hot Pot: old serving 5 grams fat; new serving 8 grams fat).

CONVERSION TABLE FOR 10g/0.3oz SERVINGS

	Grams of fat in the old serving									
	1	2	3	4	5	6	7	8	9	10
New serving	Grams of fat in your new serving size									
10g/0.3oz	1	2	3	4	5	6	7	8	9	10
30g/1oz	3	6	9	12	15	18	21	24	27	30
60g/2oz	6	12	18	24	30	36	42	48	54	60
90g/3oz	9	18	27	36	45	54	63	72	81	90
110g/4oz	11	22	33	44	55	66	77	88	99	110
170g/6oz	17	34	51	68	85	102	119	136	153	170
280g/10oz	28	56	84	112	140	168	196	224	252	280

CONVERSION TABLE FOR 30g/1oz SERVINGS

	Grams of fat in the old serving									
	1	2	3	4	5	6	7	8	9	10
New serving	Grams of fat in your new serving size									
10g/0.3oz	0	1	1	1	2	2	2	3	3	3
30g/1oz	1	2	3	4	5	6	7	8	9	10
60g/2oz	2	4	6	8	10	12	14	16	18	20
90g/3oz	3	6	9	12	15	18	21	24	27	30
110g/4oz	4	7	11	15	18	22	26	29	33	37
170g/6oz	6	11	17	23	28	34	40	45	51	57
280g/10oz	9	19	28	37	47	56	65	75	84	93

CONVERSION TABLE FOR 60g/2oz SERVINGS

	Grams of fat in the old serving									
	1	2	3	4	5	6	7	8	9	10
New serving	Grams of fat in your new serving size									
10g/0.3oz	0	0	1	1	1	1	1	1	2	2
30g/1oz	1	1	2	2	3	3	4	4	5	5
60g/2oz	1	2	3	4	5	6	7	8	9	10
90g/3oz	2	3	5	6	8	9	11	12	14	15
110g/4oz	2	4	6	7	9	11	13	15	17	18
170g/6oz	3	6	9	11	14	17	20	23	26	28
280g/10oz	5	9	14	19	23	28	33	37	42	47

CONVERSATION TABLE FOR 90g/3oz SERVINGS

	Grams of fat in the old serving									
	1	2	3	4	5	6	7	8	9	10
New serving	Grams of fat in your new serving size									
10g/0.3oz	0	0	0	0	1	1	1	1	1	1
30g/1oz	0	1	1	1	2	2	2	3	3	3
60g/2oz	1	1	2	3	3	4	5	5	6	7
90g/3oz	1	2	3	4	5	6	7	8	9	10
110g/4oz	1	2	4	5	6	7	9	10	11	12
170g/6oz	2	4	6	8	9	11	13	15	17	19
280g/10oz	3	6	9	12	16	19	22	25	28	31

CONVERSATION TABLE FOR 110g/4oz SERVINGS

	Grams of fat in the old serving									
	1	2	3	4	5	6	7	8	9	10
New serving	Grams of fat in your new serving size									
10g/0.3oz	0	0	.0	0	0	1	1	1	1	1
30g/1oz	0	1	1	1	1	2	2	2	2	3
60g/2oz	1	1	2	2	3	3	4	4	5	5
90g/3oz	1	2	2	3	4	5	6	7	7	8
110g/4oz	1	2	3	4	5	6	7	8	9	10
170g/6oz	2	3	5	6	8	9	11	12	14	15
280g/10oz	3	5	8	10	13	15	18	20	23	25

CONVERSION TABLE FOR 170g/6oz SERVINGS

	Grams of fat in the old serving									
	1	2	3	4	5	6	7	8	9	10
New serving	Grams of fat in your new serving size									
10g/0.3oz	0	0	0	0	0	0	0	0	1	1
30g/1oz	0	0	1	1	1	1	1	1	2	2
60g/2oz	0	1	1	1	2	2	2	3	3	4
90g/3oz	1	1	2	2	3	3	4	4	5	5
110g/4oz	1	1	2	3	3	4	5	5	6	6
170g/6oz	1	2	3	4	5	6	7	8	9	10
280g/10oz	2	3	5	7	8	10	12	13	15	16

CONVERSION TABLE FOR 280g/10oz SERVINGS

	Grams of fat in the old serving									
	1	2	3	4	5	6	7	8	9	10
New serving	Grams of fat in your new serving size									
10g/0.3oz	0	0	0	0	0	0	0	0	0	0
30g/1oz	0	0	0	0	1	1	1	1	1	1
60g/2oz	0	0	1	1	1	1	2	2	2	2
90g/3oz	0	1	1	1	2	2	2	3	3	3
110g/4oz	0	1	1	2	2	2	3	3	4	4
170g/6oz	1	1	2	2	3	4	4	5	5	6
280g/10oz	1	2	3	4	5	6	7	8	9	10

REFERENCES

[1]*Nutritional Aspects of Cardiovascular Disease*, HMSO, 1994.
[2]*Dietary References: Values for Food Energy and Nutrients for the United Kingdom*, HMSO, 1991.
[3]*Dietary References: Values for Food Energy and Nutrients for the United Kingdom*, HMSO 1991.
[4]The Associated Press, 29 March 1993.
[5]The Associated Press, 25 August 1994.
[6]*Nutritional Aspects of Cardiovascular Disease*, HMSO, 1994.
[7]*Food For Life*, Barnard, N., Harmony Books, 1993.
[8]Himms-Hagen, J., *Canadian Medical Association Journal*, 1979; 121: 1361.
[9]Welle, S. *et al.*, *Metabolism*, 1980; 29(9): 806–9.
[10]Kendall, A. *et al.*, *American Journal of Clinical Nutrition*, 1991; 53(5): 1124–9.
[11]*Dietary References: Values for Food Energy and Nutrients for the United Kingdom*, HMSO, 1991.
[12]*Better Nutrition*, February 1990; 52(2): 24(2).
[13]Kendall, A. *et al.*, *American Journal of Clinical Nutrition* 1991; 53(5): 1124–9.